The Methodology of Economic Thought

Critical Papers from the *Journal of Economic Thought*

Edited by Warren J. Samuels

Foreword by Robert Lekachman

Transaction Books
New Brunswick (U.S.A.) and London (U.K.)

Library of Congress Catalog Number: 78-62900
ISBN: 0-87855-645-1
Printed in the United States of America

Library of Congress Cataloging in Publication Data

Main entry under title:

The Methodology of economic thought.

Contains articles from the Journal of economic issues, 1968-1976.
Includes bibliographical references.
1. Economics—Addresses, essays, lectures.
2. Economics—Methodology—Addresses, essays, lectures.
3. Institutional economics—Addresses, essays, lectures.
4. Economics—History—Addresses, essays, lectures.
I. Samuels, Warren J., 1933- II. Journal of economic issues.
HB34.M47 330.1 78-62900
ISBN 0-87855-645-1

The Methodology of Economic Thought

Contents

Foreword

Robert Lekachman

As no one save the happily ignorant can deny, the strength of conventional economics and the source of its practitioner's prestige is an elegant methodology that sharp minds continue to refine in elegant mathematical forms. It is a platitude of the sociology of intellectual professions that the more demanding the technique, the more arcane the vocabulary, and the more inaccessible professional discussions become to mere laymen, the higher both the prestige of the specialty and the starting salaries of appropriately certified novices. Thus it is that law schools socialize young men and women of otherwise irreproachable character and aspirations into the peculiar jargon of the legal trade. Graduate schools perform a similar function in the initiation of young economists, but graduate instructors possibly even more than law teachers must fulfill a heavy, additional responsibility. Upon them devolves the task of purging the minds of their young charges of residues of common sense that might interfere with the assimilation of unworldly abstractions and theories and thus interfere with appropriate progress to the doctorate.

There is no need for me to enlarge upon this theme, dear as it is to my own heart, for the articles assembled in this volume do a splendid job of exposing the grave inadequacies of accepted economic theory and methodology. A host of theorists, for some time unclothed, should be more widely perceived in their nudity by readers of these clear-sighted essays. Candor compels me to say that the contributors are on the whole less successful in their attempts to define alternative methodologies. However, equity allows me to add that many contributors are fully aware of the need to advance beyond the demolition of received economic wisdom, essential and enjoyable as such work is, and there are included here some valuable efforts to construct institutionalist alternatives. The items in Part V, "Toward a Meaningful

Political Economy," for example, are notable attempts to expand the conceptual range and power of institutionalist methodology.

A concluding claim deserves to be made. If institutionalism were no more than an intelligent critique of mainstream economic doctrine and a series of individual studies of diverse economic phenomena and institutions, our doctrinal school ought still to be cherished even by the adherents of the modernized wisdom of Adam Smith and John Maynard Keynes, who have created the current content of price and income theory. At its best, institutionalism is already a considerably more illuminating way of inspecting the universe than the meager insights, frequently mistaken, now available to the adepts of standard price theory.

I am confident that this valuable collection will encourage further travel down intellectual paths leading to more useful destinations than most economists are now trained to reach.

Editor's Introduction

Because the economy is important to the conduct and policies of individuals and nations, economics is important. As with foreign policy, economics is indeed too important to be left to the experts alone, but that does not mean economists should not reflect upon the state of their discipline. And this they have done. From the earliest generations, economists have been concerned about the grounds and social role of what they have accepted as knowledge.

Precisely because the study of economics is important, economists must inquire into the methodology, or epistemology, that influences their study of the economy. The methodological strengths and weaknesses, or limitations, of their work have profound consequences for the probative status of their findings, that is, the significance of their analysis as a basis of description and policy.

Economics actually has three facets. One of these is knowledge. As a scientific discipline, economics is concerned with providing information, description, and interpretation of the nature of the economy in all its ramifications. Some economists study markets; others study institutions; still others the interconnections between these two aspects. They primarily use the tools of deductive theory, empirical inference, and the concepts of model and paradigm construction. The objective is positive knowledge and insight into what the economy is all about.

Economics is also social control,[1] one of the modes through which, in modern societies, a social construction of reality is formulated. Through internalization, however individualized, this construciton provides all persons with a sense of what is, what is proper, and what is possible with regard to the economy. Economics, then, has been both explanation and rationalization, and thus its ideology has come to serve some of the purposes formerly provided by religion. To control, even at several removes, the content and nuances of economic theory is to control the formation of issues (definition of problems) and of policies (solutions).[2]

The third facet of economics is its function as psychic balm. It provides us with a sense of order and sets our minds at rest.

> All we can seek is consistency, coherence, order. The question for the scientist is what thought-scheme will best provide him with a sense of that order and coherence, a sense of some permanence, repetitiveness and universality in the structure or texture of the scheme of things, a sense even of that one-ness and simplicity which, if he can assure himself of its presence, will carry consistency and order to their highest expression. Religion, science and art have all of them this aim in common. The difference between them lies in the different emphases in their modes of search. . .
>
> The chief service rendered by a theory is the setting of minds at rest. . . Theory serves deep needs of the human spirit: it subordinates nature to man, imposes a beautiful simplicity on the unbearable multiplicity of fact, gives comfort in face of the unknown and unexperienced, stops the teasing of mystery and doubt which, though salutary and life-preserving, is uncomfortable, so that we seek by theory to sort out the justified from the unjustified fear. Theories by their nature and purpose, their role of administering to a "good state of mind," are things to be held and cherished. Theories are altered or discarded only when they fail us.[3]

Inasmuch as economics is a combination of knowledge, social control, and psychic balm, the study of its methodology and its status as knowledge (that is, the nature of the combination) is complex and capable of diverse interpretation. Belief is a function of selective perception and a multiplicity of factors and forces that govern general and specific attachments of psychic importance. Because something is "known" to be objectively correct does not mean that it will win out over ideological beliefs because it is comforting in the face of anxiety of one form or another. But the study of methodology can be a mode of self-reflection and can contribute to the elevation of the discipline to more sophisiticated levels, although on those levels it may well be that ideology is only more subtly present.

Systems of orthodoxy are largely nonreflective with regard to their own limits. It is true that the foremost practitioners do tend to be cognizant of the methodological limits of their work. Indeed, one reason their work is first rate is their sensitivity both to the impact of those limits on their work and to the possible impact of their work upon those limits.

One function of economic heterodoxy is to explore the methodological characteristics and limitations of orthodoxy or of the larger economics of which both orthodoxy and heterodoxy are parts. The *Journal of Economic Issues* is the publication of the Association for Evolutionary Economics, a group of heterodox economists of diverse political and economic philosophies who have in common at least two interests: the systemic evolution of the economic system and the fundamental problem of economic organization and control, both as subjects for positive (objective) and normative (valuational) study. The journal is nonsectarian and attracts a wide range of economists, including many from within the ranks of orthodoxy interested in the above problems. Because most contributors are interested in the problems of systemic evolution and power, problems different from those of orthodoxy, the journal has attracted the attention of those interested in methodology and the status of the profession's development. By no means do all contributors agree on fundamental issues. But they have provided a sound body of diverse insights into the credentials of economics as knowledge, the forces which have governed the evolution of economic ideas, and the policy status of the substance of economic analysis.

This anthology collects materials from the journal and places them in five groups. Part I explores the relation of heterodoxy to orthodoxy in economics. Part II explores various facets of methodology or epistemology in recent economic thought. It will be obvious that the problem of ideology in economics pervades the work of both heterodox and orthodox economists. Part III explores the nature and mechanisms of change in economic thought. This is an important but widely neglected area: economists often fail to appreciate that present ideas have evolved from earlier ones and that the process of evolution has by no means been neutral or above controversy. Part IV presents materials relating to the role of economic theory as social control and a guide to policy. Part V contains materials relating to the prospects and problems of political economy in contrast to a narrower approach to economics.

The subjects this anthology covers are complicated but central to the deep understanding of economics as an intellectual discipline. The complications are many but clearly include the following: the diversity of analytical techniques employed by economists; the heterogeneity of the economy, or political economy, itself; the heterogeneity of images of the existing and future economy; and the fact that methodology, while capable of being discussed on an abstract, pure level, often is dependent upon the substantive interests and policy preferences of practitioners. Throughout, it should be evident that one person's facts may be another's prejudices. Nonetheless, it is possible to attempt an objective study of the methodology of economics while being aware of the subtle intrusion of ideology into such study. At the very least the juxtaposition of ideologies may enable us better to identify the ideological element in economic analysis and thereby better comprehend the nature and limits of our analysis and knowledge.[4]

Notes

1. *See* Warren J. Samuels, ed., *The Economy as a System of Power* (New Brunswick, N.J.: Transaction Books, 1979).

2. *See* Joan Robinson, *Economic Philosophy* (Chicago: Aldine, 1962), Chapter one.
3. G.L.S. Shackle, *The Years of High Theory* (New York: Cambridge University Press, 1967), pp. 286, 288-89.
4. *See* Warren J. Samuels, "Ideology in Economics," in *Modern Economic Thought,* ed. Sidney Weintraub (Philadelphia: University of Pennsylvania Press, 1977), pp. 467-84.

Part I

Heterodoxy vis-à-vis Orthodoxy

Introduction

In the first article in this section, Clarence E. Ayres raises the question of ideology in regard to the fundamental picture of the economy presented in orthodox economics. Ayres argues that science and technology govern aggregate production and welfare and that institutions govern the distribution of production and welfare. He believes total output to be a function of the operation of society as a whole. Rights, or claims to income by the factors of production, are seen as deriving from a mythology of productive agency implicit in the system of belief with which people in a society are conditioned. Ayres thus calls attention to the critical role of the mythological belief system (for example, that of distribution in accordance with productivity). Such a system is required for economic organization and stability and must be permissive with regard to the production of output. Indeed, the present system is not utterly irrational. Among other things, it includes or permits the redefinition of property rights. But this belief system, or ideology, misconceives the production process and fails to appreciate the role of technology. The market system's official ideology, supplied in part by orthodox economics, serves as a brake on social change and on technological progress itself. According to Ayres, it is the highest ideological responsibility of heterodoxy to study and to convey knowledge of the nature and meaning of the system's ideology, that is, to lift the veil from the system of belief. Finding the pluralism of the welfare state a working model of a creative society, Ayres cautions against overemphasis on the market: the market can be a cultural barrier to the creativity of the technological process and to the wide distribution of welfare.

Thus Ayresian heterodoxy challenges orthodoxy on the interrelated issues of responsible relevant ideology. In a comment on the Ayres article, Abraham Hirsch, a heterodox economist somewhat more solicitous than Ayres of the utility of orthodox economics, criticizes Ayres's refection of orthodoxy and cautions against the creation of a new ideology in institutional (or evolutionary) economics. Hirsch finds orthodox and institutional economics compatible and agrees with Ayres that all economists should devote careful attention to the epistemological (or methodological) limits of their analysis. Quoting John Stuart Mill, Hirsch also agrees with Ayres that income and wealth distribution depends upon legal and moral rules subject to change and that technical orthodox economics can be separated from the use of those rules that attempt to legitimize distribution on the basis of existing institutions and structure of rights.[1]

Allan G. Gruchy presents an interpretation of what he calls neoinstitutionalism, which represents for him an outlet for economic dissent.

After a critique of orthodox economics, he identifies several paths taken by dissent: the substantive analysis of factors and forces not treated by orthodox economists, such as how wants are formed under the influence of the corporate system and how nonmarket wants are aborted; criticism of the economic system and its operating consequences; criticism of conventional economics; and the formulation of a constructive alternative. In Gruchy's view, the substantive alternative interpretation of the economy provided by neoinstitutionalism involves a revision of Veblenian analysis and centers on the theory of the modern industrial system, with the central concept being the process of industrialization. Neoinstitutionalism accepts orthodox theory but goes beyond it to study both market decision making and the guidance of the larger, evolving economic system, with an appropriately enlarged view of economic reality. At least three distinctively different foci characterize Gruchy's neoinstitutional economics: attention to those interests and goals that are being served and those that are not; power and conflict in and over the economy; and problem solving.[2]

Joseph Dorfman surveys the array of heterodox contributions in the history of U.S. economic thought, with particular reference to questions of public policy.[3] Central to his survey is collective action, a topic stressed by heterodox economists. Dorfman insists that collective action involves more than government, that it governs the structure of opportunities open to individuals, that there were great changes in the economic role of government after the Civil War, and that government remains the ultimate arena in which disputes are arbitrated. Before the Civil War, laissez faire meant opposition to privilege, especially that established by law; after the war an ironic transformation took place, and governmental policy in the image of laissez faire supported the hierarchical structure of power that emerged with industrialization. Government was thereby put to a new set of uses. Dorfman considers heterodox writers to be less affected by the dogma and preconceptions of the past and therefore able to bring new insights to problems rather than merely reiterate the dominant ideology. In his view, heterodox economists overcame conservative resistance and helped produce the welfare state. Dorfman, too, stresses power and conflict over the corporation, collective action going beyond the common law and the corporation, the organization of the labor market, and the institutional organization of the economy governing the realization of values and the solution of distributive questions. Dorfman surveys the thought of the main heterodox economists: Henry Carter Adams, Thorstein Veblen, Wesley C. Mitchell, John R. Commons, John Maurice Clark, and many others.

The next two articles, by Kenneth Boulding and Richard H. Day, present somewhat different interpretations of the state of neoclassical economics. Boulding acknowledges that the boundaries of neoclassical economics are a matter of taste. He affirms the truth of both the neoclassical belief that there is an important reality to the dynamics of the relative price structure and the Veblenian view that preferences are endogenous to the system, including the system of relative prices itself. Boulding would conjoin the analysis of price structures and institutions; indeed, he would go beyond both and include the study of the political price structure. He finds it comfortable to accept both the proposition that institutions impose limits on the set of feasible market or political solutions and the proposition that production and supply functions, themselves governed in part by relative prices, govern the course of technical change. Boulding sees less of a conflict between orthodox and heterodox economics (between price and evolutionary economics) and more of an opportunity for several types of evolutionary analysis.

Richard H. Day first surveys the hallmarks and role of the orthodox economist: the beliefs that coherent principles are to be applied widely and effectively, that principles are to be mastered and applied and not created or evolved, that principles are to be defended and new and/or alternative theories are to be resisted, and that these principles characterize a state that if achieved would have certain desirable properties. The contributions of orthodoxy are its role as orthodoxy and its service as theory. However, Day finds inadequate the optimizing models of orthodox economics and suggests a spectrum of heterodox economics ranging from adaption and evolution within bounded rationality (an economic ethology of man as he is), to an existential economics representing an alliance between adaptive and institutional theorizing. Day sees institutional economics as relating to dialectical processes, the formation of individual and social preferences, conflict resolution and social control, stochastic events, real world decision making, institutional evolution, and the institutional framework of distribution. Accordingly, he summarizes the work of John R. Commons as follows: It is the study of institutions (1) functioning as the framework in which distributional decisions are made, (2) whose public purpose is defined through the working out of temporary compromises among changing and conflicting peceptions and needs, in which (3) the unit of analysis is the transaction, and (4) the fundamental task is both the study of the status quo and the design of new institutions producing, among other things, new and more effective avenues for transactions.

The Boulding and Day articles are followed by two comments by Victor Goldberg and Howard Sherman. Goldberg examines the limits of orthodox economic theory in the context of contract. Orthodox economics, he finds, tends to transfer theoretical propositions to the real world, but the linkage is fuzzy. He uses as an example freedom of contract: market economics emphasizes free contract in order to achieve gains from trade, but in doing so it neglects a number of variables crucial to actual performance. One of these is the role of contracts restricting freedom in the future. (Although the Chicago School lauds voluntary restrictions as presumptively optimal, Goldberg says the problem is not whether there will be restrictions, but which and whose .) Other variables are the lack of real world applicability of formal optimality analysis, the asymmetrical power of the parties to contracts, the asymmetrical information enjoyed by the parties, and the role of working rules. Goldberg suggests the economy has ubiquitous restrictions, not aberrant ones, and laments the failure of economics to develop an adequate theory of distribution.

Howard Sherman interprets the status of orthodoxy and delineates the development of economics in terms of a tension between realism (including conflict) and efforts to combat subversive influences. Sherman faults the neoclassical paradigm as emphasizing harmony to the neglect of class conflict, power, and the proposition that the state is the instrument of the economic power of the capitalist class, all of which function to maintain status quo institutions. Finally, he views neoclassicism as favoring incremental change and resisting fundamental change. As for liberals and institutionalists, Sherman applauds their recognition of the social determination of preferences, monopoly capitalism, monopoly of government, and evolutionary change as both possible and necessary. However, he feels that they do not really escape from neoclassical assumptions and that they see only the reform of capitalism and no reason to terminate it. This latter predicament, according to Sherman, leads the liberals and institutionalist economists to make inept policy recommendations. Alternatively Sherman applauds the radical paradigm, with its emphasis on social relations (rather than individual preferences), conflict, exploitation, the evolutionary origins of conflict, and the possibility of drastic revolutionary change when the conflict is insoluble within the system. Normatively, Sherman argues in favor of a combination of political and economic democracy.[4]

This section concludes with four reviews of Benjamin Ward's wide-ranging book, *What's Wrong with Economics?* in which Allan Gruchy stresses the viability of the neoinstitutional paradigm and Robert M. Solow presents a neoclassical defense against Ward's criticisms. Solow makes a case for the technical use of the maximizing (rationality) assumption; at the same time he defends against the argument that neoclassical economics expresses an ideological, if not also a class, bias. Solow acknowledges that positive neoclassical economics is culture bound and is not free of ideological content, but he argues that it does have relatively untainted substantive content. Siegfried Karsten, among other things, stresses the viability of both a general equilibrium and a dialectical economics. Oskar Morgenstern presents a wide-ranging review, in part juxtaposing Ward's emphasis upon general equilibrium decision making to his own work in game theory.

Notes

1. *See also* William M. Dugger, "Ideological and Scientific Function of the Neoclassical Theory of the Firm," and the comment by Abraham Hirsch, June 1976; Louis J. Junker, "Capital Accumulation, Savings-Centered Theory and Economic Development," June 1967, and Alan Nichols, "On Savings and Neo-Institutionalism," September 1969.
2. *See also* Gruchy's articles, "Law, Politics, and Institutional Economics," December 1973, and "Government Intervention and the Social Control of Business," June 1974.
3. *See also* Douglas F. Dowd, "Some Issues of Economic Development and of Development Economics," September 1967; Morris A. Copeland, "Laissez Faire, Pecuniary Incentives, and Public Policy," December 1967; Clarence E. Ayres, "The Price System and Public Policy," September 1968; and William F. Campbell, "Economics and the Machiavellian Tradition," June 1971.
4. *See also* G. K. Shaw, "In Defense of Orthodox Economics," and Howard Sherman, "In Defense of Radical Political Economy," September 1976.

Ideological Responsibility

Clarence E. Ayres

For a long time now I have been growing increasingly restive at the increasingly general use of the term "productivity." To be sure, it is most commonly used today in what is supposed to be a purely statistical sense. Increases in wages are commonly supposed to be "justified" by corresponding increases in "productivity." But what does "justified" mean? We may say that we use such words as "productivity" in a purely economic sense, meaning that we interpose the mechanisms of the market between our conclusions and the moral problems which gave rise to them. But moral considerations, being universal and omnipresent, have a way of leaking through the complexities of the market and coloring the results of even the most recondite analysis with a moral tint. This is true, and I think inescapably true, of the concept "productivity." This word suggests, whether intentionally or not, meanings which are not true and are exceedingly harmful; and all of us who know this to be the case have a public duty to repudiate these suggested meanings and to denounce the whole institutional structure they support. I propose to use this platform to try to do my public duty in this regard.

Not very long ago economists such as John Bates Clark were declaring that "Free competition tends to give to labor what labor creates, to capitalists what capital creates, and to entrepreneurs what the co-ordinating function creates." Today, only two generations later, few economists would advocate total reliance on this "tendency." But for most of them the reason for their hesitation is not skepticism with regard to the creativity of the "instruments of production." What they question is only whether competition is sufficiently brisk and sufficiently general to give effect to this salubrious tendency. The myth of "creativity" still passes virtually unquestioned.

Indeed, one of the most thoughtful, not to say philosophical, of living economists, Frank H. Knight, reaffirmed this only recently in the following language:

> The "communist" nations also must follow extensively the principle of productivity or "middle of the road," and even "marginalism," to achieve any efficiency or to make the economy function at all. And they lose much efficiency by pretending to the contrary, and especially by pretending not to recognize "capital" as productive. This is true [I assume he means that capital *is* productive] regardless of who has title to the property in which it is embodied or what the status of laborers or managers is.[1]

The author is Professor of Economics at The University of Texas. This paper is his presidential address to the Association for Evolutionary Economics, San Francisco, December 27, 1966.

[1] Strangely enough, these sentences occur in a review-article which roundly condemns Henry Hazlitt's *The Foundations of Morality*, under the title "Abstract Economics and Absolute Ethics," in *Ethics*, LXVI, 3 (April, 1966). As the title suggests, Knight chides

Such a conception of capital as productive "regardless . . . of what the status of laborers and managers is" calls to mind a picture analogous to that of the sorcerer's apprentice: vast machines, cybernized by miniature computers, spewing forth continuous streams of steel ingots and finished automobiles. But that is not what was meant by Professors Knight and Clark and the whole succession of classical economists. What they have all meant is that capital is "productive" in the same sense that labor is productive, and therefore has a valid claim on the gross product regardless of who profits by that claim.

It is interesting to reflect that capital may be productive in a sense quite different from what the classical economists have had in mind. Capital, we say, is just as productive as labor and therefore no less entitled to remuneration. This is as much as to say that the claim of capital is indefeasible, for in our society no claim is more firmly established than that of honest toil. Whatever its amount, the workman is worthy of his hire. He has earned it.

It is interesting to reflect on the claim-justifying magic of the word "earn." The *Shorter Oxford* defines this word in terms that admit of no misunderstanding: "To render an equivalent in labour for; hence to obtain, or deserve, as the reward of labour." In short, the divine right of the worker to his wage is established by his sweat. But note how language drifts! The Random House *College Dictionary* is more up-to-date. After a succinct statement of the original meaning of the word "earn," "to gain by labor or service," it continues: "To gain as due return or profit: *Savings bonds earn interest.*" In effect, we are invited to picture the bonds in the locked steel drawer of some bank vault, sweating profusely as they heave and writhe in their efforts to perform the labor or service for which their owner is about to be rewarded. Am I indulging in absurdity? Should I declare that what the savings-bond buyer is being rewarded for is abstinence from frivolity in consequence of which some wheel of industry is being lubricated which otherwise would be stuck fast? Otherwise would a box of mortar shells be arriving at the front with an empty space containing only a sad little note to the effect that the citizens whose abstinence might have filled this space went to a football game instead?

But abstinence is not the only act of piety which is signalized today by use of the verb "to earn." In a strictly contemporary spirit the September 30, 1966, issue of *Time* referred to a distinguished American as having ". . . earned more than $1,000,000 by short-selling in 1929–30." In dedicating his hard-earned dollars to this cause this citizen was of course helping to turn the market, which indeed did eventually turn.

The point I am struggling to make is this. In all these matters, even including the wages of labor, we are dealing not with opaque matters of fact but with the luminosities of spiritual conjecture. This is not to say they are

Hazlitt for taking "the vastly simplified postulates that are legitimate and necessary for the first stage of economic analysis—but which should never be taken as describing reality, and still less as normative" and, as Hazlitt does, treating them "as universal ideals."

nonsense. The mores and *manas* of any culture make very good sense indeed to the people who are governed by them. John Locke was a notably practical man. His *Two Treatises Concerning Government* were written for the very practical purpose of justifying the "glorious revolution" of 1688; and when, in the course of those essays, he undertook to provide a solid ideological foundation for the propertied class which had now in effect supplanted the British monarchy, the most potent magic he could conjure up was that of the honest sweat of labor. If, as he argued, the rights of property were established when man mixed his perspiration with the soil, what could possibly be said against them?

The truth is, of course, that involuntary servitude has been the fate of mankind since the beginning of time. This does not mean that the yoke of cultural tradition has been a galling one. Generally speaking, men have endured the discomforts and inconveniences of their way of life because it has offered some measure of security and satisfaction and because no better way of life seemed to be open to them. For example, it would surely be a mistake to suppose that the lower orders of feudal society, the bulk of the population, endured the brass collar of involuntary servitude (so vividly described in *Ivanhoe*) for centuries in a state of smoldering and barely arrested mutiny. It was only when the early medieval towns provided a sanctuary to freedmen, that escape from involuntary servitude became the *beau idéal* of modern Western civilization.

This is the magic with which we conjure when we talk about the gains of speculators as being "earned," and about "capital" as being "productive" in the same sense that labor is. All such propositions are imputations of magic potency and would be instantly recognizable as such by all of us except for the fact that they are figments of the system of make-believe to which we all have been emotionally conditioned all our lives.

Since we know this, our situation is very different from that of John Locke and his contemporaries or even that of Adam Smith and his contemporaries. Although we know it quite well, it is easy to forget how great the difference is. We have lived all our lives in a world that takes absolutely for granted the evolutionary origin and zoological character of the human species: so much so that when Veblen declares that the classical principles of economics are "pre-Darwinian," we greet that aspersion with shocked incredulity. How can the concepts we still use be "pre-Darwinian" since we, who still use them, live far down the slope on the near side of the great evolutionary watershed? We know as well as anyone that *Homo sapiens* evolved from earlier species by the same process of mutation and natural selection that produced the whale and the elephant. But, we say, what has this to do with such concepts as "productivity"—or, for that matter, Locke's property itself? And the answer is: More than we ordinarily suppose, since it involves that whole universe of discourse in which we operate.

Except within the confines of the tribal belief, there is no such thing as "inalienable rights"—of capital, or labor, or any other component of society. In every society such "rights" derive from the mythology of agency, which is implicit in the system of beliefs to which the people of that society are emotionally conditioned, beginning in early childhood. As a matter of fact, whatever any society accomplishes—however it gets its living and otherwise maintains itself—is a causal consequence of the functioning of that society as a whole. This is what anthropologists mean by insisting that all cultures can be understood only as functioning wholes. But the beliefs, to which all peoples are addicted, deviate widely from matters of fact, even from facts of common observation. This is the anomaly to which Samuel Butler referred when he represented the Erewhonians as insisting that all transactions were brought about by the exchange of the currency of the "musical banks," even though everybody knew that the actual causal process was quite different. This, too, is what Veblen meant by insisting (in his double essay "On the Nature of Capital" and elsewhere) that the achievements of industrial society are due to the combined efforts of the entire community and its entire culture, and that any proposal to assign agency to any particular individuals or functions is nonsense.

It is not true that, as Proudhon said, "Property is theft," but it is true that all property rights derive from the culture which defines and honors them. So do the rights of common labor, and so also do the rights of those who perform what John Bates Clark called "the co-ordinating function." This does not mean that culturally defined rights, privileges, and obligations are utterly nonsensical, in our society, or in any other. Whatever the mythology in terms of which rights and obligations are purportedly justified, neither the myths nor the social functions they define can be utterly irrational and obstructive: if they were, the community in question would disappear. They must be sufficiently permissive to allow the community to get its living by whatever profane means it has.

Such permissiveness may be of vital importance. Few historians would maintain that the rights of freedmen in medieval towns were devised to facilitate the growth of modern industry, or that the rights of transfer of title to hitherto entailed property were dreamed up by medieval geniuses for this same purpose. It just so happened that the freedmen were able to find juridical means to make good their escape from feudal serfdom. The ancient tradition of Roman citizenship may have helped, as Roman law may have contributed to the establishment of the rights of property. Whatever their sources these institutions did fit the requirements of emerging industry to a remarkable degree—to the very great advantage of the Western peoples and eventually perhaps the world.

I repeat: This does not mean that the institutions which have accompanied the rise of modern industry were designed for the purpose of facilitating that growth. Like all institutions, they sought to preserve ancient verities and time-honored traditions. By continuing to repeat the slogan, "A man's home is his castle," we remind ourselves that private property is an institution of medieval origin, and that its sanction derives from the past, not from the efficient operation of the industrial economy by which we now live.

In taking this line I do not mean to advocate immediate and wholesale revolution. The distribution of wealth and income is a matter too vast and complex to be encompassed by any economic planner, however wise and erudite, since it is coextensive with civilization itself, of which any economic plan can be no more than a minor and occasional manifestation. But it is the responsibility of scholars to know this. As scholars, we economists have a responsibility to understand something of the nature and functioning of the ideology of our own society, and to convey this knowledge to the intellectually less advantaged community.

This is our ideological responsibility. It is not true that free competition "tends to give" the various elements in organized society what they personally "create." Economists should know better than anyone else that no one creates anything except as a participant in the culture he shares with all the other members of the community, and that it is utterly impossible to determine how different the future of his society would have been if he had never been born. Better than anyone else economists should know that price theory is tautological: that we know what the various participants in our economy "create" only insofar as this is "revealed" by what they get. There is no independent gauge.

As every economist knows, the basic truth is that in our society, as in medieval and ancient societies, the upper classes get more than the lower classes. It is true also, and of vital importance, that the class structure of modern industrial society is very much more fluid than its forebears were. But it is also true that in our society, as in all others, the official ideology acts as a brake on social change and even on technological progress. It does so very simply by enshrining the past: by convincing the community, through the emotional conditioning of children as well as the intellectual bamboozling of the adult community, that the established ways are right and true and best.

This is a complex process. In all societies it involves the self-bamboozling of the intellectual elite. We have no knowledge of any society which has come into existence through a deliberate and conscious conspiracy of the intellectual elite to enslave simple and stupid masses. Always what the masses are taught to believe is already believed sincerely and devoutly by their mentors, and for the reasons given to all by the tribal traditions of which the elite are inheritors no less than the masses. This is the role of what Professor Galbraith has aptly called "the conventional wisdom." Adam Smith, by common consent the founder of our discipline, assumed a society in which the institution of property played a major role. That is, he assumed a class-stratified society, with ownership as the principal agent of stratification; and assuming this he undertook to show how buying and selling in the market would give effect to such a system, so that each participant, without giving any thought to the structure of society and the means of its preservation, would be "led by an invisible hand to promote an end which was not part of his intention."

In all fairness we must recognize that the preservation of the traditionally stratified order of society was no part of the conscious intention of Adam

Smith, nor of John Bates Clark, nor of Professor Knight. But such in fact is the result. Here we are, struggling to free ourselves from the shackles of the past, and we are still teaching our children that we owe all the triumphs of our advanced industrial economy to "free private enterprise," although even the children must see that the first thing we do when confronted with a major crisis, such as war or depression, is to abandon free enterprise and do our best to implement our (now clear) intentions.

What, then, should we do now? Professor Knight chides Henry Hazlitt for proposing to act on "the vastly simplified postulates that are legitimate and necessary for the first stage of economic analysis—but which should never be taken as describing reality, and still less as normative." One normative conclusion is that since economic analysis should never be taken as describing reality, and since presumably it is economic reality with which we wish to deal, we had better abandon this so-called analysis completely and forthwith. But this is a negative proposal, which therefore helps us not at all to clarify our intentions, let alone to realize them.

What are our intentions with regard to what reality? The whole theory of imputation—the imputation of causal efficacy (or ceremonial potency) to the so-called factors of production—is a distributive formula. The idea is that what people receive should be determined by what they produce, either by their own sweat or by some spiritual perspiration or other psychic output. Basically, this idea was a good one. Its intention was to stimulate production; and since production is the limiting factor, successful stimulation of production would increase the well-being of the community virtually by definition. The basic flaw in the whole theory lay in its misconception of the process of production.

What keeps the modern Western community alive and kicking is neither capital nor labor but advanced industrial technology. The physical apparatus of modern society, from which we derive food, clothing, shelter, communication, and physical mobility both local and worldwide, is not the product of sweat or abstinence or any combination of the two. It is the product of invention and discovery, science and technology. Universal, and therefore familiar, as this process is throughout the Western world, we have no single name for it. In one aspect it is a matter of physical tools, materials, and apparatus of all sorts. In another no less significant aspect it is a matter of knowledge, understanding of the materials, tools, and instruments, and generalization from the instruments to the physical universe itself. In still another, closely related to both of these, it is intellectual communication: the process by which the burgeoning material culture of the West spread like a lethal epidemic throughout the West, and now throughout the world.

This process, by which Western civilization was so quickly differentiated from all the rest of the world and from the whole of man's previous experience, began far back in our history. It may be that the situation and cultural posture of the Western peoples even as they emerged from the Roman Empire had already set them on a path no other people had as yet traversed. The journey along that path seems to have begun in what used to be called "the

Dark Ages," dark chiefly because, in the modern sense of the phrase, we "couldn't see" them. In fact, as scholars like Richard Lefebvre des Noëttes and Lynn White have established, a technological revolution had already begun in Western Europe something like a thousand years before Arnold Toynbee's "Industrial Revolution of the Eighteenth Century in England." Lynn White even declares that in terms of the discovery of basic principles the four centuries preceding Leonardo were more important than the four centuries that followed.

As everyone knows, this process is still going on, indeed faster and farther than ever. By common consent, the principal agent of change today is research and development. Or is it general, if not universal, education? Or is it the virtual disappearance from among the Western peoples of such cultural impediments as retarded the study of medicine, and indeed all the "life sciences" only a few generations ago: opposition to "vivi-section" and even to the dissection of human bodies?

In a sense "R & D" is going on everywhere today. There must be hundreds of thousands of young Americans now living who are electronics "hams," or "hot-rodders," or amateurs of some similar scientific or technological profession. Consider that if there is one in every two hundred of the population —an estimate which is by no means unlikely—there are a million altogether. Veblen insisted that economic development is the work of whole communities such as this.

If, then, we mean to distribute the benefits of industrial society in such a way as to further this process and thereby insure the continuance and growth of our society, agencies such as these should receive a generous share of the Gross National Product. Such was the intent of the classical theory. The "productivity" theory of distribution itself was a "creative" theory based on the presumption that the free market would assign or at least "tend" to assign to each "factor of production" what it "creates," thereby of course encouraging it to create more. That system of allocation has not been utterly disastrous. Obviously industrial revolution has flourished under this regime, far more, at least, than it did or could have done under feudalism or ancient despotism. But is this enough? Assuming that the market system is not utterly fallacious in theory or utterly intolerable in practice, is it sufficiently close to the truth in theory, or in actual practice sufficiently creative? Clearly the answer is negative on both accounts. We have never been satisfied to entrust our fate to the market unreservedly. For example, we realized long ago that universal (except for Negroes), free, compulsory education is a precondition of industrial progress. It is also, in the words of Sam Houston, "essential to the preservation of a free government," which is likewise a precondition of industrial progress. This is the precedent we should seek to follow.

To a degree we are already doing so. Certainly education is one of our chief concerns. The decades following World War II have been marked by a general quickening of concern for the quality and extent of education. For obvious reasons this concern has centered on scientific education. But it has spilled over in all directions. I am not one of those who worry about the fate of the humanities in a science-dominated culture. If the humanities really do make a significant contribution to civilization, civilized men will recognize it; and I think they do. For example, no part of our curriculum has received greater stimulus from recent events than language study.

Another significant development has been the progressive lowering of the barriers which have served to exclude substantial parts of the community from participation in the technological revolution. After all, half the population is female; and if we assume that woman's place is in the home, whereas our cultural frontier is the laboratory and the machine shop, we are perpetuating an institutional impediment which has come down to us from our primeval past. The same is true of racial barriers. It used to be assumed that only people with white (or rather, "flesh-colored") skins could build and operate machines. That is no longer arguable. The truth is that, within the limits of individual "talent," anybody can learn to play the piano; anybody can learn to operate a digital computer; and anybody can learn to operate an electron microscope. Hence any arbitrary exclusion is a cultural disaster.

These are not mere matters of humanitarianism. I mention them because although we have been doing the right things, we have quite generally done them for the wrong reasons. Humanitarianism is admirable, but stupid; and there is a real danger that we may be making a similar mistake with regard to "human resources" and "human capital." What is really significant in both areas is the removal of institutional barriers to the creativity of technological process. Human beings are not "resources," to be mined or otherwise harvested, and they are not "capital," to be owned and invested—even by themselves. It is the cultural process in which people are participants (or non-participants) which is relevant and significant. Understanding of that process and ideological candor with regard to it are important because what is at stake is nothing less than the life process of mankind.

Let me, by way of summary, try and state my thesis another way. In doing so may I recall again Edwin Cannan's two problems, which I have quoted so often as comprising the best definition of economics which I have ever found: why all of us taken together are as well off or as ill off as we are, and why some are better off and others worse off than the average. As we now stand, two-thirds of the way through the twentieth century, it seems clear that what determines how well off any community may be is its science and industrial arts—the knowledge and skills possessed by that community; and the reason some elements of the community are better off, or worse off, than others is to be found in the institutions by which that community is structured. These two conditions of course affect each other. A rigid and "time-honored" institutional structure will of course resist change and inhibit the growth of knowledge and skills; and a condition of chronic intellectual and technological revolution prevents institutional rigidity and induces institutional obsolescence.

As everyone knows, the latter condition has prevailed to a steadily increasing degree in Western civilization for several centuries. However, institutionalized superstitions die hard. In every society the prevailing degree of well-being is credited to the Defenders of the Faith and, in Veblen's phrase, "anointed keepers of the code." In the Middle Ages these were, of course, the feudal and ecclesiastical nobility. By the eighteenth century these gentry had largely disappeared from the scene and their place had been taken by a financial aristocracy. The doctrine which imputes creative potency to the factors of production (from which land has disappeared with the landed aristocracy while "the co-ordinating function" hails the arrival of corporate managers) is of course a myth appropriate to this condition.

As such it is already obsolete. Scarcely anybody believes it any more, since today everybody knows that all of us taken together are as well off as we are—and we are far better off than mankind has ever been before—not because of the anguished sweat of laborers or the abstinence or prudence of investors and not even because of the adroitness of managers in effecting tax-avoiding mergers, but because of the amazing discoveries which have become common knowledge and the almost incredible potency of instruments that are now in common use. We are all so well off that we are quite content to let the institutional system ride. After all it is not very ancient, and its ideology is not altogether archaic. How much easier it is to supplement the incomes of those who are worse off than to confiscate the fortunes of those who are better off than anybody has any business to be! Thus we are limning the Welfare State.

Now the Welfare State is a delightful creation. As a place to live it beats anything mankind has ever known. But as an idea it leaves something to be desired. All its emphasis is on distribution and consumption, and it is our ideological responsibility as students to recognize this defect. The defect may be only ideological. It may prove that a happy, healthy, and well-informed community is a superbly productive community: that when no one is very much worse off or better off than the common run, all will be more industrious and efficient than any previous community has even been. Nevertheless we must not rely on happenstance. Our ideal is—or should be—the Creative State, or the Creative Society. We favor the Welfare State because it tends to give the whole community what the whole community creates, and in doing so gives the community the greatest possible encouragement to create more, so that all of us taken together will be better off than anybody has ever been before. Thus the Welfare State is the working model of the Creative Society.

C.E. Ayres and the Classical Economists: A Comment

Abraham Hirsch

C. E. Ayres's Presidential Address[1] shows the kind of contribution which "evolutionary" economics can hope to make. I read it with interest and profit. Ayres is disturbed because the concept of "productivity," as often used, "suggests meanings which are not true and [are] exceedingly harmful . . ."[2] and he argues persuasively that there is reason for concern. The more I thought about the address, however, the more uneasy I came to feel, for in the course of developing his thesis Ayres takes the opportunity to attack the "classical economists"[3] in a way which is neither valid nor politic. The net effect of this is to weaken the force of his argument. Were this an isolated instance, one would probably be wise to overlook it, but I fear that it is rather representative of the style of the old "institutional" economists, a feature which makes it relatively easy for an unsympathetic critic to discredit them. This tendency to view "orthodox" economics as the "enemy" which has to be demolished before any real "progress" can be made, or true "understanding" achieved, has done a great deal of harm because it has acted as a screen hiding from the view of those who were not members of the cult the valuable insights which the institutionalists had to convey. It would therefore be well for the new "evolutionary" economists not to follow in the footsteps of their institutionalist predecessors in this regard. Ayres, unfortunately, is in the old tradition.[4] Since this issue is an important one, it is well to consider this aspect of Ayres's paper in some detail.

The author is Associate Professor of Economics at Brooklyn College, City University of New York.

[1]"Ideological Responsibility," this JOURNAL, Vol. I, Nos. 1 and 2, June 1967, pp. 3-12.

[2]*Ibid.*, p. 3.

[3]Ayres does not make clear what he means by "classical economists." Since he specifically includes in this class Frank H. Knight and John Bates Clark (p. 4), his reference is obviously broad and would seem to be synonymous with the more generally used term "orthodox economists," which includes neoclassical and Keynesian economists. It will be so used in what follows.

[4]In the Foreword (p. x) to the second edition of his pioneering book, *The Theory of Economic Progress* (New York, 1962), Ayres tells us that changing circumstances (from 1944, when the book first appeared) made him feel that the book should now begin "affirmatively, with a positive statement of the basic principles with the significance of which it is concerned." This is a step in the right direction, but Ayres does not go nearly far enough, as is shown in his address. The reasons why I feel this way are enumerated in this communication.

My first objection is that Ayres takes it upon himself to tell "classical" economists that they must change their ways. He tells them, for example, that "all of us who know this to be the case [that is, that the concept of productivity is misused] have a public duty to repudiate these suggested meanings and to denounce the whole institutional structure they support."[5] Nor is he content to tell economists that they must fight the dragon. They are, according to Ayres, allies of the dragon. Thus, he accuses economists of still adhering to J. B. Clark's "myth of creativity," and thereby being major contributors to "the preservation of the traditionally stratified order of society."[6] To the possible objection that one should not interpret economic theory in a way which, in the words of Frank Knight (quoted by Ayres), leads one to act on "the vastly simplified postulates that are legitimate and necessary for the first stage of economic analysis—but which should never be taken as describing reality, and still less as normative,"[7] Ayres answers: "since economic analysis should never be taken as describing reality, and since presumably it is economic reality with which we wish to deal, we had better abandon this so-called analysis completely and forthwith."[8] Here we have it: Ayres is not content to add a dimension to economic thought. In order to make way for the kind of insights which he has to offer, he feels constrained to denigrate an important part of the work which has been and is being done in economics. I do not think this is necessary. There is no incompatibility between economic analysis (even marginal productivity theory) and evolutionary economics. An indication of why I believe this to be so is given in what follows.

My second objection is that while it is no doubt true that *some* economists[9] hold the ideological views that Ayres attributes to economists, it does not seem at all typical of the economics profession today. Since textbooks in basic economics reveal the beliefs of economists in most unsubtle and least guarded form, I went to the most popular among them, Samuelson's famous opus,[10] to check on Ayres's accusations. I could find no positive evidence to support them. I could find nothing in Samuelson which suggests that in a market system the factors "earn" what they receive (whatever the state of competition) and are therefore

[5]"Ideological Responsibility," p. 3.

[6]*Ibid.,* pp. 3, 7-8.

[7]Quoted in *ibid.,* p. 8, from a review article by Knight, "Abstract Economics and Absolute Ethics," in *Ethics,* Vol. LXVI, 1966.

[8]"Ideological Responsibility," p. 8. Ayres merely uses this negative conclusion as a point of departure in developing his positive proposal. Happily, neither the validity nor potential fruitfulness of his thesis depends on the validity of his negative conclusion.

[9]And, of course, a large proportion of businessmen and politicians hold such views.

[10]Paul A. Samuelson, *Economics: An Introductory Analysis,* 7th ed., New York, 1967.

entitled to it. Quite the contrary: Samuelson makes it quite clear that the marginal productivity theory concerns itself with the question of *pricing* only,[11] and he takes the trouble to show how an ethically desirable distribution of income (which differs from the one brought about by market forces) might be achieved.[12] Nor do I find in Samuelson's book any suggestion that because in a market system the factors receive what they "earn," they thereby are given the greatest incentive to produce, thus making the market system the most productive one.[13] Samuelson makes clear that the "ideal" which is postulated by micro-theory is only the ideal of pricing policy to achieve the best allocation of resources compatible with given valuations.[14] In fact, were Samuelson to believe that marginal productivity theory postulates the kind of ideal that Ayres attributes to it, the large amount of material on economic growth in his text would be quite superfluous.[15]

Actually, one can find evidence to refute Ayres's broad attack even in "classical" works which are anything but contemporary. For example, John Stuart Mill tells us:

> The laws and conditions of the Production of wealth partake of the character of physical truths. . . . It is not so with the distribution of wealth. That is a matter of human institutions solely. . . . The distribution of wealth, therefore, depends on the laws and customs of society. The rules by which it is determined are what the opinions and feelings of the ruling portion of the community make them, and are very different, in different ages and countries; and might be still more different, if mankind so choose.[16]

Of course, not all economists have had this insight, and even those who did, have shown tendencies to backslide on occasion. We might then, with good reason, take it as our responsibility to call the culprits to task.[17] But is this a reason to condemn *all* classical economists and to argue that economic analysis must be thrown out?

As a third point, I would argue that Ayres leaves himself open to the charge that he has not understood some of the subtleties of economic

[11] *Ibid.*, pp. 509, 520, 611.

[12] *Ibid.*, Appendix to Chapter 32.

[13] Samuelson clearly has doubts. Cf. *ibid.*, pp. 789-792.

[14] *Ibid.*, Appendix to Chapter 32.

[15] *Ibid.*, Chapters 37-39.

[16] John Stuart Mill, *Principles of Political Economy*, New York, 1936, pp. 199-200.

[17] We might also point out how authors of traditional texts might improve their presentations. For example, Samuelson shows proper concern for economic incentives so far as taxation is concerned, but he fails even to suggest the *possibility* that even if incentives are somewhat impaired through taxation, total output on balance in the long run might be increased if the proceeds of the taxes are used productively.

theory. For one, he gives the following quotation from Frank Knight:

> The "communist" nations must follow extensively the principle of productivity or "middle of the road," and even "marginalism," to achieve any efficiency or to make the economy function at all. And they lose much efficiency by pretending to the contrary, and especially by pretending not to recognize "capital" as productive. This is true regardless of who has the title to the property in which it is embodied or what the status of laborers or managers is.[18]

On the basis of this, Ayres concludes that Knight, like "the whole succession of classical economists . . . [means] that capital is 'productive' in the same sense that labor is productive, and therefore has a valid claim on the gross national product regardless of who profits by that claim."[19] To Ayres, "such propositions are imputations of magic potency and would be instantly recognizable as such by all of us except for the fact that they are fragments of the system of make-believe to which we all have been emotionally conditioned all of our lives."[20]

This is hard to understand. Ayres seems to have fired a good missile but hit the wrong target. What Knight is talking about in the quoted passage is obviously the problem of factor pricing to achieve the best use of resources with given valuations, no matter who does the valuing. The virtue of attributing "productivity" to capital in *this* sense is that it simplifies the job of administration in the socialist state and thereby helps to avoid costly errors.[21] The "magic" which Ayres sees in this analysis is something he has read into it. There seems not the remotest suggestion in this passage, any more than there is in Samuelson's treatment of marginal productivity theory, that what we mean when we say capital is "productive" is that it has a valid claim on the gross product.

Ayres likewise leaves himself vulnerable when he concludes from Knight's admission that economic analysis does not describe reality because the analysis oversimplifies it and that, therefore, anyone truly concerned with economic reality must abandon the analysis. To an undergraduate such a conclusion might seem "obvious" but it is not very profound. Nor is it bolstered by the (correct) observation that economic analysis is tautological.[22] I would argue that to show that economic theory is tautological and why, and what the consequences are, is one of the tasks that evolutionary economists should take on. Careful analysis along these lines would *not* show, however, that because the analysis is tauto-

[18]This is quoted on p. 3 by Ayres from Knight, "Abstract Economics and Absolute Ethics."

[19]"Ideological Responsibility," p. 4.

[20]*Ibid.*, p. 5.

[21]Errors, that is, as conceived by the valuers themselves, be they consumers or government officials.

[22]"Ideological Responsibility," p. 7.

logical it is thereby useless or irrelevant, as Ayres assumes. Unfortunately, to develop this point in a meaningful way would require a rather lengthy article, and so we must limit ourselves here to a brief observation.[23] Since it is Knight who is picked on by Ayres, a telling point immediately comes to mind. One need go no further than Knight's best-known essay, "The Ethics of Competition,"[24] to see *one* important use to which "classical" economic analysis can be put; namely, it can be used to develop a devastating critique of the vary brand of ideology which Ayres is against.

My final objection derives from Ayres's statement in the last paragraph: "We favor the Welfare State because it tends to give the whole community what the whole community creates, and in doing so gives the community the greatest possible encouragement to create more, so that all of us taken together will be better off than anybody has ever been before."[25] The sentiments expressed are noble, but the passage suggests that Ayres is not against ideology *per se* but opposes only a particular brand of ideology which he wishes to replace with another. And here, perhaps, is the crux of the matter. Ayres can be so cavalier with "classical" economic analysis because he is concerned with the "big" questions.[26] There is nothing wrong with one's concerning oneself with the big questions, of course, but room should be left for those who feel that they can go further by concentrating on the smaller ones. In fact, I would argue that if most economists were to turn in Ayres's direction, it would indeed be unfortunate.[27] Our chances of making progress are far better if economists devote themselves to such questions as how income inequality and the size of output are related—in which analysis and detailed observation are involved—than in fighting the battle of ideologies. And it would help if we give up the practice of looking for ideological ghosts wherever "classical" economists fail to deal adequately with a subject. That is not to say that inadequacies should not be pointed up or that ideological bias masquerading as economic theory, *where it is found,* should not be exposed. Here is another important job for evolu-

[23]I have dealt peripherally with this question in "J. Laurence Laughlin, Wesley Clair Mitchell and the Quantity Theory of Money," *Journal of Political Economy,* Vol. LXXXI, December 1967.

[24]Frank H. Knight, "The Ethics of Competition," *Quarterly Journal of Economics,* Vol. XXXVII, 1923, reprinted in *The Ethics of Competition and Other Essays,* New York, 1951.

[25]"Ideological Responsibility," p. 11.

[26]A non-ideological approach would involve considering such relationships as that between income distribution and the size of total output, both analytically and empirically.

[27]In *The Theory of Economic Progress,* pp. 18-19, Ayres quotes Colin Clark to the effect that "there is room for two or three economic theorists in each generation, not more." Does this not hold even more for ideologists?

tionary economics. But a return to the ideological battleground would be a backward step. Our major professional responsibility, it seems to me, is to avoid the *wholesale* acceptance or rejection of *any* school of thought.

Neoinstitutionalism and the Economics of Dissent

Allan G. Gruchy

It is a pleasure to bring the honor of serving as President of the Association for Evolutionary Economics to a close with the opportunity to discuss some of the intellectual currents running through our Association. Since the Association is a very young organization, its future is quite naturally a matter of very great concern to all of us. I am not going to attempt to predict the future of our Association. However, I know that it was in the minds of its founders, when they came together in Washington, D. C., nine years ago, that this Association should have a unique function to perform—one not performed by old line economic associations. However otherwise this unique function may be described, it is clearly that of providing an outlet for economic dissent—dissent from what goes under the heading of conventional or standard economics.

If ever there was a fortunate coincidence, it was that the Association for Evolutionary Economics was organized at a time when dissent in many fields was running high. It is my conviction that this Association has a golden opportunity to provide a forum for economic dissenters at a time when old line economic associations and the economics profession in general are not providing the intellectual leadership called for by the times. Economic dissenters like Clarence E. Ayres, John K. Galbraith, Gunnar Myrdal, Adolph Lowe, Gerhard Colm, and others of a similar intellectual bent assert that conventional economics, as one sees it in standard economics textbooks and advanced economic writings, is hobbled with an excessively narrow view of the science of economics that concentrates on means and not ends; on inputs and not outputs; and on efficiency without asking the question of efficiency for what? The economics profession today directs its main energy to turning out technicians of knowledge who are experts in optimizing the decision-making process, but who do not display much concern for the purposes or goals of this decision-making. Our successful conventional economics textbook writers, following Lionel Robbins with his vintage 1925 definition of economic science, have given wide circulation to the idea that economics is concerned primarily with means and not with ends. It is not surprising then that in the current era of great crisis with respect to goals or values, conventional economics, having little to say about such ends, has become quite

The author is Professor of Economics at the University of Maryland. This paper was the presidential address for the 1968 Association for Evolutionary Economics's convention in Chicago, Illinois, December 27-29. All articles in this issue were papers presented at the same convention.

irrelevant to much of what concerns the man on the street or the student on the college campus. If ever there was a need to make economics a more relevant science, that need is now pressing for attention. Meeting this need is the aim of the economic dissent coming from Ayres, Galbraith, Myrdal, and other critics of conventional economics.

These dissenting economists, as scientists, do not propose to tell the people what goals they should seek to achieve. However, they do propose to explain to the people how their wants or goals come into being, how these wants are greatly influenced by the large industrial corporations, how collective wants in the public sector are frequently unmet because there are no strong lobbying forces at work in the public sector promoting these collective wants, how obstacles are placed in the path of meeting wants not catered to by the private market place, how the failure of the private sector to take full account of all social costs not only lowers the quality of life but also indirectly lowers the productivity of labor, and how our archaic governmental system is unprepared today to take a comprehensive view of national needs or to take the necessary steps with the cooperation of the public to make sure that these national needs are assigned proper priority.

Economic dissent falls into two categories. There are first those dissenters who criticize the way that the current economic system operates and who disapprove of many of the consequences of these operations. These dissenters usually operate outside the academic world and do not concern themselves with the inadequacies of standard or conventional economics. I am referring to such dissenters as Michael Harrington, Vance Packard, Ralph Nader, William H. Whyte, David Bazelon, and even Rachel Carson, who wondered if the day would come when our chemical companies would have achieved the miracle of a "silent spring." These dissenters have vividly and forcefully called attention to our noisy, dirty, and ugly cities, to the pollution of air and water, to the destruction of our heritage of buildings and urban areas of great historical significance, to the need to preserve the last landscape, and to the spread of what one critic has called the "materialistic Babbitism" of our affluent society.

The second group of economic dissenters is comprised of the academic world whose main concern is the inadequacies of conventional economics. Academic dissenters range from those at one end of the scale who simply want somehow to make standard economics more realistic to those at the other end of the scales who would reconstruct conventional economics into more social and less technical science. Those academic economic dissenters, who would be satisfied if conventional economics were made more realistic, argue that there should be more empirical feedback in the work of the conventional economic theorists so that conventional economic theory and economic practice would be more closely related. Dissent of this negative and unchallenging nature deplores the use of excessive abstraction and would like to see conventional economics shored up with the aid of more empirical studies.

Other economic dissenters in the academic world assert that conventional economics is too limited in scope, and that, since human problems are frequently more than economic in nature, an interdisciplinary approach is necessary if we are to tackle these problems successfully. The weaknesses or deficiencies of conventional economics are to be overcome not by reconstructing this economics, but by combining conventional economics with the other social sciences in the work of dealing with human problems. Those economic dissenters who merely want conventional economics to have more empirical feedback, or who would integrate conventional economics with the other social sciences in an interdisciplinary approach, present no basic challenge to conventional economics. This is so because the basics of conventional economics, as incorporated in its narrow definition of the nature and the scope of economic science, are left intact by the academic dissenters of the types just described.

There is a third and more fundamental type of academic economic dissent that is a distinct challenge to the view of economics held by standard or conventional economists. This type of dissent is positive and constructive in the sense that it challenges the view of economics cultivated by conventional economists and offers a different view of economics to replace that of the conventional economists. The economic dissenters who, I believe, present a constructive challenge to economic orthodoxy of both the Marshallian and Keynesian types include such well-known economists as Clarence E. Ayres, John K. Galbraith, Gunnar Myrdal, Gerhard Colm, and Adolph Lowe. Their economics I describe as neoinstitutional economics.

Perhaps some will think that I should apologize for calling attention to the institutionalist movement in economic thought. I know that in the minds of a majority of academic economists institutional economics is now regarded as something that has had its day and, as Professor Kenneth Boulding said a decade or so ago at one of these conventions, should now be placed among the museum exhibits. This attitude towards institutionalism was brought forcefully to my attention two years ago when I accidentally fell into the company of a young graduate student in economics from one of the most prestigious universities on the West Coast. Upon being introduced to me, this young student said that he was happy to shake my hand as he understood that I was the last of the institutionalists. I am sure that this young graduate was faithfully reproducing the views and opinions of the distinguished economics professors in that far western economics graduate school.

Whether or not this conventional view of institutional economics is wishful thinking—and I think it is—the fact remains that today we have a large body of economic thought that lies outside the boundaries of conventional economics. More than this it presents a significant challenge to conventional economics. My examination of the work of Ayres and others with a similar approach to economics leads me to the views that these critics of conventional economics are working in the institutionalist tradition, and that we can properly regard their work as basically an extension of the work of Veblen, Sombart, Hobson, Commons, Clark, Mitchell, and other heterodox economists of the first three decades of this century. However, the work of Galbraith, Colm, Lowe, and Myrdal is not the work of mere disciples. Thorstein Veblen has not cast his long shadow over these present-day institutionalists. None of these economists except for Ayres was influenced greatly in his formative years by Veblen and his work. For reasons to which I shall soon turn I prefer to call the work of current institutionalists "neoinstitutional economics" to distinguish it from the "old institutionalism" of Veblen.

The intellectual image that Veblen presented is significantly different from the image presented by the neoinstitutionalists. Veblen gave the impression that he would dispense with the inherited analytical or marginalist economics of his time, and that the mechanics or technics of economic decision-making would have no place in his technocratic regime of workmanship of the future. Also, Veblen did not clearly indicate what he thought were his own theoretical contributions with the result that both he and later institutionalists were criticized on the ground that they had not only dispensed with conventional economic theory, but had also put nothing in its place. Furthermore, Veblen's emphasis on the discipline of the machine process opened him to the criticism made by the conventional economists that his work was adversely affected by the acceptance of an untenable technological determinism.

The view that Veblen was an unsophisticated technocrat with little regard for the niceties of standard economic theory persists to this very day. As recently as 1968 Raymond Aron asserted that "Veblen made the mistake of thinking that the industrial order—the order of production—was sufficient unto itself," and was not subject "to the requirements of economic calculation."[1] Whether or not these views concerning the work of Veblen are well-founded—and I believe that they are not—they continue to find widespread acceptance among conventional economists. Such criticisms, however, cannot be made against the neoinstitutionalists, since they have been careful to avoid opening themselves to the criticisms to which Veblen has been subjected. The neoinstitutionalists cannot be described as anti-theoretical technocrats; they do not dispense with the basic building blocks of standard economic theory; and they avoid what is alleged to be Veblen's technological determinism. What the neoinstitutionalists do is to round out the standard or conventional economics of our time by making economics less of a technical and more of a social science. Of special importance in this connection is the neoinstitutionalists's theory of the modern industrial system with its central concept of the logic of the process of industrialization.

The neoinstitutionalists very clearly state that they have taken much

[1]Aron, Raymond, *Progress and Disillusion,* 1968, p. 187.

from the work of standard economists of the past and the present. Ayres, for example, explains in *The Industrial Society*: "This is not to say that all the inquiries of all the economists have been a complete waste of time. . . . The investigations of economists have given us a wealth of knowledge of price relationships the effect of which is to show how the various economic activities affect each other. All this is of great value."[2] Galbraith tells us in *The New Industrial State,* in referring to the work of standard economists, "I have drawn on their work, quantitative and qualitative, at every stage; I could not have written without their prior efforts."[3] Likewise François Perroux in his article on the domination effect of large industrial corporations informs us that his excursions beyond conventional economics involve no disavowal of standard economic theory.[4] Rather than dispense entirely with conventional economics, the neoinstitutionalists accept it for what it is worth, and then go beyond it to develop a broader economics which is concerned not only with decision-making in the market place, but also with the guidance of the larger evolving economic system. It is precisely at this point that the neoinstitutionalists part company with the conventional economists. The neoinstitutionalists have a larger view of economic reality which leads them to believe that their version of economics is much more relevant to the major problems of our time.

The contrast between the conventional economists and neoinstitutional economists is quite clearly indicated by inquiring into what these two types of economists think economics is all about. The conventional line, as presented in some of our most successful economics textbooks, is that, there is no consumer problem, since, as Professor Paul Samuelson puts it, "What things will be produced is determined by the votes of consumers . . . every day in their decisions to purchase this item or that."[5] In other words, student readers of these textbooks are informed that the market mechanism ordinarily satisfies consumer wants, but does not create them even though we annually spend 17 billion dollars on advertising. Furthermore, from the conventional point of view, deviations from a perfectly competitive economic system can be taken care of adequately by appropriate antitrust measures and various forms of the public regulation of industry. Since the allocation of resources in our mixed enterprise system is said to present no real problem, the only big issue is the rate of economic growth or the annual increase in real gross national product. According to conventional economists there is nothing like increases in gross national product to measure an economy's performance. Professor

[2]Ayres, Clarence E., *The Industrial Economy,* 1952, p. 36.

[3]Galbraith, John Kenneth, *The New Industrial State,* 1967, p. 402.

[4]Perroux, Francois, "The Domination Effect and Modern Economic Theory," *Social Research,* Vol. 17, No. 2, June 1950, p. 188.

[5]Samuelson, Paul A., *Economics, An Introductory Analysis,* Sixth Edition, 1964, p. 40.

Campbell McConnell tells us in his widey read textbook that national income accounting "allows us to keep tab on the economic health of society. . . . It is generally agreed . . . that the best available indicator of an economy's health is its annual total output of goods and services."[6]

According to the neoinstitutionalists this view of the measure of an economy's health does not stand up under close scrutiny. This is so because the national income accounting that is presented in our most widely used economics textbooks is an incomplete and biased form of accounting. It takes note of all the "goods" produced, but leaves out what Joan Robinson has called "negative goods," or what Ezra J. Mishan in his study of *The Costs of Economic Growth* calls the "bads." We know why conventional national income accounting accounts only for "goods," and ignores "bads" or the social costs of economic growth. The answer is that "goods" can be quantified and measured in the market place, but "bads" in the form of social disamenities frequently cannot be quantified, and so do not appear in the market place. This "goods-bads" problem is readily handled by conventional economists largely by ignoring it. One very well-known conventional economist, who felt constrained to make at least some mention of the vital difference between pecuniary and real social costs in his textbook, calls the attention of his student readers to this problem in a footnote in an appendix to a chapter.

It is all so very clear to the conventional economist: every extra billion dollars's worth of gross national product marks a step forward toward a healthier economy. As Professor Samuelson explains, "Although [economic] growth presents challenges, the subject is really a cheerful one."[7] Of course this is an unfortunate case of circular reasoning. Economic health is measured in terms of gross national product, and an increase in gross national product is regarded as an improvement in economic health. According to Colm, Galbraith, Myrdal, and other neoinstitutionalists, conventional national income accounting as it is currently used is a poor device for measuring economic health. Economic health is not something that can always be quantified. It is a condition that can be approached or improved by creating some things and by not creating other things—by creating "goods" and by not creating "bads," with the people, led by protest groups and aided by technical experts, deciding what is a "good" and what is a "bad." The neoinstitutionalists would say that an affluent society is healthy when its resources are allocated in such a way as to create not only an abundance of goods and services, but also cities free from excessive noise, pollution, and ugliness where citizens have adequate leisure, when they are fully informed about the social costs of economic growth, when nature's balance is preserved, and when industrial technology is adjusted to mankind and not mankind to technology.

[6]McConnell, Campbell R., *Economics: Principles, Problems, and Policies,* Second Edition, 1963, p. 166.

[7]Samuelson, Paul A., p. 792.

Gunnar Myrdal speaks for the neoinstitutionalists when he states that the ultimate purpose of economics is to "find out where we are heading."[8] Or, in other words, whose goals does the economic system serve, and whose goals does it fail to serve? In Myrdal's opinion, and also that of other neoinstitutionalists, the ultimate purpose of economics is to provide an interpretation of the way in which the industrial system operates with respect to the satisfaction of personal and collective wants or goals. To put the matter simply, the contrast between conventional and neoinstitutional economics is a contrast between "market economics" and "systems economics."

The main issue today in the field of economics, in the opinion of the neoinstitutionalists, is not "efficiency," but rather it is wants, goals, or values. In the past few decades standard economists have made great strides in developing the theory of optimizing or economizing. The theory of economic decision-making has been improved by important advances in both mathematical economics and econometrics. While economizing the use of scarce resources or inputs will always be a matter of great importance to all economists and to the general public, economizing or optimizing the use of scarce resources is not what is of major importance today to a large part of the population in an affluent society. The main concern today of an important section of the general population in Western Europe and the United States is not how to use scarce inputs more efficiently, but how to get the economic system to serve the people by producing what they want, or would want if they were free agents, free from dominating influence of the large industrial corporations which control much of the press, radio, and television, and so are able to impose their scheme of values on the general public. There is a growing concern today with the following three value problems which are of great interest to the neoinstitutionalist critics of conventional economics: (1) to what extent are wants or goals in the private sector of the nation's economic system created by producers and not by consumers, with the result that consumers are induced to purchase a never-ending flow of consumer gadgets and other goods of doubtful private and social utility; (2) what obstacles are placed in the path of collective want determination in the public sector by forces working from out of the private sector, and by the archaic and ineffective institutional arrangements found in our public sector; and (3) to what extent does conventional economics ignore the social costs of economic growth in the form of external diseconomies such as air and water pollution, the spoilation of the natural environment, and the destruction of the nation's historical heritage by the bulldozer and the speculating land developer—all of which lower the quality of life.

The neoinstitutionalists observe that the economic system is a goal- or want-directed system. Individuals, groups, and classes participate in the activities of the economic system with the aim of securing their wants or

[8] Myrdal, Gunnar, *An International Economy, Problems and Prospects,* 1956, p. 314.

goals. The economic system is not a monolithic system or metaphysical entity which gives expression to some vague national interest that is supposed to be common to all individuals and groups. The American economic system is not a monolithic capitalist system. On the contrary, there is in the American economy the state capitalism of the public sector, the large-scale capitalism of the big business sector, and the small-scale, laissez-faire capitalism of small business and the farmers. The economy moves to a great extent in the direction of the goals of those individuals and groups who have enough power to influence the economy and guide it towards the satisfaction of their wants.

The neoinstitutionalists define economics to be the study of the evolving pattern of human relationships which is concerned with the disposal of scarce resources for the satisfaction of personal and collective wants. What the neoinstitutionalists do is to place economizing or economic decision-making within the framework of the evolving economic system. Since the economic sytem's ulitmate concern is with human wants or goals and how they are achieved, economizing is tied up with wants or goals; and the main question confronting economists should be optimizing or economizing for what purposes or goals.

The conventional economist precludes any analysis of the existing and emerging goals of individuals and groups and the question as to whether or not these wants are being achieved, by defining economics so as to exclude the wants or goals problem. Professor Samuelson, in defining economics, states, "As a science, economics can concern itself only with the best means of attaining given ends."[9] Professor McConnell has expressed the same view much more succinctly with the observation that economics is "the science of efficiency."[10] Duplicating Samuelson and McConnell, conventional economists reduce economics to the technical subject of economic decision-making or decision theory in which, as one specialist in decision theory recently explained, "Rationality, as decision theorists think of it, has nothing to do with what you want, but only with how you go about implementing your wants."[11] The conventional economist asserts that economists have no business inquiring into the nature or origins of human wants or goals, because people are said to know what they want and to cast dollar votes for what they want. In effect, what the conventional economist says is that the market mechanism is a want-serving or want-satisfying mechanism. The neoinstitutionalists disagree with the conventional view of the nature of the market mechanism and assert that in the modern industrial society the market mechanism is in many cases a want-creating mechanism. Consumers do not always freely

[9]Samuelson, Paul A., *Economics, An Introductory Analysis,* First Edition, 1948, p. 314.

[10]McConnell, Campbell R., p. 25.

[11]Ward, Edwards, "Decision Making," *International Encyclopedia of the Social Sciences,* Vol. 4, 1968, p. 35.

express what they want through dollar votes. Instead, they buy what the large corporations induce them to buy with the aid of advertising and high-pressure or subtle salesmanship.

According to Galbraith, Myrdal, Ayres and other critics of conventional economics, the social system, including the economic system, is an institutional arrangement by means of which people seek to achieve their wants. To the social scientist people are goal-creating, goal-possessing, and goal-achieving individuals, and the social sciences, including economics, are properly concerned with the goals or wants of people. Economic goals are data which can be documented, analyzed with regard to their origins and what influences have shaped them, the conflicts among these goals, their impact on the nation's production and distribution systems, and what aids or militates against their being achieved. These goals can be treated objectively, and the scientific method can be applied to them in the sense that generalizations can be made about them. There is nothing normative about any such want or goal analysis. What is being done is to widen the scope of economic analysis to include studies of existing means and existing economic goals and their interrelationships. It is for this reason that Ayres states, "Economics is nothing if it is not a science of value."[12]

When the neoinstitutionalists, along with Ayres, state that economics is a science not of efficiency but of values, they are not raising any normative issues in the form of what "ought" to be. What they do say is that economics, viewed not as a technical but as a social science, deals with the material aspects of values or wants. The economist as a social scientist is concerned not with efficiency alone, but with efficiency in relation to the wants of the individuals and groups operating within the evolving economic system. These individuals and groups are interested in such wants as economic abundance, economic freedom, economic security, economic justice, and economic quality. The economist as a social scientist is interested in explaining how the evolving industrial system supplies these wants or does not provide them, how these wants may be achieved with the use of scarce resources, how individuals and groups are in conflict with regard to whose wants should be assigned a high priority, and how conflicts with regard to the satisfaction of wants may be reduced or eliminated.

In an affluent society consideration of people's wants or goals may take precedence over considerations of economic efficiency. A rich nation can afford at times to be somewhat inefficient if this inefficiency preserves wants or values that would be destroyed by asking for the utmost in efficiency. It may be more efficient to string power lines between poles rather than to place them underground, to put a transmission line through a Civil War battlefield rather than around it, to put a super highway through a wilderness area rather than around it, or to put former slum dwellers in unlivable 15-storied tenement buildings rather than in livable low-lying

[12]Ayres, Clarence E., *The Theory of Economic Progress,* 1944, p. 208.

garden apartments—but in an affluent society these efficiencies in the opinion of many protest groups are not worth the price in human disamenities.

The difference between the conventional view of economics as a narrow study of economic decision-making and the neoinstitutionalist view of economics as a broad study of the evolving goal-directed economic system is also the difference between a short-run view and a long-run view of the economic system. Gunnar Myrdal has severely criticized conventional economists on the ground that they are nearsighted and without a long-range view of the development of the industrial system. He tells us in the *Challenge to Affluence* that among "the things that have not changed in America and specifically in Washington during different administrations is . . . a general tendency to nearsightedness among both politicians and [economic] experts. . . . There are today an astonishing number of people in the United States who can offhand give a detailed and comprehensive analysis in quantitative terms of what is just now happening [in the business world], how all important economic indices have recently been moving, and how they are likely to move months ahead. Not only the President and Congress but also leaders in business are left without that intellectualized vision of what the future holds in store in regard to economic development in more general terms. But such a vision is needed for rational decision [-making]. . . . It is difficult to avoid the reflection that the neglect by government agencies as well as by American universities and other research institutions of the long range aspects of the American economy as a whole and the undue concentration on short-range issues . . . on timeless and by any standards less important terminological questions and unworldly [theoretical] constructs . . . all this is partly responsible for the failure of . . . economists to disseminate more economic understanding among the American people."[13]

When the economist takes a long view of the economy, he necessarily views the economy as an evolving system. The question then arises, can one develop a theory of the evolving economic system? The answer of Ayres, Galbraith and Myrdal to this question is that the evolving industrial system can be explained with the aid of the concept of the logic of the process of industrialization. The neoinstitutionalists would be the first to say that, while there are no universal economic laws governing the course of industrialization, the process of industrialization is not a haphazard, utterly random process which follows no discernible path. The neoinstitutionalists assert that there is a logic or pattern running through the process of industrialization. Clark Kerr has explained in *Industrialism and the Industrial Man* that there is a "pure logic of the industrial process" which reveals the inherent tendencies of this process. Kerr goes on to explain that: "Given the character of science and technology and the requirements inherent in modern methods of production and distribution," we may

[13]Myrdal, Gunnar, *Challenge to Affluence,* 1962, pp. 87-88.

deduce the likely characteristics and path of the evolving industrial system.[14] To the neoinstitutionalist, if not to the conventional economist, the general features of the process of industrialization are clear. These features constitute a pattern or logic through which all mature industrial nations have passed or are passing. The logic of the process of industrialization points in the direction of an urbanized society, a decline of the free competitive market, the rise of a large public sector, the separation of the managers and the managed, the emergence of conflicting economic power groups, the elevation of natural science over social science, and the development of the government as an agent mediating among conflicting economic power groups and providing guidance for the evolving economy.

The concept of the logic of the process of industrialization lies between the universal laws of pure economics and mere description. It is an explanatory device that finds a place for both quantitative and qualitative factors in explaining the nature and functioning of the modern industrial system. Conventional economists have no place in their analyses for the concept of the logic of industrialization, because by definition they exclude from economic analysis all consideration of the impact of technological change on the structure and functioning of the economy. They agree with Lionel Robbins who states that "Ends as such do not form part of this subject-matter [of economics]. Nor does the technical and social environment."[15]

The technological explosion works its way out very largely through the operations of the economic system; yet the conventional economists pay little attention to how this explosion is affecting both the economic decision-making process and the larger total economic process. The conventional economist can sit idly by without explaining how the technological revolution of the past few decades further urbanizes our society, clogs our roads and air lanes, pollutes our air and water, upsets the balance of nature, unites the nation with ribbons of concrete, dangerously raises the noise level of our environment, and fills our houses with a vast array of gadgets limited in number and variety only by the fertile and highly paid imagination of those in charge of the research and development departments of our large business corporations.

One of the major issues of today is who will harness the technological explosion, the large industrial corporation or the public as represented by the government? Who will plan the flow of technological change spurred on by scientific research, who will make certain that adequate account is taken of the social costs of technological progress, and how will the benefits of the technological revolution be shared? Will the contributions of scientific research be used largely to meet the commercial objectives of

[14]Kerr, Clark; Dunlop, John T.; Harbison, Frederick H.; and Myers, Charles A., *Industrialism and Industrial Man,* 1960, p. 33.

[15]Robbins, Lionel, *An Essay on the Nature and Significance of Economic Science,* Second Edition, 1935, p. 38.

industry or the welfare objectives of the general public? According to Galbraith, Ayres, Myrdal and other neoinstitutionalists modern industrial technology points in the direction of some form of national economic planning. Technology is a cultural imperative or "compulsion" that gives shape or pattern to the process of industrialization. As Galbraith puts it, "Technology, under all circumstances, leads to planning; in its higher manifestations it may put the problems of planning beyond the reach of the industrial firm."[16] In the opinion of the neoinstitutionalists it is no longer a question of planning or not planning, but what kind of planning and who will direct the planning. The neoinstitutionalists assert that it is up to economists to explain to the public the consequences of the alternatives of planning by private industry, or of planning by the government in cooperation with the nation's economic interest groups. Not much can be expected with regard to these issues from conventional economists, because their absorbing interest in the economics of decision-making prevents their viewing the economy as an evolving system, and also prevents their developing the long and comprehensive view necessary for analyzing the problems of a guided industrial society.

Simplistic conventional economics leads to simplistic economic policy proposals. When one looks at the superficiality of conventional economic analysis and all the important and complicating economic factors that it leaves out of account, it is not surprising that some conventional economists propose to solve our basic economic problems, as would Professor Milton Friedman and other monetarists, by simply making adjustments in the nation's supply of money relative to the changing size of the gross national product, while other simplists, the proponents of the so-called "new economics," propose to solve the same problems by simply altering tax rates in a countercyclical manner. The long, non-simplistic view of the economy held by the neoinstitutionalists suggests to them that complicated economic problems can probably be solved only in complicated ways. According to the neoinstitutionalists the "new economics" of the Kennedy and Johnson Administration can never successfully handle the long-term goals problem, because its main attention is on the employment and growth rates of tomorrow, not on the long-term national goals of the future. No one denies that full employment and rapid economic growth are important, short-run goals, but more important questions are full employment and rapid economic growth for what? It does not seem very rational to develop a finely-tuned economic engine without asking where it is going—without asking whether it is on the low road to commercialized affluence or on the high road to what Ayres calls a "reasonable society."

The industrialization process has not yet come to an end. We are now moving from an advanced industrial society to a post-industrial society. In the opinion of the neoinstitutionalists we are now entering a post-industrial era in which the economic power of the large industrial corporations

[16]Galbraith, John Kenneth, *Industrial State,* p. 20.

is being challenged by what George Kennan describes as "protest groups" which spearhead the development of public opinion and unite the weak economic interest groups. In the post-industrial society of the future the guidance of the economy will come less from the big business sector and more from the nation's educational, scientific, and artistic groups as well as from aroused citizens in general. The basic problem is, how will national priorities be determined in the post-industrial society? Before this problem can be met satisfactorily, new institutional arrangements will have to be made. We will have to substitute a new participatory democracy for our current outmoded ballot-box type of democracy which may have been adequate for the nineteenth century but which is obviously unable to cope with the problems raised by a technological society. It is now necessary to bring together representatives of all economic interest groups for the joint consideration of what should be the nation's economic and social priorities. Much progress along this line has been made in Western Europe where the United Kingdom has its National Economic Development Council, the Netherlands its Economic and Social Council, and Sweden, France, Belgium and other countries their similar joint councils.

There is no major nation so ill prepared as the United States to cope with the problem of determining national economic and social priorities. Although the Employment Act of 1946 opens the doors to the possibility of joint consultation by representatives from major economic interest groups, the Council of Economic Advisers under all administrations has consistently refused to provide for any such joint consultation, preferring to approach each interest group, if at all, on a separate basis. Consequently, national priority determination in the United States has become a running contest between the Office of the President with his troika or quadriad of governmental advisers and the Congress. The group that should provide a bridge between the President and the Congress, namely the presidential cabinet, is conspicuous for its docility and the infrequency of its meetings. The Congress has no adequate way of comparing and analyzing the nation's total resources and total needs, since, unlike most legislative bodies in Western Europe, it does not have presented to it for its consideration any annual and long-term national economic budgets of the kind recommended by Gerhard Colm, Gunnar Myrdal, Adolph Lowe, and François Perroux. In this connection the Congress does not lack the power to determine national priorities. What it does lack is an effective way of determining these priorities.

The New York *Times* recently reported that President-elect Nixon had said that national priorities are determined in the White House. This is a gross and misleading oversimplification of the national priorites problem. In fact national priorities are determined in part in the White House, but also in the Congress, in the large business enterprises, in the trade unions, increasingly in the ghettos, and elsewhere. Each economic interest group is out more or less on its own to advocate the acceptance of its own goals as something worthy of high priority consideration. But there are no well-established institutional arrangements for getting these various competing economic interest groups together for joint consultation with regard to the determination of national priorities. What we have in operation today in the United States is the outmoded advocacy concept of national priority determination which provides no adequate method of communication between the many economic interest groups at the bottom and the Congress at the top. This is an archaic way of determination national priorities that is more appropriate to the nineteenth than to the twentieth century. The neoinstitutionalists point out that the national priority determining process needs to be modernized, and related more effectively to the needs of our emerging participatory democracy. The lag between our political institutions and the rapidly changing industrial technology will have to be eliminated, before we can succeed in domesticating the technological revolution and in planning for the achievement of a life of high quality.

We can anticipate three criticisms levelled against neoinstitutional economies by conventional economists. The standard bearers of conventional economics will assert (1) that the neoinstitutionalists have made no theoretical contributions, (2) that, in assigning an imperative or compulsive character to industrial technology, the neoinstitutionalists are guilty of the sin of technological determinism, and (3) that the neoinstitutionalists, by raising the issue of wants, goals, or values, have become bogged down in normative considerations and so cannot qualify as scientists. These criticisms have been presented many times in the past, and will doubtlessly be dredged up again. If the conventional economists wish to continue to deny the validity of the concept of the logic of the process of industrialization, if they wish to deny that industrial technology is an imperative or compulsive force having much to do with the structure and functioning of our evolving industrial society, if they wish to deny that existing economic wants or goals of individuals and groups may be treated as scientific data, they are quite free to do so. But in the opinion of the neoinstitutionalists the conventional economists can do so only at the cost of keeping standard economics narrow and irrelevant with respect to much that is significant in the modern economic world.

I would like to conclude this discussion of neoinstitutionalism, the only significant academic economics of dissent in my opinion, by saying that we need both economic technicians or specialists and also what the Union for Radical Political Economists—an organization made up largely of disturbed graduate students in economics in our most prestigious universities of the northeast and far west—has described as "economic social scientists." I am fully aware of the important progress made in recent years in developing the theory and practice of economic decision-making. I am well aware of the contributions along the lines of econometric model building, linear programming, game theory, cost-benefit analysis, cost effectiveness studies, sampling theory and techniques, input-output analysis, and welfare economics with its emphasis on Paretian optimality. While this progress in the field of economic decision making has enabled us to manage ourselves more efficiently, it does not tell us whether we are moving toward Paradise or Purgatory.

While I would certainly not close the door on economic technicians, I would say that these specialists are not the best prepared to present economics as a social science in written form or on the lecture platform to the general public, or to young students who are coming for the first time to the study of economics. Also, it is my position that the general public and the political and other leaders of public opinion should see economics not through the eyes of the economic technician, but through the eyes of the economist as a social scientist.

What the neoinstitutionalists object to is not so much what is found in our widely used standard economics textbooks, but rather to what is left out of them. It was to meet these deficiencies in conventional economics that Galbraith wrote *The Affluent Society* and *The New Industrial State;* that Myrdal wrote the *Challenge to Affluence* and *Beyond the Welfare State;* and that Ayres wrote *The Theory of Economic Progress* and *Toward a Reasonable Society.* On a more popular level the Michael Harringtons, Vance Packards, William H. Whytes, David Bazelons, Bernard Nossiters, and Rachel Carsons have sought to offset the irrelevance of conventional economics by showing the public how the quality of economic life is being lowered in this age of affluence. Without these and many other economic dissenters whom I have not mentioned, economics would be still more of an irrelevant science than it now is—that is to say, irrelevant not to economic decision-making, but to issues relating to the creation and achievement of private and public economic wants, without a discussion of which economic decision-making becomes a routine without much social significance.

I would not like to close this discussion on a somewhat sour note. Neoinstitutionalists are by nature pessimistic optimists. While they are pessimistic about the immediate future, they are nevertheless sustained by a deep optimism with regard to the long-run possibility of making economics a social science that is highly relevant to the major issues not only of our time, but also of the emerging future. It is my conviction, and I believe the conviction of those unconventional economists whom I have called neoinstitutionalists, that economics will increasingly come to have more concern with what people think is the Good Society, and less concern with efficiently making decisions but never asking what the decisions are really about.

Heterodox Economic Thinking and Public Policy

Joseph Dorfman

That current American economic policy is founded in a faith in the efficacy of collective action, or more loosely, the welfare state, is almost a cliché. By collective action I am not merely referring to government but also the functioning of a host of highly organized public institutions, such as the corporation, the security and commodity exchanges, the church, the school, and the trade union. But what sets the state apart from the other institutions is its role as the ultimate arbiter of disputes backed by the physical force to maintain law and order. National economic policy over the past four decades gives ample testimony to the belief that collective action is essential, not only for the maintenance of the rights of man summed up in the term "individualism," but also to provide the best opportunities for their development through economic growth and a more equitable distribution of wealth and income. Thus, by now, for the vast majority of the American people, the basic decision of social policy has been made; namely, that collective action must be both positive and pervasive. While even the most conservative today accept a degree of government intervention that would have been decried a few generations ago, there are, of course, substantial differences of opinion as to the limits, pace, and emphasis of such action.

The shift in attitude toward the role of government which began after the Civil War accompanied many radically new problems which, in large part, were not amenable to solution within the framework of orthodox economic thinking. Thus, the heterodox writer, less fettered by the dogma and preconceptions of the past,

The author is Professor of Economics at Columbia University. This is the presidential address to the Association for Evolutionary Economics, delivered in New York City on December 28, 1969.

could bring to these problems the requisite imaginative insight. How substantial the shift in thinking had to be can only be realized if we appreciate that as traditionally understood *laissez-faire* economics had been the cornerstone of the egalitarian Jefferson-Jackson ideology which was dominant in the ante bellum era. Its advocates had sharply criticized the privileges and perquisites of feudal aristocratic society which they maintained enriched a few idlers at the expense of the industrious mass of the people. To them, the privileges established by law were the source of hated monopoly and resulted in the impoverishment of the great majority. The principle of free competition was conceived as the application of self-assertion to man's economic activity. Thus Thomas Jefferson could be an admirer of Adam Smith's *The Wealth of Nations* and its demand for "the simple and obvious system of natural liberty," and Andrew Jackson and his followers as they firmly laid the foundations of the tradition of free enterprise could advocate measures which conformed to the doctrines of David Ricardo.

As the nation, however, underwent rapid industrialization during the 1870's and 1880's, the astounding material advances came at the price of a new set of severe and far-reaching social and economic problems. For the first time the nation witnessed violent massive clashes between the wage-earning and the new capitalist-owner classes. With the increasing concentration of population in large cities came the evils of overcrowded slums, the criminal mobs, and the corrupt political machines. The established legal arrangements provided hardly any effective means for coping with the unbridled piratical activities of those in control of the newly risen industrial, railroad and financial empires. The founders of the Jefferson-Jackson liberalism with its basically humanitarian spirit had never envisioned the kind of society that accompanied the new technology. Ironically the very *laissez-faire* policies which they had advocated to free the mass of people from the enslavement of the old mercantilist doctrines resulted to a large extent in the very things that they most feared.

The economists who enjoyed the highest prestige in the immediate post-Civil War era were not unaware of the problems, but they tended to hold, in practice, that the prevailing *laissez-faire* regime was as satisfactory as could be reasonably hoped for. They maintained that most social problems had their basis in the inherent defects of human nature and were therefore ineradicable. Such other problems as developed were either the transient results of economic growth or were the result of unwise government tampering with the economic system, for example, protective tariffs, bi-metalism and so forth. They believed in an oversimplified mechanical doctrine of wages which held that the rate of wages was fixed by natural economic law; therefore any attempt to set wages by other means, such as collective bargaining or minimum wage legislation would damage society. Depressions were simply viewed as "natural tides in business" and not entirely unhealthy because they served to eliminate inefficient businessmen. There was recognition of the possibility of reducing the severity of these commercial crises but there was no agreement on specific measures.

INFLUENCE OF THE HISTORICAL SCHOOL

No account of the contributions of heterodox economic thinking can be fully understood without some recognition of the influence from abroad of the movement known as the German Historical School. During the 1870's and 1880's for the first time a large number of students interested in economics attended German universities. There they heard penetrating criticisms of the rigid restrictions of British classical economic thought accompanied by persuasive appeals for a much broader definition of the scope of economics.

At this time, in Europe as well as in the United States, the systematic gathering and interpretation of statistical and historical data, as we know them today, had hardly begun. The Historical School was among the first to recognize the promise of these methods as tools of investigation. It also attempted to give greater scope to the ethical aspect of man and to the relation of economics to the other social sciences, especially sociology and law, than the British classical school would tolerate. The members of the school in 1872 formed the *Verein für Sozialpolitik* (Association for Social Policy) with the aims of promoting the advancement of economic science, industrialization, and social reform to meet the challenge of Marxian socialism. These reforms specifically included a far-reaching program of social security legislation – sickness, accident, old age, and unemployment insurance – which was largely enacted during Bismarck's regime.

Henry Carter Adams (1851-1921), of the University of Michigan, and the first statistician of the Interstate Commerce Commission, provided a good example of the adaptation of the work of the German Historical School to the needs of the rapidly growing American society. While admiring the enlightened social reforms of Bismarck's Germany, his egalitarian background made him suspicious of the German worship of the state, and he early warned against the threat to liberty implicit in indiscriminate state intervention. In the chronology of intellectual history, Adams, who did his major work in the last quarter of the nineteenth century, may best be classified as the leading forerunner of institutionalism. His was one of the earliest, influential voices to warn that unrestrained *laissez-faire* economics, rather than being a means of achieving freedom, might have the opposite effect. In his widely-read and influential monograph, *Relation of the State to Industrial Action* (1887), he made a landmark proposal as to the government's role in the industrial area. First, the state could and, indeed, should, raise the ethical plane or level of competitive action by restricting or abolishing the worst abuses in such areas as child labor, industrial safety, public health, and industrial waste disposal. He held that action here would gradually eradicate the exploitation of human resources while preserving the essential advantages of competition. Consistent with this, he argued that those few industries in which the dictates of efficiency called for monopoly, namely, railroad, gas, water, and lighting, should be subject to extensive public control.

His most heretical contribution was in the field of labor policy. He contended in 1886, in a public address, that under the conditions of modern large-scale industry, the simple, primitive type of wage bargain between individual employee and employer was no longer adequate. In its place he envisioned a system of collective bargaining which was in effect a crystalization or codification of labor rights under common law and thus consonant with the Anglo-American concept of liberty. His was the first really fundamental challenge to the prevailing wage fund doctrine. A half century later this radical doctrine became a part of the "Law of the Land" with the enactment of the National Labor Relations Act of 1935 (Wagner Act), which threw the weight of government behind labor's right to bargain collectively.

In addition to his own work, Adams was the inspiration for many talented and creative thinkers who studied under him. Time allows only the mention of one; J. Allen Smith (1860-1924). His *The Spirit of American Government* (1907), the pioneering, systematic study in the economic interpretation of the American Constitution, was a formative influence in the launching of the mid-western Progressive movement symbolized by the Robert LaFollette family, for it supplied much of the ideological basis.

In the field of monetary policy, he was well ahead of his time. In a famous article in 1896 favoring a "multiple money standard" – in substance a constant purchasing power dollar tied to a broad index of prices – he argued that the effect of the existing gold standard was "to discourage production, and to make a bond a more desirable investment than an entrepreneur's interest in capital." To those who complained that his proposal meant fluctuating exchange rates, he answered that test of a good monetary standard was "not steady rates of foreign exchange, but the existence of a practically constant relation between the monetary unit and commodities generally." This view he based on the need of maintaining what he called "efficient demand" in a "progressive society" which is one where capital is accumulating.[1] And of course "efficient demand" has the same meaning as "effective demand" in J. M. Keynes, *The General Theory of Employment, Interest and Money* (1936).

Others who came under the influence of the German Historical School also adopted positions favoring greater government intervention in the economy. It was those associated with this point of view who formed the nucleous in 1885 for the organization which we know today as the American Economic Association. While there were some similarities between the views of Henry Carter Adams and the founders of the A.E.A., the positions of the latter were far milder. Whereas, as we have seen, it took half a century for much of Adams' position to become respectable, within a decade or two the American Economic Association and the ideas upon which it was founded had become an accepted part of the "Establishment." This probably reflected the gradual recognition on the part of the majority of the nation's leaders that some curb on the extremes of *laissez-faire* was necessary if the industrial system was to continue to function effectively.

Stemming from this recognition there followed successful agitation for major reforms in the control of business. The first substantial innovation of this nature came with the establishment in 1887 of the Interstate Commerce Commission to regulate the railroads. This federal commission became the model for subsequent national regulatory bodies. In the same period, state after state passed anti-monopoly legislation and finally this movement culminated in the Sherman Anti-Trust Act of 1890. For the first time in the nation's history, Congress, through full-scale hearings recognized as a national problem depression and unemployment in 1879-1881, and strikes in 1883-1884. Many states created bureaus of statistics, and in 1884 the federal Bureau of Labor was established to investigate industrial relations. With the establishment in 1879 of the Division of Forestry in the Department of Agriculture, a beginning was made toward a systematic conservation policy. A closely related development was the creation by Congress in the same year, of the United States Geological Survey to undertake "the classification of public lands and examination of the geological structure, mineral resources and products of the national domain." From the Geological Survey was drawn most of the technical talent for staffing the Bureau of Reclamation set up under the Newlands Act of 1902 and the Bureau, in turn, led via the Inland Waterways Commission of 1907-08 to the New Deal's Tennessee Valley Authority (T.V.A.) and subsequent multiple purpose river basin developments.

It was soon found following the creation of the various administrative commissions and bureaus that systematic implementation of policy was severely handicapped by the lack of pertinent data on which to base decisions. Fortunately there was attracted to the agencies a number of able and imaginative statisticians. Thus the Censuses of 1870 and 1880 came under the superintendancy of the heterodox economist, General Francis A. Walker, who became the first president of the American Economic Association. By making his office, to use his own words, "superior alike to partisan dictation and to the seductions of theory," he expanded the Census into a comprehensive, objective inquiry that would mirror the nation's growth.[2]

The drive for reform was not confined to the enactment of legislation. Thus in 1886 with the formation of the American Federation of Labor, there was the beginning of a permanent labor movement to protect the interests of the wage earners. This same period saw the emergence of powerful organizations of farmers and the development of employers and trade associations.

The closing decade of the century saw a reaction to the reforms of the 1880's. This was reflected in the actions of both the legislative and judicial branches of government. Not only did additional reform almost come to a halt, but in some instances the reaction resulted in an actual cutback in the role of government. Thus Congress drastically reduced the appropriation for the Geological Survey, limiting its functions to topology alone. Similarly the United States Supreme Court declared the federal income tax unconstitutional, and also sharply curtailed by its decisions the effectiveness of the Interstate Commerce Commission and the Sherman Anti-Trust Act. State courts struck down legislation protecting workers from dismissal for union membership.

For the most part, in economic writing there was a parallel reaction against reform. For example, the American Economic Association dropped its original forward looking statement of principles, and some of its leaders argued that the embarrassed financial situation of the association called for the election of officers who would attract conservatives to membership rather than men like Richard T. Ely or Simon N. Patten whose names carried "weight of so peculiar a nature as to oppress rather than invite."[3] Even the interest in statistics waned. The able first editor of the *American Economic Review*, Davis Rich Dewey, of Massachusetts Institute of Technology, had in the eighties with much enthusiasm introduced the use of historico-statistical materials in the economics course, but in the nineties, he was complaining that the crowd of students did not readily respond to this approach, and traditional lectures on theory were as much as they would absorb.

During the 1870's and 1880's in both Europe and the United States, the marginal utility theory of demand was systematically developed and became in effect an extension of classical economic theory. By the 1890's the work of synthesizing the two had been completed. The result was what came to be known as neo-classical economics. Its followers generally speaking saw in it a complete explanation of the workings of the economic system, a fully integrated model of an idealized, frictionless, automatic system. Being mainly concerned with statics, they deemed historical and statistical research as at best of secondary importance.

Meanwhile, some of the original leaders of the movement for reconstruction turned their attention to less controversial subjects, such as public finance, while others left theoretical economics and devoted themselves to administrative work and private business. Welfare proposals were considered a subject on which the economist as an objective scientist could not legitimately take a stand. In this view, the economists' pronouncements on public policy were substantially limited to monetary, banking and tariff issues.

THORSTEIN VEBLEN'S CONTRIBUTION

The reaction in the realm of economic thought was for a time so dominant that the few remaining dissenting voices went almost unheard. But with the turn of the century the pendulum again swung the other way. The complex problems of a rapidly changing industrial order did not find almost automatic solutions as had been implied by the neo-classical economists. Indeed, if anything increasing industrialization and technological advance seemed to many of the ablest young minds to be producing even more pressing and difficult problems. The most influential dissenting voices came from the group of professional economists led by Thorstein B. Veblen, his student, Wesley C. Mitchell, and John R. Commons, whose ideas became known as institutionalism. This broad term, while covering a considerable divergence, had as its common core: criticism of traditional economic theory, its presumptions concerning human motivations and the universality of capitalist institutional factors, and its unrealistic refusal to deal systematically with change. Moreover, they questioned the adequacy of the market as a means of rationally and ethically allocating scarce resources.

Let us turn first to the oldest member of the group, Thorstein Veblen (1857-1929). Paradoxically, while his thinking was in good part responsible for much reform legislation, and was also influential in many key judicial decisions, he cannot be classified as a reformer in the sense that he espoused a particular program. A strong case may be made that Veblen was the most original social thinker that the United States has produced. The basis for this contention is that he showed us new ways of looking at our everyday institutions. He was the first on this side of the Atlantic to apply the cultural approach of anthropology to the modern money economy. For example, where neo-classical doctrine saw the demand for an economic good as essentially a logical product which could be deduced from the summing up of the demands of hedonistically motivated and rational men, Veblen saw demand as a complex, often illogical consequence of emotional impulses and institutionally induced emulative desires. Thus according to him the only way to investigate the demand for a good at a given point in time was by using the tools of history and statistics.

Much of Veblen's work was concerned with two central, and closely entwined, institutions of our modern economic system; namely, the corporation and the technological process; that is the machine process. The corporation, as he saw it, was much more than an embodiment of external mechanical forces. Rather, it was a complex social organism subject to manipulation by passions and spirits which at times subvert the social benefits claimed for it by its defenders. Even more serious and fundamental, it tended to give play to and become the football of the intrigues and rivalries of inner controlling groups for their own personal gain, rather than for the benefit of either of the stockholders or the community or both. Their habit of thinking in terms of maximum money profits often placed a premium on financial maneuvering at the expense of productive efficiency. In this manner the tremendous advantages stemming from advances in science and technology, for which Veblen had the greatest respect and admiration, were in part lost. The modern corporation thus was an instance of an important general principle of institutional behavior: namely that institutions which man creates for his benefit have a way of turning around and creating a life all their own and threatening to become his masters and gods.

In evaluating the impact of Veblen one cannot point to specific policy proposals which later were enacted into law. As a result, evaluation of his influence becomes decidedly more difficult; of course in some instances, his impact was very direct. For example, on the eve of the New Deal his *Absentee Ownership* (1923) was cited by Justice Louis D. Brandeis in a famous dissenting opinion, *Lee v. Liggett* (1933) to support his well-known stand against "the curse of bigness" in unrestrained corporate growth. Less direct, but no less important, we find much of the New Deal legislation regulating corporations and security markets stemmed from a clear implication of Veblen's work that it was "the duty of the government to set up counter-forces to prevent arbitrary acts of business power."[4] Some of these measures were the Securities Act of 1933, the Securities Exchange Act of 1934, the Public Utility Holding Company Act of 1935, and the Investment Company Act of 1940. Not only were Veblen's writings influential in the drafting of these acts but a number of the outstanding early top-level administrators of the new agencies as well as the old, were strongly impressed with his writings, especially *The Theory of Business Enterprise* (1904) and *Absentee Ownership*.

Besides those in government who had a direct familiarity with his publications, there have been, and continue to be, a much greater number who, whether they are conscious of doing so or not, are expressing views in terms which are essentially Veblenian. Such is particularly the case with respect to proposals for the prevention of the waste of resources both human and material. An interesting example of the use of Veblenian conceptions by major political figures is to be found in some of former President Johnson's messages to Congress in connection with the Great Society proposals in 1965. "We do not intend to live in the midst of abundance isolated from neighbors and nature, confined by blighted cities and bleak suburbs, stunted by a poverty of learning and an emptiness of leisure." Later he draws the basic conclusion that "economic policy has begun to liberate itself from the preconceptions of an earlier day."[5] We may note the striking similarity of expression to the most technical of Veblen's famous critiques of orthodox economic thinking, "The Preconceptions of Economic Science."

Veblen had often advocated greater use of empirical data, or, to use his words, "an indispensable preliminary," to decision making, but he himself never devoted much time to such work. It lay with his intellectual heir, W. C. Mitchell (1874-1948) to develop this aspect.

Unfortunately the term "monumental" is much overused, but as applied to *Business Cycles* (1913) it is precisely appropriate. Today this work with its offshoots still provides the fundamental intellectual basis for the discussion and analysis of changes in the levels of economic activity.

THE IMPACT OF WESLEY C. MITCHELL

In the main, Mitchell's reputation is bound up with the study of business cycles. However, prior to the 1913 publication he had done important original work in the history of American monetary policy, and formed his basic social philosophy and ideas of the role of economic science. It was these same monetary investigations which caused Mitchell to doubt the empirical validity of the theoretical models advanced by the quantity theorists. In particular, he argued, that the way in which Irving Fisher used the term "normal" was misleading, because the statistical studies proved the situations to which Fisher applied the term, were rare exceptions.

While never so stringently critical as was Veblen of orthodox economics, he nevertheless made clear his belief that as he said, "to alleviate . . . the suffering and deprivation which our social organization creates . . . we need as a guide . . . sure knowledge of the causal interconnections between social phenomena."[6] To Mitchell, that sure knowledge meant in large part knowledge based upon systematic empirical observation; that is, tested knowledge. This broad approach was the one he used in constructing his landmark work *Business Cycles*. Thus the study of economic fluctuations should not be merely a technical specialty divided off from the general body of economic theory but should be treated as a part of economic dynamics, as dealing with the economic system in motion.

The impact of *Business Cycles* on the attitude of the nation's leaders came rapidly – less than a decade after its publication. The economy entered the sharp decline of 1920-1921. It was at this time, as a result of Mitchell's work that those in government, banking and the business world in general became aware of the possibility of substantially controlling and reducing the worst fluctuations of economic activity. Thus by the late 1920's, it could be said: the treatise had brought forth "an active ferment of current studies and proposals which 'carry on' and aim to utilize the knowledge gained for purposes of control."[7]

To Mitchell, the continual alternations of expansion and contraction were neither inevitable nor the outcome of modern technology; they were the product of the prevailing institutions and habits, or, in his terms, "technical exigencies" associated with the money economy. This was highlighted by the establishment of the sub-committee, Business Cycles and Unemployment, of the President's (Harding) Conference on Unemployment of 1921, of which Mitchell was a member and for which he directed the famous report *Business Cycles and Unemployment* (1923). In accordance with the logic of his treatise he publicly supported compulsory unemployment insurance, not simply as a relief scheme, as was maintained by most advocates of such legislation, but more important, as a counter cyclical measure. Concerned over the harmful cumulative process whereby lay-offs of workers led to reduction in purchasing power, resulting in lowered business activity, and, in turn, to further lay-offs, he held that "if the workers can be assured of money to buy the necessities of life during business depression, that measure will break the vicious circle which makes a depression intensify itself."[8] This thesis led logically to the effort of the government to combat the Great Depression that began in 1929 and contributed to the inclusion of an unemployment insurance system in the federal Social Security Act of 1935.

Besides its central theme, *Business Cycles* brought out the need for research in several as yet hardly explored areas. These have formed much of the basis for what in today's terminology we call macroeconomics. A partial listing would include such areas as national income and gross national product analysis, growth economics, national planning, and the special statistical tools such as economic indices, used in economic forecasting. Mitchell did more than any other economist for the advance of these subjects, especially through his work as director of research of the National Bureau of Economic Research which he helped to found in 1920. Several lines of investigation having proved their fundamental value at the Bureau have been taken over and expanded by federal agencies. These studies included inquiries on price index numbers, national income, capital formation, flow of funds, consumer credit and economic indicators. By such success he raised the dignity of quantitative economics and laid the groundwork for its acceptance as a permanent, enduring basis of economic policy. In line with this thinking, Mitchell, in the mid-1930's proposed a broadly based advisory national planning council which, drawing on the results of social science research, would be able to provide advice on social policy. Indeed, so pervasive and fundamental have the tools mentioned become that I imagine for the younger members of the audience, it is difficult to conceive of operating policy-making functions without them.

In some sense the following words of President Johnson on the state of the economy in January 1965 read almost like a paraphrase of Mitchell's words over a half century earlier. "No longer will we tolerate . . . the ravages of the business cycle . . . . I do not believe recessions are inevitable . . . . We can head them off or greatly moderate their length and force – if we are able to act promptly."[9]

Another eminent student of Veblen, Walter W. Stewart (1885-1958), in the post World War I period was one of the first American economists to recognize that the most important function of a central bank was to act as a stabilizing force. Coming to the Federal Reserve Board as director of the Division of Research and Statistics in 1922, following the severe depression of 1920-1921, he went to work to implement the two heretofore poorly understood and little used provisions of the Federal Reserve Act for stabilizing the monetary system; namely, the use of open market operations and the power to vary the rediscount rate. From the beginning he took the position that reliable basic indexes of the fluctuations in the operations of the industrial system were essential. As he said, such "fluctuations . . . must be measured before they can be interpreted or controlled."[10]

Certainly no other economist held such a large number of important advisory posts as did Stewart. In addition to his position at the Board, he advised successive secretaries of the treasury; was the first economic adviser to that most powerful of central banks, the Bank of England; was a leading architect of the Bank for International Settlements; and he served as a member of the President's Council of Economic Advisers in the Eisenhower Administration. In addition, between governmental assignments, he sandwiched in both a business and an academic career.

Yet despite his long list of top level posts, perhaps his greatest single contribution came almost at the start of his public career. I refer to the famous *Annual Report of the Federal Reserve Board for the Year 1923* (1924), in which he combined, as he put it, the statistical method with the institutional approach. An eminent, long time associate of his, the monetary authority, W. Randolph Burgess, in a recent account of the early development of Federal Reserve policy, gives an excellent summary. He said, "That Report contained a full and careful statement of principles and consequences of open market operations as a major instrument of policy, supplementing the discount rate. Of particular interest is the extent to which this discussion had moved away from the concept of the Reserve System as a mechanism responding semiautomatically to the demands made upon it to that of an organization responsible for taking the initiative. This appears in the review of guides to credit policy, which the Report recognized as including consideration of the quantity of credit (as well as the quality) to see that it is 'neither excessive or deficient in maintaining credit in due relation to the volume of credit needs for the operating requirements of agriculture, industry, and trade.' For this purpose, the *Report* said, the System must follow economic trends by the use of indexes of production, employment, trade, etc. It is revealing to see how close this review of the objectives of policy comes to the stated purposes of the Employment Act of 1946."[11]

JOHN R. COMMONS: BEYOND LABOR ECONOMICS

The last member of the founding triumverate of institutionalists, John R. Commons (1862-1945) was the only active advocate of specific economic-social reforms. Here he was successful, particularly in pioneering in social legislation in the state of Wisconsin for a remarkably high percentage of his proposals actually became law. To him, the modern industrial order if it is to function for the common good requires rational collective actions which go beyond the stringent restrictions of the common law institutions of private property and contract. The laissez-faire economists' view that the problems facing the nation were simply rare exceptions or isolated abuses amenable to easy correction was unrealistic. Meaningful solutions could only be found in substantial reform of existing institutions.

His theoretical studies including pioneering historico-sociological investigations of such major institutions as Anglo-American jurisprudence and the American trade union movement were consciously formulated in such a manner as to serve as guides to policy making. Commons was interested in dynamics. Thus to him neo-classical equilibrium theory was of very limited usefulness for in the real world, the functioning economic system was a constantly changing resultant of the conflicts and the compromises of collective bargaining processes carried on within a legal or quasi-legal framework which set limits to bargaining power.

Commons is best known as the father of labor economics in the United States, but he contributed in a much broader area. At one time or another he dealt with nearly every aspect of the science, including: monetary problems, taxation, monopoly, railroads and public utilities, immigration, business cycles, urban problems and agriculture, but he even went beyond his own discipline into such political problems as proportional representation, municipal and civil service.

In monetary policy, perhaps his most important contribution was as the *de facto* author of the bill of 1928, bearing the name of Representative James G. Strong of Kansas. The bill for the first time directed the Federal Reserve Board to perform a positive role in helping to guide the nation's economy. It stated, "The Federal Reserve System shall use all the powers and authority now or hereafter possessed by it to maintain a stable gold standard; to promote the stability of commerce, industry, agriculture, and employment, and a more stable purchasing power of the dollar, so far as such purposes may be accomplished by monetary and credit policy." To Commons, a stable gold standard did not necessarily preclude altering the existing gold standard. Thus in 1931 with the nation's economy increasingly crippled by what was to be the severest depression in the nation's history, he persuasively argued for substantial devaluation of the dollar in order to stimulate employment and recovery. The subsequent devaluation that took place in the early years of the Roosevelt administration was in some good part a result of his efforts.

Not long after coming to the University of Wisconsin (1904), he got his opportunity as an inventor of institutions; he became in effect the chief economic adviser for Governor (and later United States Senator) Robert LaFollette, who was making the state the great laboratory for social advance. The combination of Commons and LaFollette was a most effective team, which brought together both high idealism and practical political know-how. In 1905 a model civil service law was produced. In 1907 Commons helped extend public utility regulation into such areas as interurban railroads and intra-state gas, water and electric power generation. Four years later, he prepared the bill setting up the Industrial Commission to administer the state's labor laws and served as a member of the first commission. This same year he participated in drafting the state's Workmen's Compensation Act. Then two decades later under his guidance Wisconsin enacted the first unemployment insurance act in the nation (1932).[12] His former students were among the participants in the drafting of the federal Social Security Act (1935). In addition to the Social Security Act, he and his students contributed ideas for most of the social legislation enacted during the New Deal and the Truman administration following World War II.

Commons gained the label *radical* because, in his reformer's zeal, he dealt bluntly with the trouble areas of the modern industrial order. Yet in propounding solutions his guiding principle was the optimistic belief that by altering institutions conflicting interests could be largely resolved.

JOHN MAURICE CLARK AND OVERHEAD COSTS

Representing a type so closely attuned to institutionalism as often to be identified with it, was John Maurice Clark (1884-1963). While never wholly rejecting orthodox theory, Clark was keenly aware of its limitations in explaining the operations of the modern economy. It was for this reason that he sought what he called a "social-institutional-dynamic theory." Perhaps the best statement of the premises for his thinking is to be found in his correspondence with his long-time friend and colleague at Columbia, Mitchell. He wrote: "I have a theory of competition which argues that any fixed schematic laws must be misleading, because competition is an evolving thing. And I have a theory of human nature which can't be used as a basis for deductive theorizing, because it includes too many various elements and leaves too much room for personal and group differences in values and in behavior." A few days later by way of explanation he humorously added this remark, "In dealing with the evolutionary character of the mechanisms I sometimes think 'theory,' of the abstract sort, is a device for converting usefully-enlightening ideas about behavior and motivation into paper mechanisms whereby armchair theorists can grind out misleading results."[13]

Clark's treatise, *Studies in the Economics of Overhead Costs* (1923) stands as one of the landmarks of twentieth century economic thinking. It provides fundamental insights into the workings of the American economy – particularly the market system and its interrelationship with the level of business activity. Where Mitchell's studies emphasized the quantitative background for understanding and coping with fluctuations in economic activity, Clark's emphasized those qualitative, institutional factors not yet subject to precise quantitative statement, but essential for a full comprehension of the causes for the lack of full employment of the nation's resources. In this sense, the work of these two were complementary.

While never the stringent spokesman for reform Commons was, Clark early in his career was critical of the orthodox economists' refusal to take stands in certain areas; for example, as early as 1915, in an article on "The Concept of Value," he warned the profession that "theories of conservation and compulsory (workingmen's) insurance may be grafted upon the stem of marginal utility, but they will not grow there spontaneously. They represent clashes of values for which the economist has furnished no adequate common denominator. It is fruitless to claim that these are not economic values . . . . The test is that the economist must deal with them."[14]

Consistent with this stand was his concept of labor as an overhead or fixed cost. He based his contention on both humane considerations and economic efficiency. The common practice of treating labor as a variable cost, was short-sighted and self-defeating. The seeming advantage to the businessman of immediately reducing payrolls when faced with any decline in demand only produced a vicious circle in which other businessmen would do likewise, resulting in increasing unemployment, lowered purchasing power, and still further lay-offs. Clark recognized that the individual employer by himself was helpless to break this vicious circle which brought in its wake not only suffering to the individuals unemployed, but the devastation of depression for society as a whole. Thus the solution to this problem lay in acceptance of the idea that since society possesses only so much productive power, including as a major part, human beings, it could not avoid either the cost of maintaining labor or suffering from its depreciation. It was this argument by Clark which provided much of the impetus for the concept of a guaranteed annual wage, which began to be widely discussed in the late 1930's, and which reached fruition in the labor contracts of the auto industry in the 1960's. From this premise, he similarly argued that social insurance schemes should never provide simply a dole but rather should be designed to return the worker to employment as rapidly as possible so as not to lose his productive potential.

Throughout his career Clark was consulted as an expert by a large number of government agencies and private research foundations. It was while serving in one such post, with the National Planning Board of the Federal Emergency Administration of Public Works that he wrote *Economics of Planning Public Works* (1935). This constituted one of the earlier statements of what has come to be known popularly as Keynesian economics. Most significant was the analysis of the multiplicative effect of capital investment on national income.

As previously noted, both Commons and Mitchell (and even to some extent Veblen) drew to themselves a substantial group of disciples. The dedicated students of Commons even today, some two decades after his death, still identify themselves with his tradition. Likewise many, particularly some at the National Bureau of Economic Research, feel themselves intellectual legatees of Mitchell. In Commons' case, the attraction in the main was to students infused with the idealism of reform; for Mitchell, it was originally as the father of quantitative business cycle analysis, and then as a founder and guiding spirit in expanded investigation into those areas suggested by his epoch-marking tome, which became the focus for followers. Clark, on the other hand neither espoused a broad program of specific reforms, nor was his name associated with a relatively new and vital specialty, nor did he have a long time continuing association as head of a major research organization. In short, his influence was not through a group of disciples but was spread over the broad spectrum of both orthodox and heterodox opinion.

We now turn to a group of heterodox thinkers whose primary careers were outside of academic centers, and yet in each case produced highly sophisticated and original work with strong impact on public policy.

Among the advocates of socialist economics Isaac M. Rubinow (1875-1936) stands out. This physician, actuary, statistician, social worker and economist was well described in 1931 by Professor (later United States Senator) Paul H. Douglas as "the foremost American authority" on social insurance. During the 1920's Rubinow devoted a large part of his energies to the promotion of compulsory unemployment insurance and like Mitchell, he justified it not only as a relief measure but also as a counter-cyclical device "to stabilize business by preventing fluctuations of effective demand on the part of unemployed workmen." On the eve of the New Deal he served as chairman of the Sub-Committee on Research for the official Ohio Commission on Unemployment Insurance (1932-1933). This provided him the opportunity to use his training and experience as economist and actuary in the drafting of a program of unemployment compensation. The result was a sound, well-thought out proposal in this area. He played no less important a role in the establishment of the Social Security Act of 1935. "By some blind spot in official leadership, Dr. Rubinow was not called in as a technical expert" in the formulation of the measure. "But by a happy stroke his book of that year, *The Quest for Social Security*, fell into the hands of . . . President" Franklin D. Roosevelt, who was impressed and influenced by its theses.[15]

FOSTER AND CATCHINGS AS PRECURSORS

My next exhibit is the famous team of William Trufant Foster and Waddill Catchings, neither of whom had formal training as an economist. Foster (1879-1950) was the first president of Reed College. In 1920 he joined his Harvard classmate, the liberal, adventurous industrialist and financier, Catchings, (1879-1968) in producing during the 1920's, a series of influential works, expounding the general under-consumption-over saving theory of the causes of depression. This theory in its basic form was identified with the name of the heterodox British economist, John A. Hobson who was more influential in the United States than in his native land. Foster and Catchings adapted this analysis to the particular institutions of the American scene and expounded it in the area of monetary and credit doctrine. Their main argument ran as follows: a period of high business activity is generally marked by rising prices for consumer goods; this tendency continues to the point where the aggregate retail price for all consumer goods exceeds the total amount of money consumers have available to spend on such goods; as a consequence a surplus is created; while the surplus is being disposed of, production is curtailed, labor is dismissed, further reducing aggregate consumer demand, and thus accelerating the downward spiral which ends in a full scale depression.

In recent years it has become generally appreciated that the team to "a remarkable extent . . . anticipated the Keynesian theory of income determination and post-Keynesian growth economics." This is not the place for discussion of the pro's and con's of their analysis except to note that, while it did not satisfy the professional economists at the time, it helped to create an awareness of phenomena with which conventional theory did not adequately deal.

More relevant to our purpose is their scheme for meeting the problem of instability and unemployment. The plan as sketched in *The Road to Plenty* (1928), expanded and brought to the attention of a wider audience many of the proposals of Walter W. Stewart in the *Annual Report of the Federal Reserve Board for the Year 1923.* Foster and Catchings believed that scientific control of the volume and use of the money supply via fiscal policy, could do much to prevent underspending. To carry out the scheme, there should be created a coordinating board, similar to the Federal Reserve Board with the following functions:

"1. It would gather and issue information on business conditions. Special attention would be paid to indexes of retail prices and to employment, production, consumer income, the volume of money, income distribution foreign trade and the projected expenditures of private concerns and governments.

2. It would advise the government on the probable effect on economic welfare of taxes, payment of public debts, and other fiscal matters so that the government could guide its collections and expenditures in a way that would preserve stability and high levels of employment.

3. It would determine appropriations to be made for public works projects. The timing, location, and volume of such projects would be designed to correct inflationary or deflationary conditions.

4. It would determine when the government should borrow money from banks in order to inject the right amount of new money into the economic system to sustain prices and employment. This would require careful analysis of all available economic indicators."

It has been well said that "the similarity of this program to the one adopted somewhat experimentally by (President Franklin D.) Roosevelt and finally officially in the Employment Act of 1946 is rather remarkable."[16] Not only was there considerable similarity, but such portions of the plan which were not included in the Employment Act, are some of the proposed amendments most avidly supported by leading students of business cycles and of economic growth today, over forty years later.

Foster has another claim to having influenced public policy. He played a leading role in the development of the last great stage in social security legislation – health insurance. In 1932 he wrote the majority report of the Committee on the Costs of Medical Care headed by Ray Lyman Wilbur, President Hoover's Secretary of the Interior. As a first step he called for voluntary group insurance. This should be allowed to evolve to the point where it would provide medical service of high quality. When this objective had been reached, then the adoption of compulsory plans should be considered. Foster's proposal at the time was viewed as radical and drew bitter opposition from organized medicine.

WALTON HAMILTON AND NICHOLAS A.L.J. JOHANNSEN

Organized medicine long ago gave up its fight against voluntary group insurance schemes, but it continues to oppose compulsory programs. Events of the last few years, however, point toward eventual victory for the advocates of universal compulsory health insurance. The breakthrough came with the passage by Congress of the Medicare Act of 1965. And who were the pioneers in this campaign which dates back to World War I? The heterodox economists, Rubinow, Commons, and the Veblenian, Walton H. Hamilton (1880-1958) who wrote the minority report of the Committee on the Costs of Medical Care, espousing a compulsory program.

My last exhibit of an influential heterodox thinker is a man who had no college training whatever. The self-taught Nicholas August Ludwig Jacob Johannsen (1844-1928) dared long ago to espouse the greatest of heresies; namely that there could be a chronic condition of overproduction of goods, or in modern terminology, a "general deficiency of demand." Because of this, his audience among the orthodox economists was extremely limited. While he labored in relative obscurity any impression that this might give that his work was of little importance or influence would be misleading, for his limited audience included many of the best minds of the day both at home and abroad; to wit, J. B. Clark, J. M. Clark, Foster and Catchings, Friedrich von Hayek, John A. Hobson, Keynes, Mitchell and F. W. Taussig.

His major work, *A Neglected Point in the Theory of Crises*, (1908) with its clear presentation of the multiplier and of the inability of unlimited saving to find investment has been hailed as one of the earliest successful formulations of what has become known as Keynesian economics.

Johannsen followed up his intricate analysis with policy proposals that were likewise quite modern. For example, in one of his innumerable pamphlets appealing to the profession to attempt to understand his theory, he wrote that there were two alternative ways to "guard against depressions." One was to "create unlimited opportunities for building up new productive capital, so that the savings funds constantly accruing can always find investment in the beneficent way." The alternative was to "restrict or regulate the saving activity, . . . so as to keep it in healthy limits." Since "the greater the concentration of wealth in individual hands, the greater the saving power; such concentration . . . is not desirable, so far as the interests of society are concerned."[17]

Living today as we do in a society which largely accepts the welfare state, it is hard to conceive that not so long ago in our history most of the programs which go to make it up were considered radical, impractical, visionary and even subversive. After all, a hundred years ago, in the immediate post Civil War period, about the only examples of continuous, collective action on a nationwide scale, were the post office and the armed forces. It is with this record in mind that we assess the contribution of that exceedingly rare breed, the creative social thinker.

Because of the limitations of time, the emphasis throughout this address has necessarily been on the constructive accomplishments of the writers discussed and opposing views have been to some extent passed over. But to every proposal for substantial change in either the institutional structure or accepted modes of thought, powerful well entrenched forces of conservatism offered resistance. To fail to take note of the opposition encountered by the thinkers we have covered, would undervalue the quality of their achievements, for in addition to their intellectual initiative they displayed courage and determination. By and large the critical, creative thinkers and social inventors have been of the heterodox persuasion, but this perhaps is to be expected, for there is as yet no way in institutionalize creative thinking and social invention. After all Adam Smith was in his day a heterodox thinker.

FOOTNOTES

1."The Multiple Money Standard," *Annals of the American Academy of Political and Social Science,* March 1896, pp. 215, 227, 222, 232.

2.Walker to Carroll D. Wright in Massachusetts Bureau of Statistics of Labor, *Fifth Annual Report* (Boston: Wright and Potter, 1874), pp. vii-viii.

3.Worthington C. Ford to Richmond Mayo-Smith, October 18, 1893, copy in Ford Papers, New York Public Library.

4.W. E. Minchinton, "Hobson, Veblen and America," British Association for American Studies, *Bulletin,* February 1959, p.33.

5."The State of the Union," *The Congressional Record,* January 4, 1965, pp. 27-28; "The Economic Report," *The Congressional Record,* January 28, 1965, pp. 1403, 1404, 1407.

6.Mitchell to Lucy Sprague, October 18, 1911, in Lucy Sprague Mitchell, "A Personal Sketch," in *Wesley C. Mitchell: The Economic Scientist,* ed. by A. F. Burns (New York: National Bureau of Economic Research, 1952), pp. 66-67.

7.J. M. Clark, "Recent Developments in Economics," in *Recent Developments in the Social Sciences,* ed. by E. C. Hayes (Philadelphia: Lippincott, 1927), p. 284.

8."Expert Opinion on the Unemployment Fund," *The Advance*, May 18, 1923.

9."The Economic Report," *The Congressional Record*, January 28, 1965, pp. 1404,1407.

10."An Index Number of Production," *The American Economic Review*, March 1921, p. 57.

11.W. Randolph Burgess, "Reflections on the Early Development of Open Market Policy," Federal Reserve Bank of New York, *Monthly Review*, November 1964, p. 222.

12."Commons' former student, and then colleague, Harold M. Groves was his collaborator in drafting the measure. Groves, who is an authority in the field of public finance, has written a most penetrating paper on the basic role of institutional theory for his specialty. (See "Institutional Economics and Public Finance," *Land Economics*, August 1964, pp. 239-246.)

13."The Concept of Value," *The Quarterly Journal of Economics*, August 1915, pp. 663-664.

14.Clark to Mitchell, May 14, 22, 1948, in Mitchell Papers, Columbia University Libraries.

15."Social Insurance: An Approach to a New Order," *The World Tomorrow*, November 1928, p. 454; P[aul] K[ellogg], "Isaac Rubinow," *The Survey*, October 1936, p. 314.

16.Alan H. Gleason, "Foster and Catchings: A Reappraisal," *The Journal of Political Economy*, April 1959, pp. 157, 169-170.

17.*To the Economists of America: A New Depression Theory* (Brooklyn: Privately printed, [1908]).

Notes on the Present State of Neoclassical Economics as a Subset of the Orthodox

Kenneth E. Boulding

Neoclassical economics is a very fuzzy set. Almost everyone draws his own boundaries around it, and the boundaries often are determined by what we like or do not like. It almost could be described as a planetary system revolving around a doubtfully binary star: The central star, of which there is no doubt, is Alfred Marshall; the doubtful one is J. M. Keynes. In some ways Keynes is a very neoclassical economist; in other ways, of course, he represents a revolt, at least to certain aspects of the school. It is not unfair, however, to describe Keynes as a "supplement" to Marshall rather than in opposition to him, for Keynes virtually accepted all that Marshall had to say about price theory and differed only on employment theory, with which Marshall did not really deal. The theory of imperfect competition likewise can be regarded as an extension of the Marshallian system rather than a fundamental criticism of it. Indeed, a good deal of it was anticipated by Marshall himself in *Industry and Trade*.

I find it rather difficult, therefore, to understand the passion with which the great destroyers of straw men, such as John Kenneth Galbraith and Joan Robinson, go about attacking the symbol of neoclassical

---

The author is Professor of Economics and Director, Institute of Behavioral Science, University of Colorado, Boulder. *This article was presented at the Annual Meeting of the Association for Evolutionary Economics, San Francisco, California, 27–29 December 1974.*

economics. Surely they do not believe that anybody ever thought that all markets were perfectly competitive, or even that any markets were perfectly competitive. Surely they do not think that relative prices are unimportant, that any relative price set is as good as any other. Perhaps the venom of the attacks arises because the attackers believe that somehow neoclassical economics justifies a distribution of income which they regard as illegitimate. But Marshallian economics, especially, is designed in part to answer the question of what redistributions can be accomplished without a diminution of what is to be distributed. Marshall may not have had all the answers to this problem, but he certainly understood it, and unless would-be redistributers understand it, they are all too likely to do a great deal of harm in the attempt to do good. One cannot help feeling, for example, that if Allende had understood Marshall the history of Chile might have been much happier.

Two criticisms of Marshallian relative price theory strike me as having some point. The first is that of Thorstein Veblen, who argued cogently that demands and preferences were not givens of the system, but were in part, at any rate, determined by the system, even by the system of relative prices itself. This criticism seems to me a valid one in terms of long-run dynamics, although I suspect that Marshall himself would have been quite sympathetic toward it, as he certainly never believed that demands or preferences were sacrosanct. A similar criticism, of course, would be that production functions and supply functions likewise are not simply givens, but that their dynamic history is in part determined by the relative price structure itself. Inputs which are dear will be economized; those which are cheap will not, and this will determine the whole course of technical change. I have argued, indeed, that if there is a disequilibrium, either in the Marshallian sense, with some kind of "abnormal" distribution of rewards, or in the Walrasian sense, with the development of shortages and surpluses, this may operate to change the demand and supply functions just as much as it operates to change prices and outputs. Here again, however, this is an extension of the Marshallian scheme, not a contradiction of it.

The other criticism of Marshall is that of Davenport, an unjustly neglected economist at the present time, who argued that Marshall's obsession with the relative price structure led to a neglect of the forces which determine actual money prices and money wages. There is at least some validity in this criticism, although it is not one that usually is made today. It is significant, however, insofar as it explains in part the extraordinary helplessness of the economics profession in the face of inflation. A study of the actual dynamic process by which money prices and money wages are set, however, would take us far beyond the Marshallian schema. This is something which simply has not been done by anyone as far as I know.

Veblen also criticized Marshall on the grounds that his scheme was not "evolutionary." Marshall was very strongly attracted toward evolutionary theory and was very anxious to make economics evolutionary. I argue, indeed, that he came within a hair's breadth of doing this and that the Marshallian schema is an admirable starting point for true evolutionary economics. Evolution is the interaction of populations through processes of mutation by which new populations arise and through selection functions which determine the birth and death rates of existing populations and so determine whether they will be reasonably stable or whether they will decline to extinction. In Marshall's view, commodities are species; their population is, of course, the total stock. This stock is added to by production ("births"), subtracted from by consumption ("deaths"), and these processes are both regulated by the relative price structure. Marshall's equilibrium price structure, indeed, is very similar to the structure of ecological equilibrium. His long-run equilibrium corresponds very closely to the notion of a climactic ecosystem, in which the stocks of all commodities are consistent with the prevailing environment in terms of preferences and production functions, and the production and consumption of all commodities are equal, so that the stocks neither increase nor diminish with time.

Marshall certainly was aware of the importance of mutation, that is, of new inventions, new discoveries, and the kinds of social inventions involved in new organizations and in entrepreneurship. He perhaps did not pay the same attention to this that Joseph Schumpeter did, but the Schumpeterian view of "creative destruction" is a highly evolutionary one which certainly is implicit in Marshall. In a very real sense, therefore, Marshallian economics is evolutionary, despite its use of equilibrium as an essentially heuristic device. Marshall was acutely aware of the fact that no equilibrium is ever constant because the underlying parameters constantly are changing.

One perhaps might accuse neoclassical economics of being insufficiently sensitive to the extent to which different, although essential, economic functions can be performed by different institutions. Saving, that is, real capital accumulation, certainly does not have to be confined to what is done under private property. The socialist states, if anything, have oversaved, that is, sacrificed the present generations too ruthlessly for the benefit of their posterity. The theory of private saving, important as it is, which was developed with great beauty, for example, by Irving Fisher, always must be supplemented by the recognition that under given institutional conditions public saving may be a very large amount of the total. Nevertheless, the perception that saving does involve a shift between present and future consumption (or, more generally, economic welfare) is as significant for socialist as it is for capitalist states. The great importance of the relative price structure in matters of allocation of resources is also something which socialist states have had to learn very painfully. They still have not learned this lesson as fully as perhaps they might.

Most of the venom with which neoclassical economics has been attacked has been reserved perhaps for an aspect of it which was never central and which neoclassical economics was not particularly designed to evaluate. This is the marginal productivity theory of returns to labor and capital, which certainly is implicit in Eugen von Böhm-Bawerk, and was developed rather fully by Wicksteed (who, incidentally, apparently convinced Bernard Shaw that labor theory of value was a wholly inadequate dogma upon which to erect the complexities of the relative price structure). Of course, the theory particularly is associated with J. B. Clark, in whose hands perhaps it did take something of the flavor of justification of a purely market-determined structure of wages and profits, on the grounds that each party received an equivalent of the contribution made to the total product, or at least the marginal contribution. I have criticized this view rather severely on the grounds that profits emerge out of the complexity of the accounting identities and are determined much more by decisions about investment and dividend and interest distributions than by any mythical marginal productivity of capital. This is not to deny, however, that the marginal productivity of savings in terms of some kind of internal rate of return is a highly significant aspect of economic life under any institutions whatever, or to deny that rates of time preference or impatience are extremely important in explaining decisions both public and private in this area.

The relations of the relative price structure to functional distribution are extremely complex, and neoclassical economics did not really solve this problem. Radical economics, and still less Marxist economics, has not solved it either, and it remains one of the real puzzles of the complexity of the economic system. The problem of the proper limits of private property is one which goes far beyond the boundaries of formal economics and rests on questions such as the relation of private property to democracy and to civil rights, the dangers of the concentration of power under socialism, and an enormously complex scheme of evaluations of trade-offs, the nature of which is by no means wholly clear. One can see socialism as an avenue to more equitable distribution and at the same time detest the socialist state as a political monster, a brontosaur which inevitably will lead to the corruption of all decent human relations, the extinction of the arts, and the loss of a great deal that makes life valuable. One of the prime businesses of economics is how to get good things cheap and how to detect what might be called the relative political price structure and how this is related to particular institutions. We cannot expect neoclassical economics to answer these questions. Indeed, it is not designed to do so.

Neoclassical economics seems to emerge from this discussion as an absolutely essential part of a larger social theory, to be used cautiously within its self-imposed limits, but neither to be feared nor hated. Perhaps the most difficult thing is to get a proper sense of proportion about what things are central and what things are peripheral, what things are first approximations and what things are simply wrong and misleading. I would defend neoclassical economics as an extraordinarily useful first approximation in the discussion of the dynamics of that part of the social system which deals with the relative price structure, terms of trade, and the impact of this whole structure on decisions and the dynamics of other elements of the society. The terms of trade, that is, how much you get for what you give, is a crucial element in virtually all social relations, even those involving reciprocity, as in the family or in political life, and the insights which are derived from neoclassical economics in this regard may have very wide application, as the extension of the concept of exchange into sociology and political science in the last generation has demonstrated.

Neoclassical economics should not be expected to explain everything. It does not have a very good analysis of what I have called the "grants economy," that is, one-way transfers, although it is very easy to extend the apparatus of value theory to include these one-way transfers. It is not very successful in dealing with public goods and public bads, but this gets us into political science and political decision making, which is another part of the forest. Among the "trees of the forest," as Marshall saw so clearly, are all sorts of organizations in all stages of development. What Marshall is saying is that they obey certain ecological laws, although we can distort the system by public policy toward public values, just as the farmer distorts the ecosystem of his land toward crops rather than brambles. But however much we distort the system it remains an ecosystem. This I think is the ultimate meaning of neoclassical price theory.

An appendix perhaps should be added on the Keynesian contribution. It was Keynes's genius that he perceived as a question what earlier writers simply had taken for granted, that is, the "adding up theorem": Unless the total product is disposed of, either to households or to businesses or to governments or net exports, there will be unwanted accumulations, and these are likely to lead to unemployment and to a reduction in output below the optimum. Keynes saw further that adjustments in the relative price and wage structure did not necessarily solve this problem in practice. Whether theoretically there is some position of the price-wage set which always will give full employment is still a matter of some debate. What is clear, however, is that even if this set exists, it frequently is not feasible to attain it under existing institutions.

We have become acutely aware in the last year or two of the limitations which institutional arrangements such as administered prices, labor unions, and collective bargaining, as well as speculative markets, impose on the possibility of achieving full employment without inflation. Keynes was not able to solve this problem and neither are we. It may require, indeed, a return to a more micro approach and a greater understanding of the actual dynamics of absolute money-price and money-wage formation to supplement the theory of the very real pressures which disequilibrium price and wage structure in a relative sense produce. Neoclassical economics has not produced a solution to this problem, but neither has anyone else. In any case, it is hard to deny the reality of the dynamics of the relative price and wage structure, and a better knowledge of the actual dynamics of absolute money prices and money wages must be a supplement to the more fundamental forces which determine the relative structure, or at least which render each relative structure a creator of dynamic patterns which are peculiar to itself.

Orthodox Economists and Existential Economics

Richard H. Day

Adequate explanations of unemployment-inflation and of explosive population growth in impoverished economic circumstances are not to be found among the propositions of orthodox economics. This no doubt explains why coherent policies for dealing with these problems have not emerged. Something would indeed seem to be wrong with the state of orthodox economics. In these brief remarks I will try to suggest what must be done.

Hallmarks of the Orthodox Economist

By orthodox economists we should not mean W.S. Jevons, Alfred Marshall, Leon Walras, Eugen von Böhm-Bawerk, Knut Wicksell, and other founding fathers of neoclassical theory. I doubt if any of them believed they were establishing a new catechism. Rather, I imagine they felt they were contributing to the ongoing development of economics as a science. To them economic theory was to be created, not merely learned and applied. The first hallmark of the orthodox economist is an entirely different attitude. To him, economic principles may need clarification and perhaps even generalization, but they exist, are to be mastered, and then applied in solving problems.

This is not a pernicious attitude. In economics, as in any field, the or-

---

The author is Professor of Economics, Social Systems Research Institute, University of Wisconsin, Madison. *This article was presented at the Annual meeting of the Association for Evolutionary Economics, San Francisco, California, 27–29 December 1974.*

thodox, by cleaving to a coherent body of principles, prevent capricious oscillations in the way the world is understood. By resisting intellectual change they help screen out highly plausible but superficial explanations of temporary phenomena of no enduring interest. Their existence creates a barrier and hence forces competition in the marketplace of ideas. In this way they play an essential role in the evolution of science.

Practically effective theory must consist of a set of propositions that are simple in comparison with perceptions and capable of application over and over again in a great variety of settings. Neoclassical economics has such a powerful hold on the orthodox precisely because it so admirably meets this criterion. This hold is further enhanced when it is shown that the neoclassical theory can subsume and illuminate a seemingly competing theory. (We recall in this context J.R. Hicks's and Oskar Lange's incorporation of Keynesian insights within the Walrasian framework.)

Indeed, neoclassical economics now provides a virtually impenetrable armor against attack by those heretics who offer unconventional models and address problems not well suited for solution by the orthodox tools. How else are we to explain the scurrilous attacks on the builders of the so-called doomsday models? The prognoses of the latter, however, are no longer laughing matters. Although they incorporate disputable empirical hypotheses, their models are based—as I have shown elsewhere—on a coherent and valid, if novel and limited, methodology. This then is the second hallmark of the orthodox: the defense of their intellectual domain from intrusion by outsiders, even at the cost of ignoring relevant facts and effective new methods.

That too is a victimless crime. One more mischievous is the doctrine that a theory is to be judged not by its assumptions, but by its predictions. Obviously, a theory that yields accurate predictions will inspire faith, just as soldiers escaping death in answer to a pious vow become evangelists for God. But answered prayers are not definitive evidence upon which the existence of God can be founded, nor are a number of accurate predictions proof that a theory is good. Returning to the doomsday models, it is surely not on the implausibility of their predictions, which already have been borne out in part, that they are to be faulted. It is rather on the implausibility of their assumptions, and this indeed has been a focus of much of the criticism, ironically by prestigious and well-trained members of the orthodox school.

It is a short step from believing that a theory is "good" because it yields accurate predictions to believing that a theory is "good" because it yields "good" predictions, that is, predictions we would like to be true. For example, the theory of perfect competition yields the existence of an efficient social equilibrium. As the latter is desirable in a well-defined sense, it somehow makes the whole theory believable. But the theory does not, in fact, tell us how, on the basis of plausible hypotheses of behavior, such equilibria are brought about in particular, or how markets work in general. Therefore, the theory of the existence of such equilibria, which is the heartland of received doctrine, is not a scientific explanation of reality, but is *the characterization of a state* which if achieved would have certain desirable properties. This fact explains why this same equilibrium theory is supposed by some to apply equally to socialism and capitalism. But if socialism and capitalism are different, it is because they *work* differently. Plausible assumptions that describe their *working* must lead to essential differences in their theories. But for the orthodox economist, and this is his third hallmark, a theory which characterizes desirable states is believed to provide a theory of the way the world works or should work.

To summarize, orthodox economics is characterized by the following traits. (1) It has a coherent body of principles and a dedicated body of practitioners who are able to apply them effectively and widely. (2) To these practitioners, the principles are to be mastered and applied, not created or evolved. (3) The principles are to be defended. New and/or alternative theories are to be resisted. (4) The theory is held to be good in spite, not because, of its assumptions. (5) The desirable states characterized by the theory are believed to be properties of the real world that exist or can be made to exist.

Orthodox Contributions

What has been said so far has been focused on orthodox economists, not on the classical, neoclassical, and Keynesian founders of the discipline, and not necessarily on its more creative contemporary developers. The creation and extension of coherent microeconomic theory is no more an orthodox act than was the formulation of the Constitution of the United States. Effective applications are sometimes creative too, just as law may receive a novel reinterpretation in a particular case in court. No, the orthodox contribute to the evolution of ideas precisely by resisting change. They also provide a mass market for those who wish to create within the boundaries of the conventional paradigm.

These boundaries are not narrow. Although virtually all the central insights were provided by the classical and neoclassical economists, the generalization, refinement, clarification, and application of conventional theory to new problems goes on at an accelerated pace. One can doubt neither the vitality nor utility of received doctrine.

It has given us a rigorous, operational optimization theory that characterizes rational economizing and elegantly illuminates the relationship between scarcity and value. On this foundation it has built a coherent and unified theory of supply and demand and of equilibrium prices for decentrally determined allocations. By applying utilitarian concepts to risky alternatives, the economics of uncertain choices has been rationalized and brought within the conventional domain. By applying optimal control, dynamic programming, and differential game techniques to the intertemporal choice theory begun by Böhm-Bawerk and Fisher, economic development is also gathered if not squeezed into the orthodox conceptual fold.

Much of this has involved creative endeavor of a high order. But perhaps the greatest potential contribution of standard economics to wise discourse and fruitful inquiry has gone virtually unnoticed by the orthodox economists who learn and apply, defend and believe. With growing precision and clarity orthodox economics has demarcated the boundaries between analytical knowledge, the vast realm where analytical knowledge is yet to be established, and the limitless space where theory is *not* reality, where truth must be sought and action committed, not on the basis of mathematics and computation, but on the basis of dialectical discourse, persuasion, and coercion.

Adaptive Economics

It is clear that standard theory, to which the orthodox ascribe, does not tell much about how decisions are made, or how they add up within organizations and interact in transactions among competing and cooperating institutions. It tells us virtually nothing about how economies move from one point in time to another when they are out of equilibrium. Instead, the economic change accommodated by the orthodox is the economic change of optimal or balanced equilibrium trajectories.

Never mind the testimonies that agents act "as if" they optimize and economies act "as if" they were in equilibrium. Until we know how competing agents in their ignorance and in their lack of coordination bring such states to pass we do not have a convincing basis for deciding whether or when to apply optimizing and equilibrium concepts. The first order of business of creative economic theorists for the next quarter century must be an attack on this central problem. We simply have to acquire a better analytical understanding of how economies really work!

Useful and indispensable ingredients for the new models and theories will be found in the great works of our predecessors. When they do not always provide the ingredients, they often will hint at where to look. We have just been reminded by Professor Kenneth Boulding how useful and how broad some of the neoclassical fathers were. I agree with virtually all of his observations. Yet, I have great sympathy for J.K. Galbraith and Joan Robinson. The orthodox are not strawmen. They are our colleagues, and although they assuredly do not all believe "that all markets are perfectly competitive or even that any . . . [are]," they often are prepared to formulate theory and policy as if such markets did exist and were in equilibrium.

There are other sources upon which to draw. Indeed, there emerged in the past quarter century a variety of contributions to the economic theory of man as he is and of economies (or parts of economies) as they really work. One must mention Simon, Cooper, Cyert, and March, whose work has been virtually ignored by the orthodox. Of a somewhat younger vintage Sid Winter and I have in different ways tried to develop realistic economic models. Until now our quest has been lonely. Radner and Rothschild, however, recently have joined the fray, and one may venture the guess that a turning point has been reached.

The concepts of this nonorthodox school include satisficing, rules of thumb, learning, and cautious, local, approximate suboptimizing with feedback. In general, it involves adaptation and evolution with bounded rationality. This is not received doctrine. It is, however, the basis of realistic economizing. It is the economics of man as he adapts, subject to his biological limitation, to the world as he finds it and as it adapts to him. I call this emerging field *adaptive economics.*

Nothing is more important to the development of this field than the careful observation of economic agents in their natural habitat. Although one does not find its practice much used, studied, or taught by econometricians, direct observation should be regarded as a legitimate if not indispensable source of information for identifying and formulating relevant hypotheses upon which to base theoretical research. (Wassily Leontief reminded us of this just last year.) Indeed, one of the most impressive scientific achievements of this century has been the development of the field of animal ethology, not on the basis of statistical technique, but of perceptive observation and cogent rationalization. To complement our Jan Tinbergen of econometrics and economic theory, we need, for the economic agent, the counterpart of the Tinbergen of animal behavior. We need, in short, an economic ethology.

Institutional Economics

Beyond the analytical realm lies the boundless domain of dialectical thought, that domain where insights cannot be reduced to mathematical models or to propositions in the logical calculus. This is the realm where individual and social preferences are formed, where new techniques are discovered, where new organizations emerge (symbiotically more than the sum of their parts), where men coalesce in brief, vibrant, intense cooperatives for war and revolution. It is the realm of mutation, of stochastic event, of threat, of violence, and the realm of orderly disputation. It is indeed the realm where most of our conscious thought unfolds and where most of our decisions are made.

Orthodox economists have ignored this domain, although we finally have a definitive treatise on its fundamental nature in Nicholas Georgescu-Roegen's *Essays*. Marxian economics, although constrained in part by its own orthodoxy, has much to offer toward a theory that explains the emergence of conflict, irresolvable by peaceful means, and the breakdown of existing socioeconomic organization. Much of social evolution, however, is to be interpreted as the development of organizations by which dialectical conflict is controlled. When channeled through organizations the dialectical process is institutionalized. Organizations in their function as an avenue for the dialectic are *institutions*. Thus we have the institutions of economics, of law, of political process, and of revolution.

The systematic study of the creation, functioning, and demise of institutions is the concern of *institutional economics*. Such a field existed. Indeed, it emerged out of the German historical school, was established by Richard T. Ely, and in my opinion reached its zenith with the publication of John R. Commons's little read masterpiece, *The Legal Foundations of Capitalism*.

In Commons's system, institutions function in ways not recognized by orthodox economic theory. First, they provide a framework where decisions can be made that make some people better off *and others worse off*. Second, they provide a place where public purpose can be defined in the context of current situations and evolved in response to the changing perceptions and needs of the parties involved. This they do not do on the basis of a social preference ordering compatible with each individual. Rather, they proceed by forming compromises among opposing points of view that will gain acceptance for the time being. Third, the unit of analysis in Commons is not the commodity or the individual agent, but the *transaction* involving an exchange of present and anticipated opportunities and limitations between two individuals in the context of alternative potential exchanges in accordance with working rules defined, administered, interpreted, and enforced by officials of government. From this point of view, the fundamental task of the social scientist is to investigate things as they are and to design new institutions.

These must provide more effective avenues for transactions among individuals in their search for a good way of life and resolve the conflicts that inevitably arise while retaining the willing participation of those who lose in the resolution.

In recent years orthodox economists have, at the invitation of law schools and courts of law, been provided with opportunities to contribute their analytical wisdom to the resolution of conflicts and thereby to the evolution of law itself. There is also a need for economists to learn the methods of legal process and research to see if they might provide a means for interpreting the development of economic institutions and provide insights into how better institutions might be designed.

Existential Economics

Three intellectual realms have been spoken of here. The first is the realm of existing analytical knowledge. The orthodox operate from niches within this realm. There is the second realm of *possible* analytical knowledge. One's primary search here can be for territory to annex along the margins of conventional theory. I have urged, however, that explorations of a much broader nature also be launched following paths already laid down by early explorers, with the view to building a new, coherent edifice of adaptive economic theory. Finally, there is the third realm of dialectical knowledge, so unfamiliar to conventional economists. We have the tales of early pioneers in the domain. We know that they established major, yet foreign, frameworks of thought. But their paths have grown dim, and we have all but lost contact. Here, too, I have proposed major new explorations, to rediscover and to rebuild an institutional or dialectical economics.

Now I propose a permanent alliance between these two efforts in adaptive and institutional theorizing and call this the economics of man as we find him and as he is becoming, or *existential economics.* My hope is that within such a realm new regimes may be designed that will make possible the further development of man in his economic activity so that those other realms, the realms of culture and the spirit, will not perish, torn apart by hyperinstability or borne under by accumulated industrial ills.

Remarks on the State of Orthodoxy

Victor P. Goldberg

I must begin by expressing some puzzlement with Professor Boulding's identification of Alfred Marshall as the central star of the neoclassical system. Marshall is out; Walras is in. Thus, Paul Samuelson [1967, p. 109] says: "The ambiguities of Alfred Marshall paralyzed the best brains in the Anglo-Saxon branch of our profession for three decades. By 1930 the profession . . . had yet to reattain the understanding of the theory of competitive general equilibrium that Walras had achieved by 1878 or 1896." It appears that as part of their initiation rites, young theorists now are required to make an estimate of how far back Marshall had set the profession.

Orthodox economists have a tendency to transfer theoretical propositions from the pristine context in which they were spawned to a real world context. As a result, they have developed a set of homilies, rules of thumb, policy recommendations, and criteria that together loosely can be classified as an ideology. The bridge between the rigorous formal models and the ideology too often has been "Fuzzy Thought." I would like to begin by questioning one of the central elements in the ideology—freedom of contract.

Individuals are to be free to engage in exchange without restrictions and to achieve thereby the gains from trade. There can be exceptions for so-called merit good or market failure situations, but the presump-

---

The author has a joint appointment with the Institute of Governmental Affairs and the Department of Economics, University of California, Davis. *These comments were presented at the Annual Meeting of the Association for Evolutionary Economics, San Francisco, California, 27–29 December 1974.*

tion is that these are merely special cases. However, if we look closer, it becomes clear that the proposition itself is based on a very special case. First, the exchange is contemporaneous. Smith receives a widget at precisely the same instant that Jones receives his bargained-for gadget. This is the paradigmatic contractual exchange of economic theory, but it has little relation to exchange as it occurs in society. A more representative exchange would be that of Smith promising to exchange a gadget for Jones's promise to exchange a widget. Of course, theory has to simplify reality—Occam's razor and all that—and we must ask not whether the theoretical exchange accurately portrays the world, but whether the simplifications are unduly misleading in the context in which they are applied.

By promising to exchange his gadget for a widget, Smith puts restrictions on his future freedom. He must stand ready to part with the gadget and accept the widget at the agreed upon future date or suffer the legal (or extralegal) social sanctions. That is, an exchange of promises brings with it a concomitant acceptance of restrictions on the parties' future freedom to contract. The very essence of contract is the imposition on the parties of restrictions on their future behavior. Restrictions are pervasive, and while those in the example might be trivial, others are not. Franchisees, for example, can agree to restrict their freedom to alter their prices, alter their hours of operation, or purchase supplies from certain firms. (The same is true of managers of the firm—linked by an employment rather than a franchise contract—but the general tendency of the orthodox to view the firm as a monolith masks this set of restrictions.[1]) The issue is not *whether* restrictions should be imposed, but *which* restrictions should be imposed and *who* is to be the source of those restrictions—private parties or governmental units (including the courts).

Fairly complex restrictions such as franchise arrangements, promises to sell or buy over a long future period, governmental protection of the right to be served (for example, common carriers and limitations on the refusal to deal), and so on, are likely to have desirable results in many contexts. However, in orthodox economics such restrictions are aberrations viewed largely as manifestations of unwise governmental meddling or of the exercise of private market power. (Some outliers from Chicago, however, would argue that most of the "voluntarily" arrived at restrictions were presumptively optimal.)

Freedom of contract's central position in the orthodox ideology stems from its presumed effect on the efficiency of resource allocation. The conditions for efficient production in the basic orthodox model are straightforward and are satisfied, under appropriate assumptions, by freely contracting parties. But when we turn our attention to the real world, we neither know what the appropriate efficiency criteria are nor do we have the tools to determine whether resource allocation mechanisms based largely on freedom of contract perform better than alternatives. How, for example, are we to determine whether it is desirable to constrain the employer's freedom to terminate an employee, to define some form of right to job security? How are we to evaluate franchise contracts which compensate the franchisor with a percentage of the gross or complex construction contracts with cost-plus pricing?[2] Certainly, by the criteria of the basic model it is efficient to leave factor mix decisions to the employer, and it is inefficient to use percentage of the gross, cost-plus, or other forms of flexible pricing.

There are other issues related to the efficacy of freedom of contract that I only can touch on here. Power of the parties is one. While economists are apt to dismiss this issue as merely one of determining the final location of the parties on the contract curve, it is more complex, especially when power and imperfect information are simultaneously entered into the problem.[3] Imperfect information and the advantages of spreading the information costs over a large number of transactions raise other difficulties. There are tremendous advantages to consumers, employees, and business firms in delegating the task of determining the content of contracts to agents, either public (judges, legislatures, regulatory commissions) or private (unions, cooperatives, lawyers, trade associations). How much information should business firms provide to suppliers, customers, or competitors? Once we move away from the perfect information world, there is little guidance as to who should own information and on what terms.

A contract does not in itself define completely the terms on which a transaction takes place. It is conceptually useful to view transactions as being governed by a nested array of contracts, some explicit, some implicit.[4] For example, an individual employment contract is conditioned by the terms of a collective bargaining contract, and its terms, in turn, are conditioned by the public law of collective bargaining. Each transaction is thus subject to a complex array of "jurisdictions" much as an individual is subject to a complex array of overlapping political jurisdictions ranging from special districts through the federal government. Rather than beginning with the individual transaction and noting the superstructure of public and private law that governs it, we instead might focus on the question of what that superstructure should look like. That is, we have what is known somewhat presumptuously in the public choice literature as an optimal jurisdiction or optimal decentralization problem. What pattern of explicit or implicit contracts should govern particular transactions? Should these "contracts" be public or private? What should be the mix of rules and discretion? What should determine the individual's freedom to "escape" from a particular jurisdiction? This last question takes on added import when we realize that the essence of contract is to impose restrictions on future behavior and that these restrictions, in effect, define the terms on which an individual can escape from a particular jurisdiction.

This line of reasoning suggests a radically different perspective. I begin with a picture of an economy in which restrictions on behavior are pervasive and in which the source of those restrictions—public versus private—is not necessarily an important distinction. The orthodox paradigm, on the other hand, treats restrictions as aberrations, the primary source being government. While in the best of all possible theoretical worlds these perspectives might, in some peculiar analytical equilibrium, yield identical results, in practice they are apt to lead to substantially different description and prescription.

The orthodox approach can be characterized as asking: Will freely contracting individuals, behaving as hypothesized in the model, achieve the efficiency criteria defined by the model? If so, then there arises a strong presumption that freedom of contract will lead to desirable results in practice. My proposed alternative is to ask, instead: What pattern of decentralized decision making (including freedom of contract as a special case) appears desirable when set against a, quite possibly, ad hoc set of criteria? This second formulation sounds terrible until we realize that it is implicit in the apparently more rigorous orthodox formulation.

This leads us somewhat unnaturally into the question of distribution. It is a common practice to partition the allocation problem into two supposedly separable problems: efficiency and distribution. Then, since the rigorous tools of economics can give precise answers (in context) to efficiency questions and because those tools cannot give similarly rigorous answers to distribution questions, attention is focused primarily on efficiency. However, this distinction, I would argue, is illusory. The rigorous answers to the efficiency questions are the result of ruthlessly pruning the real world complications from allocation problems. Efficiency can be rigorously defined and analyzed only if we are willing to make very strong assumptions. We might then ask: Could we make equally rigorous statements concerning distribution if we were permitted to make equally strong assumptions? I do not want to get involved in the game of determining whether statements are of equal rigor or assumptions are of equal strength, but I do feel that simply raising this question is useful. It should not be terribly difficult to generate distributional statements that follow from reasonable assumptions concerning, for example, interpersonal comparisons of utility. One seldom, however, observes such an exercise. I would suggest that the lack of effort on distribution questions stems from the implicit establishment of a much higher burden of proof. In distribution questions, the crucial assumptions are often clearer and the anomalies surface more readily. We thus are quickly aware of the problem cases: Do we give the dull, unfeeling clod less than the individual with the finely-honed consumption skills? In efficiency questions the bodies are more skillfully buried, and it is more difficult to realize that trade secrets, brand names, endogenous preferences, and other complexities are rendering the basic efficiency conclusions inoperative.

We therefore could arrive at the negative position that if we cannot say anything precise about distribution, then by applying the same standards we cannot say anything about efficiency either. I prefer instead to argue that we can, with suitable caution, use some fairly rigorous theorizing to guide us in establishing criteria for evaluating alternative resource allocation mechanisms, and with similar caution, we can generate distributional propositions to serve a similar role.

Notes

1. However, see Ronald Coase [1937] and the literature spawned by that important article.
2. For an attempt to answer questions of this sort, see Victor Goldberg [1975.]
3. See Goldberg [1974] for a fuller treatment of that problem.
4. The implications of this approach are traced out more fully in Goldberg [1975].

References

[1] Ronald H. Coase. "The Nature of the Firm." *Economica* 4 (November 1937): 386–405.

[2] Victor P. Goldberg. "Institutional Change and the Quasi-Invisible Hand." *Journal of Law & Economics* 17 (October 1974).

[3] Victor P. Goldberg. "Regulation and Administered Contracts." Manuscript, 1975.

[4] Paul A. Samuelson. "The Monopolistic Competition Revolution." In *Monopolistic Competition Theory: Studies in Impact,* edited by Robert E. Kuenne. New York: John Wiley & Sons, 1967. Pp. 105–38.

The Sad State of Orthodox Economics

Howard Sherman

The classical economists, such as Adam Smith and David Ricardo, did not hesitate to present society quite realistically, class conflicts and all. They wrote at the height of the bourgeois rebellion against all feudal notions, in the period from 1776 to the 1830s, beginning with the American and French Revolution and the continuing Industrial Revolution. By the 1840s the possibly subversive implications of some of Ricardo's theory were under attack. J. S. Mill stated a theory for the transitional period of the 1850s and 1860s which claimed to be classic, but greatly modified and narrowed the labor theory of value. Finally, in the 1870s the old value theory was explicitly tossed out and the neoclassicals created a marginal utility–marginal productivity theory which was a perfect apology for capitalism.

Neoclassical theory reflected the Victorian complacency of the new ruling class; it lasted as the dominant paradigm until the shocks of the Great Depression. In that era Keynesianism was born as an attempt to state a more realistic outlook, one that could admit the possibilities of depressions under capitalism, while proposing to solve them within the capitalist system. Even this Keynesian reformism was under attack by conservatives in the 1940s. By the late 1950s and 1960s, however, the rift was healed, and Keynesian theory was mostly integrated into what Paul Samuelson calls the great neoclassical-Keynesian synthesis. This

---

The author is Professor of Economics, University of California, Riverside. *This article was presented at the Annual Meeting of the Association for Evolutionary Economics, San Francisco, California, 27–29 December 1974.*

new synthesis admits that government can (and should) take certain steps to bring about full employment, after which all the old neoclassical conclusions about the beauties of capitalism hold sway.

By the mid-1960s, this new synthesis appeared unassailable, and there was a flurry of activity to give it a more and more elegant mathematical form. Yet events of the late 1960s and early 1970s—the antiwar movement, the rise of the New Left, and a resurgent interest in Marxism—led to a many-sided attack by liberals as well as radicals on this resplendent paradigm. In his Presidential Address to the American Economic Association in 1972, John Kenneth Galbraith said: "Within the last half-dozen years what before was simply called economics in the nonsocialist world has come to be designated neoclassical economics with appropriate overtures to the Keynesian and post-Keynesian development. From being a general and accepted theory of economic behavior this has become a special and debatable interpretation of such behavior."[1]

The Neoclassical Paradigm

What are the main conservative features of the neoclassical paradigm? First, it does not begin with human relations, but with individual things and individual people. It begins with a mass of commodities with different prices. The neoclassicals make a fetish of each commodity, speaking as if it has an inherent value aside from the particular social relations involved in its production and consumption. The liberal Michael Reagan correctly criticizes this isolation or reification of economic concepts, pointing out that "property" is not a tangible thing, but a socially defined bundle of rights, based on human relationships: "The hired managers of property . . . exercised rights of use and disposition that in fact affected not just the property holders, but also the employees, the consuming public, and the community in which the firm was located."[2]

The neoclassical analysis proceeds from the relation of things to things, such as the price of tea to the price of coffee, only as far as the relation of things to individuals, such as the price of tea to consumer demand. The psychology of the individual consumer is taken to be not only fundamental, but also *given*, that is, its explanation is not considered by the economist. The neoclassical economist assumes that individual consumer preferences come from someplace—from God or innate instincts perhaps—but never considers how society shapes those preferences. It is merely assumed that the highest goal of a well-functioning economy is to follow consumer preferences, not to question their origin. They then proceed to show how consumer preferences in a capitalist economy do indeed determine the prices and amounts produced of all things (given pure and perfect competition and at least sixteen other ridiculous assumptions according to the most recent careful account[3]). Thus neoclassical theory makes individual psychology the ultimate source of the value of commodities, whereas Marxist theory sees the value of a commodity as a function of the human relationships involved in producing it.

The second major conservative feature of neoclassical economics is its emphasis on the harmonious and optimal outcome of market competition for *all* individuals, ruling out any class conflict. The center of neoclassical analysis is the mechanism by which the market functions to reach a goal of optimal equilibrium. This is similar to functionalism in sociology (although the economists' equilibrium approach came earlier), a theory which emphasizes those institutions which function to maintain the stability of the status quo. One liberal discussing functionalism in economics says: "Functional theory commonly predisposes analysis to those equilibrating forces which make for co-operation and harmony. . . . The stress of functional theories on goal-maintenance markedly reduces their capacity for dealing with conflict-ridden systems."[4] In other words, neoclassicals see nothing but a Panglossian world of harmony and equilibrium and totally ignore the social conflicts, such as racism, sexism, or exploitation.

An example of this outlook may be seen in the marginal productivity theory of income distribution, first promoted by John Bates Clark.[5] In Clark's version, still repeated in many current textbooks, each class (providers of land, labor, and capital) is paid according to that factor's marginal product, and this constitutes its fair share. It was shown long ago, most delightfully by George Bernard Shaw, that the ideological conclusion does not follow from the technical theory. Even if a piece of capital receives only "its" marginal product, a piece of capital is not the same as a capitalist. Again, neoclassical economics substitutes relations between things for relations between people. On the technical side, the marginal productivity theory has been shown to be either false or meaningless in the recent vast flood of literature called the "capital controversy."[6]

In addition to its distribution theory, the basic neoclassical paradigm leaves no room for power or conflict in its picture of the functioning of the political economy. The economy is *not* run by the monopoly corporations; on the contrary, the pattern of production is forced on the firm through the market which reflects the preferences of consumers who vote via their monetary demands (never mind that one person may have a thousand times the vote of another). The state is *not* ruled by the economic power of the capitalist class; on the contrary, decisions are made by the votes of the citizens (and never mind that one citizen may spend millions of dollars to influence a campaign directly and through ownership of the media). Galbraith points out that this flaw in neoclassical or neo-Keynesian theory is fatal. Because it lacks knowledge of power or conflict, it "offers no useful handle for grasping the economic problems that now beset the modern society. . . . Rather in eliding power—in making economics a nonpolitical subject—neoclassical theory . . . destroys its relation with the real world."[7] Indeed, realistic political economy died when neoclassical theory became "economics" and left "politics" for political scientists, with neither "science" concerned with the economic bases of political conflicts.

One last example of the prohibition on discussion of conflict in economics is the sad state of so-called welfare economics. In the nineteenth century and up to the 1920s, liberal economists, even such famous neoclassicals as A. C. Pigou, argued that an additional dollar to a millionaire is worth less than an additional dollar to an unemployed worker, so more equal distribution of income may increase total social utility or happiness. This subversive view was eliminated by the modern argument that no two people have the same psychology. In welfare economics, "interpersonal comparisions are *verboten.*"[8] Today, even if we could take ten dollars from Nelson Rockefeller and give ten dollars to a starving child, the neoclassical economist would say there is no "scientific" way to tell whether total utility or happiness is increased. Since there is no way to compare different income distributions, so-called welfare economics takes it as given, and concentrates its sole energy on the goal of "efficiency." This amounts to exactly the same goal as the functionalist goal of making *the present system* run better or smoother or more stably. Class interests and the possibility of change cannot be considered.

Resistance to consideration of change is the third pillar of the neoclassical paradigm. Whether they look at a primitive New Guinea society or at the modern U.S. economy, neoclassicals see only the possibilities of optimal efficiency through achieving equilibrium in the market. There will always be a market! Since the alternative is chaos, only small incremental changes may be made. The motto of the father of neoclassical economics, Alfred Marshall, was: "Nature makes no leaps"—and, he believed, neither should society.

The modern neoclassical, George Stigler, boasts that economic training brainwashes all young economists into conservatism: "He is drilled in the problems of *all* economic systems and in the methods by which a price system solves these problems. . . . He cannot believe that a change in the *form* of social organization will eliminate basic economic problems."[9] Thus, even if a neoclassical economist has liberal sympathies to a welfare program, such as national health care, his training (and he graduates only if he is saturated in it) makes him uncomfortable and suspicious of such a wild leap to an inefficient (by assumption) nonmarket form. Neoclassical economics is certainly the most elegant and elaborate of the conservative paradigms in the social sciences. "The only trouble is that it amounts to an ideology inherently hostile to significant change and implicitly friendly to all handy status quos."[10]

Let us look at some examples of ahistorical, functionalist (equilibrium and efficiency) approaches by neoclassicals. First, Gordon Tullock argues that legal rights should not be decided by ethics, but by efficiency;[11] therefore, to speed up the functioning of the legal process, he would end many of the procedural safeguards the poor need so badly against the police and prosecutors. Second, conservatives in international economics know all about money and commodity exchange ratios, but have never heard of unequal imperialist power relationships between countries. Third, for a century and a half conservatives have accepted Say's Law, which "proves" that general unemployment is impossible because any level of supply generates its own demand; workers are unemployed because they are lazy and "prefer" unemployment compensation and less work. Fourth, if we ask why so few blacks and women are employed in high-wage positions, conservatives such as Gary Becker tell us this *merely* reflects the preferences of employers for white males,[12] or the preferences of blacks and women for less demanding jobs, or the "fact" that blacks and women are less qualified. Milton Friedman goes further:[13] If an employer does not choose the most qualified people because of his irrational preferences, then he will lose money, and competition will put him out of business. Therefore, capitalism automatically eliminates discrimination and produces the best of all possible worlds.

Liberals and Institutionalists

Whereas most of the conservatives are neoclassicals, most of the more liberal economists are institutionalists, such as Galbraith, Alan Gruchy,[14] or Kenneth Boulding. They explicitly reject the ahistorical, harmony assumptions of neoclassical economics to a large degree. Their own paradigm, however, does not pose a consistent and theoretically complete alternative and ultimately does not escape from the neoclassical assumptions. They recognize that consumer preferences are socially determined. They recognize that competition is long gone and we live in a nation of monopoly capitalism. They even emphasize that monopoly economic power leads to dominant political power through both major parties, control of elections, the media, and many other institutions. They believe evolutionary change is possible and necessary.

Yet all of the institutionalists remain within narrow limits; they can conceive of major reforms in capitalism, but can see no reason to end it. Their economics thus has a peculiarly weak half-way feeling in analysis, but especially in proposals. Monopoly should be broken up or regulated—only Galbraith goes so far as to say a few corporations might be nationalized—by the same capitalist state which is dominated by the monopolies. Drastic reforms in favor of minorities, women, and workers may be achieved by reforming the Democratic Party, electing good nonpartisan people to Congress, and reforming congressional decision-making procedures. And what happens to the dominant power of monopoly capital over the parties and Congress? What happens to its vested interests that are under attack? Those relations, those interests and conflicts, are conveniently forgotten. An example of the neglect of class conflict and the adoration of the market is Boulding's naïve statement that "if Allende had understood Marshall, the history of Chile might have been much happier."[15] If Allende had lived to read the congressional hearings on ITT and the CIA in Chile, he would have learned more than from Marshall.

In the institutionalist view, incremental evolutionary changes are achieved by education, consciousness raising, and convincing the elites. For example, some liberals see discrimination as the result of irrational preferences so strong as to overcome the profit motive. One liberal economist says that capitalists discriminate against women because "it feels so good to have women in their 'place.' "[16] Galbraith even implies that the mistaken analyses of neoclassical economics are the major cause of continuing sex discrimination.[17] When neoclassical economics is demolished and "we" educate women and employers to raise their consciousness (and reform the Democratic Party), then sex discrimination will be ended voluntarily and by law. Never does Galbraith recognize the need to clash with the vested interests of monopoly capitalism in the exploitation of women and minorities and other workers.

The Radical Paradigm

The radical methodology first directs the researcher to social relations, not individual preferences. In the United States (and in Chile) this means recognition of the vested interests and political-economic power of the capitalist class. Second, the researcher should ask if these relations involve conflicts. In the U. S. economy, many problems can be clarified only in the light of the exploitive relations of capitalists to workers. Third, every such conflict should be approached in the context of its historical origins, its evolutionary development (for example, the emergence of monopoly and imperialism in the late nineteenth century), and the possibility of drastic revolutionary change in the future when those conflicts become insoluble within the system.[18]

On the basis of these methodological directives, radicals have carried out intensive research in many areas, including the role of capital in production and the resulting distribution of income,[19] the labor market and problems of poverty and discrimination,[20] the relation of political to economic power and the role of government,[21] the intensification of capitalist recessions and inflations resulting from the increase in monoploy power,[22] and the function of multinational corporations in U. S. imperialism.[23] Radical research has revealed that a capitalist government cannot be expected to enforce antitrust laws, regulate monopolies, close tax loopholes, or end the exploitation of cheap minority and female labor. If such a government establishes wage and price controls, it *always* will allow huge loopholes to raise monopoly prices while holding down wages (contrary to Galbraith's desires and expectations).

To achieve full employment and stable prices—as well as end discrimination and imperalist adventures—a minimal necessary condition is the establishment of public ownership of the economy by a *democratically* elected government. Neither political democracy (in the narrow sense of political forms) nor socialism (in the narrow sense of government ownership) are sufficient conditions to achieve these goals; *both* are necessary. Ending capitalism is necessary to prevent domination of government by a wealthy elite; democratic processes are necessary to prevent domination by a self-appointed and self-perpetuating bureaucratic elite. Political democracy *and* economic democracy are vital to each other and to achievement of these goals that are in the interests of most of the population.

Notes

1. John Kenneth Galbraith, "Power and the Useful Economist," *American Economic Review* 63 (March 1973): 1.
2. Michael Reagan, *The Managed Economy* (New York: Oxford University Press, 1963), p. 55.
3. See J. De V. Graaff, *Theoretical Welfare Economics* (London: Cambridge University Press, 1967), *passim.*
4. Sherman Krupp, "Equilibrium Theory in Economics," in *Functionalism in the Social Sciences,* ed., Don Martindale (Philadelphia: American Academy of Political and Social Science, 1965), pp. 65 and 78.

5. J. B. Clark, *The Distribution of Wealth*, 1899 (Clifton, N. J.: Augustus Kelley, 1966).
6. See E. K. Hunt and Jesse Schwartz, *Critique of Economic Theory* (London: Penguin, 1972).
7. Galbraith, "Power," p. 2.
8. Robert Lekachman, "The Conservative Drift in Economics," *Transaction* (Fall 1973): 307.
9. Quoted in ibid., p. 300.
10. Ibid., p. 307.
11. Gordon Tullock, *The Logic of the Law* (New York: Basic Books, 1971).
12. Gary Becker, *The Economics of Discrimination* (Chicago: University of Chicago Press, 1957), p. 5.
13. See Milton Friedman, *Capitalism and Freedom* (Chicago: University of Chicago Press, 1957), pp. 108 ff.
14. See Alan Gruchy, *Contemporary Economic Thought, the Contribution of Neo-institutional Economics* (Clifton, N. J.: Augustus Kelley, 1972).
15. Kenneth Boulding, "Notes on the Present State of Neoclassical Economics," *Journal of Economic Issues* 9 (June 1975): 223–28.
16. Barbara Bergmann, "The Economics of Women's Liberation," *Challenge* 16 (May/June 1973): 14.
17. See John Kenneth Galbraith, *Economics and the Public Purpose* (Boston: Houghton-Mifflin, 1973).
18. The methodology is briefly discussed, the whole paradigm tentatively sketched, and an extensive bibliography given in Howard Sherman, *Radical Political Economy* (New York: Basic Books, 1972). The methodology is presented fully in Oskar Lange, *Political Economy*, vol. 1 (New York: Pergamon Press, 1963).
19. See, for example, E. K. Hunt and Jesse Schwartz, eds., *Critique of Economic Theory* (London: Penguin, 1971).
20. See, for example, David Gordon, *Theories of Poverty and Unemployment* (Lexington: Lexington Books, 1972).
21. See, for example, Ralph Miliband, *The State in Capitalist Society* (New York: Basic Books, 1969).
22. See, for example, Michael Kalecki, *Theory of Economic Dynamics* (London: George Allen and Unwin, 1954). Also see Howard Sherman, *Profits in the United States: An Introduction to a Study of Economic Concentration and Business Cycles* (Ithaca: Cornell University Press, 1968).
23. See, for example, Harry Magdoff, *Age of Imperialism* (New York: Monthly Review Press, 1969). Also see entire issue, *Review of Radical Political Economics* 3 (Spring 1971); this journal carries current articles on imperialism and all other radical theoretical work.

Four Reviews of Benjamin Ward, *What's Wrong with Economics?*

The title of this important book, *What's Wrong with Economics?* suggests a missing subtitle that might have been "And What May Be Done About It." No such subtitle is provided, not only because the book is primarily a critique of what is described as neoclassical or mainline economics, but also because not much space is devoted to what might be considered to be a reconstruction of economics. Benjamin Ward criticizes mainline economics on the ground that it is the outcome of a formalist revolution. This revolution has given us a narrow technical economics that is suffused with a liberal (laissez-faire) positivist ideology, that has a methodology that forces economic reality into a rigid and static mathematico-econometric mold, and that has a narrow scope that excludes concern with the value problem.

The author explains that mainline economics has a twin brother discipline in the form of Marxist economics, which possesses two advantages over mainline economics. First, Marxist economics has a global search-mechanism that enables it to bring into economic analysis many areas of scientific interest such as technological change, class structure and related power relations, and the course of economic evolution, all of which are largely ignored by the practitioners of orthodox economics. Second, Marxist economics turns to a study of values when trying to understand the operations of the advanced industrial capitalist system, whereas mainline economics attempts to keep values and facts separated. Marxist economics finds it essential to show how values held by individuals affect their economic activities as producers, workers, and consumers. This kind of economics, however, suffers in comparison with mainline economics because it is hampered by the demands of socialist propaganda. This propaganda prevents Marxist economics from dealing satisfactorily with the detailed economic problems or puzzles with which normal economic science is supposed to deal.

What Ward is suggesting is that mainline economics is now in a state of intellectual crisis. This crisis has come about because the invisible college of mainline economists has a general scientific framework or paradigm that is no longer adequate for an explanation of current economic problems or so-called economic puzzles. What is needed is a new competing scientific framework or disciplinary matrix that would redefine a number of economic puzzles and even give rise to new puzzles. From where will this new scientific framework come, and who will be responsible for its construction? Since neither mainline nor Marxist economists are prepared to provide this new disciplinary matrix, it must be constructed, in the opinion of the author, by economists who are prepared to borrow from such extra-economic fields as language theory, existentialist philosophy, personality psychology, situation ethics, and legal theory. The author's discussion of these areas of scientific interest lying outside the field of economics buttresses his criticisms of mainline economics. He draws upon recent developments in these fields to point out that man is, after all, an existential and social being with an ideological background; a being whose preferences are culturally determined, who really does make interpersonal comparisons of utilities, and who combines facts, theories, and values in coping with human problems.

Ward's basic aim is to develop a kind of economics that makes a place within its framework for the analysis of values and their role in economic affairs. He observes that the field of legal science has made the most progress in bringing a consideration of values into the analysis of human problems. Like legal science, economics should become a moral science that accepts the ideas that interpersonal comparisons of utility can be scientifically discussed and that a system of value verification can be established. In his new version of economics the author substitutes "storytelling" for the formalistic analyses of the mainline economists. Economic storytelling is an account of an interrelated set of economic phenomena in which facts, theories, and values are mixed together. Such storytelling would, in the author's opinion, give a more realistic interpretation of the problems of the advanced industrial economies. His aim is to bring economics and economists once again close to reality.

Ward has done a very fine job of supporting long-established criticisms of mainline economics with fresh materials from other fields. Anyone already acquainted with the long history of economic dissent will find no substantially new criticisms of standard economics in this volume. However, for a generation of young economists with little or no contact with the history of economic thought, this volume provides an excellent analysis of the limitations of standard economics. When one turns to what the author describes as the constructive part of his study, he is presented only with an outline of the area in which further research is needed and with a set of guidelines for dissenters. Neither the outline nor the guidelines go very far in illuminating the reconstruction of economics as a moral science that the author has in mind. What he is attempting to do is to substitute economics as a study of evolving economic systems for the currently popular economics as a narrow and technical study of optimal economic decision making.

Ward's reduction of economics to the twin brother disciplines of mainline (neoclassical) and Marxist economics is, to this reviewer, an unacceptable oversimplification. Where in this twofold dichotomy would the author place such left Keynesians as Walter Heller, Gardner Ackley, and Arthur Okun, or such non-Keynesians as Galbraith and Myrdal? In analyzing the field of economics one surely needs a fourfold division of neoclassical, Keynesian, neoinstitutionalist, and Marxist economics, each of which has its own ideological or disciplinary matrix.

It is now becoming popular among liberated economists like Ward to think in terms of discovering "the integrated social science of the future" (p. 95). This queen of the social sciences is supposed to rise above the prevailing types of economics and to look at reality through interdisciplinary eyes. In *Beyond Economics* Kenneth Boulding has referred to the similarly elusive goal of a universal social science. It appears that the author does not wish to identify himself with any of the existing schools of economics and that he would prefer, instead, to make a somewhat independent effort to arrive at a restructured science of economics. It is hard to see where this independent effort would lead. While this volume is a critique of economics, it is not a survey of the thought of the economists who have been responsible for making economics what it is today. While economics as a science is criticized, individual economists, for the most part, are not. Consequently, the critical analysis in this study lacks historical perspective. One would like to know where Ward thinks Keynes, Friedman, Galbraith, Myrdal, Heller, Boulding, and other well-known economists stand with respect to the very basic issues with which he is concerned. With such information available one would be in a better position to evaluate Ward's contribution.

If this reviewer were forced to place Ward in one of the conventionally recognized categories of economists, he would place him in the neoinstitutionalist camp. What glimpses one gets in this volume of the economics of the future would suggest that at least Ward's intellectual sympathies are with the Galbraiths and the Myrdals and not with the Hellers and the Okuns or the Friedmans and the Stiglers. But we will have to have more intellectual fare from the author to support any final conclusion on this very interesting point.

Department of Economics ALLAN G. GRUCHY
University of Maryland

My heart sinks when I see a book or article with a title such as this one. I feel obliged to read it; after all, the author just possibly might have discovered what's wrong with economics, and I would hate to be the last to know. But in my heart—that's why it sinks—I expect a waste of time and perhaps a strain on the arteries. So it is very nice to report that Benjamin Ward's book is interesting, subtle, and seriously argued. The best thing it contains, I think, is a sophisticated application to both orthodox and Marxian economics of Thomas Kuhn's famous analysis of science as both a developing body of knowledge and a social system. These passages are miles away from the vulgar Kuhnism that circulates so freely these days and that excuses any shoddiness so long as it is in search of "a new paradigm."

I also think that the book contains some mistaken judgments, enough of them so that it is eventually unconvincing. At the risk of doing the author some injustice, I will not try to give a rounded survey of his argument. Instead, I will concentrate on a few of the points where I am inclined to argue back.

One of the things wrong with economics, according to Ward, is that it is built on a narrow and false view of how men actually are. Real people are not rationally calculating, wholly integrated, single-minded, self-interested maximizers of this or that. Since neoclassical economics assumes that they are, it is likely to give wrong answers. Moreover, it gives ideological answers by suggesting that social institutions adequate for the sort of robots that appear in the theory also are adequate for real people.

Now it is certainly true that real people are not like that. But it seems to me that the rest of the argument simply mistakes the role of these assumptions of "possessive individualism" in economics. The emphasis in economic man should be on *economic,* not on *man;* such emphasis is not so much an assumption about individual psychology as it is about social institutions of Western capitalism. Western capitalism has institutionalized the economic sphere—production, exchange, and distribution—as a sphere in which it is acceptable to be rationally calculating, self-interested, and so forth. It is a little peculiar to be anything else. It is not an insult in our culture to say that a man is not in business for love: The phrase is intended as a reminder of the obvious. Of course, even in the economic sphere, not everyone is an economic man all the time. Like any abstract assumption, this one can be more or less misleading. There is room for detailed argument about how well it works in different real-life circumstances, as well as about what, if anything persistent, those maximizers are maximizing. But general appeals to human nature are beside the point.

This means that neoclassical economics, as positive economics, is culture-bound. It is a description of the working of Western capitalism and similar societies. Whenever and wherever economic life comes to be regulated mostly by love, solidarity, ritual, or tea leaves, neoclassical economics, as positive economics, should wither away and be replaced by something else. However, to say that orthodox economics is mainly the study of capitalism is not the same as saying it is the ideological instrument of capitalism. Just as a human matter, one would not be surprised to learn that a bacteriologist who had spent a lifetime studying the gonococcus might end up with a sneaking admiration for the little devil. But that is not implicit in the science of bacteriology.

Ward is very insistent that neoclassical economics expresses an ideological bias, in fact, a class bias. But he becomes suddenly vague when it comes to saying how much ideological content there is (on a scale from zero to one, for example), or how one might recognize it and try to eliminate or diminish it, or exactly how it works, or when it comes to giving concrete examples. He does say some of the conventional things. For example, ideology enters economics through the definition of a respectable research problem, namely, one answerable using the methods of orthodox economics. Yes, it is a rare discipline that encourages its practitioners to cultivate problems the discipline cannot handle. But how is it known that the answers to most of the excluded questions are inimical to the institution of private property and fewer are favorable to it? Failing that, is one entitled to call this narrow-mindedness ideological?

Another notion: Neoclassical economics encourages the study of small variations in social arrangements but not large ones. Perhaps, although there is more to the subject than marginalism. It seems to follow that a marginalist training would be perfectly safe for the economists of a socialist society. They too would be inclined to study only small variations in social arrangements. Is that ideology? The soldier of fortune, who would be equally at home fighting for either side, usually is described as nonideological.

Another common notion: Neoclassical economics discourages the study of income distribution, presumably because that is where the bodies are buried. But does it? The theory of distribution, whatever its merits, is a standard textbook topic. The journals would be glad to publish interesting papers. It is not clear to me that students are warned off, by word or deed, because the subject is politically dangerous. What is true, I think, and as Ward points out, is that orthodox economics is mostly about efficiency and has no sharp way of dealing with equity; when presented with social institutions A and B, economics is capable of indefinite elaboration of minor differences in efficiency between them but has no accurate way of saying that A is unjust and B just. This is a limitation of the subject, and one might talk about getting around it, but simply to label it ideology seems to me slipshod.

Ward has a positive suggestion to make here. It is that economics try to incorporate equity and other values explicitly by becoming more like the study of law. He is not very clear about this analogy, at least not to me. I think he has in mind that economists should try to figure out what is "right" in a situation just as legal scholars try to figure out what course of action best serves "justice." In this way of doing economics, what would take the place of the Constitution or common law? I suppose one could try to interpret the shared ethical tradition of the society as it applies to concrete cases. That might be interesting, although I doubt that the ability to do it well is likely to be associated with the other talents an economist needs. There also might be a problem if the ethical tradition of the society contains contradictory strands. Consistency may not be characteristic of ethical traditions.

Please, I am not arguing that neoclassical economics is free of ideological content. I suppose most neoclassical economists are disinclined to make a root-and-branch attack on the social institutions of Western capitalism. In this they resemble most other middle-class citizens, and indeed most other citizens. The system is not obviously breaking down, and no compellingly attractive and available alternative has presented itself. On top of this, many economists think they know little ways to make the system work better. One hardly would expect the Revolution to begin in the pages of *Econometrica.* That statement is not high caliber sociology of knowledge, and it hardly will bear the weight of dark implications that economic science is necessarily loaded with ideological distortion.

In his application of Kuhn's schema to economics, Ward described the Keynesian revolution as a true scientific revolution in Kuhn's sense, and there I agree with him. (Although I was astonished to read that "the notable thing about both the *General Theory* and the massive discussion in the leading economic journals that followed its publication is the dearth of empirical studies." I would have thought that the important thing to say about the *General Theory* was that it triggered an absolute flood of empirical work. If the remark is to be limited to the years immediately after publication of the *General Theory,* then it is only fair to take some account of the fact that time series of the national accounts were just beginning to become available. The econometric tradition was just beginning to take hold, and comsumption functions were not long in coming. Furthermore, the empirical fact of the depth and persistence of the Great Depression was in everyone's mind.)

Ward also goes on at length about the "formalist revolution" in economics, dating from the early 1950s. By this he means not only the rapid increase in the use of mathematical methods and formal econometrics, but also the self-conscious adoption of a strict positivist methodology complete with hypothesis, data, test, rejection, and so forth. He regards this revolution as a scientific failure and points out, with some puzzlement, that it appears to have been a revolution entirely in technique and not at all in substance. I think he is incorrect to characterize this development as a scientific revolution in the first place. At least I do not recognize any real break in continuity, except perhaps in style. (I differ with him about the merits, too, but I am making a different point now.)

Perhaps this will be clear if I mention another of Ward's positive methodological suggestions. He favors a way of doing economics that he calls "storytelling," by which he means, roughly, informal and persuasive argument. But apart from the very top of formal economics, which engages only a handful of people, that is exactly what the modern economist does. In fact, he uses exactly the same word: "The story I'm trying to tell is this . . .," only the story is told in calculus. P. B. Medawar has argued that working scientists in all fields operate this way; the positivist apparatus may be a rationalization of the process, but it does not describe what actually happens.

Ward detects a tendency in modern "formalist" economics to judge the merit of a particular piece of work by the cleverness of its technique and not the social value, nor even the intrinsic scientific value, of its results. Students absorb this standard of professional quality and the accompanying definition of what constitutes a good research topic. They look for theorems, not solutions to problems. There is much truth in that observation. I know of no serious attempt to understand why it happens and how one could move to something better. I think Ward chalks it up to ideology again; a concern with technical puzzles keeps economists tame. He has more confidence than I in how savage they would be if they did not have technical puzzles to work on. It would be interesting to see a comparative study of busywork in different disciplines; it might teach us something.

Department of Economics ROBERT M. SOLOW
Massachusetts Institute of Technology

Benjamin Ward gives a lucid account of the problems facing contemporary economics. He points out that the emphasis on positivism and formalism (quantitative economics) has resulted in a serious neglect of the interrelationship of human, social, and cultural phenomena, their interdependence, and their effect on the science of economics in particular. The high level of abstraction employed, the extreme emphasis on methodological rather than on substantive refinements, have led economists to ignore human and social interrelationships and value judgments, thus making the economist a narrowly specialized technician rather than a profound social scientist. Ward thus presents a serious indictment of economics by pointing out that the prevalent high level of abstraction has resulted in abstracting from everything that is really meaningful to man and society. The result is primarily to serve the status quo in the form of the so-called liberal tradition, tying the science to an ideology within which areas of disagreement and research are understood. Ward calls on economists to emancipate themselves and to transform economics into a more integrated social science which uses its positivist and formalist aspects as means toward an end rather than as an end in economic analysis.

Of course, economics has contributed greatly to the understanding of social and cultural phenomena by its research into those aspects which are readily quantifiable. However, the question arises whether the science has made equal progress in the perception of man's inner nature in relationship to all natural and social phenomena. The answer is no. One must conclude that every adaptation to changing conditions brings with it both a further development, at least in some parts of the science, and an inhibition in other areas.

The general theme of this highly interesting book, then, is that what economists often consider as unimportant or even primitive aspects of their discipline, such as the history of economic thought, is based on the relatively unknown and uncomprehended phenomena of the economic process into which they have not attempted to penetrate. Whether one likes it or not, no one can escape making value judgments about himself, his fellow man, nature, or society at large. Thus one cannot help but be prejudiced in one way or another about his own or other cultures. Processes of value formation and conflicts, as well as the interrelatedness of economic relations, therefore demand the economist's attention.

Colligation, the process of interweaving facts, theory, and idea formation, invalidates the deductive and inductive methods of analysis and the criterion of conceivable falsifiability on which neoclassical economics is built. The author's treatment of the value problem, language and change, man and society, and the learning process call attention to the common elements to be depicted in social behavior and in the process of change, which are thought to be conceived differently by men than by economists as such. Elements of institutional aspects in both neoclassical and Marxian economics, the verification of theories, the properties of storytelling, to mention a few, all provide the reader with a greater perception of a more relevant methodology and with valuable insights into fundamental aspects of economics.

Ward proceeds by employing Thomas Kuhn's criteria for a normal natural science to determine the existence of a social science and under what conditions the latter is to be found in a state of crisis, which is essential for its further development. Kuhn's method of paradigms is designed as a pattern of development for mature sciences. In the process of evolution, an existing paradigm is replaced by a completely new one, which does not contain elements of the old paradigm. Kuhn denies that various paradigms or even elements thereof would coexist at a given time. The transition from one paradigm to another he pictures not as smooth but rather as discontinuous and noncumulative in nature, brought about by a sudden and unstructured crisis or revolution.

Ward's discussion with regard to Kuhn's concepts of a normal science, of a paradigm, and of a puzzle lacks clarity. It is not evident whether or not the author considers only a single paradigm to be characteristic of economics or what he pictures the current paradigm in the science to be. What does the author mean by *neoclassicism?* It seems that all orthodox theories are included under this label. Are neoclassical, Keynesian, and Marxian economics puzzles of the same paradigm, or do they constitute separate paradigms? The latter would have to be the case if Marxism is considered as a promising alternative science for neoclassical economics. But, following Kuhn, Marxism could not represent a viable alternative, as is indicated. Thus the applicability of Kuhn's method of paradigms to explain the development of economic theories is highly questionable. This reviewer is of the opinion that Kuhn's approach is essentially the dialectical method of analysis, which is more appropriate for the evaluation of economic theories.

Ward, using Kuhn's methodology, shows that neoclassical economics meets the criteria for a social science and for states of crises rather well. Marxism, on the other hand, does so to a lesser degree. The main reason for this less satisfactory performance of Marxian economics is due to the fact that Marxist scholars generally are inhibited by political constraints, in both the capitalist and the so-called socialist countries, to critically analyze societies, irrespective of their political orientation. Of course, such restraints are placed not only on Marxists but also on all scientists. An attack on orthodox thought, questioning the status quo, is not looked upon favorably by the various *hierarchies*, as the author labels them, or the political apparatus. It is correctly implied that an evaluation of contemporary times is hardly possible by ignoring Marxism.

One shortcoming of this interesting book is that the author does not present a concrete solution, as he himself points out. His primary concern is to call attention to problem areas and to indicate steps that might be taken to correct the situation. As an example of an alternate route that economics might try to follow, Ward discusses the science of law. He points to the interrelatedness of all phenomena to which judges and lawyers must address themselves. The legal science, by its very nature, is forced to make decisions in the context of interpersonal comparisons of gains and losses, which so far have eluded the positivist school in general and welfare economics in particular. Furthermore, he shows that law is capable of handling the problems pointed to by the Walrasian, Heisenbergian, and Velikovskyan principles, which in essence state that everything is in a state of flux and is interrelated.

Even though Marxism is considered as a promising alternative to neoclassicism, once it reasserts itself as a true science the author does not consider the dialectic nature of Marxism in sufficient detail. If he had done so, much of his critique of Marxism, as a science, would have been removed. The function of the dialectic process in Marxian analysis is to point to the dynamics of change and to the interrelatedness of all phenomena. It must be viewed in its aspect of relations; all Marxian terms are descriptive of social relationships. The essence of Marxian analysis thus is to examine the manifold ways in which all phenomena are mutually interdependent or interrelated in terms of the past, present, and future. According to Marx, the theorist not only should view his work in terms of a coherent construct, but also should examine the theoretical system in the context of men and society, their problems as he sees them, and the impact which his ideas would have upon them. But this is in essence the approach which Ward suggests in order for economics to become a viable science which addresses itself to relevant problems of substance rather than of methodology.

Department of Economics
University of Utah

SIEGFRIED G. KARSTEN

It is notoriously difficult to write a book review that gives a good account of the contents of the work, places it within the framework of existing literature, and gives fair criticism, that is, some sort of evaluation useful for the reader and perhaps even the author. This task is particularly difficult if the work under consideration is of broad general scope and also touches on work the reviewer has done himself. Having quite recently published two papers which set forth my own views, one on the critical state of economics and the other on methodology,[1] I may be permitted to refer to them because there Professor Benjamin Ward, as well as the reader, will find the necessary amplification and justification of some remarks that follow. But I shall refrain from giving a lengthy account of the contents of Ward's book because the topics are so important that they are easily characterized. They are, after all, in the mind of everyone who strives to advance our knowledge in one way or the other.

There is first of all Ward's contention that economics is in a state of crisis. I wonder how strongly this feeling is shared by the many who continue calculating more and more correlations, lag distributions, and so forth, with data whose properties they tacitly assume to be sure, but which in fact are only vaguely known. A feeling of crisis ultimately must be a very personal matter; it will depend upon one's expectations of what the science is all about and to what extent they can be fulfilled if one continues in the present manner. The expectations may be exaggerated, and there may be impatience. I wonder whether physicists and astronomers, before Newton published his great work, felt that there was a crisis in those fields, what "puzzles" they identified, to use Thomas Kuhn's not very furtunate term to which Ward pays so much attention. Clearly, from time to time one has to sit back and ask what it is all about that economists are doing; one then will discover that the unrestrained adherence to one kind of procedure has led into a cul-de-sac.

So it was with labor value theory, hopelessly enmeshed in self-contradictions: exceptional situations demanding exceptional explanations, and so forth. Marginal utility came then as a revelation, and a new burst of activity occurred. This then became what Ward calls the "neo-classical economics" of today. It is confronted by Ward, or almost put on a par, with Marxism, a confrontation I fail to understand. I do not see that there exists any Marxist theory concerned with the same problems dealt with by neoclassical theory. Marxist thought—one hardly can say "theory"—deals mostly with goals, gives broad generalizations of alleged historical and social processes, but has nothing to say about duopoly, exchange rates, inflation, preferences, and so forth. What it says about value has been laid ad acta one hundred years ago and is as devoid of scientific interest as the value theories of Adam Smith, David Ricardo, and Jean Baptiste Say. These theories are part of the history of economics, but not of its living body. Incidentally, I agree warmly with Ward that today's economists would do well to study the history of their science, if only to see the recurrence of the same themes and their often ineffective similar treatment over the ages: This is, indeed, an aspect of crisis or at least of lack of progress.

In his dissatisfaction with present-day economics, Ward clearly shows one trait he shares with most economists, whether pleased or dissatisfied: There is a failure to realize the enormous difficulties our science offers which, when at some distant day they are overcome, will make economics as complex as, indeed even more complex than, the most developed physics of today. We are far from that state. One should compare this attitude with that taken, for example, by one of the most distinguished neurophysiologists of our time, John C. Eccles. In his admirable book, *The Understanding of the Brain*

(1973), he displays our neurological knowledge, which is stupendous in comparison with what we call economic theory. Yet Eccles says that it will take hundreds of years before we really can explain the brain. Is economics that simple that we now can make the tremendous claims and demands we constantly encounter? The view of the complication and difficulty of the subject matter determines largely what one should and can expect. Ward is dissatisfied that there were poor predictions, that econometric models have gone wrong, and so forth. That happens in all sciences—in cancer research, in biology, in medicine. Some economic models have cost a million dollars. Granted, this is a nice sum, but it is nothing compared to the cost of physics equipment that had to be discarded or is being built in the vague hope that something of relevance might be discovered.

So we come to the critical point, unfortunately not seen by Ward: A crisis has to be recognized (and the author does help us see that there is one), but—and this he does not seem to see—it is overcome *only* if a new basic thought, a new *concept*, appears which throws new light on existing problems, perhaps shows that the real problems lie elsewhere than generally assumed, that our very empirical description must be changed. I greatly doubt that the continuation of current econometric work, no matter how sophisticated its techniques, will produce that new insight. I am constantly reminded of Albert Einstein's remark, made several times to me, that most scientists naïvely think they know what they should observe and how they should measure it.

Applying this to economics, it is *not* more "data gathering" that is crucial, as Ward seems to think (p. 241). Rather, we must know what data are needed and how good they are (there is in this book not one word on accuracy, on how to determine it, how much to insist on in relation to theory and application). It is here where a peculiar gap opens which one would think Ward would at least have pointed out: He stresses (p. 96) as a most important recent development the construction of "decision models" (not specified by him in any detail) which, however, are seriously flawed because of a "high degree of interdependence among decisions" (presumably of different individuals).

Indeed they are interdependent! As a consequence it is necessary to develop new concepts and methods to take care of this situation. In addition, one might add that all of economic behavior is nothing but the making of decisions in the face of uncertainties and of the interests of others whose interests are sometimes parallel to one's own, sometimes opposite. Information is of primary importance, that is, the gathering of it and, sometimes, preventing it from falling into the hands of opponents. There are expectations of future states of the economy which resolve into expectations of the behavior of others. Thinking these matters through should make it immediately clear that our science is vastly different from all natural sciences, where nothing of this sort occurs. Yet in "neoclassical," that is, contemporary, economics as well as in Marxism, nothing of this is incorporated, nor can it be incorporated without bursting apart the whole edifice. Here the true crisis emerges. It is not seen by Ward. The mathematical formulation of contemporary economics is not of the essence. On the contrary, the mathematics which merely formulates concepts that must be replaced by others only makes the reversal that much more difficult because it hides the true issues below an increasingly complicated formalism. I agree with Ward that many bright young men are now strongly attracted to economics by the recent extensive use of mathematics. I also agree with him that there is a tendency toward theorem construction versus problem solving.

Current economic theory has not come to grips with the interdependence of decisions made by many individuals. But at this point I must register surprise and dismay: Has the author never heard about game theory? That theory is mentioned once by him, but there is no trace of any acquaintance with its aims, purpose, method, and accomplishments.[2] Granted, the theory is difficult, comprehensive, and in rapid development, but one would think that by now it deserves attention and evaluation (and possibly conscious rejection). A bibliography by Mr. F. Kelemen of the Technical University of Vienna lists, up to the end of 1970, not less than 6,200 publications from all over the world since the work by John von Neumann and myself was published in 1944. Many deal with crucial problems of economics. Most go far beyond the implied linear programming duality. I clearly should not and could not attempt to describe the theory here,[3] but I must emphasize that it deals not only with oligopoly, or bargaining, but rather questions the entire orientation of contemporary economics so far as the latter conceives of its task as merely being concerned with maximum or minimum problems. Yet, on page 251, Ward quotes approvingly D. Gordon, who in 1965 still could write: "The basic maximizing model has never been replaced." Of course, Paul Samuelson is of the same opinion, as most recently was demonstrated in his Nobel lecture (*American Economic Review*, June 1972). Game theory is a truly social science profoundly different from the image of physics which has dominated economics for so long. There is a true break here of a fundamental philosophical nature as I have tried to describe in my recent contribution to the *Dictionary of the History of Ideas* (1973, vol. 2). The theory also touches on problems of utility and preferences and as is well known, a new utility theory that takes care of the fundamental fact of uncertainty has been developed, a theory that surely will replace current notions of utility, culminating in self-contradictory indifference curve analysis. I agree with Ward that the present views of utility are too simple, that interpersonal comparisons offer great problems which simply have to be faced. But it is easy merely to point out their existence. As far as I can see, Ward has no suggestions on how to approach them.

Another matter of great importance and much concern to economists is taken up by Ward in an interesting manner in the last part of his book. This is the question of value judgments. Ward describes how legal theory and procedure might offer ways to get out of the dilemma so that we should be able to construct social welfare functions without violating the logic that "ought" propositions do not follow from "is" propositions. This is, indeed, a troublesome area, and much thinking will have to go on before a consensus is obtained. The law does say what ought and what ought not to be done. The law relates norms to facts, and not all such norms derive from some basic norm. Rather, they originate—not only in law but also in general social behavior—in the acceptance of some institution by the people (a question of *fact!*) such that then these institutions *imply* that certain behavior ought or ought not to take place. This is called "logical extension" (from fact). Space forbids me to elaborate on these matters, and I may refer to my "Thirteen Critical Points" and also to John Rawls's *A Theory of Justice* (1972). In the latter book, interestingly enough, game theory reappears in a significant manner, a connection that deserves to be explored further. Clearly, here is an area of which one can say with confidence that surprises are not to be excluded. But even if we learn how to construct logically acceptable, intellectually satisfactory, social preference functions, it still will be a long time before these will play a role in the theory of economic policy, let alone in applications. Yet, this should not dampen our efforts, although one has good reasons to be skeptical. It suffices to look at the current world inflations and monetary disorders—which are surely nothing novel or exceptional—and the ineptitude with which they are treated. Nevertheless, at the bottom of all policy lie such seemingly abstract matters as the interpersonal comparison of utility and the question as to how to derive normative statements from facts!

I conclude these remarks with the statement that I am grateful to the author for having forced me once more to look critically at economic science. Agreement and disagreement with Ward's own appraisal have added to my perception of the present issues. Other readers will not fail to gain new insight too.

Department of Economics OSKAR MORGENSTERN
New York University

Notes

1. Oskar Morgenstern, "Thirteen Critical Points in Contemporary Economic Theory: An Interpretation," *Journal of Economic Literature* (December 1972): 1163-89, and "Descriptive, Predictive and Normative Theory," *Kyklos* (December 1972): 699-714.
2. This is particularly surprising since Ward teaches at Berkeley, where his colleague, John Harsanyi, has made many valuable contributions to that field.
3. Oskar Morgenstern, "Game Theory," *Dictionary of the History of Ideas*, vol. 2 (New York: Scribners, 1973), pp. 263-75.

Part II

Methodology

Introduction

One of the major methodological controversies within economics has involved the conflict of induction and deduction. Almost all work done by economists represents subtle blends of each, but the substantive procedures utilized in research and analysis differ markedly. One of the subsidiary controversies involves the question of whether theories are to be judged by the realism of their assumptions or by their predictive power. The controversy is not strictly one of deduction versus induction but of the level or stage (assumptions or conclusions) at which empirical testing is to be undertaken. In the first article in this section, Eugene Rotwein surveys and evaluates the number of recent views on the nature of scientific validation dealing with that question. The article criticizes positivist methodology, is especially critical of permissive empiricism, and defends the requirement for continuous testing of both assumptions and predictions.[1]

Abraham and Eva Hirsch present an interpretation and critique of Frank Knight's assumer and Milton Friedman's predictor approach to methodology. The Hirsches stress that Knight and Friedman have held essentially the same methodological position, both agreeing that mainstream economic theory is not mere analysis but has empirical significance and that it tells us what actually happens, although it is accurate only in broad and general terms. According to the Hirsches, the assumer and predictor postures are weapons with which to defend economic theory against the attack on the realism of premises. They point to Knight's position that general economic behavior cannot be easily controverted and that it is positive and normative at the same time, abetting the clarification of value choices in liberal society. One receives the impression that a key to the entire story is the continuing search for an acceptable defense of economic theory, not for epistemological purity and credentials. The twists of methodological defense have been in response to (1) developments in methodology and epistemology in philosophy and (2) perceived criticism within economics, as well as (3) the desire for the self-satisfaction that economics is truly a science, whatever that means. The key is the defense of orthodox theory based on the strong conviction that economic theory has value in dealing with important social problems. The Hirsches' article also explores the subtle interconnections between the positive and the normative in economics.[2]

Similar material is covered by Charles Wilber and Jon Wisman in their critique of Milton Friedman's methodology. They maintain that his claim for a *Wertfrei* (value free) positivism ends up as a defense of a laissez faire economic system. Furthermore, Friedman's technical positivism (the predictor position) is compromised. The Hirsches suggest this when they point to his position as including an assumer element, namely, the propriety of status quo economic theory which ends up *de facto* with Knight, relying upon the position that truth is a function of the logic of the theory, that is, the assumption *ab initio* of the paradigm from which all else follows.

After a survey of the origins, nature, and limits of positivism, Wilber and Wisman indicate the limits of positivist methodology for the social sciences in the instability of data and a subject matter which creates an open system not amenable to controlled experimentation. They conclude that positive economics is perfectly insulated from refutation by the dominant role of the paradigm, which is never seriously questioned. That is to say, confirmation is largely a matter of consonance with the underlying paradigm. Science is a facade for what is essentially metaphysics.

The resulting body of theory is best identified, they argue, as an ideal type that idealizes one facet of a complex reality and functions largely as a prescriptive device. Friedman's positive economics thus is deemed to function to restrict the scope of scientific economic inquiry and to legitimize certain aspects of the status quo in whose image it would mold society. With regard to restricting the scope of economics, Wilber and Wisman point to the emasculated treatment of externalities, the presumed value free facticity of market-generated data (including prices), the camouflaged existence and exercise of power, and the limited range of explanatory variables in explaining income distribution so that in Friedman's analysis it seems "that personal inequality is due to free choice—by the rich and poor alike".

Wilber and Wisman reason that "since the Chicago School's theory is left essentially unscathed by both the unrealism of its assumptions and its inability to provide successful prediction, the ideal type has an independent life of its own. Rather than repairing the model to better conform with the real world, the burden of conformity is placed on the real world. And thus, the policy stance of the Chicago School is characterized by proposals to change the real economic world according to the requisites of its ideal type—laissez-faire capitalism." For them "positivism becomes a facade; faith wins out." Here deep within methodological controversy, once again, there are fundamental normative conceptions that become tautological in relation to the policy conclusions of the body of theory. Policy conclusions are foreshadowed by the normative conception of reality and values adopted by the theorist.

Vincent Tarascio inquires into the nature of the value judgments found in economic science. He feels that economic science may be able to exclude *normative judgments* regarding what is best for society, but that it cannot exclude *methodological judgments,* including the scope of study, the problem studied, and so forth. The nature and scope of analysis is profoundly influenced, channeled, and limited by cultural influences that govern both methodological and normative judgments. He finds that the professional stake in knowledge inhibits innovation outside the received paradigm and is a factor in producing scientific revolutions. (See Part III for several views on whether scientific revolutions have taken place in economics.)

Melville Ulmer argues that values are not, cannot, and should not be excluded from economic science. Value judgments, he finds, are inevitable and are not necessarily merely emotive in character, lacking reasoned deliberation. The proposition, for example, that tastes are to be taken as given is a key value judgment of neoclassical economics, and, in Ulmer's view, it is an incorrect assumption: tastes are not given by either biology or factors external to the economic system. Wants are largely a function of the performance of the system; tastes are endogenously generated, in part deliberately shaped by business. Such an assumption is one example of the ways in which value judgments are hidden in neoclassical economics. Such judgments, Ulmer argues, are virtually inherent in the nature of the subject. Arguing that values can be tested by the quality of our experience with them, Ulmer primarily advocates that economists make their values explicit and thereby subject to scrutiny. By so doing, they will disclose the consequences of choices, and both decision and policy will be informed.

In a comment on Ulmer's article, Robert Lekachman considers the sociology of the economics profession. He focuses on several deficiencies of orthodox theory: neglect of the fact that markets mirror status quo income and wealth distributions; neglect of egalitarian values; neglect of an economic theory of political influence; and neglect of economic power. Power, Lekachman believes, is important in governing markets and therefore in understanding how markets operate. Power, he says, is the "guilty little secret" of economic theory. The economy as a system of power, it may be noted, is the subject of a companion anthology.

The final group of materials in this section is comprised of four, wide-ranging reviews of Nicholas Georgescu-Roegen's *The Entropy Law and the Economic Process* by one physicist and three economists. Together they probe the possibilities and limits of the author's searching application of physical concepts and theorizing to social phenomena. The reviews raise such issues as the utility of dialectical analysis, the importance of the fallacy of composition for economics, the probabilistic character of economic theorems, the irreversibility of change, environmental limits, systemic evolutionary change, and the theory of conflict. One reviewer points to a paradox of rationalism: greater deliberativeness lessens the nondeliberative basis of science. Another cites Niels Bohr for the insight that minor truths, whose opposites are false, must be contrasted with major truths, whose opposites are also true. Paradox upon paradox!

Notes

1. *See also* Robert B. Ekelund, Jr., and Emilie S. Olsen, "Comte, Mill, and Cairnes: The Positivist-Empiricist Interlude in Late Classical Economics," September 1973.
2. *See also* Warren S. Gramm, "Chicago Economics: From Individualism True to Individualism False," and John McKinney, "Frank H. Knight and Chicago Libertarianism," December 1975.

Empiricism and Economic Method: Several Views Considered

Eugene Rotwein

In the present period with its unparalleled emphasis on the empirical testing of hypotheses, the demands that the standards of science impose on economics are of obvious moment. Accordingly, it might be expected that writings on the methodology of economics generally would reflect these standards. This, however, is not the case. Insofar as economics is regarded as a "science," no one, of course, is flatly opposed to empiricism. Yet, the constructions of empiricism or of its applications to economics vary considerably and in ways which significantly affect both general perspectives and the treatment of important controversial questions within the field.

Some time ago, procedures employed in the empirical testing of economic hypotheses were attacked severely by Milton Friedman in his essay "The Methodology of Positive Economics."[1] Friedman's position, which branded much such empirical testing as a misguided use of scientific method, has been criticized in some detail by myself and others.[2] It is the principal purpose of this article to examine several more recent writings which deal with questions of a general methodological character within the context of economics. Either explicitly or otherwise these raise the same issue considered by Friedman, and, as I shall seek to show, they contribute in various

The author is Professor of Economics, Queens College of the City University of New York, Flushing.

ways to a perpetuation of error regarding the application of empirical principles to the area of economics.

Empiricism and the Background Controversy in Economics

Before considering these writings it will be helpful if brief attention is given two questions: What are the foundations of empiricism and, in light of this, the shortcomings of Friedman's position? What is the nature of the general methodological background, historically speaking, in which the issue raised by Friedman is to be viewed?

To turn to the first question, empiricism rests on an analysis of the manner in which human "belief" is formed. Since this is fundamental, it is ultimately on the acceptability of this analysis that the empirical method stands or falls. There is, of course, no single ground on which belief rests. Man has been transported to a state of belief on the basis of pure emotion, astrology, palmistry, and messages from crystal balls. He confuses dreams with reality, and he hallucinates. Were there nothing beyond such diversity, however, "science" would be impossible; for it is the hallmark of science that its methods of verification can *compel* general agreement. It is the kind of thinking that underlies science—but which in everyday affairs is far more common—that the empiricist takes as the basis for his position on the requirements for establishing belief. Needless to say, although it may have uncomfortable consequences, one may persistently reject even the most compelling empirical evidence. But insofar as the procedures employed in testing any view depart from the testing procedures of science, that view must be acknowledged to remain (more or less) private. It manifestly cannot be argued on scientific grounds that the view should be accepted as valid.

Science seeks general relations between matters of fact, or those general empirical relations that can be couched in the hypothetical form "if A then B," where A is the event denoted by the assumption (or antecedent) of the hypothesis, and B is the prediction (or consequent). When we speak of establishing belief in the context of science, we are then speaking of the method of validating or gaining acceptance of such propositions. In dealing with the question of validation, a basic premise of the empirical position is that it is not permissible to assert that, in the nature of things, relations conflicting with those observed *cannot* occur. If we could make such an assertion, this would imply that relations between matters of fact were logical, which is to say that the opposite of any such relation would violate the principle of noncontradiction (that is, the principle that nothing can be in and out of existence at the same time) and for this reason would be inconceivable or impossible. The opposite of any statement concerning matter-of-fact relations, however, is always conceivable simply because the entities or events related are conceptually separable and therefore can be imagined to assume any form we may choose. This, and only this, is the reason why—as distinct from propositions that are logically related—no proposition concerning empirical relations can be treated as "certain."

Rejecting certainty within the world of empirical relations, the empiricist concerns himself with the probable and argues that, for purposes of ascertaining this, there is ample evidence to be drawn from experience. Here the empiricist accepts the view (which must be treated as a faith) that it is through an understanding of the past that the future may be foreseen. If empirical predictions cannot be made with certainty, what is most likely to occur, in a word, is a repetition of the regularities between events already observed. In other words, our confidence in the occurrence of any prediction B is contingent on the occurrence of another event A, where evidence indicates that the two are invariably related. Our ability to foresee the future—or the transformation of the chaos of "possibility" into the more orderly stuff of "probability"—thus rests on a continuing refinement and improvement in the procedures for ascertaining such regularities.

To consider Friedman's central thesis, this arose out of criticism of certain doctrines fundamental to orthodox economic analysis, specifically, the theory of perfect competition and, more broadly, the principle of marginalism. The criticism centered on the realism of the assumptions underlying these doctrines. Seeking to rebut this attack, Friedman argued that the concern with assumptions represented a total misdirection of effort since, properly construing scientific method, the validity of a theory depended solely on the accuracy of its predictions and not on the realism of its assumptions. For example, the validity of the theory of perfect competition, Friedman contended, did not depend at all on the nature of the markets in which the theory was used for predictive purposes.[3]

As is clear, this argument totally brushes aside the rationale for empirical modes of testing in science. On probability grounds, the belief that any prediction will occur depends on the occurrence of another event (denoted by the assumption) which evidence indicates is invariably related to the prediction. Validity is an index of the confidence we may repose in the belief, and its test involves assertions with respect to the "realism" of both the assumption and the prediction.

Friedman thus ignored the essential condition in science for establishing the validity of a probability statement; he was asserting that confidence in a theory for predictive purposes was unaffected by an *observed absence* of association between the conditions specified by its assumptions and the event predicted.[4] The point may be stated in terms of the requirements for scientific explanation. Although there may be substantial variation in the explanatory content of accepted hypotheses, evidence of a constancy of association between the events related in the hypothesis is likewise essential (as it is for prediction) to the explanation of one of the events by the other.[5] It manifestly cannot be said that the conditions unique to a perfectly competitive market "explain" some given price or output phenomenon in cases where the market is monopolistic. Although Friedman applied the term *explanation* to cases of this latter nature, in arguing that the realism of the assumptions of a theory was irrelevant to its validity his analysis disregarded the requirements for *explanation* as this term is used in science and, commonly, outside the context of science as well.[6]

It should be noted that nothing in the foregoing implies that a prediction drawn from assumptions that are erroneous may not prove accurate. In the realm of relations between matters of fact anything is conceivable; it might turn out that the predicted phenomenon, to use Friedman's phrase, behaved "as if" the assumptions were true when they were, in fact, false. What is implied, rather, is that, to the degree that the prediction depends on the use of erroneous assumptions (which is, of course, what necessitates the employment of the "as if" formulation), it loses plausibility. Accordingly, the evidence concerning the prediction which is required to gain acceptance of its own probability will grow, which is but another way of saying that falsity in any assumption (even if it should, by chance, lead to a true prediction) is an "invalid" element in the hypothesis.[7]

We have been dealing with the foundations of empiricism. But this leads directly to our second question, which concerns the general background of contemporary methodological discussion. For since the principles considered are of general applicability, they are fundamental to the empirical tradition in economics and also go far toward setting the scene for current debate over economic methodology. This is not to say, of course, that in the past the practices of economists typically have been thoroughly empirical. Nor is it to say that formal methodological theory in economics traditionally has taken full account of the central implication of empiricism, that is, the need for repeated testing of all empirical generalizations by reference to experience and the progressive modification of the theoretical apparatus of the discipline in the light of such tests. However, in one basic sense which is of special relevance here—the recognition in principle that realistic assumptions are essential to the validity of theory—the empirical tradition in economics has a venerable lineage. The major classical economists, for example, relied heavily on deduction and argued that this was indispensable to the development of economics as a science. With an eye toward this, it has indeed been asserted—and approvingly—that various nineteenth-century classical economists believed, as does Friedman, that the realism of their premises was irrelevant to the validity of their theories.[8] The evidence is entirely to the contrary. Representing the more general view of the period, not a single classical economist who dealt extensively with methodological theory (for example, Nassau Senior, or J. S. Mill, or J. E. Cairnes) ever doubted that unrealistic assumptions would impair the validity of their theoretical analysis.[9]

This empirical standard, however, has been a constant source of difficulty. For the failure to meet the standard has been one of the most important general grounds on which both the classical and neoclassical economists have been criticized. And owing to its importance, both schools of economists have themselves given much attention to this issue. Considering all views, however, the positions taken have differed. Some of the classical economists, among others, acknowledged the lack of realism in the basic premises and the subsidiary assumptions they employed for deductive purposes and, in conformity with their methodological theory, stressed the need to keep these departures from realism in mind when applying the conclusions of their deductive analysis to experience.[10] Although similarly recognizing the pervasive importance of realism, others stressing the importance of deduction in economics have slighted or rejected the need for repeated and careful testing of the basic premises of their analysis on the ground that experience already had established their universal and immutable truth.[11] A third and quite different position—stated in its most extreme form by Ludwig von Mises and representing an outgrowth of the Austrian approach—has posited a separate deductive world of "pure theory" in which the basic assumptions of economics, although regarded as fundamental to an understanding of the real world, are held to be apprehended *a priori* and are hence alleged to be true independently of any empirical tests.[12]

The requirement that assumptions be "realistic" has indeed long been a heavy cross for the economic theorist to bear. And in propounding his new version of empiricism (a form of "demi-empiricism" which acknowledges the empirical nature of theoretical assumptions but denies the relevance of tests of their realism for "validity") Friedman was seeking to cast off this burden once and for all. In doing so, Friedman was concerned to defend his own brand of theory. Nonetheless, his position has had a broader appeal. It stressed tests of predictions. But pending such tests, it afforded *carte blanche* for the disregard of any and all varieties of "unrealism" in theoretical model-building and so appeared to provide a new and sweeping warrant for a practice which theoretical economists of many persuasions have not found uncongenial to their inclinations. To many (although clearly not all) it seemed that Friedman had made the breakthrough: In boldly proclaiming the "irrelevance" of the long gnawing criticisms of traditional empiricists, he had at one stroke gained for unrealistic economic theorizing a measure of scientific respectability that it previously had not enjoyed. It is scarcely surprising then that others dealing with economic methodology subsequently should have used his analysis, in one fashion or another, to defend the extensive use of "theory" in empirical inquiry.

An Eclectic View

To turn to these post-Friedman writings, let us consider first an essay by Martin Bronfenbrenner which, among other things, is pointedly concerned with the "Friedman controversy," or "the battle of the assumptions."[13] Notwithstanding his own deep interest in economic theory, Bronfenbrenner is an eclectic—in practice as well as in principle. Much of his essay reflects this open-mindedness and his unwillingness to bind himself to any orthodoxy. But in his treatment of the controversy it is largely this eclecticism that leads him astray.

Specifically, Bronfenbrenner contends that in their selection of hypotheses theorists are willing to sacrifice predictive efficiency and explanatory power for simplicity, whereas institutionalists are willing to sacrifice these same objectives for realistic assumptions. In his view both these approaches are legitimate. The particular approach which one adopts, he argues, is wholly a matter of personal preference. The Friedman controversy is thus to be regarded essentially as one concerning personal tastes, and it is misleading to suppose that the issues raised can properly be treated in terms of general methodological standards.[14] This position may appear to afford an inviting way out of the controversy touched off by Friedman's view since it offers something to everyone. But it should be apparent that this overextends eclecticism.

For the hallmark of science lies precisely in its employment of procedures which are based on general methodological principles.

The objectives of these procedures consist in nothing other than the discovery of propositions with predictive efficiency and explanatory power. Once attained, these are never sacrificed for anything else. As noted, it is likewise a characteristic of science that the evidence which its procedures yield (that is, evidence indicating a constancy of association between events) is capable of compelling general agreement. Were this not the case, science typically would have yielded little beyond the cacophony of interminable squabbles between rival personalities. Properly altered, there is manifest truth in Bronfenbrenner's view. Purely personal preference (depending on the character and background of the investigator) certainly will influence the choice among alternative hypotheses when the evidence for any one of the alternatives is not considered satisfactory. However, in treating predictive efficiency and explanatory power as matters subordinate to the indulgence of personal preferences, Bronfenbrenner not only misstates the ultimate objectives of scientific inquiry but also, through this misstatement, neglects the basic issue in the controversy. That issue is the evidentiary requirements for achieving predictive efficiency and explanatory power themselves. In substance this central question is not discussed.[15]

In his general statement Bronfenbrenner also misrepresents the essential methodological difference between the approaches of the theorists and the institutionalists. This flows from a misidentification of the issue of "simplicity versus realism" as it arises in Friedman's analysis with the issue as it arises in the context of disagreement between theorists and institutionalists. In the latter context the distinction between *simplicity* and *realism* refers to the degree and pattern of abstraction involved in the statement of a hypothesis. Theorists differ from institutionalists in the sense that, when treating the same problem area, they generally are disposed to "simplify" by rejecting as irrelevant various "realistic" considerations concerning institutions which the institutionalists regard as crucial. Nonetheless, they both agree insofar as they accept as essential the process of abstraction itself—or the omission from the assumptions of a hypothesis of factors considered irrelevant to the problem under analysis. Were this not recognized, one would be obliged, in treating any problem, to deal with everything in the universe at once (something which no institutionalist, however comprehensive and scrupulous his eye for detail, has yet undertaken or ever deemed necessary). Although differing in the character of their abstractions, both institutionalists and theorists can likewise agree—and as scientists are indeed constrained to agree—that the resolution of their differences regarding these assumptions depends ultimately on evidence concerning the extent to which the conditions specified in the rival assumptions do *in reality* form parts of regularly recurring relationships within the problem area under study. In this sense there is no methodological controversy between the two at all.

When considered in the context of Friedman's central argument, the distinction between simplicity and realism has a very different meaning. Although he was speaking of theory, Friedman's main point did not involve the question of abstraction or the legitimacy of confining theoretical assumptions to a relatively small number of facts surrounding a problem while *excluding* large numbers of others. As Bronfenbrenner recognizes, Friedman was arguing that it was legitimate (or did not affect validity) to *include* specifications in theoretical assumptions which contradicted or falsified the circumstances surrounding a problem.[16] The assumption (for the sake of "simplicity") that a given case was perfectly competitive when it was, in fact, monopolistic would, in his view, have no bearing on its validity either for purposes of prediction or explanation. This is a quite special view. In its disregard of the nature and test of a probability statement it sets Friedman methodologically in opposition to theorists and institutionalists alike insofar as both the latter pursue the objectives of science.

Science as Preeminently "Pure Theory"

A second view which warrants attention is the position taken by Fritz Machlup. Although Machlup has long been a defender of theoretical economic analysis, the nature of his defense has undergone change. In his well-known debate with R. A. Lester concerning the validity of the principle of marginalism, Machlup recognized that the realism of theoretical assumptions was a matter of central significance in evaluating economic theory.[17] But since that time, and specifically since the appearance of Friedman's essay on methodology, he has drawn away from his earlier concession to catholicity. In the treatment of the routes to the understanding of economic experience, Machlup's more recent methodological tracts (more fully reflecting the Austrian influence) increasingly have emphasized the difference between the world of "exact laws" or "pure theory" and the world of empirical generalization—to the advantage of the former and the disadvantage of the latter. His methodological theory, however, is not entirely in the Austrian mold but represents an attempt to amalgamate aspects of the Austrian position with the position taken by Friedman. Through portions of his treatment, moreover, there runs an empirical element that Machlup never attempts, much less manages, to harness to the rest of his analysis. His latest general methodological essay, in which his position appears in its fullest form, is of special interest because it well serves to highlight the difficulties inevitably encountered by anyone seeking to preserve a place of superiority for pure theory in the world of science.[18]

In Machlup's view, *theory* consists of the pure constructs of human reason; and, while such constructs bear a relationship to reality, the distinguishing characteristic of pure theory is said to lie in its reliance on "idealization, hypothecation and heuristic fictions" which are introduced for purposes of "analytical convenience." This is contrasted with "inductive generalizations," which are based on operational (empirical) constructs. If theoretical generalizations are regarded as "fictitious" or "ideal," Machlup has recognized that they are drawn from experience. Nonetheless, like von Mises, he sees pure theory as something basically different from inductive generalization. Despite any similarities, they differ "in kind." As such, the superiority of theoretical over inductive generalization is to be found in the logical relations within theoretical systems. For these enable us, through deduction from broad generalizations, to explain and interpret wide ranges of empirical phenomena. Theoretical systems make it possible for us to move from "causes to consequences" so that theoretical conclusions are "logically necessary." Inductive generalizations, on the other hand, are only "correlation statements." As such they are usually "narrow" and yield only "some more or less definite probability value."[19]

In its treatment of the relation between theoretical (or logical) systems and inductive generalizations, this statement is internally inconsistent and misleading. On the one hand, theoretical systems yield cause and effect relations, which means that they yield statements concerning matters of fact. On the other hand, theoretical generalizations—the basis of the logical systems—are sharply distinguished from "correlation statements." This implies that the theoretical generalizations do not themselves take the form of matter-of-fact statements, which leads us to wonder how these generalizations can form part of, or explain, any causal relation. Manifestly, if the material of logical sequences is to form part of a causal relation, the major premises of these sequences must contain the basis for establishing the relationship; and these premises (as in the theoretical proposition: "Entrepreneurs maximize profit") reduce to nothing other than "correlation statements" or statements of association between events or entities. A related difficulty is found in Machlup's treatment of the conclusions of logical systems. If these conclusions are statements of causal relations, they are probability statements, as are the matter-of-fact propositions that comprise the premises. No amount of deductive reasoning can alter this (although the showing that an empirical statement is deducible from more general and true premises enhances its own probability value). Yet, contrasting these conclusions with the probabilistic nature of inductive statements, Machlup treats the former as "logically necessary."

Also indefensible is Machlup's contention that empirical propositions are generally "narrow" and therefore cannot be employed as the major premises of logical systems. An empirical proposition, in Machlup's definition, is one that does not contain fictitious or ideal elements, but this has no bearing on the breadth or the degree of generality of the proposition. Is the empirical proposition: "All living things are mortal" narrower than the theoretical proposition: "All entrepreneurs maximize profit"? Propositions may be narrow and fictitious or broad and realistic and vice versa; and it is precisely the breadth of the empirical generalizations and the extent of their logical interrelations with lower order propositions that constitute the distinguishing characteristic of the most advanced sciences. Machlup argues that, owing to errors of observation and measurement alone, empirical propositions generally cannot, in fact, be logically interrelated. "The impurities and inaccuracies inherent in most or all practicable operations with sensory observations and recorded data," he states, "destroy the logical links between different concepts."[20]

The implication is that the "laws" of science, taken as statements which do not include error terms, contain fiction and presumably, therefore, must be classified as theories. Even allowing for the many relatively unrefined empirical generalizations (where there are no errors of observation), this would indeed entail an extensive reclassification. However, the errors in question are designated "errors of observation and measurement" precisely because the evidence (including evidence concerning the nature of measuring instruments, and so forth) creates a strong presumption that they spring from imperfections in experimental techniques. In other words, it may be presumed that, were it not for such imperfections, the laws would be seen to operate as stated, or that for purposes of the general analysis of experience they confidently can be used as they stand. This is quite different from Machlup's theories which contain "real fiction," or misrepresentations of experience which, for the sake of analytical convenience, are introduced deliberately. It may be added that when the laws are corrected to allow for observational errors the magnitude of the errors is small enough to permit for reliable predictions covering wide ranges of events, including events involving relatively precise measurement.

It has been observed that Machlup's analysis raises serious questions concerning the place of his theoretical systems in the (empirical) area of science because he treats the premises and conclusions of these systems as statements which differ from probability statements. Machlup's essay, however, throws further light on the issue, for it also deals explicitly with the test of theoretical propositions within the context of science. Since theory is said to contain fiction, here one encounters the crucial question: How can a proposition that is fictitious (and we are speaking of "real fiction") be regarded as valid either for purposes of prediction or explanation in the world of real experience? It is possible to argue—and indeed often has been argued—that fictitious theory, although invalid, is useful as a first approximation to experience because it simplifies complex phenomena and thus renders them more tractable to analytical treatment. A progressive rectification of the fictions and the conclusions drawn from them may then provide a fruitful basis for developing more satisfactory hypotheses. So viewed, the value of the first approximation would vary with the extent of its falsifications and with the difficulty, accordingly, in progressing through successive approximations to the real dimensions of the problem without substantially sacrificing the analytical advantages of the initial theoretical framework.[21]

Machlup, however, does not consider pure theory in its role as a first approximation; his statements imply that, as it stands, it has considerable scientific value.[22] But his treatment of the text by which its value is established is curious. Speaking generally, he points out that the constructs of a theory cannot be too fictitious because this would impair their value in explaining real phenomena.[23] This appears to be a recognition that theoretical generalizations *are* matter-of-fact statements and are so to be judged. The implication then, clearly, is that in appraising the validity of a theory it is appropriate to consider whether and to what extent its assumptions are fictitious, or to treat the realism of its assumptions as essential in evaluating both its predictive reliability and explanatory value.[24] In pointedly considering the test of a theory, Machlup, however, retreats from this implication. He contends, rather, that in testing a theory attention need only be given the realism of the initiating change in the problem under study (such as the imposition of an excise tax on an industry) and the accuracy of the consequences (with respect, say, to commodity price) which flow from the theoretical apparatus employed to analyze the effects of the change.[25]

An examination then of the realism of the theoretical assumptions themselves (in the above case those regarding the structure of the industry in question) is not, in fact, to form part of the test by which we judge the validity of a theory.[26] This turns out to be the same as Friedman's test of a theory, although the approach to it is somewhat different. Seeking to establish the validity of theory despite the falsity of its assumptions, Friedman spoke as though the fictions of theory did not at all impair its explanatory value. In contrast, Machlup acknowledges the functional relationship between the realism of theoretical assumptions and their value in explaining experience. But—persuaded nonetheless that theoretical generalizations somehow differ "in kind" from correlation statements and that a substantial measure of self-sufficiency can be claimed for theoretical systems solely on the basis of their "logic"—he then proceeds as though tests of theoretical hypotheses can disregard this critical relationship between "realism" and "explanation."[27] A final accent on this note of self-sufficiency appears in Machlup's concluding comments on the test of a theory. Disregarding the role of "repetition" in the testing process, he here contends that only "occasional" verification of its hypotheses suffices to establish confidence in the whole theoretical system.[28]

Accepting Questionable Assumptions as "Expedients"

A methodological position which differs from those already considered is that of D. V. T. Bear and Daniel Orr; for in this case it is argued unqualifiedly that tests of assumptions are relevant in testing hypotheses.[29] The analysis here, however, is also concerned with a special problem, namely, the testing of hypotheses when the realism of assumptions is difficult to ascertain; and it is this portion of their treatment that is open to criticism.

The authors argue that this problem is generally a vexing one because the testing of assumptions is always "hard" and typically far more difficult than the testing of predictions. However, where the assumptions "do not flatly contradict anything observable," it is legitimate, they point out, to treat their specifications as correct and proceed directly to a test of the predictions. In their view, on grounds of "expediency" there is a "powerful justification" for employing this method in economics, as elsewhere, because it enables us to "get on with the generation of testable prediction statements." Adducing the model of perfect competition as an illustrative case, the authors contend that "it is wrong categorically to disregard predictions from a perfectly competitive model on the ground that any of the four to five inadequately rationalized intermediate theory textbook conditions of perfect competition do not hold. Such a rejection is erroneous because of the difficulty in establishing how widely or how significantly the actual situation varies from perfect competition."[30] Although the rationale for the approach is basically different from Friedman's, and the scope and pattern of its application likewise would differ, Bear and Orr thus advocate a testing procedure which, presumably over a large range of cases in economics, is the same as that supported by Friedman. In these cases (where it is difficult to test certain assumptions relevant to particular hypotheses) our choice among existing hypotheses should depend wholly on the predictive findings; and (until the assumptions are tested) the theory with the greatest predictive success is to be given preference over the rest.

Setting aside the issue of its applicability to economics and considering the question on general methodological grounds, there is nothing objectionable in this mode of testing hypotheses when assumptions are unobservable. While the test is not as complete as one which also covers the assumptions, favorable findings on the observable implications of the assumptions support a presumption that these assumptions are correct and thus enhance our confidence in them.[31] Employed commonly on the frontiers of natural science (where it is especially likely that the hypotheses will contain unobservable assumptions), this method of testing may provide a basis for assessing rival theories (for example, different theories of light) and for the selection of a single theory as preeminent in explaining the class of phenomena involved.

In the natural sciences the procedure has indeed proved powerful. But is it likely to prove generally powerful in economics? To begin with, when certain assumptions of a hypothesis are unobservable the acceptance of the hypothesis on the basis of observable predictions requires highly imposing evidence of success in prediction simply because the experimental evidence must be drawn *wholly* from such findings. The importance of this consideration in a nonlaboratory field such as economics—where serious problems often are encountered in performing crucial experiments on predictions—should be apparent.

The authors' case for concentrating attention on predictions, moreover, is scarcely strengthened by their arguments concerning assumptions. There is no foundation for their view that assumptions (the specifications of the "if" clause of hypotheses) are generally more difficult to test than predictions (the specifications of the "then" clause). The nature of the assumption and the prediction (and hence the relative difficulty of testing each) varies with the particular analysis;

moreover, the assumption of one hypothesis may serve as the prediction of another.

Similarly, Bear and Orr present no substantial argument to support their view that economic assumptions in particular are commonly unobservable. The case drawn from the nature of market structure assumptions in the area of price theory, if anything, constitutes evidence of a contrary nature. On the basis of such considerations as the number of firms in the industry, the importance of product differentiation, and the conditions of entry into the industry (as affected by product differentiation and other factors), there are numerous departures from the assumption of perfect competition that—given the whole spectrum of theoretical departures—would be regarded as "wide" by virtually everybody.[32] There are also numerous cases where the nature of the market is difficult to ascertain in the sense that the question evokes disagreement. But here, contrary to the view of the authors, the relevant circumstances cannot simply be treated as "unobservable," since many observers believe that the cases in fact reveal a considerable measure of noncompetition.

There also is reason to believe that this kind of case is not at all atypical in economics. In a large proportion of the instances, statements appearing as assumptions in economic hypotheses are at least partially observable, or are commonly believed to be so. Included would be assumptions of a "subjective" character (for example, the profit maximization assumption) since these are to some degree testable by introspection and communication. Under these circumstances an evaluation of the plausibility of predictive findings on the basis of the "realism" of the assumptions is frequently unavoidable. In the area specifically of industrial organization (where there is abundant ground for doubting that any *one* existing model, or therefore its predictions, can be applied to all cases), the task of gaining acceptance of the general applicability of the perfectly competitive predictions would indeed require successful predictive evidence of monumental proportions. When consideration, furthermore, is given the difficulty in economics of conducting controlled experiments on predictions which are free of ambiguous results, the procedure urged by Bear and Orr is seen in a very different light. Economics is not physics, much less physics on the frontiers; and while evidence on predictions is basic to progress in any area of science, there is little reason to expect that in economics broad-scale progress can be made without a continued and concomitant examination of the assumptions which are germane to the predictions.

Concluding Comments

Among the deficiencies in formal treatments of economic methodology, the most general and significant (as revealed over a considerable time span) has been the uncritical acceptance of procedures that do not meet the stringent empirical standards of science. This shortcoming may be attributed to a tendency to view methodology within the context of the difficulties encountered in the area of economics, a pattern clearly apparent in the writings discussed. All deal with the role of deductive process in economics which, typically based on "analytically convenient" oversimplifications of reality, has been the principal mode of accommodation to the methodological difficulties of the discipline. Although this procedure has been of value within limits (and the limitations have not gone unrecognized), in practice the extensive dependence on the method has engendered a disposition to treat economic theory as though its validity could be established without full and repeated reference to experience. Again, as on occasions in the past, this perspective has prompted an attempt at justification through the use of formal methodological theory. On the contemporary scene the principal new attempt of this nature—Friedman's—has taken the form of a claim that the deductive process need only be opened to empirical test at the "prediction" end, but in one fashion or another the influence of his position is evident in the other writings considered.

Observing the difficulty in resolving controversy in economics, Bronfenbrenner accepts as correct methodology the unrestrained indulgence of personal proclivities in the choice of assumptions and hypotheses. (One wonders whether this is not an archly disguised statement of resignation to an unpalatable and presumably unalterable reality, or a wry way of saying that, given the nature of the field, an interminable clash between subjectively inspired views *is for economics* "scientific method.") Machlup—arguing for the superiority of unrealistic theoretical analysis while seeking to make allowance for empirical considerations—is led into a maze of insupportable and internally conflicting views (including the Friedman position) only to withdraw eventually into a substantially self-justifying deductive world of "pure theory." Bear and Orr explore the requirements of empiricism more thoroughly, but, similarly confronting the issue of conflict concerning "assumptions," they transform this into a demi-blessing by consigning the realism of a wide range of economic assumptions to the domain of the "unknown" and by supposing that, as such, they can be handled as science handles "unobservables." For an extensive variety of cases the way is thus to be opened for shifting emphasis to the process of deducing predictions at the expense of a concern with the realism of the assumptions employed.

The formal methodological analysis developed within a discipline affords one kind of overview of the discipline itself. Such an overview may be misleading, since methodological prescriptions may be honored in the breach—and often by their own authors. But it also may be significantly illuminating since (as one among several forces) persuasions of a methodological nature may lend momentum to intellectual movements by endowing them with a highly general rationale. The heavy reliance on deductive analysis in economics was the outgrowth of many influences, not the least of which were the vexing investigatory problems encountered in the field, but the sanction provided by methodological argument has helped perpetuate this type of approach. The more recent concern with the empirical testing of hypotheses, whatever its variants, is likewise the product of many forces, but it owes some of its momentum to persistent methodological criticism of the weight traditionally given deduction.

No science progresses in an "ever onward and upward" fashion. In the social sciences, where the subject matter is highly complex and the discipline of the laboratory is wanting, movements both backward and downward are particularly likely to occur, and perhaps especially so in the area of formal methodology. The standards of science in social fields are so difficult to meet that in these realms there is an ever-present susceptibility to more permissive versions of "science." Formal views on methodology thus generally are vulnerable to the winds of controversy over substantive doctrine, the prevailing climate of opinion, and the professional fashions of the period, all of which shape the special permissiveness that is legitimized. It is not at all paradoxical, then, that contemporary methodological tracts should contain errors that writers of a much earlier period—including the classical economists—would not have made.

Methodological theorizing that loses an eye for the full demands of empiricism may succeed in affording some sort of sanction for virtually any practice. Even inadequately justified lines of analysis and inquiry may not prove entirely sterile. But, in affording them sanction, methodological theory abets the perpetuation of practices whose costs are not small. These entail the continuing diversion of intellectual effort into channels that produce little of importance for new knowledge and the impairment of perspective and judgment in making use of knowledge we already possess.

Notes

1. See Friedman's *Essays in Positive Economics* (Chicago: University of Chicago Press, 1953), pp. 3 ff.
2. My criticism is contained in my article "On 'The Methodology of Positive Economics,'" *Quarterly Journal of Economics* 73 (November 1959):552-75. For other criticisms of Friedman's position, see Ernest Nagel, "Assumptions in Economic Theory," and Paul Samuelson, "Problems of Methodology—Discussion," *American Economic Review* 53 (May 1963):211-19 and 231-36, respectively; and Jack Melitz, "Friedman and Machlup on the Significance of Testing Economic Assumptions," *Journal of Political Economy* 82 (February 1965):37-60.
3. See Friedman, *Essays*, pp. 8-9, 14, 16-18.
4. Friedman argues that it is not the realism of all but only of "theoretical" assumptions that is irrelevant in testing hypotheses. He states, in fact, that in testing the predictions of a theory it is essential to observe and specify the conditions under which these predictions occur (see ibid., p. 19). Indeed, the predictions of science, as conditional general statements, always contain "assumptions," so that realistic assumptions are essential to valid scientific predictions themselves. A recognition of all this, however, is inconsistent with Friedman's position regarding the test of a theory. In stressing the necessity for observing and specifying the conditions under which a prediction occurs, Friedman is implicitly recognizing that in the future we will look for the reoccurrence of these latter *real* conditions to tell us when the event predicted will reoccur, which is to say that, insofar as they are unrealistic, the assumptions of the theory *lack* validity for purposes of prediction. To argue that it is the unrealistic assumptions of the theory that are valid whenever its predictions are accurate while stressing the importance of ascertaining the actual conditions under which the predictions occur is much akin to asserting that "in curing disease it is but necessary to rub a rabbit's foot, provided one takes the proper drugs." Cf. Rotwein, "On 'The Methodology,'" pp. 560-61.
5. Although typically there would be agreement on whether a particular association of events had explanatory content, the explanation afforded is a matter of degree; for it depends on the degree to which the conditions contained in the assumption can be related to other experience. The prediction: "Aspirin will alleviate headaches" would gain explanatory content if it were related to a broader condition which specified the manner in which the chemical properties of aspirin affected the brain. In turn this would become more explanatory if the chemical properties of aspirin were shown to have similar effects on other parts of the body, or if aspirin were shown to be a subgroup of chemicals having such effects, and so forth. For a discussion of the relationship between prediction and explanation and the range of variation between the two see Carl G. Hempel, *Aspects of Scientific Explanation* (New York: Free Press, 1965), especially pp. 364-74.
6. Cf. Friedman, *Essays*, pp. 8, 12-15, 20, 41.
7. Sometimes in support of the Friedman view that the realism of theoretical assumptions does not matter, cases are cited in which there is already

abundant evidence for belief in the prediction itself. This plainly begs the question since, for purposes of drawing the prediction or establishing belief in it, there is no dependence on the assumption whose falsity is said to be of no significance. For example, one can introduce any one of an indefinite number of false assumptions into an hypothesis whose prediction is that man is mortal without affecting our belief in the latter. Needless to say, however, as soon as we wish to explain man's mortality in terms of broader considerations, the realism of the assumption employed becomes crucial. Moreover, although we may believe that man is mortal independently of any explanation, such explanation—in principle—enhances the probability value of the belief.

8. Cf. below pp. 371-72 and n. 26. It should perhaps be pointed out that nothing in our argument implies that deduction is not important in the process of empirical inquiry. The question at issue concerns the significance of the realism of any proposition employed—whether deductively or otherwise—in exploring experience.

9. In the detailed attention given the realism of economic assumptions, the writers mentioned make unequivocally clear their belief that unrealistic assumptions would adversely affect the accuracy of their predictions. To cite but one of many of Mill's comments (which appear in his treatment of the "Logic of the Moral Sciences"):

> All the general propositions which can be framed by the deductive science, are therefore, in the strictest sense of the word, hypothetical.
>
> They are grounded on some suppositious set of circumstances, and declare how some given cause would operate in those circumstances, supposing that no others were combined with them. If the set of circumstances supposed have been copied from those of any existing society, the conclusions will be true of that society, provided, and in as far as, the effect of those circumstances shall not be modified by others which have not been taken into the account. If we desire a nearer approach to concrete truth, we can only aim at it by taking, or endeavoring to take, a greater number of individualizing circumstances into the computation.

System of Logic (London: Longmans, 1865), pp. 489-90. See also chap. 5 in Mill's *Essays on Some Unsettled Questions of Political Economy* (London: London School of Economics and Political Science, 1948); and J. E. Cairnes, *The Character and Logical Method of Political Economy* (London: Macmillan, 1878), especially pp. 45-57. In his treatment Senior raises objections to the use of unrealistic assumptions which are worth repeating on the present scene. He points out that such assumptions are objectionable because (1) their use renders a science "unattractive" since it renders it irrelevant to "what is actually taking place"; (2) anyone starting from arbitrarily assumed premises is "in danger of forgetting, from time to time, their unsubstantiated foundation, and of arguing as if they were true"; and (3) reasoning on the basis of unreal assumptions is especially susceptible to logical error since anyone dealing with an imaginary world is less likely to be startled by strange conclusions which might have alerted him to his mistakes. See N. W. Senior, *Four Introductory Lectures in Political Economy* (London: Longmans, 1852), pp. 63-65.

For a general treatment of the economic methodology of the period, see J. N. Keynes, *The Scope and Method of Political Economy* (London: Macmillan, 1917), especially pp. 11-20, 211-20.

10. Among the classical economists Mill and Cairnes best represent this point of view. It is for this reason that both—anticipating the later position taken by Alfred Marshall and others—emphasized that the conclusions of economic reasoning constituted only statements of "tendencies" subject to correction for errors of omission and commission in the treatment of reality in the reasoning process. Cf. Mill, *System of Logic*, pp. 487 ff.; and Cairnes, *Character and Logical Method*, pp. 48 ff. This view is an early statement of the position that the deductive analysis of economic theory represents but the first stage in a process of successive approximations. See below p. 371.
11. Senior's comments on the basic premises of economics are of this character. See his *Political Economy* (London: Griffin, 1873), p. 3. Among neo-orthodox economists, several statements of Lionel Robbins are of a similiar nature. See his *An Essay on the Nature and Significance of Economic Science* (London: Macmillan, 1932), especially pp. 78-92 and 83-86.
12. See Ludwig von Mises, *Human Action, A Treatise on Economics* (New Haven: Yale University Press, 1963), pp. 7-8, 32-41, 64, 351, 868.
13. See his "A 'Middlebrow' Introduction to Economic Methodology" in *The Structure of Economic Science*, ed. Sherman R. Krupp (Englewood Cliffs, N.J.: Prentice-Hall, 1966), pp. 5-24.
14. See Bronfenbrenner, "A 'Middlebrow' Introduction," pp. 17-18.
15. Although he does not amplify or seek to support his statement, Bronfenbrenner asserts that he does not agree with the view that a preference for realistic assumptions is "inherent in normal human nature" or that such realism is essential either to prediction or explanation (ibid., p. 18). With respect to human nature, as has been noted there is no single basis on which human belief is formed. The main issue here, however, concerns the procedures for validating propositions *within the context of science*. The "realism" which is essential to establishing the regularity of association between events on which scientific belief is based is, of course, also found to a substantial degree in "normal" human behavior. Otherwise, science itself would have little or no place in human affairs.
16. Notwithstanding the basic difference between these two positions, Friedman draws on the argument for the necessity of abstraction in support of his main thesis concerning the irrelevance of falsity in assumptions. Cf. Rotwein, "On 'The Methodology,'" pp. 564-65.
17. See his "Marginal Analysis and Empirical Research," reprinted from *American Economic Review* 36 (September 1946), in *Essays on Economic Semantics* (Englewood Cliffs, N.J.: Prentice-Hall, 1963), pp. 147-90. The acceptance of the importance of the realism of assumptions is evident throughout the article. Speaking of all aspects of theory, Machlup concludes that "the correctness, applicability and relevance of economic theory constantly needs testing through empirical research" (p. 190).
18. See his article, "Operationalism and Pure Theory in Economics," in *Structure*, ed. Krupp, pp. 53-67.
19. Ibid., pp. 57-58, 67.

20. Ibid., p. 61.
21. What is sought in the first and simplified approximation is a determinate solution, and the more this approximation falsifies experience the more difficult is it to preserve the elements of determinacy as the unrealistic assumptions are modified in successive approximations. It can be argued that first approximations themselves may afford valuable insights into experience. Insights, however, are not validated hypotheses and are usually the subjects of considerable controversy. See Rotwein, "Mathematical Economics: The Empirical View and an Appeal for Pluralism," in *Structure,* ed. Krupp, pp. 111-12.
22. Machlup, "Operationalism and Pure Theory in Economics," in *Structure,* ed. Krupp, p. 66.
23. Ibid., pp. 57-58.
24. In addition to assumptions whose specifications are demonstrably false, Machlup (in opposing the position of those who insist on operational definitions of theoretical constructs) argues for the legitimacy of using theoretical assumptions whose specifications are either unobservable or very difficult to observe. In these latter cases, the degree of falsification involved, if any, cannot, of course, be ascertained, or, if so, only imperfectly at best. This raises special questions which are considered below. See pp. 372-73.
25. Ibid., p. 65.
26. In an earlier article Machlup asserts that this was the position of Mill, Senior, and Cairnes and credits Mill with its original formulation. "The point to emphasize is that Mill does not propose to put the *assumptions* of economic theory to empirical tests, but only *the predicted results that are deduced from them.*" See his "The Problem of Verification in Economics," *Southern Economic Journal* 22 (July 1955): 7 [italics his]. Cf. the treatment of this question above on pp. 364-65 and n. 9. In light of the full nature of the evidence on the issue (Machlup cites but one statement by Mill taken out of context), his interpretation must be regarded as one instance of the not uncommon practice of misreading the past out of a zealous desire to discover support for the views of the present.
27. In view of the central significance of this inconsistency in Machlup's argument, it is not surprising to find that it should lead to vagueness and ambiguity elsewhere in his analysis. For example, while Machlup's test of a theory makes no place for an examination of the realism of theoretical assumptions, he subsequently states that it is necessary that there be "links" between empirical data and "*some* of the crucial theoretical constructs." Ibid., p. 66 [italics mine]. This same difficulty appears in even more striking form in Machlup's Presidential Address before the American Economic Association. Here he states: "The model of the firm in traditional price theory is not, as so many writers believe, designed to serve to explain and predict changes in the behavior of real firms; instead, it is designed to explain and predict changes in observed prices (quoted, paid, received) as effects of particular changes in conditions (wage rates, interest rates, import duties, excise taxes, technology, etc.). In this causal connection the firm is only a theoretical link, a mental construct to explain how one gets from the cause to the effect. This

is altogether different from explaining the behavior of a firm." "Theories of the Firm: Marginalist, Behavioral, Managerial," *American Economic Review* 57 (March 1967): 9.

The inescapable difficulty which the question of "explanation" poses for the Machlup-Friedman approach is conspicuously apparent in this struggle with ambiguity. The theorist's reference to any fictitious constructs he may have used of course "explains" what *he* did—or his own mental processes—in relating the variables here described as "cause and effect." But Machlup's view that these mental processes, insofar as they deal with constructs that falsify what we know about firms, can serve to explain *actual relations involving firms* (that is, relations between cost and price) is something which itself defies explanation. It is precisely because this procedure is "altogether different from an explanation of the behavior of the firm" that it *cannot* explain such price-cost relationships. If the "false" is to be regarded as in any sense explanatory of reality, then plainly a new term is needed to denote what is usually meant by *explanation.*

It is noteworthy that Machlup himself considers the behavior of *real* firms in a competitive industry and argues that, with respect to its impact on the direction of market changes, it does not significantly depart from what would be expected of the fictitious firm, that is, one that single-mindedly pursued maximum profits. (Cf. Machlup, pp. 12 ff.) This of course is to descend from the level of pure theory to an attempt at genuine explanation. But then what purpose is served by treating industry behavior as the product of single-minded maximizing agents? One can simply replace this with the statement: "*Some* firms in a competitive industry maximize profit" (while others, of course, do not seek losses). Or, probably more realistically, one can abandon reference to profit maximization altogether. With respect to the prediction of the *mere direction* of market changes, there is no inference that can be drawn from the maximization assumption (whether applied to some or all firms) that cannot be drawn from the assumption that competitive firms simply seek to "make money"—meaning that they exploit advantages to increase their profit in degrees unspecified. Nonetheless, with respect to the prediction as stated, Machlup not only insists on the retention of the concept of the maximizing firm as "a postulate in a web of logical connections" but also seeks to preserve the notion that mental processes employing such fictitious constructs "explain" experience.

28. Machlup, "Operationalism and Pure Theory in Economics," in *Structure,* ed. Krupp, p. 66.
29. D. V. T. Bear and Daniel Orr, "Logic and Expediency in Economic Theorizing," *Journal of Political Economy* 75 (April 1967): 188-96. The argument considered below is found on pp. 194-96.
30. Ibid., p. 195.
31. I discussed this point in my article "On 'The Methodology,' " pp. 570-73. In the literature of the philosophy of science the term *theory* often is reserved exclusively for the hypothesis with unobservable assumptions. This contrasts with a *law,* where all elements of the hypothesis are observable.
32. Bear and Orr give no justification for their assertion that the conditions

of perfect competition are ''inadequately rationalized'' or, more precisely, for the view that the model is so inadequately rationalized that no standards are afforded for determining when significant departures from the model exist. This extraordinary view is indeed contradicted by their own phraseology, that is, their reference to ''the predictions from a perfectly competitive model.'' .If the model were as inadequately rationalized as their treatment implied, there would be little or no basis for *drawing* predictions from the model.

The Heterodox Methodology of Two Chicago Economists

Abraham and Eva Hirsch

In the area of methodology, the "old" and "new" Chicago School seem literally poles apart. Frank Knight, spokesman for the old, was the archenemy of positivism; Milton Friedman, representative of the new, is its great champion.[1] Yet, in at least one respect they are alike. In relation to the Nassau Senior/J.E. Cairnes tradition which has dominated mainstream Anglo-Saxon economic methodology,[2] both Knight and Friedman are heterodox. It is this heterodoxy to which major attention will be devoted in this article. First, the major characteristics of the Senior/Cairnes methodology will be considered as a context for what follows. Knight's views, and then Friedman's, will be examined. It is not our purpose to cover the subjects' work comprehensively, nor to undertake a detailed critique of their views on methodology. Occasional reference is made to the work and ideas of Knight and Friedman which fall outside the area of methodology, but only where this material is relevant to methodology. Where questions are raised it is primarily for the purpose of illuminating differences between vision and its rationalization. The last part of the article will consider whether Knight and Friedman are as far apart as they appear to be and whether, despite any difference, there can be distilled from their work a set of ideas

---

The authors are, respectively, Associate Professor of Economics, Rutgers University, Newark, New Jersey, and Professor of Economics, Brooklyn College, Brooklyn, New York.

which might be characterized as the methodological preferences of the Chicago School.

The Senior/Cairnes Methodology

Methodologists in the Senior/Cairnes tradition argue that economics is a "science."[3] Skeptics dismiss this as window dressing, and in a sense the criticism hits the mark. What skeptics overlook, however, is that the association of economics with science shows a real intention, a choice to follow a predictive rather than an assumptive approach and to make economics one of the family of predictive disciplines.[4] The assumer determines validity by correct logical deduction from premises which are necessarily true, the predictor in the correspondence of the predictions of theory with the real world. The assumer may feel that his work has predictive relevance since true premises lead to conclusions which are at least part of the truth. The predictor is not necessarily unconcerned with the truth of his premises since untruth affects the quality of predictions.[5] But an assumer does not judge theory on how well it predicts, nor does the predictor on the basis of self-evident premises. Thus methodologists compare economics with physics rather than with metaphysics because, reflecting a view that long has prevailed in the community of economists, their objective is to attain the kind of predictive power the physicist has, rather than to derive the kind of explanations that are characteristic of metaphysics.

But having chosen the predictor family, methodologists have found it very difficult to remain inside its bounds. First, they generally ruled out the possibility of deriving premises for theorizing from detailed observation of specific experience, as is done in the other predictive disciplines.[6] This choice could be defended on the ground that what counts is not how the premises are derived, but how well they predict.[7] Fair enough. But having ruled our the a *posteriori* method,[8] they then appealed to the truth of their premises in defending economic theory! Nassau Senior, J. E. Cairnes, John Neville Keynes, and Lionel Robbins all followed this course.[9] They did so because economics is really political economy, and if the economist had offered policy proposals and given as his authority the record of his past predictions, he would have looked rather silly.[10] It was easier to be disloyal to the prediction family and appeal to the truth of premises. (Not so John Stuart Mill. He was a reasonably consistent predictor who earned a reputation as black sheep of mainstream methodology because of it.[11])

This inconsistency in the position of mainstream economic methodology posed a problem. Since theory oversimplifies, even if premises are unqualifiedly true, as Mill pointed out, the conclusions will predict only if "disturbing causes" are unimportant.[12] In other words, in order to be able to predict, the premises not only must be true but also must include all the forces that "operate in a predominating way," as J. N. Keynes put it.[13] Few mainstream economists today believe that this condition is fulfilled,[14] but until relatively recently most economists felt that it was, and methodologists reflected their consensus, including Lionel Robbins [50, p. 152] in 1933 and Benjamin Higgins [17, p. 27], in a work on methodology, as late as 1951.

Frank H. Knight

Frank Hyneman Knight was reared in the same rigid, narrow-minded, dogmatic environment as the institutionalists, an environment in which the common prejudices of the community were elevated to the status of premises for academic ("common sense") philosophizing,[15] and the foundations of economic thought were said to be on a par with the teachings of Christianity.[16] It was an environment in which contradictions between what economists did and what they said they were doing appeared to a sharp observer even greater than generally has been the case. Institutionalists, such as Wesley Clair Mitchell, saw through the methodological inconsistency of the Senior/Cairnes tradition, wrote off economic theory as mostly a misguided enterprise, and opted for an economic theory that was truly predictive.[17] Knight recognized the inconsistency, too, but reacted differently. He saw value in the theory, finding fault only in its misuse.[18] To achieve consistency, Knight removed economics from the predictor family altogether,[19] a bold stroke which had much to recommend it as far as representation of what actually prevailed in the past was concerned, and perhaps even as guide for the future. But being so out of line with the trend of the times put Knight beyond the pale, a philosopher who had insightful things to say on assorted subjects, but hardly one to follow in the area of methodology.

The benefits that Knight could show from putting economics into the assumer family were impressive, among them the fact that he unselfconsciously could appeal to premises and argue about them in a most persuasive fashion. The thesis that the validity of the behavioral foundations of economic theory could be established by observation might be relatively easy to demolish.[20] The notion that there is an aspect of our behavior which corresponds to the behavioral assumptions of neoclassical economic thought and that is necessarily true cannot be so easily controverted.[21] One could ask, of course, whether this made for a discipline which is very meaningful or useful, but that is another question, and one to which Knight had an answer.

The reason Knight could deal so adeptly with the question of significance was that he viewed economics as being an assumer rather than predictive discipline. A true assumer does not see a contradiction between theory which is both positive and normative, nor need he avoid introducing his own value scale in building his system. Thus, Knight saw the chief role of economic theory—what he called "pure theory"—as the clarification of value choices in a liberal society. He did not argue that economic theory "proves" the case for liberal policies. Quite the other way around. It is only in a liberal society, Knight felt, that economic theory finds its true significance.[22] Belief in liberal society rests upon freedom as value, according to Knight, and it is supported by an understanding of how limited is our ability to predict human behavior.[23] Knight did not apologize, as did Alfred Marshall, for example,[24] for the intrusion of political values into the economic theorizing of his predecessors. He felt that it was the correct procedure, and one that should be carried on in the present.[25]

This was only one side of Knight's views on methodology. He also believed that economic theory has instrumental value, that is, that it can help us find the means to achieve desired ends.[26] In this, the portion of his methodology which deals with what generally is regarded as the province of methodology as such, Knight comes closer to the Senior/Cairnes tradition, but even here there are significant differences. As already observed, Knight is more direct and unselfconscious in basing his arguments on the self-evident nature of the premises. More important, being very well aware that we deal in economic theory with only part of man's nature, a part which may not predominate in any situation or area, and recognizing that there are "disturbing causes" which cannot be identified and measured in any systematic and objective manner, Knight does not give "verification" of theory any role in his system, nor does he need to duck the issue. This, of course, follows to a large extent from Knight's unashamed assumer stance. It gives his methodology, even the part dealing with the instrumental side of economics, an entirely different flavor. Although economists until quite recently pretty much neglected the verification aspect of the methodology to which they supposedly subscribed, methodologists either had to give it a definite role or gloss over the issue, else economics would have lost its link with the predictor family.[27] Knight was under no such constraint.

Since Knight makes economics an assumer discipline, and since the term *science* generally has been associated with the predictor family, one might have expected Knight to argue against the notion that economics is a science. We find, in fact, that he does. In page after page Knight embellishes and reiterates this thesis. Man is an animal who responds in a predictable fashion to stimuli, he admits. But he is also a knower whose knowledge of predictions will upset predictions; he is a calculating animal whose calculation of the best means to achieve ends leaves its mark; he is a romantic searcher after new values, a problem solver, a maker of mistakes. As a consequence, Knight feels, one could not expect to deal successfully with human behavior in the way one deals with material which does not have these complicating characteristics. Knight observes, for example, that

> human phenomena are not amenable to treatment in accordance with the strict canons of science. They will not yield generalizations which can be used as the basis of prediction and the guidance of policy, because there are no generalizations about them which are true. . . . It seems to us that science is a special technique developed for and applicable to the control of physical nature, but that the ideal constantly preached and reiterated, of carrying its procedure over into the field of the social phenomena rests on a serious misapprehension.[28]

Yet, having said this much, Knight backtracks and argues that economics *is* a science. He states flatly that "there is a science of economics, a true, and even exact, science, which reaches laws as universal as those of mathematics and mechanics."[29] One is tempted to resolve the paradox by saying that Knight believed that in *form* economics is a science, but this would be incorrect; for a true rationalist such as Knight, form without content has little usefulness or meaning. In fact, we see no way of resolving this paradox, but we can note some of Knight's arguments and observe why we feel they are unsatisfactory in the context of his own frame of thought.

One argument Knight uses is that the laws of economics are like the laws of mathematics, which are "characteristics of the world we live in, but characteristics so obvious that it is impossible to escape recognizing them and so fundamental that to think them away would necessitate creating in the imagination a different type of universe." One could argue with this conception of mathematics, but more to the point is the purpose for which Knight uses it. Were he unconcerned with practical usefulness, the matter would be academic. But the very purpose for which the relation is made is to show that since mathematics is useful, although abstract, economics must have the same kind of usefulness. Of mathematics he says that "its conclusions are descriptive of reality and are indispensable in predicting and controlling the phenomena of the physical world."[30] The problem here is that mathematics as such has no usefulness whatsoever; a particular calculus (or model) of mathematics may be useful when applied (or interpreted) in a particular area, but it must be *demonstrated in each area* that the application works. We have by now had enough evidence of the usefulness of different calculi of mathematics to agree *in general* that mathematics is useful. But does this carry over for economic theory, a specific calculus? Above all, what does the whole argument tell us about economic science, particularly economics as an *empirical* science?

A second argument Knight uses is that economics is like classical mechanics (and theoretical physics generally) because the conclusions of mechanics hold true only for an "ideal" universe, in the case of mechanics a frictionless world.[31] Friction, of course, is identifiable and measurable, and it can be demonstrated that the less friction, the better the predictions. This makes it possible to give "verification" of predictions such a central role in physics. In fact, the role is so fundamental, as Knight himself seemed to believe, that theory in physics which did not predict would not be given an important place in the science for very long. As Knight observes, "science, then, is merely the *technique of prediction*."[32] Arguments that premises are necessary truths are not convincing to the physicist. As a result, economists such as Mill, impressed with this state of affairs and desiring to make economics a "true" science, have argued that theory should be judged on how well it predicts.[33] Not so Knight, of course, who grounded theory on necessary truths.[34] Then what sense does it make to argue that economic theory is like theoretical physics?

It is true, of course, that both theoretical physics and economic theory oversimplify and therefore must be supplemented when applied. But the significant point is that the way theory is applied is so different, according to Knight himself. Knight was annoyed because economic theory was criticized for oversimplifying, whereas physics was not,[35] but such criticism against economics arose at least partly because its theory, no matter how applied, did not yield reliable predictions. The criticism of oversimplification was merely an attempt to find reasons for the failure. To answer the criticism Knight would have had to demonstrate that if simplifications are properly allowed for, the theory does give reasonably good predictions which are not dependent upon the unique intuitive skill of the particular predictor. As Knight observes, "in general, truth cannot be considered scientific unless it is demonstrable, which means that it must be alike for all observers and accurately communicable."[36] Knight instead gives the distinct impression in most of his writings that he felt that, even if properly applied, economic theory could not do this. Typical are statements such as these: Applied economics is inherently "at least as much an art based on general knowledge and sound judgment as a science with accurate premises and rigorous conclusions," and "it is not conceivably possibly to 'verify' any propositions about 'economic' behavior by any 'empirical' procedure, if the key words of this statement are defined as they must be defined to be used with relevance and precision."[37]

Knight uses still another argument in this same area, a thrust apparently aimed at the common criticism that physicists generally agree, but economists do not. Knight observes that, even in physics, "truth" is determined by the consensus of the fraternity of competent physicists, as in agreement on the results of experiment.[38] Of course, this is true. Yet to say that the difference between economics and physics in this respect is a matter of degree, even if it is admitted that the degree is large, does far more to mislead than to point up a significant connection. In the predictive disciplines such as physics, some disagreement does occur, of course, and in the rationalistic disciplines such as metaphysics, men in the field sometimes do agree about what is supposedly self-evident. What seems significant about this, however, is the difference in kind between the two processes of trying to reach agreement, not the fact that agreement and disagreement are possible in both areas.

More can and should be said about Knight's views about economics as science. The questions asked here, however, merely were raised to show that this is the most vulnerable portion of Knight's methodological formulations, to suggest that it is not an inherent element in the methodological vision which Knight was trying to rationalize, and to argue that even an admirer who accepted all else that Knight taught, but came of age a generation or so later and absorbed notions about science which were taken for granted by then, likely would have had difficulty going along with Knight in this area. We only can speculate whether Friedman found himself in this position as a student of Knight's and note that the conjecture that he did does not seem incompatible with the available evidence.

Milton Friedman

At first glance Friedman's methodology seems to represent a revolt of student against teacher, for Friedman does nothing less than turn Knight's methodology inside out. But more careful reading shows that this is not at all the case. In fact, Friedman in his methodology is manning the same barricades in defense of economic theory. The common enemy is the critic of traditional theory who attacks the validity of premises.[39] A major mission of Knight's from the first was to parry such threats by admitting that the premises of economic theory were "unrealistic," but then going on to argue that it was the very unrealism of the theory which made it valuable. Thus, as Knight saw it, "the makers and users of economic analysis have in general still to be made to see that deductions from theory are necessary, not because literally true—that in the strict sense they are useful *because not* literally true—but only if they bear a certain relation to literal truth and if all who work with them constantly bear in mind what that relation is."[40] Friedman, too, argues that unrealism can be a virtue,[41] a feature of his methodology which has generated a great deal of argument, but he modifies its character by putting the argument in a different context, as will be shown in what follows.

Friedman, too, came of age when traditional economic theory was under attack, but the critics were now not institutionalists attacking from the "outside"; they were members in good standing of the economics fraternity who had begun to have doubts about the assumptions of traditional theory. Since the ability of theory to predict, according to mainstream methodology, depends not only upon the truth of the premises, but also upon whether the forces taken account of in the premises have a predominating effect, it seemed clear that what was needed was to erect new theory on more adequate premises. The result, as everyone knows, was a series of revolutions which have made economic theory very different from the way it was in Alfred Marshall's day. Not only was new theory developed, but also the way theory was envisaged underwent radical change. Theory now tended to be seen as "models" which were entirely analytic (not empirical or synthetic), and it was posited that such models could be fruitfully applied only where the assumptions of the model corresponded with what prevailed in fact.[42] That Marshallian theory as such did not have the requisite "realism"—much as it might be useful in some undefined way as "analysis"—generally had come to be accepted. It was to show that the new trends represented retrogression rather than advance that Friedman's methodology was formulated.

Knight himself had argued against the new trends, but his arguments lack the force of his earlier broadsides.[43] Perhaps this is because weapons fashioned for one purpose do not serve as well for another. It may also be that the arguments seem less effective because we ourselves have been affected so directly by the new trends that arguments against them do not convince so easily. In any case, Friedman resumed where

Knight left off, and instead of renovating the Knightian structure, he chose to erect a new, more contemporary one, a methodology which was consistent, as Knight's was not, with the prevalent view that economics was a mature science. In developing his methodology Knight used science negatively; his positive references are peripheral and, as we have tried to show, somwhat puzzling. Friedman puts "science" at the center of his analysis.[44] As did Knight, Friedman rejected the Senior/Cairnes methodological tradition, wherein economics takes on the dual character of being ostensibly predictive, but mostly assumer in fact. But whereas Knight resolved the dualism by putting economics squarely into the assumer family, Friedman resolved it by making economics a member of the predictive group. His methodology, in effect, attempts to draw the implications from this choice.

Friedman downgrades analysis as such to the status of mere language,[45] which is its role in the predictor family. He argues that theory be judged primarily by how well it predicts. He even goes so far as to welcome back the *a posteriori,* which had been banished from economics since before Mill's time, and seems to be suggesting that the derivation of theory from specific observation is not only the way it should be derived, but also the way it always has been derived. He tells us that

> Theory can be used in two very different ways in the development of a science. The approach that is standard in the physical sciences is to use theory to derive generalizations about the real world. The theorist starts with some set of observed and related facts. . . . He seeks a generalization that will explain these facts. . . . He tests this theory to make sure that it is logically consistent, that its elements are susceptible of empirical determination, that it will explain adequately the facts he started with. He then seeks to deduce from his theory facts other than those he used to derive it and to check these deductions against reality.[46]

All of this is fully consistent. Problems arise when Friedman begins to argue within this context, as Knight had within his, that the lack of realism of premises can be a strength rather than a failing.

Critics of Friedman point out that he gets himself into fundamental problems of logic,[47] that he seems to rule theory out altogether in favor of empirical generalizations,[48] that contrary to his argument there is a vital connection between the truth of premises and the ability of a theory to predict.[49] Friedman's formulations invite such criticism. A more sympathetic reading, however, suggests that, *within the context of the predictive disciplines,* theory that does not in time yield testable predictions is considered of little value, that theory whose assumptions are not entirely true (or whose truth or falsity is not known) may yet be exceedingly valuable,[50] that the choice between a theory which has more realistic assumptions and one which gives better predictions probably would be made in favor of the latter. But since so much debate has ensued in this area, it would be to little purpose to cover this ground yet once again.[51] There are, however, other questions that Friedman's formulations raise which have not been asked and that are more germane to our purpose.

First, Friedman presents his methodology not only as an ideal, but also as the rationale of economic science which is implicit in work of the past.[52] It is an intriguing thesis and worth more attention than can be devoted to it here. Suffice it to note that, at least on the face of it, it does not seem to be borne out by the facts. For example, do we judge advance in economics by theories' power to predict? Is neoclassical considered to be superior to classical theory because of its greater predictive power? The solution of the "paradox of value" is considered a matter of some importance in the history of economics. Does it represent much of an advance in the power to predict? If we reject Friedman's references to the past and argue that this is the way things should be rather than the way they have been, his thesis stands on firmer ground, but questions still remain.

If economics is taken to be a member of the predictor family, we must be able to demonstrate objectively that the theory which we accept does, indeed, have some minimum of predictive power. It was the failure to be able to do so, we have suggested previously, which led methodologists of the Senior/Cairnes tradition away from predictive moorings. Has the situation changed that much today? Not on Friedman's showing. In arguing for the maximum-of-returns hypothesis, for example, Friedman does not demonstrate predictive power; rather, he admits that "this evidence is extremely hard to document; it is scattered in numerous memorandums, articles and monographs concerned primarily with specific concrete problems rather than with submitting the hypothesis to test."[53] If the data are really there, and if we are committed to Friedman's methodology, would it not be of vital importance to gather it together as the only real support for the hypothesis? When we do, of course, we might be in for a surprise. Until more work is done, might not the declaration of a methodological revolution be premature?

Not having the data, Friedman resorts to the classic argument in favor of the maximum-of-returns hypothesis. He argues that it is inconceivable to think differently from what we know about the world.[54] Here is an assumer argument somehow lost in the midst of Friedman's predictive methodology.[55] In this instance the matter is not merely one of formulation; it points up a fundamental question: Is a true predictive economics an attainable ideal? Fritz Machlup, staunch defender of mainstream economic thought, admits that "the test of most of our theories will be more nearly of the character of *illustrations* than of the kind possible in relation with repeated controlled experiments or with recurring fully identified situations."[56] Under such circumstances is the kind of "mature" science of economics, which Friedman ostensibly champions, attainable? Some of Knight's arguments certainly leave one in doubt. One wonders, in fact, about Friedman himself. Might he, in his enthusiasm to formulate a methodology that was consistent with prevailing views in philosophy of science, have made statements whose implications he would not be ready to accept?[57]

The Chicago Core

So far we have tried to show how the methodologies of Knight and Friedman differed from those in the Senior/Cairnes tradition and how they differed from each other. The latter difference is obviously great, and we here can reiterate the observation made in the introduction, since examination does indeed show that the two are poles apart.[58] Yet, it could be argued that on a deeper level the basic feelings about the character of economic theory of Knight and Friedman are essentially the same and to suggest as an hypothesis that these notions validly can be described as belonging to that group of economists who have been identified as members of the Chicago School.[59] The two basic notions are: (1) Mainstream economic theory, which was developed from Adam Smith to Marshall, is not mere analysis; it has empirical significance, that is, it tells us what actually happens in the real world. It may be only part of the truth, but it is the truth nonetheless; and (2) while economic theory tells us what actually happens, it gives us a picture that is true only in the most broad and general terms. Thus, if we hold the theory too closely to account for detailed observation, it may appear to be falsified, even though, on a broader view, it is generally valid.

Friedman's emphasis is stronger on the first point, Knight's on the second, but one finds evidence that Knight and Friedman adhered to both. Thus, Friedman argues very vigorously against abstract theorizing and holds up Marshall as an example of one who properly developed the kind of theory which helps us to discover tendencies in the real world.[60] That Marshall himself half succumbed to the sin of mere analysis in his formulations of demand theory, Friedman admits, but Friedman tries to convince us of the superiority of a side of Marshall on demand which is more empirically oriented.[61] Friedman's criticism of Léon Walras, Oskar Lange, and Abba P. Lerner, specifically, and of most trends in contemporary economic thought, generally, centers on this point.[62] Furthermore, Friedman takes on a defense of the maximum-of-returns hypothesis even though, as we have shown, it gets him into difficulty. Such a defense was necessary because without it neoclassical thought is left mostly an analytic shell. Some would say that even as analysis this theory can be exceedingly useful, but not Friedman. His criterion of acceptability is that theory be in some sense descriptive of the real world.

There is less obvious stress in Knight on the first point, but it is quite clear that he adheres to it just as fervently. As assumer he has no use for analytic bones without the flesh of reality attached to them.[63] That is at least one reason why very early he dissociated himself from mathematical economics.[64] His arguments for economic "science," if they have any purpose at all, are to support the contention that economic theory is as "real," even if abstract, as is theoretical physics.[65] Telling, too, is Knight's association with his fellow Chicagoans during the Great Depression in urging government action through spending to increase the money supply. Knight was not as explicit as were others who more directly concerned themselves with money,[66] but at Chicago, according to Friedman, "the quantity theory was connected and integrated with general price theory and became a flexible and sensitive tool for interpreting movements in aggregate economic activity and for developing relevant policy prescriptions."[67] Methodologically, this contrasts sharply with A.C. Pigou's view, for example, that "the 'quantity theory' is often defended and opposed as though it were a definite set of propositions that must be either true or false. But in fact the formulae employed in the exposition of that theory are merely devices for enabling us to bring together in an orderly way the principal causes by which the value of money is determined."[68]

With regard to the second point—that is, the one having to do with the limitations of theory—little need be added to what already has been said concerning Knight. From the beginning to the end it was a central theme in his work. Friedman has said little directly on this score, and one must admit that the spirit of his positivism on the face of it does not seem to go very well with notions about limitations. However, a careful reading of Friedman does show that he is very specific about the need to explore where and to what extent the theory does or does not hold,[69] and it is hard to believe that his general endorsement of Marshall as guide in today's times does not have attached to it implicitly the kind of cautions about which Knight was so eloquently explicit. Friedman's policy conclusions from his monetary work are also pertinent in this regard. Although a fervent believer in the relationship between changes in the quantity of money and income, he does not draw from the (positivist) results of research the conclusion that there is a basis in this for close control. Rather, he urges that the results best can be used as general guide in the formulation of policy in a manner which is reminiscent of the use of the quantity theory by others from Chicago in the 1930s.[70]

Both Knight's and Friedman's methodological formulations founder on their attempt to link up economics with science. Knight got into difficulty because the rationale of economics he developed does not fit with science; Friedman is unconvincing because he established an ideal from which he himself, even at this late date, is forced to back away. One must distinguish, however, between a vision and its rationalization. The vision that seems common to both men needs more careful formulation by its adherents and more serious scrutiny by its critics. We strongly suspect that further examination will show that it was this vision which guided mainstream economic thought until relatively recent times. The vision was accepted too uncritically at one time and tends to be rejected too cavalierly today. To judge it more intelligently and more fairly we must try to understand what the vision is. Knight and Friedman not only can help us understand, but also can show why understanding in this area is so difficult to achieve.

Notes

1. Knight and Friedman use the term *positivism* somewhat differently. To Knight [24, p. 226], positivism involves using the methods of physical science, which excludes the kind of concern with means-ends calculations with which economic theory deals. Friedman [12, pp. 3–7] uses the term merely to exclude concern with norms. As will be seen in what follows, however, the difference in methodological formulations is more than a matter of semantics.
2. Lionel Robbins [50, p. 82] speaks of the Senior/Cairnes tradition, with which he identifies.. J.N. Keynes [21] differs from the others in some respects, but on the whole is in conformity with it. John Stuart Mill [43; 44], for reasons suggested below, does not belong. T.W. Hutchison [20, p. 745], too, refers to the Senior/Cairnes tradition.

3. For example, Cairnes [5, pp. 16–20]; Keynes [21, pp. 149–52]; Robbins [50, pp. 78–79]; and Higgins [14, pp. 9–22].
4. We would have preferred to use more familiar labels, but terms such as *rationalist* and *positivist* have too many meanings and too many complex associations attached to them to serve well for our purposes. John Dewey [8] makes the comparison we have in mind when he analyzes what he calls "the natural history of thinking," referring to the first (assumer approach) as the "discussion" mode and to the second (predictor) as the "inference" mode. He observes (p. 844): "What makes the essential difference between modern research and the reflection of, say, the Greeks, [is] the presence of conditions for testing results." However, Dewey has no doubts but that the "inference" approach is superior to that of "discussion"; so far as theoretical economics is concerned, we feel that this is very much an open question. The reason for our doubts will be apparent in the part of the article dealing with Friedman's contribution.
5. Melitz [41] shows this clearly.
6. Cairnes [5, pp. 60–87]; and Robbins [50, pp. 104–21]. Mill [43, pp. 423–35] argues this point persuasively. Keynes [21, pp. 227–36] is somewhat ambiguous, but in the areas of traditional theory (pp. 207–15), he is very much in line with the others.
7. Popper [49, p. 31].
8. Mill [43, pp. 423–24] stacked the cards, so to speak, by defining the *a posteriori* method as one in which only empirical generalizations are derived from detailed investigation of the facts. We include the derivation of postulates for theorizing. Both uses conform to the traditional philosophical conception of the term, but ours, we feel, is more in conformity with common usage.
9. Bowley on Senior [1, p. 43]; Cairnes [5, pp. 39–45]; Keynes [21, pp. 223–26, 240]; and Robbins [50, pp. 78–80].
10. Senior notes, as quoted in Cairnes [5, p. 51]: "No one listens to an exposition of what might be the state of things under given but unreal conditions with the interest with which he hears a statement of what is actually taking place." This illustrates, if indeed illustration is needed, that methodologists were not unconcerned with the policy issue in formulating methodological principles.
11. For criticism of Mill see Keynes [21, pp. 233–34, 115–19]; and Robbins [50, p. 150]. Mill particularly irritated Alfred Marshall, who spoke of "the baneful spell of Mill's logic." (The quote is from an unpublished letter by John Whittaker in an article to appear in the *Journal of Political Economy*.)
12. Mill [43, p. 429] introduced this term.
13. Keynes [21, pp. 223–24].
14. For example, J.R. Hicks [16, p. 23] talks of "the assumption, at the beginning of every economic argument, that the things to be dealt with in the argument are the only things that matter in some practical problem." He adds: "This is always a dangerous assumption, and nearly always more or less wrong—which is why the application of economic theory is such a ticklish matter."
15. Compare, for example, Dorfman [10, chapter 2].

16. For example, Laughlin [34].
17. For example, Mitchell [45, pp. 342–55].
18. See, for example, for the earliest statement, Knight [32, pp. vii–ix]. (Since Knight keeps repeating the same themes in his writings, sometimes almost verbatim, we cite only examples of his views. The reader who is interested in more complete citations is referred to the very excellent article by Gonce [15].)
19. For example, Knight [22, pp. 105–35]. Knight [30, p. 751] notes: "I, for one, do not particularly care whether economic theory is regarded as science or not."
20. For example, Hutchison [19].
21. Methodologists often have appealed to "consciousness" as the basis for premises in economic theory, but they do not make clear what they mean by this and invariably go on to fudge things up by speaking of assumptions as "facts," running together different aspects of behavior, and not recognizing the implications of what they are saying. Knight is in a class by himself for clarity and consistency.
22. Knight [22, pp. 286–88].
23. Knight [28; 21, chapter 11].
24. Marshall [39, p. 756].
25. Knight [22, pp. 285–86, 279].
26. Ibid., pp. 135–47.
27. Cairnes [5, pp. 80–81]; and Keynes [21, pp. 232–36]. With Mill [43, pp. 431–33], for reasons that have been indicated, verification has a more genuine role. (This does not mean that Mill's practice necessarily was consistent with his methodology. Compare De Marchi [7].) Robbins is quite definite in the belief that economics is a science like physics [50, pp. 104–106] and has no doubts whatever about the predictive power of economic theory [50, pp. 121–26], yet he says nothing about verification. The omission is either an oversight or an irrationality.
28. Knight [22, pp. 129, 133].
29. Ibid., p. 135.
30. Ibid., pp. 136, 137.
31. Ibid., pp. 138, 94.
32. Knight [25, p. 109, italics in original].
33. Mill [44, p. 585].
34. Knight seemed to have difficulty in making up his mind about verification and prediction. Three careful readers (Gonce [15, p. 555], Macfie [36, pp. 783–84], and Shackle [57, p. 65]) come to the conclusion, on the basis of good evidence, that it was Knight's view that prediction was impossible in economics. Yet, Knight [25, p. 260] does say that the principles of economic theory "have great value in the prediction of the effects of changes." It is not surprising that readers were thrown off. Statements about prediction such as the above come out of the air and are in a spirit quite opposed to that in Knight's work generally. One would expect that if theory can predict, it should be possible to verify such predictions. But verification is something Knight will have none of; he tells us [25, p. 163], for example: "It is not conceivably possible to 'verify' any proposition about 'economic' behavior by any 'empirical' procedure." Is it then on the *authority* of the economist that we must

rely? James Buchanan [4] tells us that Knight was not interested in prediction, which we think sums it up quite well.

35. Knight [32, p. 16].
36. Knight [22, p. 118].
37. Knight [22, p. 143; 21, p. 163].
38. Knight [23, pp. 264–65; 26, pp. 751–52]. We do not have to rely on the *authority* of a physicist on matters of prediction as, apparently according to Knight (see note 34), we do in economics.
39. Friedman [12, pp. 15–16].
40. Knight [32, pp. 14–15].
41. Friedman [12, p. 14] tells us that "the more significant the theory the more unrealistic the assumptions (in this sense)."
42. Joan Robinson [51, p. 2], for example, argues that "the best the economist can do is . . . to take the utmost pains to make clear what assumptions about the nature of the problem are implicit in his answer. If these assumptions are near enough to the actual conditions to make the answer serviceable the practical man can accept it."
43. Knight [27; 29; 25, chapter 9].
44. Friedman [12, pp. 3–12].
45. Ibid., pp. 7–8.
46. Ibid., pp. 8–9, 282–83.
47. Rotwein [52; 53]; and Samuelson [54; 55; 56].
48. Nagel [46].
49. Melitz [41].
50. Melitz (ibid., p. 59) admits this, and Nagel [46, p. 219] ends his critique with the statement that "I have therefore tried . . . to indicate why the main thesis he is ostensibly defending is nonetheless sound."
51. A very large literature on this issue has been created, and it continues to grow. Compare, for example, in addition to those cited above, Bear and Orr [1]; De Alessi [6]; Koopmans [33]; Lerner [35]; Machlup [37; 38]; Massey [40]; and Wong [59].
52. Friedman [12, pp. 41–42].
53. Ibid., pp. 22–23.
54. Ibid., p. 22.
55. Knight [25, p. 206] gives this kind of an argument, but it more appropriately fits with Knight's assumer orientation. However, the argument that "it suffices that men largely behave 'as if' they were trying to conform to the principles" seems to involve a switch on Knight's part from the notion that the premises of economic theory are necessary truths to the idea that they are a fiction needed for prediction.
56. Machlup [37, p. 191, italics in original].
57. We say this not only because of the lapses already noted, but also because there are a number of very significant escape clauses in Friedman which make it possible to come up with very different interpretations of his position. For example, as does Knight, he argues that only "experts" can determine whether predictions are consistent with theory [12, p. 25]; he has an impressionistic, empirical "rules of application or interpretation" part, telling us how and where the hypothesis legitimately can be applied, which he takes to be an integral part of the hypothesis; and he argues (p. 31) that "legitimate" criticism must be accompanied by

an alternative hypothesis which yields better predictions than the one criticized, implying that theory does not have to predict at all well, only less badly than any other. Such qualifications, we believe, while they make Friedman's position ambiguous, do make it more defensible. In effect, Friedman's qualifications can be interpreted to make him an aggressive disciple of John Stuart Mill, who felt constrained to show that economic theory was a mature science.

58. This is true even if, for reasons cited in the last footnote, we soften the sharp lines of Friedman's analysis.
59. Discussions about the Chicago School—for example, Miller [42]; Stigler [58]; Bronfenbrenner [3]; Davis [9]; Humphrey [18]; and Patinkin [47]—do not deal explicitly with methodological issues. Cursory examination suggests the proposed hypothesis, which we feel is worth exploring.
60. Friedman [12, pp. 11–12, 91, 283, 300; 13].
61. Friedman [12, pp. 47–99].
62. Ibid., pp. 91, 300, 319, and [11].
63. That is why, as noted above, Knight insists on a descriptive (rather than analytic) interpretation even of mathematics.
64. Knight [32, pp. 5–6].
65. Knight [28, p. 72] tells us: "The statement that economics describes the way the economic order works refers to its working as a mechanism; that is the meaning of being scientific."
66. Davis [9].
67. Friedman [11, p. 937].
68. Pigou [48, p. 38].
69. See note 57 above.
70. Friedman [14, p. 23].

References

[1] Bear, D.V.T., and Orr, Daniel. "Logic and Expediency in Economic Theorizing." *Journal of Political Economy* 75 (April 1967): 188–96.

[2] Bowley, Marion. *Nassau Senior and Classical Political Economy*. New York: Augustus M. Kelley, 1949.

[3] Bronfenbrenner, Martin. "Observations on the 'Chicago School(s).'" *Journal of Political Economy* 70 (February 1962): 72–75.

[4] Buchanan, James. "Frank H. Knight." *International Journal of the Social Sciences* 8: 424–28.

[5] Cairnes, J.N. *The Character and Logical Method of Political Economy*. 2d ed. London: Macmillan, 1875.

[6] De Alessi, Louis. "Reversals of Assumptions and Implications." *Journal of Political Economy* 79 (July–August 1971): 867–77.

[7] De Marchi, N.B. "The Empirical Content and Longevity of Ricardian Economics." *Economica,* N.S.37 (August 1970): 257–76.

[8] Dewey, John. "The Natural History of Thinking." In *Intelligence in*

the Modern World: John Dewey's Philosophy, edited by Joseph Ratner. New York: Modern Library, 1939. Pp. 837–50.

[9] Davis, J.R. "Chicago Economists, Deficit Budgets and the Early 1930's." *American Economic Review* 58 (June 1968): 476–82.

[10] Dorfman, Joseph. *Thorstein Veblen and His America.* New York: Viking Press, 1934.

[11] Friedman, Milton. "Comments on the Critics." *Journal of Political Economy* 80 (September–October 1972): 906–50.

[12] ———. *Essays in Positive Economics.* Chicago: University of Chicago Press, 1953.

[13] ———. "Leon Walras and His Economic System." *American Economic Review* 45 (December 1955): 900–909.

[14] ———. *A Program for Monetary Stability.* New York: Fordham University Press, 1960.

[15] Gonce, R.A. "Frank H. Knight on Social Control and the Scope and Method of Economics." *Southern Economic Journal* 38 (April 1972): 547–58.

[16] Hicks, J.R. *Value and Capital.* 2d ed. Oxford: Clarendon Press, 1946.

[17] Higgins, Benjamin. *What Do Economists Know?* Melbourne: Melbourne University Press, 1951.

[18] Humphrey, T.M. "Role of Non-Chicago Economists in the Evolution of the Quantity Theory in America, 1930–50." *Southern Economic Journal* 38 (July 1971): 12–18.

[19] Hutchison, T.W. *The Significance and Basic Postulates of Economic Theory.* New York: Augustus M. Kelley, 1960.

[20] ———. "The Significance and Basic Postulates of Economic Theory: A Reply to Professor Knight." *Journal of Political Economy* 49 (October 1941): 732–50.

[21] Keynes. J.N. *The Scope and Method of Political Economy.* 4th ed. New York: Augustus M. Kelley, 1955.

[22] Knight, F.H. *The Ethics of Competition and Other Essays.* New York: Augustus M. Kelley, 1951.

[23] ———. "Fact and Metaphysics in Economic Psychology." *American Economic Review* 15 (June 1925): 247–66.

[24] ———. *Freedom and Reform.* New York: Harper, 1947.

[25] ———. *On the History and Method of Economics.* Chicago: University of Chicago Press, 1956.

[26] ———. "Immutable Law in Economics: Its Reality and Limitations." *American Economic Review, Papers and Proceedings* 36 (May 1946): 93–111.

[27] ———. "Imperfect Competition." *Journal of Marketing* 3 (April 1939): 360–66.

[28] ———. *Intelligence and Democratic Action.* Cambridge, Mass.: Harvard University Press, 1960.

[29] ———. "Realism and Relevance in the Theory of Demand." *Journal of Political Economy* 52 (December 1944): 289–318.

[30] ———. "A Rejoinder." *Journal of Political Economy* 49 (October 1941): 750–53.

[31] ———. "Review: Robbins, L.C. *The Nature and Significance of Economic Science.*" *Ethics* 44 (April 1934): 358–61.
[32] ———. *Risk, Uncertainty and Profit.* New York: Augustus M. Kelley, 1964.
[33] Koopmans, T.C. *Three Essays on the State of Economic Science.* New York: McGraw-Hill, 1957.
[34] Laughlin, J.L. "Political Economy and Christianity." In *Latter Day Problems.* New York: D. Appelton and Co., 1866.
[35] Lerner, Abba P. "Professor Samuelson on Theory and Realism: Comment." *American Economic Review* 55 (December 1965): 1153–55.
[36] Macfie, A.L. "Review: Knight, F.H. *On the History and Method of Economics.*" *Economic Journal* 68 (December 1958): 780–86.
[37] Machlup, Fritz. "The Problem of Verification in Economics." *Southern Economic Journal* 22 (July 1955): 1–21.
[38] ———. "Professor Samuelson on Theory and Realism." *American Economic Review* 54 (September 1964): 733–35.
[39] Marshall, Alfred. *Principles of Economics.* 8th ed. New York: Macmillan, 1920.
[40] Massey, Gerald J. "Professor Samuelson on Theory and Realism: Comment." *American Economic Review* 55 (December 1965): 1155–63.
[41] Melitz, Jack. "Friedman and Machlup on the Significance of Testing Economic Assumptions." *Journal of Political Economy* 73 (February 1965): 37–60.
[42] Miller, H.L. "On the 'Chicago School of Economics.'" *Journal of Political Economy* 70 (February 1962): 64–69.
[43] Mill, J.S. "On the Definition of Political Economy and on the Method of Investigation Proper to It." In *John Stuart Mill's Philosophy of Scientific Method,* edited by Ernest Nagel. New York: Hafner, 1950.
[44] ———. *A System of Logic.* 8th ed. London: Longmans, Green & Co., 1965.
[45] Mitchell, W.C. *The Backward Art of Spending Money and Other Essays.* New York: Augustus M. Kelley, 1950.
[46] Nagel, Ernest. "Assumptions in Economic Theory." *American Economic Review, Papers and Proceedings* 53 (May 1963): 211–19.
[47] Patinkin, Don. "On the Monetary Economics of Chicagoans and Non-Chicagoans: Comment." *Southern Economic Journal* 39 (January 1973): 454–59.
[48] Pigou, A.C. "The Value of Money." *Quarterly Journal of Economics* 32 (November 1917): 38–65.
[49] Popper, Karl. *The Logic of Scientific Discovery.* New York: Basic Books, 1961.
[50] Robbins, Lionel. *An Essay on the Nature and Significance of Economic Science.* London: Macmillan, 1949.
[51] Robinson, Joan. *The Economics of Imperfect Competition.* London: Macmillan, 1948.
[52] Rotwein, Eugene. "Empiricism and Economic Method: Several Views Considered." *Journal of Economic Issues* 7 (September 1973): 361–82.
[53] ———. "On 'The Methodology of Positive Economics.'" *Quarterly Journal of Economics* 73 (November 1959): 552–75.

[54] Samuelson, Paul. "Problems of Methodology: Discussion." *American Economic Review, Papers and Proceedings* 53 (May 1963): 231–36.
[55] ———. "Professor Samuelson on Theory and Realism: Reply." *American Economic Review* 55 (December 1965): 1164–72.
[56] ———. "Theory and Realism: A Reply." *American Economic Review* 54 (September 1964): 736–39.
[57] Shackle, G.L.S. "Review: Knight, F.H. *On the History and Method of Economics: Selected Essays*." *Economica* 25 (February 1958): 65–66.
[58] Stigler, G.J. "On the 'Chicago School of Economics': Comment." *Journal of Political Economy* 70 (February 1962): 70–71.
[59] Wong, Stanley. "The 'F-Twist' and the Methodology of Paul Samuelson." *American Economic Review* 63 (June 1973): 312–25.

The Chicago School: Positivism or Ideal Type?

Charles K. Wilber and Jon D. Wisman

The economics profession recognizes the University of Chicago as the fountainhead and guardian of a distinct, although by no means homogeneous, school of thought (with branches at UCLA and VPI). It can be characterized by both its methodology for analyzing "what is" and its policy stance on "what ought to be." Its methodology is a form of logical positivism which strives to make economics as *Wertfrei* or objectively scientific as the physical sciences. Its policy stance is founded on the belief that the theoretical model of competition can be utilized to provide empirical proof that laissez-faire capitalism maximizes both personal freedom and economic welfare.

The purpose of this article is to investigate the degree to which the Chicago School's methodology and policy stance are related. We argue that hypotheses generated from a logical positivist methodology in economics are, in practice, nonfalsifiable. As a result, when combined with a commitment to a policy of laissez-faire, the "positivist" economic theory of the Chicago School tends to be transformed into an ideal type. As such, economic analysis becomes more a prescriptive than a descriptive theory. Ironically, what starts off as a *Wertfrei* positivism ends up a

---

The authors are, respectively, Professor and Chairman, Department of Economics, University of Notre Dame, South Bend, Indiana, and Assistant Professor of Economics, The American University, Washington, D.C.

value laden tool for the defense of a particular socioeconomic system. We conclude with a brief discussion of a certain paradox between the Chicago School's espousal of a positivist methodology and its commitment to laissez-faire. Furtherance of the former may be inimical to crucial elements of the latter.

Even though the Chicago School is characterized by both methodological and policy stance heterogeneity, its internal differences are less marked than its differences with the outside world. In fact, under scrutiny, many of the differences tend to disappear. For example, Frank Knight held that empirical verification of theory is unnecessary, that truth lies in the logic of the theory. Despite an explicit espousal of positivism, this is where, *de facto,* Milton Friedman ends up. This is our main argument. However, to avoid overly gross distortions of those internal differences, we confine our investigation principally to Friedman, the Chicago School's currently best known spokesman.

Positivist Methodology

How can we know reality? How can we explain what happens in the physical and social worlds? Before the advent of modern science, the appeal was to authority. Sorcerers, popes, kings, and tradition were looked to for explanation of reality. With the growth of modern science two major opposing trends developed in the philosophy of science. On the one side were the rationalists, such as René Descartes, who argued that we can know the world through reason alone. For Descartes, the real world is characterized by order and rationality, and thus it is best apprehended through an appeal to human reason alone. Descartes's lineal descendants in economics include Ludwig von Mises, Frank Knight, and sometimes Lionel Robbins.[1] Truth about reality lies in the logic of the theory. Opposing the rationalists were the empiricists, such as John Locke, who argued that we can know reality only through experience. Direct descendants of Locke include the German Historical School in the nineteenth century and T. W. Hutchinson in the twentieth.[2]

Those economists in the rationalist tradition believe that economic theory is not amenable to verification or refutation on purely empirical grounds. Instead, they believe that economics is a system of *a priori* truths, a product of pure reason, a system of pure deduction from a series of postulates. The difficulty is that there is an infinite number of possible logical systems. Without some empirical means of choosing one over another, logical systems tend to degenerate into ideologies (or, less pejoratively, ideal types).

Empiricism also faces a telling objection, one that has become known as the problem of induction.[3] If reality can be known only through experience, then generalizations are impossible. Simply because *X* follows *Y* the first 1,000 times measured does not necessitate that it will follow the 1,001st time.

Immanuel Kant wanted to prove that scientific explanations are true and, at the same time, answer both the rationalists and empiricists. Rationalists *assumed* that reality is rational, and the empiricists denied that it is anything more than a collection of discrete experiences. Kant argued that to experience anything we must give it order by synthesizing those experiences in terms of categories such as time, space, substance, and causality. That is, we create synthetic, *a priori* truths. They are *a priori* assumptions, *but* they, or at least their implications, can be tested against experience.

The grand synthesis that Kant constructed serves as the foundation for logical positivism. The classic modern version of this logical positivism is found in the work of Carl Hempel and Paul Oppenheim.[4] They attempted to construct a model of scientific explanation that codified how, in effect, physical science explained reality. Their argument that scientific explanation always requires the use of general laws led them to develop what they call the covering law model. The following diagram will help clarify their model. The C's are statements of antecedent conditions, since they describe facts about the world which are relevant in explaining the observed phenomenon. The L's are general laws of the particular science (in economics, maximizing behavior would be one, for example) which form the core of the model used to explain the observed phenomenon. Using the rules of logic, an explanandum or hypothesis is deduced from the explanans. This explanandum is then subjected to empirical verification by either direct observation or statistical inference. The hypothesis is then either accepted as confirmed or rejected as disconfirmed. The result is that every explanation is covered by (subsumed under) one or more general law. This is what makes an explanation a *scientific* explanation instead of merely an *ad hoc* one.

COVERING LAW MODEL OF EXPLANATION

Logical deduction	$L_1, L_2, L_3 \ldots L_n$ General laws $C_1, C_2, C_3 \ldots C_n$ Antecedent conditions	Explanans
	→ E Description of the empirical phenomenon to be explained (hypothesis)	Explanandum

In the covering law model, explanation and prediction are seen as symmetrical. That is, explanation occurs when the explanandum is derived after the event, and prediction occurs when the explanadum is derived before the event takes place. Explanation is not considered adequate unless it could have served as the basis of prediction.

Logical positivism, with its covering law model of explanation, has found wide acceptance among economists since the publication of I.M.D. Little's *Critique of Welfare Economics* and Friedman's *Essays in Positive Economics* during the early 1950s.[5] Both Paul Samuelson's revealed preference theory and Friedman's demand for money function can be seen as attempts to restructure economic theory into a logical positivist form.[6] This acceptance has become so widespread that an overwhelming number of current textbooks contains an introductory chapter in which a positivist methodology is espoused.[7]

The goal of positive economics, according to Friedman, "is to provide a system of generalizations that can be used to make correct predictions about the consequences of any change in circumstances. Its performance is to be judged by the precision, scope, and conformity with experience of the predictions it yields."[8] Predictability, then, is the crucial element in positive economics. Since explanation and prediction are symmetrical, correct predictions imply correct explanations. Economic science is carried forth by logically deducing an explanandum from an explanans. These explananda or hypotheses act as predictions of correlational relationships in the real world. That is, the positive investigator pursues a testing of the degree of correspondence between his or her predictions and the empirical evidence provided by the real world. A high degree of correspondence, or a "good fit," acts to confirm or verify the theory. A low level or lack of correspondence indicates a flaw in the theory. It is by testing that disputes are resolved, and testing leads to the accumulation of general laws that constitute theory. If the predictions derived from one model prove "better" than the corresponding predictions drawn from another model, the former is tentatively selected as preferable. In every case the theory preferred is the one which best explains the observable phenomena of the economic world.

Furthermore, Friedman argues that the validity of an hypothesis is to be judged *solely* by its predictive ability, regardless of whether or not the initial assumptions are realistic. A model cannot, by definition, capture or reproduce the whole of reality. Therefore, assumptions and hypotheses must of necessity be unrealistic. Consequently, one hypothesis is to be chosen over another "not because its 'assumptions' are more 'realistic' but rather because it is part of a more general theory that applies to a wider variety of phenomena"; and the more general theory "has more implications of being contradicted, and has failed to be contradicted under a wider variety of circumstances."[9] Indeed, assumptions are often best presented "as if" they were true. For example, it may be sufficient to assume that economic agents behave "as if" they were maximizing.

A second related criterion for the selection of one hypothesis over another involves the principle of simplicity, or maximum use of Occam's razor. Thus, for Friedman, "the choice among alternative hypotheses equally consistent with the available evidence must to some extent be arbitrary, though there is general agreement that relevant considerations are suggested by . . . criteria [such as] 'simplicity'. . . . A theory is 'simpler' the less the initial knowledge needed to make a prediction within a given field of phenomena. . . . A hypothesis is important if it 'explains' much by little."[10] Theory, by definition, involves the simplification of reality, and thus in the interests of economy maximum simplification is justified. Simplicity also serves the function of warding off value judgments which might seep in unnoticed amid unnecessary complexity.

Although the goal of prediction is no mean task, especially in a social science such as economics, the end sought by positivism is notably a humble one. Positive methodology does not strive to assert causality. Rather, it is satisfied to establish a high probable correlation between two events. An event is explained by citing an earlier event with which it correlated and establishing a generalization which relates the two. The generalization is validated through repeated empirical testing. Causality cannot be observed empirically. The world of facts offers the investigator only events in contingent sequences. General laws can exist only as the consequence of repeatedly observed correlation.

The final major distinguishing characteristic of positivist methodology is that its orientation is ahistorical. Positive theory is conceived of as a timeless analytical construct. Not only does it deny values in its framework, it denies that as a method it represents values, or that it is culture bound. And, in addition to denying its own historicity, positive methodology relates to historical issues in a quite restricted manner. It is not concerned with either the evolution of ideas or the motivations behind historical events, since such phenomena are not amenable to empirical verification. Its interest in history is bound by the degree to which historical investigation promises to confirm ahistorical, general laws.[11]

Positivist Insularity

The task of positive economics, then, is to apply to the realm of economic phenomena the same methodology which has yielded such impressive fruits in the physical sciences. The position of positive economics is that knowledge, whether in the physical sciences or in a social science such as economics, is to be distinguished solely on the basis of the empirical subject matter and not by the methodology. The crucial issue, then, is whether the subject matter of economics is of a comparable nature to that of the physical sciences, so as to permit profitable application of a positive methodology. In other words, is the subject matter of economics such that the generalizations which can be formulated about it lead to successful predictions?

The social sciences and the physical sciences are by nature different because of "the inherent instability of the data with which the discipline is concerned."[12] These data can be classified into two different categories: The first relates to "the physical nature of the production process," whereas the second relates to "the behavioral response to economic stimuli."[13] Robert Heilbroner argues that although behavioral responses tend to exhibit a significant degree of long-run stability due to the influence of " 'habits,' customs, traditions and usages of societies . . . the long-run production functions of the economy are . . . awkward or impossible to predict."[14] On the other hand, whereas it may be "within the bounds of plausibility that it would be possible to construct a set of production functions that would mirror with a fair degree of accuracy the actual production possibilities open to society in the short-run,"[15] short-run behavioral responses tend to be highly unpredictable.[16] Consequently, prediction in economics is severely limited because of the nature of the subject matter.

A related limitation on the possibility of deriving successful predictions of economic events stems from the fact that the discipline deals with open rather than closed systems.[17] In the physical sciences experiments can be controlled such that an "artificially closed system" is created in which it is possible to correctly identify the chosen variables. Because the subject matter of economics is not amenable to controlled experiments, "economics has resorted to the use of partial equilibrium analysis in an attempt to reduce the complexity of economic phenomena to manageable proportions."[18] The potential random behavior of certain factors requires extensive use of the *ceteris paribus* technique to give the model, although not the subject matter itself, a degree of determinedness.

Because of the reasons given above, we conclude that successful prediction is extremely difficult to achieve in economics. Experience in the past several years with unemployment, inflation, the energy crisis, and so on, highlights this inability to predict. However, positive economists have achieved a high degree of insularity from the failure of their predictions. This is due to the highly conditional nature of economic predictions, which are dependent upon the *ceteris paribus* clauses holding and upon the data's being representative of economic reality. These conditionals give the positivist an escape clause for rationalizing the failure of a prediction. When his model repeatedly fails to predict correctly, the physicist blames his model. The positive economist, on the other hand, is tempted to blame the *ceteris paribus* conditions, the data, or the specific testing procedure itself. Consequently, for the positive economist, hypotheses are seldom disconfirmed and general theory rarely or never disproved. Positive economics thus becomes perfectly insulated from refutation: It cannot be harmed by demonstrating its assumptions to be unrealistic, and it is not rejected when its predictions fail to fit the facts.

Since Friedman places so much weight on the ability to predict as the main verification of the truth of a theory, this insulation of predictions from refutation is worth exploring further. Why do positive economists resist disconfirmation of their hypotheses? At the heart of the issue is Thomas Kuhn's concept of a paradigm.[19] A scientist normally has some general theory that guides the choice of problems, provides the analytic tools, and supplies a general vision of how reality is structured. This general theory—whether it be neoclassical economics, Marxism, or some other—is usually so much a part of the very thought processes that empirical disconfirmation of some particular hypothesis is almost automatically rejected. Three specific problems, briefly mentioned above, make it easy to reject a disconfirmation as invalid and, thus, protect the scientist's basic theory or paradigm.

First is the *ceteris paribus* problem. Hypotheses in economics must always be stated in the form of "if . . . then" propositions. Since the "ifs" do change, an econometric test that disconfirms the theory can always be rejected as "misspecified."[20] In addition, since explananda or hypotheses are stated in probabilistic terms, a *non*occurrence of the predicted event cannot be used as a refutation of the general law from which the particular hypothesis was deduced.[21]

Second is the difficulty of constructing a clear-cut test of an hypothesis in economics. Most of the traditional statistical tests, for example, null hypotheses, are very weak ones which a large number of different theories are capable of passing. The choice among alternative theories, therefore, cannot be settled on empirical grounds. Instead, the desirable qualities of a logical model—simplicity, generality, specificity, and aesthetic quality—are used, and the relative evaluation of these qualities is probably determined by one's own paradigm.[22]

Finally, both the methods of collection and construction of economic data are unreliable. Furthermore, the data that are statistically constructed frequently are not conceptually the same as the corresponding variables in the theory. Therefore, econometricians engage in data "massaging." If a test disconfirms an hypothesis, the investigator can always blame the data—they have been "massaged" either too much or not enough.

The Ideal Type

When a theory has achieved such a high level of insularity from falsification, we contend that it might be best termed an ideal type. Implicit in such theories (or abstract formal models, as Paul Diesing refers to them) "is an idealization of one facet of a complex reality, while the verbal language of the theory disguises the abstractions of the model and makes it look like a simple empirical description."[23]

When a theory becomes an ideal type it functions more as a prescriptive than as a descriptive device. That is, theory functions as a parable to elucidate the ideal toward which we should strive. For economists such as Paul Samuelson, Robert Solow, and Wassily Leontief, neoclassical economic theory has become the "grand parable" that is still defended against nonbelievers but is not taken too seriously as a scientific explanation of "what is."[24] Rather, attention is focused on the development of a set of "engineering tools"—linear programming, input-output analysis, cost-benefit analysis, and so on. Economics has come to be conceived in engineering terms: How do you maximize some objective function in the face of various constraints?

For the Chicago School, however, particularly as exemplified by the work of Milton Friedman, neoclassical economic theory (including the pure competition version), while in fact an ideal type, is treated as if it were a highly confirmed theory of "what is." Ironically, Friedman the avowed positivist ends up *de facto* in company with Frank Knight. Knight held that empirical verification of theory is unnecessary, and Friedman, through his insistence on prediction as the sole form of verification, renders empirical falsification virtually impossible. All that remains is theory as ideal type.

As an ideal type, Friedman's version of economic theory serves two essential and related functions. It acts to restrict the scope for "scientific" economic inquiry, and it serves as a policy stance for molding society in its image, while legitimating certain aspects of the status quo.

On the level of restricting or defining the scope of economics, the neoclassical theory of the Chicago School acts as a set of "exemplars" which guide the pursuit of normal scientific research. The complexity of the real world is to be viewed through the lenses of supply and demand, equilibrium, and maximization subject to constraints. As such, universally applicable hypotheses are devised which transcend institutional and historical variations. These lenses focus potential economic research upon and, in effect, constrain attention to the behavior of atomistic agents. Such agents are assumed to act rationally and exclusively on the basis of market given information. Hence, one of the most challenging areas for current economic theory—the issue of externalities—seldom merits more than a passing reference. Market generated data have the aura of value free facticity, whereas imputing valuations of extramarket phenomena is clearly more open to the influence of the researcher's own values. Thus, the challenges of social critics such as Ezra Mishan,[25] namely, that human welfare may be decreasing even as per capita market values increase, are excluded from serious "scientific" scrutiny.

But more important yet is that concentration on the presumed "rational" actions of atomistic actors camouflages the existence and exercise of power. The firm is assumed to be ultimately subordinate to the consumer. Advertising functions merely in providing the rational consumer with market information. And although some firms are admittedly larger than others, and some consumers richer than others, power is assumed to be widely diffused and vested solely in the atomistic, sovereign consumer. Firms do not collude and form cartels, nor do consumers exert power through social class membership. A perfect example of this myopia, induced by being a prisoner of an ideal type, is Friedman's attempt to connect personal and functional income distribution.[26] The latter is explained, of course, by marginal productivity theory, and the former is attributed to risk, chance, natural ability, and inheritance. Differences in power and sociocultural environment are never mentioned; differences in wealth play but a minor role. In fact, his conclusion seems to be that personal inequality is due to free choice—by the rich and poor alike.

The Chicago School's ideal type "explains" economic reality in a very restricted sense. Only those phenomena which can be represented in its laissez-faire, capitalist model merit investigation. For example, most members of the Chicago School have ignored the question of monopoly, both empirically and theoretically. Theories of imperfect competition have been dismissed out of hand,[27] and no real attempt has been made empirically to test noncompetitive theory.[28] Since the Chicago School's theory is left essentially unscathed by both the unrealism of its assumptions and its inability to provide successful prediction, the ideal type has an independent life of its own. Rather than repair the model to better conform with the real world, the burden of conformity is placed on the real world. Thus, the policy stance of the Chicago School is characterized by proposals to change the real economic world according to the requisites of its ideal type—laissez-faire capitalism.

This orientation is most clearly exemplified in the public policy pronouncements of Milton Friedman. This stance is commensurate with a neoclassical vision of an economic reality in which externalities are of minimal importance, power is widely diffused, and economic agents behave independently in a rational manner. Since externalities are "marginal," markets should be unfettered so as to provide optimally efficient resource allocation. Monopoly power, if existent, is not viewed as institutional or endemic to modern industrial society, but is largely traceable to governmental interference in the economic system. Indeed most, if not all, of the ills afflicting contemporary society are to be traced to the existence of an overgrown government. But the growth of government is not seen as functional to the economic system, that is, as stemming from an increase in externalities, as a force countervailing other growing power concentrations, or as representing particular class interests; rather, it stems from misguided political philosophy.

Individuals are viewed as self-interested maximizers who function with a timeless sort of reason, unbounded by any cultural or institutional artifacts other than the available choices provided by the market itself. Thus, it is not relevant that Americans might be culturally prone to seek fulfillment through consumption rather than in creative work environments. Since markets assume overwhelming importance in rational, individual decision making, maximizing behavior will eradicate all vestiges of racism and sexism in a laissez-faire capitalism. And failure to recognize that rationality is culture and class bound leads to a proposal that education also be allocated by the market system.[29]

Somewhat ironically, although Friedman's version of theory emphasizes both prediction and rationality, it places no faith in the possibility of discretionary, macroeconomic stabilization policy. Successful prediction is not deemed possible in this realm, and it is implied that policy makers are not quite capable of behaving rationally in the interests of society. In a *Newsweek* column on national economic planning, Friedman argues that "we are suffering from inflation and recession produced by government attempts to promote full-employment."[30] He goes on to say that government planning cannot work and then outlines his alternative.

> The central planners want planning by them for us. They want the government—by which they really mean themselves—to decide "social priorities" (i.e., tell us what is good for us); "rationalize production" (i.e., tell us where and how we should work); assure "equitable distribution" (i.e., take from some of us to give to others of us).
>
> Such planning, from the top down, is inefficient because it makes it impossible to use the detailed knowledge shared among millions of individuals. It undermines freedom because it requires people to obey orders rather than pursue their own interests.
>
> I am for planning, too, but planning by each of us separately in light of our individual, though shared, values, coordinated by voluntary exchange in free markets. Such planning, from the bottom up, enlists the interests of each in promoting the well-being of all. Government has its role—to provide a stable legal and monetary framework, enforce contracts and adjudicate disputes and protect us from coercion by our fellow citizens.[31]

Adam Smith could not have said it better. Two hundred years of change in the economic world is irrelevant to the economic theory of the Chicago School. No Rockefellers, no multinational corporations, no imperialism, no environmental destruction; just many small buyers and sellers engaging in exchange and thus maximizing their freedom and economic welfare. If we could only get government to tend to its proper business, all would be well. This vision of the world may be beautiful, but it *is* a vision. It has no established basis in empirical reality. Positivism becomes a facade; faith wins out.

Conclusion

As seen above, positivism tends to insulate the Chicago School's version of neoclassical economics from falsifiability. What remains, therefore, is an ideal type from which policy prescriptions for the "good society" are derived. But this ideal type seems particularly inappropriate to provide solutions to today's socioeconomic problems. The modern economy is characterized by *interdependence* of its economic actors. Externalities are the rule not the exception. Firms are not simply price takers; they are dependent upon each other's price and quantity decisions. Power is necessary to market new products, attain government favors, and compete internationally. General Motors, ITT, and IBM, not the corner newspaper dealer, typify the "representative firm" of today.

The perfectly competitive model of the Chicago School has little of relevance to say in the face of today's urgent socioeconomic problems other than to exhort us to believe that they all will go away if we simply return to a laissez-faire government policy. Technological change will not undermine competition, external diseconomies will transform themselves into minor "neighborhood" effects, power will dissolve, bureaucracies will break up, and to eliminate job dissatisfaction people will equate the disutility of work with the utility of income.

Finally, we want to make some brief comments on an apparent paradox between the Chicago School's espousal of a positivist methodology and its commitment to laissez-faire. Ironically, the methodology of positive economics might be inimical to the social values which are so highly esteemed in the Chicago version of neoclassical economics.

Friedman, the Chicago School, and the liberal tradition which they represent place ultimate importance on the freedom of the individual to determine his or her own fate. However, free human choice is only emphasized within a given institutional framework. Thus, the approach tends to direct attention away from what could conceivably constitute the most important realm of human choice—creating meaningful changes in social institutions.

Perhaps more crucial yet, by striving for the predictability of economic phenomena, the methodology of positive economics creates a powerful instrument of social control. Predictability holds forth the potential for social control in two essential ways. First, predictions, when issued by those with power and authority, sow the seeds of their own fulfillment by influencing expectations. Humans, unlike atoms and celestial bodies, are capable of understanding predictions and changing their behavior in conformity with them. The success of such predictions may rely less on "scientific truth" than on the power—as represented by prestige, wealth, or politics—of those formulating them.

Second, prediction provides those possessing power with a more readily rationalized justification for social manipulation. Of course, it could be countered that prediction might provide the powerless with the arms to discredit the powerful. However, such a retort has overtones of a produce-bombs-for-peace argument, and such a stance presumes that there is a widely dispersed ability to gain access to data, generate predictions, and make them known. Such is not the case: Government and large corporate interests underwrite, either directly or indirectly, most of the social science research which leads to predictions. Furthermore, those who collect the data from which most economic predictions are made are generally either government agencies or corporate entities. Faith in the possibility of the successful prediction of social phenomena leads to an increased demand for data. Since data gathering probably admits of economies of scale, the industry might therefore be a case of "natural monopoly." Not only does the collection of data pose a serious threat to personal liberty, but also its potential for "scientifically" rationalized social control is more frightening yet. Thus, for example, whereas the Chicago School has persistently opposed the implementation of national planning, its epistemology promises to take us ever closer to it. This is not because predictability has been proven, but because an ever increasing portion of the American people have been led to believe that we can predict and thereby control our social destiny.

The glory of the Chicago School is its insistence on maintaining a vision of a "good society" and its refusal to become mere technicians at the service of whoever is in power. Thus, the ethos of the Chicago School would seem to plead for a methodology which, rather than providing us with predictions, would provide us with an understanding of our past and present such that we might more rationally and freely choose our own destiny. Our social sciences must not constitute what Ben Seligman referred to as a "mere scientism"—"the attempt to impose a unified method on all disciplines . . . that is confusing form with substance."[32] Ultimately, it is the intrusion of human freedom and responsibility that renders the social sciences different in substance from the physical sciences and thereby makes human behavior largely unpredictable.

Notes

1. See Ludwig von Mises, *Epistemological Problems of Economics* (Princeton: Princeton University Press, 1960); Frank Knight, "The Limitations of Scientific Method in Economics," in *The Ethics of Competition* (New York: Harper, 1935); and Lionel Robbins, *The Nature and Significance of Economic Science* (London: Macmillan, 1935).
2. See T. W. Hutchinson, *The Significance and Basic Postulates of Economic Theory* (London: Macmillan, 1938).
3. See Martin Hollis and Edward Nell, *Rational Economic Man* (London: Cambridge University Press, 1975).
4. Carl G. Hempel and Paul Oppenheim, "Studies in the Logic of Explanation," *Philosophy of Science* 15 (1948): 135–75.
5. I.M.D. Little, *A Critique of Welfare Economics,* 2d ed. (Oxford: Clarendon Press, 1957); and Milton Friedman, *Essays in Positive Economics* (Chicago: University of Chicago Press, 1953).
6. Paul A. Samuelson, *Foundations of Economic Analysis* (Cambridge,

Mass.: Harvard University Press, 1947), chapters 5 and 6; and Milton Friedman, "The Demand for Money: Some Theoretical and Empirical Results," *Journal of Political Economy* 67 (August 1959): 327–51.

7. See particularly Richard Lipsey and Peter Steiner, *Economics* (New York: Harper & Row, 1966). Lipsey published an earlier version in England under the title *Introduction to Positive Economics.* Oddly, the ascent of positivism in economics has coincided with a decrease in its popularity among professional philosophers.
8. Friedman, "The Methodology of Positive Economics," in *Essays,* p. 4.
9. Ibid., p. 20.
10. Ibid., pp. 10, 14.
11. This can be seen in much of the "new" economic history, where history is treated as merely a laboratory for testing economic models. See, for example, Robert Fogel, *Railroads and American Economic Growth* (Baltimore: Johns Hopkins Press, 1964).
12. Alfred F. Chalk, "Concepts of Change and the Role of Predictability in Economics," *History of Political Economy* 2 (Spring 1970): 109.
13. Robert L. Heilbroner. "On the Limits of Economic Prediction," *Diogenes* 70 (April 1970): 36.
14. Ibid., p. 37.
15. Ibid., p. 33.
16. Note that Friedman's concept of "transitory income" in his permanent income hypothesis would tend to substantiate this view.
17. Chalk, "Concepts," p. 114.
18. Ibid.
19. T.S. Kuhn, *The Structure of Scientific Revolutions* (Chicago: University of Chicago Press, 1970).
20. See Fritz Machlup, "The Problem of Verification in Economics," *Southern Economic Journal* 22 (July 1955): 1–21.
21. Ibid.
22. See Jeffrey B. Nugent, "Methodology in Economics: Some Implications of Pessimism and Some Suggested Alternatives," *American Economist* 11 (Fall 1967): 49–55; and Jack Melitz, "Friedman and Machlup on the Significance of Testing Economic Assumptions," *Journal of Political Economy* 73 (February 1965): 37–60.
23. Paul Diesing, *Patterns of Discovery in the Social Sciences* (Chicago and New York: Aldine-Atherton, Inc., 1971), p. 121.
24. Under the onslaught of the theory of second best, the Cambridge controversy in capital theory, Koopman's dissection of econometric method, Little's attack on welfare economics, the competitive model as a theory of "what is" was quietly shelved. See Martin Shubik, "A Curmudgeon's Guide to Microeconomics," *Journal of Economic Literature* (June 1970): 405–34.
25. Ezra J. Mishan, *The Costs of Economic Growth* (New York: Praeger Publishers, 1967).
26. Milton Friedman, "Choice, Chance, and the Personal Distribution of Income," *Journal of Political Economy* 61 (August 1953): 277–90.
27. E.H. Chamberlin, *Towards a More General Theory of Value* (New York: Oxford University Press, 1957), pp. 296ff.

28. Ben Seligman, *Main Currents in Modern Economics* (Glencoe: The Free Press, 1962), p. 728.
29. See the essays in Milton Friedman, *Capitalism and Freedom* (Chicago: University of Chicago Press, 1962).
30. Milton Friedman, "National Economic Planning," *Newsweek*, 14 July 1975, p. 71.
31. Ibid.
32. Ben B. Seligman, "The Impact of Positivism on Economic Thought," *History of Political Economy* 1 (Fall 1969): 262.

Value Judgments in Economic Science

Vincent J. Tarascio

The problem of values and its implication for economic science has been a source of methodological controversy ever since logical positivists distinguished between positive and normative economics. A casual inspection of the literature on the subject would seem to indicate that current opinion ranges from the view that economics cannot be anything but an ethical discipline to the view that "positive" economics is independent of any ethical position or normative judgment. For instance, T. W. Hutchison [4, 14] has recently argued that Joan Robinson, G. Myrdal, and A. Smithies hold the former opinion, while G. Haberler, M. Friedman, G. Stigler, and L. Robbins are of the latter opinion. He further states that the point of view which claims that "positive" economics is independent of any ethical or normative judgments is the "orthodox" view [4, 14]. Also, he takes the stance that the possible separation of "positive" economics and "normative" economics "was almost a basic tenet of the "orthodox" methodology of economics for about a hundred years from Nassau Senior and J. S. Mill, through Cairnes, J. N. Keynes, Pareto and Max Weber, down to Robbins and Friedman" [4, 18]. Finally, he tells us that there has been a recent "wave of criticism and scepticism" regarding the orthodox view. Specifically, this "recent scepticism" is said to doubt that value judgments can be completely eliminated from "Positive" economics [4, 44-45].

The major purpose of this note is to clear up a source of confusion regarding the problem of ethical neutrality which continues

The author is Associate Professor of Economics at the University of North Carolina.

to persist in the literature. This confusion stems from the failure to distinguish between what I shall call *methodological* judgments and *normative* judgments. In order to make the distinction clear, I shall take up the case of Friedman, whom Hutchison calls an "orthodox" methodologist.

METHODOLOGICAL AND NORMATIVE JUDGMENTS

To support his claim that Friedman is an "orthodox" methodologist, Hutchison quotes from Friedman: "Positive economics is in principle independent of any particular ethical position or normative judgments" [3, 3-4]. Yet Friedman admits that value judgments are involved in the choice of criteria for judging the validity of a theory, the selection and interpretation of data, the adherence to the canons of formal logic, and so forth [3, 7-16]. What Friedman seems to be saying is that some value judgments are a necessary part of all positive science, while others can be dispensed with.

Here again, the vagueness of the term "values" leads to confusion. In order to attach significance to its meaning, it will be necessary to clarify whose values are referred to and which of various meanings of the term, used on different planes of discourse, are being employed.

To begin, when we speak of values, do we mean those of the observer or those he encounters in the subjects of his analysis? The latter gives rise to considerations of individual values and social choice.[1] My main concern is with value judgments as they enter scientific analysis—that is, those of the observer. Suppose we select the observer as our reference. And suppose also that we classify value judgments in terms of the various planes of scientific discourse:

> I. Methodological judgments: (a) the choice of scientific principles to be followed; (b) the scope of study; (c) the choice of methods; (d) criteria for accepting or rejecting theories; (e) professional norms; (f) theoretical assumptions; and so forth.
>
> II. Normative judgments: (a) personal ethics of the observer; (b) normative principles; and (c) policy views.
>
> The crucial difference between the two types of judgments is this: judgments involved in positive economics are *methodological,* pertaining to the philosophy of science and mainly concerned with investigations into the nature of society, what is, whereas judgments in normative economics are concerned with what is best for society, what ought to be, from the observer's point of view.[2]

THE ROLE OF CULTURAL INFLUENCE

Cultural influence play a role in *both* methodological and normative judgments.[3] Indeed, if cultural influences were absent in *methodological* judgments serious questions would arise regarding the relevance of theory. And it is precisely differing cultural influences acting upon methodological judgments which caused the theoretical systems of the classicals, neo-classicals, and Keynes to differ. At the same time the development of economics as a science witnessed the attempts of economists to supress the normative elements in their theoretical systems.

Today cultural factors are influencing intellectual thought as they have in the past. The relevance of positive economics in dealing with social problems is being increasingly questioned. In such an environment there is a tendency to become more normative-oriented. As long as the empirical and normative aspects are kept in their proper relationship, the scientific nature of the discipline can be preserved. During periods of political and social ferment, there is a temptation to supress the positive elements so that the normative elements hold sway;[4] the eighteenth-century "heavenly city" becomes a substitute for social science. In such an environment there is also the intrusion of ideology. It is not contradiction of ideology by events that counts, but contradiction by ideals and preconceptions. As long as attitudes remain intact, no degree of historical contradiction will shatter the ideology.

If economics is to avoid such a fate, economists must make clear where the source of the problem of relevance lies, and hence where the solution to the problem lies. The problem of relevance exists not so much because economics is not normative enough but because the *methodological* judgments implicit in positive economics prevent it from dealing with many problems outside the scope of its analysis. The central issue, then, is not the inability of positive economics to study the nature of value systems but the narrow scope of economics, which precludes such studies as being outside its purview.[5]

In summary, the progress of economics as a science does not involve solely the elaboration and modification of existing theories, the development of new concepts within the framework of the existing scope of the discipline, improved techniques, or better sources of data. These factors are very important. However, there exists an additional means for progress—a widening of the scope of economics to include other social phenomena.

SCIENCE AND IDEOLOGY

The problem of ideological intrusion in economic theory becomes much more complex when the discussion is extended to social and cultural change. In particular, there remains the continuing problem of altering methodological judgments to conform with changing institutions and values. Professional training in economics is very time consuming, and individuals tend to have a psychological stake in what they have learned as well as in what they have contributed to the discipline. Hence there is often the desire to "conventionalize" thought. Such attempts have been successful in the short run, but with time either internal or external forces exert pressures for change.[6] This is what the marginalist and Keynesian revolutions were all about. But intellectual revolutions, like political revolutions, are divisive and costly; the wounds heal slowly. Also, like political revolutions, intellectual revolutions are evidences of the failure of individuals to respond successfully to a changing social and cultural environment.

FOOTNOTES

1. This aspect of values has been investigated by Bergson [2] and Arrow [1].

2. Both Pareto [7, p. 3] and Weber [13, p. 11] advocated the subjective minimization of ethical judgments. What they had in mind was the elimination of *normative* judgments from economic *science,* at the same time fully realizing that methodological judgments were a necsary part of positive science. As regards Weber, this fact is not understood even today. Leo Strauss [10, pp. 35-80], completely misses the point when he insists that Weber argued for a completely value-free social science. For a more detailed discussion regarding the problem of ethical neutrality see Tarascio [11, pp. 30-55].

3. The influence of culture and subjective experience upon what I have called methodological judgments has been the concern of the sociology of knowledge. In Stark's [9, p. 188] terminology the sociology of knowledge involves a study of the relationship between the "axiological layer of the mind" and the "objects of knowledge." By the axiological layer of the mind, "Stark means the prejudgments or value positions of the individual which lead him to select among objects of knowledge those elements which he feels to be important. It is out of the relationship between the objects of knowledge and the axiological system of the individual that new ideas are created, which in turn become a part of the axiological system of subsequent generations" [6, p. 79].

4. One such example is Seligman, whose critique of positive economics leads him to welcome the possibility that "all economics is apt to become normative" [8, p. 278]. Seligman seems to overlook the fact that it is difficult to conceive of a normative economics without a positive economics since the distinction itself stems from positivism (unless he means by normative economics, a kind of economic philosophy). Although Seligman points to the

alleged ideological aspects of positive economics, he neglects the more serious problems of ideological intrusion associated with a purely normative system.

5. For a more detailed discussion on this point, pertaining to Pareto's sociology see [12, pp. 1-4].

6. Kuhn [5] describes the process as a displacement of one scientific paradigm, or way of seeing the world, by another fundamentally different. Since scientists are influenced by their environment, I prefer to view paradigm change as part of a more general process of cultural and social change.

REFERENCES

1. Arrow, K. *Social Choice and Individual Values.* New York: John Wiley & Sons, 1951.

2. Bergson, Abram. "A Reformulation of Certain Aspects of Welfare Economics," Q.J.E. LII (February, 1938), pp. 310-34.

3. Friedman, Milton, "The Methodology of Positive Economics," in *Essays in Positive Economics.* Chicago: University of Chicago Press, 1953, pp. 3-43.

4. Hutchison, T. W. *'Positive' Economics and Policy Objectives.* Cambridge, Mass.: Harvard University Press, 1964.

5. Kuhn, T. S. "The Structure of Scientific Revolutions," Vol. 2, no. 2, of *Foundations of the Unity of Science, International Encyclopedia of Unified Science,* Chicago, 1962, chap. ix.

6. Nabers, Lawrence. "The Positive and Genetic Approaches," in *The Structure of Economic Science,* S. R. Krupp, ed. Englewood Cliffs, N.J.: Prentice Hall, 1966, pp. 68-82.

7. Pareto, Vilfredo. *Manuel d'economie politique.* Paris: Giard et Briere, 1909.

8. Seligman, Ben B. "Positivism and Economic Thought," *History of Political Economy* I (Fall, 1969), pp. 256-278.

9. Stark, Werner. *The Sociology of Knowledge.* London: Routledge, 1958.

10. Strauss, Leo. *National Right and History.* Chicago: University of Chicago Press, 1953.

11. Tarascio, Vincent J. *Pareto's Methodological Approach to Economics.* Chapel Hill: University of North Carolina Press, 1968.

12. ——————— . "Paretian Welfare Theory: Some Neglected Aspects," J. P. E. 77 (Jan./Feb. 1969), pp. 1-20.

13. Weber, Max. *The Methodology of the Social Sciences.* Translated and edited by E. Shils and H. Finch. Glencoe, Ill.; The Free Press, 1949.

Human Values and Economic Science

Melville J. Ulmer

A few years ago twelve leading economists were convened at New York University to discuss the relationship between "Human Values and Economic Policy," a title almost identical with that of the present article.[1] It might appear, therefore, that we are wasting our time in exploring a territory already well mapped and traveled, particularly since the group included two Nobel Prize winners, Paul Samuelson and Kenneth Arrow, together with Milton Friedman, Kenneth Boulding, and other very bright stars of our profession. But the curious fact is that the proceedings of that colloquium, despite its title, had almost no connection with the central problem that concerns me today, and that I believe is of primary interest to you: that is, the relationship between value judgments and the methodology of economics. The NYU discourse was confined almost entirely to the determination of market values, under ideally competitive conditions, with a brief side trip to Arrow's theorem concerning majority votes at the polls.[2] Mention of value judgments, in the usual sense of that term, was as carefully avoided as sex at a Sunday school spelling bee.

That outcome, except for the ever hopeful, should have been expected. For orthodox economists contend that value judgments have been, and should be, effectively excluded from their science. As though it had been liberated from the deadly embrace of invading

---

The author is Professor of Economics, University of Maryland, College Park, and contributing editor of the New Republic. *This article was presented at the Annual Meeting of the Association for Evolutionary Economics, New York, 27-29 December 1973.*

barbarians, they proclaim that economics is "value free." The argument is familiar.[3] There are two general questions, they say, that we may ask about economic affairs and, I am sure, about a lot of other things, to wit: What is? and What ought to be? The first question is the proper subject of scientific investigation. The second question extends beyond the realm of our science. Thus economists are instructed to obtain their values, or goals, from other authorities, presumably from voters or their political representatives. So goes the reasoning that, today as well as yesteryear, can be reproduced verbatim by most college sophomores.

Although it might appear to be so, this position—this circumscription of what economists properly can and cannot do—is not a mere arbitrary or politically convenient rule. It is a deduction that follows logically from an underlying notion of what a value judgment is. The classic statement of the matter, in modern economic literature at least, is that of Friedman.[4] He views a *value judgment* as an emotive reaction about which, as he says, "men can ultimately only fight." He further supports his position by reciting that precious gem of ancient wisdom, *De gustibus non est disputandum.* Judgments of value therefore are asserted to be beyond the realm of reason, impervious to fact or logic, and on *that* ground must be excluded from the business of economists. It is this assertion about the fundamental nature of values that is arbitrary.

Certainly, Friedman's interpretation does violence to the meaning that most people, and some philosophers, attach to the word *judgment,* which to them conveys something more than an emotional seizure, more than an irrational prejudice, or an inchoate "gut reaction." Thus, one outstanding authority on the philosophy of science, Ernest Nagel, defines a *value judgment* as "a reasoned approval (or disapproval) of something by someone, in the light of deliberation concerning what is desirable."[5] I would wish to underline the words *reasoned* and *deliberation.* If a judgment has those characteristics it must necessarily take account of relevant facts and general principles. If the situation being evaluated is economic, then the relevant empirical and theoretical evidence must relate in considerable measure to economic matters. In such instances, on that ground alone, value judgments would seem to fall within the science of economics. Nevertheless, after all the evidence is in, and after it has been distilled and redistilled with the most painstaking professional care, a nagging question persists: How can a generally satisfying, verifiable *conclusion* be reached in problems of evaluation? How can an objective decision be secured that one situation is better than another? We shall have to return to that question. First, it will be useful to look further into the claim that neoclassical economics is value free. Is it actually so in practice?

Consider the neoclassical assumption that we must take the tastes of consumers, or the populace in general, as given constants. Few of us would object to that postulate as a tentative device—a convenient fiction—for achieving specific objectives, such as the derivation of a demand curve. But I have used the imperative advisedly. We *must* take the tastes as given in neoclassical economics, and not only as given data but also as the ultimate standard for analyzing and evaluating the operation of the economy. Tastes, too, are considered outside the purview of science, a sacrosanct enclave in the economic environment that one must observe and obey, but never question. Here we have the central, even though unacknowledged, value judgment of neoclassical economics. It rates that situation unequivocally better that more fully satisfies prevailing wants, whatever they may be. It bears with it a normative corollary concerning the output of industry and national consumption, of "the more, the better," indiscriminately, or what one writer has termed the "pig principle."[6] I think that it is easy to show that this value judgment is both illogical and empirically wrong.

In the first place, like some other propositions in orthodox doctrine, this one rests solidly on an assumption that is flatly contrary to fact, viz.: that tastes are a basically stable set of propensities determined by biological and other factors external to the economic system. Since this proposition is a keystone in the structure of the neoclassical edifice, the abundant facts that oppose it, as you might expect, have been overlooked with exceptional determination.

One uncomfortable fact, for the orthodox, relates to the obvious flexibility of tastes. A measuring rod must be independent of the things to be measured. If it expands or contracts each time it is applied, it can be of no service. Mere casual observation is sufficient to show that tastes represent that kind of perversely flexible measuring rod. What people want, and the intensity of their wants, are determined largely by the performance of the economic system; hence their wants cannot measure that performance. Shaped primarily by economic events and experience, tastes are, in other words, endogenous to the economic system, not exogenous.

Thus, the very act of consumption changes our tastes. Everyone outside our profession knows that. In the words of an old song, "how're you gonna keep them down on the farm, after they've seen Paree." The experience of one way of life, as even Tin Pan Alley recognized, quickly alters our attitude toward another. We may live, contentedly, with frankfurters, radio, and dishcloths for a time, and later, with a change in income and prices, move up to beef, TV, and electric dishwashers. But can we then move back, if required, to the old regime—frankfurters and the rest—and *regain the old contented preference level?* If presented once again with the same prices and incomes that had prevailed in the first or earlier situation, would not people borrow, or take two jobs, to maintain the second, more expensive level of living? Since in comparable situations they frequently do, it follows from the facts that tastes change when consumption changes. And since, therefore, the scale itself has been altered, how can it be used to measure relative well-being over time?

The fact that tastes are dependent variables, economically determined, becomes even more evident when we take into account that they are individually interrelated. I do not mean simply in the superficial sense of "keeping up with the Joneses," but more fundamentally, more inexorably, more commonly. In multitudinous ways each of us is influenced by what others do. Let me cite some of my own observations of this matter since by chance they occurred at intervals that were particularly significant. In the medium-sized town of Leiden, Holland, about a decade and a half ago, most people rode to work on bicycles and appeared to like it. It provided daily exercise and a breath of the outdoors for old and young alike. Even Princess Beatrix rode to her classes at the university on a bike. Visiting there at seven-year intervals later, I noticed the following: As incomes rose, about half the people shifted over to automobiles. Then most of the other half, as the streets became more dangerous, were forced to do the same, or if they could not afford that, shifted to motorbikes. With nearly everyone using autos, inner city transportation became slower than ever, noisier, more congested, more nerve-racking, and of course more expensive. At present, now, can any individual in Leiden shift back to the bike and regain his old, simpler, and very likely more satisfying preference level? Clearly he cannot, and would not try, because his tastes—by which I mean of course his utility function or indifference map—have been changed by his own prior acts of consumption and even more by the acts of others. Since the measuring rod has altered its dimensions, can we accept without question the neoclassicist's appraisal that the people of Leiden are better off now, with respect to transportation, than they were fifteen years ago? For the orthodox economist that quaint conclusion is unavoidable. He reasons that the men, women, and youth of Leiden now have *more*—expensive automobiles, that is—and, as always, the more, the better.

I would not want anyone to suppose, from my two examples, that I oppose either automobiles or dishwashers. I favor them both, along with electricity and indoor plumbing. All I am saying is that material things cannot properly be abstracted from their social context—from the way they are used, and the way others use them, and from our changing attitudes and expectations. That means that we cannot, with accuracy, relate particular goods and services to specific levels of satisfaction that are comparable for people at different points in time, any more than we can do that for people living in different places. Comparing levels of welfare in that way, by merely counting up the value of goods purchased, may be an advertising man's dream and an orthodox economist's hang-up, but it cannot yield meaningful, verifiable conclusions.

I have saved for the last the most familiar reason for holding that our tastes are economically determined, that is, the argument presented so prominently by John Kenneth Galbraith. He conceives of big business as the driving force in our entire economy, influencing, in ways that serve its own interests, both consumers and government. It is the concern of big business, he says, to induce people to want more and more endlessly, particularly of the things that the "technostructure," from time to time, finds it profitable, secure, and convenient to produce. The technostructure—meaning the technicians who actually run the great corporations—is mainly concerned with perpetual growth. That preoccupation requires, above all, that they must continuously excite the hunger of the population for an ever expanding flow of output. If that implies planned obsolescence, limited durability, and appeals to purely artificial, fictitious, or even harmful needs, as they say on Madison Avenue, so be it. In a nutshell, Galbraith's point is that the tastes of consumers are in part deliberately shaped, not to their own needs, but to the needs of big business. Maximizing the output of goods and services under these terms, in accord with the orthodox value criterion, would in this view maximize business welfare instead of human welfare.

Up to this point I have concentrated on the neoclassical attitude toward tastes because of its central importance. In his most recent book, Galbraith has called attention to a variety of other value judgments that have somehow insidiously penetrated into the body of orthodox economics.[7] In *What's Wrong With Economics?* Benjamin Ward has mentioned still others.[8] Elsewhere I have described additional examples,[9] but I do not think it would serve a useful purpose to review them. I wish to remark only on two general aspects of these findings.

First, it is not the presence of value judgments in standard economics that is reprehensible, but the fact that they are unacknowledged, hidden, the fifty-third card in the casino deck, the medium's helper behind the arras, the sacred unmentionable that never can be exposed in the forum of public opinion. Such value judgments have a capacity only for harm, for distortion, for retarding or obscuring knowledge rather than advancing it. Second, the presence of value judgments—preferably openly proclaimed as testable hypotheses—is virtually inherent in the nature of our subject. I say "virtually" because I am reluctant to waive the possibility that a crudely empirical approach to economic activity could accumulate facts, figures, and even functional relationships in a formless jumble that conceivably could be called economics. It would be value free, but it also would be substance free. It would not be a science because it would lack order and objective, while its practitioners were drowned in a sea of meaningless trivia. No science can be created by exposing the blank sheet of an undirected human mind to the infinite stimuli of reality, each element of the universe of inquiry accorded an exactly equal chance of making its impression. One or more particular views of the economic system are required in order to bring intellectual order from chaos, and behind every view, as Gunnar Myrdal has said, there must be a viewpoint, a frame of reference that enables us purposefully to select, analyze, and appraise. In economics, and in any other social science, such viewpoints must be shaped and energized by values.

The reasons, it seems to me, are obvious. In the social sciences we deal with the behavior of human beings. Their activities in society are mutually interacting, mutually influential, and derive from causes or enabling circumstances, as perceived by men and women. Social decisions, necessarily, exercise an impact on people. It is of the essence of these activities, particularly in the economic sphere, that they enrich or impoverish, degrade or uplift, alienate or unite, persuade, abuse, exploit, befriend, and so on. A full, objective analysis of society requires that such interactions be recognized. Merely to describe them, meaningfully, implies at least an elementary process of evaluation. If a certain method of production serves to rob workers of their creativity, dignity, and intelligence, if it reduces them to routinized robots, alienated, surly, perhaps brutalized, it is a relationship at least as worthy of note as the estimated lag between a change in the quantity of money and a change in the GNP. It is also an observation that is clearly and necessarily motivated by a value judgment. It is ignored in standard economics not because value judgments are abjured—for we have seen that in practice they are present although unacknowledged—but because human values are buried and embodied in commodities, in the simple proposition that the more goods and services the market turns up, the better. Human values are equated with market values, the beneficiary being, of course, the status quo.

How can we distinguish what is good from what is bad? Is it, as Friedman has suggested, merely a question of taste, in the noneconomic sense of that word, like a preference for apples over oranges? Must we then, as he would have it, simply accept the majority vote on what is better or worse? If that were true we would indeed have little cause for complaint against the majority vote of the Germans in 1932. The selection of Hitler would have to be accepted as a standard of goodness provided by the highest source—the voice of the people. We would have no complaint at all, I suppose, so long as Arrow's conditions for consistency in voting were satisfied. Or, as an alternative to Friedman, are there certain *ultimate* values to which we can appeal, that will guide us always and unerringly to the right decisions? If so, what are their sources? What are the operations by which we can achieve such ultimates as "the ideal society," when will we get there, and whose version shall we accept? By their very nature, it would seem, ultimate values must be taken on authority, a great convenience in totalitarian countries, but surely the opposite of scientific procedure.

Value judgments become operative and part of science when they are formulated in more humble terms, when they are penultimate rather than ultimate, when they are specific and relate to particular problems, not to vague and distant goals; when they can be *tested by ongoing experience.* One situation or policy can be adjudged better than another on the basis of its scientifically determined consequences.[10] Let me cite an example.

Census Bureau figures show that family expenditures per person for medical care increase enormously with income, a relationship that is modified but by no means broken by Medicare and Medicaid. This result obviously does not stem from an inherent tendency for the rich to sicken. In fact, analysis by age group suggests that, in considerable measure, the medical care received varies inversely with need.[11] The upshot is that the lives of poorer people are much less adequately protected than others. In this respect the situation of the working, lower middle class seems to be even worse than that of the very poor. Their children have a much smaller chance for survival than do those of others. If we agree with the value judgment that all have an equal right to life, as well as liberty and the pursuit of happiness, we must agree also that the market system in the medical field has miserably failed. We have a basis then for concluding that something else would be better. We in the United States are now trying to shore up the market system with insurance schemes, in belated recognition of that failure. It may well be that economic science can show, particularly if it deigns to refer to foreign experience, that socialized medicine can achieve the stated objective most fully, and at the least cost of all available alternatives. If such is the case, economics has an obligation to bring its conclusions to the forum of public opinion. In the final analysis, to be sure, only the electorate can make an *effective* decision on what is better, but for accuracy the electorate must be fully informed, empathic, and unprejudiced, particularly in this instance, by the machinations of the AMA.

Note that astronomers do not ask the populace to vote on whether the universe is expanding, contracting, or remaining the same. As much as the astronomers, we have an obligation to seek the truth independently concerning the effect of economic institutions on people, regardless of what some majority may believe, and to make the truth known. Transforming the finding into public policy requires education, not simply nose counting; it requires controversy in a truly open forum, unbiased by vested interests, and *then* the critical vote.

The market, including especially its pecuniary calculations, is now the touchstone of standard economics. In the temple of the Pareto optimum, human values are sacrificed the way flies are swatted in a candy shop—quite dispassionately, of course—on the altar of profits. Once human reactions and needs are brought to the foreground, the structure of economics necessarily will change. Let me cite another example.

The replacement of an obsolescent machine or tool by a more efficient model is a frequent occurence in business and is commonly judged to be one sign of progress. It is considered even more progressive if the new equipment renders some human beings obsolescent. Indeed, one calculation that enters critically into the decision to purchase an improved model is nearly always the saving in labor costs gained from the dismissal of workers. The full wages of the discharged men and women enter into the accounts of the firm as a saving. The reckoning is only fair by conventional standards, quite impartial, since it also counts the full cost of maintaining a machine as a saving when *it* is scrapped. But a little thought shows that the calculation is neither fair nor accurate from the economy's point of view. Unlike the machine, human beings cannot be scrapped, and their costs of maintenance go on even after they are unemployed and are necessarily met in one way or another by society—through welfare payments perhaps, through unemployment insurance benefits as long as they last, through private charity, or, in some instances, through crime. Add to this the cost of retraining, where that is feasible, the cost of moving the family, when and if new jobs are found, and the psychic blow to the individual who is suddenly classified as obsolete.

The point is that technological unemployment is typically expensive in a variety of ways that do not enter business calculations. Were they taken into account, it would no doubt turn out that much of the world's so-called technological progress had in fact been regress; that, in other words, new laborsaving devices had in general been introduced too abruptly and too fast and that the net gains to society were in the aggregate much smaller than generally supposed and in some instances were probably negative. It also shows, as I have argued elsewhere, that there is a better case than is commonly assumed for a policy of guaranteed jobs backed by a strong program of public employment.[12] The case rests also on another value judgment with significant repercussions for economics as well as for education: Society has an obligation to offer each individual an opportunity to utilize his capacities fully, or more broadly, in the words of one social philosopher, to find and follow his "vocation."[13]

The latter point has to do with the nature and content of human labor. Work in standard economics is counted fully as a cost, but that rests on its own unacknowledged value judgment associated with the maximization of profits. Labor in that format becomes strictly a means to an end, and human values are once again, in this instance, submerged. Of course, it is true that man-hours enter as an input in the output of goods and services, as the orthodox view it. But that is only *part* of the truth. If we are concerned with human welfare, and not simply commodities, then work must be reckoned as an output as well as an input. The output is measured by the satisfaction the human being obtains from his work activity, from his creativity, from the utilization of whatever capacities he may have. If the satisfaction is negative in one productive process and positive in another, this would represent a powerful count in favor of the second. In practice workers do not have such choices, and in a society in which concentrated control over the means of production rests in private hands, no business firm is motivated to enter the quality of work experience into its accounts. But this is a lesser sin than that of orthodox economics, which does not permit such calculations to enter its thinking. In the imaginary world of the standard practitioners, there are innumerable firms in every industry offering innumerably different types of work experience, and the attitude of labor toward these alternatives is reflected in its supply curves. We have here another familiar legend that solves a problem by assuming it away.

We have in the legend, also, another illustration of the way in which neoclassical economics subordinates individuals to the needs of production, instead of the other way around. That perverse subordination is inherent in its narrow definition of efficiency, and in its tautological equation of maximum efficiency with maximum welfare. The more we pursue the consequences of that position, the more conflicts we uncover between its tenets and generally accepted human values. Thus, efficiency in the food industry in the United States, free competition has determined, lies in highly concentrated facilities for production and distribution. This centralization in turn requires considerable long-distance transportation and in general a lengthy time period for output and marketing. Food additives of various kinds, including preservatives and artificial coloring, become imperative. The ingestion of some of the additives, recent experience has shown, is toxic, and about some of the others it can only be said that we do not yet know—engaging the population, willy nilly, in a kind of chemical Russian roulette. The view of orthodox economics on this matter is characteristically hard-nosed; we have a trade-off here, say its proponents, between the quantity of poison on the one hand and the cost of food on the other. Greater purity *could* be obtained, but only at a price. The present situation reflects, simply, the decision provided by free competition. The people have spoken with their dollar votes, the market has functioned in response, and efficiency has been maximized. But does the housewife shopping in the supermarket, or any of us, have the range of choices this view supposes, even if she takes the trouble to read the fine print and has the knowledge to interpret it? Is not the entire food industry, barring the off-beat health foods, organized so that all brands of canned goods, all meat cuts and sausages, and all other produce have more or less the same doses of sodium nitrite, tartazine, cyclamates, and the rest?

Consider the decisions that business firms now make, as a matter of course, to reduce or expand their output, or to change the locale of their operations. The decisions are fateful in numerous ways for the workers who may be fired or hired, as well as for the communities that serve them. But the decisions on such matters, as well as on the organization of the food industry, are made by corporate bureaucracies on the basis of *their* version of efficiency. Their version also happens to be that of their faithful rationalizer, orthodox economics. I am not implying in these examples that cutbacks in output are never justified, or that costs of production are unimportant. I am leading to the proposition that the lack of democracy in economic decisions levies a tremendous, uncalculated cost on all of society. The value judgment I am implying is that a greater participation of workers and consumers in business decisions, either directly or through representatives, would make for a better economic world. At a minimum it would expand the range of data on which a broader and more accurate calculation of efficiency could be based.

I earlier mentioned the sacred position occupied in orthodox economics by prevailing tastes. In rejecting that role, I do not suggest that tastes can or should be ignored. Following them slavishly and uncritically is no more irresponsible, scientifically, than ignoring them completely. The remaining alternative to those extremes is to treat the community's tastes as an object of active scientific attention. This means that economic research must be directed, in important part, toward seeing to it that the community's tastes are informed, undistorted by the propaganda of business or other vested interests, unprejudiced by the irrational, self-serving appeals to which they so frequently fall victim. Thus, when individual wants are mutually self-defeating, that fact must be discovered and disclosed, even if it does mean lower sales and profits for some, and even if it violates, as I am sure it does, the hallowed Pareto criteria for an optimum. We cannot wait until the rising number of cars and people ring the globe with highways swirling above the underground cities of the human race, in which people live on tiny but nutritious, and only slightly carcinogenic, patticakes produced exclusively by DuPont. All of the foregoing implies that economics must not flee from values, but must bring to bear the most powerful tools of scientific method it can muster to analyze them, to explore their meaning and repercussions, to make known the full range of possible alternatives in policy, to distill through unrestricted controversy the relative merits of those alternatives, and, above all, to disclose the consequences for human beings of the choices they may make.

Notes

1. Sidney Hook, ed., *Human Values and Economic Policy: A Symposium* (New York: New York University Press, 1967).
2. The major papers of the conference were given by the twelve leading economists. Nine philosophers participated as discussants, and nearly all, particularly the chairman, Sidney Hook, indicated their disappointment with the direction of the discussion.
3. It also has an extensive history in economics and, of course, a longer

one in philosophy. See Robert B. Ekelund, Jr., and Emilie S. Olsen, "Comte, Mill, and Cairnes: The Positivist-Empiricist Interlude in Late Classical Economics," *Journal of Economic Issues* 7 (September 1973): 383–416.

4. "The Methodology of Positive Economics," in his *Essays in Positive Economics* (Chicago: Chicago University Press, 1953).
5. "Preference, Evaluation, and Reflective Choice," in *Human Values and Economic Policy*, Sidney Hook, ed., p. 76.
6. Sidney S. Alexander, "Human Values and Economists' Values," in *Human Values and Economic Policy*, Sidney Hook, ed., p. 110. Alone among the conference economists, Alexander recognized what the problem was.
7. *Economics and the Public Purpose* (Boston: Houghton Mifflin Co., 1973).
8. (New York: Basic Books, 1972).
9. "Toward Public Employment and Economic Stability," *Journal of Economic Issues* 6 (December 1972): 149–70.
10. John Dewey, *Theory of Valuation* (Chicago: University of Chicago Press, 1939). See also the excellent discussion in Sidney Hook, *John Dewey: An Intellectual Portrait* (New York: John Day, 1939), chap. 7, to which the present analysis is indebted.
11. Average family income, by age of head of household, reaches a peak in the age group 45–54 years and then declines markedly. Health expenditures per person in the family follow the same pattern, even though other evidence suggests that the need for medical care increases after the age of 54.
12. Ulmer, "Toward Public Employment."
13. Sidney Hook, *Education for Modern Man*, 2d ed. (New York: Dial, 1963).
14. I pass over here an additional theoretical alternative, which in the present context I do not consider it useful to mention. Instead of ignoring tastes, or, as I would propose, attempting to inform them in an open educational forum to enlighten and uplift them, some writers would *suppose* that a group of individuals could be found whose tastes were fully informed, unbiased, and otherwise ideal. The standards of this select group would serve to determine the relative value of alternative situations. Since such a device is obviously nonoperational, I have relegated it to this note. See John Rawls, *A Theory of Justice* (Cambridge, Mass.: Harvard University Press, 1971).

Comment

Robert Lekachman

I read with admiration and empathy Melville Ulmer's eloquent interpretation of why mainstream economics is, to the distress of people like us, an essentially conservative subject, less and less interesting to speculative and imaginative students, and more and more devoted to hypertechnical refinement of received opinions.

In what follows I do no more than note an additional implication or two of our profession's dominant intellectual sociology. Here is one strategic effect. Since the unstated values of approved scholarly inquiry include general acceptance if not actual endorsement of existing market arrangements as well as the patterns of production and distribution which flow from them, we accurately can anticipate small rewards of publication, fame, and academic advancement for independent souls who, cursed by different valuations, devote themselves to unpopular lines of research. The pressure upon the ambitious young is substantial to exercise their intellects upon safe raw material. It is no surprise then that the body of standard research swells and that of dissident traditions can, with some justice, be criticized as slender.

It is well to be specific. A malcontent might start, as to confide the guilty secret I do, from the value premise that income and wealth in the United States are far too unequally distributed. Such a claim

---

The author is Distinguished Professor of Economics, City University of New York, New York. These comments were presented at the Annual Meeting of the Association for Evolutionary Economics, New York, 27-29 December 1973.

is only an opinion to which one might aspire to gain adherents by deploying literary and forensic skills. But the premise is full of potential consequences for the conduct of professional study. Thus an egalitarian confident that more equality is a good greatly to be desired and earnestly to be promoted might follow the recent example of Herbert Gans, who, although a mere sociologist, has thoughtfully explored in his recent *More Equality* some of the possible results of narrowing income differentials as reflected in production patterns, incentive structures, and the quality of public and private services.[1]

Such a researcher is likely at the very threshhold of his inquiry to be dismayed by the scantiness of available information about distribution. As the Marxist friends of my youth were accustomed to charge, it scarcely can be an accident that until publication of some of the valuable recent work of Joseph Pechman and Benjamin Okner at Brookings and of Lester Thurow at MIT, one was compelled to go back to Robert Lampman's classic study, based on data now a generation old, in order to say anything quantitative about who owns the United States. The gap has been more or less filled by free-lance intellectuals of the Left like Ferdinand Lundberg.

An egalitarian endowed with the tools of modern price theory could do worse than look closely at the ways in which markets mirror existing income and wealth disparities. "Scientific" economics seldom focuses upon the origins of large fortunes and thus is unable to ask how much these fortunes appropriately reward the vision and administrative skill of our millionaires and billionaires and how much, to the contrary, these vast hunks of cash spring from the black arts of political corruption, market manipulation, and deployment of market power.

Where is the economic theory of political influence? Surely some of our Chicago friends, busy at this very set of meetings in the demonstration that the market for ideas is just like the market for cereal, could take a moment or two to explain just how a Harold Geneen allocates his time among personnel selection, managerial conferences, analysis of operating results, and the application of personal pressure upon Washington officials so as to equate at the margin the pecuniary benefits of the last seconds devoted to each of these activities.

It may be that I risk frivolity. However, I now approach a second, unquestionably serious topic to which ITT and its mahout inevitably conduct us. This is the neglected theme of economic power. The poverty of conventional economic explanation which skirts this embarrassing subject is glaringly highlighted in much economic discussion of current energy problems. Nixon economists, operating according to free market criteria, evidently are moving to a "solution" which allows prices and profits vastly to increase. Presumably these incentives to exploration will in due course evoke all the oil and gas even Detroit might hope for. The "solution" is, to start with, glaringly inequitable. One need not attend graduate school to appreciate that when essential commodities are rationed with price, the working poor either must skimp upon gasoline or divert expenditures from food, clothing, and other necessities. The market is a mean model for sharing out universally required items. Better models are available: the family, the fraternal society, even, Lord help us, the team.

Market solutions are technically weak as well as socially unfair. How can anyone be really certain that cash bounties will evoke new energy supplies from giant petroleum corporations until we find out a good deal more than economists have thought it worth their while to discover up to now about the way these business monsters deploy their vast market power? This is only to say that the old-fashioned, low status study of industrial organization is likely to become a major interest of economists who realize that the history of markets is indispensable to comprehension of how these markets currently run, the timeless universe of theorists to the contrary notwithstanding.

It is another nonaccident that oligopoly theory persists in its traditional disarray. Thus it is that on pp. 513-14 of Paul Samuelson's ninth edition up pops, as an explanation of pricing in concentrated industries, Paul Sweezy's bright idea of the 1930s, the ever-kinked demand curve. I doubt, from my occasional reading of the *Monthly Review*, that Sweezy, the dean of U.S. Marxist economists, now attaches, if ever he did, any great explanatory value to his youthful *jeu d'esprit*.

Why has power become the guilty little secret, to adapt Norman Podhoretz to our present purpose, of economic theory? It is genuinely a remarkable feat of professional avoidance if not actual evasion that endless energy continues to be expended on the analysis of market behavior without serious, concrete investigation of the style in which the major actors on the market stage play their roles.

One might hazard the guess that conventional theory, starting from an enduring love of competition,[2] leaps to the conclusion that since competition is so splended a mode of organization and the U.S. economy is so successful, it must follow that U.S. economic affairs, trifling exceptions aside, must be conducted competitively.

Hence no one need do the grubby work of describing the actual conduct of businessmen. Indeed, much danger attends such inquiries.

Unwary economists, lured into history, sociology, and politics, might neglect the austere intellectual beauties of economic analysis.

If Watergate—I nearly concluded without mentioning the word—contains a moral for economists, it obviously has to do with the relations among politics, power, and profit. I have yet to read anything illuminating about the Watergate drama as an exercise in entrepreneurial maximization.

Enough. My excuse for continuing as long as this has been the impact of Ulmer's excellent article upon my own speculations in related realms of criticism.

Notes

1. (New York: Pantheon, 1972).
2. Cf. John Stuart Mill, writing in 1848: "Only through the principle of competition has political economy any pretension to the character of a science. So far as rents, profits, wages, prices, are determined by competition, laws may be assigned for them. Assume competition to be their exclusive regulator, and principles of broad generality and scientific precision may be laid down. The political economist justly deems this his proper business: and as an abstract or hypothetical science, political economy cannot be required to do, and indeed cannot do anything more." See *Principles of Political Economy* (London: Longmans Green, 1909), p. 242.

Four Reviews of Nicholas Georgescu-Roegen, *The Entropy Law and the Economic Process*

One of the great generalizations of physical science tells us that in any isolated system the changes which occur are always those which bring about an increase in the *entropy* of the system. The prescription is one form of the Second Law of Thermodynamics, which can be given as simple a statement as: "Heat always flows only from hot bodies to cold ones," that is, never "uphill." But in this form the law loses the wide applicability and richness that it has as a statement of entropy increase.

The thesis of Professor Georgescu-Roegen's book is that the basic concern of the economic process is with entropy; and, as a corollary, he wishes to see economics established not after the model of a mechanical science (as in so-called classical physics), but as a science that can accommodate the complexity, indeterminism, and human factors of economic process. His book is not to be regarded as an attempted philosophical gloss on economic science; rather, he is essaying a deep and central construction on the level of foundations.

It might be well to refresh our minds about the entropy concept. It is not one that is easily explicated, since it refers to a ratio of two quantities, heat and temperature, rather than to a single, directly measured variable. In 1865 Rudolf Clausius introduced entropy into physics with the following definition: for a system a change of entropy, ΔS, is equal to an element of heat, ΔQ, added to or taken from the system, divided by its Kelvin temperature, T, at the moment of transfer of the ΔQ. A simple example shows us why S increases. Suppose our isolated system consists of two bodies in contact, one at temperature T_1 and the other at a higher temperature, T_2. Heat

ΔQ will flow from the hotter to the colder body, until the two temperatures are equal. The colder body gains entropy, $\Delta S_1 = +\Delta Q/T_1$, and the hotter body loses entropy, $\Delta S_2 = -\Delta Q/T_2$. But since T_2 is greater than T_1 for any flow ΔQ, ΔS_1 is a larger absolute number than is ΔS_2, and hence $\Delta S_1 + \Delta S_2$ always will be positive. Therefore, in coming to thermal equilibrium the system of two bodies gains entropy.

The entropy-increase law has been found to be valid in a generalization from explicit heat transfer to chemical processes of all kinds, for macroscopic systems of many constitutent entities (such as atoms or molecules). Thus, the rusting of iron gives iron oxide, which has a higher entropy value than does its separated constitutents, oxygen and pure iron. Likewise, the chemical processes of biological organisms must, we believe, proceed always with a total increase of entropy in the total system of organism plus its surroundings. The suffusiveness of the law of entropy increase is indicated by the association that is often made between the forward direction of time (time's arrow) and the increase of entropy: The succession of past to future is matched by the development of states of successively greater amounts of entropy in the total natural world.

Georgescu-Roegen argues that the concern of economics is primarily with the struggle for low entropy; not, he says, that "the intimate connection between the Entropy Law and the economic process" will aid us in better managing a given economy, but that by improving our understanding of the economic process we will learn what aims are better for the economy of mankind. In order to gain appreciation of his point we must, as he does, consider entropy from another point of view. Several years after Clausius' pioneer discussion, Ludwig Boltzmann showed that entropy could also be defined, quite independently of $\Delta Q/T$ considerations, as a measure of the order or disorder of a system. Low entropy, he showed, is equivalent to a relatively ordered system, and high entropy to one that is relatively disordered. We may define order in a system as limitation of possibilities for location or motion of the particles of a system.

Suppose, for example, the molecules of a flask of gas to be contained by an internal partition in one-half of the volume of the flask; there is then a state of relative ordering of the molecules, and hence of lower entropy, compared with a state in which the molecules occupy the entire flask. With removal of the partition the gas will expand into the entire flask; there is then less order and more entropy for the gas, either on the order definition or the $\Delta Q/T$ definition (heat would flow into the gas as it expanded if it is to keep a constant temperature). To take another example, suppose heat is removed from a liquid until it freezes into a crystalline solid. It is in a state of lower entropy, as a solid, because the molecules of the former liquid are now restricted in their possible positions to appropriate places in a crystal lattice. Heatwise, the entropy is less for the solid because of the heat that was withdrawn to bring about the freezing, giving a negative $\Delta S = -\Delta Q/T$.

Construed in terms of order, the entropy principle tells us that the natural development of any total system is toward states of greater disorder. When Georgescu-Roegen says that economics is about low entropy, he is referring to the efforts of mankind to maintain the order that is necessary for life. A human being is a highly ordered assemblage of atoms; also, both growth and learning imply further increase of order, and hence a decrease in entropy. Such a decrease can occur—by the law of entropy increase—only at the expense of compensating increases in the surroundings with which the biological organism interacts. Hence, a person must have a steady supply of food, perhaps fuel, and, in many cultures at least, various types of ordered surroundings for his life. These are all low-entropy elements, and, Georgescu-Roegen tells us, the procuring or devising of them, and their ultimate conversion to high entropy *for the sake of the enjoyment of human life,* is what economics is all about.

There also is a First Law of Thermodynamics, which prescribes that energy is neither destroyed nor created; nor is matter destroyed or created, considering the mass-energy equivalence that relativity theory has disclosed. Hence, there is only so much of energy, or of anything else, in the world. The author points out that economists—Alfred Marshall, for example—have accepted and understood the First Law, but generally have assumed that the economic process can go on, and even grow, without being continuously supplied by a flow of low entropy into the system. He asserts that there is a general practice of representing the material side of the economic process by a mathematical model which is a closed system "in which the continuous flow of low entropy from the environment is completely ignored." But in fact, the processes of economics are not at all circular, since there is an inevitable and irrevocable production of high entropy as waste (or, we might say, pollution).

The neglect of the entropy law leads to a grave oversight in the judgment of the overall economic potentialities of the earth. To take two salient factors, consider the supplies of fuel and of fertilizer. Each of these contributes low entropy by virtue of its specific molecular arrangements. Georgescu-Roegen suggests that eventual utilization of solar energy may give an abundant substitute for fuel, but that the supply of earth's molecular resources puts a limitation on the total number of human lives that are possible during the entire time span of our species. It is a task of economics, therefore, to adjudicate between the use of resources and low entropy for machines, on the one hand, and for the necessities of human life, on the other. There are criticisms to be made, I am certain, of some of the author's specific statements relating to limitations on resources, but his general entropic approach to human economics through the Second Law cannot but be a valid one.

It would be a gross oversimplification of Georgescu-Roegen's thesis to leave it as I have so far reported it. A large fraction of the book is devoted to a discussion of that departure of physical science from classical mechanics which is concomitant with the establishment of the entropy law. His treatment is prolix and, especially in several long appendices, both technical and erudite. It becomes apparent why he wishes to discuss the departure, as far as economics is concerned, but I shall suggest that much of what he says is misguided with respect to the basic physical and philosophical questions that are involved.

We again must review some purely physical concepts. The classical mechanical physics that we term Newtonian is one of systems of forces and motions of single (or a few) bodies, be they atoms or planets. It is a prime characteristic of the Newtonian equations of motion that they are *time reversible:* The motions they describe are fully possible in a reversed sense, with all original velocities in the opposite direction from those first assigned (or, equivalently, with time running backward). The to and fro swinging of a pendulum, or the orbital motion of a planet, are two examples of the time-reversible motion that pervades the processes of change that are described by classical physics. Furthermore, the equations are *exact.* In principle, location and motion of bodies may be described as a function of time with unlimited precision, and with a course of development whose direction depends only on the given initial conditions. We all well know that the physics based on these principles had an immense success, both for understanding motions of astronomical bodies and for a wide variety of terrestrial phenomena. It is this deterministic, mechanical physics—simple in that it describes processes that have only a small number of constituent entities—which has been generally taken, Georgescu-Roegen writes, as the model for economic science.

The development of thermodynamics and statistical mechanics in the latter half of the nineteenth century gave physics an extension to systems made up of many, many constituent particles: 6×10^{23} molecules, for example, in a mole of gas. The basic laws of Newtonian physics were assumed and used in the statistical mechanics (the particle-analytic version, one might say, of thermodynamics) that describes many-particle systems. But a profound problem then arose. The entropy law of thermodynamics clearly is *not* time reversible. This we can readily appreciate: Thermodynamic, macroscopic processes in nature generally will go only one way in time. Iron ore does not spontaneously separate into iron and oxygen, molecules do not naturally gather themselves under high pressure into a tank, and the pieces of a broken bottle do not reassemble themselves into the original whole vessel. We have noted, indeed, that the increasing-entropy direction of thermodynamic processes is associated with the forward, nonreversible direction of time. And yet, the individual molecular motions and collisions in many-particle, thermodynamic processes *do follow* Newtonian time-reversible laws. How can large-scale time irreversibility be formed from individually reversible processes?

The answer to this question was given, at least for the case of gases, by Boltzmann in his celebrated H-theorem. Professor Georgescu-Roegen argues, however, that Boltzmann, and statistical mechanics generally, are trying to preserve the exact determinism and time reversibility of Newtonian physics, in contrast with the irreversibility and less than exact description that comes with the thermodynamic entropy law. He is persistently quarrelsome with Boltzmann's work on this topic throughout the book. He would, I believe, have done better not to enter into the issue in detail, particularly for a readership that is not likely to be expert on the issues involved. In any event it is difficult for me to see the justification for his truculence. Even Boltzmann came to accept the inherently statistical-probabilistic aspect of the H-theorem. Certainly for physicists generally, statistical mechanics, in its achievement of the results of thermodynamics on a basis of classical physics, does bring probability intrinsically into physics, even before Werner Heisenberg's introduction of quantum-theoretic indeterminism.

In a more positive vein, the author stresses that the many-particle physics of macroscopic systems can well serve as a better model for economics than do the time-reversible Newtonian mechanics. The appearance of properties that are distinctive for the assembly of many particles and not obviously consequences of individual-particle properties (the whole is greater than its parts), the inherent statistical-probabilistic factor, and the irreversibility of change, all are characteristic of thermodynamic systems, and likewise are appropriate, we are told, for economic systems and processes. So, Georgescu-Roegen not only sees the specific content of the entropy law as a foundation statement for economics, but also recommends the form of thermodynamic science as a model.

Another element of physics that is of interest to Georgescu-Roegen is the degree to which the observer has become a part of the natural reality that is described. This partial subjectivism is a feature, in the established physics of today, not of macroscopic systems, but of physical description on the microscopic level of atomic and subatomic particles; a parallel with the systems and societies of economics is therefore not an exact one. However, in a general way the author is justified in saying that physics gives support to his assertion that we should not demand complete objectivity in science. That is, the older notion of a natural reality whose properties, as described, are completely independent of the observer's existence is strongly discredited by quantum physics. Indeed, in the past decade or so a microscopic subjectivism in physics somewhat stronger than that referred to by Georgescu-Roegen has been demanded both by experiment and theoretical discussion. The values of microscopic physical variables depend not on the limitations of observation, as he asserts, but on the necessary *physical* superposition of different values for a variable until the act of observation-interaction selects the value that appears in an actual event. Which value is physically manifest is guided only by probability considerations, which give the traditional approximate physical determinism only for ensembles of many events or particles. There is, then, a contributive role for human observation in natural reality on the quantum physics level, and, I assume, no comfort is forthcoming for the economist who would hope to expunge the *Geist* or *Weltanschauung* from his science.

The ideal of economics as a quantitative science, built wholly with rigorously defined terms, takes further punishment from Georgescu-Roegen in a language distinction that he uses throughout between *arithmomorphic* and *dialectic* concepts. The former, which are quantitative and exact, have a utility which is not to be denied, but the latter are necessary for thought, even though "they are surrounded by a penumbra within which they overlap their opposites." Thus, at a particular moment a nation may be both a *democracy* and a *nondemocracy*. (Here too, I might add, there is a precedent in physics: Niels Bohr liked to make a distinction between minor truths, whose opposites are plainly false, and great truths, whose opposites are also true.)

The book ends with a long chapter wholeheartedly devoted to economics and to some general conclusions about it. This final discussion does not explicitly make much use of the entropy-law theme; conversely, most of the material in the preceding chapters is not explicitly about technical economics (with some notable exceptions). It is not for me to state what Professor Georgescu-Roegen has contributed to economic science, but I have tried to report on what he has brought to it from physics. Considering that economics does study events that are in the natural world, and judging from the understanding and liveliness of mind with which the author has carried out an application from basic natural science, I would opine that he has brought forward a fruitful and helpful guiding principle.

Department of Physics
Michigan State University

RICHARD SCHLEGEL

Economists in recent years have displayed an increasing interest in philosophical methodology and its relation to their subject. Professor Georgescu-Roegen's book is a contribution of great importance and interest in this area of thought. But it is a difficult book to review precisely because it deals with scientific fundamentals in an exact and sophisticated way. It ranges over a wide array of basic subjects in the physical, biological, and social sciences; it offers new insights, arguments, and interpretations. Consequently, it is not a book to be read and immediately evaluated and labeled. One wants time to rethink, to mull over and digest the book; one would like to discuss the book with others, especially with Georgescu-Roegen; but editorial deadlines do not allow a reviewer time for such maturation.

The theme of the book is that economic processes are a manifestation of the entropy law. Entropy and the entropy law are complex subjects which have been the basis of a great deal of scientific controversy, but some grasp of the basic principle can be obtained rather easily. An automobile uses the energy in gasoline to do mechanical work, that is, to move. Before combustion the energy of the gasoline is free energy, or energy which can be used, but as it is used and is dissipated it becomes bound energy which cannot be used. A system which has a great deal of free energy has low entropy, while a system with a great deal of bound energy is characterized by high entropy.

Two further points about the entropic process should be noted. First, it is irreversible; the energy of the gasoline cannot be used over and over. Second, the process goes on whether or not human agents are present. The sun's radiance continues regardless of whether crops are grown; the energy of the gasoline ultimately would be dissipated even if it were left in the ground.

Thus it is logical to argue that economic resources are those with low entropy, and that economic processes are characterized by the conversion of low entropy to high entropy. The author points out that low entropy is a necessary but not sufficient condition for anything to have value. Necessity is required on physical grounds, but to have economic value a thing must also be wanted by individuals. As a result, it can be argued in a very general sense that resources featuring low entropy are the fundamental economic resources of the earth. Since the entropic process continuously converts low to high entropy, and since the process is irreversible, the useful endowment of the earth ultimately must be exhausted, and mankind's career must come to an end.

This outcome might be prevented by what the author calls "entropy bootlegging." For example, what is now high entropy might be viewed as low entropy after technological advancement. But Georgescu-Roegen argues both vigorously and cogently against this possibility. There is no succor in this direction.

In developing the concept of the entropic process and in applying it to economic matters, the author discusses a most impressive number of subjects in the physical, biological, and social sciences as well as in mathematics, probability, and the philosophy of science. These subjects are not merely discussed in the sense of explaining them, but their fundamentals are examined, and concepts and arguments are criticized and evaluated. It is difficult to convey any sense of the flavor of the book without going into these varied matters, yet to do so in a brief review is clearly impossible. An unsatisfactory compromise can be reached by giving one example.

The author distinguishes arithmomorphic entities from dialectic concepts. The former are discretely distinct or clearly distinguishable—a number is an example. A dialectical concept is meaningful but not clearly distinguishable because it lacks arithmomorphic boundaries—it is spanned by a penumbra of meaning. Concepts such as justice or democracy are dialectical. This dichotomy of arithmomorphic and dialectical is applied by the author not only to the entropy law, but also to the positivistic view of scientific investigation and directly to economics itself. In the latter subject there is clearly a dialectical area as well as a mechanical area, although in Georgescu-Roegen's view the second area is, unfortunately, dominant at the present.

The arithmomorphic and dialectical concepts are typical of subjects developed and used by the author in that they are matters of interest in themselves and are developed as such. Yet, they also are used to further the chief theme and main burden of the book. In other words, the great array of diverse subjects treated does not merely impress the reader with the author's richness of scholarship and add to the reader's general knowledge (although they did both in my case): This array is present because it supports the case the author is making. In short, in spite of the great variety of subjects covered, there is a fundamental unity and coherence to the book which emerges very clearly.

The economist who reads the book may wonder whether Georgescu-Roegen's arguments, especially with regard to the physical and biological sciences, are correct. I am the wrong reviewer to give a definitive answer. His knowledge of the physical sciences goes beyond mine, and I felt especially at sea in the sections dealing with biological matters. I doubt that the question is as significant as it may appear.

Even if some of the arguments were incorrect, indeed even if the main theme were unsound, this would still be an important book because of the questions that it raises and because of the subthemes that it develops.

Department of Economics RALPH W. PFOUTS
University of North Carolina, Chapel Hill

Nicholas Georgescu-Roegen, "a scholar's scholar and an economist's economist,"[1] has made unique contributions to the epistemological problem of economics, a field usually ignored by members of the profession. His latest book, *The Entropy Law and the Economic Process,* in which he develops the revolutionary view that economic activity is an extension of man's biological evolution, is an impressive achievement. Drawing on Georgescu-Roegen's profound knowledge of mathematics and statistics, the book ranges widely through the physical, biological, and social sciences. Its central theme is that economic activity, rather than being a mechanical analogue as represented by standard economic theory, is an entropic process of qualitative change which eludes arithmomorphic schematization and can be understood only by using dialectic concepts without precise arithmomorphic boundaries. There is no need for economists to suffer from an inferiority complex as they note the supposed exactitude of the natural sciences; their efforts to make the social sciences value free and ethically neutral are futile as they strive in vain to make economics akin to mathematics and physics. In the language of Blaise Pascal,[2] economics eludes *l'esprit géométrique* and can be approached only by *l'esprit de finesse.*

Emphasis on the fundamental nature of the entropy law permits Georgescu-Roegen a scholarly discussion of the limits to economic growth, a topic which has received so much popular, and often sensational, attention in the recent literature. The exceptional importance of the entropy law for our epistemological orientation stems from the fact that its recognition comes from the science whose point of departure is that matter is not subject to change. Yet, every physical activity inexorably decreases the total amount of energy available in the universe and is associated with the conversion of matter from a state of higher available energy (low entropy, less disorder) to a state of lower available energy (high entropy, more disorder). The economic process thus consists of a continuous transformation of low entropy into high entropy, that is, into irrevocable waste or pollution, a statement identical with that proposed by Erwin Schrödinger for the biological process of a living cell or organism.[3] The price of technological progress has been a continuous shift from more abundant sources of low entropy (the solar radiation) to less abundant ones (the earth's mineral resources). "If we stampede over details, we can say that every baby born now means one human life less in the future. But also every Cadillac produced at any time means fewer lives in the future" (p. 304).

Readers of this journal will be pleased to see a signal defense of institutional economics coming from the pen of such an eminent theorist. He laments that the "problems in which the romantic economists—Marx at his best, the historical school, or the institutionalists—were interested as well as their methods of research are practically forgotten, often treated with high scorn" (p. 121). Evolutionary elements predominate in every concrete economic phenomenon of some significance. "If our scientific net lets these elements slip through it, we are left only with a shadow of the concrete phenomenon" (p. 320). "The much better faring of standard economics notwithstanding, it is the position of the historical school that is fundamentally the correct one" (p. 342). In Georgescu-Roegen's view, the sin of standard economics is the fallacy of misplaced concreteness, by which Alfred North Whitehead understands "neglecting the degree of abstraction involved when an actual entity is considered merely so far as it exemplifies certain [preselected] categories of thought."[4]

As economics is a science not only of "observable" quantities but also of man, it must rely extensively on dialectical reasoning, which Georgescu-Roegen defines somewhat differently from Hegel. Although dialectical concepts are not discretely distinct and therefore defy precise arithmomorphic boundaries, they do not overlap with their opposites throughout the entire range of denotations. As David Hume already had observed in his discourse "Of Refinement in the Arts,"[5] just because the bounds between two opposing qualities, such as virtue and vice, cannot be exactly fixed, we cannot refuse to study moral subjects. Far from being unscientific, the infinite regress of the dialectical penumbra reflects the most essential aspect of change. Exact arithmomorphic analysis retains the obvious merit—acknowledged by almost every criticism of mathematical economics—of bringing to light important errors in the works of literary economists who reason dialectically. But it has no value unless there is some such dialectical reasoning to be tested (p. 341). Arithmomorphic models offer the great advantage that "Irrtümer nicht lange unentdeckt bleiben könnon."[6] Or, in the words of Frank Knight, "economic theory . . . is a first step, and chiefly significant negatively rather than positively, for showing what is 'wrong' rather than what is 'right' in an existing situation and in any proposed line of action."[7]

The predicament of any evolutionary social science derives from the fact that mankind has no access to observing other "mankinds." As Karl Popper has argued,[8] the study of the evolution of human society includes the study of that study itself and thus leads to an irreducible paradox of infinite regress in the problem of evolution. Or, to put it somewhat differently, the variety of historical hypotheses consistent with any given body of evidence is limited only by the values and ability of the human observer who constructs them. It is here, I think, that Georgescu-Roegen's epistemological approach has come full circle. True enough, any analysis of the economic process "must . . . proceed by some heroic simplifications and totally ignore their consequences" (p. 212), with "some additional heroic steps all aimed at assuming away dialectical quality" (p. 215). But as dialectical concepts themselves are subject to all the failures and frailties of the human mind, how do we know that they are more pertinent or close to reality than our analytical abstractions?

Georgescu-Roegen himself admits that he may be fighting a straw man in his objective "of proving that the economic process as a whole is not a mechanical phenomenon" (p. 139). Few economists indeed would subscribe to such a narrow view, notwithstanding the sanguine hopes of accomplishment each profession must express for its own peace of mind. Wide disagreements about policy confirm only too well the indisputable verdict: "No social science can subserve the art of government as efficaciously as physics does the art of space travel" (p. 16). "Nor does the intimate connection between the Entropy Law and the economic process aid us in managing a given economy better" (p. 18), the traditional purpose of most economic analysis.

Georgescu-Roegen relates Jeremy Bentham's misgivings about the possibility of a community welfare index: "'Tis in vain to talk of adding quantities which after the addition will continue distinct as they were before, . . . you might as well pretend to add twenty apples to twenty pears." But he fails to quote Bentham's conclusion on the same manuscript sheet: "This addibility of the happiness of different subjects, however, when considered rigorously, it may appear fictitious, is a postulatum without the allowance of which all political reasoning is at a stand . . . ."[9] Similarly, he repeatedly refers to Marshall's famous dictum that "the Mecca of the economist lies in economic biology rather than in economic dynamics,"[10] although this insight did not prevent Marshall from pursuing his brilliant partial equilibrium analysis.

Georgescu-Roegen could have added that these soul-searching reappraisals have gone on throughout the history of economic thought. To name only some of the eminent founders of mathematical economics, both F. Y. Edgeworth and Vilfredo Pareto spent the latter years of their lives trying to disassociate themselves from the exaggerated claims they themselves originally had made for mathematical physics.[11] It is among the many ironies in the history of economic thought that Pareto,[12] in his later sociological writings, moved far away from his own optimality concept long before it had become a standard tool of modern welfare economics.

"Even though Einsteinian physics supersedes Newtonian physics as an explanation . . . of the universe, the Newtonian framework remains quite adequate at the level of application for which it was intended."[13] In a similar vein, Georgescu-Roegen could have emphasized recent contributions of standard economics to recognize the limits of its own application. Just as the exceptional importance of the entropy law for an understanding of evolution stems from its very recognition by a formal science stressing the sameness of matter, so stand out recent economic insights stemming from the very application of formal mathematical analysis. The existence problem of a general equilibrium system, the impossibility theorem, the general theory of the second best, the questioning of traditional hypotheses by the "new economic history," the refutation of historicism, all attest to the usefulness of standard economics in defining more sharply the very bounds of our knowledge. Georgescu-Roegen shares Whitehead's complaint that "the self-confidence of learned people is the comic tragedy of [our] civilization." But this fact, in no way unique to economics, has its roots in the universal danger of any scientific abstraction. "Wherever there is the sense of self-sufficient completion, there is the germ of vicious dogmatism. . . . Our conscious thought is an abstraction of entities from the background of existence. Thought is one form of emphasis."[14]

Fundamental to all economic reasoning is the assumption of rational behavior, and Georgescu-Roegen's central concern, therefore, is with finding a proper definition of this term. Human behavior eludes prediction because it is subject to biological as well as cultural evolution and novelty; Georgescu-Roegen proposes to call phenomena of this category "rational of the third order": "Indeed, by the very fact that they are actual they cannot violate any law of elementary matter (or of organic matter, if they are superorganic); hence, there is no reason whatsoever for taxing them as irrational. But let us not fail to note that this peculiarity separates by a broad line the sciences of life-bearing structures from those of inert matter" (p. 117).

Here again, Georgescu-Roegen deplores the enthusiasm for mechanistic epistemology and its impact on the evolution of standard economics (p. 40). He reminds us of Kant's teaching that "the understanding does not draw its laws (a priori) from nature, but prescribes them to nature."[15] Georgescu-Roegen is particularly concerned with the political implications of Percy Bridgman's pronouncement that "we will not have a true social science until eventually mankind has educated itself to be more rational,"[16] an idea "near the hearts of the worshippers of a thoroughly planned society, of Marxists in particular" (p. 347). Or, as the theme has been expounded by Adolph Lowe: "Public control has by now become a prerequisite not only for the stability and growth of industrial systems but also for their scientific interpretation."[17]

True enough, "when a social scientist speaks of irrational behavior, he generally refers to a normative criterion" (p. 346); the eighteenth-century founders of our discipline freely interchanged *rationality* with *morality*. To the Age of Reason, irrational behavior signified madness and justified confinement to hide away unreason,[18] as political deviance is often dealt with today in the totalitarian state. Yet none of this should obscure the fact that economics had its origin not only in "the sanguine hopes raised by Newton's success in transforming mechanics into such a [theoretical] science" (p. 39) but even more so in the faith that "our most solid judgments . . . with regard to right and wrong are regulated by maxims and ideas derived from an induction of reason."[19] Rational man, therefore, could "assume . . . the separate and equal station to which the Laws of Nature and of Nature's God entitle" him.[20] In their enthusiasm for the Heavenly City of rational man, the eighteenth-century philosophers (with the notable exception of Hume[21]) forgot "that to ascertain that a behavior is free from normative irrationality we would have to know all its possible consequences—which, of course, is beyond our intellectual reach" (p. 346). But, then, they had the good excuse to know from their personal experience the shortcomings of a society still dominated by the political and religious dogma of dialectical concepts.

To put all this somewhat differently, rational consistency of choice—apart from trivial cases of consumer behavior—is a useful *a priori* assumption only as long as individuals are guided by a common image of history, by essentially the same universal set of imaginable events, by that community of interest the eighteenth-century moral philosopher took for granted. It is the great paradox of the human condition in modern times that the individual freedom and tolerance which were the ultimate goal of eighteenth-century morality, and which alone made possible rational market behavior, also have undermined the common world outlook which gives more precise meaning to the very concept of rational behavior.

Georgescu-Roegen scorns the eighteenth-century dream of a mechanistic perfect world and its judgment that tradition is an obstacle to progress: "Had it not been for the inertia of tradition, every power-hungry dictator and every overconfident and overambitious scientist would have had no difficulty in subjecting mankind to their vast plans for a 'rational' society, with the probable result that the human species would be defunct by now" (p. 360). Social conflict is an inevitable "outgrowth of the struggle of man with his environment" (p. 307), what Georgescu-Roegen calls "the struggle for entropy" (p. 306). As Pareto already had suggested in his theory on the circulation of the elites,[22] every elite is overthrown by a jealous minority which stirs the masses by denouncing the abuses of the establishment and finally replaces it. In this process the intellectuals may play a crucial role of "rationalizing" the shift in power.[23] To quote another distinguished economist: "Since it is their role to interpret values in all fields of culture, the intellectuals are very well placed for identifying the aspirations that express the deepest trends in social feeling."[24]

To remake himself and to create the Heavenly City of the eighteenth-century philosopher, man needs both a knowledge and a power well beyond his reach. "That is why, in the future as in the past, the human society will pass from the control of one elite to another and why each elite will have to influence not the genotypes of people, but their beliefs with the aid of a seemingly different, yet basically homologous, mythology" (p. 359). These are wise words, yet they do not follow from the entropy law. Rather, they reflect Georgescu-Roegen's philosophy of history, a hypothesis full of "meaning" in the sense of a rational search for the understanding of the past and the present, but nevertheless a hypothesis which—as Georgescu-Roegen himself emphasizes again and again—eludes rigorous testing. It belongs to the many cyclic theories of history, whether we think of Vico's *ricorsi,*[25] Nietzsche's *ewige Wiederkunft,*[26] or Pareto's circulating elites. Unwittingly, Georgescu-Roegen confirms the extraordinary difficulties encountered in any attempt to heed his call and to interpret the values which determine quality and change, an effort necessary to move economics from its mechanistic epistemology to an evolutionary science.

The last two centuries, since the origin of modern economics, certainly have lain under the spell of a linear, rather than cyclical, conception of history; they hardly can be understood without some reference to the relentless drive for economic growth and development, abetted by corresponding changes in the idelogy, or "mythology," of progress and power. A society without conflict would indeed cease to be human, yet so would, in the prevailing view of contemporaries, a society without some sense of purposeful direction, some concept of man's meaningful destiny, or "progress." Neither one can be ignored in its impact on human action and economic evolution.

It may be instructive to compare Georgescu-Roegen's interpretation of an evolutionary economic science with Jacques Monod's "Essay on the Natural Philosophy of Modern Biology." Both of these eminent scholars are concerned with implications of the entropy law, and both wrote their books simultaneously but quite independently. While Georgescu-Roegen appears to deduce from entropy the inevitability of social conflict and elitist cycles, Monod pleads for a normative epistemology as "the one at once rational and resolutely idealistic attitude upon which a real socialism might be built."[27] The polar contrast of these conclusions suggests the immensity of the task in any attempt to move beyond the confines of scientific objectivity as construed by standard economics.

Georgescu-Roegen's central theme is the futility of trying to separate the social sciences from the humanities, the means from ends, the economic process from normative judgments, values from knowledge. In this regard, both Georgescu-Roegen and Monod fully agree. Organic versus mechanical, picture versus formula, imagination versus system—these are the distinctions which indeed are current wherever a romanticism of feeling seeks to balance a period of successful scientific formulation. Georgescu-Roegen combines in one and the same person the two complementary attributes of analytic rigor and creative understanding. Perhaps it has been his very eminence as a theorist which has prevented him from stating the obvious: The economist's enthusiasm for mechanistic epistemology does not stem from his shortsightedness; rather, it reflects an awareness of his own limitations and a fear of losing his scientific objectivity. If this objectivity—at least for all the "big" questions involving evolutionary change—has been an illusion anyway, as both Georgescu-Roegen and Monod claim and this reviewer agrees, new vistas are opened for a humanistic political economy, for the "ethic of knowledge" Monod proclaims.[28] Even more important, it heightens the responsibilities of the economist not to subsume his personal prejudices for scientific fact and to humbly recognize the limits of his craft. For, to repeat Georgescu-Roegen's warning, to define behavior as "rational" we would have to know all its possible consequences, which is beyond our intellectual reach.

Department of Economics WERNER HOCHWALD
Washington University

Notes

Page numbers without name in the text refer to the book reviewed.

1. Paul A. Samuelson, "Foreword," in Nicholas Georgescu-Roegen, *Analytical Economics* (Cambridge, Mass.: Harvard University Press, 1965), p. vii.
2. Blaise Pascal, *Pensées sur la religion et sur quelques autres sujets* [1670], vol. 1 (Paris: Renouard, 1803), p. 189.
3. Erwin Schrödinger, *What Is Life?* (Cambridge: the University Press, 1944).

4. Alfred North Whitehead, *Process and Reality, an Essay in Cosmology* (New York: Macmillan, 1929), p. 11.
5. David Hume, *Political Discourses* (Edinburgh: Kincaid, 1752), quoted from Eugene Rotwein, ed., *Writings on Economics* (Madison: University of Wisconsin Press, 1955), p. 19.
6. Knut Wicksell, *Über Wert, Kapital und Rente nach den neueren nazionalökonomischen Theorien* (Jena: Gustav Fischer, 1893), p. vii.
7. Frank H. Knight, "What Is Truth in Economics?" *Journal of Political Economy* (February 1940), quoted from *On the History and Method of Economics* (Chicago: University of Chicago Press, 1956), p. 177.
8. Karl R. Popper, *The Poverty of Historicism* [1936] (London: Routledge & Kegan Paul, 1957), p. 80.
9. Jeremy Bentham, MSS U.C., No. 14, entitled *Dimension of Happiness* [1780], quoted in Elie Halévy, *The Growth of Philosophic Radicalism* [1901] (Boston: Beacon Press, 1955), p. 495.
10. Alfred Marshall, "Preface to the Eighth Edition," *Principles of Economics* (London: Macmillan, 1920), p. xiv.
11. F. Y. Edgeworth, *Mathematical Physics, an Essay on the Application of Mathematics to the Moral Sciences* (London: Kegan Paul, 1881).
12. Vilfredo Pareto, *Trattato di sociologia generale* (Florence: Barbera, 1916).
13. Trout Rader, *Theory of Microeconomics* (New York and London: Academic Press, 1972), p. 11.
14. Alfred North Whitehead, "Mathematics and the Good," quoted from Paul Arthur Schilpp, ed., *The Philosophy of Alfred North Whitehead* (Evanston: Northwestern University Press, 1941), pp. 670–72.
15. "Der Verstand schöpft seine Gesetze (a priori) nicht aus der Natur, sondern schreibt sie dieser vor." Immanuel Kant, *Prolegomena zu einer jeden künftigen Metaphysik die als Wissenschaft wird auftreten können* (Riga: Hartknoch, 1783), p. 72.
16. Percy Williams Bridgman, "The Strategy of Social Sciences," quoted from *Reflections of a Physicist* (New York: Philosophical Library, 1949), p. 313.
17. Adolph Lowe, *On Economic Knowledge: Toward a Science of Political Economics* (New York: Harper & Row, 1965), p. xviii.
18. Michel Foucault, *Histoire de la folie* (Paris: Librarie Plon, 1961).
19. Adam Smith, *The Theory of Moral Sentiments* [1759] (London: Bell & Sons, 1892), p. 470.
20. Declaration of Independence [1776].
21. David Hume, *Dialogues Concerning Natural Religion*, published posthumously by Adam Smith [1779] (Aalen: Scientia Verlag, 1964).
22. Vilfredo Pareto, *Les systèmes socialistes*, vol. 3 (Paris: Giard et Brière, 1902), p. 30.
23. Edward Shils, *The Intellectuals and the Powers* (Chicago: University of Chicago Press, 1972).
24. Celso Furtado, *Diagnosis of the Brazilian Crisis* (Berkeley: University of California Press, 1964), p. 37.
25. Giovanni Battista Vico, *Principi di una Scienza Nuova* [1725] (Napoli: Riccardo Ricciardi Editore, 1953), Libro Quinto.
26. Friedrich Nietzsche, *Also sprach Zarathustra, Ein Buch für Alle und Keinen* (Chemnitz: Schmeitzner, 1883).

27. Jacques Monod, *Chance and Necessity* [1970] (New York: Vintage Books, 1972), p. 179.
28. Ibid., p. 176.

This important volume needs to be reviewed by physicists, biologists, philosophers, sociologists, political scientists, and anthropologists as well as economists. Professor Richard Schlegel, Department of Physics, Michigan State University, is publishing a current review in this journal, as are two other economists. I will review the book from the standpoint of an agricultural production economist with a substantial interest in both economics and philosophy. Persons needing assistance on the physics of the book are advised to read Schlegel's review.

Professor Nicholas Georgescu-Roegen has produced a fundamental work dealing in new, creative ways with a number of topics. Partly because it is new and creative (at least to economists), it is also incomplete, at times inconsistent and both over- and underemphasizes different topics. It should be read carefully by many economists, although reading it is not easy. It draws fundamentally on concepts from physics, biology, philosophy, chemistry, and various philosophies of science. Furthermore, while written carefully and in a scholarly way, the sentence construction is often complex, while somewhat rare English words are used repeatedly. Examples of the latter include the word *entropy* itself as well as *hysteresis, ergodic, endosomatic, exosomatic, ektropy, entropometer, algeny*, and many more. Several of these words seem to have somewhat unique meanings; this includes the word *entropy*, which, as indicated in discussion starting on page 4, has a rather unique meaning in the context in which Georgescu-Roegen uses it. Because of its great content, it is a difficult book to review. This effort may cover some unappropriate topics while neglecting more appropriate ones. In any event, it is impossible to do the volume justice in a short review.

The basic idea introduced into economics by the book is the entropy law. That law states that the physical world moves irrevocably from lower to higher states of entropy, or from greater to lesser levels of available energy, and/or from more to less organized states of matter. According to this law, production processes which make energy available or which produce order (form, place, institutional, technological, and human capacity utility) use up at least as much (and generally more) low level entropy than the low level entropy they bring about, the excess being high level entropy or waste. The laws of conservation of matter and energy are consistent with the entropy law. See Schlegel's accompanying review for more discussion of entropy.

The entropy law has several consequences for economics. Conversion from low to higher entropy is not totally reversible. Thus, *production of available sources of energy and order within any system* depend eventually on sources of low level entropy from outside the system. Georgescu-Roegen asserts that this fact is unduly neglected by classical and neoclassical economists. Conservationists have long agreed with this point, and present-day ecologists and environmentalists will heartily approve this conclusion whether or not they understand entropy. However, this reviewer does not agree that the neglect has been quite as complete as Georgescu-Roegen indicates. Many neoclassicists have questioned whether "the market" properly prices our exhaustible low-entropy resources. Furthermore, this reviewer feels that even the classical and neoclassical models and work which have neglected this fact have been more useful than Georgescu-Roegen implies at some (pp. 334–36) but not at other (p. 341) points.

Another consequence for economics is in the realm of value theory (chapter 10). Clearly, low entropy has value as a source of free energy and of the different kinds of physical, institutional, and other order man desires. With the passage of time, levels and kinds of entropy change. These changes change values—thus, normative concepts about goodness and badness depend on physical phenomena. Understanding this fact helps amplify and clarify the labor and other value theories followed by such economists as David Ricardo, Jeremy Bentham, John Stuart Mill, Karl Marx, and Alfred Marshall. But such entropically induced changes in values, in turn, change the definitions of variables, categories, classes, and class intervals important to and acceptable by physical scientists. Thus, even for physics, recognition of the entropy law has made the relevance of positive, *man-made* concepts dependent on the relative values *to man* of different kinds and levels of entropy and vice versa. The result is a special case of the interdependence between normative and positive concepts stressed by pragmatists and a fatal blow to philosophic positivism *from physics,* the original showpiece of positivists. Georgescu-Roegen correctly wastes no tears over this destruction of the usefulness of philosophic positivism even for physics and chemistry. In fact he rejects positivism at several points (see, for example, pp. 44, 50ff., 80ff., and 342), although tacitly accepting it elsewhere as will be pointed out later.

The irreversibility of the entropy law combines with the pragmatic interdependence between normative and positive concepts discussed above to cause Georgescu-Roegen to place great emphasis on dialectical in preference to analytical reasoning. Recognition of the entropy law makes it necessary that time or process be explicitly considered in economics. The role of entropy in the determination of value, which, in turn, makes the relevance of any time interval a function of time-consuming, problem-solving processes, means that *analysis* of data for preconceived time intervals loses meaning. Thus, concludes Georgescu-Roegen, *dialectics* are needed so that we can study the process whereby entropically influenced values reveal dialectically the relevant time intervals (p. 62ff.).

A student of American pragmatism recognizes at once that the special interdependence noted by Georgescu-Roegen between entropically determined concepts of values *and* positivistic concepts is but part of the more general pragmatic assertation that the truths of all normative and positive concepts are interdependent in problem-solving contexts of processes. Indeed, recognition that the relevance of a positive concept depends upon entropy-based values is but a special incidence of the workability "test of truth" long followed by pragmatists.

Unfortunately, Georgescu-Roegen dismissed pragmatic American institutional economics after Thorstein Veblen with a footnote on page 321; however, he places great stress on the closely related German historical school (p. 342). Although he cites the American pragmatist Peirce in an insignificant way (p. 125), he does not make any reference to John Dewey, who drew on Peirce in becoming a founder of American pragmatism. It was Dewey's influence on John R. Commons that made the Wisconsin school of institutional economics pragmatic. Like Georgescu-Roegen, the Wisconsin institutionalists are concerned with dialectics. The institutionalists, however, appear to have had the advantage of basing their logic on a *general* interdependence among normative and positive concepts without specialization in entropically determined values. Elsewhere, this reviewer has argued that positivism (which rejects the interdependence of normative and positive concepts and, indeed, rejects the possibility of objective normative knowledge) has demonstrated, historically, its usefulness. Similarly, forms of outright normativism have demonstrated their usefulness,[1] a case in point being utilitarianism as expounded by Jeremy Bentham and elaborated by Vilfredo Pareto, J. R. Hicks, and Kenneth Arrow. Thus, it seems to this reviewer that, in addition to avoiding emphasis on a limited form of pragmatism, Georgescu-Roegen advantageously could make more allowance for a discriminating use of positivism and various forms of normativism.

For example, Georgescu-Roegen's emphasis on his entropic pragmatism is so strong that he rejects the possibility of a theoretic economics (p. 322ff.) in a manner quite similar to the "scorn" with which he says, in a footnote on page 321, American institutionalists reject theory and for apparently similar reasons. In doing so, he is considering a *positivistic* kind of theoretic economics based on definitions, class intervals, categories, and variables whose definitions are independent of the normative questions and answers arising out of the entropic process (pp. 42, 50ff., 334). In this connection it is worthwhile reading his distinction between theoretic science and science beginning on page 42. His argument leads, of course, to a similar rejection of positivistic theoretic chemistry and theoretic physics (chapter 2); however, he does not reject the possibilities of more general sciences of physics, chemistry, and economics which go beyond a positivistic theoretic science. This reviewer believes that a "theoretic" economics (of a more general nature going beyond positivism) could be justified to conserve the use of scarce (low entropy) research and academic resources. In such a more general theoretic economics this reviewer would agree with Georgescu-Roegen's conclusion on page 341 that "arithmomorphic models—are indispensable in economics, *no* less than in other scientific domains." But positivistic arithmomorphic models alone would not be adequate; nonpositivistic arithmomorphic models also could be considered.

It seems necessary to discuss dialectics in a somewhat more general way in reviewing this book. The classes, class intervals, categories, variables, and so forth, which we define to use in doing descriptive and analytical work are typically relative to a particular problem or set of problems and, hence, to the normative components of that problematic situation. Because of this relativity, normative and positive *concepts* are interrelated whether or not the corresponding positive and normative realities (whatever they are) are interrelated. This is true with respect to concepts of a great variety of values, not merely the entropically based ones. This interdependence *of* intervals, classes, categories, and variables *with* values introduces penumbra or uncertainties about the definitions of intervals, classes, categories, and variables. These penumbra exist with respect to many different variables, not only the time variable. By *dialectics* Georgescu-Roegen seems to mean the unraveling of the interdependencies *among* the meanings of definitions of classes, categories, intervals, and variables *and* the meanings of normative concepts of elements in the problematic situation as we go through the process of solving the problem (pp. 46–47) and discovering penumbra with respect to those meanings.

A difficulty which has bothered this reviewer in reading Marx, the Wisconsin institutionalists, philosophic literature, and, now, Georgescu-Roegen is the question as to whether analytical and dialectical reasoning really are different. This question is a debatable one, and many philosophers, including Karl Popper, Richard Rudner, and Carl Hempel, would argue that the difference is illusionary. As we change class intervals, categories, and classes (the definition of a variable being itself a definition of a class) in a problem-solving process, it is abundantly clear that, in general, *analysis* of preconceived classes, categories, class intervals, and variables does not produce solutions to problems; instead we must use flexible definitions. Room must be allowed to discover the vaguenesses—the fuzzinesses—of our preconceptions. However, it is not clear that the processes of redefining classes, categories, class intervals, and variables are nonanalytical except on the assumption that only *reasoning with positivistic concepts is analytical.* The same is true of the analysis of the redefined categories, classes, and variables and of further redefinition. To recognize the difference between the discovery of penumbra and doing something about them is to recognize the distinction between the contexts of "discovery and validation." Discovering penumbra dialectically seems to be no more unanalytical than any other method of discovering. And validating the meaning of the dialectical discovery is obviously aided by analysis.[2] Georgescu-Roegen seems to identify positivism with analysis when contrasting analysis with dialectics, much as he identifies theoretic with positivism in discussing theoretic science and science (p. 42ff.) and theoretic economics and economics (p. 322ff.). And it seems abundantly clear to this reviewer (also an experienced researcher) that the process or redefining can be regarded as normatively and pragmatically, as well as positivistically, analytical. Furthermore, analysis or ordinary logic is used in dealing with each successive set of redefinitions. This reviewer almost concludes, along with certain philosophers, that what is got out of dialectics comes from analysis employing the usual forms of logic. All that is needed for this is an objective analytical normativism dealing with endogenously determined variables (both normative and positive). Georgescu-Roegen has not eliminated this possibility from our hope chests by furnishing us an impossibility proof for the normative case.

There is a very desirable, in my view, paragraph at the end of the book (pp. 363–64) in which Georgescu-Roegen takes exception to the positivistic inclinations of the behavioralists to weed out of scientific inquiry all information which human beings can obtain from themselves by introspection and from others by empathy. In my view, Georgescu-Roegen correctly refuses to ignore the important sources of information (actually normative as well as positive) provided by introspection and empathy (see also pp. 85, 194–95).[3] Human behavior is at least partially determined by human conceptions, both positivistic or normative, whether those concepts do or do not have pragmatic origins. An attempt to study human behavior solely from a positivistic point of view would be like a three-armed man fighting with two of his three arms tied behind his back, the two behind his back being normative and pragmatic while he fights with only his free positivistic arm! In this connection, the section on purposive activity is particularly good (see pp. 187–95), as is a section at the top of page 336.

Georgescu-Roegen makes a great deal out of an asserted inadequacy of the principle of contradiction (p. 46). He also cites the Marxian concern with conflict and tends to identify classical and neoclassical economics with capitalistic societies (pp. 321, 325) while denying their applicability to noncapitalist societies (pp. 321, 329). This reviewer merely notes that validity of Georgescu-Roegen's interpretation of the principle of contradiction is one about which competent philosophers disagree and leaves further evaluations on this matter to the philosophers he hopes will review the book.

Like Marx, Georgescu-Roegen is concerned with conflict. However, he regards conflict as having a physical basis in entropic change which would prevent all social, political, and economic programs and policies (including Marxist ones) from resolving the conflict (p. 306ff.). Even if Marxist programs and policies would eliminate conflict, Georgescu-Roegen predicts the consequences of doing so would be the end of humans as humans through degrading them to animal status (pp. 306–307). Georgescu-Roegen seems to feel that the neoclassicists have neglected change, conflict, and dialectics and that there is a more constructive contribution to make than either the neoclassicists or the Marxists have made. In this connection, Georgescu-Roegen treats the German historical school more kindly than the neoclassicists, while, as noted above, he ignores American institutional economists. These latter also were concerned with change, conflict, and dialectics and were about as distrustful of theoretic economics as is Georgescu-Roegen.[4] The constructive success of American institutional economists in working on agricultural problems suggests that Georgescu-Roegen's views are productive, if not entirely new.

Readers not acquainted with the author's quantitative skills and work could find considerable reinforcement for any antiquantitative biases they hold in Georgescu-Roegen's realistic hard appraisals of arithmomorphism, mechanics, computers, and mathematics. Similarly, his criticism of theoretic science and his position that a theoretic economics is impossible could reinforce antitheory biases of some readers. Yet the book itself is both theoretical and quantitative (in the sense of using mathematics), although virtually no empirical data are to be found in it.

This reviewer would have been pleased had Georgescu-Roegen extended his inquiry into the use of the computerized, systems science, simulation approach used interactively (some might say dialectically) with decision makers to solve problems involving institutional, technical, and human change. This reviewer's experience with this approach is consistent with much of the argument Georgescu-Roegen has begun.[5]

Persons familiar with Georgescu-Roegen's Ely lecture, his joint AAEA/AEA 1971 lecture in New Orleans, and his *Analytical Economics* would expect to find the substance in this book with respect to stocks, flows and funds, and production which appears in chapter 9. Like his earlier works, this chapter contains much that is excellent. This reviewer would have liked more on the user cost problem, investment and disinvestment, and the relationships among opportunity cost, replacement cost, and salvage values as these relationships influence the generation of services from durables.

I began this review by stating that this book should be reviewed by persons from several different disciplines. I close the review by stating that the hours I have expended on it were well spent. They will make me a better teacher of production economics and research methodology. They also will make me a better, more confident applied researcher on problems involving environmental quality, resource ownership patterns, institutional change, technical change, and improvement in the human agent. I also enjoyed reading the volume and feel that many of my colleagues should read it as well; it opens up many new ideas and legitimizes interests in previously questionable areas. At the same time, the book is sufficiently inconsistent and incomplete to challenge the reader to do further work on the topics.

Department of Agricultural Economics
Michigan State University

GLENN L. JOHNSON

Notes

1. Glenn L. Johnson and Lewis K. Zerby, *What Economists Do About Values* (East Lansing: Department of Agricultural Economics, Center for Rural

Manpower and Public Affairs, Michigan State University, 1972).
2. Richard Rudner, *Philosophy of Social Science,* Foundation of Philosophy Series (New York: Prentice Hall, 1966), p. 58.
3. Ibid.
4. Earl O. Heady et al., *Agricultural Adjustment Problems in a Growing Economy* (Ames: The Iowa State College Press, Iowa State College, 1958). See also chapter 18, by Kenneth H. Parsons, "The Value Problem in Agricultural Policy."
5. Thomas J. Manetsch et al., *A Generalized Simulation Approach to Agricultural Sector Analysis With Special Reference to Nigeria* (East Lansing: Department of Agricultural Economics, Michigan State University, 1971); and George E. Rossmiller et al., *Korean Agricultural Sector Analysis and Recommended Development Strategies, 1971-1985* (East Lansing: Department of Agricultural Economics, Michigan State University, 1972).

Part III

The Development of Economic Thought

Introduction

Economists study the economy, and the thought of economists itself is a proper and fit subject for study.[1] This section presents articles that raise and take positions on a number of important problems generic to such study.

Many students of the development of economic thought have concluded that its course has been profoundly influenced by both ideology and the power structure.[2] Warren Gramm's article analyzes the workings of this influence. Any body of theory, he writes, actually represents a spectrum of possibilities. Each may be interpreted in a number of substantially if not fundamentally different ways. For example, there may be, and indeed was, right-wing and left-wing Ricardian economics. The development of economic thought is characterized both by conflict between these alternative formulations of a body of theory and by a filtration among them with the resulting accepted version being a function of both ideology and the social power structure subtly operating through the profession. Theoretical systems have both positive and normative origins, but Gramm argues that they are transformed in the process of being made compatible with the status quo social system through filtering out the unsafe versions of the theory. Indeed, the system may even derive ideological and intellectual legitimacy from the parts of the theory that remain after filtration. Gramm's analysis is developed using the reception and revision given the work of John Maynard Keynes, the founder of modern macroeconomics. Keynes's theories not only have been scientifically developed and refined but also have been reinterpreted so as to blunt the radicalism (the governmental fiscal activism) that conservatives in the profession saw in his work. Left-wing Keynesians, if they be so called, generally have lost the conflict. There is, of course, inevitable controversy over what a particular writer "really meant." What Gramm urges is that this conflict itself is part of, or is conditioned by, the larger conflict over the "proper" attitude to take toward government and the uses to which it is to be put, a conflict in which the development and interpretation of economic theory is fundamentally involved.

There are echoes of Ulmer's articles in Ben Seligman's critique of the role of philosophical perceptions in the history of economic thought. He believes there is an inevitable "ought" element in economic science. Among other things, Seligman finds two different world views: scarcity and affluence, the latter relatively new. Seligman favors a positive approach to the problem of continuity versus change, recognition of the role of human choice in evolutionary patterns, investigation of the factors and forces governing want formation, and an instrumental economics that would study the relation of means to chosen ends. He finds, however, that the development of economics has been dominated by a quite different philosophical perspective.

Robin Linstromberg's article considers a set of thorny interpretive problems that confront historians of economic thought. These center on the conflict of absolutist and relativist approaches to economic reality and thereby to economic theory and the history of economic thought. He is concerned with such problems as whether there is an underlying order, the existence of certainty, the status of values and institutions, continuity versus change in relation to a determinate science, and the relation of existentialism to social science. Linstromberg himself takes a philosophical relativist position, but his exposition can serve as an introduction to some truly fundamental questions. One's attitudes toward currently dominant theory, vis-à-vis both earlier and rival current theories, and the relation of theory to the economic system, as well as, indeed, the nature of economic reality itself, are profoundly influenced by one's position on these issues.

The next three articles present differing interpretations of the relevance to economics of the work on scientific revolutions by Thomas Kuhn. J. Ron Stanfield analyzes the history of Keynesian economics in an essentially Kuhnian framework, arguing that there has been at least this one scientific revolution in the discipline.[3] Michel De Vroey reaches a similar conclusion regarding the transition from classical to neoclassical economics. Quite aside from whether the Kuhnian model is appropriate to economics, both Stanfield's and De Vroey's articles offer additional insight into Gramm's analysis of the role of the ideological, or political, factors in the development of economic theory. For example, De Vroey concludes that Ricardian economics was discarded as unsafe in favor of an analysis of static phenomena within the system, an analysis that remains political in its role however obscure the role is made. Stanfield insists that "social science is forever a potential weapon of propaganda." In the final article, however, Jorg Baumberger argues that there have been no Kuhnian revolutions in economics. He insists, interestingly, that a dialectical approach is more promising. In his view, the proper focus of interpretive attention should be on an internal dialectic between a holistic "political economy" that desperately resists the atomization of social sciences and an "economics proper" that confines itself to refining the representation of an ever-narrower province of reality. He also points to a basic ambiguity concerning membership and nonmembership in a discipline as a factor inviting the misapplication of Kuhn's analysis to economics.

As the articles in the section suggest, whatever one's position on the substantive issues, the development of economics itself has been a function of a number of variables and forces whose presence and role must be juxtaposed to the viewpoint that currently believed and taught doctrine (having gone through a process of eliminating error and producing truth) represents an objective analysis consonant with underlying economic reality. The lesson, of course, applies to both economic orthodoxy and all economic heterodoxies. Empirically, of course, school has succeeded school, and doctrines firmly advanced as descriptive and interpretive of reality have been adopted and later discarded. The role of the increasing sophistication of the defense of the system, from one orthodox school to another, and similarly with heterodoxy's critiques, is another factor in the evolutionary dynamics of the discipline.

Notes

1. *See* Joseph J. Spengler, "Economics: Its History, Themes, Approaches," March 1968; "Was 1922-1972 a Golden Age in the History of Economics?," September 1974; and "Institutions, Institutionalism: 1776-1974," December 1974.
2. *See also* John P. Henderson, "The History of Thought in the Development of the Chicago Paradigm," March 1976.
3. *See also* Richard X. Chase, "Keynes and U.S. Keynesianism: A Lack of Historical Perspective and the Decline of the New Economics," September 1975.

Natural Selection in Economic Thought: Ideology, Power, and the Keynesian Counterrevolution

Warren S. Gramm

This brief, interpretive article deals primarily with the nature, causes, and significance of the historical revision of the political economics of J. M. Keynes as presented in *The General Theory of Employment, Interest and Money.*[1] A general thesis on the epistemology of economic analysis is introduced and applied to Keynes. The focus is on explanation—elucidation of the nature and causes of the Keynesian counterrevolution. The key relationship is the distinction between Keynes's economics and the Keynesian economics that has evolved since the mid-1940s. The conceptual setting is Joan Robinson's observation that economics "has always been partly a vehicle for the ruling ideology of each period as well as partly a method for scientific investigation."[2] Insofar as this is true, it is relatively uninteresting unless the apologetic portion can be specified. The general thesis presented here provides a conceptual or analytical base for examining how and why the proportion of science and ideology changes over time for given individuals as well as for analytical systems in relationship to particular environments.

The author is Associate Professor of Economics, Washington State University, Pullman.

Summary of Epistemological Thesis

The thesis is that in the history of economic analysis over approximately the past two centuries several observations can be made. First, major contributors and their analytic systems have interrelated normative and positive elements. Second, in its initial formulation the positive analytic content of the new system has been directly related to and supportive of its normative element. Third, the system has undergone a transformation in which those ingredients of the system most compatible with the existing power structure have come to be regarded as the essence of the system, regardless of their initial relative significance. Furthermore, with respect to the final point, the succeeding system draws both ideological and intellectual legitimacy from those ingredients of previous systems that are most appropriate.

For example, in the case of David Ricardo, with respect to the first and second observations, the major positive elements of diminishing returns to agriculture (the extensive margin) and the subsistence theory of wages led directly to the normative argument for repeal of the Corn Laws as a necessary means for increasing the profit share and promoting economic development. With respect to the last observation, neoclassical economics draws on Ricardo as a precursor of marginalism and an advocate of free trade (laissez-faire), and rejects or ignores his arguments concerning the normal existence of an unearned distributive share to landholding and labor as the major source of value. Clearly this selection process was consonant with power relationships in late-nineteenth-century England.

In general, the elaboration of the first and second items is essentially descriptive, with elements of fact and judgment clearly identifiable and debatable. Within this contextual, factual setting, the third item involves the functional, causal dimension which presents an explanatory basis for major changes in economic theory. The dynamic process of epistemological change—the discovery, acceptance, and discard of ideas—is undeniable. Still, it remains essentially unexplained. On the one hand, the relativist points out that the operational application and acceptance of a major idea in a given setting validate that it was right for its time. On the other hand, the absolutist—commonly of positivistic, pure science persuasion—takes a naturalistic, even deterministic position on scientific progress. What is, is true; present truths have been developed on the basis of clearing away the demonstrable errors of the past. Neither position presents an explanation of the process of change whereby accepted truths develop for a given time and place.

Two main dimensions of epistemology are the origin of new ideas and the way in which they change over time. The former, of course, is an aspect of the process of invention for which there is apparently no single satisfactory theory or explanation. Formally, as C. E. Ayres has pointed out, the new idea is a new combination of two older relationships. But, particularly in the realm of social invention, that is, of new ideas pertaining to social relationships and organization, there is no explanation of the basis for the rise and decline of a given concept. It is this second epistemological dimension which is the basic concern here. Its general, historical frame of reference is the sociology of knowledge, a direct extension of the sociology of invention.

The life-cycle analogy of institutional change provides a useful conceptual base for analysis of the dynamics of changing ideas. The invention, the new idea that finds contemporary use, that catches on, develops in response to a problem. It necessarily has socio-historical roots, although initially it is perceived as radical and is subject to critical scrutiny. It becomes conservative as it gains acceptance and simultaneously becomes and reinforces what is. It works, it produces payoffs for the problem to which it is addressed. Finally, it becomes obsolescent and archaic. New problems appear to which it may adapt, but, ultimately, positive returns evolve into negative payoffs.[3] Insofar as the process of adaptation becomes blended with resistance to a new idea or institution more appropriate to the new problem, the old, established one becomes reactionary, which is a self-defensive end in itself.

Economics now has sufficient history as a discipline for these relationships to be examined through one full, major cycle and two recent, minor ones. The major, long-run cycle, of course, had the marginalist revolution, or the transition from classical to neoclassical economics, as its turning point. The Keynesian revolution and the contemporary counterrevolution are identified as minor cycles, as transitional to an eventual culmination in a new major development analogous to the marginalist crisis.[4] The present purpose is to present an illustrative statement of the last or the present phase. Very generally, all the major issues considered here are encompassed in the interpretive use of Keynes's closing sentence in *General Theory:* "But, soon or late, it is ideas, not vested interests, which are dangerous for good or evil."[5] Keynes is concerned with how much effect his book will have, with the relative power of the interests served or thwarted by the ideas he has presented. Ignoring this context, the quotation repeatedly has been employed to deny the relevance of economic or political power—of vested interests—compared with the power of ideas. This ultimate section of *General Theory*, like earlier key passages, raises more questions than it answers. Keynes's short-run analysis (essentially the first twenty-three chapters) has been subject to the most searching scrutiny and criticism; yet increasingly his long-run perspective is ignored and the book's last sentence accepted as dissociated, self-evident truth.

Ideas, Schools, and Power

Power is the ability of one individual or group to effectuate (impose) its interests over that of another. The means of effecting or administering power range from pure force to persuasion, necessarily supported over time by positive payoffs. A key element in persuasion (which shades into propaganda and thought control) is the ability of the power group to define the terms, to establish the meanings of words that serve its ends. For example, the needs of patriarchy appear to have been the basis for change in the meaning of *bawd, concubine, coquette, hag, harlot, hoyden, shrew, termagent, wench,* and *witch.* Originally denoting either sex, these are now demeaning words for women only.

Such transformation of meaning is the fundamental relationship to be examined. In particular, with respect to economics, concepts and theories come to mean what the power group wants (or needs) them to mean. Power, like freedom, cannot be absolute. To identify a dominant power group is not to deny the presence of other elements in the society or economy that limit or condition the exercise of power, nor to deny that they ultimately may reverse the role of dominance, that is, the exploited become the exploiters. Similarly, with respect to the epistemological relationship under consideration, there is no allegation of conspiracy, of collusion, overt or covert, between the locus of power and economic analysis. Rather, the relationship unfolds as a natural process wherein the analysts feel themselves part of (for example, see no conflict with) the power group. This relationship is characterized by mutuality of understanding and values concerning ends and means.

This particular power relationship necessarily pertains only to the modern era (since perhaps the fifteenth century in the West), the period in which economic analysis arose. It relates only to the associations between economic analysis and capitalism and socialism. There exist, however, direct linkages to feudalism and mercantilism when the analysis is applied to the initial phase of economics as a discipline. The use of ideas or belief as a means of social control is as old as formal human organization. The relative importance of the role of economic concepts is a function of the dominance of economic factors in Western capitalist society as compared with other social relationships.[6]

A common element in the development of new analytic systems in economics is rebuttal of the old alongside presentation of the new. The clearest and most commonly recognized case prior to Keynes was Adam Smith's critique of mercantilism in Book IV, "Of Systems of Political Economy." Keynes introduced *General Theory* with his rejection of the classical theory of employment, citing as "classical economists" the followers of Ricardo—Alfred Marshall, F. Y. Edgeworth, and A. C. Pigou. The purpose of Keynes's acknowledged exaggeration and of the overstated attack on Pigou which followed was to clear the way for consideration of the new, fundamentally stagnationist proposition, namely, that underemployment equilibrium was the *general* or normal condition for industrial capitalism.[7] The general epistemological thesis is illustrated in the following diagram. In extending and applying his attack on Say's Law, Keynes averred that "Ricardo conquered England as completely as the Holy Inquisition conquered Spain." Of course, this rhetorical assertion begged the factual, historical question, "Which Ricardian tradition?" and the more important interpretative question, "Why did one aspect of Ricardo become *the* tradition?"

Three Ricardian and Keynesian streams or schools can be identified. These range from left to right, from radical to conservative or reactionary on the basis of their position *vis-à-vis* reform or revision of capitalism. There is a direct philosophical and conceptual link between Ricardian socialism, stemming from the classical labor theory of value, and the leftist Keynesian diagnosis of stagnation and prescription of social priorities planning which shades directly into liberal or Fabian socialism. The right, or conservative-cum-reactionary stream, includes supporters of moderate, gradual expansion of public economic policy and philosophical noninterventionists. The center line may be characterized as the Cambridge tradition; the key connection from Smith to Robinson is humanist, socially oriented individualism, which is "primarily a *theory* of society, an attempt to understand the forces which determine the social life of man."[8]

The terms *radical, conservative,* and *reactionary* are used here in relation to the economic philosophy and accompanying normative

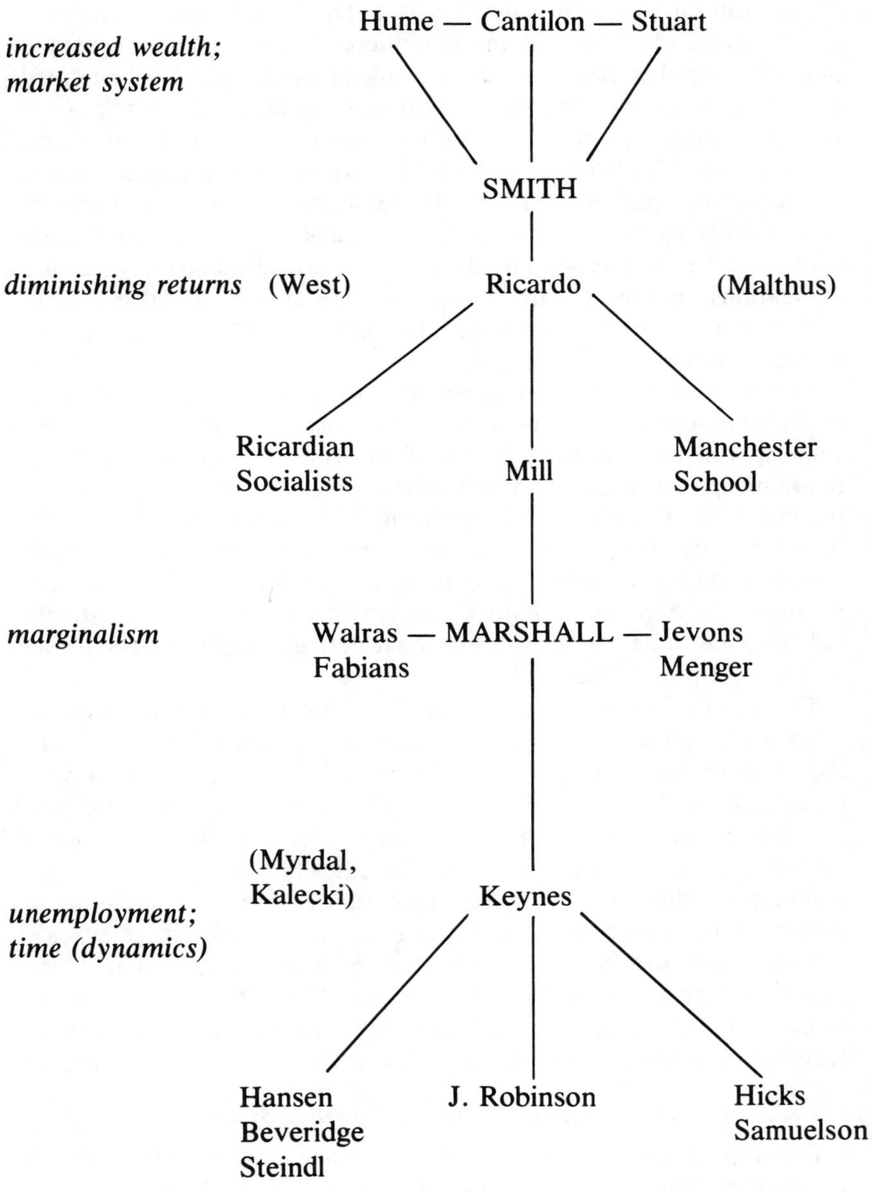

Figure 1. ***The Selection Process: Which Ricardian (or Keynesian) Tradition?***

or policy positions of a given economist concerning capitalism (the private enterprise system) and socialism. The basic frame of reference for the present analysis of the evolution of Keynesian thought and policy is the public policy spectrum, which ranges from the conceptual extremes of a complete to a zero governmental economic role. In the technical context of twentieth-century industrial capitalism, with its extensive elements of market imperfection, interdependencies, and environmental impact, the laissez-faire end of the spectrum is identified as reactionary. In the political context of conflicting economic philosophies—capitalism versus socialism—policy recommendations in the private market society are regarded as more radical the closer they approach the government intervention end of the spectrum.

The conservative position is oriented to resolution of the dilemma of "change amid order and order amid change." Hence, it accepts some appropriate, changing degree of government intervention. These relationships are necessarily relativistic; like beauty, they vary with the beholder. There is, then, no alternative to invoking the principle of employing reasonable judgments by reasonable men—reason encompassing a common base of ethics or values.[9] In this light Keynes is judged as a political conservative with some relatively radical ideas, one "who offered constructive dissent always ahead of practical possibilities."[10]

This duality in Keynes, tied to the fundamentally different implications of his short- and long-run perspectives, provides the key to the fragmentation process (see Figure 1). In terms of politics or ideology it involves a shift from left to right in terms of a predominant selection by orthodox economics of those elements in Keynes most compatible with private capitalism. Specifically, identification of the counterrevolution as the takeover of conservative, predominantly monetary Keynesianism is examined in terms of comparing Keynes's analysis with the Keynesianism that developed after him. Marx was provoked to comment "I am not a Marxist" in response to propositions claiming his parentage. The underlying question is, if Keynes were alive today, which of his progeny would he deny?

Major Elements in Keynes's Analytic System

General Theory, like other comprehensive classics (*The Wealth of Nations, Capital,* the Bible), is a large canvas drawn in broad strokes, presenting something for almost everyone. It is similar, too, in its inclusion of ambiguities and contradictions from which partisans may choose. While possessing significant positive, analytic content, *General Theory* rests essentially on nondeterminant (non-quantifiable) psychobehavioral relationships and on at least one metaphysical proposition—full employment.[11] In 1936, Joseph Schumpeter observed that the book was full of *dei ex machinae* (that is, in a sense, fictions).[12]

Despite these complications, defensible generalizations concerning Keynes and *General Theory* are possible, but necessarily are in relationship to his other writing. This volume is the capstone, the culmination of his mature thought which began with *The Economics of the Peace.*[13] His position on ends or values did not change in any significant way during this development, but his normative position on means underwent a basic shift between the 1920s and 1930s to acceptance of "a positive policy of collective action through government."[14] The latter move is reflected directly in the analytical core of *General Theory,* in particular in the concepts of underemployment equilibrium, deficit spending, the multiplier,[15] and the several psychological variables.

Keynes's long-run position consisted of: (1) the chronic, increasing deficiency of private investment (the stationary state perspective of Smith-Ricardo-Mill); and (2) the necessity of more equal income distribution (in relation to equity, social stability, and oversaving). Underlying both these long-run elements were (3) the diminishing marginal propensity to consume and (4) remedy of these problems by reform capitalism. Consistent with item four, his short-run, normative position, early and late, involved marginal adjustments in the system, the resolution of an unfortunate, unnecessary muddle. This was to be achieved, first, through the monetary reform of the 1920s and then through the more urgent, and controversial, depression stimulated measures of increased public expenditure and debt. The latter, which introduced the issue of systematic, rational, or planning oriented fiscal policy, is the normative essence of the Keynesian revolution. A major element in the counterrevolution is the reversal of primary emphasis, or the reinstatement to a prime place in Keynesian policy of monetary, as compared with fiscal, relationships.

The Normative Base of Keynes's Thought

Keynes was a late-nineteenth-century British conservative, a scholarly critic schooled in the eclectic climate of Cambridge catholicism and the British liberal tradition. Maturing in the twilight of the British century and the climactic disillusionment of Versailles, Keynes understood or intuited the deep-seated institutional adjustments required for the transition from individualistic to corporate capitalism. As a philosophic, economic conservative he recommended serious, functional reform of capitalism in the midst of its major crisis. Like Smith and Ricardo, his analytic system combined radical ideas with a conservative program. It was radical to reject Say's Law: To argue that oversaving was the rule questioned the social desirability of the existing degree of income inequality. His arguments on underemployment equilibrium and planned deficit spending denied existing economic and fiscal orthodoxy, and his view that the long-run rise in the relative importance of the public or social investment sector (and the related euthanasia of the rentier) clearly was Fabian in perspective. But his program was conservative and favored reforming rather than eliminating or displacing capitalism as a system. Private ownership and individual decision making were to remain strategic, although attenuated, for the foreseeable future.

Such a combination of radical ideas with a conservative program is paradoxical, but not contradictory. However, it provided the basis for opposite judgments concerning the radicalism of Keynes and *General Theory.* At one extreme is the "Keynes at Harvard" syndrome which associates all elements of the new economics of *General Theory* with socialism, hence with Stalinist statism.[16] The other extreme, represented for the most part by monetarist oriented economists, denies that *General Theory* was radical in any significant sense: "Whatever his real attitude was, my point is that the radical schemes hitched to the Keynesian bandwagon have nothing to do, logically speaking, with the *General Theory.* From the point of view of the *General Theory,* what is needed to prevent mass unemployment is monetary policy and, at the most, a mild form of fiscal policy."[17]

Keynes's early empathy for humanistic, Fabian, or guild socialist solutions was consistent with his distaste for the Conservative (that is, Tory or reactionary) Party.[18] There is a direct connection between his short-run advocacy of an increased role of government as a means to the end of improving the climate of private investment (and reducing unemployment) in Britain and his general acceptance of ultimate atrophy of the strategic nineteenth-century role of private saving and investment.

Finally, Keynes's thought is significantly nationalistic. While presenting a general analytical system for advanced private market economies, his policy orientation was toward Great Britain. The generality of the analysis was necessarily limited since "Keynes's advice was in the first instance always English advice, born of

English problems even where addressed to other nations." The observation that "practical Keynesianism is a seedling which cannot be transplanted into foreign soil" foreshadows the counterrevolution.[19]

Keynes's Analytic System and the Revolution

Which Keynesian tradition has been effectuated in Britain and the United States since World War II? Has it been the same in both countries? If the positive and normative elements in Keynes's own system are Siamese twins, what are their chances for survival upon separation? The nature and significance of such a partition is encompassed in the distinction between the Keynesian revolution and the counterrevolution. The former, the undeniable revolution, lies in the impact of his analytics—the positive economics of *General Theory*—on the corpus of formal economics through incorporating aggregate relationships, uncertainty, and money into the private exchange model. The counterrevolution, the process of selection and emphasis that evolved into post-Keynesian aggregative economics, essentially involves the normative dimension, or the elimination of the radical elements and implications of Keynes's ideas.

The selection process stemming from the influence of ideology and power structures works like a sieve to screen out undesirable thoughts. This process must be sharply distinguished from that of development and refinement, whereby the errors, ambiguities, or heuristic elements of an analytic system are respectively eliminated, clarified, or refined. The latter is scientific progress; the ideologically based sieve is retrogression.

General Theory was concerned primarily with the short-run cyclical problem of unemployment and its remedy through publicly stimulated increase in effective demand, particularly private investment; fiscal policy and public deficits were to be the catalytic agent. Keynes does not extend the argument for public works and an increasing role of public investment to public or social planning. His policy base is, rather, an *ad hoc* response to a particular depression or recession. It is conservative in spirit. However, it is radical both in its support of deficit spending and in its rejection of the existing degree of income inequality (private saving) as being excessive or incompatible with full employment through unassisted private investment. Thus Keynes's argument of structural deficiency in aggregate demand is the basis for the Keynesian stagnation thesis in particular and leftist Keynesianism in general. It is radical even in the short run because rational, programmed public expenditure means social planning; it requires analysis of the comparative welfare implications of public and private expenditures and of military versus nonmilitary outlays.

The wide variation in specific fiscal policy measures is the key relationship in distinguishing betweeen radical and conservative Keynesianism. In general, conservative economic policy in a free enterprise system involves minimal interference with private market decisions and minimal discretionary political judgments. By definition, policy as such is discretionary; for example, fiscal policy must be distinguished from necessary fiscal *effects* of any public action. Still, it is possible to distinguish between the degrees of discretionary impact with respect to private allocation of resources. (In the full radical-conservative-reactionary policy spectrum the conceptual extremes would be public ownership and laissez-faire. Major, specific monetary-fiscal policy alternatives may be ranked from left to right as follows: discretionary fiscal policy, built-in stabilizers, and discretionary monetary policy and monetary rules, or built-in monetary policy.)

Built-in or automatic stabilizers are relatively nondiscretionary. They incorporate the macro goals of full employment and/or stability into regular fiscal legislation. Such fiscal policy orientation is relatively conservative in its indirect impact on private resource allocation decisions and involves minimal policy extension beyond pre-Keynesian understanding.[20] In this sense, and in direct contrast, discretionary fiscal policy is relatively radical. However, in terms of its political basis and impact on existing property and power relationships, the latter may be *either* radical *or* conservative. The latter is exemplified by direct government subsidy expenditures to major businesses (for example, the Penn Central railroad and Lockheed Aircraft in 1971).[21] Radical or leftist Keynesian discretionary fiscal policy is Fabian in spirit and objective. Reflecting the principle that considered government action can be beneficial and the Galbraithian argument on social balance, it leads directly to social priority analysis and public works planning.

Radical fiscal Keynesianism follows directly from Keynes's perspectives on rational application of deficit expenditures and long-run socialization of investment. In this sense it is argued that the Keynesian revolution in fiscal policy was essentially stillborn, especially in the United States. *General Theory* provided potent intellectual support for both discretionary monetary *and* fiscal policy, but only monetary policy has been applied in a general and sustained manner. The principle of comprehensive discretionary fiscal policy was accepted by orthodox Keynesians alongside their development and use of Keynes's analytics. It had achieved textbook orthodoxy by the late 1940s, for example, in A. G. Hart's 1948 "gong and whistle" formulation. But there are two fundamental questions. To what extent has this initial professional conviction *vis-à-vis* the desirability of discretionary, public planning fiscal policy remained in the textbooks, and to what extent has it been transmitted from the groves of academe to the boardrooms where political and economic policies actually take form? In other words, to what extent has the *idea* of radical fiscal policy actually been powerful in the sense of leading to concrete, general welfare oriented economic policy measures?

The Keynesian era reached its apogee in the early 1960s. Its celebration—the confident expression of its permanent takeover—is manifested in Robert Lekachman's elaboration in "The Triumph of an Idea."[22] In this view, the effective application of discretionary fiscal policy, that is, Keynesian economics, to counter both recessions (depressions or stagnation now being a thing of the past) and inflations or overheating is no longer a controversial proposition. " 'Everyone' had become a Keynesian—and, by assumption or implication, a left-Keynesian, at that." The celebration was premature, or out of order.[23] While most Western economists had come to accept the idea of the efficacy of positive fiscal policy, only in Britain (and perhaps the Scandinavian countries) had it been applied at all systematically. Under the aegis of conservative and anti-Keynesian arguments, and of the sympathetic conservative-reactionary political climate in the United States, monetary remedies (and military expenditures) evolved as the most politically acceptable and generally employed measures for achieving economic stability. Conservative fiscal and monetary Keynesianism shades almost imperceptibly into non-Keynesian monetary emphasis. This is the meaning and significance of Milton Friedman's piquant observation: "We are all Keynesians now and nobody is any longer a Keynesian."

Of equal importance during the post-World War II decades (1946-1970) has been the fact that the Keynesian problem of chronic unemployment stemming from deficiency in aggregate demand has been minimal. From 1946-1958 two major sustaining elements were post-World War II replacement demand and federal outlays for the Korean and cold wars. Following the recession of 1958-1962, the economy was stimulated once again by heavy military expenditures. In the inflationary setting of relatively high employment the Keynesian fiscal remedy has been less pressing, or uniquely appropriate. In the early 1960s under President John Kennedy it came briefly to the fore. For "the new economists of the Kennedy administration. Their finest hour was the tax cut of 1964."[24] Like all golden eras the high point of Keynesian economics came when it was in its declining phase. This is indicated by the rapidity of its demise in the last half of the 1960s.

"The most striking development in Keynesian economics in the last decade has been the retrogression in its general understanding and acceptance. Ten years ago it seemed [that it had passed] from being considered something wrong and revolutionary [to] something right and natural. . . . So successfully has [Keynesian economics] been disguised as 'what we have known all along' that the ancient fallacies have been able to creep back on the stage, pretending that they are the new 'common sense.' "[25] With the reinstitution of Say's Law, Keynes becomes "defunct";[26] *General Theory* moves from the live world of theory to the limbo of intellectural history.

This perspective concerning the decline in understanding and application of what was central in Keynes is sharply opposed to that of Lekachman, Herbert Stein, and many others. The fiscal Keynesian believes his position is established as dominant orthodoxy; the monetarist on the right and the radical economist on the left regard this as an illusion. The situation is reflected in the two general varieties of new economics: relatively radical reform on the one hand and the several variations of post- or neo-neoclassicism (the revival of full employment equilibrium analytics) on the other. The counterrevolution develops as a sequence of Keynesian fractioning and coalescence into the neoclassical resurgence.[27]

The Keynesian Counterrevolution

The two main aspects of the counterrevolution parallel the revolution. Lacking a more satisfactory terminology these aspects have been identified as the analytic (positive, theoretic) and public policy (normative) dimensions. In simplest terms, as noted above, the revolution identified capitalism as an unemployment equilibrium system to be corrected by public fiscal catalysts. While the problem and the solution were viewed in short-run perspective, clearly both had long-run structural dimensions. The counterrevolution, in parallel, emphasizes general and full employment equilibrium and monetary policy. The counterrevolution began immediately following the presentation of the revolutionary manifesto—*General Theory.* Its genesis may be identified with the transformation of J. R. Hicks and the publication of his "Mr. Keynes and the 'Classics'; A Suggested Interpretation."[28] Employing the revolutionary language and functional context of its analytical relationships, the investment-saving and liquidity preference-supply of money (IS-LM) formulation shifted the economic question back to the determinants of neoclassical equilibrium. Keynes was faulted for failing in a realm of dynamics that neither he nor Hicks actually entered. Illustrating the rule of schools,[29] Hicks's followers ignored his closing strictures concerning the severely limited purview of his "little apparatus."

In accepting the reality of unemployment equilibrium, initial Keynesian orthodoxy logically accepted the fiscal remedy in political as well as analytic terms. But the contemporary fiscal Keynesian, as noted, essentially overlooks or denies that his professional advice concerning discretionary fiscal policy has been ignored for the most part. In their post-Camelot literature, Keynesian economists have assumed that "the major economic question which faces Americans in the Keynesian era is no longer a matter of whether modern fiscal policy should or should not be employed."[30] Another question is more relevant in both political and epistemological terms: To what extent have major fiscal decisions reflected basic economic and political power and interests, rather than the professional advice of Keynesian economists?

The answer to the latter question is to be found in the context of historical experience as well as in the logic of economic power and rationality or self-interest. In 1903 Edwin Seligman analyzed the intellectual takeover of the laissez-faire "edifice erected by Ricardo and elaborated by McCulloch and Mill" at the expense of voluminous opposing opinions. He concluded that "the practical issues of the time were so momentous that the economic science which taught a doctrine in harmony with these practical demands was accepted as infallible. The economists in England, indeed, were not responsible for free trade and industrial development. . . . but when the demands of the dominant social and political classes were reinforced by the teaching of the scientists, economics leaped with a bound into the position not only of a popular, but almost of a sacrosanct, science."[31] Economic interests effectuate economic policy; understandably, the virtually unanimous opinion of professional economists on free trade had no discernible effect on U.S. reversion to protectionism in either 1930 or 1970. In direct parallel, the logic of a leftist Keynesian case for price controls in the militaristic, cost-push setting of the 1960s was politically irrelevant. Controls arose out of a politico-intellectual context that propounded doctrines of nineteenth-century laissez-faire until the moment of their application.

The function and the operational rationale for this conservative or reactionary fiscalism is neomercantilist—the protection of existing private property positions. It is the opposite in political and economic philosophy from a radical Keynesian fiscalism based on the rational humanism of economic possibilities for our grandchildren. Its historical precendents are in Otto von Bismarck's state welfare measures and a half-century of public subsidy for U.S. agriculture; its most likely future is a configuration patterned on the Italian *Istituto per la Ricostruzione Industriale* (IRI) established in the 1930s and the Japanese *Zaibatsu.*[32] Its deepest implications are suggested in Schumpeter's observation: "Nothing shows so clearly the character of a society and of a civilization as does the fiscal policy that its political sector adopts."[33]

The social application of discretionary fiscal policy, especially in the United States, was burdened from the outset by the breadth and depth of individualist, capitalist ideology. A generally successful fiscal program depends on Smithian-Fabian sympathy with government as a constructive social instrument. In the United States the business community's fear of creeping socialism, that is, of the socially oriented planning perspective necessarily attending radical fiscal policy discussion, provided a dampener of business expectations, a built-in retardent for private investment stimulated by nonmilitary, public outlays.

Consistent with the logic of the economic system, dominant property interests have been the most strategic determinant of U.S. fiscal decisions in the aftermath of Keynes, as they were before. The operation of this strategic relationship is detailed by Stein in his discussion of the tax cut of 1964. President Kennedy's December 1962 "Economic Club speech was not a case of the administration selling the conservatives liberal Keynes-and-Heller doctrine, either 'straight' or 'under the familiar colors,' presumably the colors of Herbert Hoover. They thought . . . they had persuaded the opposition to relax its resistance to expansive fiscal policy. But by 1962 this was not the issue [for the conservatives of the business community to be found in the Economic Club of New York; rather it was] reduction of those taxes which affected the return to investment most directly, and expenditure restraint as a means to future tax reduction."[34]

The only fundamental change in fiscal attitudes of the business community in the Keynesian era has been acceptance of federal deficits as not incompatible with their interests; they may be a necessary accompaniment to their desire for tax relief (and public debt as a risk-free income source for cash flows). In 1967 the effect of the self-interest bias was noted in the *Economist:* "the mortal defect in the application of Keynesian economics in the United States is that it will always be a one-way street, used only when the economy needs stimulation, not when it requires restraint."[35] This learning experience was essentially a release from the balanced budget dogma that had been tied to the Say's Law perspective of defunct neoclassicism. Continental and British businessmen had known for well over a century that a large, even growing, public debt could be good for business. More generally, it involves a basic rejection of fiscal policy in the general Keynesian sense of an economics of control. It is simply overt recognition of fiscal effects in relation to particular economic interests.[36]

The undeniable impact or contribution of the Keynesian revolution was to solve the problem of the nineteenth-century trade cycle, particularly deep and extended depression. Pervasive involuntary unemployment is incompatible with liberal capitalism, as is social planning. It has not been established, however, that the necessary reduction of the former can be accomplished without the latter. Given this dilemma, the revolution was simultaneously absorbed and defused in the neoclassical resurgence—in the development of two interlocking neoclassical syntheses. The positive or analytic synthesis blends into the monetarist counterrevolution: "It represents the final rejection of Keynes' every claim to being a major theoretical innovator . . . [as] the outcome of the long 'Keynes and the Classics' debate."[37] The postneoclassical analytic takeover rests fundamentally on a return to the neoclassical question of the frictional determinants of equilibrium, which is a rejection of the Keynesian question of the institutional or structural changes required for attainment of full employment.

When the second, the essentially normative, neoclassical synthesis was introduced, it achieved almost immediate orthodoxy in the 1955 edition of Paul Samuelson's widely used introductory text. By the fifth edition (1961) the subject had expanded from a long note to a recurring theme. The Keynesian revolution had succeeded, it had "validated their [the classicists' Say's Law] premise of adequate demand" in that economists and statesmen now knew what they must do to maintain stability and full employment.[38] The case was not so clear with respect to the remaining problem of inflation, given monopolistic, cost-push market elements. In any event, acceptance of macro policy was a war that had been won and economic analysis could concentrate once again on the neoclassical problem of efficiency in a basically viable private market system. In its subsequent reiteration and refinement this synthesis was reinforced with the concepts of fine tuning and the full employment surplus, based on the key assumption (the necessary condition) of closely coordinated *discretionary* monetary and fiscal policy. The related, seldom articulated, assumption was that of classical and neoclassical natural harmony, that is, in the assumed pluralistic nonconflict setting, fine tuning would find no deep-seated political barriers. The postneoclassical, monetarist argument that there was nothing really new in Keynes's theory now is being supplemented and reinforced in the normative realm. It is argued that Keynes's fiscal remedy of full employment derived from unbalanced budgets also was not new, that it had been anticipated and initiated by Jacob Viner and other neoclassicists in the early 1930s.[39]

In its counter- or antireform function, the monetarist counterrevolution removed once again from consideration the two fundamental long-run problems of capitalism as understood by Keynes: chronic, structural unemployment of men and machines, and unequal, inequitable income distribution. "The outstanding faults of the economic society in which we live are its failure to provide for full employment and its arbitrary and inequitable distribution of wealth and incomes."[40] In the context of the normative neoclassical synthesis, the counterrevolutionary process received strong, probably necessary, support from fiscal Keynesians as the crisis-ridden thirties evolved into the self-satisfied fifties. Nonmilitary full employment equilbrium became, once again, the thinkable norm. Most rejected the leftist Keynesian argument that the continuing problem of inflation should be met by extending the principle of public utility regulation to the oligopoly sector as a supplement to monetary and fiscal measures.

With respect to concern for less inequality of income and wealth, two major elements may be noted. First, the literature on income revolution and constancy of relative shares satisfied most economists that this aspect of the Keynesian problem had been resolved by the 1940s. Second, there is the normative significance of the analytical shift from Keynes's consumption function—from a diminishing marginal propensity to consume (MPC)—to an accepted convention of a constant MPC in relation to changes in income. Whether this shift is attributed to the pedagogical and analytical convenience of linear functions and/or to substantive interpretations of empirical consumption functions, it is highly relevant for both macrodistribution, wherein the deflationary gap will increase relatively as well as absolutely at higher levels of aggregate income, and for variations in relation to personal distribution structure.[41]

The effect was a fundamental revision of Keynes's vision and long-run goal of income redistribution. It is necessary to recognize the fundamentally euphoric Millsian stationary state perspective that underlies Keynes's equable attitude toward both the long-run diminishing MPC and the parallel diminution of private investment opportunities in advanced industrial capitalism. This vision is based on the reality of satiation, of limits, with respect to human consumption of material goods; of the place of leisure in human welfare; and of the secular decline in necessary rates of material growth with the increase in average living standards.[42] This satiation perspective, which is also the base of John Kenneth Galbraith's affluent society, is fundamentally subversive, of course, in undercutting the maximization rules for both neoclassical welfare (price and equilibrium) theory and the private profit system. In terms of income distribution, the concept—the reality—of a decreasing MPC reinforces the oversaving, underconsumptionist position of Keynes. Maximum stimulation for private investment via the multiplier will be provided by an equalizing income shift to the poor, those having the highest MPC.

Why the Counterrevolution?

The general epistemological relationship examined here is the process of development and change of ideas in relation to their environment. Granting the purely intellectual dimension of social science, major social concepts or ideas develop and change in relationship to the real world. Hence, the atrophy of leftist Keynesian analysis and programs (that is, those relating to chronic unemployment, monopoly, poverty, stagnation, and capitalist reform), especially in the United States, was not due to their inherent inadequacy or error, but primarily because they were socialistic. They had no more prospect of survival in the McCarthyite, antisocialist setting of the 1950s and 1960s than did their Veblenian and Fabian counterparts during and after World War I.

This key aspect of the thesis applied to Keynes's thought rests upon the historical proposition that at the end of World War II capitalism as a system was on the defensive and that this was deeply felt by its leading decision makers (industrialists, bankers, and their professional advisors). The great fear was that the United States itself would "go socialist" or become a capitalist island in a socialist world. The end of laissez-faire perspective and literature of the 1920s (for example, Pietro Sraffa, Lionel Robbins, and Keynes), the reality of economic breakdown in the 1930s, and war-induced recovery was capped by the survival of the socialist Soviet economy. Capitalism now had a functional-institutional competitor with respect to organization of industrial technology; it had been established that a socialist economy could work. While the question of relative efficiency remained, memories of capitalism's performance in the interwar period, especially during the depressed 1930s, were still fresh. The key remaining issue was the freedom question, but the liberally based, minimally socialistic middle course of Sweden made democratic socialism at least thinkable.[43]

In this historical setting the defense of capitalism, especially in the United States, came to rest primarily on the ideological base of anticommunism with associated opposition to social planning. This was a cold, inhospitable climate for leftist Keynesianism and fundamental reform in Western market economies. The important analyses of Lerner, Kalecki, and Steindl, which dealt with the vital dynamic link between aggregate income distribution and micro monopoly, were relegated to the underworld, experiencing the fate of Cournot and all others whose meaningful ideas have not been right for their times. Thus, the problem of structural change, of "realizing or trying to remedy, the industrial, even cultural arteriosclerosis that is the real source of the problem,"[44] was supplanted by remedies oriented to late-nineteenth-century laissez-faire.

Counterrevolution is necessarily reactionary, a step backward from the revolutionary purpose and achievement. If the revolutionary program was desirable, retrogression from or reaction to it necessarily involves some social cost. The nature and locus of the Keynesian counterrevolution is clarified when one recognizes the varying relevance of Keynesian policy for different national-cultural settings. Schumpeter's proposition that "Keynes' advice was in the first instance always English advice" was validated in Paul Streeten's observation that by 1955 Great Britain "[had] been thoroughly transformed by the Keynesian revolution."[45] In Great Britain, in the seedbed of liberal-humanist compromise that permitted a relatively viable socialist political movement, a reformed, liberal, industrial capitalism was not only thinkable but also possible.

That the revolution was not permanent or irreversible even in England is suggested by recent arguments that it should emulate U.S. emphasis on monetary policy.[46] Acceptance of counterinflationary monetary policy (high interest rates) in the name of Keynes may be characterized as "how bankers learned to love monetary policy and businessmen the public debt." The high interest rate stabilizer is attractive for those who have money to lend (bankers and the rich or rentiers in general), and it is no large problem for those who either need not borrow or can raise their prices to match or exceed rising finance costs (for example, many oligopolists and others able to finance internally).

Thus, a crude but relevant measure of the takeover of rightist or monetary Keynesianism is the movement of the interest rate. It is now hard to remember the 1940s discussion of a 1 or 2 percent war. By the late 1960s, post-Keynesian macro policy—heavy reliance on the restrictive impact of high interest rates (with increased taxes, minimal reduction in public expenditure, and formal disavowal of direct price controls)—had contributed to the worst of all possible worlds: continuing inflation with increased unemployment and either a budget surplus or deficit. This is the new world of stagflation.

Monetary policy historically has been conservative. That is, in providing minimal interference with micro market decisions it is most compatible with the laissez-faire ideology of private capitalism. But in reinforcing the neoclassical resurgence and in supporting minimal monetary restraints as the basis of macro stabilization policy, monetarism becomes reactionary. Applied in the world of oligopolistic, corporate capitalism it has served to prevent conservative, Keynesian institutional adaptation. Perhaps a halfway house could have been constructed between minimal restraint and the central, micro intrusions of its philosophical opposite, state capitalism.

Keynes and Epistemology: The Interrelation of Ideas and Power

A major use of Keynes in the counterrevolution has been to obfuscate or deny the functional relationship between ideas and vested interests. Neoclassical economics, in both the original and the contemporary resurgence, assumes away the issue of economic power in its sublimation of distribution questions. It is now widely held that Keynes provides unqualified support for the position that ideas are dominant over other elements of power: This is a serious misunderstanding.

Keynes as political economist was acutely aware of the mutuality, the interaction, between ideas and vested interests. In concluding *General Theory* he introduced this question: "Are the interests which they [his ideas in the book] will thwart stronger and more obvious than those which they will serve?"[47] In the following paragraph he observed that the ideas of economists are powerful "both when they are right and when they are wrong." It may be assumed that Keynes believed his ideas were correct and had a reasonable prospect of catching on. But while recognizing the time lag involved, he ignored the selection process in which a vested interest could choose those ideas that it could use. There is nothing to prevent the world from being ruled by the gradual encroachment of the *wrong* ideas, by "madmen in authority . . . distilling their frenzy from some academic scribbler of a few years back." Distillation is a fractional selection process. Keynes was acutely aware of the use of archaic, socially perverse ideas by those in authority. Since scientific concepts as such are politically neutral, the basic political and epistemological point is their context—the use to which they are put, the group whose ends they serve. The political use of ideas establishes their functional interconnection with administration and maintenance of power, their role as means to that end.

No positive quantitative base has been established here for judging the changing proportions of ideology and scientific investigation in economic thought or in a given analytic system. However, at least one general relationship may be drawn from the epistemological analysis of Keynesianism: The master or originator of a school has a significant normative element in his analysis, but, given the radical aspect of his ideology, a minimum of the apologetic. Here the definition and usage of ideology is that of Schumpeter, but a different general inference is drawn with respect to the relationship between masters and followers.[48]

Ideology is based on the social class identification or empathy of the individual; everyone has an ideological element in his thought and being. In terms of the present thesis, the ideology of major contributors involves a class identification significantly antagonistic to interests or beliefs of the dominant group. This stems from the critical, dissenting, normative element of their vision and thought. Schumpeter argued that Keynes's precognitive vision or creed of capitalist stagnation (that is, oversaving and underemployment equilibrium) "petered out with the situation that made it convincing."[49] Apparently, he felt that the secular stagnation problem had been solved; capitalism's demise would be generated from the Schumpeterian contradiction of creative destruction. The ideology in post-Keynes Keynesianism rests on acceptance or rejection of the factual proposition that capitalist reform has been realized and that an actual scenario of effective full employment has supplanted the stagnationist vision. Contemporary Keynesian revolutionists believe that Keynes's 1919 vision was correct; that, for example, military based full employment or prosperity is manifestation of a dying civilization or end of an era, rather than a mark of viable, adaptable, liberal capitalism.[50]

In general, as social critic or dissenter, the master's class identification or ideology reflected in his ideas concerning the problems and possibilities of social adaptation have radical connotations embodied in a moderate or conservative program. A politically viable power structure can absorb or co-opt the latter and subdue the former. In this process the ideology of the followers comes to coincide with the dominant group; the school loses the radical element of its founder. In present perspective it seems that the timeliness and substance of his work will assure Keynes's posterity. But the Keynes clouded by counterrevolutionary derogation, the Keynes of neither "significant contribution to theory," nor pioneer of compensatory policy, soon could join the humanist limbo of Mill, Marshall, and Marx. For Keynes's future the key consideration is whether or not the counterrevolution will be the last word. As George Stigler has observed, "if a theory once acquires an established meaning, each generation of economists bequeaths this meaning to the next, and it is almost impossible for a famous theory to get a fresh hearing."[51]

The breadth and depth of the counterrevolution is important not only for Keynes's posterity, but also for the timing and humanist substance of the genuine new economics to come. The positivistic, neoclassical resurgence presents an economics devoid of ethics, divorced from substantive social, human welfare content. Those elements of Keynes which have been selected out and assimilated as worthwhile by Alex Leijonhuvud and his precursors and cohorts are those which fit the analytical and normative needs of the counterrevolutionary, market equilibrium perspective. The social economics required for the late (twentieth-century) problems of spaceship earth will not evolve from this essentially reactionary base. It will develop out of the conservative, humanistic welfare perspective of Keynes, built on the Smithian foundation of socially grounded individualism. In terms of the natural process considered here, it will be oriented to fundamental contemporary problems and will be radical in its intellectual content.[52]

Notes

1. Use of the encompassing Darwinian paradigm in the article's title is supported by Cournot's analogy: "Even if theories relating to social

organizations do not guide the doings of the day, they at least throw light on the history of accomplished facts. Up to a certain point it is possible to compare the influence of economic theories on society to that of grammarians on language. Languages are formed without the consent of grammarians, and are corrupted in spite of them, but their works throw light on the laws of the formation and decadence of languages; and their rules hasten the time when a language attains its perfection, and delay a little the invasions of barbarism and bad taste which corrupt it." Antoine Augustin Cournot, *Researches into the Mathematical Principles of the Theory of Wealth* (New York: Augustus M. Kelley, 1960, reprint), pp. 171-72.

2. Joan Robinson, *Economic Philosophy* (Chicago: Aldine Publishing Co., 1962), p. 1. The contemporary significance of the relationship is indicated in Manuel Gottlieb's statement concerning a full-circle movement from the late-nineteenth to the mid-twentieth century: "In its American habitat economics recently has thrown all caution to the wind in its association with elite groups. It has evolved into the comfortable role of policy advisor for the upper crust circle of the great foundation executives, for leading politicians, for corporate and union elite, and for the agencies of the state headed by these or their political agents." "Mukerjee: Economics Become Social Science," *Journal of Economic Issues* 5, no. 4 (December 1971): 45.
3. See Kenneth E. Boulding, "The Legitimacy of Economics," *Western Economic Journal* 5 (September 1967): 300-301.
4. For a formal statement of these relationships see Thomas S. Kuhn, *The Structure of Scientific Revolutions* (Chicago: University of Chicago Press, 1962).
5. John Maynard Keynes, *The General Theory of Employment, Interest, and Money* (New York: Harcourt, Brace and Company, 1935), p. 384. The opposite position is suggested by Cournot (see note 1).
6. A workable private market system "means no less than the running of society as an adjunct to the market." Karl Polanyi, *The Great Transformation* (Boston: Beacon Press, 1957), p. 57 (see also, pp. 40-41 and 101-92).
7. Overstatement is a virtual necessity if a new idea is to gain attention. "New ideas are even harder to sell than new products." Outspoken persuasion has "preceded and accompanied the adoption on a large scale of almost every new idea in economic theory." George Stigler, "Originality in Scientific Progress," *Economica* 22, no. 88 (November 1955): 5.
8. Friedrich von Hayek, "Individualism: True and False," in *Individualism and Economic Order* (Chicago: University of Chicago Press, 1948), p. 6. This is what Hayek regards as true individualism. The other variety, stemming from Benthamite utilitarianism or earlier Cartesian rationalism, he rejects on the ground that it "always tends to develop into the opposite of individualism, namely socialism or collectivism." Paradoxically, it is precisely this rationalistic individualism that has become the philosophical base of positive economics—the individualist, rationalist base of ethic-free, Paretian-Hicksian welfare economics. Certainly this economics presents no theory of society in contrast to

the philosophically grounded systems of *both* Smith and Marx. In terms of historical process this poses the vital question of whether the Cambridge center way is more weighted to the leftist, humanist-socialist position (as reflected in the socialist empathy of Mill, Marshall, Keynes, and Robinson) or the rightist, the private market, individualist rationalism of Lionel Robbins and Hicks.

9. Consider, for example, the position taken by Cournot on this kind of relationship in *An Essay on the Foundations of Our Knowledge* (New York: The Liberal Arts Press, 1956). In the translator's preface Merritt H. Moore observes: "Claiming nothing more than probable truth, the coincident use of Cournot's metaphysical and epistemological principles frequently brings us to conclusions whose probability is of such an order that any reasonable being must accept them as practical certainties concerning both the nature of things and the nature and conditions of knowledge."
10. Gottlieb, "Mukerjee," p. 45.
11. Keynes, *General Theory*, pp. 245–47.
12. Joseph A. Schumpeter, "A Review of *The General Theory of Employment, Interest and Money*," *Journal of the American Statistical Association* 31 (December 1936): pp. 791-95. For a major criticism of *General Theory* in this regard, see Wassily Leontief, "Implicit Theorizing: A Methodological Criticism of the Neo-Cambridge School," *Quarterly Journal of Economics* 51, no. 2B (February 1937): 337–51.
13. "Keynes' vision [of a stagnating, decaying capitalism] . . . appeared first in . . . the *Consequences of the Peace* (sic.)." Joseph A. Schumpeter, "Science and Ideology," *American Economic Review* 39, no. 2 (March 1949): 355–56.
14. Leo Rogin, *The Meaning and Validity of Economic Theory* (New York: Harper & Brothers, 1956), pp. 619-20.
15. For their initial statement, see John Maynard Keynes, *The Means to Prosperity* (New York: Harcourt, Brace and Company, 1933), pp. 5-9. Axel Leijonhuvud presents a relatively extended discussion of these positive and normative interrelationships in *Keynesian Economics and the Economics of Keynes* (London: Oxford University Press, 1968), pp. 15-24, 403–7.
16. The most pertinent reference here is Zygmund Dobbs, *Keynes at Harvard: Economic Deception as a Political Credo,* rev. ed. (West Sayville, N.Y.: Probe Research, Inc., 1969). Keynesian economics is seen as Fabianism, part of the international communist conspiracy. More broadly, the author establishes to his satisfaction that Marshall and Schumpeter were undercover socialists (pp. 154–58).
17. Gottfried Haberler, "The General Theory," in Seymour E. Harris, ed., *The New Economics* (New York: Alfred E. Knopf, 1950), p. 286. The first sentence is correct in the sense of the essential normative neutrality of any given analytic proposition. However, the second involves a quite different interpretative relationship.
18. Attribution to Keynes of a doctrinaire antisocialist orientation by Samuelson and others is not supported by a full reading of Keynes (see, for example, his essays "A Short View of Russia" and "Am I a Liberal?" in John Maynard Keynes, *Essays in Persuasion* [New York: W. W. Norton &

Company, Inc., 1963]). Keynes's position seems to have been very similar to that of Mill on communism (and Marshall on Marxism and socialism). See note 8 concerning the ethical base of the Cambridge school.

19. Schumpeter, "John Maynard Keynes, 1883-1946," *American Economic Review* 36, no. 4 (September 1946): 505-6.
20. See J. Ronnie Davis, *The New Economics and the Old Economists* (Ames: Iowa State University Press, 1971).
21. Since discretionary fiscal policy, as such, is antithetical to laissez-faire—to the economic philosophy of nineteenth-century liberal capitalism—such "radical" fiscal policy from the political right is neomercantilistic. It is either perverse or reactionary in terms of capitalism as a free market system.
22. Robert Lekachman, *The Age of Keynes* (New York: Random House, 1966), pp. 266-301. See also Herbert Stein, *The Fiscal Revolution in America* (Chicago: University of Chicago Press, 1969).
23. See, for example, Harold Wolozin, "Is Fiscal Policy Dead?" *Journal of Economic Issues* 4, no. 1 (March 1970): 23-34. His answer is that it is moribund.
24. Milton Friedman, *The Counter-Revolution in Monetary Theory*, Occasional Paper No. 33 (London: The Institute of Economic Affairs, 1970), p. 14.
25. Abba P. Lerner, "Keynesian Economics in the Sixties," in Robert Lekachman, ed., *Keynes' General Theory* (New York: St. Martin's Press, 1964), pp. 222-23.
26. "The piquant situation today is that Keynes himself is now a defunct economist: and in this matter of the money supply, post-Keynesians (mostly Americans) seem to be allied with elderly pre-Keynesians (mostly European central bankers), in opposition to ordinary Keynesians (still a majority influence in Britain)." *The Economist*, 26 October 1968, p. 16.
27. Clower was perhaps the first to use the term *counterrevolution* in this context; he associates its beginning with Hicks's classic 1937 article and subsequent refinement in *Value and Capital* (London: Oxford University Press, 1939). Hicks's 1937 analysis focused upon the issue of equilibrium as does Clower's discussion (compared with the monetary or policy element). Robert Clower, "The Keynesian Counterrevolution: A Theoretical Appraisal," in F. H. Hahn and F. P. R. Brechling, eds., *The Theory of Interest Rates* (New York: St. Martin's Press, 1965), pp. 103-25.
28. J. R. Hicks, "Mr. Keynes and the 'Classics'; A Suggested Interpretation," *Econometrica* 5, no. 2 (1937): 147-59. It appears that between his June 1936 review in the *Economic Journal* and the 1937 article Hicks's orientation toward *General Theory* underwent a drastic change. From acceptance of Keynes's relatively strong public policy prescriptions he reverted to competitive market equilibrium as the only thinkable base for viable capitalism. The latter position subsequently was reinforced in depth in *Value and Capital*.
29. Simply stated by Friedman: "You must never judge a master by his disciples." *Counter-Revolution*, p. 8.
30. Lekachman, *Age of Keynes*, p. 286.

31. Edwin R. A. Seligman, "On Some Neglected British Economists II," *Economic Journal* 13, no. 52 (December 1903): 534.
32. The development of the IRI is reviewed in Ernesto Rossi, "Nationalization in Italy," in Mario Einaudi, Maurice Bye, and Ernesto Rossi, *Nationalization in France and Italy* (Ithaca: Cornell University Press, 1955), pp. 195-200.
33. Schumpeter, *History of Economic Analysis* (New York: Oxford University Press, 1954), p. 769.
34. Herbert Stein, *Fiscal Revolution*, p. 420. See pp. 412-21 for a discussion of the political process under the headings "The Basis for Agreement," "The Appearance of Agreement," and "McKinley, Hoover, Keynes, and Heller."
35. *The Economist*, 23 September 1967, p. 1093.
36. The highly complex issue of conscious and overt versus unconscious and/or covert elements in the pursuit of self-interest by a power structure or its components and its relation to both aggregate employment and sectoral profits is considered by Richard England, "Capitalism and the Military-Industrial Complex: A Comment," *Review of Radical Political Economics* 4, no. 1 (Winter 1972): 118-22.
37. Leijonhuvud, *Keynesian Economics*, p. 8. This judgment must be compared with others. See, for example, Joseph A. Schumpeter, *History of Economic Analysis* (New York: Oxford University Press, 1954), p. 1178.
38. Paul A. Samuelson, *Economics*, 5th ed. (New York: McGraw-Hill Book Company, Inc., 1961), p. 375. Earlier he had observed: "As everybody knows once an idea gets into these [the elementary textbooks] however bad it may be, it becomes practically immortal." Lekachman, *Reports of Three Decades*, p. 317.
39. Davis, *The New Economics*.
40. Keynes, *General Theory*, p. 372.
41. See, for example, Dudley Dillard, *The Economics of John Maynard Keynes* (New York: Prentice-Hall, 1948), pp. 79-85.
42. The vision is elaborated in Part V, "The Future," "Economic Possibilities for our Grandchildren," *Essays*, especially pp. 363-66.
43. Milton Friedman, *Capitalism and Freedom* (Chicago: University of Chicago Press, 1962), pp. 18-19.
44. David McCord Wright, Discussant, "The *General Theory* after Twenty-five Years," *American Economic Review* 51, no. 2 (May 1961): 19.
45. Paul Streeten, "Opium Eaters and Opium Abstainers," in Robert L. Heilbroner and Paul Streeten, *The Great Economists* (London: Eyre & Spottiswoode, 1955), p. 270. See also note 27.
46. See, for example, Friedman, *Counter-revolution*, p. 21.
47. Keynes, *General Theory*, p. 383.
48. Schumpeter, "Science and Ideology," pp. 349-51. Schumpeter's usage of ideology is restricted to the positive, analytic sphere—to its role in the creative thinker's cognitive, prescientific vision. Here, the ideological relationship is extended into the normative sphere.
49. Ibid., p. 356.
50. "Instead of being a ruinous burden on a highly developed economy, the apparent economic waste of armaments is really a method of

maintaining prosperity.'' Joan Robinson, *Collected Economic Papers*, vol. 2 (Oxford: Basel and Blackwell, 1960), p. 11.

51. George Stigler, ''Ricardo and the 93% Labor Theory of Value,'' *American Economic Review* 48, no. 3 (June 1958): 367.

52. To cite just two entries in a rapidly growing literature, see Harold Wolozin, ''Environmental Control at the Crossroads,'' and Anatol Murad, ''Comments on Wolozin,'' *Journal of Economic Issues* 5, no. 1 (March 1971): 26–46. Wolozin observes that the environmental problem is a ''challenge to our values'' and Murad adds: ''What is called for is a theory of social value, not based on market value'' (p. 45).

Philosophic Perspectives in Economic Thought

Ben B. Seligman

Seeking a purely scientific study of income and wealth, the economist became the first of the social scientists to abandon philosophy. Yet try as he might, he could never completely sever his intellectual roots in philosophic discourse, for even the most rigidly scientific system in ecomonics still displays its views of how the world *should* function. For the economist is always "absorbed in the behavior of [his] fellow man, first as he created worldly wealth, and then as he trod on the toes of his neighbor to gain a share of it"[1] However, he might twist and turn, ethical and other philosophic questions keep intruding into the economist's ratiocinations, behaving quite like unwanted week-end guests.

Ancient writers did not mind such intrusions: indeed, they were most welcome, for ethics supplied the major criteria for judging economic behavior. Economics could be understood only in the context of social, political, ritualistic, moral, and even aesthetic considerations.[2] Kinship relations and status governed exchange, and social norms determined the nature of lending and whatever investment may be said to have existed. Of course, I refer to pre-capitalist times when society was less complicated, less interdependent, and when markets — not yet *the* market — reflected direct personal relationships more than they now do.[3]

The late author was Professor of Economics at the University of Massachusetts. This is Ben Seligman's presidential address to the Association for Evolutionary Economics and was read in Detroit by his son Robert Seligman on December 28, 1970. "I should like," Ben Seligman wrote on completing this paper, "to express my gratitude for helpful comments to Professors Robert S. Heilbroner, Harold Wolozin, and Solomon Barkin."

But as the economy became more complex, shifting from an agrarian base to an industrial one, a new model or paradigm was needed to grasp what was taking place. Here I borrow T. S. Kuhn's useful concept.[4] It may be recalled that Kuhn spoke of a paradigm as a shared set of rules and standards for the conduct of scientific research. Such rules made sense of the great mass of facts that an investigator had to confront and they gained acceptance because they were more successful than other rules in solving pressing and acute problems. Kuhn's classic example is the displacement of the Ptolemaic system of astronomy by Copernicus in the 16th century.

Employing a model like Kuhn's, it would not be difficult to demonstrate that pre-18th century economic doctrine gradually became "Ptolemaic" in its incapacity to deal with newly evolving fact. Adam Smith was so well received — even eagerly awaited — because he offered in place of earlier theory a new conception that seemed to exhibit a Copernican power to explain the wealth of nations. It was a new paradigm in economics that successfully incorporated new facts into its model and gave economists new rules for research. Though challenged later by Karl Marx and others, the classical paradigm appeared invulnerable, especially after it was buttressed by the Austrians and by such "analysts" as Cournot, Walras, Jevons, Pareto and Wicksell.[5] It seemed that their economic analyses most effectively and realistically described what occurred in the market and that their theories suggested an extraordinary capacity to predict the most likely outcome of any course of action. These theories were declared valid because they could ingest the universe of economic fact. Quite simply, the economic order functioned autonomously once the Prime Mover had acted. A kindly providence insured corroboration everlasting for the lucubrations of the economist.

But, as Adolph Lowe has recently demonstrated, Classicism and its near-cousins began to be discomfited by facts that failed to meet the standards of 19th century economic paradigms.[6] Competition underwent significant alteration; unemployment interfered with the circular flow of income; and the automaticity that the economist demanded was not always manifested. Disarray in the real world led to disarray in economic theory, reluctantly compelling the economist to concede that the world of fact did not "obey" the rules of those elegant and internally consistent models he was wont to construct.

The paradigm had to be altered. Increasing disarray meant that economic institutions and their behavior remained unexplained, an intolerable scientific situation for many, impelling them to voice a certain measure of dissent. Norms of action, purpose, and even prescription — decisive elements in pre-classical theory — once again began to merit attention. Sectors of the economy that had received relatively short shrift in classical doctrine — largely the public sector — assumed more weight, for it became increasingly clear that if theory was to be meaningful, it would have to explain their functioning. And the more one became concerned with these troublesome sectors, the greater the need for philosophy to define standards of economic behavior and social purpose.

Hence, it would seem most appropriate at this meeting to sketch philosophy's relationship to economics and to attempt to outline some of the intellectual questions that are bound to arise. This may be done either historically, that is, vertically, or in terms of problems, or horizontally. My own taste in the matter accords with the historical approach. However, whatever method is adopted, the exploration must be undertaken, else what we seek to accomplish in the public sector will remain largely ill-defined. We are confronted by a society in which scarcity as a goad to achievement need not be of as great moment as it once was; in which producers long ago decided to replace rivalry with gentlemanly cooperation; where consumers are mercilessly cuckoldized; where the welfare state can, if it only so desired, redistribute the blessings of affluence; where the Puritan ethic is now a quaint standard of behavior; and where growth, regardless of cost, is deemed to be a proper requirement for reaching a state of grace. Modern technology has reduced the fluidity of capital and labor to a mere trickle, and the inflexibility of the economy forces decision-makers, whether they like it or not, to peer into that famous glass through which one sees only darkly. All we really know is that we live in a new economy blessed, or cursed, (depending on when and where one has learned his economics) with an immense public sector. New facts are continuously generated and these can only be absorbed in a new paradigm in economics. One ingredient of that paradigm must be philosophy.

PLATO, ARISTOTLE AND SOCIETY

If I return to Plato and Aristotle for a moment, I do so for illustrative purposes and to bolster my case. The texture of their society — Ancient Greece — compressed an intricate web of social relationships in which exchange, risk-taking, and competition were but minor strands. Economic action was conditioned by higher social needs and requirements. Markets were primarily local (foreign trade was governed by state treaties) and price was often established by convention. It was expected that the rule of equivalency would prevail which in most cases satisfied the parties in a transaction.

By Plato's day, this archaic society was undergoing severe stress. Men paid less and less attention to social needs, as they crowded into cities seeking riches. For many the sole aim in life became an unceasing quest for wealth. The philosophers sought in vain for incorruptible standards of behavior.[7] It was not surprising that one of Plato's major concerns should focus on the decay of the Greek polis. The Athens of his own lifetime bore witness to an oppressive oligarchy, succeeded by a democracy that then destroyed his beloved Socrates. The descent into a raging individualism constituted for Plato retrogression and the destruction of social unity and order. He saw a corrupt society and was revolted.[8]

Plato concluded that mortal men could not prevent community collapse, a contingency in which the gods would simply leave mankind to its own stupidities. If there was to be a renascence, its fundamental elements would have to be situated in the community: the individual was hopeless. And inspiration would have to come from a recent past that had been peaceable and had been governed by moral standards that transcended the judgment of ordinary men.[9] As a consequence, Plato's social thought — and, by implication, his economic ideas — rejected the competitive struggle for gain and all that accompanied it.

None of this suggests that economics as we know it today can be discovered in Plato, or for that matter in any of the Greek philosophers (except for some hints in Aristotle). Economics was embedded in broad social and philosophical concerns emphasizing ethics and politics. Thus, insofar as one can detect any economic thinking at all in ancient Greece, it reflected certain relationships among men rather than things. Even Aristotle's model of exchange involved primarily transactions among parties of disparate skill, with the goods they offered being essentially vehicles of "justice".[10] But if justice was to be achieved, then private relationships were to be governed by the same ethical precepts that held for the community. The public and the private were virtually identical.[11]

As elements of his political philosophy, Plato's economic ideas were more than just guides to household management — they were intended to help in the proper functioning of the polis. If, as some would have us believe, the *Republic* and *Laws* described a planned society, such planning surely must have sought to enhance what was valuable in life.[12] It was meant to produce a good and virtuous existence, one that the polis could insure only by carefully balancing society's contending forces. Hedonism as a spring to action was rejected; if pains and pleasures were indeed expressions of human psychology, they would have to be manipulated and controlled by the guardians.[13]

Whatever else there may be in Plato, we must recognize his insistent demand for justice. And its attainment had to start in the individual soul, for only then would it be possible for the guardians to move toward the harmonious balance that a properly constituted society should reflect. And, as an essential element in the political viability of the polis, each member of society was expected to perform his specialized tasks in careful, authentic, and rational manner.[14]

A theory of exchange was a minor element in Greek thought. Exchange itself was but begrudgingly acknowledged by the philosophers and was to be rigidly controlled, for the market place could only lead to excess and corruption. Plato wanted a "good" human nature, unsullied by the hurly-burly of the agora. And the order of his perfect society was to stem from inherited tradition. Alas, like all utopias, of which his was perhaps the first, it was but a dream filled with the shadows of the past.

Aristotle was more practical-minded. Though disturbed as much as Plato was by the decaying moral fibre of civilization, he nevertheless recognized the constraints that institutions imposed on individual behavior: ethics had to consider the potentialities of men living in a setting of practical politics.[15] Virtue was not a natural acquisition, but had to be inculcated through education. A major facet of virtue was the exercise of prudence, which dictated the pursuit of a happy mean. For Aristotle this was the mean of the middle class, lending to the state the sort of stability necessary to the good society. Comprised of equals, the middle class could supply a requisite moderation; it was not overly ambitious; and its actions were molded by the prudence and rationality of household management.[16]

Attached to Aristotle's prudence and moderation was a glimmering recognition of the market. Why else would he have gone to such pains to explicate the nature of exchange, which it seemed was increasingly important in the determination of justice? Improper pricing could create an immoral situation, violating justice by its distortion of reciprocity. A just exchange, based on an equality of the ratios involved, was one way of relating natural forces to each other and maintaining social equilibrium. Such were some of the Aristolian dicta on economics; and they exerted an important influence on men's minds well into the 18th century. But they failed because they attempted to straddle two camps — the traditional concern with the time honored values of the polis and the emerging "rationality" of the market.[17]

Implicit in this philosophy was a concern with nature. Knowing nature made it conceivable that man might escape the pain engendered by human wants. With Stoics and precepts of nature dictated a turn to man's inner soul, and consequently, a rejection of the turbulence of the market place. It was argued that such rejection meant accomodating oneself to the laws of nature. Yet in later centuries the same laws of nature would be transformed to support the market and convert its activities into natural pursuits. History's irony would make virtue an ingredient of trade and business perfection a personal attribute to be assiduously cultivated, thus giving a quite different twist to the concept of natural law.

As we know, the complete identification of virtue with trade was not accomplished until the Reformation. In the meantime, it was necessary to transform the idea of natural law so that it might offer a suitable setting for the new paradigm that was to come. With Cicero, for example, the ethics of natural law was divorced from the ethics of economics, so that it was possible to preach high minded morality while doing whatever one wanted to in economic matters. He had no difficulty in making the distinction. In essence, Roman philosophy restricted the scope of ethical inquiry, refusing to examine behavior in the market because it was so undignified, thereby denying to economics a legitimate place in the spectrum of philosophical questions. It was a perverse act that was to be repeated two millennia later when economists decided that it was undignified to flirt with philosophy.

CANONISTS AND SCHOLASTICS

Yet the tradition of natural law persisted and in the Middle Ages was strengthened by Canonist and Scholastic writers. To scholars of the time the old paradigm, modified by the Christian faith, still seemed useful. The traditions of the ancient world were kept alive, as the Church became the primary, if not the only, transmitter of culture.[18] And while over the decades philosophy followed a line of development from the faith of St. Augustine to the formal doctrine of Peter Lombard to the divine reason of Aquinas, the underlying theme and reliance on natural law remained untouched. For example, Gratian's 12th century codification of court decisions, theological commentaries, and papal pronouncements relied on natural law as a unifying moral principle.

Ethical standards were derived from the law of nature and man naturally tended to know what was good. However, the meaning of these ideas was soon diffused, so that it became unclear whether the notion of the natural was meant to be applied to man's origin or to his destiny. One thing was evident: behavior had to be shaped by something more general than the practical needs of man. Its source lay in the demands of a Supreme Ruler whose will was to be obeyed once perceived. As the world consisted of things placed in it by the Supreme Ruler, one learned what to do simply by observing how things moved. Yet following nature did not always provide suitable guides to conduct, resulting in some philosophic confusion.

Seemingly the confusion was clarified by St. Thomas Aquinas. By fusing the principle of "following nature" with precepts derived from reason, he made natural law once again palatable. The teleological ends of existence, which were inherent in nature, could be accepted by all men, he argued. Hence, one could speak of certain social functions, or allude to higher levels of development as natural.[19] The implications of such thinking for economics were not exposed until many decades later when Thorstein Veblen cast a mordant eye on the concept of the natural. [20] The natural law approach, argued Veblen, merely issued in a set of logically consistent propositions what had little to do with what went on in the real world. It led to the use of conjectural history, a belief in an ideal state, and, eventually, to apologetics.

But we move too rapidly. May I once more emphasize that we are wrestling here with changing paradigms in social analysis. Even in philosophy the paradigms were shifting. The Thomistic system was seriously questioned by Duns Scotus who, in effect, separated theology from philosophy. Roger Bacon avoided appeals to authority, preferring rather to study phenomena directly. With William of Occam, theology could still rely on scripture, but science required a different order of inquiry. Concepts became perceptions or symbols of objects in the external world, making science a matter of ordering concepts. Here one observes the beginnings of the positivism of a later era. In any case, the medieval paradigm was no longer useful for a Europe eager to move on to new achievements. Scholasticism, which had sought to infuse a sense of ethics into the practices of the market, urged rules of conduct that were inappropriate for a rising capitalism. For example, the usury doctrine, though continually modified, could not survive. In the

16th century, merchants were sufficiently irritated to evade it with strategems; bu by the 18th century no one paid much attention to its proscriptions.[21]

Yet throughout these shifting emphases, the theme of natural law remained a hardy one. It told men that ethical goals could be reached through the faculty of reason, enabling men to apprehend what was good; and what was good now shifted from the social to the individual. The Scottish moral philosophers, borrowing from Hugo Grotius and Samuel Pufendorf, incorporated natural law in its new guise into their system of thought; later it became an integral element of Anglo-Saxon economics as founded by Adam Smith.[22]

Thus, by the 18th century natural law had been given a reverse twist, one that supported individualistic trends in moral philosophy and in economics. Individuals became the ultimate units of account in human relationships and all social action was explained as the sum of their actions. Whether the philosopher argued from benevolence or from self-interest, it was the individual who was the focus of attention. Economic discussion began with atomistic assumptions, making it possible for self-interest to become the fundamental moral principle

The connections between individuals, however established, were all part of nature, for the way in which one person accommodated himself to another had been set forth in the Great Design: they were part of the rational order of nature, timeless and immutable. Yet all this was a flexible enough philosophical system, employed to justify various and sundry political arrangements, even underpinning the revolutionary assertion of the rights of man.

Yet some questions were raised. Montesquieu, in his *Spirit of the Laws* thought that institutions were relative to the needs of those they presumably served. David Hume gravely doubted the efficacy of natural law rationalism[23] and such writers as the Earl of Shaftesbury and Frances Hutcheson preferred an appeal to benevolence rather than self-interest as a basis for human relationships. Indeed, Hume's "principle of communication", according to which human association sustained social unity, suggested the abandonment of individualism as an ethical precept.

ADAM SMITH: BENEVOLENCE OR SYMPATHY?

These developments reach their climax in Adam Smith. Yet with Smith there seems to appear an unresolved tension between benevolence or sympathy, and self-interest. The apparent clash was striking enough for some scholars to speak of the problem of Adam Smith.[24] *The Theory of Moral Sentiments* employed the idea of sympathy, defined as the capacity of a person to enter into another's situation and thus establish accord with him, an idea that crops up in modern phenomenology. The *Wealth of Nations,* however, is based on self-interest as the motive force in social behavior. In the *Moral Sentiments* one detects the influence of Shaftesbury and Hutcheson; in the *Wealth of Nations* it is the notorious Bernard de Mandeville who provides the inspiration. One is a vindication of certain spiritual values; the other, an assertion that social ends are attained only through the unintended consequences of self-interest.

But we must recall that Smith thought of spiritual value as a compound of prudence, justice, and benevolence. If prudence is a derivative of rational self-interest set within the constraints imposed by justice and benevolence, then the clash between the earlier and later Smith evaporates, for self-interest would be implied by man's primary sentiments.[25] Hence, it was not too much of a task for those who followed Smith to maintain that his system was consistent: they could discourse on an economic man governed by certain moral sentiments in which those defined by criteria of self-interest did not clash too seriously with a concern for the common weal.

And it all stemmed from nature. The social order was "admirably contrived to serve all needs of the individuals who compose it..."[26] Whenever individuals pursued their own aims they contributed to the social order. The theory revealed not only a sublime faith in the benign order of the universe, but it was as well a paradigm that suited quite satisfactorily the needs of a rising middle class and its political and economic demands. Natural law was thus commercialized, focussing on market transactions. Its substance was to specify the rules of behavior among men of means.

English economic success was thus vindicated by a system of natural law that was as inviolable as the laws of Newtonian physics. Hobbes might view society as a war of all against all, necessitating the imposition of a social compact, but Locke knew that men were social by nature, and that their individual rights were insured by natural law. There was no need, therefore, for a strong central government: the only proper function of the state was to secure middle class claims. And when the state failed to protect that most natural of all rights, property, then a revolution was permissable — provided it was a middle class revolution.

But the emphases of paradigms do change, especially when circumstances alter. By the end of the 18th century some shift could be detected. With Jeremy Bentham, for example, the discussion moved from natural law to utility. Bentham weighed institutions by a pragmatic test and was ready to discard those that failed. The mainspring of action was the pleasure-pain nexus, a criterion that led to the sum of individual happiness as the prime social good. Happiness for the greatest number became the touchstone of social ethics and the guiding principle of economic behavior. It is a concept that is still persuasive enough to move many people, though we now know that human motives are infinitely more complex than any "net" sum of pleasures and pains would indicate.

But the concept of happiness could be used to support general rights, lending a tone of humanitarianism to economic theory. A vague yearning for amelioration gradually began to manifest itself in classical writings: Alfred Marshall, you may recall, hoped that knowledge and progress would rid the world of poverty and ignorance.[27] Philosophers and economists began to praise the universality of toleration and it was anticipated that a gentle spirit of accommodation would soon transcend national boundaries. Progress became a natural phenomenon, inherent in society, always moving upward in ascending spirals, and totally self-sufficient. Writers were blissfully unaware that such luminous optimism represented little more than a class-centered doctrine rooted in the belief that middle class careers always rise higher and higher. They made history predictable and beneficient and men became happy subjects of a kindly fate.

However, such thinking did not diminish the stress on the individual, even though there might be a few occasions when it might be employed to support state action. The individual was still the best judge of his own interest. While Adam Smith might have rejected utility, preferring the sentiment of sympathy as a way of explaining social experience, his epigones had no difficulty in assimilating the new utilitarianism into their justification of the sort of economy they preferred. Free trade and the "spontaneous identification of interests" were all they required; even the infrequent action of government could now be discarded.[28]

In essence, post-Smithian writers stressed standards of usefulness as the basis of esteem. What a man did, rather than his inheritance, became the criterion of judgment. The stress on individual achievement was crystal clear. And as rewards were apportioned according to individual contributions, economic success became the wedge that the bourgeoisie could employ to gain a place in society, establish its identity, and eventually become the first order in the polity. As all citizens were deemed equal and endowed with the same natural rights, the privileges of older ruling groups could be challenged. Natural rights now emanated from the market. It was not enough that a man might express high ethical intentions: that only supplied him with the garb of a saint. It was economic results that counted, results that flowed from a rational evaluation of actions in the market. Natural law was thus wedded to individual performance.[29]

There was a reaction, of course, especially on the Continent. So mechanical an individualism seemed repugnant, for it missed the emotional side of man and ignored the true richness of the human personality. Everything that man felt and witnessed testified to the complexity of experience. Man had ideals and there had to be a way of expressing them. The sort of economics that had been developed in England, with its mechanistic precision, offended the sensibilities of Continental critics, especially in Germany. Such was the Romantic protest, one that was flexible enough to support religion, the soul of man, revolution—and political reaction.[30] While it had some value, this paradigm was unacceptable to most reasonable men. It was far too redolent of youthful *weltschmerz* to be useful for scientific analysis.

MARXISM AS A UNIFIED ORGANON

Yet there was a more useful approach to economic problems that had its origins on the Continent to which attention must be paid, much as Anglo-Saxon economists might not want to. I refer, of course, to the rough, grand system developed by Karl Marx.[31] As a unified organon Marxism, as we know, had its roots in German philosophy, French utopian socialism, and English economics. As such, it became not only an economic theory, but a philosophy of history, a sociology, and a prescription for politics. It was, above all, a *weltanschauung,* a world outlook, which recognized change, not as the progressive blandness of the Victorian era, but rather change through strife.

Only when standard economics began to acknowledge the growth of monopoly and the possibility of such disturbing phenomena as unemployment did the contempt for Marx begin to dissolve. More and more, social scientists began to acknowledge that his effort to look at the economic system in its totality was relevant to the problems at hand. They noted that Marx had tried to work out carefully and analytically the relationships between the various social and economic components. He even set up "models", so dear to the hearts of modern theorists, and dealt with technology, underconsumption, unemployment, and the concentration of capital. These were big questions and Marx sought to supply the big answer. That he was not always able to come up with the right one is beside the point. The fact is that he was a serious thinker who dealt with serious problems. That so many of his supposed intellectual descendants assert all the Marxian phrases as absolute truth is merely sad, for this reveals them to be precisely the sort of fools that Marx abhorred.

Whatever else we may wish to say about Marx's economics, I submit that the problems of circulation and accumulation as he explored them were perhaps the most spectacular parts of the doctrine, for they represented in a fundamental way a theory of economic development. The central theme of *Das Kapital* was precisely what the title implied — man-made means of production and the social relations that governed their use. Since the latter were rooted in the wage relationship, capital had to be defined by alienation from tools and ownership of property. Workers not only were legally free but also free from the means of production. And because of this, capital began to assume a monopolistic aspect, for it was the capitalist who, upon hiring the means of production, came into possession of the entire product which he then distributed to the factors of production. The Marxian schema, then, may be visualized as a flow analysis of income, one of the most analytically effective ones in the history of economics.

Accumulation and growth were central, for this was the locus of all fundamental contradictions of the capitalist order. Involved in this process was the fall in the rate of profit and the periodic eruption of economic crisis. And superimposed on all this was group conflict, class consciousness, and the whole sociology of revolution — the political elements in the story which have served, unfortunately, to obscure the economic analysis. Basically, the economic problem was to discover how the continuous reduction of labor requirements affected accumulation and the changing structure of capitalism. English history provided Marx with many striking illustrations of this inexorable process.

Marx's analysis of accumulation and growth was internal to the economic order and did not require any outside stimulus to get it going. This is the basic message of his theory, one that is frequently overlooked. Further, the values of Marx may be seen in his emphasis on technology and the central role of the capitalist. Stability could be attained only if economic growth was properly balanced between the producers' and consumers' sectors of the economy—an unlikely contingency by virtue of capitalism's essential nature. And the under scoring of political power was an element that other economists might have acknowledged a good deal sooner than they did.

We must agree with Schumpeter when he said that Marx's economic ideas could not be easily dismissed. Despite the enormous handicaps under which Marx worked, he was able to carve out a significant body of theory. The errors and false trails notwithstanding his ideas cannot be blithely ignored, as is all too often done, for their numerous indights can provide useful leads to an understanding of the real function of the economy.

A PARADIGM HARSHLY REJECTED

But such a paradigm was harshly rejected; there were errors in it, and perhaps more important, it threatened the status quo. It seemed that ideas of organic growth, as suggested by the theory of evolution, would be a more effective counter weight to the old mechanistic models. Applied to the world of man, growth, of course, implied the use of foresight to counteract social entropy.[32] But it also meant a continual climb to perfection. The blatant Hegelianism, the reach for political virtue displayed in such a concept was challenged by Darwin's theory of evolution which was later applied to economics with brutal precision by Veblen. For all evolution could investigate were the cumulative effects of increments of change. The idea of wholesome progress really had no place in it. Change might mean advance: it might mean retrogression.

Futher, by responding so enthusiastically, and so erroneously, to the theory of evolution, economists, and other social scientists, often manifested an invidious egocentricity. The later stages of the process were always preferable; that which came earlier was depreiated as "primitive". Yet to judge by present day experience, it is difficult to say for certain that one society, or one economic system, is superior to another.[33] To assert such superiority, and to base it on a movement toward perfection, simply provides new trappings for ancient natural law.

Evolution is continuity, a process of becoming, in which society is alway confronted by an assortment of alternatives. Often the direction of change is a matter of happenstance: often that direction leads into a blind alley. Who is to say that now with our technology, our politics, and our environment, we are not at the entrance to one of those blind alleys, leading to the same evolutionary impasse that long ago confronted the dinosaur and the saber-toothed tiger?

But let us leave these flights of morbid fancy and shift to a brief consideration of the social uses to which evolutionary theory has been put. It seemed inevitable that a victorious middle class would demand an ideology that would serve also as a paradigm for its conception of the good society. The philosophy—and the economics—of natural law, laissez faire, and individualism performed that function most satisfactorily. For example, the ideas of Herbert Spencer, adopted with great alacrity especially by the American middle class, rejected aid to certain groups in the polity as an outright desecration of the law of nature and of laissez faire. Spencer's views have been rightly described as anarchy plus the cop on the beat.[34]

Spencer's brand of Social Darwinism, published some years before Darwin's *Origin of the Species,* was a compound of the Puritan ethic and crude Malthusianism. It produced some rather odd notions of freedom and the precept that only the fittest will survive. The principles were divine in origin, reflecting little more than elementary justice. The government was not to be trusted: the only good legislature was the one not in session. The state had no business educating the young, carrying the mails, minting the currency, providing charity, regulating industry, operating a lighthouse, improving sanitation, or being concerned with outbreaks of the plague. (Curiously, there are some academic centers that still give voice to these quaint ideas.) If nature functioned unimpeded, it would expel those lacking merit. The state should not come between man and his suffering, Spencer seemed to say. His philosophy ignored man's role as a social being, concentrating only on his economic performance. It was a philosophy for those who knew no other.

So optimistic a people as Americans quite readily digested Spencerian perorations on unceasing progress and how to achieve it. The implied hint that Americans would eventually march to domination over others was most palatable. Individualism and self-interest became a positive good. Trade unionism was a foolish venture, for workers had merely to surrender to the predestination of natural law without a murmer. And economists, notably John Bates Clark, proved beyond doubt that the economy rewarded everybody justly.

The middle class grasped this philosophy to its bosom in all its vulgarity. It was quite comfortable with so self-serving a paradigm. It enjoyed the assurance that success was to be attributed to simple virtues and that the poor lacked its qualities of heart and mind. The idea that those who survived the economic jungle were indeed the fittest was an agreeable piece of self-congratulation sustained by the pieties of political economy. Indeed, for some members of the middle class economics was good because it "hardened men's hearts".

MARGINALISM AND THE SOCIAL CONTEXT

Thus economic science offered few genuinely new ideas to explain what was happening, nor was it able to predict the course of events. Most writers, particularly those in the academy, were retailing the same brand of natural law that had been advanced a hundred years before.[35] There were modifications and changes in economic theory, to be sure: marginalism, propounded by Jevons and the Austrian school of economists around 1870, was absorbed into the text books by the turn of the century;[36] Alfred Marshall stressed concepts of elasticity and time; and Leon Walras developed an elegant model that was attractive to those who wished to explain economic action with but a few principles. But I should contend that from a philosophic standpoint very little had been added. I shall pass over the utilitarianism still evident in many writers, the latter day positivism of Milton Friedman, the apodictic or apriorism of Ludwig von Mises, the moment-in-being of G. L. S. Shackle and the operationalism of Paul Samuelson. I regret that time does not allow a more detailed discussion of these writers, for their paradigms do imply, as much as they might deny it, prescriptive models. Let us rather focus on two other contemporary economists — Frank H. Knight and Friedrich A. Hayek.

I have chosen them, not only because they are important economists, but because they exhibit a greater awareness of philosophic foundations than most. Indeed, in Knight's case, a thorough grounding in philosophy and theology makes him a formidable adversary. Yet his approach to the relationship of philosophy to economics has been somewhat indecisive. Initially, he restricted economics to supposedly objective data; later, he thought that these data had to be related to a broader metasystem from which they derived their characteristic shape.

But, I should argue, there was not much advance in Knight's formulations over Adam Smith, for ultimately he was compelled to resort to some conception of natural law. Individualism was still a fundamental precept, making Knight's version of the economic process little more than a subtle restatement of 18th century philosophy. Indeed, he has argued that man is social because he pursues individual interests.[37] Human society is to be distinguished from an anthill he says, because it presents problems to man as an individual, making him a "motivated" person. Thus Knight has endeavored to carry on his analysis on two levels, but without success. For if there is purpose in action, as he has argued, then it must be recognized that individual purpose and social purpose are frequently at odds with each other. When this happens, as it so often does in our own time, then a paradigm that incorporates such a contrast should specify modes of reconciliation. Unfortunately, in Knight's paradigm the reconciliation moves easily toward the individual since his "social purpose" is little more than a mask for what the latter seeks. That hardly represents a gain over Adam Smith.

The consequence is indecision, an indecision that is self-defeating. In order to pass judgment on matters of economic policy, for example, such judgments must be based on "defensible" criteria of values, that is, on ideals. But these, according to Knight, are not economics, which is "science" and cannot be related to arguments on goals and ends.[38] Thus, consideration of what are matters of science and what are matters of philosophy are kept apart, although he had earlier conceded that the economic analysis of wants could proceed from the level of wants to an investigation of the ethical framework of wants.

Should economics, then, be pure analysis or should it be set within a broader framework of institutional description? Knight cannot decide: on the one hand individual economic behavior is a factitious notion because such behavior is part of the total cultural environment; on the other, scientific economics studies the behavior of abstract atomistic units.[39] Such a safe position may be a desirable one for those who wish to be traditionalists when arguing with institutionalists and at the same time rip-roaring institutionalists when confronting a traditionalists, but that it would enable us to know where we are headed is dubious.

If economic behavior is embedded in culture—a truism that needs frequent iteration—and if culture is shaped by those who comprise it, then social change is possible. Thus Knight's paradigm is inconsistent and Ptolemaic. Moreover, his violent attack on John Dewey's instrumentalism, which did stress the need for change, can be interpreted only as a preference for the purportedly scientific side of economics, that rooted in the philosophy of individualism.

While Knight recognizes that some limitations on the individual may be necessary, in reality he would go no further than Herbert Spencer.[40] Thus the instrumentalities of society are precluded from dealing with what are fundamental social problems. In the modern context this invites disaster. The social problems I have in mind are precisely those we have been discussing at these sessions — the city, its environment, its transportation, its people, and a host of others. To appeal to "law and order" — in the philosophic sense — is to appeal to archaic notions of what is natural, offering only a set of homilies that would do justice to Dr. Pangloss.

The alternative to this dilemma is to avoid any consideration of the social. This is the path taken by Hayek and it leads to odd destinations. As I have remarked elsewhere, Hayek's psychological studies offer a good starting point for an examination of his philosophical biases.[41] For Hayek, perception, located in the individual nervous system, is the basis of mental constructs, so that meaning and experience represent nothing more than ordered perception. Mind is but a sequence of events unrelated to external environment; thus, one can never really know objective reality. Social analysis is not possible, according to Hayek, for all that mind can do is to seek new relationships between mental constructs. But Hayek has evaded the problem of intersubjectivity, the connection of one mind to another, and thereby has converted economics into nothing more than a heterogeneous collection of disembodied spirits who float past each other like amoeba on the water's surface.

Investigations of what is real are dismissed by Hayek as forms of "scientism", an ostensibly fatal mode of thinking that employs materialism in a patently unsuccessful attempt to discover the nature of human action. Accordingly, such concepts as "society" or "capitalism" are presumably unamenable to analytic treatment. With mental constructs the only proper basis for analysis, Hayek thus reduces social science to sense perception, and nothing else, thereby evading the possibility that these mental constructs might establish connections between human beings. Quite simply, he avoids the now familiar idea of intersubjectivity.[42] If people classify experiences in the same ways — about as far as Hayek allows himself to go — how do they learn these common patterns? There is no answer.

Facts become mere opinions, argues Hayek, and knowledge

offers no guide to action, since what we know exists in incomplete form, dispersed among many minds. Yet for Hayek even such bits-and-pieces knowledge somehow produces order. Somehow social facts arise Phoenix-like out of scattered items of knowledge. Somehow Adam Smith's providential hand has sneaked in the back door. And all this has taken place without connectibility and without intersubjectivity. But surely, the latter require antecedent study if we are to grasp the nature of social and economic action.

Hayek's philosophy, so crucial to his economics, denies that ideas and consciousness are functions of social involvement, which is itself firmly planted in intersubjectivity. Only if this relationship is accepted, does it become possible to investigate ideas and their situations. These situations are not artificial; they are rather genuine settings for weighing, evaluating, accepting, or rejecting ideas. We communicate ideas and aspirations and fears because we function in a social context. These are important areas of exploration, if we are to learn why man behaves as he does.

THE SOCIAL DIMENSION OF MEANING

Economics is not exempt from this task of exploration. Economics is not merely a set of propositions tautologically derived from a priori concepts. Meaning has a social dimension that arises only in the context of human connectibility. Thus institutional abstractions such as capitalism can be analysed, permitting an understanding of division of labor, income, and other categories of analysis without always resorting to the putative psychology of individuals. Consequently, capitalism implies certain sociological and economic performances that together condition — and illumine — the behavior of individuals.

I should argue, therefore, that all the paradigms offered to date by received economics no longer serve our needs. Decisions once made by individuals have been transferred to groups, organizations, governments. The parameters of action, to employ a favorite term, have been altered. Moreover, the areas of performance are no longer strictly economic. To assume that groups, organizations, and governments will behave exactly as individuals do has been shown to be fallacious. Organizations have quasi-political objectives, and their motivation and direction shifts depending on the relative strength of contending internal forces. They have a logic of their own that is as distinct from that of neo-classical theory as a tropical forest is from a moonscape.

What then are the elements of the new paradigm that economics now demands? The basic element is the acknowledgement that those who built our economy and perform roles in it — craftsmen, merchants, manufacturers, farmers, financiers, legislators, rag-pickers, teachers, and toll-takers — are actors in a social system and that their acts are not only economic but political as well. Whatever decisions they affect take place in a social setting that conditions more mightily than we know the sort of behavior described as economic. Goods and services are not only commodities and performances with price tags attached to them but are directions and actions and are significantly related to human actors who control them.

Thus the paradigm of the pure market has little relevance to the problems we are discussing at these meetings. The city, the environment, medical care, welfare — the public sector — are in many ways not subject to the criteria of the market. Yet we lack adequate tools of analysis that would enable us to comprehend the turbulent political economy of the public sector. Someone once said that economists are blockheads who design fancy band-aids to cover the sores in the body politic: they do not seem to know that a nation can be sick. And what we fail to do is evidence of that sickness.

To be sure, refined economic theory offers numerous suggestions — Pareto optima, turnpike theorems, and dynamic stability. But propositions of this sort often turn out to be counsels of quiescence, suggesting that nothing be done about such problems as distorted income distribution, external diseconomies attendant to growth, or inflation mixed with unemployment. Economists do on occasion turn their attention to these latter questions, only when reminded that Emperors often dress in invisible garments.

CONSTRUCTING A NEW PARADIGM

Constructing a new paradigm in economics will be achieved by relating a relevant and meaningful theory to practical policy. This suggests a concern with *political* economics and *social* economics and with the public sector. In this context, meaning and goals must precede analytical elegance. If economics is to be a science of fact rooted in the human condition it will have to check its theory against political policy and social unrest. Relevance demands that the economist make his theory a meaningful way of perceiving reality. Unless this perception is available, theory cannot perform its primary function — that of guiding empirical inquiry.

A new paradigm must be constructed because pure competition

no longer describes the realities of the market; private capital accumulation has lost it religious imperative; resources and factors are less mobile; technology, a dominant element in change, is often malign; scarcity is no longer a prod to achievement, having been displaced for many by at least a modest affluence, the Puritan ethic does not convince anyone; natural law is now a matter of educated superstition; and primarily because the public sector now conditions much of our daily lives. We need a paradigm that embraces these new facts of human existence; one that will explain and hopefully predict the consequences of social action; that will provide understanding of motivation and aetiology and relate these to economic analysis; that views the market as an institution of significantly reduced importance; that acknowledges the role of corporate behavior; that recognizes the urgency of giving direction to science and technology; that specifies correctives for the failure of affluence to spill over into the public sector (exclusive of defense); that is, as Professor Heilbroner has said, holistic or global in its aim and above all, one that will be genuinely instrumental in its application of human intelligence.

It is against this background that one must establish the need for a fresh approach to the science of economics. Basic to such an approach would be the realization that there really are no *a priori* behavior statements: everything must be specified and always subjected to critical examination. Investigation must start with an aetiology or a statement of what exists initially. Then one can shift to a consideration of what would be desirable, employing propositions about moving the economy from the initial state to the desired one. There is a marked difference between so radical an approach and traditional methodology in that behavioral premises cannot be merely accepted, but must be subjected to continual test.[43]

The hypotheses involved would acquire fresh significance, for there would be an attempt to relate them to goal-seeking behavior. In a sense, one works regressively, as in solving a problem in plane geometry, by moving backwards to establish the instrumentalities that might be employed to reach an economic goal. To be sure, there are many unknowns in this approach. We need to know the behavior patterns of individuals and firms; we need to know the motivations that give rise to these patterns; we need to know the path that the system will take in reaching the specified goal; we need to know the character of the parameters that are embedded in the meta-economy.

Needless to say, the goal itself is not subject to empirical observation, and indeed if the economy fails to attain its objective, the goal may never be observed. Clearly this takes us into the judgmental area, but it is one that economists need not fear to explore. For, it is perfectly possible to specify the conditions for a social decision process based on some sort of collective rationality stemming from a social ordering of preferences.[44] There are problems, certainly. Questions may be asked as to who decides on the nature of the social ordering. Or what is the metaeconomic set by which the orderings may be confirmed or tested? And how do the institutions of the society exert their influences on choice?

Now, we do have some understanding of the technical means by which resources and facilities can be arranged to obtain optimum results. Thus the relation of goals to instrumentalities is mainly a "technological" matter. But our society is inhibited in clearly establishing these relationships by the exigencies of politics or by the ideology of some defunct economist. Assuming that our "technical" information is fairly advanced, then it ought to be sufficient to describe the paths available to a rational society. Embedded in this approach would be an appreciation of the motivations and psychology of the economic actors. These notions presuppose that economics is concerned not only with the confrontation of man and matter but also by the confrontation of man and man, for surely the latter relationships are also economic.

If the relationship of man to machine is fundamentally a question of technology and its impacts, then the confrontation of man and man is a matter of the behavior to which the confrontation gives rise. In a stationary economy it takes little more than following established rules of production to maintain equilibrium. The motivations for such routine behavior would stem from inelastic expectations based on a kind of stabilizing feedback mechanism. The behavior patterns and motivations can be rigorously defined in such a model.[45]

But in a complex world such a model is simple-minded. One needs rather information on motivations, social organization, rules of production, and above all where we want to head. With these data we can describe a path that brings us close to the target. One does not suggest that such an approach would display full predictability. It cannot be assumed that all the forces at play will move the economy along desirable paths unless specific action is taken to provide the necessary motivations and behavior patterns.

My argument essentially is an appeal for a social economics. More and more, the so-called free goods of our society demand a price tag. The scarcities today are pure water, clean air, privacy, mental health, space, cities that are liveable, highways that are not parking lots — everything that the population explosion, industrialism, and urbanism are undermining and threatening to destroy. These are not mere esthetic scarcities: their lack vitiates our ability to enjoy rising levels of material abundance. How much utility does the consumer obtain when he must crawl in and out of town each Sunday in search of green pastures?[46]

If one wishes to describe such concerns as *political* economics, that will be acceptable, for social goals must be pursued in a context of political decision-making. The fact is that so many services are required in the public sector that we have already made large parts of the market mechanism otiose. I repeat, the choices in the public sector are political rather than economic. If this means active intervention in economic affairs, so be it. Haven't we been doing just that in greater or lesser degree ever since Alexander Hamilton's Report on Manufacturers? What were tariffs, land grants, and government subsidies for canals and railroads, if not interventionism? The War on Poverty, despite its patent failures, represented a shift from the market to the political process.

What sorts of cost would be generated as the economy moves along these paths? Great sums of money would have to be allocated to clean the air, purify the water, wipe out the slums, improve traffic flows, provide urban transportation, and control population densities. There will be auxiliary costs as well: industry might have to be relocated and livelihoods disturbed. But set against these costs would be the immense and perhaps immeasurable value of more healthful living, both physical and mental, decent recreational space, and the mitigation of the festering sores that now plague the cities.

Constraints abound, of course: there are numerous elements in society that tend to cancel each other. Human behavior at times confounds the best-intentioned of social scientists. But surely the goals of the public sector would be sufficiently in harmony with individual aspirations so that conflict between the two levels of behavior would be minimized. In any case, as the external diseconomies of the private sector become more and more intolerable, is it not likely that public sector macro goals and individual micro goals will have to come together?

Let me close with an anecdote about John Dewey. At the age of 90 he returned to Columbia University, where he had taught for many years, to lecture to a group of post-graduate students. In his address, he developed sadly the theme that philosophers had retreated to purely technical matters, while the world was facing violence, irrationality, and dogmatism. It was a difficult time, he said, to be a philosopher. Then he sat down, but quickly rose to his feet to add that he was afraid he had been too discouraging to young scholars just starting out. Perhaps it was a good time to be a philosopher, he remarked, for the old formulas, the old paradigms were not working. The challenge was to create a bold, new analysis, to venture creatively in thought. All it required, said Dewey, as he turned to take his seat once more, were ideas, imagination, and, he added, guts.[47]

FOOTNOTES

1. R. L. Heilbroner, *The Worldly Philosophers*, New York, 1953, p. 6.

2. cf. J. Robinson, *Freedom and Necessity*, London, 1970, p. 24.

3. cf. M. Gluckman, *Politics, Law, and Ritual in Tribal Society*, Chicago, 1965 and R. Firth, ed., *Themes in Economic Anthropology*, London, 1967.

4. T. S. Kuhn, *The Structure of Scientific Revolutions*, Chicago, 1962.

5. cf. P. A. Samuelson, *Collected Scientific Papers*, V. 2, Cambridge, 1966, pp. 1499 ff.

6. A. A. Lowe, *On Economic Knowledge*, New York, 1965, pp. 165 ff.

7. cf. R. Firth and B. S. Yamey, eds., *Capital, Saving, and Credit in Peasant Societies*, London, 1964, pp. 20-23; M. Rostovtzeff, *A History of the Ancient World*, V. 1, London, 1925, pp. 197, 218, 316.

8. cf. E. Voegelin, *The World of the Polis*, Baton Rouge, 1957, p. 333.

9. Plato, *Laws*, 679.

10. Aristotle, *Nicomachean Ethics*, 1133.

11. Plato, *Statesman*, 259, 285.

12. cf. J. Wild, *Plato's Theory of Man*, Cambridge, 1948, pp. 101 ff.

13. *Laws*, 709 a-e, 732 e, 733 c; *Republic*, Bk. 9, 583 ff.

14. *Republic*, 443 c, d, 590 c; *Laws*, 918 b; *Philebus*, 55, 56.

15. cf. Voegelin, *Plato and Aristotle*, Baton Rouge, 1957, pp. 289 ff.

16. Aristotle, *Politics*, 1259 b ff, 1304b.

17. *N. Ethics*, 1131 a 30 ff, 1132 b 33; *Politics*, 1257 b 15, 1261 a 14, 1263 a ff, 1266 b 5, 1330 a.

18. cf. W. Jaeger, *Early Christianity and Greek Paideia*, Cambridge, 1961; H. O. Taylor, *The Medieval Mind*, V. 1, London, 1911, pp. 11 ff.

19. cf. H. Meyer, *The Philosophy of St. Thomas Aquinas*, London, 1944; D. J. O'Connor, *Aquinas and Natural Law*, London, 1967.

20. T. Veblen, *The Place of Science in Modern Civilization*, New York, 1919; cf. also D. Hamilton, *Evolutionary Economics*, Albuquerque, 1970.

21. J. Gilchrist, *The Church and Economic Activity in the Middle Ages*, New York, 1969.

22. R. de Roover, "Scholastic Economics: Its Survival and Lasting Influence", *Quarterly Journal of Economics*, March, 1955, pp. 188ff.

23. cf. P. Gay, *The Enlightenment*, V. 2, New York, 1969, p. 457.

24. cf. A. L. Macfie, *The Individual in Society*, London, 1957, pp. 71ff; J. Viner, "Adam Smith and Laissez-Faire", *Journal of Political Economy*, April, 1927, pp. 198ff.

25. G. R. Morrow, *The Ethical and Economic Theories of Adam Smith*, New York, 1923, p. 8.

26. *ibid,* p. 41.
27. A. Marshall, *Principles of Economics,* Variorum Edition, 1961, Bk. 1, ch. 1.
28. cf. E. Halevy, *The Growth of Philosophical Radicalism,* London, 1949, pp. 479ff.
29. A. W. Gouldner, *The Coming Crisis of Western Sociology,* New York, 1970, pp. 61ff.
30. cf. F. Stern, *The Politics of Cultural Despair,* Berkeley, 1961.
31. cf. R. L. Heilbroner, *Between Capitalism and Socialism,* New York, 1970, pp. 117ff.
32. cf. A. O. Hirschman, *Exit, Voice, and Loyalty,* Cambridge, 1970.
33. cf. C. Levi-Strauss, *Structural Anthropology,* New York, 1963.
34. R. Hofstadter, *Social Darwinism in American Thought,* Philadelphia, 1944, pp. 31ff.
35. cf. J. Dorfman, *The Economic Mind in American Civilization,* Vol. 3, New York, 1949, pp. 188ff.
36. E. Kauder, "The Retarded Acceptance of Marginal Utility Theory", *Quarterly Journal of Economics,* Nov. 1953, pp. 564ff.
37. F. H. Knight, *Freedom and Reform,* New York, 1947, pp. 231ff.
38. *idem, Ethics of Competition,* London, 1935, pp. 40, 42ff.
39. cf. *idem,* "Economics and Anthropology", *Journal of Political Economy,* June, 1941, pp. 247ff.
40. *idem, Intelligence and Democratic Action,* Cambridge, 1960, p. 124.
41. cf. F. A. Hayek, *The Sensory Order,* London, 1952.
42. cf. A. Schutz, *The Phenomenology of the Social World,* Evanston, 1967, pp. 97ff.
43. cf. A. A. Lowe, *On Economic Knowledge,* New York, 1965.
44. K. Arrow, *Social Choice and Individual Values,* New York, 1951.
45. Heilbroner, *Between Capitalism and Socialism,* pp. 165 ff.
46. cf. J. K. Galbraith, *The Affluent Society,* Boston, 2nd edition, 1969.
47. I. Edman, "America's Philosopher Attains an Alert 90", *New York Times Magazine,* October 16, 1949.

The Philosophy of Science and Alternative Approaches to Economic Thought

R.C. Linstromberg

In 1935 Lionel Robbins stated that the appropriate area of concern for economists is that provided by the scarcity of means by which given ends can be achieved.[1] He added that no economist is by profession qualified to choose among ends. As Lawrence Nabers pointed out, Robbins played a role in purging economics of a concern with ends, and this has led to increased emphasis "upon the logical structure of economic science abstracted from questions of morality and policy."[2] An important result has been the transformation of the history of economic thought from a crucial component of the discipline to the status of an "important embellishment," a transformation Robbins himself decried in 1955 (apparently without recognizing that elimination of concern with ends must lead to this result).[3]

This transformation testifies to the position of strength currently held by the absolutists *vis á vis* the economic profession. The technically oriented, mechanical view of reality that characterizes the absolutist approach now appears to have been accepted by the profession.[4]

Absolutists typically insist that the scientific purity of economics requires that its propositions be value free, and that its theorems be analyzed and evaluated only in terms of internal consistency and ability to describe objective reality. While some absolutists recognize the temporality of objective institutions, all reject the notion that norms might be subject to change. The absolutist approach to economic thought can be characterized by four propositions:

The author is Associate Professor of Economics at Bradley University, Peoria, Illinois.
He renders his thanks to Douglas Thorson, William Henderson, Kalman Goldberg, William Belmont, and Linda Metzler for their comments and criticism but emphasizes that any remaining deficiencies are solely his own responsibility.

[1]Lionel Robbins, *The Nature and Significance of Economic Science*, second edition, London, 1935, p. 24.

[2]Lawrence Nabers, "The Positive and Genetic Approaches," in *The Structure of Economic Science*, Englewood Cliffs, New Jersey, 1966, pp. 70-71. As Nabers indicates, such questions have been traditional concern of economists.

[3]Lionel Robbins, *The Theory of Economic Policy*, London, 1955, p. 1.

[4]Although there are a few economists who regret the fact, as this statement by Sumner Slichter attests: "aversion to appraisals" is one of the major reasons "to which is to be attributed the failure of theorists to perceive the supreme importance today of the problem of organization and control of economic activity."

1. Economic theory deals with facts that are verifiable, either by observation or by experiment.
2. The only method to be used is that of logical inference from facts so verified.
3. The scientific character of analytic work is independent of the motives for undertaking it.
4. The only criteria available to analysts of past economic thought are those provided by analysis for congruence with reality and for internal consistency, using contemporary standards as a yardstick. (Failure to consider ends almost inevitably leads to judgment on the basis of congruence of that thought with contemporary ends.)

Development of economic thought is perceived by absolutists as movement from error to truth. Old theory is either internally inconsistent, based upon erroneously perceived fact, or may be still relevant. (In the latter case no movement is involved.) In short, a theory valid at one time is valid for all time. As Blaug put it, "The absolutist looking down from present heights at the errors of the ancients, cannot help but conclude that truth is concentrated in the marginal increment to economic knowledge."[5] Fittingly, Blaug opens his book on past economic thought with the statement "This is a study of the theories of the past, not of theorists and their time."[6] Neither the conditions existing at the time the theorist worked nor the experiences, predilictions, influences, or training of the theorists can have any meaning to the absolutist. Hence, according to Stigler, environmental theories are little more than platitudes, social and development theories are untenable, and economics generally is fittingly unaffected either by social change of a contemporary nature or by developments in other fields.[7]

Relativists urge a more eclectic approach, an approach that introduces values explicitly into the analysis. They argue that the narrower approach of absolutists render those theories incapable of dealing with theorems possessing a normative base, making it necessary for them to ignore important aspects of the development of economic thought. In addition, relativists insist that the temporality of objective institutions necessitates changing norms.

Thus one of the leading relativists, Leo Rogin, opened his book on past economic thought with the statement that "the claim to validity of economic theory is best explored not in terms of a direct appeal to fact but by appeal to fact through the requirements of practice—of economic

[5]Mark Blaug, *Economic Theory in Retrospect*, Homewood, Illinois, 1962, p. 4.

[6]*Ibid.*, p. 1.

[7]George Stigler, *Essays in the History of Economics*, 1965, pp. 16-22. It must be added that his "proofs" are less than powerful.

policy."[8] He pointed out that economic science had not been dedicated to discovery of new facts, but rather had been concerned with derivation of the implications of a relatively small number of known facts.[9] Also, according to Rogin, systems developed in economics have typically been conceived in terms of a degree of homogeneity, simplicity, and discreetness foreign to the real world. Both the definition of problems appropriate for study and the method used in classifying facts have contributed to this result. And, no less important in later discussions, the requirement that a determinate conclusion must follow from the analysis imposed a further constraint upon the data.[10] From this Rogin drew two conclusions: First, systems constructed within this context reflected data incapable of any but relatively simple and unambiguous implication; second, the data, and their organization, form the premises of deductive models, with conclusions following neatly from the premises.[11]

It was but a step further to Rogin's insistence that "mere correspondence between the premises of a theory and the complex and devious flux of historical experience is hardly the criterion of a theory's pretentions to validity."[12] The only meaningful criteria of a theory, as Rogin saw it, are (1) that the premises of a theory must relate to and be adequate to all relevant facts, and (2) that the theory must be relevant to guidance of policy as related to some practical issue in which the interest of society is involved. Use of other criteria makes is impossible to evaluate normative models, and such models constitute an important part of those developed over the years.

Normative models have been used traditionally as a means of classifying real world institutions as normal or abnormal. Those institutions classified as abnormal are treated as perversions, the result either of external nature or of perverse human nature. Recommendations flowing from normative theory are usually aimed at elimination of those perversions. But, as I. M. D. Little pointed out, speaking in reference to welfare theory, "I know of no serious attempts to test its realism, perhaps because there are no obvious tests."[13] Little suggested that since empirical tests

[8]Leo Rogin, *The Meaning and Validity of Economic Theory,* New York, 1965, p. 2.

[9]*Ibid.,* p. 2. And Stigler has said that the boundaries of economics have not widened appreciably since Smith. (It is probably more nearly correct to say that the boundaries have narrowed.)

[10]Data suggesting instability, discontinuity, and so forth, must be excluded in models to explain their opposites. Anything of a qualitative nature must inevitably be excluded.

[11]Rogin. Hans Brems makes this last an integral part of his definition of theory. Hans Brems, *Output, Employment, Capital, and Growth,* New York, 1959, p. 1

[12]*Ibid.,* pp. 2-3.

[13]I. M. D. Little, *A Critique of Welfare Theory,* London, 1957, p. 4. None of this is meant to imply that normative theorists are relativists. In fact, the contrary is usually more accurate.

of the conclusions of welfare theory are not practicable one is forced to evaluate the assumptions. Little comes close to the relativist position.

The relativists go further arguing that descriptions of reality provided by welfare theory can be best judged through use of two tests. First, is it really possible to eliminate the perversion specified by the theory, given existing political, social, and technological conditions? Second, if it is possible to eliminate the perversion, would positive action in the real world occasion the result specified by the theory?[14] Negative answers to either or both questions would be sufficient to cast doubt upon the validity of the theory.

It seems clear from the foregoing that Blaug's charge that, for relativists, all theory is at least in principle justified as partially correct.[15] The relevance of policy depends upon the needs of society at a moment in time. Those needs change as the structure and circumstance of society change. Since the test of theory is its policy relevance, an economic theory valid at one time may be irrelevant and invalid at other times, and vice versa. Thus the validity of theory is relative to time, place, and condition. For the relativist, the skill of an economist lies at least as much in his ability to select the right theory for the right problem as in his ability to develop theory. For the relativist, the study of past economic thought is as much study of the conditions under which theory was developed and applied as of the theory itself.

Of perhaps greater importance, as the ends of society change so must the theory. This follows since the underlying ends of a society condition the assumptions underlying the theory. Only if one assumes immutability of ends is one able to adopt the absolutist approach.

ADAM SMITH AND THE DEVELOPMENT OF ECONOMIC THOUGHT

The statement by Stigler that economics has been fittingly uninfluenced by developments in fields outside economics is quite provocative. It also has relevance to analysis of the debate between the absolutists and relativists. While it is probably correct to say that it has been some time since the main body of economic thought has been directly influenced by other fields, it was not so in the earlier years of the discipline; and those influences still affect its form and method. Adam Smith, for example, was strongly affected by developments in the natural sciences, scientific method, philosophy, political thought, and so forth. And, through Smith, these influences permeated economics and its method. Consequently, they are important determinants of judgment in the debate under analysis.

The economy Adam Smith described was a "rational Capitalist" econ-

[14]Little raised both questions, and placed himself squarely in the relativist camp on this point.

[15]Blaug, p. 2.

omy in which the perversions of feudalism and monopoly had been removed. In this sense, he described an ideal economy rather than a real one; and his model was normative. As Herbert Thomson so aptly suggested, this designation is reinforced by Smith's identification of consumption as the "final cause," of economic activity.[16]

Smith adopted from Aristotle the notion of purposeful nature, and so the conception of consumption as the final cause of economic activity was crucial to analysis of Smith's worth (and, to the extent that this bias carries over into subsequent work, to analysis of post-Smithian theory). Aristotle held that things develop toward ends internal to their own natures. Therefore, a full explanation of anything requires an analysis of not only the material, the formal, and the efficient causes of the thing, but also the purpose for which the thing exists or was produced. That is, an account must be given of the thing's final cause; its end. Thus, there is a natural teleology; a purpose in nature. By implication, one has only to identify the final cause and the force which propels toward the final cause if one is to identify the unifying force in nature. Smith identified the final cause of economic activity as consumption, and found the propelling force in man's "natural" desire to improve his position according to his own self-interest.[17]

The systematic form of Smith's work derived from Newton. Newton created a theory of celestial mechanics that gave rise to the concept of a "world" machine. Classical physics conceived of the universe as a mechanical system, and propounded "natural laws" regulating the motion of physical bodies within the context of this system. According to Lensen, philosophers, under the influence of the mechanical view of the universe that Newton's theories engendered and expanded a theory of the mechanical universe into a theory of materialism as a theory of reality.[18] And, as Thomson demonstrated, Smith was one of the philosophers so influenced.[19] Smith viewed systems as little machines; in which apparently disconnect-

[16]Herbert Thomson, "Adam Smith's Philosophy of Science," *The Quarterly Journal of Economics*, Vol. LXXIX, No. 2, May 1965, p. 230. Notice, however, that this constitutes a reinforcement; not, as Professor Thomson implies, the entire basis for the characterization.

[17]When economists talk of excluding consideration of ends from their analysis, they frequently seem to forget that ends such as this one are a basic part of their analytic framework. Now this is not to say that perspectival statements are incorrect if their proponent both recognizes and allows for their partial nature. The danger lies in the fact that ends not made explicit may lead to assumptions that the theories are a complete representation of the phenomena under examination.

[18]Victor Lensen, "The Philosophy of Science," in D. D. Runes, *Living Schools of Philosophy*, Ames, Iowa, 1958, p. 160.

[19]Thomson.

ed phenomena were tied together by one central connecting principle—defined in terms of material status.[20]

Aristotle provided teleology, Newton provided systematic form, but Descartes and Montesquieu provided method. In the *Discourses* Descartes set forth five methodological precepts:

1. Never accept anything as true not known to be so.
2. Divide the analysis into as many parts as possible and as might be necessary for adequate solution.
3. Conduct the examination in such a way that, by starting with the easiest to understand, one is able to move to the increasingly complex.
4. Order must be assigned even to those objects which do not, in themselves, possess antecedence or sequence.
5. Always make enumeration so complete and review so general that one is reasonably certain nothing has been overlooked.

The precepts of most interest to us are the third and fourth. The third precept implies that one must abstract simple models before one can successfully develop those that are more complex. There is some reason to believe that much of what passes for normative economics, including parts of Smith's work, is really the abstraction involved in the "first step" simple model. The fourth precept suggests that scientific work will always have a tentative and temporal quality. If one is to assign order to things not possessing an inherent order initially, as new facts become available, either through discovery or through change, the nature of the assigned order is subject to change.[21]

This brings us to Montesquieu. *The Spirit of the Laws,* an exposition of the historical and evolutionary development of legal and political forms, provided Smith with a model of the historical method. In addition, Montesquieu reinforced the impact of Descartes upon Smith (for Montesquieu, too, was a devotee of the Cartesian method); his major contributions to Smith being his historical approach to science and a particular view of social development.

In *The Spirit of the Laws,* Montesquieu dealt with historical development of societies and with changes within those societies in the light of a variety of objective factors. This approach, as Schumpeter suggested,

[20]See H. Becker and H. E. Barnes, *Social Thought From Lore to Science,* New York, 1961, p. 364. English Diests and French Philosophers based their theories upon the notion that natural laws govern both the physical and the social universe.

[21]If this interpretation is correct, then the position taken by the absolutists, for example, that economic science moves from error to truth, is quite tenuous. Rather, economic theory involves movement from old truth to new truth; or, at best, from partial truth to fuller truth. In any event, changes in the order assigned to internal variables bring about necessary alterations in theoretical structures over time.

yielded realistic explanations and potential analytic theories, but no simple nor rationalist general theory.[22] Schumpeter went on to point out that this was a new departure and significant break with natural law ideas, being based upon individual temporal and local patterns rather than merely upon general properties of human nature.[23]

According to Montesquieu, each society has a specific structure; a structure that derives from the society's own inner logic. Facts are necessary if one is to grasp this inner logic, but a society cannot be viewed simply as an aggregate of facts. That is, it cannot be comprehended simply by collecting data and sifting that which is relevant from that which is irrelevant. Rather, a societal type is an expression of a structure that can only be understood by reading into the facts a meaning that reveals the principles underlying their place in the structure called society. Each type of society was viewed as possessing one unifying and integrating principle, and all phenomena were to be interpreted in terms of this principle.

It follows, then, that historical laws of change flow from this structural concept. Change in one element of the structure results in change of the total structure. Hence, society is both an agent of change and the result of change. And laws are seen as the logical extension of the internal logic of a given societal type. There are, however, no laws of a general nature covering all societal types.[24]

Both Marx and Marshall spoke approvingly of the marriage of history and theory that was integral to Smith's method.[25] Rogin also praised Smith for having provided a "theory of natural economic development which he imposes as a norm upon the historical career of nations since their emergence from the feudal period."[26] And James Bonar said, with reference to the *Theory of Moral Sentiments,* "What Smith proposed to achieve was not merely a treatise on political philosophy and a treatise on economics, but a complete moral and political philosophy in which the two elements of history and theory were to be closely conjoined."[27] This suggests that Smith thoroughly understood the Montesquieuan point, namely, that while economic science involves study of facts, facts are so

[22]Joseph A. Schumpeter, *History of Economic Analysis,* London, 1948, p. 136.

[23]*Ibid.*

[24]It is clear that if the system should change from one type to another, the internal logic of the system should also change. Change in the internal logic requires discovery of the new connecting principle. The relativist implications are striking.

[25]It is interesting to note that only Smith and Marx used the historical method consistently. Perhaps unfortunately, the profession did not absorb this aspect of Smith, although the relativists have typically urged it.

[26]Rogin, p. 76.

[27]James Bonar, *Philosophy and Political Economy,* London, 1927, p. 5.

complex that their direct study is fruitless until they have been interpreted in their historical context.[28]

Absolutists argue that philosophic influence are irrelevant for judgment of an economist's work and, so, these influences are ignored by them. But Smith provides us with an excellent example of the way understanding of philosophic influences may clarify economic understanding. One of Smith's close friends was David Hume, and most economic historians agree that Hume exerted some influence upon Smith's thought. Hume urged utilization of a free market system on the basis that only such a system could raise the material level of living conditions, and only improvement in living conditions could bring about desired improvement in the moral tone of society. Only so could the "coarse and baleful aspects of acquisitiveness be made to disappear and honor and justice be allowed to take their place."[29] For Hume, the end of economic activity was development of a more moral society, with the development of free markets was viewed as a means to higher economic development. In turn, the latter was the means to the higher end.[30] There is evidence that Smith concurred in this view. *The Theory of Moral Sentiments* suggests that moral society depends upon economic development, the idea that economic development requires free markets is explicit in *The Wealth of Nations*.[31]

This points up one of the major areas of difference between the absolutists and the relativists. According to the latter, it is impossible to reach a valid judgment concerning a theory without consideration of its ends. Would the system Smith envisioned lead to improved living standards or would it lead instead to perpetual regeneration of the aspect of human

[28]Given Smith's recognition of the evolutionary aspects of economic systems, his view that his work represented an attack upon the mercantile system—by his time dying and of doubtful validity for contemporary England, and hence unrealistic—is not inconsistent with the view that his work was descriptive. Thomson, for example, urged that this was the basis for Rogin's insistence that Smith's work was essentially normative. In the light of what has been said above, this seems to be unfair to Rogin.

[29]Charles W. Hendel, *David Hume's Political Essays,* New York, 1953.

[30]This view of morality is quite different from that typically held prior to Hume. The previous view was that a source of *immorality* was concern with economic activity. In fact, morality was seen as based in ability to rise above worldly concerns.

[31]This is not a contradiction of the previous statement that Smith viewed consumption as the end of economic activity, for improvement in the capacity of the economy to produce consumption goods is the object of economic development, and rising living standards were to provide the fulcrum freeing men from the pressures of economic want. Absolutists argue that Smith's reasons for advocating free markets are irrelevant. What matters to them is the extent to which his theories "hang together" and describe reality. But relativists insist that this can lead to faulty conclusions.

nature selected by Smith as the unifying principle of his system?[32] The answer hinges upon the ability of competitive markets to remain competitive, and to bring about innovation and growth capable of improving living conditions.[33] If the answer to *either* or *both* of these questions is negative, Smith's model is invalid. If the answer to both is affirmative, then, other things remaining equal, his model is valid. Thus, if Joseph Schumpeter were correct in his assessment of the results of perfect comptition (with reference to its innovative aspects and its ability to generate meaningful economies of scale), the response to the second criterion is negative.[34] Smith's model would lead to little more than regeneration of the acquisitive aspects of self-interest by perpetuating the conditions under which this aspect of man is promoted. And, if an assessment made by Kalman Goldberg and myself of the tendency for economic power to coalesce is correct, the reaction to the first criterion is also negative.[35] In either case, Smith's model fails the test of policy. It would lead neither to attainment of welfare maximization over time nor to a more moral society (given the assumed nexus between morality and improved living conditions). Hence, by relativist standards, Smith's model is invalid.[36]

Economics has been influenced, through Smith at any rate, by a number of other fields. These influences have been exerted in ways that have had a direct effect upon the direction and form of analysis. Some of these influences have shaped the economist's view of the economic universe, some have conditioned his method of analysis, some have helped to form his concept of man.[37]

The introduction of the Newtonian view of the universe into economics has led to adoption of a mechanical approach to the subject, thus providing justification of the absolutist approach. One either explains how a machine runs or one does not. Even a complicated machine has only one pattern of operation. Speed can be varied, perhaps, and the flow of out-

[32]This raises an interesting question. Do social scientists, by describing man as he is in a particular social context, help create—or at least perpetuate—that kind of man. Floyd Matson, in his interesting book *Broken Image,* New York, 1966, suggests they do.

[33]It is important to note that Smith's advocacy of free markets was based upon his appreciation of the role played by enlargement of markets and application of the methods of specialization and division of labor.

[34]Joseph A. Schumpeter, *Capitalism, Socialism, and Democracy,* third edition, New York, 1950.

[35]Kalman Goldberg and Robin C. Linstromberg, "A Revision of Some Theories of Economic Power," *Quarterly Review of Economics and Business,* Vol. 6, No. 1, Spring 1966, pp. 7-17.

[36]First, it is impossible to eliminate perversions of competition; second, even if the perversions could be eliminated, projected results would not follow.

[37]It is clear that the full range of influences have not been covered. The Stoic influence on concepts of individualism, the impact of the Protestant Ethic, the Utilitarian outgrowth of Natural Law doctrines, and the influence of Darwin have all been ignored.

put altered, but the machine itself is invariant. If one has explained its operation correctly at one point in time, that explanation holds with only minor variation for all time. Since a machine is a static structure, its analysis is appropriately conducted in static terms.[38]

Of perhaps greater importance, although not entirely unrelated to the foregoing, the notion of an internal teleology leads to a search for central principles. This search conditions one to utilization of equilibrium concepts, especially when coupled with a concept of universal order. In consequence, one is led inescapably to analysis with internal logic. Ends become irrelevant because the inexorable working out of the universal order has its own end.

The Montesquieuan notion of identification of a specific structure for each specific type of society has its counterpart in economics. Economists have typically concentrated their attention upon an economy organized around free markets and have bent their efforts to the explication of a perceived structure for that type of economy. In consequence they have been led to attempts at cataloguing elemental changes leading to different structures. Thus, they speak of a "spectrum" of structures, ranging from perfect competition on the one hand to perfect monopoly on the other. But only seldom does one find explicit discussion of the forces causing structures to change;[39] nor, in the absence of consideration of ends, is one likely to. Further, a failure to utilize the historical approach poses an additional barrier.

On balance, given the orientation of contemporary and relatively contemporary economics, the absolutist approach has become the dominant mode in the discipline. But, if economics is viewed in a different light, the relativistic approach becomes more relevant.

THE "NEW" SCIENCE AND EXISTENTIALISM

Classical and neo-classical economic thought has traditionally centered around study of the impersonal mechanism understood to lie at the heart of an economy. And, in spite of important modifications, Keynesian and neo-Keynesian economics have retained their orientation.[40] This sym-

[38]It can be argued, I think, that at least a part of the difficulty in developing a "dynamic" explanation of economic activity stems from the fact that the overall view of economists has been static in the above sense.

[39]In fact, if one overlooks the Institutionailsts and the Historicists, one must conclude that the profession is uninterested in such problems.

[40]Harvey Bunke, "Economics, Affluence, and Existentialism," *The Quarterly Review of Economics and Business*, Vol. 4, No. 2, Summer 1964, pp. 9-16, suggests that Keynes represented a first step away from the old concepts in that he pointed out that the automaticity of the market mechanism was an historical fiction, that the market was nothing more than an unruly machine without purpose or goal except as man's intellect gave it direction and meaning. Bunke also recognized that the profession largely ignored the philosophic meaning of Keynes' work.

bolizes the felt relationship between the world of Newtonian physics and the world of man that has permeated the discipline since its inception. Newtonian physics posited certainty of knowledge and, particularly, the certainty of causal relationships and their effects. And, of course, it follows in this view that there is logic and meaning in these relationships.

But a new science has developed during the past one hundred years, a science that uses such terms as "uncertainty," "indeterminacy," "complementarity," "personality of knowledge," and so forth. New philosophy has arisen, one that contradicts the philosophic premise of absolutist economics, namely, that essence precedes existence. And these two forces have led to increased understanding of the basic distinction between the natural and social sciences, that is, that the natural sciences deal with causal processes objectively perceived while the social sciences are concerned with meaningful relations that become comprehensible only through understanding based upon insight. The new science is arising out of developments in the field of physics; the new philosophy is Existentialism.[41]

From the time of its inception the machine concept of the universe had its critics. But they were typically from "outside" science, and their objections were beaten back as simply expressions of "anti-scientific" attitudes.[42] Toward the end of the nineteenth century, however, criticism began to arise from within science itself. James C. Maxwell's theory of electro-magnetism shook the foundations of the notion of absolute certainty, and Maxwell was led to suggest that the study of "singularities and instabilities" might cause scientists to drop their prejudice in favor of determinism, a prejudice deriving from the mechanical view.[43]

The Newtonian view was limited still further by publication of Einstein's special and general theories of relativity. Now space and time could no longer be viewed as conceptually absolute and independent entities; and science could no longer propose to be both an explanation for nature as a whole and of the essence of things. "The propositions of nature acquired their validity only from the limited aspects of nature they described."[44] The non-mechanical, non-material view of the universe had begun to find its way into the main body of scientific literature and

[41]One gets to many of the same conclusions through examination of the implications of Darwinian concepts as through examination of new physics, but limitations imposed by space force these similarities to be omitted. This means, of course, that the work done by Institutionalists, motivated as they were by Darwinian concepts, is unfortunately slighted here.

[42]This was the fate of the Historicists in Europe, and the attack of the Institutionalists—based largely upon Darwinian influences—was blunted by the continued appeal to Newtonian concepts.

[43]Maxwell's work generally raised the possibility that all scientific knowledge, even that concerning familiar Newtonian entities, consisted only of an understanding of the mathematical structure of things.

[44]Matson, p. 117.

knowledge and Sir James Jean was led to suggest that "the universe begins to look more like a great thought than a great machine."[45]

But the final blow to the mechanistic view fell with Dr. Max Planck's formulation of the proposition that energy, once thought to be emitted in a continuous stream, is emitted instead in discontinuous "quanta." For it was now perceived that not only was energy incapable of representation in the mechanical model, but that there is a basic discontinuity at the heart of things. The Newtonian concept of a continuous chain of causally related events was seen to be a chimera.

Out of these developments emerged two crucial principles: the principle of uncertainty and the principle of complementarity.[46] Two important conclusions flow from the uncertainty principle. First, it is impossible to determine whether initial states determine future states. Therefore, the existence of rigorous casual connections cannot be tested, and scientific statement becomes statement of probabilities, not certainties. Second, attempts to define data change them. Newtonian physics was based upon a notion of nature apart from man. Man could observe nature, therefore, without affecting it.[47] But now the act of observation had to be viewed as an act of participation. The thing observed became an ineffable part of both the observer and the observation. In essence, the Heisenberg principle stipulated that the course of nature cannot be observed without disturbing it, and the choices of the observer determined the form in which nature appears.

The principle of complementarity deals with the relationship between mutually antagonistic but cognate phenomena. It suggests that there are complementary but mutually exclusive situations incapable of being described by the same concepts, and requiring, therefore, two separate kinds of expressions. In the words of Matson, "the crucial meaning of complementarity in the context of human affairs . . . is that of the mutually exclusive but peculiarly cognate relationship between the traditional scientific method of 'cause and mechanism' and the traditional humanistic method of purposes and reasons."[48] It is impossible to describe reality with either method in isolation, but it is also impossible to use both simultaneously.

The principle of uncertainty indicates that there are limits to our ability to know and predict aspects of nature. It suggests that nature may even be irrational and chaotic; it stresses the personality of science and of the

[45]Sir James Jean, *The Mysterious Universe,* as cited by Matson, *Ibid.*, p. 122.

[46]The first is attributed to Werner Heisenberg; the second to Niels Bohr.

[47]This same view is expressed in the dictum that economics describes, not human behavior, but the behavior of economic variables. The implication is that these variables, being insensate, do not respond to the explanation.

[48]Matson, p. 135.

scientist.[49] The principle of complementarity implies that we cannot know all things at once. In fact, it suggests that a choice to know more about one thing bars us from knowledge of another aspect of that thing. The *hubris* of Newtonian physics collapses. And this had led to what Existentialists have referred to as the encounter with nothingness. As they have seen more clearly than most people, if we are unable to expect certainty in the physical universe how much less likely it is that certainty exists in human affairs.

It is clear that Existential thought does not stem merely from a notion that *God* is dead. *Certainty* is dead, and the death of certainty is part of the Existential theme.[50] With the death of certainty has come awareness of the finitude of man; and out of this awareness has come understanding that man's existence is posited in untruth as well as in truth.[51] And the Existentialists have been quick to point out that man's institutions are *man's* constructs. There is nothing "natural" about them; they work because man wills them to work.

When certainty died so did stability and security as well as the easy assurance that rationality provided a sound base for value systems and modes of judgment. Notions of inner dialectics, working out of logical possibilities, and of historical laws lost relevance, and emphasis shifted to the role of existential factors in the formation of thought. And awareness increased that thought cannot be judged apart from those factors. This suggests that man's ideas can best be explained and evaluated in terms of social ideals, fears, aspirations, and the objective possibilities open to both the individual and his society.[52] All of these must be considered within the context of existing modes of production, class structures, stage of development, and legal structures. As Karl Mannheim has suggested, one is able to characterize a human situation only when one understands the view participants have of it, when one understands the kind of tensions they feel in that situation, and when one understands the way

[49]This forces us to hark back to an earlier question. By describing man as he is, or seems to be, in particular settings and situations, do social scientists help to create or perpetuate that kind of man? The implication here is that they do.

[50]It can be argued that the death of God and the death of certainty are the same thing. I suggest, however, that Enlightenment Man possessed a sense of certainty apart from a God concept, deriving as it did from science.

[51]William Barrett, *Irrational Man,* New York, 1962, pp. 267-280. As he says on page 279, " . . . it is not his reason that makes man man, but rather that reason is a consequence of that which really makes him man. For it is man's existence as a self-transcending self that has forged and formed reason as one of its projects."

[52]This does not suggest or imply historical determinism in the usual sense. There are no rules, no predictable causes and effects that enable us to predict future courses. The past can help us only by adding to our understanding of the reasons for adopting specific ways of viewing things.

they react to that situation.[53] Carried one step further, this implies that the same kind of understanding is required for comprehension of the characterization and for common judgment of its validity.

Yet, as Nabers pointed out, existential factors sometimes give rise to inconsistencies that result in the development of thoretical structures which delineate reality erroneously.[54] If a theoretical structure possesses implicit norms that result either in an orientation of analysis or in a selection of data leading to proposals for action incapable of justification in the context of existing social, political, or economic settings, that structure is false in consciousness, and is invalid.

The bodies of thought that have influenced the relativists stress the temporality and spatial limitations of theory. Relativists judge a theory on the basis of its relevance to the ends it is designed to serve, suggesting that those ends are subject both to change and to critical review. Most striking is the awareness that the observer is not nor can be neutral in his observations, and that his observations change that which he observes so that his method of observation has its own impact upon his object.[55]

All of this implies that understanding of man, his time, and the conditions and problems facing him are essential to understanding of his work. From this arises the need to expose the norms within the concepts, for they delineate the shape reality is expected to take.

CONCLUSION

The absolutist approach rests upon the fundamental assumption that a "natural" underlying order exists in human affairs. It is an assumption that enables absolutists to take norms as given. There appears to be a fundamentalist belief in the *externality* of both ends and norms, a belief which accords well with the mechanistic view of the universe typical of the absolutist. The acceptance of this view has led most absolutists to ignore the impact of changing institutions upon the phenomena they are attempting to explain. For example, most of Western economic analysis

[53]Karl Mannheim, *Man and Society in an Age of Reconstruction,* New York, 1950, pp. 39-40.

[54]Nabers, "The Positive Genetic Approaches." There are a wide variety of things which may lie at the heart of inconsistency. Lagging values, changing modes of production, changes in class structures, movement to a different stage of development, and so forth, all tend to create views of reality differing from objective facts.

[55]At a positive minimum the questions an observer decides to study are influenced by factors outside himself (apart from the questions themselves). Cultural factors, social factors, levels of technology, philosophic influences, and international events all act to call certain problems to the theorist's attention, and cause him to ignore others. All these forces cooperate to bring a theorist to a method of attack, and, potentially, to a conclusion.

takes private property as a given. The explanation offered for doing so is usually that Western economics aims at a explanation of an economic system based upon privacy in property. But it is rare indeed to find recognition in the literature of the fact that private property today is seldom the same thing as private property one hundred years ago.[56] Yet if the institution has undergone substantial change, it is unlikely to play the same role now as it did in its original form.[57]

Relativists start with the proposition that ends, norms, and institutions are all variables. They suggest, therefore, that at least part of the analysis of economic ideas ought to be directed at understanding man's ability to effect change and to the discovery of the impact of such changes upon the system. More than this, however, they argue that the theorist's biases, implied values, and attitudes must inevitably enter into his analysis. These determine the form of his observations, and these, in turn, help shape the thing observed. Hence the need to analyze the man as well as his work, that is, his ends as well as his means.

[56]A reading of David Bazelon, *The Paper Economy,* New York, 1963, will make this point more persuasive.

[57]This is a point that Schumpeter makes most explicit in *Capitalism, Socialism, and Democracy.*

Kuhnian Scientific Revolutions and the Keynesian Revolution

Ron Stanfield

"The most obvious way in which sciences advance is by new departures, that is, by the discovery of new facts, or new aspects of old facts, or new relations between facts. . . . But there is another way. When we use the concepts and theorems that we have inherited from our predecessors . . . [w]e add here and correct there and so this apparatus slowly develops into a different one."[1] It is the thrust of this article that the history of science paradigm provided by Thomas S. Kuhn is a useful framework for understanding the two developmental paths to which Joseph Schumpeter alludes.[2] In this view, the gradual development of the apparatus or paradigm is seen as a process of articulation, of exhausting the potential of that paradigm. In the process, the way is cleared for a new departure or scientific revolution—the installation of a new paradigm.

The procedure is to demonstrate the applicability of the Kuhnian paradigm to the new departure called the Keynesian revolution. To do so, the basic Kuhnian model is reviewed and compared with phenomena leading to and flowing from the watershed appearance of Keynes's *General Theory*.

The author is Assistant Research Environmental Economist, Center for Marine Affairs, University of California, San Diego. *He wishes to thank Tom Curtis of the University of Oklahoma, Norman, and a particularly thorough and tenacious anonymous reviewer for helpful comments on earlier drafts.*

The Structure of Scientific Revolutions

The basic stages of Kuhn's history of science paradigm are the following:[3] preparadigm; normal science; crisis and, possibly, extraordinary science; and normal science again once the crisis is resolved. The preparadigm stage is characterized by the existence of several competing schools of thought, each offering a potential paradigm, none of which are persuasive enough to gain the (near) universal acceptance associated with normal science. There is a lack of direction as to the research which should be done and as to the appropriate methods for doing it. Each competing group tends to seize upon a set of problems, facts, and methods. Published works take the form of extensive treatises which define and justify the scope and method of the research. There is thus a fundamental insecurity which is exemplified by the tendency to limit fact gathering to existent or easily accessible data. There is little incentive to exhume recondite data since there is no guide to assure its relevance once attained.[4] In short, although those in each school may be practicing science, taken as a whole, the sum of these schools does not form a science.[5]

When one of the competing schools, or a synthesis thereof, begins to attract ever larger shares of practitioners, the transition to normal or mature science is begun. Paradigms gain this acceptance by being considered more capable of solving a set of problems which have come to be accepted as the most important. The transition to normal science is marked by a withering away of competing schools, caused by conversion of old adherents, lack of recruits from a new generation, or simply *defining out* of the science the diehards who refuse to convert. The discipline also is given a narrower, more rigid definition. This more rigid definition changes the nature of scientific publications, as general books (except textbooks) are replaced by shorter articles or research reports addressed to the discipline which assume prior knowledge of the paradigm on the part of the reader. The textbook tradition also arises: Students learn from texts, not by using original sources. The discipline grows more insular, with its own standards and communications system, increasingly separated from the lay public.[6]

Normal science is achieved when the discipline more or less universally accepts the dominant paradigm, which then directs the practitioner as to the key questions and appropriate methods of normal research. Normal science is a period of paradigm articulation involving the manipulation of fact and theory to expand the scope and precision and resolve ambiguities of the paradigm.

Significantly, normal science is characterized by a *lack of intent* to uncover phenomenal or theoretical novelties. The accepted paradigm defines the appropriate problems to pursue and the procedures to be used for this pursuit, and it guarantees that solutions exist to the problems using these procedures. Normal science is puzzle-solving; when an experiment fails to produce the anticipated result, the puzzle solver, not the puzzle (paradigm), is considered inadequate.[7] This point is important because, as is shown below, scientific revolutions are rejections of paradigms which do not make good their guarantees.

A situation of crisis is the interruption of this normal science pattern. The existence of one or several anomalies is the first stage of such a crisis. An *anomaly* is a "violation of expectation" or failure of a set of paradigm puzzles to come out right. As such, an anomaly may be associated with conflicting experimental or empirical discoveries or with an insistent theoretical ambiguity which defies resolution by paradigm articulation. An anomaly may not lead to crisis; it may exist and be recognized but be considered peripheral. Or, the paradigm may be adjusted to resolve the anomaly. To evoke a crisis, an anomaly must, for example, question explicit, fundamental generalizations of the paradigm, be important to the solution of a pressing practical problem,[8] or involve a long history of persistently defying resolution within the paradigm.[9]

When, for these or other reasons, an anomaly becomes recognized as more than merely a difficult problem, the transition to crisis and extraordinary science occurs. More attention is afforded the anomaly, and it may come to be recognized as *the* subject matter of the discipline. The period of extraordinary science is similar in many ways to the preparadigm stage. There occur a relaxation of the rules of normal science and more speculative, random research. Increasingly divergent articulations occur which may involve the formation of schools of thought. This pattern often leads to an increase in discoveries and a shift to philosophical analyses or explicit methodological debates on the rules of the paradigm.[10] In essence, then, a disequilibrium state exists in which the discipline, as would any stable system, exhibits a search behavior by questioning structural institutions, evaluating received doctrine, and the like.

The period of extraordinary science ends in one of three ways. The anomaly may be resolved by normal science; it may resist all offered approaches, in which case the discipline accepts it as insoluble given the state of the arts; or a new paradigm may emerge and a battle for its acceptance ensues. In the last case, the ascension to dominance of a new paradigm is, of course, the consummation of a scientific revolution.

Several interesting features of scientific revolutions should be noted. First, the old paradigm is retained until and unless a new paradigm arises to replace it. To renounce that which defines the discipline without a redefinition is to renounce the discipline itself.[11]

Second, the new paradigm is not simply a cumulative process of attaching a new layer to the old foundation. Rather, it is the construction of a new foundation involving new fundamental laws, generalizations, and behavioral functions, often new methods and applications, and a redefinition of the character and standards of the science. The new paradigm is a change in world view to the extent that the world itself is changed: The perception and cognition of data and even the data to be collected are redefined.[12]

Third, scientific revolutions frequently are invisible due to the textbook tradition. Textbooks generally include only that past scientific work which is relevant to the current paradigm. This creates the accumulated knowledge illusion of a science since past scientists are seen as sharing the same world view, that is, as studying the same puzzles, data, and phenomena as current scientists, albeit somewhat less accurately.[13]

Several features of the paradigm battle are of interest. The new paradigm arises in the minds of one or a few individuals whose research usually is concentrated in the anomaly area and who generally are young or new to the discipline. The true testing in a science occurs within the paradigm battle. Normal science does not involve testing the paradigm with fact; it is a matching of fact and theory with the burden of failure resting upon the tool user, not the tool. Testing occurs in the paradigm battle as competing paradigms are tested for the allegiance of the discipline. This testing cannot be done by "proof," either of the falsifiability criterion or the probability of accurate prediction types, since competing paradigms are incommensurate. That is, holding different world views, standards, delineations of the science, and connotations of terminology, the practitioners with different paradigms cannot agree on a precise *test* of the paradigms.

Rather, the testing and conversion process is one of *persuasion.* Frequently, members of the old generation remain unpersuaded and either are defined out of the discipline or manage to stave off conversion of the discipline until their deaths. There are three principal persuasive arguments for a new paradigm: that it is capable of resolving the crisis-producing anomaly, that it permits the admission of new phenomena which are inadmissible under the old paradigm, or that it is aesthetically more pleasing, "neater," "more suitable," or "simpler" than the old paradigm. More generally, to gain acceptance the new paradigm must be seen as preserving most or all of the problem-solving capacity of the old paradigm while offering additional capacity of its own. Of course, its chances for success are greater the more the importance that can be attached to this additional capacity.

The choice between competing paradigms is then an act of faith, based upon the paradigms' comparative *future potentials.* The conversion process is a cumulative shifting of the distribution of allegiances. The relative volume of experiments, research, curricula, and publications based upon the new paradigm increases until the new paradigm becomes dominant, then finally universal.[14] Universal acceptance of the new paradigm, of course, culminates the revolution and commences a new period of normal science.

Overview of the Keynesian Revolution

The basic anomaly of the pre-Keynesian heritage is found in the area of automatic full employment based upon Say's Law and the quantity theory, which deny the possibility of general market gluts. Say's Law is, of course, the contention that production creates equivalent income which creates equivalent spending or aggregate demand. The crucial linkage is the income-spending one wherein all saving is considered to find its way into investment. This follows from the contention that hoarding is irrational and the assumptions that money illusions and price inflexibilities are absent. Full employment also is assured with flexibility because the price of resources, some of which are unemployed, will fall to secure full employment. Furthermore, flexibility and the quantity theory assure that adjustments will be made to avoid gluts even if hoarding does occur.

The inconsistency of these tenets with empirical fact and the need for alternative macroeconomic conceptions long had been recognized by theorists. Schumpeter notes that Johann Becher, as early as 1668, and later Pierre Boisguillebert and G. Ortes, stressed aggregate demand as the prime motivator of economic activity, thereby anticipating the later work of Thomas Malthus and J. M. Keynes, not to mention Lord James M. Lauderdale, Jean Sismondi, and Karl Marx. Schumpeter also notes that John Stuart Mill, Ludwig von Mises, Edwin Kemmerer, and Irving Fisher recognized the store of value function of money, although principally as a *consequence* of crisis or recession.[16] However, these interests remained peripheral or "underworld" to mainstream economics since classical economics concentrated on distributive shares given full employment, and neoclassical economics on the optimum use of fully employed resources.[17] That is, pre-Keynesian orthodoxy "assumed, as Ricardo did, that the amounts of the factors of production in use were given and that the problem was to determine the way in which they would be used and their relative rewards."[18] Moreover, both classical and neoclassical monetary theory "[were] concerned primarily with the theory of the price level, the determination of the general level of prices [and were] not directly concerned with the level of employment."[19]

To this point then, there was no crisis. However, around the turn of the century, more and more work became concentrated in the anomaly areas. Cycle theories, although still peripheral, grew in number with the sunspots, monetary, and innovational theories offered by Edward Huntington, William Jevons, R. G. Hawtrey, John Hobson, Schumpeter, Wesley Mitchell, and others. Knut Wicksell and Léon Walras tried to link the real and monetary sectors, dealt with aggregate quantities such as income and spending flows, and stressed the differences between the saving and investing roles. There arose competing saving/investing schools of thought such as the Stockholm *ex ante* and *ex post* process analysis of Gunnar Myrdal, E. R. Lindahl, Erik Lundberg, and Bertil Ohlin; D. H. Robertson's period analysis;[20] and Keynes's "vision" in the *Economic Consequences of the Peace* of a mature economy suffering secular stagnation due to an excess of saving relative to investment opportunity.[21]

Keynes succinctly summarizes the situation: "Contemporary thought is still deeply steeped in the notion that if people do not spend their money in one way they will spend it in another. Post-war [World War I] economists seldom, indeed, succeed in maintaining this standpoint *consistently;* for their thought today is too much permeated with the contrary tendency and with facts of experience too obviously inconsistent with their former view. But they have not drawn sufficiently farreaching consequences; and have not revised their fundamental theory."[22]

Prior to the Great Depression, then, there was a crisis in evidence. It probably was caused by the sheer momentum of the time period in which the anomaly resisted resolution and by the articulation of the existing paradigm by the neoclassicists. The Great Depression probably accelerated the crisis and shortened the paradigm battle after the appearance of the *General Theory*. As Paul Sweezy notes, ". . . the opportunity to which Keynes responded was essentially a crisis in traditional economics, a crisis both accentuated and laid bare by the Great Depression."[23]

Turning to the *General Theory,* one can first see that its revolutionary content lay not solely in the advocation of counter-cyclical fiscal policy, the use of aggregate analysis, the store of value function of money, the possibility of money illusions or gluts, nor the distinction between savers and investors, all of which had been mentioned before. Rather, Keynes combined these factors in a way that altered the focus of the discipline. He found employment, not efficiency of employment, to be the primary problem: ". . . I see no reason to suppose that the existing system seriously misemploys the factors of production which are in use . . . . When 9,000,000 men are employed out of 10,000,000 . . . [t]he complaint against the present system is not that these 9,000,000 men ought to be employed on different tasks, but that tasks should be available for the remaining 1,000,000 men. . . ."[24] After Keynes, the center of macroeconomics was to be the level of employment of resources, the primary role of aggregate demand in determining this level, and the role of government in underwriting the adequacy of aggregate demand.

That is, the essence of the Keynesian revolution is a change in world view. Keynes promised in a 1935 letter to G. B. Shaw that the *General Theory* would "revolutionize . . . the way the world thinks about economic problems. . . ." In the new view, not saving or thrift, but aggregate demand determines the prosperity of a nation, and the government is given a consistent theoretical rationale for fiscal intervention. The primary puzzles of the economist changed from distributive shares or optimum resource allocation given full employment to those puzzles related to the determinants of the level of employment and policies to achieve full employment.

A Kuhnian Scientific Revolution?

Does this scenario fit the Kuhnian paradigm of a scientific revolution? First, the period of crisis and extraordinary science was a gradual process in which a growing number of the discipline began working in the anomaly area. Second, the rules of normal science were blurred, and research became increasingly speculative and random (sunspots). Third, there was demonstrated an insecurity concerning definitions of approach and terminology, similar in many respects to the search for rules and assumptions which Kuhn refers to as philosophical analysis.[25] Fourth, as noted above, competing paradigms arose, each offering its own resolution of the conflict. Keynesian theory was one of these alternatives; it gradually became *the* alternative paradigm, then gained sway in the discipline.

With respect to the revolution itself, first, the old paradigm lingered until a new one appeared to replace it. Note that a majority of economists favored public works expenditures while still using the old paradigm, which offered no rationale for such intervention.[26] Second, Keynes provided new fundamental behavioral functions and tools of analysis, such as the consumption and liquidity functions and the multiplier,[27] and new applications of the discipline in the areas of policy and econometrics. Third, as we have seen, the Keynesian revolution was a change in world view, a redefinition not only of the purposes, tools, and problems of the discipline, but also of the world itself. The social happiness derived from laissez-faire, thrift, and competition was replaced by the social specter of stagnation and/or cyclical depression and the vice of oversaving.

In the paradigm battle, rather than being convinced by proof, conversion was an act of faith. For example, the question of whether unemployment derives from rigid prices (including wages and interest), given some differential between potential output and aggregate demand, or from the adjustment of the level of output to aggregate demand was (is) a matter of assumption. One analyst, given that aggregate demand is less than potential output, might say: *Ceteris paribus,* prices will fall. Given the same situation, another analyst might say: *Ceteris paribus,* actual output will fall below potential output. It was, in Benjamin Ward's terms, a matter of "stylized facts,"[28] a matter of selecting the potentially more useful axiomatic position.[29]

Then, too, Schumpeter believed that, aside from its practical utility, Keynesian analysis derived much of its appeal from its apparent simplicity relative to the highly complex, esoteric neoclassical theory.[30] Note also Schumpeter's view that Keynesianism was first adopted by the young in the profession and that many of the older generation never converted.[31] Among the latter, note the emotion with which A. C. Pigou admitted conversion in 1949, after he had retired and Keynes had died.[32]

As for the universality of these conversions, there are frequent utterances, from conservatives and liberals alike, that "we are all Keynesians now." Nor should the monetarist counter-revolution be viewed as a negation of this point.[33] Linkages between the pre-Keynesian monetarists and the modern monetarists are not so strong as the term *monetarist counter-revolution* suggests.[34] The *fundamental* change in world view evoked by the Keynesian revolution is the attention centered on the level of employment, income, and output, not on any particular explanation of this level nor on any particular policy to achieve a desirable level.[35] Indeed with "stagflation" the primary anomaly, the current scene is best viewed as a new period of extraordinary science with the monetarist and structuralist paradigms challenging the Keynesian orthodoxy.[36]

As for Keynesian normal science, despite its fundamental simplicity, Keynes's theory was sufficiently open-ended to allow substantial articulation. For example, note the surge of econometrics and national income accounting, the consumption function debates, the stagnation theories, and the portfolio balance approaches to liquidity preference. Furthermore, the textbook tradition after Keynes largely has made the Keynesian scientific revolution invisible. Macroeconomics texts and, to some extent, history of thought texts imply that pre-Keynesian analysts studied the same problems as Keynes, but less adroitly. In fact, Keynes's contribution sometimes is reduced to the practical one of rationalizing government fiscal policy by demonstrating "special cases" or institutional irregularities which allow unemployment to occur.

Concluding Notes

I shall note what I think are some implications of the foregoing. First, for the history of economic thought discipline, absolutist or validity of theory approaches tend to contribute to the invisibility of revolutions and, therefore, to the science-as-accumulation illusion. It would seem that viewing only a writer's analytical work would increase the tendency to impose a foreign world view upon him and that, however imperfectly, a more relativist or historical context approach would allow more opportunity for correctly assaying a past world view.

Second, progress in economic science does not involve a teleological movement toward truth, but an increase in the number of puzzles provided and those solved and an increased precision in matching fact with theory. This is rather positivistic, but remember that a commitment to a paradigm is more an act of faith than an objective decision.

Finally, I believe the importance of viewing commitment to a paradigm as an act of faith cannot be overstated, nor can the analogy of scientific revolutions to political revolutions. The opposition of one group seeking to change institutions they see as of less relative promise to another group seeking to maintain the status quo due to inertia, faith, vested interest, loyalty, or whatever, could not be more starkly drawn.

There always exists the possibility that a paradigm will resist revolution and simply decay. That is, a paradigm may be sufficiently institutionalized to *suppress* alternative paradigms, even to the point of glossing over fundamental crises. The competitive market model has withstood myriad attempts to inject into it elements of power, polity, or class struggle. Both Donald Gordon and A. W. Coats note the tenacity of the basic market/maximizing model in economics.[37] Sweezy makes the same point and explains it through the interplay between social theory and social reality.[38] That is, to a more pronounced degree than the hard sciences, social science is a reflection of underlying social ideology and forces. As such, social science is forever a potential weapon of propaganda, and this facet is in continuous tension with that of man's desire to know himself.

Notes

1. Joseph A. Schumpeter, *History of Economic Analysis* (New York: Oxford University Press, 1954), p. 1141.
2. Thomas S. Kuhn, *The Structure of Scientific Revolutions*, 2d ed., enlarged (Chicago: University of Chicago Press, 1970).
3. The term *paradigm* is basic to all that follows. A paradigm is a world view, a set of implicit and explicit guides or examples defining the world and the questions and methods for analyzing the world. Or, in Stigler's terms, a paradigm of a science is ". . . [t]he corpus of theoretical knowledge and analytical and empirical techniques which is accepted by the dominant group of members of the science. . . . The paradigm provides the consensus necessary for the existence of a group of scholars. The paradigm is open-ended and thus allows the continuous utilization of its apparatus to deal with an essentially unlimited number of unsolved problems. . . ." George J. Stigler, "Does Economics Have a Useful Past?" *History of Political Economy* 1 (Fall 1969): 223.

   It should be noted that Stigler's "main quarrel with Kuhn" is the lack of sufficient specification of the term *paradigm* to allow empirical testing. Concretely, Stigler argues that the marginalist revolution did not affect the "essential elements" of the classical theory (ibid., p. 225). In view of the shift from "political economy" to "economics" that occurred around this time, I find Stigler's concrete example inexplicable. However, *paradigm* is a slippery concept, and there is substance to Stigler's point, even though one does not quite know how to interpret "empirical testing" after reading Kuhn.
4. Thus, technological advances in the professions and crafts which increase the store of easily accessible data are of fundamental importance to the birth of new sciences.
5. Kuhn, *Structure,* pp. 13–18.
6. Ibid., pp. 18–23.
7. Ibid., pp. 23–42, 80.
8. Kuhn notes that instrumentality toward the solution of a social problem probably can merely time and not cause a crisis since irrelevance to practical affairs per se does not constitute an anomaly. This point well could need revision *vis-à-vis social* science.
9. Kuhn, *Structure,* pp. 67–82.

10. Ibid., pp. 82-89.
11. Ibid., pp. 77-80.
12. Ibid., pp. 84-85, 103-35.
13. Ibid., p. 138. Even history of thought texts create this illusion, especially if they take an absolutist approach.
14. Ibid., pp. 144-69.
15. Schumpeter, *History*, pp. 283-85.
16. Ibid., pp. 622, 1087-88.
17. This is not to deny the existence of theoretical interest in the question of unemployment. (Cf. Warren J. Samuels, "The Teaching of Business Cycles in 1905-1906: Insight into the Development of Macroeconomic Theory," *History of Political Economy* 4 [Spring 1972]: 140-162.) Rather, the point is that mainstream theory had no interest in such phenomena, although an otherwise mainstream theorist might dabble in cycle theory.
18. J. M. Keynes, "The General Theory of Employment," *Quarterly Journal of Economics* 51 (September 1937): 209.
19. H. G. Johnson, "Monetary Theory and Keynesian Economics," in H. G. Johnson, *Money, Trade, and Economic Growth* (London: Allen and Unwin, 1964), reprinted in R. W. Clower, ed., *Monetary Theory* (Baltimore: Penguin Books, 1970), p. 226.
20. Cf. Bertil Ohlin, "Some Notes on the Stockholm Theory of Saving and Investment," in *Readings in Business Cycle Theory*, Howard S. Ellis, ed. (Homewood, Ill.: Richard D. Irwin, Inc., 1951), pp. 87-130; and William Fellner, "Employment Theory and Business Cycles," in *A Survey of Contemporary Economics*, Howard S. Ellis, ed., vol. 1 (Homewood, Ill.: Richard D. Irwin, Inc., 1948), esp. pp. 49-59.
21. Cf. Schumpeter, *History*, pp. 1171-72.
22. J. M. Keynes, *The General Theory of Employment, Interest, and Money* (Harbinger Edition; New York: Harcourt, Brace, and World, 1964), p. 20.
23. Paul M. Sweezy, *The Present as History: Essays and Reviews on Capitalism and Socialism* (New York: Monthly Review Press, 1953), p. 278.
24. Keynes, *General Theory*, p. 379.
25. Kuhn, *Structure*, p. 88. As evidence of such insecurity in economics, the reader is referred to *Readings in Business Cycle Theory*, Ellis, ed., chaps. 5, 6, 7, 15, and Part III-A of the bibliography.
26. Mark Blang, *Economic Theory in Retrospect*, rev. ed. (Homewood, Ill.: Richard D. Irwin, Inc., 1968), p. 654. It should be noted that the revisionist thought concerning the revolutionary nature of the *General Theory* as to policy (cf. J. Ronnie Davis, *The New Economics and the Old Economists* [Ames: Iowa State University Press, 1971]) does not contradict the *General Theory's* Kuhnian revolutionary nature. Cf. the review of Davis's book by Robert L. Heilbroner, *Journal of Economic Literature* 10 (September 1972): 813.
27. Whether or not R. F. Kahn developed the multiplier for Keynes is not relevant here.
28. Benjamin Ward, *What's Wrong With Economics?* (New York: Basic Books, 1972), pp. 20ff.
29. It seems that this interpretation accords well with the recent study by Axel Leijonhufvud, *On Keynesian Economics and the Economics of*

Keynes (New York: Oxford University Press, 1968). According to Grossman, Leijonhufvud's point is that Keynes meant to depart from the traditional market theory which postulated equilibrium market clearance and to develop "an alternative analytical paradigm which would focus upon the inter-relation of markets which chronically failed to clear." Cf. Herschel I. Grossman, "Was Keynes a 'Keynesian'? A Review Article," *Journal of Economic Literature* 10 (March 1972): 27.

30. J. A. Schumpeter, *Ten Great Economists* (New York: Oxford University Press, 1965), p. 290, and *History*, p. 1144.
31. Schumpeter, *History*, p. 1180n.
32. Joan Robinson, *Economic Philosophy* (Garden City, N.Y.: Anchor Books, 1964), pp. 81-82.
33. See H. G. Johnson, "The Keynesian Revolution and Monetarist Counter-Revolution," *American Economic Review/Papers* 61 (May 1971): 1-14.
34. See Don Patinkin, "The Chicago Tradition, the Quantity Theory, and Friedman," *Journal of Money, Credit, and Banking* 1 (February 1969): 46-70.

    The monetarist revival is a faction within Keynesian normalcy. The monetarists attend to the question of aggregate demand and its determination of the level of income, employment, and output. They offer distinct explanations of the process of income determination and distinct policy proposals. The point is, however, that the question of aggregate demand and the level of employment is posed. Pre-Keynesian mainstream analysis did not pose this question. (See also notes 34 and 36.)
35. Martin Bronfenbrenner, "The Structure of Revolutions in Economic Thought," *History of Political Economy* 3 (Spring 1971): 137-38, cites the monetarist resurrection as well as contemporary examples of medieval and mercantilist thought as anomalies *vis-à-vis* the application of the Kuhnian paradigm to economics. However, contrary to Bronfenbrenner's interpretation, the current author finds nothing in Kuhn that would imply the impossibility of once ebbed ideas flowing again. Bronfenbrenner's basic contention is that "a crude Hegelian dialectic" is more applicable to the history of economic thought than the Kuhnian paradigm. Yet it would seem that the Kuhnian paradigm is highly dialectical.
36. Perhaps some elaboration is needed here. Stagflation, the simultaneous occurrence of unemployment and inflation, is an anomaly to the Keynesian income-expenditure model. This is so since aggregate demand cannot simultaneously exceed and fall short of potential output. Of course, that in reality structural frictions prevent instantaneous adjustment long has been recognized. So long as the trade-off involves small inflation-unemployment percentages, these frictions are considered minor. However, as the percentages grow, the anomaly becomes more acute and bids to create a crisis.

    The monetarist alternative à la Milton Freidman and the structuralist alternative à la J. K. Galbraith offer versions of resolution. The monetarists point to the absence of emphasis on the supply of money and the presence of a meddling, fine-tuning government. The structuralists point to unemployables, strong unions, and price administering corporations. Each alternative would substitute a new set of "stylized facts."
37. Donald F. Gordon, "The Role of the History of Economic Thought

in the Understanding of Modern Economic Theory,'' *American Economic Review/Supplement* 55 (May 1965): 124; and A. W. Coats, ''Is There a 'Structure of Scientific Revolutions' in Economics?'' *Kyklos* 22 (1969): 292.

The Transition from Classical to Neoclassical Economics: A Scientific Revolution

Michel De Vroey

The success of Thomas Kuhn's work, *The Structure of Scientific Revolutions,* in circles to which it was not initially addressed is particularly striking in the case of economics. In the last years, studies applying the Kuhnian framework to economic science have flourished, and no discussion about the history of economic theories takes place without at least a reference to Kuhn.[1] Undoubtedly, his ideas have provided the basis for a fresh look at the sociological factors affecting the development of economic thought. This is developed by Benjamin Ward in the following way:

> Economic science develops along a sharply constrained trajectory. The motive-force for development is the emergence of puzzles, which in turn is caused by the proposing of solutions to previous puzzles, and by transforming the issue of the time into the language of economic science. Constraints to the path of development come from the focusing devices, including the evolving tradition of accceptable stylized facts, the underlying worldview economists have in common, and the constraints imposed by power in the normal social science system and its environment [Ward 1972, p. 31].

The author is Chargé de Recherches FNRS, University of Louvain, Belgium.
He would like to thank Mr. de Souza and two anonymous referees for their helpful comments on a previous draft.

This article does not intend to criticize Ward's view, but to enhance it by focusing on those aspects to which Ward alludes when he speaks of constraints imposed by power in the environment.

More specifically, two theses will be defended. First, in the social sciences, the process of scientific construction necessarily includes a political dimension, which plays a pervasive role in the orientation of scientific activities. Second, in a class society, the ruling class cannot be indifferent to the type of social science developing in the society in which it holds power.

In an effort to illustrate these theses in the case of economic science, the factors which led to the transition from classical to neoclassical economics will be examined. The analysis will be structured in Kuhnian terms, but supplemented with the political connections which will be outlined hereafter. We will argue that this transition exhibits the characteristics of a scientific revolution, in the Kuhnian sense, and we will defend the view that the occurrence of this revolution is fully understandable only if account is taken of its political dimension.

Introduction

The Political Dimension

To support the first thesis, let us start by looking at the way in which scientific models are built, as described by Ronald Meek in his essay, "Marx's Economic Method."

> The model-builder usually begins, on the basis of a preliminary examination of the facts, by adopting what Schumpeter has called a "vision" of the economic process. In other words, he begins by orienting himself towards some key factor or factors which he regards as being of vital causal significance so far as the structure and development of the economic system as a whole are concerned. With this vision uppermost in his mind, he then proceeds to a more thorough examination of the economic facts both of the present situation and of the past situations which have led up to it, and arranges these facts in order on what might be called a scale of relevance. . . . Taking the facts which he has placed at the top of the scale as his foundation, the model-builder proceeds to develop certain concepts, categories and methods of classification which he believes will help him to provide a generalized explanation of the structure and development of the economy. . . . The particular analytical devices which he employs—his tools and techniques, as it were—are thus by no means arbitrarily chosen. To quite a large extent they are dependent upon the nature of his vision, the nature of primary facts which they are to be used to

explain, and the nature of the general method of analysis which he decides to adopt [Meek 1967, p. 93].

Implicit choices are made at the onset of theoretical construction, and they impinge upon its whole development.[2] First, the way one defines the object of economics contains a choice that is full of consequence. Thus, to assert, as is often done, that this object is efficiency is to narrow one's view to a technocratic approach to economics and the economist's role. It excludes all reference to the analysis of the transformation of economic structures from the scope and heart of the science. This order of priorities is not neutral. The effects on scientific development of the way of asking questions further can be shown in the case of two basic economic categories, the units of analysis used in a theory and the rationality of action attributed to economic agents.

Concerning the units of analysis, one of two approaches can be adopted. In the first case, one considers that social classes, that is, groups of people aggregated according to their specific relationship to the means of production, are the effective actors, shaping social and economic developments. Thus, theoretical construction must be framed in terms of classes. This is the Marxist view of historical development. It was also that of the classical political economists. The other approach, on the contrary, considers that it is the individual, with his aims and tastes, who constitutes the basic unit upon which economic theory should be built. Individuals are seen as the atoms of society, and no intermediate structure between them and the aggregate society is deemed relevant.

The same duality concerns the rationality of actions. Indeed, it may be assumed either that economic units are free choosers or that their behavior is socially determined. In the first case, human action is made equivalent to the act of a choice among alternatives. One premise here is that actors are rational. But this is only of secondary importance, since modifications easily can be introduced in order to integrate uncertainty or the possibility of foolish goals. The central premise is, rather, that behavior is regarded as the result of an individual decision. For example, if someone presents himself on the job market as a miner, this would then be explained exclusively in terms of his preferences, his utility and disutility function, his attitude toward risk and abstinence, and so forth. On the contrary, the second conception considers that social behavior is best explained in terms of social belonging and the constraints flowing from the exigencies of the system's functioning and self-reproduction, and that free decision occurs only within narrow limits.

Of course, choices about units of analysis and types of rationality are closely linked. Intentional rationality (the first aspect depicted above) is connected to the idea that individuals should be considered as the proper units of analysis, and, conversely, social rationality fits in with the conception that classes are the forces active in shaping historical development. In the latter interpretation, individuals are seen as "personifications of economic categories, embodiments of particular class-interests," to borrow Marx's expression [Marx 1967, p. 10].[3]

The problem is not to state in abstracto whether people are completely free or fully determined. Everyone admits that both dimensions play a role in reality. But the question is one of methodological choice. One of the two grids of analysis has to be used as the basic category of apprehension of reality.

This choice is of the utmost importance and pervades the whole scientific reasoning since it directs inquiry in quite opposed directions. Differences between paradigms lie not so much in the fact that they provide different answers to the same questions, but in the fact that they ask different questions. Once their premises are different, paradigms speak different languages. Likewise, the policy conclusions derived from analysis are predetermined by the way in which the conceptual system is framed. Because of these preliminary options about the social vision and the basic categories of analysis, social science cannot be neutral.

Class Interests

Our second thesis flows from the first one. If, as just described, scientific construction includes a political dimension, then, in a class society, the ruling class is not indifferent to the type of social science developing in the society in which it holds power. Hence Kuhn's view that the progress of science can be restrained by extracognitive factors, such as conservatism within a profession,[4] must be enlarged in order to include factors relating to the power structure within society as a whole. More specifically, one should assume that a ruling class utilizes its power to influence scientific construction, either directly and blatantly or, as is more probable today, indirectly. A paradigm, the social vision of which corresponds to the interests of the ruling class, will see its developments encouraged, while, on the contrary, an approach leaning against these interests will be overthrown or stifled in its growth. Class interests must be introduced in the process of scientific construction. Knowledge does not limit itself to a disinterested quest for truth. It is also a political confrontation where opposing views of society fight each other.

The views defended here should not be labelled too quickly as relativist. They represent, rather, a combination of the relativist and absolute view of the development of economic thought. The two are joined together in the following way:

(1) Theories of the social sciences contain a political dimension that flows from the social vision on which they are founded. This vision influences the choice of units of analysis, the object they treat, and the ones they do not;

(2) the efficient development of a science does not require those professing it to be aware of these implications. One does find "schizophrenic" cases of scientists who are oriented toward the left in politics while undertaking conservative scientific work;

(3) once the framework of analysis is set up, science develops according to its internal logic; and

(4) the development is socially controlled by the ruling classes, as already stated above, because of the political consequences of scientific statements. This leads to the encouragement of apologetic, inoffensive, and technocratic theories and to the dissuasion of those that criticize the existing social order.

Kuhn's Normal Science

Central in Kuhn's framework is the notion of normal science.[5] It refers to the specific state of development of two related but distinct realities, namely, science as a social system and science as a system of ideas.

Science as a social system refers to the community, sometimes called an "invisible college," formed by scholars of a like discipline. It exists through a series of institutions, which act as support for the development of interactions and education (departments, reviews, meetings). These institutions are penetrated with social values, for example, criteria for rigorous scholarship or for admission within the profession. There is also a specific distribution of prestige bearing upon institutions as well as upon people. In this regard, the judgment of colleagues is more important than that of the general public. Likewise, there is a structure of power, linked with the prestige elements and based upon past achievement and the holding of strategic position. Scientific communities thus constitute a well-structured in-group.[6]

The notion of paradigm expresses the unity and the coherence of a system of ideas. It encompasses the social vision, methodological principles and categories, theories, techniques and stereotyped examples, all of which together make up a particular system of ideas, the content of which is reflected in textbooks. The paradigm enables scholars to concentrate on narrow fields of research without, however, losing the feeling that their specialized activities are integrated in a wider context. The system of ideas, about which there exists a general consensus in a given scientific community, is called the *paradigm in dominance*. Thus a normal science consists of two articulated elements: a specific scientific community and a specific paradigm.

Kuhn's main thesis is that a change of the paradigm in dominance occurs in a rather brutal way, comparable to political revolution. The signs of a crisis are the appearance of anomalies, that is, puzzles which the existing paradigm cannot resolve. A general uneasiness about the relevance of the framework of analysis then arises. If the anomalies are not resolved and the uneasiness tempered, and if approaches involving a radically different way of looking at the problems are suggested, then the chances of a revolution will grow. However, cognitive factors are not sufficient in themselves to cause the move. Indeed, such a change does not occur in a social vacuum. The power elite within the profession is linked to the existing paradigm. Since they feel, rightly, that changes within the power and prestige structure probably will follow a scientific revolution, they may very well use their power to oppose the changes. Thus a scientific revolution is the result of forces in tension. On the one hand there are forces, usually of a cognitive order, pushing for a break; on the other there are forces, either cognitive (the ability of an existing paradigm to broaden its scope in order to integrate anomalies) or social, which will work against the successful occurrence of the scientific revolution.[7]

Given this interpretation of Kuhn's view, we enter the heart of our subject. The classical and neoclassical paradigms will be described in turn, and the factors explaining the transition from the former to the latter will be discussed.

The Classical Paradigm

The classical period in economics generally is delineated by two occurrences: the publication in 1776 of Adam Smith's *Wealth of Nations* and the publication in the 1870s of the fundamental works of the marginalist theory constituting the core of the neoclassical period.[8] During the classical era, economics was firmly erected into a distinct science. Joseph Schumpeter's judgment about what happened in this regard reveals a prescience of the notions of paradigm and invisible college.

> The study of economic phenomena was not yet a full-time job and few people were economists and nothing else: many were businessmen, or public servants, or journalists, and even the academic teachers of economics, in many if not in most cases, also taught cognate—or even completely different—subjects. Nevertheless, we have a right to speak of a rapid process of professionalization that

> went on during that period: from the first, economics had established its claim to a definite field of research; it had become a definite specialty; it used definite methods; its results gained in definiteness; and economists, even though fractional personalities, recognized one another and were recognized by the public, more definitely than before. New political economy societies were founded; new journals, new dictionaries and new bibliographies appeared—all of which, however, meant only continuation of previous practice. The study of the history of economic thought made a vigorous start and there was, of course, a rising tide of textbooks [Schumpeter 1954, p. 384].

To translate Schumpeter's view in the Kuhnian framework, the rise of classical economics witnessed the formation in England of a normal science, although still at an incipient stage. On the one hand, a distinct scientific community of economists was developing and becoming recognized as such, even if not yet professionalized. On the other hand, a consensus existed among these people about the field in which they inquired, the questions they asked, and the main concepts and categories which they used in order to answer these questions. Thus, one already may speak of a "paradigm in dominance." In order to describe it, the following features will be outlined: (1) the object of economics; (2) the general aim for engaging in scientific activities; (3) the institutional framework and the units of analysis; (4) the core of the conceptual framework; (5) the conception of value; and (6) the conception of profit.

The Object of Economics

As stated by Schumpeter, classical authors had a precise idea of the field assigned to economics. It may be called a substantive view as opposed to the formal one, which later on would characterize their neoclassical followers. For the classicists, the object of economic science was to determine the genesis of wealth and the laws governing its distribution. Since they regarded accumulation of capital as the main cause of the increase in wealth, their analyses primarily were aimed at explaining the nature and effects of the accumulation process.

The Aim

This definition of their field of interest must be related to the goal for which they engaged in scientific activities. According to Meek, "classical political economy was primarily concerned to assist those policy-makers who aimed to increase the wealth of nations. Its main task was to discover the relevant laws relating to the origin and increase in wealth and to propound them in such a way as to define the 'areas of decision' open to the policy-makers" [Meek 1973, pp. 83–84]. Their objective was not at all to set up a general theory which purported to be universally valid. Rather, they sought to explain the workings of the system in which they were, *hic et nunc*, involved. Therefore, they really do deserve the denomination of political economists.

The Institutional Framework And the Units of Analysis

The importance which classical authors attributed to the institutional framework follows as a logical consequence of their aims. On the one hand, they generally indicated the institutional contexts in which the economic processes were supposed to occur; on the other hand, they also normatively worked out the institutional conditions necessary to foster accumulation. With regard to the choice discussed above of a unit of analysis, their stand was clear. Social classes constituted one of their fundamental categories. As is well known, three classes were retained, the landlords, the workers, and the capitalists, each receiving a specific revenue, that is, rent, wage, and profit, respectively. Capitalists were assigned the dominant role. As Robert Eagly states: "Capitalists lead; all other groups in society follow. Laborers and landlords, though naturally indispensable for economic activity, are assigned negligible roles as decision makers. Analysis is conducted in terms of aggregate or class units. Although allusion is not infrequently made to individuals (generally for purposes of illustration), classical economic theory had no place for the common man" [1974a, p. 135]. Relationships between classes were at the core of their analyses.

Their Conception of Capital

Given their interest in accumulation, the notion of capital was quite naturally central to the classicists' whole conceptual framework. To demonstrate this centrality was Eagly's main objective in his recent work, *The Structure of Classical Economic Theory*. According to him, the unity of the theory, in its internal structure, was the direct consequence of the capital concept. "Capital provided the central schema or analytical structure that gave a sweeping overview of economic processes and provided a mode of analysis that served as the main vehicle for progress in economic theory from 1759 to the end of the 19th century" [Eagly 1974a, p. 34].

Strikingly, the classical authors defined *capital* in a comprehensive way (in comparison to the neoclassical definition). Capital included machinery as well as raw material and labor, and one of their leading problems consisted precisely in the allocation of the total capital stock between fixed (machines) and variable (raw materials plus a wage fund) capital. "The basic Classical model concentrated on working out the details of the production process. Output was specified to be a function of previously accumulated capital stock. . . . At the outset of this process the economy's total stock of commodities is in the form of capital stock; and at the end of this process the total stock of commodities takes the form of fixed capital plus (unmarketed) inventories of commodities" [Eagly 1974a, p. 4]. Thus, the classicists used a "period-analytical structure," or "compartmentalized analysis," in which they singled out production and exchange for separate and sequential treatment. The factor market and the product market tended to be treated as largely independent of each other. "Capital accumulation is regarded as prior to production and production as prior to exchange of commodities" [Eagly 1974a, p. 131].[9]

Their Conception of Value

Given the purpose of this article, the classical theory of value deserves particular attention for two reasons. First, as Meek asserts, "the particular theory of value with which an economist begins is almost invariably a sort of shorthand expression of the basic attitude which he is going to adopt towards the phenomenon he seeks to analyse and the problems he seeks to solve" [Meek 1973, p. 244].[10] Second, change in the value question brought about the scientific revolution from the classical to the neoclassical paradigm.

No unique theory of value can be ascribed to all the classical authors. Nevertheless, their treatment of the subject exhibits some common features enabling one to contrast their approach to that of their neoclassical followers. First, the determination of value was explained in terms of production rather than exchange. Thus they emphasized cost and supply rather than utility and demand.[11] Second, the view underlying their analyses was that the economy must be regarded as a social process and that value is to be linked with the division of labor within society. To borrow Meek's terms, "the classical labour theory grew up in direct association, not so much with the Lockean theory of property rights as with the concept of the social division of labour. In essence, it was another way of saying that the relations between things which manifested themselves in the sphere of commodity exchange were dependent upon the relations between men which manifested themselves in the sphere of commodity production" [Meek 1973, p. 126].

Within these boundaries, however, there were marked differences in the classical treatment. As is well known, Adam Smith believed that a pure labor theory of value was valid in a primitive state of economic development, but not in modern times. In the latter case, in Meek's interpretation of his thought, "the 'regulator' of value was no longer the quantity of embodied labour: it should rather be sought by enquiring into the manner in which the equilibrium levels of wages, profits and rent which make up the 'natural price' were determined. And his own inquiries into this problem seem to have been conducted on the assumption that the constituents of the natural price could legitimately be regarded as *independent* determinants of value" [Meek 1973, p. 71].

David Ricardo's reflections on value were directed at criticizing Smith's position, and undoubtedly he took an important step in the direction of a pure labor theory of value. However, his views were rather ambiguous. On the one hand, as argued by Piero Sraffa [1961] and Meek [1973], he persisted to the end of his life in "his deep-rooted feeling that in spite of all appearances to the contrary, embodied value did in some significant sense constitute and regulate the 'value' of a commodity" [Meek 1973, p. 119]. He entirely rejected Smith's view that the labor theory was valid only in primitive times and had to be replaced by some sort of "cost of production" theory, once capital accumulation had taken place. On the other hand, he had to admit that his law of value held only under the drastic assumption of similarly constituted capital (same durability of fixed capital and same proportions of fixed to variable capital). This restriction paved the way for a cost theory of value, if not in his eyes at least in those of subsequent interpreters.[12] As wittily noted by Mark Blaug, "Ricardo was the first to show just why a labor-cost theory cannot fully account for the relative prices of reproducible commodities under perfect competition" [1968, p. 96].

In the light of the aims of this article, these more recent interpretations of Ricardo's writings are not as important as those made in his time. In this regard, two features should be noted. First, Ricardo's ideas dominated the economic scene in England, at least until 1830. From this date to the end of the century, they declined progressively before finally being overthrown by the neoclassical revolution.[13] Second, Ricardo's ideas received radical extensions, which he himself certainly did not expect. One such extension was that of the so-called Ricardian socialists, like William Thompson and Thomas Hodgskin, who wrote in the 1820s and 1830s. They presented a simplified interpretation, ready-made for political action, according to which labor was the sole cause of value and thus deserved the entire value of production. Another extension with deeper theoretical effects was that of Marx, who put his theory of value under Ricardo's paternity. It is not our purpose to expose in detail these extensions of Ricardo's theory of value. What matters here is that they were made in a radical perspective. This fact is important for assessing the causes of the scientific revolution which overthrew the whole classical construction.

Their View on Profit

In the classical view, capitalists' contribution to production consists of an advance of wages made necessary by the division of society into classes. Indeed, as the workers were not provided with wealth, they could not subsist during the period between production and commercialization of the finished products and therefore needed advances from the capitalist. Profit was viewed as the reward for these advances; its level depended upon the consumption habits of capitalists, which determined the amount that they were able to invest in wage funds and the price at which labor was paid. However, the classical authors did not condemn the profit the advances yielded. For them, it was rather the propulsive force of economic growth. As Joan Robinson puts it, the basis of the classical view is that "in a hard-headed way [it] recognized exploitation as the source of national wealth" [1962, p. 58]. Acting in their own self-interest, capitalists automatically would lean toward an increase in the collective wealth.

The Neoclassical Paradigm

During the classical period economic science had not yet reached the stage of a fully developed normal science. The community of economists was still small, and its boundaries were vague. Consequently, intellectual production was neither abundant nor specialized. This is not the case for the neoclassical period. In the 1870s the founders of the new school published their main works.[14] However, it was not until the very end of the nineteenth century that the neoclassical paradigm became dominant. Thus, the turn of the century witnessed at the same time both a rapid development of the economic profession and a change of paradigm.[15] These two developments should not be confused, contrary to the view sometimes held that the "marginal revolution" was nothing more than a process of professionalization.[16] This point will be dealt with in the last part of the article. First, let us outline the characteristics of the neoclassical paradigm according to the criteria used for defining the classical approach.

The Object of Economics

This rise of the neoclassical paradigm was accompanied by a change in the field of study assigned to economic science. Attention no longer was focused on economic growth, as in the classical perspective, but on efficiency, that is, on optimal allocation of scarce resources among alternative uses. As Stanley Jevons said, the "problem of economics" was: "Given, a certain population, with various needs and powers of production, in possession of certain lands and other sources of material: required, the mode of employing their labor which will maximize the utility of the product" [quoted in Blaug 1968, p. 300].

The Aim for Engaging in Economic Research

Breaking with their predecessors, neoclassical economists no longer were interested in helping policy makers. As G. J. Stigler has noted [1972, p. 577], they turned their backs on the "journalistic crisis of the day or the decade" and focused on more abstract objects of research. Assuredly, this shift was influenced by the major triumphs in the natural sciences in the nineteenth century.[17] What they were looking for was a general theory, universally valid, applicable to all social systems. The specification of the institutional framework, which was so important in the eyes of the classicists, was neglected. The political aspects of economics also gradually became separated from the so-called scientific aspects, the latter being limited to the observation of reality. Neoclassicals advocated laissez-faire, but without specifying, as the classical authors did, the social conditions necessary for allowing its correct working.[18]

The Institutional Framework And the Unit of Analysis

To borrow Eagly's expression [1974a], the new paradigm involved a "complete recasting of the *dramatis personae* of economic analysis." The capitalist class was removed from the center of the stage. Capitalists, defined as mere owners of capital stock and as distinct from entrepreneurs, were put on the same level as laborers and landowners. As a matter of fact, the analysis no longer was framed in terms of classes, which no longer figured in this approach. Individuals were the only units of analysis, and their behavior was explained solely in terms of subjective rationality.

The neoclassical paradigm reduces all the elements entering the explanation to a common denominator. Only one aspect of actual phenomena is retained, their economicity, that is, the fact that they bear utility or disutility and are thus exchangeable. The classical framework consisted of irreducible categories, as social classes with their specific revenues, factors of production, production and distribution. In contrast, the neoclassical paradigm transcends specificities. Due to the introduction of new analytical tools (notions such as marginal increase or marginal rate of substitution) and to the use of algebraic reasoning, the explanation is made in terms of one unique principle: the maximization of subjective satisfaction.

If the social structures vanish from the scene, then there only remain what Eagly calls the "general public." Through its votes in the market it becomes the real decision maker.

> By specifically setting down decision criteria or behavior guidelines for members of the general public, the marginal utility approach permitted a calculus in which the vast majority of the general population would participate in voicing their preferences and voting their income in the market place. It provided the basis for analysis of demand decisions in the commodity market as well as the basis for study of supply decisions in the factor market. In a sense, the marginal utility approach democratized economic theory and made every person influential, to some degree, in the outcome of economic activity [Eagly 1974a, p. 137].

Thus exchanges are supposed to occur in a social vacuum. Several decades ago Maurice Dobb pointed out the underlying premise of such a model: "It implies that economic phenomena are ruled by a series of contractual relations freely entered into by a community of independent individuals, each of whom knows well what he wants and has access to and knowledge of all the available alternatives" [Dobb 1972, p. 65]. Is this assumption correct? What are its ideological implications? These are questions to which we will have to return in the last part of the article.

The Central Concept of the Neoclassical Paradigm

On the conceptual level, the neoclassical paradigm shifted emphasis from the notion of capital, which was central to the classical paradigm, to that of price. Indeed, the determination of the equilibrium relative prices of goods and factors becomes the main task of economic analysis.

This relegation of capital to a secondary position has been ably described by Eagly.

> The Walrasian definition of capital originated in the analytical character of the instantaneous general equilibrium system. Specifically, Walras eliminated the variable capital component from the classical concept of capital. The goods that made up variable capital (wage goods and raw materials) were merged with the income flow of a single time period. For Walras, capital consisted narrowly of fixed capital: i.e., goods which enter production but are not used up in a single time period. Prior acccumulation of the commodities which constituted variable capital was thus no longer required by economic theory. Accordingly, the responsibility formerly assigned the capitalist class dropped from sight and received no further attention beyond the Austrian school. It was, in other words, Walras' new definition of capital, not any recantation by John Stuart Mill, that killed the wages fund component of classical theory. The period analytic approach of the basic classical model no longer served as the means for dealing with the allocation of the total capital stock. The allocation of total capital stock no longer existed as a theoretical problem. Wage income, for instance, became transformed into a flow from current productive activity rather than a division of an already accumulated capital stock for current production. The close identification between labor's current productive activity and labor's wage, which was made possible by Walras' instantaneous system, was a short step removed from the marginal productivity theory. In the classical system, labor is paid a wage that is determined through the equilibrium measure of marginal (value) productivity. Labor is paid out of current, not past, output [Eagly 1974a, pp. 7–8].

Thus, the sequential approach of the classical authors was removed and replaced by the idea of a simultaneous interdependence culminating in the notion of general equilibrium. To quote Eagly again: "Walrasian general equilibrium, in its essential aspects, joins together the factor market and product market in a system in which equilibrium in both markets is simultaneously established. Time lags, such as existed in classical analysis, are eliminated" [Eagly 1974a, p. 132].

The Concept of Value

The originality of the neoclassical paradigm in respect to its classical predecessor also appears clearly from the examination of its treatment of value. As is well known, in the neoclassical approach the value of a good is determined by the marginal utility of its buyers. Later, the concept of utility itself was abandoned, but fundamentally its subjective underpinnings were retained. This change in the theory of value involves, in fact, a radical transformation in the vision of the economic process. In the classical paradigm, economic action was, before all, viewed as a social process. Value was analyzed within the framework of production, viewed itself as a social process whose features are the result of a specific social system. On the contrary, in the neoclassical paradigm, the origin of value is searched for in a mental process. Value depends upon the consumer's desires.

The Concept of Profit

Capital and labor now are considered on the same level. Both are productive factors. Profit no longer is equated with an exploitation made possible because of the unequal distribution of wealth between classes, but is viewed as the remuneration of a subjective cost which is as real as wages. Profit becomes the reward for the capitalists' abstinence and thus receives an explanation in purely subjective terms.

The Political Foundation of Neoclassical Economics

After having outlined the main features of the two paradigms, we will devote the last section of this article to the examination of three questions. The first concerns the nature of the change between classical and neoclassical economics. Does it manifest the thorough change of perspective linked with the idea of a scientific revolution? Was it, in other words, really a scientific revolution? The second question bears on the time span over which the change occurred. The third concerns the causes of the change.

The Nature of the Change

It seems clear from the above discussion that classical and neoclassical economics each constitute a coherent and specific paradigm. To repeat an earlier statement: They do not provide different answers to the same questions; they ask different questions. Table 1 summarizes the main characteristics of the two approaches. The transition actually concerned really the premises of analysis, and, thus, it must be regarded as a scientific revolution à la Kuhn rather than as a scientific advance in a Popperian way through a process of criticism and falsification of existing laws or assumptions.[19]

Table 1. ***A Comparison of the Main Features of the Classical and the Neoclassical Paradigm***

	Classical paradigm	Neoclassical paradigm
The object of economics	Accumulation and distribution	Efficiency
The aim for engaging in economic research	To assist policy makers	The discovery of universal laws
Institutional framework and unit of analysis	Specification of the institutional framework, especially in terms of the division of society between social classes. Behavior expresses class belonging.	No classes, but a "general public" making decisions through votes (individually) in the market. The idea of choice is central.
Core of the theoretical structure	Capital, defined in a comprehensive way, is at the center of the theoretical structure.	Prices form the central concept.
Conception of value	A production theory of value, in which value is viewed as the expression of the social division of labor	Value flows from the subjective mental evaluation of the individual agents.
Conception of profit	Profit results from the unequal distribution of wealth between classes; it is the source of growth.	Profit is the reward for abstinence.

The Time Span of the Revolution

One must avoid a naïve interpretation of the Kuhnian concept of revolution, which would equate a revolution and a coup d'état, to borrow a political analogy. In our opinion, it does not distort Kuhn's view to regard scientific revolutions as processes rather than instantaneous events. In this perspective, the following turning points and phases can be pointed out in the case under study.

The first and, in our view, main blow against the classical paradigm came in the 1830s. The targets of the attacks were some pillars of the Ricardian theory: the class connotation of the economic categories, the concepts of value which viewed work and profit as a kind of surplus, and the limits of the progress of capitalism.[20]

These attacks were quite successful. According to Meek, they led to the result that "Ricardo's system was purged of its more obviously disharmonious elements, particularly those which might have been used to suggest that there was a real conflict of economic interest between social classes under capitalism, or that progress under capitalism might be limited for some other reason" [1967, pp. 72–73].

The rapidity with which Ricardian views, until then commonly accepted, were abandoned is amazing. As elliptically depicted by Schumpeter: "Ricardo died in 1823. In 1825, Bailey launched his attack that should have been decisive on the merits of the case. Actually it was not, for schools are not destroyed so easily. But the decay of the Ricardian school must have become patent shortly after, for in a pamphlet published in 1831 we read that there are some Ricardians still remaining. In any case, it is clear that Ricardianism was then no longer a living force" [1954, p. 478].

Schumpeter's view about the end of Ricardianism has not been shared by everyone, and many authors would rather place the turning point between classical and neoclassical economics in the 1870s, during which decade the marginal utility theory was formulated.[21] However, these two conceptions easily can be reconciled by regarding the 1830s as the landmark of the negative or destructive phase of the revolution and the 1870s as that of the constructive phase.

In between there was a long period of hybrid equilibrium. It was a sort of interregnum between the *ancien* and the *nouveau regime*. The dominant figure was J. S. Mill, whose *Principles of Political Economy* "functioned as the undisputed bible of economists during the second half of the 19th century," to borrow Blaug's expression [1968, p. 180]. Mill himself thought he was only qualifying Ricardo and was not aware of the long-term consequences which would result from the infiltration of subjective elements into the Ricardian system. More precisely, he did not realize that the labor and the subjective theories of value, which he tried to synthesize, belonged to opposed methodological approaches. Indeed, the labor component of his theory of value was linked to a definition of economic processes as relations between classes. On the contrary, the subjective component depended upon a vision in which the object of analysis was the relation between the individual and his desires.

The subjective approach, first introduced in explaining the rewards to capitalists for abstinence, received its full theoretical elaboration in the 1870s. Jevons, Menger, and Walras discovered simultaneously but independently the principle of diminishing marginal utility, which was to become the fundamental building block of the new microeconomics. However, as pointed out by Blaug, "the significance of the marginal utility theory was that it provided the archetype of the general problem of allocating given means with maximum effect. It was not long before the same approach was extended from the household to the firm, from the theory of consumption to the theory of production. The theory of utility supplied most of the excitement of discovery in the seventies and eighties, but it was the introduction of marginal analysis as such that marked the true dividing line between classical theory and modern economics" [1968, p. 299]. Hence it is not utility theory in itself which is central for grasping the essentials of the neoclassical paradigm (and this specific theory has lost much of its prominence today). What is central are the categories on which it was built, namely, the definition of the economic process as a relationship between the individual and his needs, the absence of class consideration, the identification of economic behavior with an act of individual choice. The object of our attention must be the rise of subjectivism, a new social vision and set of methodological principles, rather than the particular form in which this subjectivist approach became embodied, that is, the theory of marginal utility.

The Causes of the Scientific Revolution

What were the causes of the transition to neoclassical economics? One popular position identifies neoclassical economics with "modern economics," the connotation being that only the latter is really scientific.[22] The passage to modern economics is then regarded as an entry of economics into the very select club of modern science, the criterion for admission being a high level of generality and of conceptual rigor. This attitude was probably in the back of J. M. Keynes's mind when, in his *Essays of Biography,* he wrote about Jevons that he was "the first theoretical economist to survey his material with the prying eyes and fertile, controlled imagination of the natural scientist" [quoted in Collison Black 1972, p. 369].

A related type of explanation is advanced by writers focusing on the professionalization of economics, which took place at the turn of the century. One prominent example of this position is provided by Stigler, who explains the adoption of the marginal utility theory in terms of the rise of new values as the discipline became increasingly academic. "What utility contributed was precisely the values we attribute to the academic world and in particular to the academic science" [1972, p. 578] (these values mainly being generality of major results and cultivation of scholarly techniques).

However, it appears that this explanation remains at the surface of the problem and cannot be accepted. First, it minimizes the differences between the two paradigms, as revealed in the following quotation, extracted from Stigler: "The marginal utility revolution of the 1870's replaced the individual economic agent as a sociological or historical datum by the utility maximizing individual. The essential elements of the classical theory were affected in no respect" [1969, p. 225]. As the reader will easily understand, this view is at the opposite pole of the interpretation developed here. Stigler regards the passage toward the subjective theory of value as a Popperian progressive change, while we take it as a radical discontinuity that implied a complete reversal of the social vision involved and the methodological categories used.

Furthermore, and this is our second criticism, we would consider that the approach in terms of modernization does not provide an explanation in depth of the reasons for the change. Indeed, it evades what appears to us as being the heart of the matter, namely: What was the rationale behind the sudden abandoning of the Ricardian concepts in the 1830s? Once this question is raised, a new field for conjecture opens, and the political dimension of scientific discussions comes to the front as a new explanation for the shift in paradigm. This has been shown by Meek in his well-documented study, "The Decline of Ricardian Economics in England," reprinted in *Economics and Ideology*.

The context of increasing social trouble in which the attacks against some of the main aspects of the Ricardian system developed has been described by Marx in the following way:

> With the year 1830 came the decisive crisis. In France and in England, the bourgeoisie had conquered political power. Thenceforth, the class-struggle, practically as well as theoretically, took on more and more outspoken and threatening forms. It sounded the knell of scientific bourgeois economy. It was thenceforth no longer a question, whether this theorem or that was true, but

> whether it was useful to capital or harmful, expedient or inexpedient, politically dangerous or not. In place of disinterested inquirers, there were hired prize-fighters; in place of genuine scientific research, the bad conscience and the evil intent of apologetic [1967, p. 15].

The labor theory of value and the origin of profit were at the center of the debate. Ricardo had built up his theory of value from the idea that it was the expenditure of energy by the workers which conferred value on commodity rather then the capitalists' expenditure on subsistence goods for their workmen. Now, as already has been noted, socialist authors pushed this theory to its more radical conclusions. They argued that if one considered labor as the only source of value, it appeared logical that workers be entitled to receive the totality of the product of their work. Nothing justified an important portion of produce, namely profit, accruing to the capitalists. Thus the Ricardian doctrine provided an important intellectual argument to the socialist movement, which was in full development at the time and which questioned the moral validity of the existing social order. It also did not take long before the conservative forces discovered the political content of the Ricardian doctrine. It therefore became imperative for the bourgeoisie (to which most of the economists belonged) to eliminate these views. Meek writes: "It is hardly too much to say that every new development in economic thought in England about this time had the objective effect of cutting the ground under the feet of writers like Hodgskin and William Tompson" [1967, p. 70]. He adds that "it seems not too unfair to say that economists like Scrope, Read and Longfield, in varying degrees, tended towards the view that if a doctrine inculcated pernicious principles, if it denied that wealth under free competition was consigned to its proper owners, or if it could be so interpreted as to impugn the motives or capacity of the Almighty, then that doctrine must necessarily be false. Their fundamental approach, in other words, was determined by a belief that what was socially dangerous could not possibly be true" [1967, p. 71].

Conclusion

These are the opposing views about the causes of the transition from classical to neoclassical economics. The author adheres to Meek's analysis because it provides a coherent answer to the central question as to why the classical approach was dropped. The other view does not even consider this question, for it assumes, by definition, that the new theory of value is more scientific.[23] Thus, in our opinion, the deep rationale underlying the attack against the Ricardian theory of value was that it led to radical conclusions. The urgent task was to discard a theory which was justifying a radical transformation of society. We face here a clear example of a contradiction between a theoretical framework leading to radical conclusions and the power structure within society, in which the bourgeoisie had become the dominant class. The stumblingblock or anomaly within the classical paradigm lay in its political consequences. Therefore, it was necessary both to discard the disharmonious elements of the Ricardian approach and to propose a justification for profit.[24]

This was exactly the function played by the neoclassical scientific revolution. The new paradigm was especially attractive because it looked as scientific as the natural sciences theories, while it eluded the dangerous topics of class interests and transformation of the system. It left aside the theoretical categories which could apprehend the specific characteristics of the capitalist mode of production. Thus, it simply was unable to frame any question about a possible change in the structures of the system. It provided tools for the management of the economy in the framework of the existing social order, as if this was the only possible object of economics. This inoffensiveness was and is, from the viewpoint of the capitalist ruling class, the main quality of the neoclassical paradigm. Political economists are transformed into engineers.

The new paradigm, in which the term *political economy* is replaced by *economics*, does remain political, in the sense that by hiding the political dimension of economics, it plays a very definite political role. This was shown, a long time ago, by Dobb.

> [The assumption is] that each individual had free range of opportunities and had only taken the road he had after surveying and estimating the range of existent alternatives. This is what can*not* be postulated of capitalist society; and it is the absence of this assumption—indeed, the existence of the direct opposite, namely class division—which forms the necessary starting point for any understanding of the specific character of capitalist society [1972, p. 70]. The very form in which abstract postulates about individual choices are put constitutes them a distorted description of the actual forces which control economic phenomena in capitalist society, unless they are radically qualified by statements concerning the social relations by which individual choices are governed and the choices of *classes* are differentiated in capitalist society. The mere absence of any such qualification means that the statement that individuals *choose*, as soon as it is made concrete in the form that individuals choose in a particular way, becomes the false statement that individuals choose *freely* and that the events which are the outcome of these individual actions are unaffected by those basic productive relations—class relations connected with

ownership of economic property—which are the distinguishing characteristic or capitalist society [1972, p. 75].

Notes

1. See A. W. Coats [1969], D. F. Gordon [1965], *Review of Radical Political Economics* [1971], Benjamin Ward [1972], Robert Heilbroner [1973], Hyman Cohen [1973], Martin Bronfenbrenner [1971], Leonard Kunin and F. S. Weaver [1971], Siegfried Karsten [1973], and R. D. Collison Black et al. [1973].
2. See Gynnar Myrdal's book, *The Political Element in the Development of Economic Theory:* "Facts do not organize themselves into concepts and theories just by being looked at; indeed, except within the framework of concepts and theories, there are no scientific facts but only chaos. There is an inescapable a priori element in all scientific work. Questions must be asked before answers can be given. The questions are an expression of our interest in the world, they are not bottom valuations. Valuations are thus necessarily involved already at the stage when we observe facts and carry on theoretical analysis, and not only at the stage when we draw political inference from facts and valuations" [1954, p. vii]. The same view is also developed by Lucio Colletti [1972]. For an opposite view see Stigler's article, "The Politics of Political Economists," reprinted in his *Essays in the History of Economics* [1965].
3. The same theme is developed by Maurice Godelier in his book, *Rationality and Irrationality in Economics* [1973].
4. Examples of this can be found in Robert Merton [1972] and Michael Mulkay [1972.]
5. Kuhn himself often has been accused of conceptual confusions. See Imre Lakatos and Alan Musgrave [1970].
6. For the sociology of scientific communities see Barry Barnes [1972], Robert Merton [1973], Diane Crane [1972], Joseph Ben-David [1971], and Bernard Barber [1952]. Interesting remarks are also to be found in Ward's book, *What's Wrong With Economics?* [1972] and in Eagly's article, "Contemporary Profile of Conventional Economists" [1974b].
7. For further development and application of these ideas to economics, see Ward's *What's Wrong With Economics?* [1972].
8. The above delineation is, of course, somewhat arbitrary. In his important book, *The Structure of Classical Economic Theory* [1974], Eagly regards François Quesnay's *Tableau économique* as the start of the classical theoretical structure.
9. Adam Smith did, however, sometimes refer to the impact of changes in product prices on factor markets. See Smith [1904], chapters 7 and 8.
10. The same view is held by Myrdal [1954, p. 15].
11. Thomas Malthus and Nassau Senior were exceptions in this regard.
12. See Stigler's well-known article, "Ricardo and the 93 Per Cent Labor Theory of Value," reprinted in his *Essays in the History of Economics* [1966].

13. See Joseph Schumpeter [1954], Ronald Meek [1967], Marc Blaug [1968], Frank Fetter [1969], and D. F. Gordon [1965].
14. Carl Menger [1871], Stanley Jevons [1871], and Léon Walras [1874–1877].
15. See Stigler's "Statistical Studies in the History of Economic Thought," in his *Essays in the History of Economics* [1965].
16. See Stigler [1972].
17. See Collison Black [1972] and Stigler [1972].
18. The changes both in the object of economics and in the general aim of research possibly could be explained by the state of develpment of the capitalist system. During the classical period, the capitalist class was still emerging as the new ruling class and needed intellectual support to back its ascension. At the time of neoclassical economics, its power position already was well established, and this support was no longer needed that much.
19. For a confrontation of scientific progress à la Popper and discontinuities à la Kuhn, see Lakatos and Musgrave [1970].
20. See Schumpeter [1954, p. 552] and Meek's "The Decline of Ricardian Economics in England," reprinted in *Economics and Ideology and Other Essays* [1967, p. 72]. For an opposite view, according to which the concept of value was not central in Ricardo's theory, see Fetter [1969].
21. See the special issue of *History of Political Economy* on the "Marginal Revolution in Economics" [1972].
22. Examples of this position are to be found in Schumpeter [1954] and Blaug [1968; 1972].
23. A good example of this attitude is again given by Stigler: "It is indeed true that a believer in the labor theory of value could not get a professorship at a major American university, although the reason would be that the professors could not bring themselves to believe that he was both honest and intelligent." Stigler, "The Politics of Political Economists," in *Essays in the History of Economics* [1915, p. 58].
24. As Joan Robinson wittily says: "Adam Smith's hard-headed view that the landlord and the master muscle in and take their share will not do for a more pious generation. Capital must be allowed to create the value that it receives" [1962, p. 34].

References

Barber, Bernard. 1952. *Science and the Social Order.* New York: Free Press.

Barnes, Barry, ed. 1972. *Sociology of Science.* London: Penguin Books.

Baumol, William J. 1974. "The Transformation of Value: What Marx Really Meant (An Interpretation)." *Journal of Economic Literature* 12 (March): 51–61.

Ben-David, Joseph. 1971. *The Scientist's Role in Society, A Comparative Study.* Englewood Cliffs, N. J.: Prentice-Hall.

Berger, Peter L., and Thomas Luckmann. 1967. *The Social Construction of Reality. A Treatise on the Sociology of Knowledge.* London: Allen Lane.

Blaug, Mark. 1968. *Economic Theory in Retrospect.* Rev. ed. Homewood, Ill.: Irwin.

———. 1972. "Was There a Marginal Revolution?" *History of Political Economy* 4 (Fall): 269–80.
Bose, Arun. 1971. "Marx on Value, Capital and Exploitation." *History of Political Economy* 3 (Fall): 298–334.
Bronfenbrenner, Martin. 1971. "The 'Structure of Revolutions' in Economic Thought." *History of Political Economy* 3 (Spring): 136–51.
Bukharin, Nikolai. 1972. *Economic Theory of the Leisure Class.* New York: Monthly Review Press (1927 first edition).
Coats, A. W. 1969. "Is There a 'Structure of Scientific Revolutions' in Economics?" *Kyklos* 22, pp. 289–95.
Cohen, Hyman R. 1973. "Dialectics and Scientific Revolutions." *Science and Society* 37 (Fall): 326–35.
Colletti, Lucio. 1972. *From Rousseau to Lenin, Studies in Ideology and Society.* London: New Left Books.
Collison Black, R. D. 1972. "W. S. Jevons and the Foundation of Modern Economics." *History of Political Economy* 4 (Fall): 364–78.
———, A. W. Coats, and Craufurd D. W. Goodwin, eds. 1973. *The Marginal Revolution in Economics.* Durham: Duke University Press. (Special issue of *History of Political Economy* 4 [Fall 1972]).
Crane, Diane. 1972. *Invisible Colleges. Diffusion of Knowledge in Scientific Communities.* Chicago: University of Chicago Press.
De Vroey, Michel. 1972. "Une explication sociologique de la prédominance du paradigme neoclassique dans la science économique." *Economies et sociétés, Cahiers de l'I. S. E. A.* 6 (August): 1655–701
———. 1974. "The 'Structure of Scientific Revolutions' and the Economic Science." *Communication and Cognition* 1, no. 1: 153–61.
Dobb Maurice. 1973. *Theories of Value and Distribution since A. Smith—Ideology and Economic Theory.* London: Cambridge University Press.
———. 1972. "The Trend of Modern Economics." In *A Critique of Economic Theory*, edited by E. K. Hunt and Jesse Schwartz. Modern Economic Readings. London: Penguin. Pp. 39–81.
Eagly, Robert V. 1974a. *The Structure of Classical Economic Theory.* Oxford: the University Press.
———. 1974b. "Contemporary Profiles of Conventional Economists." *History of Political Economy* 6, no. 1: 76–91.
Fetter, Frank F. 1969. "The Rise and Decline of Ricardian Economics." *History of Political Economy* 1, no. 1: 67–84.
Godelier, Maurice. 1973. *Rationality and Irrationality in Economics.* London: New Left Books.
Gordon, D. F. 1965. "The Role of the History of Economic Thought in the Understanding of Modern Economic Theory." *American Economic Review* 55 (May): 119–27.
Heilbroner, R. L. 1973. "Economics as a Value-Free Science." *Social Research* 40 (Spring): 129–43.
History of Political Economy. 1972. Special issue, "Marginal Revolution in Economics." 4 (Fall).
Howey, R. S. 1960. *The Rise of the Marginal Utility School 1807–1889.* Laurence: University of Kansas Press.

Jevons, Stanley. 1871. *The Theory of Political Economy*. London: Macmillan.

Karsten, Siegfried G. 1973. "Dialectics and the Evolution of Economic Thought." *History of Political Economy* 5 (Fall): 399–419.

Kuhn, Thomas. 1967. *The Structure of Scientific Revolutions*. Chicago: University of Chicago Press.

Kunin, Leonard, and F. Stirton Weaver. 1971. "On the Structure of Scientific Revolutions in Economics." *History of Political Economy* 3 (Fall): 391–97.

Lakatos, Imre, and Alan Musgrave, eds. 1970. *Criticism and the Growth of Knowledge*. Cambridge: the University Press.

Marx, Karl. 1967. *Capital*. Volume 1. New York: International Publishers (1st English edition 1887).

Meek, Ronald L. 1967. *Economics and Ideology and Other Essays*. London: Chapman and Hall.

———. 1973. *Studies in the Labour Theory of Value*. 2d ed. London: Laurence and Wishart.

———. 1974. "Value in the History of Economic Thought." *History of Political Economy* 6 (Fall): 246–60.

Menger, Carl. 1950. *Principles of Economics* (1871). Glencoe, Ill.: Free Press.

Merton, Robert K. 1972. "The Institutional Imperatives of Science." In *Sociology of Science*, edited by Barry Barnes. London: Penguin Books. Pp. 65–79.

———. 1973. *The Sociology of Science, Theoretical and Empirical Investigations*. Chicago: University of Chicago Press.

Mulkay, Michael. 1972. "Cultural Growth in Science." In *Sociology of Science*, edited by Barry Barnes. London: Penguin Books. Pp. 126–42.

Myrdal, Gunnar. 1954. *The Political Element in the Development of Economic Theory*. New York: Simon and Schuster.

Review of Radical Political Economics. 1971. Special issue, "Scientific Paradigms and Economics" 3 (July).

Robinson, Joan. 1962. *Economic Philosophy*. London: Watts.

Schumpeter, Joseph A. 1954. *History of Economic Analysis*. New York: Oxford University Press.

Smith, Adam. 1904. *The Wealth of Nations*, edited by Edwin Cannan. London: Methuen and Co. (1st. ed. 1767).

Sraffa, Piero, ed. 1961. *David Ricardo: Works and Correspondence*. Cambridge: the University Press.

Stigler, George J. 1965. *Essays in the History of Economics*. Chicago: University of Chicago Press.

———. 1969. "Does Economics Have a Useful Past?" *History of Political Economy* 1 (Fall).

———. 1972. "The Adoption of the Marginal Utility Theory." *History of Political Economy* 4 (Fall): 571–86.

Walras, Léon. 1954. *Elements of Pure Economics* (1874–1877). Homewood, Ill.: Irwin.

Ward, Benjamin. 1972. *What's Wrong With Economics?* New York: Basic Books.

No Kuhnian Revolutions in Economics

Jorg Baumberger

A rapidly rising number of scientists seems to regard Thomas S. Kuhn's theory of scientific revolutions as descriptive of the way their discipline is evolving. Lately, Michael De Vroey, in "The Transition to Neoclassical Economics: A Scientific Revolution" [1975], has applied it to economics. Many of these applications, especially to economics and the social sciences in general, seem less than warranted by the letter of Kuhn's famous essay. On the other hand, the misinterpretations owe quite a bit to Kuhn himself. Although it would be grossly unfair to blame Kuhn for all genuine inadequacies in his followers' writings, some subtle ambiguities clearly attributable to Kuhn seem particularly apt to attract the more conspicuous errors of other science historians.

From a Logic of Science to a History of Science

An informal group of teachers at an American university, whose background ranged from the humanities to the sciences, recently was surprised that they all independently had elected Kuhn's work as the one

---

The author is Research Affiliate, Massachusetts Institute of Technology, Cambridge. *In preparing this article he benefited from comments by Donald A. Schon, Massachusetts Institute of Technology, and Thomas Vietorisz, The New School of Social Research.*

most relevant book in modern thinking about science. No one familiar with the way the progress of science had been depicted up to Kuhn should be particularly astonished about this result. Under the influence of an essentially positivistic philosophy of science, which dismissed psychology, sociology, and history of science from its subject matter, we have long taken for granted that the context of discovery, the context of application, and, in the last analysis, the context of justification are redundant in the description of scientific change. The only valid concern was the *logic of justification.* Although this philosophy of science never claimed to be more than a logic, and in particular never claimed to be a sociology, history, or psychology of science, it nevertheless shaped the prevailing conception of the history of science.

Even though the title of Karl Popper's famous book insisted that it was "but" a *logic* (*The Logic of Scientific Discovery*), publications such as his had a major effect on the historiography of science and on the self-perception of scientists. And this effect was far from being purely accidental. It was due in part to the fact that the advocates of the Vienna school of philosophy, through their pedantic insistence on the distinction between history, sociology, and psychology of science, on the one hand, and the philosophy of science, on the other, clearly aimed at, and partly succeeded in, denigrating all not strictly nomological research in these fields. These fields certainly were no integral parts of the Viennese school's philosophy of science. In fact, they were at best allowed to play the role of nonscientific footnotes to the one and only scientific inquiry into science, namely, the logic of science. The only admissible scientific study of science, the only science of science, the only metascience with any claim to scientificity, was their own formal logic of science. In their hierarchical conception of science this logic was the superstructure which logically controls the admissible "object" sciences, the so-called formal and the nomologically oriented "real" (or "special") sciences.

But despite itself, the positivistic pure logic of science also became the prevailing sociology and psychology of science of the day, and it was bound to. To begin with, the advocates of the positivistic logic of science proscribed any other inquiry into the wheelings and dealings of science except their own. Thus, it was natural that a model very much akin to their logic of science started trickling down into the void their criticism had produced. But there are more compelling reasons for its becoming the *de facto* ruling history, sociology, and psychology of science. Indeed, a pure logic of science (any pure logic whatever, for that matter) means nothing unless and until it is enriched with a behavioral connotation. All the abstract conceptual demarcation criteria and definitions of science, of the concept of explanation, and of whatnot, mean rigorously nothing unless they are given a behavioral content. On the other hand, the rigorous and highly restrictive definition of science that resulted from the adoption of the rigid demarcation criteria was bound to reflect itself in a limitation of the possible scope of a historiography of science. In other words, the necessity to give some behavioral content to the logic, on the one hand, and the rigid limitation of behavior to be subsumed under the class of "scientific behavior," on the other, combined to produce a *de facto* historiography, sociology, and psychology of science that were almost indistinguishable from the logic of science itself. Since in many circles this was the only conception available, it was freely projected onto the scientific process.

Moreover, it was somehow flattering to scientists to view themselves, and the past of their discipline, in terms of a Popperian logic of experiment, observation, and falsification, or in terms of a Carnapian logic of increasing inductive probability of hypotheses. The projection of this logic favored a perception of science as evolving through a series of discrete and disconnected decision points, each of which is the locus of a purely formal logical decision calculus, the calculus itself having the function of rationally producing, or at least simulating, the rejection or acceptance, in short, the logical assessment of hypotheses. In all this it was, of course, presupposed that the inputs into the logical calculus are, and can possibly be, of the most unbiased possible kind (leaving the question open what this means in terms of behavior), and that the output somehow faithfully bears upon concrete behavior as well.

In such a context, Kuhn's essay was bound to be a bombshell. After decades during which science had been viewed as a series of disconnected logical decision calculi (which may ultimately be performed by computers, and thereby be totally rationalized), there comes a fellow who dares say that, after all, *science is genuinely and basically human*. There can be no doubt that, metaphorically speaking, for many an observer of science Kuhn was the author who brought man back into the picture and reminded people of a few conspicuous facts that tended to be overlooked by philosophers and scientists alike. Indeed, it was high time to point out that theories are believed, disbelieved, made, tested, liked, disliked, interpreted, attacked, amended, improved, and not least of all *needed* by people talking and living among other people. In other words, he reminded everyone of the then not so trivial fact that *science is social* in every one of its manifestations. Likewise, it was necessary to spell out the pervading fact that what confers the seeming cohesion to the whole or a part of a scientific discipline is not anything approaching a thoroughgoing and explicit axiomatic structure; rather, it is a complex conceptual *and* behavioral structure replete with self-reinforcing, and at times insulating, logical and behavioral mechanisms. For some it came as a shock to be told that what was being taken as something like an aristocratic hierarchy of propositions with axioms forming the top was really a relatively self-contained, circular structure mediated and enforced by circularly rationalizing human beings. It was also disturbing to hear someone clearly state that, according to the empirical evidence, scientific inquiry is not basically truth-functional, that scientists in practice do not even bother too much about falsification or abstract inductive probabilities. It was certainly necessary to show that science, to the extent that it *is* controlled, is controlled by very complex and malleable, largely self-developed, and more often than not self-confirming, standards which, in practice, are genuinely indistinguishable from the whole of the human behavior displayed by the people engaged in science.

All this was certainly news for some people, and Kuhn deserves full credit for getting the message across.

The Meaning of "Revolution" and "Normal Science"

But it is well known that the key ingredients of the Kuhnian message are of an infinitely more specific nature, namely, they comprise also the "revolution"/"normal science" dualism. And it so happens that his dualism amounts to combining a badly needed rectification with a conceivable and appealing, but not very likely, extra-model about the way science undergoes change. In order to pinpoint the problem we must examine what this dualism really means. Several interpretations are conceivable.

I. Every single piece of scientific work is either "revolutionary" or "normal science" depending on its *internal propositional structure.* That is, the two terms are the two possible "values" of a property of the propositional appearance of a scientific utterance.

II. "Revolution" and "normal science" denote a *relationship between the propositional structures of a pair of scientific utterances* or of a pair of two *sets* of scientific utterances. Thus, such a pair can either be or not be in a relationship of "revolution to normal science." This version of the dualism admits two concrete interpretations:

IIa. The "revolution to normal science" relationship can obtain between any such pair, no matter whether, historically, they occur simultaneously or in sequence; and

IIb. the relationship can obtain only between the components of pairs that occur one after the other.

III. The concepts "revolution" and "normal science" do not, or not primarily or exclusively, refer to the propositional content of a science, but rather to two *complex behavioral modes of operation* of the scientific community, namely:

IIIa. The relative historical positions in which these behavior modes occur do not matter;

IIIb. the two modes cannot coexist, since "by definition" they constitute *stages* corresponding to roughly identifiable historical *periods*. They involve a scientific discipline as a whole.

Unfortunately, Kuhn is not very outspoken in this regard. It is not easy to uncover his conception. To arrive at a "testable" version of his theory one is partly forced to argue through the absurd. Thus, if I or II would adequately reflect his idea, the whole theory would boil down to the assertion that in scientific revolutions there occur important propositional changes and that, consequently, scientists have to "unlearn" and learn many things; conversely, if ostensibly scientists have to unlearn and learn a great many things, there is a scientific revolution. Yet, this story would be a relatively trivial one and would certainly tell us nothing over and above what was commonplace before Kuhn. It would be trivial because the specific dualistic morphology of the social learning and unlearning would largely fall outside the scope of the theory. From the point of view of the history and sociology of science this theory would be hollow. Such, clearly, is not the author's intent. To begin with, he speaks about "revolutions," thereby ostensibly trying to evoke at least some of the behavioral features of social upheaval. Moreover, he asserts [1970, p. 8] that his "generalizations" (and we are entitled to assume that the dualism is part and parcel of his generalizations) are about the "history and sociology of scientists." This being so we must take his assertions concerning the modalities of behavior very seriously. We must take it that breakdown of both communication and mutual intelligibility, the desperate search for *ad hoc* amendments of existing theories, the disruption of the social fabric of a discipline, and the increased reliance on extrascientific standards, increased behavioral uncertainty, and so forth, are what mark off a revolution from normal science. Lacking further historically and sociologically relevant information regarding the dualism, we have to assume that these characteristics define the historically and sociologically relevant content of the dualism.

On the other hand, Kuhn seems to think in terms of *periods*: "What is surprising . . . is that such divergences should ever largely disappear. For they do disappear to a very considerable extent and once and for all" [Kuhn 1970, p. 17]. In another passage he asserts that crisis is a "prelude to new theories" [Kuhn 1970, p. 85]. His repeated reference to "periods," not just "functions," strongly suggests that there is a *period* of normal science (not just a pocket) during which the revolutionary mode does not obtain for the discipline in question. In this period the victorious paradigm reigns sovereign and ensures a peaceful and piecemeal development within an agreed upon framework. The two modes seem to be discipline-wide behavioral and sociological phenomena. There is not just a propositional change together with an undefined social process, for he seems also to place some emphasis on the assertion that the revolutionary propositional change is accompanied by a revolutionary social and behavioral mode of operation clearly distinct from the mode of operation that prevails during periods of normal science. Revolutions also come to an end. The revolutionary crisis "is the only historical process that ever actually results in the rejection of one previously accepted theory or in the adoption of another" [Kuhn 1970, p. 8]. All this strongly argues in favor of something like the second portion of the third version that we mentioned above.

The first problem that arises in connection with this interpretation is that, ostensibly, the examples of scientific revolutions (Copernican and Einsteinian) on which Kuhn places greatest weight fail to illustrate his thesis. The revolutionary disarray and turmoil simply cannot be detected in physics, as Stephen Toulmin [1972], in his seminal work on the evolution of scientific concepts, has very aptly demonstrated. Rather, the transition occurred in a highly orderly, more often than not even gentlemanly, fashion and within a general atmosphere of intense and highly effective communication. There was certainly no breakdown in discipline-wide intelligibility, rationality, or sobriety during these two "revolutions." Most important of all, however, is Toulmin's observation that the historical material failed to support the thesis of a major behavioral discontinuity between the revolutionary and the supposedly nonrevolutionary normal science periods that preceded and followed the revolutions. To be sure, there did occur an important shift in the propositional structure and also in the general outlook of the scientists. But in all this the distinctive behavioral ingredients of a revolution seem to be conspicuously missing. The revolution metaphor seems at best to be a colorful exaggeration.

Pressed by his critics, Kuhn, in his 1969 Postscript, has retreated to a position very much in the neighborhood of II with extremely few behavioral connotations. What remains of these is of the type: If one propositionally revolutionary theory replaces another one there *has to be* a certain behavior mode. Somehow he confines himself to inferring the behavioral implications from the presupposed validity of the dualistic scheme. The social process of a "revolution" may now be very much like the social process of normal science. It takes little perspicacity to notice that such a *volte-face,* although it no doubt adjusts the scheme to the facts of physics, nevertheless strips the model of its possible sociological and historical message. It must be clearly understood that the relevance of the Kuhnian dualism rests on its peculiar fashion of connecting each of the two types of propositional change (large or small) with one, and only one, social mode of behavior. In other words, Kuhn's thesis is significant from a historical and sociological point of view (although perhaps not adequate) insofar as it claims that the revolution on paper occurs together with something like a revolution among people. We thus have to adhere to the IIIb version in assessing *Kuhn*'s relevance for transitions in economics, in particular the passage to neoclassicism with which De Vroey is dealing. This strategy is sensible since it would be much ado about nothing if the application of Kuhn's theory to economics would boil down to the assertion that the transition meant an important change in writing and speaking about economics. That much we have known all along (and we have also known the numerous traits that the neoclassics have inherited from the classics). By trying to apply the IIIb version of Kuhn's story in an unbiased fashion to the transition from classical to neoclassical economics we are bound to make some very astonishing observations. Incidentally, these are exactly the opposite of De Vroey's conclusions. In the Kuhnian account it is fairly explicit that the periods of revolution sooner or later come to an end so that the canvas is cleared for another period of normal science that then develops piecemeal and in a more or less cumulative fashion on the basis of a common consistent paradigm.

Permanent Dialectic Instead of Revolution

What was the course of events during and after the emergence of the neoclassical approach? To begin with, any historical analysis of the rise of neoclassicism is bound to present serious lacunae by neglecting Marx.

Regardless of one's assessment of Marx, the fact remains that he represents the *other* major event in the history of economics in that era (and not only in that one). His work is a pivotal event that happened to occur in very much the same epoch as the rise of neoclassicism. It is rather easy to construct a defeat of the classical school if one sets Marx outside the scope of one's analysis. However, in a comprehensive historical study of the evolution of the economic science in the 1870s one has to account for the fact that Marx is the legitimate heir of the classical tradition. No one was more vividly aware of the fact than he, himself. He consciously uses the basic apparatus of classical economics in his criticism, and more revealing in this context is the striking observation that, when criticizing Adam Smith or David Ricardo, he usually abstains from the furious Cicero-like contempt and sarcasm that are characteristic of his attacks on what he calls "vulgar economics." In fact, very few would argue that he is not firmly rooted in the classical tradition, so much so that a famous neoclassical economist recently called him "a minor post-Ricardian." We may argue about the rating, but it would be difficult to deny his theoretical affiliation. This judgment is confirmed by Joseph A. Schumpeter: "Ricardo was Marx's master, and . . . Marx, though he transformed the theoretical material he found, yet worked with tools that he found and not with tools that he created." And in a footnote he is even more specific: "So far as theory is concerned, this makes Marx an English economist. And he was one" [Schumpeter 1954, p. 390]. The "English" here clearly stands for "classical." It would also be fallacious to believe that the Marxian interpretation and transformation of the Ricardian system came entirely off the top of Marx's head. Rather, Ricardo's followers, and very likely Ricardo himself, were "alarmed by the vistas which were opened up to them" [Sweezy 1970, p. 38].

We might also be tempted to argue that Marx can be dismissed in the historiography of the rise of neoclassicism on the grounds, first, that he was dead when the neoclassical movement actually began and that, second, he could not possibly be considered a participant in the debate because he was unaware of the subjective value theory. The first assertion, of course, cannot be denied, but the second one is positively incorrect. Stanley Jevons himself was perfectly aware that his generation of economists was not the inventor of subjective theory [Jevons 1970, p. 94], and he gives Jeremy Bentham explicit credit for it. Indeed, the static Benthamite pleasure/pain calculus which, despite many "improvements," constitutes the conceptual foundations of the neoclassical approach up to this day had already been around for half a century when it was picked up by the emerging school of economics. And, more important, Marx had been sensing all along that Bentham's was a doctrine that was bound to be eagerly adopted by some economists. That is why he explicitly rejected it with the whole eloquence of his colorful contempt [Marx 1973, p. 146, pp. 599–600]. This, by itself, should be sufficient evidence in support of the contention that he, qua the intellectual movement, was a party in his own right in the debate that ensued.

The fact that Marx did not confine himself to paraphrasing the classical tradition, but instead transformed it and combined it with his own version of Hegelian dialectic, does not invalidate this thesis.

After Marx, "Marx" could not possibly be overlooked in any discussion of classical economics. He certainly set a new standard within this tradition. One may well venture the conjecture that the fact that a revolutionary rather than an inoffensive German *Geheimrat* henceforth represented the most recent branch of the classical tree greatly helped to establish the dignity of the comparatively sectarian neoclassical movement. In this context it is well known that Eugen von Böhm-Bawerk's capital theory was primarily destined to refute Marx. The minister of finance of the Austro-Hungarian monarchy was hardly guided by purely scientific motives. The opposition to "Marx the revolutionary" stimulated a lot of neoclassical work which formally took the shape of attacks against "Marx the scientist" and his classical ancestry. It may not be too far off the mark to say that, had it not been for Marx, today's mainstream economics could much more comfortably relate to the classical tradition.

But although Marx clearly is an offspring of classical economics, he fails to provide a convincing example of puzzle-solving normal science. We will have to keep that in mind later on.

On the other hand, "classical-economics-including-Marx" by no means died after Marx. Just as there is a clear genealogical line from Smith to Marx, there are multiple lines leading beyond them that no less clearly carry on the tradition. To be sure, this tradition is much more dynamic than a rigid Kuhnian "paradigm," but this "tradition in progress" nevertheless constitutes a historical whole. The classico-Marxian ancestry cannot be denied, and its descendants are well known. The first that comes to mind is the Marxist tradition with all its orthodox and revisionist factions, but there is also American institutionalism as exemplified by Thorstein Veblen. Then there is contemporary neo-Marxism. The peace of the neoclassical era has also been somewhat disrupted by the Cambridge post-Keynesians, where the classical tradition is mediated by a group of post-Ricardians.

Is this an undue inflation of the classical tradition? Not at all! The fact that that tradition does not fit into the Procrustean bed of a Kuhnian normal science paradigm and the fact that it turns out to be more vigorous than we would superficially have suspected is no reason to whittle it down to size so that it becomes comparable to the neoclassical tradition, with its much greater homogeneity and discipline. Such a procedure would be like pointing to one segment of an ongoing conflict in order to demonstrate that one of the participants won it. Historiography can do a better job, at least if we assume that the purpose of historiography of science is not to provide footnotes to Kuhn but to produce an intelligible and instructive account of the way science evolves, that is, of the laws of motion of science, so to speak.

These remarks, although sketchy, suffice to demonstrate that there has been less than complete peace in economics ever since the neoclassical "revolution." By any standards, the classical paradigm (if we may call the content of the tradition by that name) has been around all the time, and the battle is far from finished. If there was something like a revolution a hundred years ago, the intervening century clearly was not sufficient to consolidate it.

In a sense, economics provides the counter-example *par excellence* to physics. But, as does physics, it fails to illustrate and support Kuhn's schema. Whereas in physics we look in vain for the period of the revolutionary mode of behavior, in economics we are at a loss to find the period of the normal science mode of behavior.

Now, no one would argue that there is not a great deal of puzzle-solving, limited scope science in economics, especially in the wake of the neoclassical "revolution." This is all too plain. But its presence cannot be taken as an indicator for Kuhnian normal science; because Kuhnian normal science, in the only nontrivial (IIIb) sense, is not just any puzzle-solving science, but a whole *period* of it, that is, a period when the scientific community as a whole is operating within a common paradigm with respect to a wide range of questions. The puzzle-solving science which we have been witnessing in the wake of the neoclassical "revolution" is not the Kuhnian normal science which follows a successful revolution; it is simply the expression of the sheer scale of institutionalized science. In order to keep this huge and fast-growing machine busy there is bound to be a lot of niggling, even in the midst of the fiercest of revolutions, so to speak. No one denies that this machine generates its own dynamic, but this dynamic is not adequately describable in terms of the Kuhnian dualism. What we have been witnessing in economics also fits poorly into the mold of a Kuhnian revolution. A revolution that is never completed may well be a permanent one in a colloquial sense, but it certainly is not a Kuhnian one.

By refraining from looking at things through the Kuhnian looking glass we notice that (1) both of the traditions in question have been around ever since the birth of the neoclassical approach; (2) the conflict between the two has flared up in various shapes at different moments and is still with us; (3) there has been puzzle-solving work along both tracks, although admittedly more in neoclassics due to its limited scope and large number of adherents in the United States, the home of large-scale institutionalized science; (4) both traditions have undergone and produced qualitative and quantitative change. One has evolved more along the lines of mathematics, the other more along the lines of political economy proper; and (5) the changes in both camps were not independent from each other. Rather, they occurred within a tough and continuing *bataille rangée*.

In point of fact, De Vroey, who claims that the rise of neoclassical economics was a Kuhnian revolution, does not really succeed in making his point watertight. In order to do this he would have to show persuasively, first, that the period preceding the neoclassical "revolution" was one of normal science in the Kuhnian sense; second, that the emergence of the neoclassical approach was a full-fledged revolution in the Kuhnian sense; and, finally, that the shift was followed by another period of normal science. This he does not attempt to, and cannot, demonstrate, because it did not happen. It is of no avail to point out that there is no Popperian changeover either. We may grant *cum grano salis* that "the transition concerned really the premises of analysis" [De Vroey 1975, p. 429], but this is not enough to turn the whole into a full-fledged Kuhnian revolution in the IIIb sense. What this observation shows is simply that there surely was a revolution of the historically and sociologically trivial II type. It neither proves that there was more nor that, *if* there was more (which happens to be the case), the "more" was a Kuhnian revolution.

In sum, the case for scientific revolution in economics seems to boil down to something like this: (1) Since the period in question displays a large propositional change, (2) since there is evidence for puzzle-solving science before and after the period in question, (3) since the paradigms in question, during this period, served and reflected political and ideological positions and processes, and since the whole transition occurs in the midst of a politics-laden atmosphere, there has to be a Kuhnian scientific revolution somewhere along the way. Even though

I am far from arguing about these assertions, I do believe that it takes a great deal of eclecticism to infer from them that we are faced with anything like a genuine Kuhnian revolution in economics, today no more than a century ago.

These points fail to show (and no one can show it) that *before* and *after* the period of the rise of neoclassicism economics was operating in a normal science puzzle-solving way under a unique paradigm. They also fail to demonstrate (and no one will ever be able to demonstrate it) that *during* the supposed revolution the behavioral, social, and psychological mode of operation was markedly different from what it used to be before the period of transition and has been since.

The Struggle about the Boundary

Despite all this, I must admit that the case against the revolution thesis is not yet completely watertight, and cannot be made such. Indeed, the objection can be raised that the opponents of the neoclassical paradigm placed themselves, or were placed by their fellows, outside the discipline proper. Such a thesis finds some support in Kuhn's essay: "To desert the paradigm is to cease practicing the science it defines" [Kuhn 1970, p. 34]. "The new paradigm implies a new and more rigid definition of the field. Those unwilling or unable to accommodate their work to it must proceed in isolation or attach themselves to some other group" [Kuhn 1970, p. 19]. It is clear that if we regard the adversaries of neoclassicism as drop-outs from economics, all our arguments concerning Marx and other post-Marxian and postclassical trends would turn out to be beside the point, and De Vroey's thesis thereby would be validated. I refrain from attempting to close this gap because *this* particular riddle points less to a weakness in my argument, or in De Vroey's for that matter, than it touches upon a very sensitive point in Kuhn's theory. The quoted sentences are absolutely crucial ones, and Kuhn may not have paid enough attention to their significance. As did Wallenstein, we might say: *"Du sprichst ein grosses Wort gelassen aus!"*

Indeed, the above statements by Kuhn are an extremely dangerous and distortive device in the hands of historians who use them to chop off major pieces from the history of science or from the history and current inventory of their disciplines. There is nothing in Kuhn to prevent such a use. We will presently see that there is much in his essay that is apt to enhance it.

For the time being we may note that in scientific conflicts such as the one at hand the very question: "Is or is not this or that movement part of the discipline, and thus part of a historical account of the discipline's possible revolutionary change?" is likely to lead us astray because it suggests answers that inevitably out-define the issue. It is of paramount importance to keep in mind that in all serious large-scale and long-standing conflicts and competitive processes the parties tend to acquire a set of "secondary sexual characteristics" whose implicit function consists in producing and maintaining identity *vis-à-vis* the adversary. Thus, we often observe marked differences between the contending factions as to their modal way of clothing, talking, and defining the boundaries of the discipline. Quite often there are significant differences in such mundane things as the use of neckties, the size and age of cars, the average incomes. According to their allegiance, scientists also tend to be politely locked out of certain journals and tend furiously or complacently to lock themselves into their own set of publications. Moreover, periods of ostensible clash often alternate with periods in which the scientific landscape locally looks as peaceful and as neatly subdivided as a field of trenches in World War I. There are *drôle de guerres,* guerrillas, and full-fledged wars in science as well. The list of configurations and possible changes in configurations of these "secondary features" could be indefinitely expanded; and as we would proceed we would be bound to notice that form and substance do not come neatly separated, that the secondary and the primary features occur together in the shape of an inextricable whole. This renders the identification of conflicts and of the objects of conflicts extremely difficult. Nevertheless, such are the essential features of large-scale conflict, no matter whether scientific or "real." The two spheres of life are not hermetically sealed off anyway, as the history of science even of this enlightened century clearly demonstrates. In particular, it is a pervasive fact of this ambiguous kind of warfare in science that one or both of the contenders often attempt to place the opponent outside the scope of the discipline or outside of science as such. Inclusion and exclusion are not so much the unambiguous outcomes of settled conflicts as they are the weapons *and* the stakes in an ongoing manifest or latent confrontation. The definition of the battlefield and of the admissible participants are both stakes and weapons. After all, this is what all the *Methodenstreite* in economics have always been all about: to liquidate scientifically some school of thought by associating it with poetry rather than science. To ignore this is to neglect the properly historical, sociological, psychological, and ultimately also the scientific dimensions of the scientific process.

From these reflections it follows that what is and what is not part of a discipline is not only difficult to determine but also is a question that cannot be answered in simple terms at all. The historian who considers the demarcation as something that can unambiguously and undialectically be determined in terms of "in" or "out," or even in terms of a quantitative scale, is reminiscent of the historian who expects a purely one-valued, geographical answer to the question: "What is the Israeli border?" Such questions cannot be answered except in terms of the conflicting claims and the concomitant action. The whole process, and all that supports it, is the boundary, so to speak.

The Boundaries

Now, it is one thing to state that the opponents differentiate themselves and differentiate each other (by expelling each other from science or from the discipline), sometimes to a very considerable extent (in fact, to such an extent that all the attributes of coexisting disciplines and subcultures start emerging); but it is quite another thing to rely on the testimony of one, or both, factions in the demarcation of the field of historical inquiry. In other words, it is one thing to say (metaphorically) that an Arab country which establishes friendly relations with Israel places itself outside the Arab world and quite another to dismiss such a country from a study on the evolution of the Arab world, that is, actually to regard it as non-Arab and thus rely on the single-valued, partisan testimony of the conflicting parties. Just as, in political history, such an omission backfires in the form of an exaggerated coherence of political entities, in science it backfires in the form of illusions about the coherence and discreteness of disciplines. But is not this exactly what Kuhn does all along: exaggerate the coherence of the disciplines by ignoring the concrete nature of the compartmentalization of science and implicitly give the benefit of the doubt to the faction with the narrowest definition of the field? The idea does not occur to him that many, if not all, the clusters that we label "disciplines" might fruitfully be regarded as mere factions.

Although his theory stands and falls with certain very specific boundaries between science and nonscience, between mature, historic, paradigmatic science, on the one hand, and immature, prehistoric, nonparadigmatic science, on the other, between one specific science and another, between one specific discipline and another, and finally between the periods of normal science and the periods of crisis and revolutionary science, he completely fails to face the *demarcation problem* in any systematic fashion. The very nature of that problem seems to escape him, and it does so for an obvious reason. The entire exposition rests on the hidden assumption that there are *discrete "discipline-atoms"* separated from each other by fairly large amounts of empty nonscience space. In principle, these atoms are assumed to be classifiable one by one in terms of the Kuhnian schema. Some of them are tightly knit, well-defined, highly self-contained, mature discipline-atoms. Others are large, fuzzy, and logically and behaviorally unhandy and unsatisfactory. These are the immature ones. As a matter of fact, the immature atoms are as unhandy as most other things in the world, for example, art and politics. That is why it is often utterly unclear whether or not an immature atom is really a science at all. Of course, this way of reasoning pulls the rug from under any in-depth treatment of the demarcation problem. The problem becomes a purely "semantic" one, into which "often great energy is invested, great passion aroused," but where the "outsider is at a loss to know why" [Kuhn 1970, p. 160]. Kuhn's notion of science is derived from a one-sided interpretation of everyday language usage [Kuhn 1970, p. 160], at which he arrives by deliberately ignoring the fact that the ambiguity of the term "science" in the vernacular is a rather faithful mirror-image of a concrete and ongoing conflict within science; it therefore does not "mean" anything simpler than this very conflict in all its complexity.

Based on this background theory Kuhn takes for granted a sweeping theory of scientific development. Science, according to him, is engaged in a secular process of maturation, that is, a process whereby immaturity (in the sense defined above) is gradually replaced by maturity. To a large extent this is a purely definitional tenet. The single discipline-atom attains maturity once it displays the properties outlined above. "Ever since prehistoric antiquity one field after another has crossed the divide between what the historian might call its prehistory as a science and its history proper" [Kuhn 1970, p. 21]. Kuhn fails to deal with the question of whether the totality of all science-atoms as a whole also undergoes a maturation process. Presumably he thinks that the maturation of science as a whole consists in the ever increasing number of atoms on the maturity side of the boundary. However this may be, maturation of science, or just of the science-atoms, in Kuhn's hands, becomes a secular process producing *ever increasing discreteness,* or more precisely, a process in which the essential underlying discreteness of the as yet not perfectly discrete discipline-atoms tends to become manifest in the scientific process, thereby presumably expressing the essential discreteness of the object of science itself. To Kuhn this seems to be a pure statement of a historical law. It has no value connotation whatsoever.

Disciplines as Interacting Historical Wholes

If we evaluate this atomic conception of science in the light of our findings from economics and those that, for example, Toulmin has contributed from a host of other sciences, we are led to suspect that there might be something wrong with the whole conception. Indeed, Kuhn ignores or plays down the fact that the conceptual and behavioral process in which a scientific generation engages is, as a whole, a *transmit from* and a *transform of* what preceded them, revolution or no revolution. In other words, the historical whole constituted by a scientific generation, or a generation of a discipline, is contingent upon, but never identical with, what went before. On the other hand, this transmit, at whatever level we may look at it, never displays the placid consistency and discreteness of a Kuhnian normal science paradigm or a Kuhnian discipline-atom. All the discreteness, constancy, and self-sufficiency that Kuhn ascribes to his entities are abstractions. Now, there is nothing wrong with abstractions *per se,* but we should be very suspicious of historians who, after mortgaging their concepts with heroic assumptions concerning constancy and discreteness, start creating sweeping theories of history destined to "explain" the discontinuities that they are bound to encounter once they start projecting their abstractions onto their subject matter. In actual fact, the transmission constituted by a discipline, or science as a whole, is a *population of far from discrete process fields* or activity areas that are competing and conflicting in many different, but interdependent, complex fashions. Pockets of this whole may well, and are bound to, in an era of large-scale institutionalized science, in an oblique sense, approach the process characteristics of a normal science à la Kuhn. But the whole, even the whole of a subdiscipline, never displays these properties, least so in economics.

One reason, among many, for this state of affairs resides in the fact that these pseudo-Kuhnian pockets, however large they may be in terms of personnel, not only affirm something but also negate and attack other things. Every paradigm has its gatekeepers. They are the institutions that ultimately give shape to the paradigm. But they cannot help giving shape to other things as well, among them to the people and theories they negate, or to the disciplines to which, by projection, they assign all the problems with which their own discipline does not deal. This is all too plain in economics. A great deal of the content of the conflicting or complementary "paradigms" draws its very shape from the presence, and is literally responsible for the presence, of divergent and complementary paradigms in the population.

The *conflict-symbiosis* between political economy proper, on the one hand, and neoclassical economics and all the specialized social sciences, on the other, is a case in point of such a negative but mutually supportive relationship. The *complementarity-symbiosis* between neoclassical economics and all the other specialized social sciences is an example of a positive, mutually supportive relationship. Indeed, as early a neoclassicist as Jevons was urging the creation of a whole range of specialized social sciences, a range that was not long in cropping up wherever neoclassical economics flourished, in particular in the last forty years in the United States: "It is by subdivision, by recognizing a branch of economic sociology, together possibly with two or three other branches of statistical, jurial or social science, that we can rescue our science from its confused state" [Jevons 1970, p. 89]. It is clear also from these two related examples that the nonconflict in the latter case, which, by the way, Kuhn, in his excursion into the realm of the social sciences, promptly misinterprets as indicative of the relative "maturity" of economics in his sense [Kuhn 1970, pp. 160–61], is really a highly partisan nonconflict. Its nature cannot be adequately understood without reference to the ongoing conflict between the specialized social and historical sciences and political economy proper.

The Kuhnian discreteness assumptions are not just slight exaggerations or "ideal types." They are the foundations of a static and atomic universe wherein all sorts of tricks must be invented to account for change.

The whole of a discipline cannot possibly be adequately described by the Kuhnian apparatus because the demarcation process is always part and parcel of this whole, whether or not there is ostensible conflict. This process is crucial for the shape and content of the discipline; and its concrete nature accounts for the concrete type of fuzziness displayed by every science and by the mosaic of science as a whole. Where the demarcation process is inconspicuous at first sight, it would be a serious mistake to take this as evidence for the absence of such a process. In point of fact, it requires a highly orderly and timely, and thus extremely improbable, process to achieve locally such a state of affairs. This alone should be a sufficient incentive to devote the utmost attention to such phenomena.

By thus discarding the rigidity of the Kuhnian scheme we can see that disciplines decisively interact and shape each other even though, at some specific level, there is little formal interaction. Sometimes disciplines are similar to divided countries. An observer without a holistic understanding would be inclined to "see" two discrete, barely interacting, entities, whereas, in fact, the two "independent" modes of operation and paradigms arise from a mutual negation and would hardly be the same were there no antagonism. To some observers political economy proper (not only, but including, the Marxian variant), in the sense of the study of the total social, political, and economic household, may formally look like a discipline distinct from economics, if political economy is, or can be regarded as, a discipline at all. Yet, even though at times political economists only talk to each other, and "straight" economists only to other "straight" economists, it would amount to shallow historiography to ignore the antagonism in theorizing about the evolution of the two factions.

To deal with disciplines atomistically amounts to misunderstanding the very nature of differentiation in science and everywhere else. Differentiation enhances independence only in a dialectical sense. The significant aspect of differentiation in science is not that disciplines *are* differentiated, whatever such a "state" may mean, but rather the fact that, and the manner in which, the concrete differentiating process and the concomitant *concrete integrating process occur, that is, reproduce themselves and/or change, with and without apparent conflict. Some* concrete way of integrating always occurs in science, whether or not it was planned, because integration and differentiation are but the obverse and reverse of one and the same coin. In science, as in international politics, stabilized boundaries are something less than perfectly stable boundaries and should not be mistaken for such. Even less are they boundaries where "nothing happens." Nothing requires more change and activity than to achieve local stabilization.

Very few could be more critical than I am of the multifaceted scientific-ideological whole that is usually labeled "Marxism." However, as I argued above, this is no excuse for rewriting history in a distortive manner. I would now like to add that there also is no valid reason to reject the intellectual approach that permeates Marx's thought, namely, the tradition of Heraclitean dialectic. Indeed, the refutation of the Kuhnian scheme for economics strongly suggests that a holistic and dialectical mode of historiography might offer a more effective tool for describing and understanding the evolution of science than do the cyclical theory of revolution and normal science and the underlying atomic theory of the maturation of science. The toolbox of dialectic would even produce the additional payoff of shedding some light on the notion of revolution itself and thus produce valuable insights into the ambiguous and dialectical nature of every kind of seemingly sweeping discontinuities. Among other things, it might give rise to a few interesting reflections on the thus far ambiguous and controversial Keynesian revolution that some regard as abortive, others as consummated, others as not yet completed, still others as completed and having led to disaster. But first and foremost, dialectic seems to be *par excellence* a theory of continuous dynamic social disequilibrium fields in which competition and conflict, differentiation and integration, innovative variation and elimination play predominant roles. It is a theory of nondiscrete, intimately interlocked historical wholes in process. Dialectic, so it seems to me, is not only an interesting way of thinking about the motion of capitalism, but also a highly instructive manner of theorizing about the motion of the economic science. Just as the classics of economics may, in many respects, still have some potential for grasping today's economy, the classics of the motion of mind may still retain some potential for promoting the understanding of the motion of science, perhaps more than much of contemporary historiography of science.

Proliferation of Revolutions

Before concluding, I would like briefly to raise the question of what accounts for the immense popularity of the Kuhnian thesis among the scientific community, especially among social scientists. Part of the reason certainly resides in the fact, mentioned earlier, that it emerged after a rather long period of "Dark Ages" in which, in some circles, an incredibly dull and dry story had been told about the evolution of science. Suddenly, there was a new story that many practicing scientists were immediately able to recognize as strikingly similar to their own experience in the institutional process of organized science. But I dare conjecture that there is an additional appeal as well, especially for younger scientists. Indeed, a cursory reading and/or the ambiguities arising in the course of a more thorough study of Kuhn's essay make it relatively easy to stretch the concepts a little so as to confer a revolutionary aura to many things in the scientific universe, not least to one's own struggle within the tough and extremely "human" environment of bureaucratized science. It undoubtedly offers some comfort to view oneself as the lonely revolutionary who is fighting against a fossilized normal science establishment. Given today's history-less scientific training, scientists may well be unaware of the evolutionary, populational (that is, ecological), and conflict-laden character of the history of their discipline and of science as a whole. The Galileo, Lysenko, and Nazi science episodes may be the only, and unfortunately only the most extreme, historical examples of the essentially "human" nature of science that they are aware of. On the other hand, their daily struggle in which scientific and "extrascientific" problems do not come neatly separated, but are inextricably intertwined, does not leave the slightest doubt that, here and now, there are competing and conflicting people, schools, theories, sciences, vested and nonvested interests, and so forth, and that, here and now, fairness and rationality are problems rather than facts. Equipped with the Kuhnian looking glass they are only too inclined to assume that their period is an instance of the revolutionary part of Kuhn's dualism. In some sense the Kuhnian scheme is being misused as a valve for many a scientist's frustration. Just as the Popperian scheme tends to be the stereotype of a self-content science, the Kuhnian scheme tends to take on the function of a stereotype for the discontents within science. I personally am convinced that for the understanding of these phenomena another theory of the history of science would be much more effective and would tremendously enhance the perspicacity and awareness of the historian and scientist alike.

References

De Vroey, Michel. 1975. "The Transition from Classical to Neoclassical Economics: A Scientific Revolution." *Journal of Economic Issues* 9 (September): 415–40.

Jevons, W. Stanley. 1970 [1871]. *The Theory of Political Economy*. Harmondsworth: Penguin.

Kuhn, Thomas S. 1970. *The Structure of Scientific Revolutions,* 2d enlarged ed. Chicago: University of Chicago Press.

Marx, Karl. 1973 [1867]. *Das Kapital, Kritik der politischen Oekonomie,* Band I: *Der Produktionsprozess des Kapitals,* 5th ed. Frankfurt am Main: Ullstein.

Popper, Karl. 1965. *The Logic of Scientific Discovery*. New York: Harper & Row.

Schumpeter, Joseph A. 1954. *History of Economic Analysis*. New York: Oxford University Press.

Sweezy, Paul M. 1970 [1942]. *The Theory of Capitalist Development*. New York: Modern Reader.

Toulmin, Stephen. 1972. *Human Understanding,* vol. 1, *The Collective Use and Evolution of Concepts*. Princeton: Princeton University Press.

Part IV

Critique of Economic Theory as Social Control and a Guide to Policy

Introduction

The question of the role of economic theory in social control is considered directly by David Dale Martin. As to whether economic theory provides useful insights with regard to changing legal rules, Martin's answer is mixed. Orthodox economic theory has elements of the theory of social control of a business society, for example, maximizing and conflict resolution through markets. A nondogmatic application of the theory can be helpful. But certain characteristics of our society are likely to result in the abuse of economic theory when used in developing and changing legal rules: unneutral, nonmarket mechanisms are required to produce redistribution of income and wealth, and these are almost systematically excluded by theory; business is important in determining the relative degree and distribution of scarcity that exists in society; and economic theory fails to consider important consequences of the corporate system insofar as it portrays conflict resolution through markets. Martin discusses several fundamental limits to economic theory as a guide to policy. He recognizes that the "efficiency" argument tends to build in the status quo power structure as proper; business power (and not the market *per se*) governs preferences, relative scarcity, technology, products, markets, and product standards; and the corporate power system forms the market but is taken by orthodox theory as merely a peaceful system of voluntary exchange. As Lekachman asserts, and as is treated in depth in *The Economy as a System of Power,* the chief limitation of economic theory is its neglect of the fundamental structure of social power, the rationalization of which is a chief service (as social control and psychic balm) performed by theory.

Martin's analysis is, in effect, further developed by William H. Melody's discussion of the use of marginal analysis in the formation of public policy. Melody makes a number of important points. He believes there are no standard microeconomic solutions to policy issues, although microeconomic theory is usually employed to reinforce status quo institutions and power structure. Marginal analysis and optimization require a specification of content, and that specification is selective and manipulable (thus, for example, the reinforcement of status quo institutions and power structure is selective). Melody illustrates this through a critique of marginal cost pricing in principle and in application, focusing especially on its use to rationalize positions predetermined on strategic grounds. He argues that marginal cost is a function of the power structure governing decision making. (On this point, see the review articles by A. Allan Schmid, below.) Moreover, marginal analysis assumes a competitive market structure yet is used to support monopoly and restrictive practices. Accordingly, Melody finds that the terminology (conceptualization) of marginal analysis is sterile but is nonetheless available for selective use. He calls for accountability, believing that facts asserted by theory will continue to seem like facts until they are challenged. In other words, the use of economic theory in public policy formation requires an adversary system challenging the presumption of orthodoxy that it has a monopoly of technique and insight, if not also of truth.

Alfred E. Kahn, himself a distinguished analyst of power in economic affairs, presents a critique of the Martin and Melody articles. Kahn does not consider Martin's analysis in itself a sufficient guide to policy. We need to know more about the precise relation of our economic institutions to the nature of conscious choice. Also the search for efficiency (in the economists' sense) is not all that bad: it possibly can eliminate dysfunctional redistributive schemes. As for Melody's views, Kahn agrees that marginal cost pricing can be predatory. But Kahn argues that disregard of marginal costs and adoption of a return-on-the-past investment rule mean using sunk costs as the decisive criterion, which is contrary to the traditional understanding that sunk costs are gone and should not enter current decisions. He presents a quite detailed critique of Melody's arguments against marginal cost pricing. In general, Kahn agrees that there are serious dangers of misuse but insists that it does not follow that marginal cost theory should not be used at all.

Marginalist analysis is central to welfare economics, the subject of the remaining articles in this section. Sherman Krupp's analysis applies to all theoretical systems in its stress on the critical role of axioms. With regard to welfare economics specifically, Krupp argues that "efficiency" is a relationship that cannot be observed (with the implication that all designations of real world phenomena as efficient are subjective and selective). He maintains that efficiency analysis is tautological with meaning acquired only within the larger theory (a point also made by Wilber and Wisman). Krupp believes that deduced efficiency is a function of the terms of postulated efficiency (including the premises on power structure and whose interests ought to count); that theorists' use of efficiency analysis in partial equilibrium situations often, if not usually, neglect externalities; and that standard analysis, which takes distributional variables as given, tends to rationalize and reinforce existing distribution. In general, Krupp argues both that efficiency analysis lacks the capacity for confrontation with experience, except insofar as selective specification of efficiency postulates and premises is made, and that that is presumptive, such that efficiency conclusions are a function of the specification and use of the underlying efficiency axioms and premises as to rights.

G. Warren Nutter also is critical of welfare economics, finding it narrow, bankrupt, and pseudoscientific. He finds Pareto optimality, the heart of the so-called new welfare economics, sterile in the face of change. The central problem that welfare economics should be facing, and, in his view, is not, is that of determining the decision-making process and structure, namely, the rules for making rules. Such a task would require, he recognizes, a revival of the notion of progress as a subject of inquiry.

The next four articles present extended critiques of various aspects of applied welfare economics. The effort is important because applied welfare economics comprises a main use of economic theory as social control and a guide to policy. Victor Goldberg argues that the ostensibly positive analysis of welfare economics actually contains and indeed requires deep and selective normative choices and that distinctive normative biases characterize much of the literature. He points to a paradox found in the writings of many users of applied welfare economics, namely, their assertion that individual preferences should count but their failure to develop normative rules based solely on that criterion. Goldberg finds that orthodox analysts place severe boundaries on the utility functions that they use in their work. They take tastes as exogenously given (which means giving effect to the structure of power in the market that endogenously produces tastes and preferences). They tend to treat ethical and commodity preferences differently, especially preferences operative with regard to political action. They tend to permit only certain preferences and certain persons' preferences to count and not others. Finally, *inter alia,* they support certain forms of hierarchical decision making while repudiating others. Goldberg also examines the unanimity and compensation principles and the theory of constitutional choice and in each case finds ambiguity, selectivity, and the inevitable role of often disguised value judgments as to whose interests, or which preferences, ought to count. Ostensibly positive and objective theory is seen to become a brief for selected interests and a certain policy perspective.[2]

In two review articles, A. Allan Schmid examines the same literature as Goldberg and reaches similar conclusions. He finds that both public choice and property rights theory make inplicit assumptions as to whose interests should count, and only then is it possible to reach policy conclusions. With regard to public choice theory, Schmid argues that the theory neglects the fact that costs (that is, which effects are a burden to whom) are a function of and indeed the essence of public choice. He finds public choice theorists making implicit assumptions as to rights and thereby who counts, which is to say, whose interests become a cost to others. The theory, always with varying degrees of normative evaluation, does enable us to make limited predictions of behavior under different public choice rules, but it is no guide as to who should have what rights or to the choice of rules themselves. As for the ostensible use of the Pareto criterion in public choice theory, Schmid finds broad policy inferences are being made that only constitute presumptive optimality reasoning without regard to losses incurred by the adoption of the rule(s) in question.[3]

Regarding property rights theory, Schmid notes much of the literature argues that the creation of property rights can make markets work. In his view this is essentially a tautology. Since the market working means individual valuation and adjustment, property is instrumental; property carries out the logic of the market, and the market carries out the logic of property. Schmid is critical not of the regime of markets, but of that approach to choosing among alternative assignments of property rights that maintains one can allocate rights so as to minimize costs, including transaction costs. He argues that this is fallacious and permits implicit judgments as to whose interests should count as costs to others. He insists that cost is not something that exists independent of the property rights system and thus cannot be a guide to choice of that system. The problem is to determine whether rights now held, or held under any right-definition-and-assignment system, are the "correct" ones, an issue on which the Chicago-influenced property rights literature is weak. Schmid reasons as follows: "The point is that there is a cost minimization for each alternative property rights distribution. Cost minimization then cannot be a guide to the choice of that distribution." Furthermore, alternative cost minimizations cannot be compared meaningfully inasmuch as they each affect different bundles of interests, that is, different registrations of costs; to choose between them requires judgments as to whose interests are to count as costs to others. The typical orthodox analysis in this area, Schmid finds, "is not addressed to the broader questions of the original and subsequent vestures of property rights among people. It speaks only to the secondary question of carrying out the logic of the costs implicit in a given rights distribution," which may be that of the status quo (selectively defined) or some other implicit structure.[4]

Some of the reasoning of applied welfare economics has found its way into policy-oriented undergraduate texts. In a review of several of these works, Alan Randall finds positivism (objectivity and neutrality) mixed with selectivity and normativism. The basic economic analysis itself is unable to produce the policy answers stressed by the authors; the policies stem from implicit antecedent normative premises introduced by the authors. Randall finds that the efficiency stressed by these writers is severely limited by their neglect of the distribution of income, wealth, and power, distributions governing whose interests count in efficient solutions.[5]

In the concluding article in this section, E. K. Hunt and Ralph C. d'Arge offer a guide to policy in what they call a contextualist framework as an alternative to the mechanistic neoclassical applied welfare economics. Hunt and d'Arge are concerned that overemphasis upon acquisitive desires may lead U.S. society toward environmental catastrophe and that neoclassical analysis, useful for analyzing the operation of the system but unconcerned with the systemic conditions required for its existence, is unable to deal with problems of systemic change required to avert such catastrophe. In their contextualist alternative, stress is placed on process, holism, temporality, the relational, and synergism, rather than on partial static equilibrium and related formal optimality conditions. In contradistinction to the policy theorems of applied welfare economics, Hunt and d'Arge offer alternative propositions. These deal with maximizing through nonmarket transactions (the use of the state), maximizing the number of nonmarket transactions, maximizing the values associated with nonreciprocal externalities, and a decision rule that one cannot make anyone more miserable without making others less so. Using their propositions as a guide to policy, they suggest strategies for externality solutions. They urge that in order to avoid environmental catastrophe, consumption gratification must be checked, and fundamental changes in the structure of power must be brought about.

Notes

1. *See* issues of December 1975 and March 1976, which have been combined, together with several additional chapters, in Warren J. Samuels, ed., *The Chicago School of Political Economy* (East Lansing: Division of Research, Graduate School of Business Administration, Michigan State University, 1976); and the multiple reviews of Martin Hollis and Edward J. Nell, *Rational Economic Man* (New York: Cambridge University Press, 1975).
2. *See also* Goldberg's article, "On Positive Theories of Redistribution," March 1977.
3. *See also* Daniel W. Bromley, "Economics and Public Decisions: Roles of the State and Issues in Economic Evaluation," December 1976; H. H. Liebhafsky, "Price Theory as Jurisprudence: Law and Economics, Chicago Style," Victor P. Goldberg, "Toward an Expanded Economic Theory of Contract," and S. Todd Lowry, "Bargain and Contract Theory in Law and Economics," March 1976.
4. Thus, Schmid holds that slavery does not permit a slave the right to ownership of his labor; efficiency conclusions based on slavery neglect this interest and give effect only to the rights structure implicit in slavery itself. Similarly, regulation (the so-called attenuation of rights) represents implicit rights and benefits to certain other parties; policy ultimately is a matter of whose interests, whose rights, and whose costs. Thus, showing that one institution's costs are lower than another's does not mean that society is better off because of it. Only certain interests are registered as costs, in part reflecting certain rights. With a different structure of rights, different interests and therefore different costs would be registered. This is true whether the rights are explicit or implicit. Interests exist in any case. Measured costs are specific to the structure of rights; in each case, some interests will be given effect and not others. The issue is not market versus no market, but whose interests are to be given effect in and through the market. The economic theory of applied welfare economics can be a guide to policy largely only insofar as it makes

implicit judgments as to whose interests are to be a cost to others, a procedure laden with presumptiveness.

5. A similar review is to be found in Lawrence H. Officer and Leanna Stiefel, "The New World of Economics: A Review Article," March 1976.

The Uses and Abuses of Economic Theory in the Social Control of Business

David Dale Martin

Economic theory consists of a body of propositions deduced from alternative sets of premises. Few, if any, of these propositions have been tested and accepted, even tentatively, as scientific laws in the sense in which the natural sciences have "discovered" laws of nature. The propositions of economic theory are statements about the behavior of human beings within a social structure. Those economists whose philosophical underpinnings permit an element of "free will" in human behavior are likely to consider even those empirically tested and accepted hypotheses to be limited to particular societies subject to change by human actions.

The philosophical proposition that mankind's nature gives rise to universally true and discoverable economic laws is perhaps gaining acceptance among economists. Even the purest positive economists, however, have come forth with so few persuasive claims of empirical verification that we will not be concerned here with the uses and abuses of economic science in that sense. Rather, this article addresses the question of the usefulness of the process of theorizing as generally practiced by those who "do economics."

The author is Chief Economist, Senate Judiciary Subcommittee on Antitrust and Monopoly, on leave from Indiana University, Bloomington. *This article was presented at the Annual Meeting of the Association for Evolutionary Economics, New York, 27-29 December 1973. The views expressed herein are the author's alone and in no way represent the views of the members or staff of the subcommittee.*

The term *social control of business* is used in the title with the deliberate intent of conjuring up in the minds of those with long memories, or an historical bent, the literature of a bygone era.[1] Although a generation of economics graduate students has grown up with "industrial organization" labeling their specialty, social control of business never died as a characteristic of the society itself. With or without the participation of economists, society continues its attempts to control business, and, I might add, vice versa.

The topic, therefore, really does not require consideration of all the philosophical questions associated with the proper role of value judgments in economics.[2] The question is, rather, whether we gain useful insights or mislead ourselves and others when we use the tools of our trade as citizens participating in the political and governmental processes through which legal rules are developed and changed. And changes are advocated by almost everyone and perhaps most vigorously by those most committed to the withdrawal of government from what is called interference in private business decisions.

Those who have studied those ideas called "economic theory" that have evolved primarily over the past two centuries have something in common with each other. Essentially, there exists a common language, a language with which to think about certain aspects of human behavior. Economic theory consists of some "packages of logic." Conversations move along much faster if the conversing parties can make mutually acceptable "big leaps" in the logic. Economic theory is much like mathematics, except that the variables are much less abstract.

These packages of logic can be arranged under three main groupings: (1) a theory of maximizing behavior of households and firms; (2) a theory of conflict resolution through markets; and (3) a theory of aggregate economic activity within the system. Each is used in the social control of business. Some persons tend to use them dogmatically, and it is from dogmatic use that abuses arise.

The dogma of economic orthodoxy can be summarized in a few sentences, which should suffice to call to mind much more for anyone who has been exposed to a good principles course. Economic activity is directed by heads of households, or consumers with "given" preference functions, the nature of which is revealed by their behavior and determined by forces beyond the scope of economics. A subset of these households, singly or in combination, takes on the character of business firms that acquire the services of human and nonhuman agents, organize production, and distribute produced goods and services to households. Each household and each firm is a goal directed entity that maximizes its objective function subject to constraints placed on it by nature and all other entities. The entities deal with each other primarily through voluntary market transactions mutually agreed upon. Government and the political process are used for limited purposes to maintain the peace and keep the lighthouses lit for the fishermen. This dogmatic approach teaches that government intervention should meet the test of whether it makes someone believe he is better off without making anyone believe he is worse off. Although such questions are beyond the scope of economics, each citizen is free, in this scheme of things, to advocate government intervention to achieve a more equitable distribution of income and/or wealth so long as the transfer is not effected by means that interfere with incentives "at the margin."

Some adherents to the dogma would allow the "weak welfare principle," whereby even intervention that injures someone is welfare increasing if those gaining gain enough to compensate those losing from the government action.

If not applied dogmatically, these ideas can be helpful in searching for public policy proposals. It is good politics and good government, as well as good economics, to do good whenever possible without incurring anyone's wrath. The packages of logic on which these welfare principles are based, however, include a number of specific premises of which we need to be aware when jumping to conclusions about the "efficiency" effects of alternative public policy proposals. Because I treat the body of theory as theory rather than as a set of empirically verified propositions of economic science, I am unwilling to accept the irrelevance of testing the premises.[3]

The structure of the society in which we live differs in many important respects from the skeleton laid bare in economic theory. With no attempt to be exhaustive, this article will consider a few characteristics of our society, neglect of which is likely to result in abuse of economic theory by those citizens participating (qua economist or otherwise) in developing the legal rules through which society at large attempts to control that subset of itself we call business. These characteristics are: (1) the necessity of unneutral mechanisms to achieve redistribution of income and wealth; (2) the role of business in the determination of relative degree of scarcity; and (3) the consequences of "combinations in the form of trust or otherwise" for the existence of maximizing entities resolving conflict through market mechanisms. The last of these has to do with the failure of economic theory in the past century to adapt its premises to take into account the rise of the corporate form of business organization.

Mechanisms for Income Redistribution

The most powerful argument brought to bear on government policy makers by economists is the efficiency argument. Almost all proposals to change legal rules are perceived by some groups as damaging to their own interests. Advocates of change often are motivated by a desire to enhance the welfare of a subgroup of which they are members. Each side gains strength in the political conflict resolution system by showing that its own interests are really consistent with the public interest.

The *public interest* is not easy to define. Most of us hold values that prevent us from accepting a simple majority rule. We not only do not wish to risk being in the minority in such a system, but also, I think, we are unwilling to be part of a 51 percent majority that enslaves the other 49 percent. Our democratic principles of government rest very much on legal rules designed to protect the "civil liberties" of each individual. Perhaps the greatest threat to democracy is use of the majority rule principle in matters affecting the vital interests of individuals. A decentralized, competitive market system offers much to a society desiring to assure individual freedom.

Freedom, however, is multidimensional. Freedom from want as well as freedom from fear are important to us. Each person is born into a society in which wealth and income are, in fact, distributed. He does not start in a new game. Each new baby is part of a family whose older members have been participating in the struggle against scarcity. Their status very much affects the economic prospects of the new family member. Those who enter the on-going economic system as part of a family with a relatively larger stock of material, legal, and intellectual capital are doubly blessed.[4] They not only are better off, but also have the means to defend and enhance their advantages and those of their children. In a market system the rich will get richer unless the political conflict resolution mechanism redresses the balance.

Will Rogers is alleged to have told a group of Boston bankers that if they did not give back about half of what they had stolen they would lose it all. Voluntary restraint in the uses of power may help preserve it, if not carried too far.

What role does economic theory play in conflict over legal rules? Sometimes economists are able to help decision makers assess the claims of interested parties by forecasting the true consequences of alternative actions, not only on the active participants in the dispute, but also on other parties. Skill in such forecasting, however, is not limited to economists. Indeed, in most specific cases, engineers or businessmen are more likely than economists to have command of the facts necessary to judge consequences.[5]

Unfortunately for policy makers, the best qualified forecasters are likely to be interested parties. For this reason adversary proceedings play an important role in the nonmarket conflict resolution system. Third parties tend to be left out, however, and that gap is beginning to be filled by the developing public interest pressure groups. Public servants, of course, also are supposed to look after the public interest, but in many cases they operate under rules requiring them merely to resolve conflict between two contending parties.

Economic theory is useful in forecasting, if it is used flexibly. Its practitioners, however, often tend to use it dogmatically. The easy way to measure the effect on the public is simply to ask whether a government action would interfere with the market's "Pareto-optimal" results. If so, it lessens "efficiency." But what about the effect on the distribution of income, wealth, and power? A dogmatic economist will wash his hands of that matter and say: "You can do anything you wish with the income distribution so long as you do not use a government measure that is inefficient." All government measures to redistribute income and wealth, however, are inefficient when judged in terms of the economist's welfare criterion. No one has yet devised a neutral tax and spending scheme.[6]

Dogmatic use of economic theory, therefore, is inherently conservative. It comes down on the side of the status quo. That may not be a truly conservative position, of course, if Will Rogers was right. Perhaps that fact accounts for the existence of an "Eastern liberal establishment."

The distribution of wealth did not arise from economically efficient public policies in an egalitarian society of the past. Today's wealth and income distribution is the result of yesterday's power struggles. Measures used by our ancestors as participants in those power struggles included war, enslavement, and forced migrations; industrial sabotage, strike breaking, monopolization, restraint of trade, and unfair methods of competition; and manipulations of government policy. To accept the distribution of wealth, income, and power now existing, and to argue that measures to redress the unbalance must be consistent with the Pareto optimality condition or else be economically "inefficient," are, to me, abuses of economic theory. To invoke that proposition as if it were a scientific finding devoid of value judgment is at best a delusion. As a minimum, a positive economist should ask: What is the next best method actually available for achieving redistribution of income?

Business Power and Relative Scarcities

A fundamental weakness in economic theory as a guide to government policy is its premises of "given" consumer preferences, "given" technology, and "given" resources. Economic theory abstracts from all the institutional characteristics those forces that determine the manner in which consumer preferences are brought into consistency with relative scarcities. In so doing, the theory focuses on only a small part of the actual role played by both business and government in the workings of the economic system.

That "business" plays a major role in the determination of household preferences has been clearly recognized.[7] Household preferences not only are influenced by advertising, but also in many ways by public policies and legal rules that are determined in large measure by business participation in the political process.[8]

Perhaps more important is the failure of the theory of consumer behavior to take into account the learning process. Each person's preference function in reality is very much influenced by his pattern of want, satisfaction over time, and even by his family's pattern before his birth. Preference itself evolves within a social system in which the degree of scarcity and the distribution of power in past periods play a major role.

One might dismiss the relevancy of this evolving nature of consumer preferences with the observation that, however determined, today's preferences are all we have with which to judge what is good or bad, and each person's current preferences can be known collectively only through the market process without government intervention. That argument is very persuasive. Yet, today's public policy issues very often have to do with the distribution of power to affect tomorrow's preferences.

Business power affects the demand side of relative scarcities other than by its effect on consumer preferences. In spite of the derived nature of the demand for goods and services by governments and businesses, much opportunity exists for business intervention in the processes of derivation of demand for such intermediate goods and services. Mention of a few such opportunities will suffice to suggest the nature of this problem.

Reciprocity is a term well known to businessmen and antitrust experts but not often used in economic theory. The multiproduct, multimarket firm may have opportunities to tie its transactions in some markets to its bargaining in other markets in ways that distort the demand for its outputs or the prices of its inputs. Both offers of rewards and threats of retaliation in unrelated markets can be used in negotiation of terms in a particular transaction.

Standards for product design are set by processes given very little consideration in the literature of economic theory.[9] Products as well as preferences for them usually are assumed to be given.[10] Yet decisions about standards play a major role in the determination of relative demands for intermediate goods as well as in determining the set of products among which consumers may choose to allocate their budgets.

Standards often are reversible only at great cost because of the necessity of either scrapping useful equipment or multiplying the varieties during transition. For example, any change in television transmission processes that requires a change in television receivers could make obsolete the existing stock of receivers and perhaps even require duplication of equipment at both ends. Standards are set by a wide variety of decision-making processes ranging from completely governmental to completely private, but in most cases the process involves interaction among governments and businesses. Economic theory is abused, it seems to me, if it is used to denounce the governmental role in standardization without adequate consideration of the relative power of the business participants in any nongovernmental alternative standard setting mechanism.

For example, those who criticize the recently growing role of the federal government in automobile design should, at least, apprise themselves of the structure of control of the Society of Automotive Engineers, its role in years past in deciding such things as the design of bumpers, and the consequences of bumper design on the demand for "crash parts" and the rate of scrapping vehicles.[11]

Technological change effects relative scarcities on both the demand and the supply side. All goods and services are substitutes for or complements to other goods and services to some degree. Technical change, like standardization, affects both demand and supply of all products in, or potentially in, the system. The course of technical change may be exogenous to the theory of markets, but it is not exogenous to the structure of control of industry. A major role of business management is in making decisions concerning not only the allocation of research and development budgets but also the many questions associated with innovation. The existing structure of power affects, for example, whether resources are devoted to such energy demand reducing research as that on windmills or sailboats. The degree of vertical integration plays a major part in determining whether "creatively destructive" technical changes will be adopted.

A basic paradox of economic activity is that the ultimate achievement of the goal of economic growth would reduce GNP to zero and destroy all capital values. Without scarcity, market values do not exist. Therefore, a social system that encourages individuals, acting alone or in coalition, to enhance the value of their property, also may encourage actions that increase scarcity for society as a whole. A theory that takes the degree of scarcity as "given" must be used very carefully as a guide to government intervention in a business system in which business firms can gain by restricting the supply of productive services. Contrived scarcity is the basic issue of antitrust. The purpose and the effect of restraint of trade is literally to restrain trade. To the recipient, rent is income whether or not it results from contrived scarcity.

Unfortunately, the distinction is very difficult to make in practice between scarcity that stems from the niggardliness of nature and that which results from such practices as the ancient crimes of forestalling, regrating, and engrossing. The contriving that takes place in a highly industrialized, corporately organized, "new industrial state" is particularly difficult to identify. Only decentralization in the structure of control can offer much assurance that perceived scarcity reflects the state of nature sufficiently accurately to warrant a laissez-faire policy.

The effects of centralization of control of pricing and output decisions in particular markets have, of course, been the subject of much of the literature of microeconomic theory. Much less attention has been given, however, to the centralization of investment decisions or the preemption of resources.[12] In the short run, scarcity in plant capacity is very real whether or not contrived. Government failure to intervene to prevent contrived scarcity of either resources or capital equipment vitiates any economic grounds for a government hands-off policy in the future short-run price-output decision process. The current controversy over deregulation of natural gas pricing is a good case in point.[13]

The fact that scarcity is, in part, contrived gives rise to three additional common abuses of economic theory that will be mentioned here with little elaboration. One is the tendency to cope with the very real unemployment-inflation dilemma by defining full employment to be whatever level results from monetary and fiscal policies restrictive enough to stabilize average prices. The theoretical foundations for concluding that appropriate macro policies can be found to achieve simultaneously full employment and price level stability include the assumption that all particular markets are adequately decentralized in structure to be competitive. Rather than simply assuming that condition to hold and defining full employment to be that level that results from the workings of the system with price-level stabilizing monetary and fiscal policies, an economic scientist could as easily view the fact of unemployment with price stability as empirical evidence that competition is inadequate.

If one's economic theorizing leads him to the latter conclusion, it can be very useful in suggesting policy measures to achieve the macroeconomic goals without the necessity of direct government intervention in short-run price and allocation decisions.[14]

The fact that scarcity is, in part, contrived, if ignored, also can mislead a policy maker into believing that government intervention would interfere with "efficient" location of economic activity. Much recent controversy over U.S. foreign trade policy stems from dissatisfaction with the market system dominated by giant multinational firms as an appropriate way to determine the location of plants and jobs. Economists tend to use their theory to come down on the side of no government intervention without any concomitant opposition to essentially nonmarket "private government" regulation of international trade by multinational corporations with power surpassing that of many national governments.

For example, writing in the magazine for Volkswagen owners in the United States, Paul A. Samuelson very persuasively makes the comparative advantage case for free trade and argues against the need for government quotas, tariffs, and surcharges to maintain employment in the United States. He says: "The give and take of international competition can be a great policer of monopoly. It has been well said in our political history: The tariff is the mother of trusts.[15] No mention is made of international cartels, "voluntary" export restraint arrangements, or multinational corporations. Yet, a U.S. Department of Commerce survey for 1970 showed that 298 responding "American" multinational corporations accounted for over one-third of all U.S. imports, and 46 percent of those were transfers from majority-owned foreign affiliates.[16]

A third example of the policy implications of applying economic theory as if no scarcity were contrived has to do with the tendency of antitrust economists to first define markets and then look for evidence of monopoly. The notion that products and markets are "given" is so deeply rooted in economic theory that it is easy to ignore the fact that those with power to contrive scarcity often have the power to determine the extent of the market. Specifically, we can expect a monopolist to raise his price high enough to invite competition from greater spatial distance and greater "distance" in the spectrum of product qualities than would be the case if no monopoly power were exercised. This simple fact was obvious to William Howard Taft when he wrote the lower court opinion in 1898 in the Addyston Pipe and Steel case.[17] Yet, economists still suggest that courts should ascertain the boundaries of a market before asking whether the structure is competitive, or argue that interindustry or international competition is adequate to protect the public interest from contrived scarcity.[18]

Combinations: Trusts or Otherwise

The method of economic theorizing is to abstract from the multifaceted and rapidly changing social structure those few more or less persistent characteristics thought to be crucial in the ordering of economic activity.[19] If the theory attempted to tell the truth, the whole truth, and nothing but the truth, it would not be a theory. The resulting description of the economic system would be as complex as the social structure itself, and no useful insight would result. Economic theory should not be criticized for abstraction; rather, it should be questioned from time to time about the continuing appropriateness of its choice of premises.

By 1874, with the publication of Léon Walras's general equilibrium theory, economics had taken on those essential characteristics that give it an identity separate from other branches of philosophy.[20] Economists have taken ever since a "systems approach." The theory has sought to explain not only the behavior of producers and consumers, but also their interrelationships with each other as part of a system of economizing in the use of scarce resources and distributing the scarce goods and services among the members of society. The foundations of economic theory were then and remain today in the hedonistic psychology of Jeremy Bentham.[21] Each person is assumed either to be a maximizing entity or to have all decisions made for him by such an economic animal. Resolution of conflict about goals within the household or family was considered "home economics" and was not the concern of political, social, or national economy.

The economic system all along has been viewed by economists as a social structure that accomplishes peaceful resolution of conflict among the separate and clearly defined households and firms. Although the theory of household behavior and the theory of the firm were not brought together explicitly until Samuelson's *Foundations* was published in 1948, the method of economics all along was to explain the maximizing behavior of only those entities characterized by what Jacob Marshak called "solidarity" and to explain conflict resolution only in terms of the theory of markets.[22]

Most teachers of microeconomic theory, I conjecture, would be very happy to have their undergraduates understand the market system as well as Alfred Marshall did in 1890 when the first edition of the *Principles of Economics* was published.

What has happened to the actual structure of control of the American economic system since the basic underpinnings of the theory were settled upon?

Something other than competitive market structures had, in fact, evolved as a major part of the conflict resolution mechanism as early as the 1870s with the rise of the trusts as a device for forming coalitions among small numbers of wealthy capitalists. The trusts were outlawed by the Sherman Act in 1890. Despite the statute's use of the phrase "in the form of trust or otherwise," combinations have persisted and grown in importance as part of our system's conflict resolution mechanism.

In 1887 the New Jersey legislature enacted a statute providing "that it shall be lawful for foreign corporations to acquire, hold, mortgage, lease, and convey such real estate in this state as may be necessary for the purpose of carrying on . . . business."[23] In 1889 New Jersey's general incorporation law was further amended to provide that "any company . . . may carry on part of its business out of state, and have one or more offices and places of business out of this state, and may hold, purchase and convey real and personal property out of this state the same as if such real and personal property were situated in the state of New Jersey."[24]

In 1893 New Jersey specifically authorized horizontal mergers without limit.[25] In 1888 the New Jersey legislature had authorized its corporations, for limited purposes, to purchase and hold stock in other corporations. In 1893 all limitations were removed, and the New Jersey holding company was born.[26] One week later, the legislature removed New Jersey's last obstacle to unlimited centralization of control of the world's economy by providing that "subscriptions to the capital stock . . . may be paid wholly or partly in cash, or wholly or partly in property."[27] The medium of exchange with which a New Jersey holding corporation could acquire ownership of other corporations, without limit, was not only money, but also its own stock certificates, which could be issued in unlimited numbers.

In 1895 the United States Supreme Court, in the sugar case,[28] held that the Sherman Antitrust Act did not prohibit any combinations created under the authority of and with the legal sanction of a state legislature. Between the E. C. Knight decision in 1895 and the Northern

Securities Company dissolution in 1904, no legal constraints limited consolidation of control for purposes of market control, and the structure of control of the American economy underwent revolutionary changes. These changes by coincidence took place at the time when the number of years since the birth of Jesus rolled over from 1899 to 1900 and, in our conventional reckoning, the twentieth century arrived and the third millenium began. But we should guard against the very strong temptation to conclude that big business, the corporate revolution, and the new industrial state were caused, therefore, by "modern technology." The legislature of New Jersey and the United States Supreme Court—the same Court that sanctioned racial segregation—with deliberate speed overrode the policy embodied in the Sherman Act and set us on the road to the corporate state. The full implications of the change in the structure of control of the economy have taken some years to work out. The slow but steady decline in the relative magnitude of the agricultural sector has played a major role, it seems to me, in delaying until recent years some of the inevitable consequences of the structural changes that occurred three-quarters of a century ago.

What has happened to economic theory since 1890 to keep it relevant to questions of social control of business? Most of us would admit, it seems to me, that very little has happened to the theory to reflect the radical changes in the structure of control. Despite the contributions of E. H. Chamberlin, Joan Robinson, J. M. Keynes, and John von Neumann, economic theory remains fundamentally a theory of conflict resolution among maximizing entities brought about through voluntary market transactions.

Despite the antitrust laws in the United States and similar restrictive practices laws in many other countries, corporations have made possible the evolution of very complex organizations that overlap and interrelate with each other and with governments. Some corporate groups have taken on characteristics very much like those we generally attribute to governments. Meanwhile, the proliferation of nation states and the development of socialist economic systems have given to many governments the characteristics generally attributed to business firms. The behavior of the existing economic system of the world cannot be understood adequately with a theory that treats giant multinational corporations and complex financial interest groups as if they were "ma and pa" grocery stores.

Society still controls business largely through law, and vice versa. Economic theory is useful to those persons who share in the responsibility for development of the law as it relates to the structure of control of economic activity. To some extent each member of society shares that responsibility—even the positive economists. Citizens participating in the development of the law as it affects the constraints under which business managers, qua manager, make their decisions undoubtedly are helped by knowledge of the probable consequences of alternative legal rules. Because false knowledge may be worse than none, however, we must ask whether economic theory helps those who have knowledge of it. Some wise man once said: "It is better to not know and know you do not know than to not know and think that you do." Economic theory is more useful to those who know its weaknesses than it is to the true believers. The process of theorizing is more useful than the propositions of economic theory, if those propositions are misconstrued to be laws of nature.

Notes

1. See J. M. Clark, *Social Control of Business*, 2d ed. (New York: McGraw-Hill Book Co., Inc., 1939).
2. This author's views have not changed on this fundamental issue since writing "Value Judgments in Economics: a Comment," *Southern Economic Journal* 23 (October 1956): 183-87. See also John Dewey, "Theory of Valuation," *International Encyclopedia of the Unified Science,* vol. 11, no. 4 (Chicago: University of Chicago Press, 1939); and Gunnar Myrdal, *Objectivity in Social Research* (New York: Pantheon Books, 1969).
3. See Fritz Machlup, "The Problem of Verification in Economics," *Southern Economic Journal* 22 (July 1955): 1-21.
4. By assuming that each new consumer enters the economy with an exogenously determined set of attributes, economic theory abstracts from all those forces through which new members of society are related to their families and to larger social groups. Much recent literature in psychiatry and social psychology focuses on the importance of family systems in individual behavior. See Jack Oldham Bradt, M.D., and Carolyn Johnson Moynihan, ACSW, eds., *Systems Therapy; Selected Papers: Theory, Technique, Research* (Washington, D.C.: Groome Child Guidance Clinic, 1971).
5. For example, the author's work on the problem of seasonal unemployment in the construction industries led him to engineers, architects, contractors, and labor leaders for judgments on the consequences of alternative policy proposals. See David D. Martin, "Construction Seasonality: The New Federal Program," *Construction Review* (May 1970): 4-7.
6. See Paul A. Samuelson, "The Pure Theory of Public Expenditure," *Review of Economics and Statistics* 36 (November 1954): 387-89; and George M. von Furstenberg and Dennis C. Mueller, "The Pareto Optimal Approach to Income Redistribution: A Fiscal Application," *American Economic Review* 61 (September 1971): 628-37.
7. The consequences of advertising have been well treated in the literature

at least since the appearance of Edward H. Chamberlain, *The Theory of Monopolistic Competition* (Cambridge, Mass.: Harvard University Press, 1933). The implications for welfare theory of corporate power to influence public policy, technological change, and the social context in which consumer preferences are formed more recently has been articulated in John Kenneth Galbraith, *The New Industrial State* (Boston: Houghton Mifflin, 1967); and Kenneth Boulding, *Economics as a Science* (New York: McGraw-Hill, 1970). Also see Philip Klein, "Demand Theory and the Economist's Propensity to Assume," *Journal of Economic Issues* 7 (June 1973): 209-40. But little has been added to the contributions contained in C. E. Ayres, *The Theory of Economic Progress* (Chapel Hill: University of North Carolina Press, 1944), chap. 4.

8. Undoubtedly, consumers have interacted with government as well as business in recent years in forming preferences for such goods as cigarettes, drugs, pollution control devices, and rapid transit facilities. Market and nonmarket information flows are treated in Joseph F. Brodley, "Massive Industrial Size, Classical Economics, and the Search for Humanistic Value," *Stanford Law Review* 24 (June 1972): 1155-78.
9. See Edward H. Chamberlin, "The Product as an Economic Variable," *Quarterly Journal of Economics* 67 (February 1953): 1-29; David D. Martin, "Monopoly Power and the Durability of Durable Goods," *Southern Economic Journal* 28 (January 1962): 271-77; and Peter L. Swan, "Durability of Consumption Goods," *American Economic Review* 60 (December 1970): 885.
10. But see Kelvin Lancaster, "A New Approach to Consumer Theory," *Journal of Political Economy* 74 (April 1966): 132-57; and Irvin M. Grossack and David D. Martin, *Managerial Economics, Microtheory and the Firm's Decisions* (Boston: Little, Brown and Company, 1973), chap. 8.
11. See Motor Vehicle Information and Cost Savings Act, Public Law 92-513, 92nd Congress, 20 October 1972; Donald A. Randall and Arthur P. Glickman, *The Great American Auto Repair Robbery* (New York: Charterhouse, 1972), chap. 7, "High Repair Costs by Design"; and Subcommittee on Antitrust and Monopoly, Committee on the Judiciary, United States Senate, 91st Congress, 1st sess., Hearings, *Automotive Repair Industry* Part 3, 6, 8, 9, 14, and 16 October 1969.
12. See David D. Martin, "Resource Control and Market Power," in *Extractive Resources and Taxation*, Mason Gaffney, ed. (Madison: University of Wisconsin Press, 1967), pp. 119-37.
13. Subcommittee on Antitrust and Monopoly, Committee on the Judiciary, United States Senate, 93rd Congress, 1st sess., Hearings, *Natural Gas Industry*, 26, 27, and 28 June 1973.
14. See *Studies by the Staff of the Cabinet Committee on Price Stability* (Washington, D.C.: Superintendent of Documents, January 1969); Subcommittee on Antitrust and Monopoly, Committee on the Judiciary, United States Senate, 92nd Congress, 2d sess., Hearings, *Symposium on the Economic, Social and Political Effects of Economic Concentration*, 18, 19, 20, and 21 January 1972; and *Congressional Record*, 92nd Congress, 2d sess., 24 July 1972, remarks by Senator Philip Hart and text of the Industrial Reorganization Act, pp. S. 11494-505.
15. Paul A. Samuelson, "Imports and America's Prosperity," *Small World*, Fall 1973.

16. See Betty L. Barker, "U.S. Foreign Trade Associated with U.S. Multinational Companies," *Survey of Current Business* 52 (December 1972): 20–28, Table 2, p. 23.
17. *United States* v. *Addyston Pipe and Steel Co.,* 85 Fed. Rep. 271 (1898).
18. See Bryce J. Jones, "The Brown Shoe Case and the New Antimerger Policy: Comment," and David D. Martin, "Reply," *American Economic Review* 54 (June 1964): 407–15.
19. The notion that economic principles were useful abstractions rather than laws of nature was first brought home to this writer upon first reading Frank Knight's *Risk, Uncertainty, and Profit* (Chicago: University of Chicago Press, 1921).
21. Léon Walras, *Éléments d'économie politique pure* (Lausanne: L. Corbay & Cie, 1874).
22. See W. Stark, *Jeremy Bentham's Economic Writings* (London: George Allen & Unwin Ltd., 1952).
23. Jacob Marschak, "Towards an Economic Theory of Information and Organization," in *Decision Processes,* R. M. Thrall, C. H. Coombs, and R. L. Davis, eds. (New York: 1954), pp. 187-220.
24. *Acts of the One Hundred and Tenth Legislature of the State of New Jersey, and Forty-Second under the New Constitution,* C. 124, 11 April 1887.
25. *Acts,* C. 265, 9 May 1889
26. *Acts,* C. 67, 8 March 1893
27. *Acts,* C. 171, 14 March 1893
28. *Acts,* C. 254, 21 March 1893
29. *United States* v. *E. C. Knight,* 156 U.S. 1, (1895).

The Marginal Utility of Marginal Analysis in Public Policy Formation

William H. Melody

In times past, neither the development of economic theory nor the activity of economists took place in an environment where there was a direct involvement in the formulation of economic policies by government and business. For the most part, economists and their theories stood outside the real world of practical decision making as exogenous observers and descriptions of economic behavior. However, over the past generation or so, both economists and their theories have become increasingly involved—for better or worse—in the economic policy decisions of government and business. The involvement has been most obvious and direct in macroeconomics and the formulation of aggregate economic policies by national governments. The Keynesian revolution virtually required involvement, and economists have been placed in positions where they are responsible, and sometimes held accountable, for the development and application of economic policies.

At the microeconomic level, there has been no Keynesian revolution that has thrust microeconomics into an equivalent role in the formulation of real world economic policies. Nevertheless, a marked increase in the involvement of the profession in the microeconomic decisions of government and business has occurred, either by means of direct

---

The author is Associate Professor of Communications Economics, University of Pennsylvania, Philadelphia. *This article was presented at the Annual Meeting of the Association for Evolutionary Economics, New York, 27-29 December 1973.*

employment of economists by government and industry, or through consulting and advisory relationships.

The neoclassical theory of the firm has provided economists with very little to say on matters of microeconomic policy. Given an optimal income distribution and perfect knowledge, counsels the theory, optimal resource allocation and maximum consumer welfare will be achieved in a perfectly competitive market system where the government follows a policy of laissez-faire. But a moment's observation clearly demonstrates that there are no real markets approximating perfect competition; many markets are heavily concentrated oligopolies; some are monopolies; many goods and services are not supplied through traditional market mechanisms; and government involvement in many areas of economic activity is extensive. In the face of a clear contradiction between theory and practice, what can economists say to policy makers on microeconomic problems?

Some economists continue to recommend laissez-faire, extending the tradition of earlier economists who counseled Say's Law at a time of world-wide economic depression. Others recommend a more vigorous application of antitrust policy to bring the structure of real markets closer to the perfectly competitive structure of neoclassical theory. Still others conclude that the theory is irrelevant to policy issues and it should be abandoned as being more harmful than helpful.[1]

Unfortunately, as the involvement of economists in real world microeconomic problems has increased, most theoretical work has become directed more and more narrowly, as if to attempt to save the theory by means of more elaborate and elegant "proofs." But this pursuit of positivism through rigor has tended to foster more rigor mortis than enlightenment. The result has been that all issues of microeconomic public policy involve problems that turn out to be *exceptions* to the general neoclassical theory. Recommended policy solutions depend upon how much, if any, weight is given to selected elements of the neoclassical theory. Hence, there are no standard theoretic solutions to microeconomic policy issues.

At the microeconomic level, economists are seldom in positions where they are responsible and accountable for the development of public policy. They are almost universally advisers who generally take great pains to separate their pure economics from areas where societal value judgments are involved. Yet, we must recognize that advisers are hired by clients with vested interests who have a very good idea of what any adviser is going to say on any particular public policy issue and what the consequences are likely to be for the client. Thus, both the economic theories and the economists selected become part of the advocacy of a client's position. The aggregate strength of that advocacy depends upon the significance of the policy issue for the client and its position of economic and political power. Disturbing for economics is the fact that its use in such public policy formulation is primarily as cannon fodder for vested interests, a role that only can serve to reinforce the inherited structure of economic institutions and the maintenance and extension of monopoly power.

Marginal Analysis

The major area of microeconomic public policy development has been in the social control of business, either by means of antitrust policy or direct governmental regulation of firms and industries uniquely "affected with a public interest," such as public utilities and transportation. Most public policy issues are heavily involved with problems relating to pricing, costing, or profits. Although these firms and industries are clear exceptions to the neoclassical theory, the theory has provided an elegant framework from which economists can advise that decision makers should look to the marginal conditions, most specifically marginal costs, in order to optimize their objectives. This general standard can be recommended sweepingly to all problems in all possible circumstances at all times. Firms can use marginal analysis as a means of maximizing profits. Government agencies can maximize net social benefits. Regulatory agencies can force regulated firms to set prices so as to optimize resource allocation and maximize consumer welfare.

A recommendation that decision makers employ the mathematical methods of optimization may not be viewed as containing a high level of economic content. Indeed, the economic substance of the matter does not begin until the economist begins to define his terms in light of the public policy issue at hand, to place values on alternative courses of action, and to pour content into the empty mathematical functions. Unfortunately, economic theorists generally have declined to assume the responsibility for providing the economic substance, leaving the factual calculations on these matters to the specialists who are familiar with operational details. As a result, the marginal principles have acquired the status of doctrinal slogans, so internalized to economic thinking that failure to employ them calls for a brief recitation on the mathematics of optimization.

Economists have not been much concerned about what practitioners actually do, or how they go about actually trying to measure such things as marginal cost. Rather, the important thing has been what they say. Concern has been devoted almost entirely to the terminology that practitioners use. Failure to adopt the terminology of marginal analysis elicits the appropriate reflex response. But, as Gunnar Myrdal has observed, "terminology, and the meaning given to terms, do matter. They represent, if not subjected to continual scrutiny, temptations and opportunities for the logical gliding of our thinking in unrealistic directions."[2]

Claimed applications of the marginal analysis have been guided generally by a series of mythological impressions about the meaning of the term and the nature of its applications. The myths are created both by economists, in their careless or expansive interpretations of the theoretical concepts when attempting to apply them to real world problems, and by practitioners, in developing methodologies directed toward the calculation of desirable results. The logical gliding of thinking on marginal analysis in public policy formulation seems to have glided quite far in unrealistic directions, despite its limited use in the application of public policy.

Resource Allocation: Theory and Practice

Alfred Kahn has observed in his recent work, *The Economics of Regulation,* that "the central policy prescription of microeconomics is the equation of price and marginal cost. If economic theory is to have any relevance to public utility pricing, that is the point at which the inquiry must begin."[3] Yet, inquiry by corporate managers and government regulators has seldom, if ever, attempted to begin at the point where price equals marginal cost. Resource allocation in practice is characterized by the almost complete absence of prices set equal to marginal costs. Moreover, in an economy characterized by imperfect markets where, according to neoclassical theory, all prices should be expected to deviate from their respective marginal costs, neoclassical economists rarely recommend that prices be set equal to marginal costs. Even in the directly regulated public utility sector, economists seldom recommend that marginal cost pricing be employed. Rather, they recommend that marginal costs, however defined, be used as reference points from which optimal deviations of prices from marginal costs can be calculated.[4] In essence, they recommend that the inefficient deviations of prices from the theoretical marginal cost optima be minimized.

But why should public policy depart from a theoretical optimum and attempt to achieve inferior results that only can be calculated by reference to that optimum? What overriding constraint possibly could be acceptable as a legitimate cause for injecting such allocational inefficiency into an optimal pricing system? The overriding constraint is the financial revenue requirement of the firm. In the real world, those who actually allocate resources base their decisions upon financial parameters such as rate of return on investment. Public policy makers also have directed their attention to these financial parameters as a principal basis for policy decisions.

Yet, what is it about the nature of marginal cost that tells us that marginal cost pricing will yield a deficient amount of revenue to the firm? It is the overwhelming assumption that the firm is operating under continuous long-run decreasing costs within the static framework of the neoclassical model. However, such an assumption has no validity as a basis for public policy analysis of real world problems. As Ralph Turvey has stated, "an a priori statement about the relationship between long run marginal cost and total cost is possible only if the system lacks history—i.e., in practically no real system. Thus, simple statements of the sort that, since the industry is one of increasing returns, marginal cost pricing would involve a deficit, are irrelevant."[5]

The assumption that marginal cost pricing *in reality* would involve a financial deficit reflects an imposition of the artificial limitations of theory upon the policy issue under examination. In addition, this assumption has fostered the myth that marginal costs are always lower than average or fully distributed costs. Indeed, Kahn has noted that a lesson to be learned from our long experience with intercarrier competition is that "not all rates will be set as low as long-run marginal costs, because competitive pressures will differ between different customers, classes of service, and localities; nor can all rates be set as low as LRMC and still cover average total costs."[6] Under this set of circumstances, however, the neoclassical theory would lead us to conclude that all firms in the economy would suffer financial deficits if they employed marginal cost pricing. Moreover, it would tend to indicate that the most efficient allocation of resources could be achieved by having a single firm supply all goods and services in the industry, if not the entire economy. Clearly, one cannot begin the analysis of public policy issues with a presumption that the marginal costs of neoclassical theory are necessarily less than average costs, or that marginal cost pricing would yield a financial deficit, without adopting an enormous unjustified bias in the approach.

Nevertheless, there is no *a priori* reason to believe that the marginal cost standard for resource allocation would yield results similar to the return on investment standard. This raises the question: Which standard is superior as a guide to efficient resource allocation? The return on investment standard is viewed almost universally in practice as the appropriate economic one for allocating resources, especially when a firm is attempting to attract capital in competitive capital markets. Capital is allocated to applications that offer higher rates of return and away from applications that only offer lower rates of return. Those users that cannot earn rates of return sufficient to cover their respective costs of capital do not obtain the resources.

Both the rate of return on investment standard and the marginal cost standard are founded upon the basic economic idea of opportunity cost. Neoclassical theorists generally approve of a rate of return standard for allocating resources among industries and among firms within an industry. However, in allocating resources among product lines or services within the firm, the marginal cost standard is viewed as crucial, while the return on investment standard, which now has become labelled as a fully distributed cost standard, has sunk to the depths of "arbitrary allocation." According to neoclassical economics, if services A and B are supplied by different firms, then a return on investment standard is an acceptable basis for efficient resource allocation. But if services A and B are supplied by the same firm, the return on investment standard is in error. Marginal cost becomes the standard for efficient resource allocation within the firm.

This dividing line between the rate of return on investment and marginal cost standards at the level of the firm is not justified by any economic criteria. Indeed, the neoclassical theory states quite clearly that all prices should equal marginal costs for optimal resource allocation. Rather, advocates of the neoclassical theory have fallen back to the level of the firm in advocating marginal cost and have accepted any revenue requirement constraints imposed by return on investment criteria at higher levels of resource allocation.

It must be emphasized also that the return on investment criterion is applied where there is a market exchange of resources between firms and suppliers of resources. The marginal cost standard is advocated most strongly for intrafirm product line or interservice resource allocation, which does not require submission to an external market test. Hence, marginal cost is advocated principally where real resource allocation decisions are not at issue because the firm acts as a single unit in attracting resources. Individual products and services do not have to attract resources from external markets on their own merits. The internal issue is the distribution of resources attracted by the firm among the products or services.

As a practical matter, tests of the efficiency of resource allocation have tended to apply the return on investment standard to intrafirm as well as interfirm decisions. Most firms have established product line, cost responsibility center, or profit center classifications as a means of measuring and comparing the profitability of particular products or services within the firm. Similarly, government policy makers have tended to rely on the return on investment criterion for policy relating to intrafirm resource allocation decisions. Moreover, such a criterion has been recommended by economists directly involved in public policy analysis. This author concluded that if the Federal Communications Commission is to fulfill its regulatory responsibilities, it must adopt a return on investment standard as a basis for reaching policy decisions relating to efficient resource allocation among the Bell Telephone System's major interstate service classifications.[7] Recently, the Bureau of Economics Staff of the Federal Trade Commission proposed an annual line of business report program for large corporations as a means of determining relative returns on investment. In its Statement of Purpose, the staff stated:

> Given the purpose of the FTC, a guiding principle in providing solutions to the allocation problem is that all costs must be finally allocated. . . . The reason for this necessity is that a major concern of the Commission is the overall allocation of society's resources in such a way that the benefits to society are made as large as possible. Without descriptive data on how the totality of the pool of resources at the disposal of society have been allocated, it would not be feasible to comment meaningfully on how well resource allocation has been carried out. Nor would it be possible to analyze the effects of changes in underlying structural or behavioral characteristics of the economy on the allocation of resources.[8]

In sum, as a guide to public policy directed to encouraging efficient resource allocation, the marginal cost standard of neoclassical theory has been a resounding failure. Its advocacy on public policy issues appears largely opportunistic, dictated primarily by firms with vested interests in certain public policies. Regulated firms prefer a return on investment standard for determining their profit levels and revenue requirements. But marginal cost, as the standard for pricing individual services, preserves maximum flexibility to the firm in pricing its individual services. This flexibility does not derive from the neoclassical theory of marginal cost, but from the mythology of marginal cost and from a recognition by the regulated firms that they will have complete control over the calculation of the marginal cost values. It is a tribute to public policy makers that they generally have not succumbed to the superficial rationality of the neoclassical model and the marginal cost slogan.

Marginal Cost: Theory and Interpretation

Kenneth Boulding has observed that the essential principles of marginal analysis are almost trite. The firm in neoclassical theory is viewed essentially as an input-output process where, given the principle of maximization of something, the marginal conditions follow as simple mathematical tautologies. Boulding has stated: "The firm is thus an aggregation of capital and labor rather than an organization, and most of the problems which are connected with it simply do not arise."[9] Thus, criticism of the neoclassical theory and its applicability as a guide to public policy is not directed to pointing out logical flaws in its analysis but rather to demonstrating that the enormous constriction of its explicit and implicit assumptions renders it, for the most part, irrelevant for solving the economic problems of the real world.

The term *marginal cost* is so general that the variety of interpretations of its meaning is virtually infinite. To give it a somewhat more specific content, economists must apply further definitional restrictions such as *short run* and *long run.* But even these terms do not provide restrictions upon the interpretation, selection, and valuation of marginal costs. There are as many marginal costs as there are conceivable sets of alternatives to be considered, and their values can range from very high to extremely low. The important issue in marginal analysis is always the *selection* of the alternative courses of action between which the marginal conditions will be measured.

One is reminded of the story of the young man who told his father that he had walked home from school instead of taking the bus and saved $.25. The father replied that his son should have walked home instead of taking a taxi because then he would have saved $3.00. The son's marginal cost was $.25; the father's was $3.00. Had the son evaluated the alternatives of taking the bus home instead of a taxi, he would have concluded that the marginal cost of taking a taxi was not $3.00, but $2.75. If he considered a limousine ride at $5.00, he would have concluded that the marginal cost relative to walking was $5.00; the marginal cost relative to taking the bus was $4.75; and the marginal cost relative to taking a taxi was $2.00. The marginal cost depends crucially on the relevant decision alternative that will *not* be followed. He who selects this decision alternative will determine the marginal cost. Clearly, public policies affecting vested interests cannot be based upon such subjective assessments by vested interests.

In addition, the framework for marginal cost analysis assumes a planning horizon sufficiently distant that all the effects of all alternative decision possibilities can be taken into account. But all of this information is hypothetical and subject to the forecasting ability of the decision maker. Once the optimum alternative is selected and pursued, the firm must await the judgment of reality to see if its decision was good or bad. If the firm correctly perceived and made perfect forecasts for all alternative decision possibilities, its decision indeed will have been optimum. If it did not, its marginal cost calculations will have been inaccurate. As a practical matter, we know in advance that our hypothesis of optimization will be disproved by reality.

As a theoretical construct, the long-run marginal cost concept does not come to grips with the problems created by the continuity and incomplete nature of the firm's activities. The concept assumes that the decision to be made involves a single complete venture. At the time the decision is to be made, there are no constraining conditions of past decisions and events that will influence the decision alternatives. The firm is in a completely uncommitted state. Moreover, the evaluation of the alternative decision possibilities reflects all effects through the completion of the activity under consideration. Hence, the framework for decision is closed. The firm is considering a venture in which it can both start fresh and complete the activity. At this theoretical level, there is no need for an evaluation of the state of affairs before the effects of the decision are complete. There will be no modification of the decision as reality unfolds. An accounting is required neither during nor at the completion of the venture.[10]

Indeed, theoretical optimization can be a very misleading concept. In the neoclassical model, the decision maker is deemed to have optimized if he does what he thinks is best in light of the alternatives he perceives. But if his best turns out to be in reality an obviously wasteful investment that has no use whatsoever, the decision was still optimal according to the marginal criteria. For most matters of public policy, a static mathematical test that asks whether management believes that it did what it thought was best on the basis of what it knew at the time is not a relevant policy standard. What is generally more important is the market test of whether management decisions made in an uncertain environment with limited information turned out to be prudent, responsive to consumer demands, and tolerably efficient in light of the reality that developed. Rate of return on investment is such a test that can be applied not only prospectively for planning purposes, but also retrospectively for purposes of tracking, accountability, and improved future decision making.

At any point in time, a real firm is highly constrained by its past decisions. It is a going concern involved at different stages of decision making with respect to many interrelated and interdependent investment decisions that relate to different combinations of output for various services in different localities. The characteristics of the investments, including the amount of the expenditure, the types of facilities to be added, and the timing of additions, depend directly upon the quantity and structure of the capacity elements inherited from the past as well as plans for related investments in the future. The firm is in a continuous process of partial adaptation to changing events, and its planning into the future is severely limited by its inability to forecast future events accurately and to perceive all the effects of its alternative investment possibilities.

In any real world situation, the firm has an infinite variety of marginal costs, marginal cost functions, and families of marginal cost functions with values covering a wide range of cost variation. Different marginal costs can be derived for every pair of alternatives being considered; for every conceivable increment in output; for every difference in the amount and/or structure of inherited capacity; for every difference in the actual planning period employed in the analysis; for every change in the relative proportions of the various products or services being supplied; for every different forecast of future events; and for every different perception of the timing, location, and impact of the marginal effects. In addition, since units of output are far from homogeneous, different marginal cost functions will be obtained as the dimensions of the output unit are varied.

In the final analysis, it must be recognized that marginal costs (as well as revenues) are entirely bound up in the personal judgment of the analyst, the "arbitrary" decisions that he makes in defining his problem, and his changing expectations. In fact, we should expect that the optimists in a firm could have quite different marginal costs than the pessimists. Marginal costs cannot be viewed as facts for which objectively valid values can be known. The marginal cost values will depend upon who applies the theory and the incentives under which he works in the environment in which it will be applied. The nature of marginal cost illustrates Myrdal's conclusion that "valuations determine not only our policy conclusions but all our endeavors to establish the facts, from the approaches chosen to the presentation of our results."[11]

In addition, it should be noted that the information requirement for measuring marginal costs in imperfect markets and multivariable production functions is overwhelming. Boulding has observed: "As a theory which purports to represent actual behavior, the maximization theory suffers from the almost fatal defect of failing to consider the information which is available to the decision maker. A theory that assumes knowledge of what cannot be known is clearly defective as a guide to actual behavior.[12] Finally, there is no indication that consistent measurements over time of any single definition of marginal cost by the same individual would have any degree of necessary *stability* from one measurement to the next.

Marginal Cost and Industry Structure

The neoclassical theory of the firm provides no *a priori* basis for concluding that any particular marginal costs are lower than, higher than, or equal to the firm's total cost or revenue requirement. The theory illustrates situations where short-run marginal cost may be higher than short-run average cost, long-run marginal cost, and long-run average cost. The only real constraining relationship is that short-run average costs never can be less than long-run average costs. Moreover, none of the theoretical cost functions have any necessary relationship to actual expended costs that are recorded in the books of account.

Nevertheless, when it comes to measuring marginal costs, practitioners almost invariably address their attention to the books of account, allocating the firm's total costs between fixed and variable. The variable costs are classified as short-run incremental costs. The addition of some fixed capacity costs raises the figure to the level of long-run incremental costs. The inclusion of all costs raises the figure to average total costs. The incremental unit cost figures are deemed applicable to *all* relevant output increments. This additive methodology reinforces the myth that marginal costs are always lower than average costs because you do not allocate the common overhead costs to the former. Under this methodology, all incremental and marginal cost estimates must be less than their companion average cost estimates, a circumstance that can find no support in the neoclassical theory.

The theory of the firm does not directly address the issue of determining the optimal industrial structure. Rather, it is accepted as given for purposes of the marginal analysis. The rationale described above, that marginal cost is always lower than average cost, provides large firms with substantial ammunition, in the name of theoretical economic efficiency, to thwart the entry of potential competitors into their markets, to justify extension of their markets, and to support discriminatory pricing practices. In the communications industries, the American Telephone and Telegraph Company is attempting to reestablish, and the United States Postal Service is attempting to maintain, public policy prohibitions against the entry of competition into some of their traditional monopoly markets. Their principal argument is that their relatively low marginal costs demonstrate that economic efficiency rests in monopoly and not competition. Moreover, since they are using the "correct" terminology from microeconomic theory, their assessments become "generally acceptable" to theorists. Somehow forgotten is the fact that the implementation methodologies adopted would require very low marginal cost calculations when applied anywhere. And the fact that economic entities with vested interests to protect, and with powerful economic incentives to arrive at very low marginal cost figures, are doing the calculating on the basis of personal, subjective valuations for which there can be no accountability is naïvely assumed away.

On matters of competition and industry structure in regulated industries, policy change often occurs when the burden of proof is shifted from one opposing position to another. For example, historically in telecommunications, a new firm could not obtain entry to a communications market without first demonstrating that the existing certified carrier, usually a telephone company monopoly, could not, and would not, provide the service. There was no entry. In its landmark decision permitting the entry of new certified carriers into data and other specialized telecommunications markets,[13] the FCC shifted the burden of proof to those who would oppose the entry of new firms. Now the established carriers must prove that specific entry applications are not in the public interest if new entrants are to be denied certification.

Competitive rate reductions based upon the established firm's assessment of its own relevant marginal cost, in a market environment where traditional monopoly services automatically will provide all residual revenue requirements, has proven to be an effective tool for the established monopoly to take the industry structure policy away from the regulatory authority. The established monopolist assesses its relative efficiency in the market and implements its industry structure policy through its marginal cost determinations. If and when new entry begins to threaten the established market structure, new valuations are placed on new alternative prices, and new marginal costs are calculated. Marginal cost of neoclassical theory provides an effective weapon by which the regulated monopolist can usurp the real power to make the relevant judgments necessary to the implementation of public policy. Thus, the significance of economies of scale, the scope of natural monopoly, and the dimensions of competition become determined by the monopolist, whether natural or unnatural.

Despite their claims of economies of scale as a substantial efficiency advantage, both AT&T and the Postal Service appear to fear a market test of these claimed efficiencies as something equivalent to the bubonic plague. They continue to petition for policy barriers to entry, lest a real market test embarrass them. In sum, the myths of marginal cost have provided a universally applicable efficiency rationale for the preservation and extension of concentrations of economic power in the creep toward monopoly structures in many industries.

Conclusion

It is somewhat ironic that the marginal analysis of neoclassical theory, which was developed to explain how perfect competition could provide optimal resource allocation, has been adopted principally by monopolistic firms to thwart competition and justify the allocational efficiency of monopoly. From a public policy viewpoint, the economic substance of the economic opportunity cost notion has been wrung out of the terminology of marginal analysis. What remains is sterile terminology available for appropriation and implementation in an unlimited variety of applications.

Moreover, the mythology surrounding the terminology of marginal analysis has made it extremely vulnerable to misapplication. We clearly have passed the point of diminishing returns in terms of the benefits of the marginal analysis to effective public policy formulation, and we probably are operating in the area of negative returns. It is time to dispense with the slogans of marginalism. General sweeping recommendations for the use of marginal cost or marginal analysis must be recognized as nothing more than the exhortation of neoclassical theory for decision makers to do their best. The neoclassical theory of the firm should be recognized as essentially irrelevant to the analysis of public policy issues. Economic analysis must return to the rudiments of the opportunity cost concept and its specific meaning for particular public policy issues in an environment of uncertainty, incomplete information, and monopoly power, where the largest constraints on today's policy decisions are the conditions inherited from the immediate past.

Finally, if economic theory is to approach that dangerous area where it would be really useful in the formulation of public policy, it must go beyond the task of providing terminology that is supposed to help decision makers select what they think is best from a predetermined number of alternatives. It must provide a basis for the improved assessment of the efficiency of decisions in light of the market reality that develops. The ultimate economic test is not whether decision makers state (or believe) that they have done their best; it is whether their best is an efficient allocation of resources in the satisfaction of consumer demands. Without accountability, public policy is a sham.

Notes

1. See, for example, John Kenneth Galbraith, *Economics and the Public Purpose* (Boston: Houghton Mifflin, 1973), and "Power and the Useful Economist," *American Economic Review* 63 (March 1973): 1-11.
2. Gunnar Myrdal, *Against the Stream: Critical Essays on Economics* (New York: Pantheon, 1973), p. 159.
3. Alfred E. Kahn, *The Economics of Regulation: Principles and Institutions* (New York: Wiley, 1970), p. 65.
4. See, for example, W. J. Baumol and D. F. Bradford "Optimal Departures from Marginal Cost Pricing," *American Economic Review* 60 (June 1970): 265-283. See also testimony of Baumol on behalf of the American Telephone and Telegraph Company in FCC Docket 16258, 1968; and testimony of W. Vickrey for the United States Postal Service before the Postal Rate Commission, 1973.
5. Ralph Turvey, *Optimal Pricing and Investment in Electricity Supply* (Cambridge, Mass.: The MIT Press, 1968), p. 59.
6. Kahn, *Economics*, p. 160.
7. See W. H. Melody "Interservice Subsidy: Regulatory Standards and Applied Economics," in *Essays on Public Utility Pricing and Regulation*, H. M. Trebing, ed. (East Lansing: Institute of Public Utilities, Michigan State University, 1971), pp. 167-210.
8. "Statement of Purpose, Annual Line of Business Report Program," Bureau of Economics Staff, Federal Trade Commission, 1973.
9. K. E. Boulding "The Present Position of the Theory of the Firm," in *Linear Programming and the Theory of the Firm*, K. E. Boulding and W. A. Spivey, eds. (New York: MacMillan, 1960), p. 1.
10. Melody, "Interservice Subsidy," pp. 181-86.
11. Myrdal, *Against the Stream*, p. 54.
12. Boulding, "Present Position," p. 5.
13. First Report and Order, Docket 18920, 29 FCC 2d 870 (1971).

Economic Theory as a Guideline for Government Intervention and Control: Comment

Alfred E. Kahn

I react to David Martin's article with a mixture of pleasure and dismay—pleasure from hearing congenial and familiar truths that take me back to my childhood as an institutional economist, and dismay because of the impression it leaves that evolutionary economics has itself evolved so little in the intervening decades. At times I felt like the Indian who is said to have remarked, after watching the smoke puffs bursting forth from a distant erupting volcano, "Gosh, I **wish** I had said that." At other times I feel like the Pope who, having granted an audience to the then Ambassador from the United States, Clair Booth Luce, in which she did all the talking, intensely and long, was reported finally to have broken in: "But madam, I already am a Catholic!"

Consider the times. Reputable economists can advise a President, in the circumstances of 1969, 1970, or 1971, that the wage-price guidelines of the Kennedy-Johnson years, or more thoroughgoing wage and price controls, were or would be futile, mischievous, or both! They can argue that deflationary macroeconomic policies would bring inflation to a halt at a tolerable cost, or that the "maximization of economic welfare" calls for avoiding gasoline rationing and freeing

---

The author is Dean, College of Arts and Sciences, Cornell University, Ithaca, New York. *These comments were prepared on the basis of remarks as delivered at the session and were presented at the Annual Meeting of the Association for Evolutionary Economics, New York, 27-29 December 1973.*

the price of natural gas. Under these circumstances, one can hardly argue it is superfluous for economists like Martin to expose and question—even though in very familiar terms—the assumptions and value judgments underlying these prescriptions, namely, that the implicit definition of economic welfare completely ignores the distribution of income; that no public policy can be justified on purely economic grounds if the polity regards its results as unacceptably unjust; that policies aimed at letting the market cater to the unfettered expressions of preference by sovereign consumers must be weighed in the light of the fact that the consumer's complement of wants and preferences, and the kinds of alternatives presented to him for selection, are themselves heavily influenced by our economic institutions; or that there is indeed such a thing as stagflation, and it has something to do with market power.

But these reminders and retorts are not a sufficient guide to public policy either. One hardly can quarrel with Martin's concluding observation that "economic theory is more useful to those who knew its weaknesses than it is to true believers," but it does not tell us very much either.

How far does it carry us forward to be reminded that the giant corporation is not the same as a mom and pop store, if we have read Thorstein Veblen, Adolf Berle and Gardiner Means, or Robin Maris? Or that man is not merely a rational calculator of costs and benefits who comes into the world with a fully developed set of preferences for underarm deodorants, food additives, color television, and 150-horsepower engines mounted behind fragile bumpers, if we have read Veblen, or Ruth Benedict, or John Kenneth Galbraith?

The really important questions are the *next* ones and the ones after *those,* and these Martin does not address. What exactly is the relationship between our own particular set of economic institutions and the nature of consumer choices? It is surely a parody to pretend that they are simply molded by the large corporation, even one so large as General Motors or Ford. How else does one explain the Volkswagen and the Edsel and the appreciation of automobiles by the Russians? And what are the acceptable limits of efforts by an imperfectly democratic government to write some other messages on that *tabula rasa?* Exactly to what extent and in what ways does the theory of monopoly behavior lead to erroneous inferences about the behavior of the giant corporation; what are the implications of those differences?[1] How important and prevalent is the power to "contrive scarcity," and how do we go about identifying it? How exactly do we balance the demands of economic efficiency and distributive justice? Answers to all these questions must be sought both in general terms, with respect to the economy at large, and in each specific context. To take but one example, I wish I knew to what extent Martin is right when he cites natural gas as a case of "contrived scarcity."

I do not see what is wrong with an economist approaching income distribution policy from the standpoint that Martin attributes to his archetypical dogmatic theorist: "You can do anything you wish with the income distribution so long as you do not use a government measure that is inefficient," provided the search for alternatives does not end there. It was that kind of reasoning that led a conservative economist like Milton Friedman to a powerful advocacy of the negative income tax, and a New Dealist Secretary of Agriculture, Charles Brannan, to advocate direct income supplements to farmers in preference to the manipulation of prices, both, I think, policies that Martin would applaud. Surely, economic history is replete with examples of prices being held far above marginal cost—farm prices toward parity, oil prices under prorationing, distributive margins under resale price maintenance—purportedly in order to help the small producer or seller, but with big producers and sellers reaping most of the advantage. There are also examples of other prices held far below marginal cost, purportedly to help the poor but inevitably helping more those who buy much than those who buy little. All of these help us see the desirability of trying to accomplish income redistribution in less inefficient ways.

I recognize that such happy solutions reasonably consistent with both economic efficiency and income redistribution are not always available or politically feasible, and I agree with Martin's conclusion that we then should look for "next-best methods actually available." It was in precisely that spirit that I designed and recommended a two-price system for regulating the field price of natural gas, but always with the caveat that I would have preferred a tax on economic rents and with a challenge to the industry that if it were willing to give up prorationing, percentage depletion, and import quotas on oil I would advocate deregulating natural gas. And it seems to me at least arguable that the inefficiencies of holding the field price of domestic gas in recent years far below the costs of the alternatives to which pipeline and distribution companies are in fact turning, and so low as to encourage burning vast quantities as boiler fuel, may well outweigh the income distribution benefits of doing so.

This is particularly so now that society has become much more concerned than it was as recently as ten years ago about our historic profligacy in the use of our natural endowment. The most effective and pervasive instrument for conserving scarce resources and preserving the environment is a system of prices fully reflecting the incremental costs of production, internal and external, private and social. The challenging task before us is to meet these requirements of economic efficiency while assuring that the distribution of our newly discovered poverty accords with the community's conception of justice. Perhaps this can be done by such means as excess profits taxes, direct controls on home insulation and automobile horsepower, and possibly some device for cushioning the impact on the poor of the sudden changes in the conditions of supply more selective than simply holding price below marginal cost for *all* customers.

These observations lead me directly to William Melody's article. Before turning to it, however, I must admit that these critical comments on Martin are fundamentlly unfair: I have been chiding him for not having written the article *I* want to write. I should, instead, thank him for having stimulated me to think about that next article, which should begin with an acknowledgment to him.

I am simply appalled by William Melody's article.

Most notably in proceedings before the Federal Communications Commission, Melody has played an enormously useful role in recent years in pointing up the problems and dangers of permitting regulated companies to adopt marginal cost pricing in competitive situations. The danger is that such a policy can be effectively predatory, thereby reflecting a genuine conflict, in those situations where marginal are below average costs, between the requirements of static efficiency and good dynamic performance. These dangers, he has argued eloquently, are accentuated by genuine problems of measurement: Once one turns from short-run to long-run marginal cost as the floor for competitive price, there enter inevitable elements of arbitrariness in defining the unit or class of service and in specifying the pertinent time frame for which the costs are to be measured.

His present article once again effectively, although not always in my judgment accurately, describes these problems. But it also does much more: It proceeds to generalize those observations in such a way as to raise economic know-nothingism to the level of an ideal. In a world economy characterized by fantastic inefficiencies, he simply would throw out a critical element in the entire conception of economic efficiency.

Do I exaggerate? Our cities are clogged and decaying in large measure because automobiles are not charged their full marginal costs, including marginal congestion costs. We confront the possibility of a new world of energy shortage, over years and perhaps permanently, in large measure because we have not priced energy at its full marginal costs. We have become increasingly concerned about the destruction of our environment by a market system that fails to reflect marginal external costs in price. Large portions of our transport system are atrophied and unresponsive and run wastes estimated at billions of dollars a year, in large measure because of our failure or unwillingness to let traffic be distributed on the basis of marginal costs, just exactly as electricity power pools take energy from all the interconnected sources of supply, from one instant to the next, on the principle of equalizing cost at the margin. This case is particularly ironic since it is the result largely of the ICC's historical policy of determining the low-cost carrier on the basis of average or fully distributed cost, the very standard under which Melody urges us to rally.

It is in circumstances such as these that Melody would resurrect as our new standard of efficiency the realized return on investments made in the past. In so doing, he not only would ignore the pervasive phenomenon of marginal costs differing from average, but also would base pricing and resource allocation on historic costs rather than current; in so doing, he would turn economics upside down. Sunk costs are no longer bygones, best ignored, but are brought to the center of the decision process.

"Economic analysis," he says, "must return to the rudiments of the opportunity cost concept." But the only opportunity costs that have any current significance are present or future costs. Sunk costs represent alternatives already and irretrievably foregone; they, and the return on investments made in the past, have no proper role to play in current allocative decisions except as, by chance, they happen to correspond to current costs and prospective returns on incremental investments.

I wish I had time to point out all the errors of fact and logic on which Melody constructs this case. Instead, I can only list a few, with the briefest of comments, on each.

(1) The "neoclassical theory of the firm" and marginal costs, he declares, have virtually no application in the real world. (True, what he says on the last is that prices are almost never set *at* marginal cost; but what he advocates is complete rejection of that standard.)

Yet the firm of National Economic Research Associates is introducing testimony in regulatory proceedings in which it is specifically trying to test electric rate schedules against its measurements of long-run incremental costs,[2] and it is doing similar analyses for other electric companies. Great Britain and France sell electricity at time-of-day rates that are based roughly on an upwardly sloping short-run marginal cost function. Power pools draw power automatically from alternative sources on the same basis. The central issue in the famous *Ingot Molds* and Southern Railway grain cases was the right of railroads to base charges on their computed incremental (rather than fully distributed, or average, or historic) costs.[3] Standby youth airplane fares were based on the fact that the incremental costs of standby service are lower than those of reservation service. The increasing spread between charges for operator-assisted and direct-distance-dialed, and between day and night, telephone calls is based on similar calculations, and the efforts of telephone companies to introduce usage-sensitive pricing (rather than flat rates, based on *average* costs, for unlimited local calls) springs from a recognition of the fact that the marginal costs of additional calls, while below the average, are more than zero. Conservationists are insisting that electricity rates be based on current rather than historic costs, and the Environmental Protection Agency has introduced variable effluent charges reflecting the rising external costs of air pollution.

Some of these differentials could be justified to some extent on the basis of differences in average costs and even historic costs properly computed; others could not.

(2) There is something in the marginal cost concept, or the way it is measured, that tends inherently to make it come out below average cost. That is simply not true of many of the illustrations I have just given; in consequence, a great deal of energy has been devoted in recent years to finding ways of returning the *excessive* revenues that would be produced by uniform marginal cost pricing, with a minimum loss of efficiency.[4]

(3) Economists are inconsistent who advocate application of the marginal cost standard for "allocating resources among product lines or services within the firm," while looking to rate of return on investment as the "standard for allocating resources among industries, and among firms within an industry." This observation seems to betray almost total confusion. Marginal cost is the proper beginning point for efficient pricing of *all* goods and services, whether produced in a multiproduct firm or by several firms and industries. Return on *incremental* investment is the proper basis for allocating capital *both* between firms and industries *and* within the multiproduct firm. Comparative rates of return on past investments, by different industries, firms, or product lines within a firm, are *possible indicators* of comparative efficiency, profitability, and the presence or absence of monopoly power. The rate base of a regulated firm is a convenient

basis for computing allowable profits; it is *not* a sound basis for determining individual prices.[5] Where is the inconsistency?

(4) The definition and measurement of marginal cost is wholly arbitrary and assumes that the firm begins with a clean slate, unencumbered by the effects of past decisions. Not so. The marginal cost that is pertinent is the addition to (or saving of) total cost that will in fact be incurred (or reaped) by a firm, whatever its current situation, as a result of a *particular pricing* or output decision under contemplation.

Applied microeconomics is the exciting new frontier of public policy. The policies are going to be made, in one way or another. Martin and Melody supply useful reminders of the pitfalls of entrusting the task to people who know only economic theory. They provide no convincing reason for entrusting the task instead to people who know none.

Notes

1. See Robert F. Lanzillotti, "Pricing Objectives in Large Companies," *American Economic Review* 48 (December 1958): 921-40; and A. E. Kahn, "Comment," ibid. 49 (September 1959): 670-78.
2. See the testimony of Irwin M. Stelzer, Jules Joskow, Charles H. Frazier, and Leo T. Mahoney before the Public Service Commision of Wisconsin in the Madison Gas and Electric Company Rate Case, Docket No. 2-U-7423, August 1973.
3. *American Commercial Lines* v. *Louisville & Nashville Railroad*, 392 U.S. 571 (1968); and Interstate Commerce Commission, *Grain in Multiple-Car Shipments—River Crossings to the South*, 325 ICC 752 (1965).
4. See, for example, Paul L. Joskow, "Applying Economic Principles to Public Utility Rate Structures: the Case of Electricity," draft ms., Massachusetts Institute of Technology, July 1973; and A. E. Kahn, "The Economics of the Electricity-Environmental Issue: A Primer," P.I.P. National Environmental Press Seminar, Minneapolis, 31 May 1972 (copies available on request).
5. Melvin G. Dechazeau, "The Nature of the 'Rate Base' on the Regulation of Public Utilities," *Quarterly Journal of Economics* 51 (February 1937): 298-316.

Axioms of Economics and the Claim to Efficiency

Sherman S. Krupp

Some of the logical relations between formal micro-economic theory and the claim of this theory to provide an explanation of the "efficient allocation of resources" will be discussed in this paper. Of course, qualifications of the efficient allocation of resources is an old story in economics. Indeed, much of the development of modern economics is such a qualification. Monopoly, Keynesian theory, welfare economics, distinctions between wants and needs, less than perfect mobility, imperfections in knowledge, differences between short- and long-run planning, consumer irrationality—all qualify the tradition of an optimum resource allocation both theoretically and empirically. What is less familiar, however, is that the language of the theory itself introduces qualifications on understanding allocation.

Some of the basic qualifications arise because micro-economic theory is mainly a deductive science. This means that its more complex theorems are logically compounded from simpler statements so that the entire theory, in turn, is finally reducible to a set of fundamental axioms. This reduction is what gives deductive explanation its analytical power, precision, and generality. The first link in this chain of derivations are the axioms which provide the concepts, definitions, and relations of the theory and which also delineate its domain. Fundamental to a deductive science, therefore, is the crucial shaping influence of the axioms.

Specifically, the postulates and axioms define and classify the basic properties and units of economics, state the fundamental relations between the units, delineate the domain of the theory, and provide or suggest some of the rules of correspondence by means of which the abstract terms of a theory can be applied empirically. The basic properties of micro-economics are stated in the postulates concerning "scarce goods" and "human wants"; the fundamental relation or law of the system is that of the maximization of utility or profits. The domain is a field of independent individuals and firms compounded into a market and the rules of correspondence define the way in which properties, relations and domain can be associated with the empirical world. That is, they construe the extent to which theoretical terms, such as "the individual," "the firm," "maximization," or "efficiency" can be made descriptive of reality.

Although the axioms provide explanatory premises, the economic theory tries to explain the efficient allocation of resources. Thus, economic theory

The author is Professor of Sociology at Queens College, City University of New York and Adjunct Professor of Bernard Baruch School of Business, City University of New York.

orders its descriptions towards an explanation of the efficiency of the economic system. "Efficiency," however, is not a descriptive term but a highly abstract theoretical term whose meaning must be understood by its relation to the theory as a whole. Like the sub-atomic particles of physics, "efficiency" cannot be directly formulated or observed. This is because it is a relationship rather than a thing; it is discriminated by thought rather than by the senses. Consequently, the claim that economic theory is the analysis of the "efficient allocation of resources" is as much a statement of theory as it is one of experience.

I propose to point to difficulties in the language of economics that increase the tautological and circular character of efficiency as the term is used in economic theory, and the difficulties which qualify its application as a descriptive or prescriptive term. The tautological element in "the efficient allocation of resources" arises in at least three different ways. The first concerns the inner structure of the basic maximizing unit. The second concerns the problem of summating these units into a deductive aggregate. The third involves the conformation of the deductively derived system with experience. Although economic theory is the subject matter being discussed, the terms I will be using depend heavily on the philosophy of science. The importance of this reference language rests on its complete neutrality with regard to the subject matter and theory of economics. The world of experience is understood through the language of economic theory. Consequently, there is a continual interdependence between the perceiver and the thing perceived. By freeing us from the conventional metaphors of economic theory, the philosophy of science permits some degree of detachment from traditional beliefs in economic matters.

I. Micro-economic theory uses the postulate-deductive form as its strategy for theoretical explanation. A highly simplified system of axioms and rules of combination is introduced at the most elementary level of the theory. The scope of inquiry is thereby limited to a very small set of properties and their relations. The way the parts are related to one another is determined by axioms of combination. A basic combination axiom is that of the maximizing, independent unit. Like gravity in Newtonian physics, maximization is postulated as the fundamental elementary force of the system. Theorems of "substitution" which related the parts to one another are derived from this elementary axiom.

Postulates are chosen because of their logical form, so that deductive techniques, such as equilibrium analysis, can be applied. This emphasis on logical form means that descriptive realism is not an ingredient of the fundamental premises. A deductive theory, however, does not necessarily lack empirical content. Empirical content and descriptive fullness can be introduced through limiting conditions imposed on the derived system. It need not be contained in the initial formulation of the axioms and assumptions. Nor need the absence of realism in the postulates create a significantly distorted system. The postulate-deductive form does not by itself distort. Distortion occurs because the theorist assumes a higher correspondence with experience than is justified by the empirical content of later elaborations of the theory. Since the independent maximizing unit of the firm is an elementary starting point in micro-economic theory, one form which major derivations are obtained, it is especially useful to examine the logical function of this unit.

The law of maximization is the single universal law or force of theoretical microeconomics. It applies equally to the internal behavior of the elementary unit of the firm and to combinations of all units, the competitive system as a whole. When applied internally to the unit of the firm, the maximizing postulate becomes the conventional statement of a firm equating its margins. This marginal cost-marginal revenue equality is, in effect, a logical derivation, a corollary of the postuate. Indeed, it is merely another way of saying that the firm maximizes. Maximization, therefore, by postulate implies efficiency in the internal relations of the firm.

Theoretical derivations from the maximizing firm inevitably assume its internal relations. Therefore, any theorem in competitive equilibrium that concerns the efficient allocation of resources must take the inner combination of resources for granted; that is, the internal elements of the micro-units have already been mixed as to eliminate any question as to the internal efficiency of the unit. For purposes of the theorem, the unit is assumed to have arranged its inner structure in an optimal manner. Since optimality is equivalent to asserting the efficiency of the unit, the optimal firm has, by postulate, comprehended a crucial property of efficiency of the entire system takes for granted the micro-efficiency of the unit. The efficiency of the aggregate, therefore, must be expressly understood to have removed the possibility of one area of possible inefficiency in the systm: the less-than-maximizing firm. In the real world less-than-maximizing behavior has traditionally been looked upon as a modification of the realism of the maximizing assumption. I believe this is ultimately a minor controversy. What is probably more significant is that the qualification of the maximizing assumption reduces the efficiency implications for the economic system as a whole. To put the problem in another way: If firms do not maximize, then each unit will really be a less than perfect efficient unit. The sum of abstract postulated maximizing firms has theoretically eliminated this possibility and takes unit efficiency for granted. Consequently, the argument that the allocation of resources is an efficient one is essentially a tautological arugment to this extent. I do not mean to say that economic theory does not explain efficiency in the system as a whole. Rather, I am suggesting that efficiency is circulary defined. Circularity occurs in that efficiency of the whole also summates the efficiency of the units taken as individual entities. The theory has postulated efficiency and at the same time it suggests that the efficient allocation of resources is a logical deduction from the postulates. When we apply the efficient allocation of resources of conventional theory to the world of experience, it must be understood to have removed from possible confrontation with experience the efficiency of the micro-unit. Efficiency thus takes on the character of an implicit definition.

This tautology cannot be eliminated without devastating the logical fertility of the axioms. That all tautologies be removed from a theory is not necessary. It is important, however, to know what they are. The concept of efficiency in economic theory is circularly defined by the theory itself and must be understood in terms of this restriction.

II. The way the units are combined introduces a second tautology which has important implications for the question of efficiency. The power of a deductive system depends on its ability to extend the fundamental laws that apply to the units and to larger combinations of these units. The postulates that permit this extension of the fundamental axioms are known as composition rules or laws. An example from traditional geometry is the rules permitting the addition of lines and spaces; similarly, the modifications in vector space of the laws of commutation define new composition rules. A composition law is implied when the theory of the firm is used to explain the industry or when the economy is treated as a collection of firms and industries. The underlying assumption is the possibility of summating the micro-properties of the basic units. Keynes brought this summation into question when he argued that the achievement of optimality by individuals and firms need not bring about either full employment or efficiency in the economy as a whole.

Composition laws are also basic to any discussion of externalities. If a theorist uses price theory to explain the social and economic costs of racial discrimination, he is extending micro-economic analysis to a new sphere of inquiry. He thereby modifies a law of composition. Composition laws permit free use of deductive apparatus within some delineated domain. Some of the crucial composition laws of micro-economic analysis, necessary as they are for theoretical purposes, help make an "efficient allocation of resources" a logically necessary outcome from the postulates. The law of substitution derives from profiit maximization and the independence of the units; this implies that more efficient combinations will always replace less efficient in the economic system. That is, the composition rules have helped put the conclusions in the premises.

Composition laws can appear implicitly within the inner logic of a theory. Often they are hidden within the postulate. At other times they may be compounded into the explicit statements and definitions delineating the boundaries of a theory. An example of an internal composition rule tied to the logic of economic theory is the assumption concerning the independence of the firm; more explicit rules might be those that limit economics to the examination of market behavior and the pricing system. Axioms of independence or interdependence can act as composition laws. Axioms of independence, for example, lead directly to the laws of substitution; interdependence can lead to complementarity. Where substitutability prevails a change in a small sector will usually be offset by neighborhood compensating changes and adjustments. These compensating changes reduce the scope of the individual change. Where complementarity prevails a given change may magnify through the system. The composition rules of economic theory directly affect the way efficiency within the system is explained.

Independence means that the behavior of the elementary unit can be described without reference to the behavior of other units. To discuss a unit, *X*, it is not also necessary to discuss another unit, *Y*. Both *X* and *Y*, however, can be analyzed as members of the same class of things, possessing similar properties and described by similar relations. Although *X* and *Y* have similar properties, independence means that the specific properties found in *X* do not affect the specific properties found in *Y*. If we designate the common properties and relations by *alpha,* then *X* has the properties, $alpha_X$, and *Y* has the properties, $alpha_Y$. In interdependence, *X* and *Y* will reveal a second property, *beta,* which was not contained in the initial formulation of either *X* or *Y* but which characterizes both in relation to one another. That is, both *X* and *Y* in relation to one another will be characterized by another common property, *beta.* This second property must be added to the thorems that are derived from *X* and *Y* in their joint relation. Thus, the predictions from *X* and *Y* will also include some new property which was not directly predictable from *X* and *Y* as separate units but which characterize them in combination. If this new property cannot be included in the postulates, it can be thought of as emergent. With interdependence, *X* and *Y,* together with the new property, *beta,* constitute a field different from that bounded by *X* and *Y* as independent units. This new field includes both *alpha* and *beta.* Any deductions from *X* and *Y* must now comprehend the new relations of this more complex field. Adding the new property, *beta,* has increased the complexity of the relation and thereby reduced the domain of the application of the simple law of combination. Independence, in contrast, permits a compounding or addition of the basic units under the same law until a limit has been reached. The limit is usually some *beta* which was not directly compoundable from the initial properties or from an unknown or emergent property. The axiom of independence assumes *alpha* to be characteristic of combinations, permitting the same laws to apply throughout all deductions and additions within the system, (for example, substitution). The axiom thereby encourages high deductive genality. Assuming independence reduces the likelihood of investigating possible interdependencies or for discovering new emergent properties. Thus, the axiom of independence in economic theory exercises a strong constraint on the way we view the efficient allocation of resources. In particular, negative implications for efficiency tend to be overlooked. In addition of *alphas* into a macro-composition may even create a new interdependence which brings about a transformation in the property, *alpha.*

A specific *beta* in economic theory is that of externalities. Externalities can be defined as a *beta* not directly deductible from the initial postulates but not excludible except for purposes of generality in composition. Clearly, the "efficient allocation of resources" is a collective term derived from the unit of the firm and, by the aggregation of firms, extended to a larger system. Consequently, any limitation on this deduction will affect the meaning of efficiency. Fundamental to efficiency as a collective term in conventional economics is the assumption that the *betas*—the emergent properties, the side-effects, and the externalities of micro-theory—are negligible. But the universe of discourse in conventional theory does not include explicit analysis of externalities. Therefore, it cannot predict or legislative on the emergence or importance of these *betas*. The dilemma for conventional theory, of course, is that if externalities were not negligible, the basic postulates would not provide adequate premises for explaining the efficient allocation of resources. Deductive fertility has been obtained by maintaining the postulate of independence in the fundamental units, thereby implying the *beta* to be either negligible or non-existent. As a result, the quality of efficiency has been tautologically built into the theory in still another way.

III. Finally, there are problems in the conformability of micro-economic theory with experience. The simplified abstractions of economic theory create special difficulties in relating the theory to observable. Simplification makes a few properties the focus of analysis and treats all other factors as complex surrounding conditions. These complexities are contained in the *ceteris paribus* assumptions, the statement that other things are equal. The *ceteris paribus* pound contains all other factors, stated as side conditions. These are either kept constant or introduced into the discussion, depending on whether the inquiry is kept abstract or permitted specific kinds of complexity. Usually, the variables determining economic events are exceedingly numerous, so that the practice of providing explanations from the main theorems is consistent with simplification. When this is done it is assumed that the factors in the *ceteris paribus* box have little influence on the phenomena being explained.

The conditions of the pound—all the specific contingencies—always provide a reserve for more complete explanations and for new explanatory premises. A more complete explanation can always be provided by adding properties and relations that were omitted in the promary abstractions; rival theoretical explanations can be obtained by elevating these new explanatory factors to significance and by giving them systematic form. So long as the explanatory premises released from the *ceteris paribus* box are of the same order as the conventional premises of the theory, no significant logical problem need arise. The new relations can be fitted into a common theoretical framework. The introduction of monopoly and oligopoly into conventional theory was such a modification. When an influence or rival explanation is offered that does not fit into the conventional framework, however, serious difficulties can arise. Since the *ceteris paribus* pound contains all cultural, political, and institutional factors, rival explanations can be suggested that stress different properties and relations and derive from unconventional behavioral assumptions. When this occurs one is outside of the main stream of postulate-deductive derivation and the conventional theory offers no way of adjudicating between rival theoretical explanations. Still more serious consequences are involved. The existence of conditional give the theoretician a way of rationalizing his failure in prediction. He can always blame "outside conditions," the empirical framework that this theory has left unexplored.

Because of the highly conditional nature of the economic theorems, it is often very difficult to make the theory operational. The simple properties and relations of the theory rarely match the complexities of reality. The theoretical formulations of time, for example, the short and long run, are undated and bear little resemblance to the clock-time of the actual world. The actual economic system is part of a cultural setting, which is also changing over time. The contingencies of culture and time provide important escape clauses for the predictions in economics; when predictions fail, culture or time can always be made liable.

The concept of time enters economic theory as an illustration. It is usually introduced as the period necessary for forces producing specific effects to work themselves out. Instantaneous market period, the short run, and the long run, are abstract concepts used in relation to particular forces believed to be operating in certain inquiries. The time span within which the laws of substitution operate is practically never specified. This highly generalized concept of time leads to serious difficulties in prediction. In practice it is never clear how much actual time must be allowed for any set of forces to fulfill prediction. Consequently, the theorist can always continue to maintain his theory and claim that time allowed was not long enough. Time is especially problematic when market solutions are applied to underdeveloped areas. In the very long run the free market may result in a world allocation of resources that is optimal, but in the short run, international inequalities may be increasing. Since theoretical time cannot be matched with historical time, the theory can escape confrontation with experience.

Furthermore, consider the explanation given relating the distribution of income to an efficient resource allocation. The marginal productivity explanation of factor returns makes the explanation of distribution depend on the efficient allocation of resources. If distribution depended on the efficient allocation, it could be explained by, but could not itself explain, this allocation. The efficient allocation of resources could be discussed independently of distribution while superior and inferior distributions become matters only for practical or ethical decision. Although distribution is determined by market forces, it also has cultural and institutional determinants. These factors could be released from the *ceteris paribus* pound to offer a rival explanation. But even a political redistribution of income would not vitally affect the purely economic explanation of resource allocation, because allocation has been treated as though it were independent of distribution. The Pandora's box of institutional determinants can be kept closed as long as this independence is taken to prevail.

The new interest in poverty and development has made the interdependence between distribution and allocation evident. Clearly, the supply of skills depends on income distribution, just as human energies depend on class structure. Empirically, an efficient resource allocation could not take distribution for granted. Distributions might be ranked in accordance with their affect on an efficient allocation. Moreover, if distribution is determined by the institutional arrangements of society, then the *ceteris paribus* pound may contain among other things, major determinants of efficiency or inefficiency. These considerations suggest that the postulate-deductive framework cannot explain an efficient resource allocation without significant help from non-economic external influences.

The problem of conforming theory to the actual world may be carried even further. When predictions concerning efficiency fail, the theorist can always call on the *ceteris paribus* pound to provide him with an excuse for failure. If a supply of skills is not produced by market forces, outside factors can always be called upon to rationalize their absence. It is always possible to blame the institutional deterrents to mobility. Cultural factors can thus be used to explain an existing state despite the fact that they cannot provide an optimum allocation. According to convention, the optimum allocation is finally determined by the free flow of market forces. But the difficulty of relating the theory to observables insulates the theory from refutation. Problems connected with the matching of theory to experience significantly affect the meaning of the efficient allocation of resources.

The "efficient allocation of resources" is a highly tautological term with only very indirect correspondence with the actual world and with mainly theoretical meaning and application. I have suggested three reasons why this is so. The first concerns the efficiency put in the premises through the axiom of maximization. The second involves the total inapplicability of conventional micro-economic theory to the problem of externalities. The third results from the difficulties of including any but a few simple properties in the picture of reality. This restriction encourages the theory to insulate itself from refutation. Moreover, these difficulties are not disparate; they may reinforce one another at various points in the theory. This, however, does not mean that economic theory as a whole is not valuable. It is enormously useful as an organizing framework for description and for occasional prescriptions where the actual world fits the exacting limitations in its conditions; the analysis of inflation could be such a case. What is more tenuous, however, and all too frequently mixed in with the descriptions are norms for the correct allocation of resources. Common-sense and the vast array of empirical qualifications have taught us not to accept too easily its prescriptions. What I have tried to do is to show the logical foundations, and thereby to qualify, one of its main applications—the optimum allocation of resources.

Economic Welfare and the Welfare Economics

G. Warren Nutter

Economics, a child of the Enlightenment, was born as moral philosophy or the science concerned with how to build the good society. In that age of optimism and enthusiasm, leaders of thought in the West looked forward to unimagined progress through reason and liberty. The Enlightenment marked a fundamental revolution in outlook, in which hope for the future and faith in freedom displaced endurance of the present and worship of authority. It was an exciting age of great expectations.

Adam Smith gave concrete form to the vision of his age in the *Wealth of Nations,* one of the most influential works in man's history and the foundation of economics or, more properly, political economy. Yet, as a necessary product of its time, Smith's treatise—as its title proclaimed—was concerned overwhelmingly with the problem of improving material well-being. A rising standard of life in its narrow sense was viewed as the first order of business if mankind was to progress, and this rising standard was to be brought about by greater efficiency in the use of resources and by accumulation of wealth.

Over the years, those who call themselves economists have studied a widening circle of problems, but in the main they have kept material welfare as the central issue of their discipline. Although there have been notable exceptions, these have not pointed the direction of study for the profession as a whole.

One is perhaps justified in characterizing economics today as the study of how to create the comfortable life, not how to build the good society. By and large, the word "progress" has disappeared from the economist's vocabulary to be replaced by "growth," which means "more of the same." Curiously, many economists seem to believe that, by thus restricting their range of interests, they have become more scientific, that they avoid value judgments by being concerned with the comfortable life rather than the good society. There is even recurrent talk of establishing a purely objective, value-free theory of economic welfare which would tell us how to make society better off while maintaining ethical neutrality.

It is sufficient to say that all such thinking is wrong. Economics cannot be purged of moral content if it is to be concerned with the question of welfare; and economists must be concerned with this question, at least implicitly and indirectly, if economics is to be anything more than

The author is Paul Goodloe McIntire Professor of Economics, University of Virginia.
This essay is based on a lecture presented at Bethany College in a series on "Some Unsettled Questions of Political Economy" supported by the Relm Foundation.

an intellectual game. This is not to say that economists are obliged to advocate their own versions of the good life, or that they should confuse matters of fact and normative assertions, or that every aspect of economic study must be tied directly and explicitly to a specific issue of social welfare. Rather, it is to say that the subject as a whole takes on meaning only as it keeps in contact with real social problems, which by the nature of man and society have ethical content. Economics can escape moralizing, but it cannot escape morals.

To avoid misunderstanding, let me be clear: this is not an essay on what economists should or should not do. They should do whatever they want to do and can find a market for. I am leading up to a different point, namely, that the narrowed vision of economists is largely responsible for the poor state of welfare economics.

Let me be more specific. According to modern welfare economics, an economy is in an ideal state if no one can be made better off without making someone else worse off. This state is often referred to as the Pareto optimum. Conversely, the state of society is said to be improved if someone can be made better off without making anyone worse off, even though some may have to be compensated by others for this to be so.

The trouble with this approach is clear: the optimum state is never achievable. Society is not only never there; it can never get there. In the first place, the optimum state is constantly changing as wants, resources and technology undergo change. In the second place, and more importantly, such a state cannot be defined independently of the path through which it is to be approached. Hence such theorizing is utopian and sterile. For example, suppose analysis of an economy leads one to conclude without a doubt that, by the "Paretian" welfare standard, to tax one industry and subsidize another would be desirable. Let this be done. An immediate consequence is that the structure of durable assets in the economy is altered, thereby changing the structure of costs relevant for any practical purpose. The Pareto optimum corresponding to this revised state of affairs will be different from the one corresponding to the earlier state. In the course of trying to move toward the optimum, the economy moves the optimum itself.

In addition, of course, the optimum moves of its own accord, in response to any significant change in the "givens" of the economic system. It is literally impossible to keep up with these changes analytically. What makes sense as a policy today, viewed in terms of the "Paretian" standard, will make no sense tomorrow.

Why, then, do economists persist in this utopian analysis? Although some have obviously grown uneasy, they seek a curious way out. They have created a theory of the "second best" which seems to say that the "best" policy in the optimum state of affairs is not necessarily the "best" policy for moving toward the optimum. Hence some other, or "second best," policy should be followed.

But if the "best" is not the "best," why call it the "best"? Or, more to the point, if the "second best" is really the "best," why call it the "second best"? The answer seems to be that these economists, too, are victims of utopian theorizing. They are judging the "betterness" of a policy on the basis of how far it advances a society toward an unattainable, inconstant goal. If we were to think this way about nature, what would we deem to be the "best" weather and what the "second best"?

Let me emphasize that I am not taking economists to task here for dealing with normative issues. Nor is the question that of whose norms are the right norms. Instead, I am challenging the vision of the problem, the mode of analysis, the outlook of economists.

To rephrase the question raised earlier, how did economists fall into this habit of thinking, and why do they find the habit so hard to shake off? One important reason is that economists have been preoccupied with the notions of efficiency, optimality and growth, conceived in the context of an unchanging world. Too little attention has been given to change itself, in large part because there is no simple and easy way to analyze and assess the effects of change. But the economy changes at least as much as it grows, and an appraisal of performance that takes no account of this fact is bound to be misleading if not irrelevant.

Economic change in the main is the product of expanding knowledge, and neither change nor knowledge can be optimized. Future knowledge is unknown and unknowable now, and that is that. It is utter nonsense to speak of optimum knowledge or optimum change. Both come from a process of exploration, chance and discovery. What sense does it make, then, to think of improvement in economic welfare as movement toward an optimum state of affairs?

More concretely, a society is surely made better off, in any ordinary sense of the term, as much by discovery and introduction of new products as by growth in the volume of old ones. The automobile, airplane, radio, television, computer, medicine, and countless other innovations are what make our standard of living today incomparably higher than it was a century ago. These innovations enter our lives continuously and unpredictably. They work out their effects pervasively and unpredictably in the economy. Theories of welfare economics that abstract from the very nature of modern economies are bound to give the wrong answers.

In short, we need a fresh approach. I do not pretend to know what it is, but I will try to suggest some of the ways in which our thinking needs to change.

Economists must, first of all, grasp the fact that where an economy goes depends on how it gets there. There are no practical alternative policies that will lead to the same state of affairs. Once any significant economic decision is made, it leaves its imprint on society, and conditions can never be restored to their original configuration. Any given imprint can be erased only by leaving other imprints. We must therefore give up any notions we may have of casting the economy as a whole into a preconceived structure.

We must think, instead, of changing a little bit here and a little bit there while taking the rest for granted and as beyond our immediate control. Similarly, we must be content to appraise the changes in terms of their primary effects and not their total impact on social welfare, which we can never know. Perfectionists may wish to argue that piecemeal improvements in welfare, however defined, are likely to lead to less total improvement than a policy that takes all interactions into account; but they must face the fact that the course they advocate is simply impossible. Society is condemned to a certain amount of drift, no matter how much conscious control is exercised over its activities. Too much control, in fact, merely magnifies the drift, because the task of directing social behavior grows disproportionately faster than the extent of control.

In any case, the problem of welfare economics is essentially the problem of choosing and implementing social policies. The first task is to decide who is to make the decisions. Put more broadly, it is to choose the economic system. I would argue that this is the foremost task, to which all others are quite subservient. Viewed in this context, the fundamental problem is not one of making the rules to guide social activities, but rather one of making rules for making rules. The constitution comes first, and then specific laws and policies.

There is much to be said for encouraging economists to abandon altogether the field of welfare economics as it has developed and to substitute more sophisticated study of alternative economic systems. Let economists raise the question of what system works best, all relevant considerations being taken into account, and not what specific policies are desirable regardless of the system.

At least two difficulties must be expected with regard to this approach. First, utopian theorizing is even more tempting when an entire system is to be chosen than when only specific policies are at issue. Analysis may degenerate into search for the perfect system instead of choice among attainable alternatives. The second difficulty is closely related to the first. In choosing a system, the bad features must be accepted along with the good, and remedy must come through evolutionary change in the social structure if it is to come at all. But one is likely to be impatient and try to have his cake and eat it too. Before long, economists will begin to advocate monkeying with the operation of the system, no matter what it is, to try to give it characteristics which it cannot have; and we are back where we started, approaching the problem from the point of view of specific issues and specific solutions.

Once again, a fundamental change in outlook and attitude is required. If welfare economics is to be something more than bickering about day-to-day actions on the part of government in carrying out its role in the economy, it must focus on constitutional issues. It must be supplanted, in other words, by political economy in the classical sense:

a science for building the good society. The first step, it seems to me, is to revive the notion of progress as the test of a good society. Leaving aside the ethical content to be given progress as a goal, we may illustrate how much difference it makes to broaden our vision of the economic process.

Consider the large volume of loose talk these days about the "optimum path of growth" for an economy. We are told that there is some best way of achieving a given expansion of productive capacity in the shortest time with a given rate of investment. Once that way is discovered, policies should be enacted to bring it about.

I find it difficult to take this line of reasoning seriously. How, in the first place, are we to determine the goal toward which society is supposed to move as quickly as possible? Is it to be a particular state of affairs, specified in advance? If so, why? Or is the objective simply to be to move as far as possible in a given period? If so, what does that mean? Furthermore, if we know in advance where we are trying to head, how are we to find the quickest way to get there? And even if we were sufficiently omniscient to mark out the path, what happens when we try to control growth to conform to it? Deliberate social control can be achieved only by creating political instruments for that purpose, and those instruments have other effects on society, inhibitory as well as stimulative to "growth." The institutional framework must change in the course of implementing policies formulated on the assumption that it would not change. The nature of the problem is altered in the process of solving it.

Most important of all, to predetermine "growth" is to forestall it in the most meaningful sense. As already noted, the economy changes at least as much as it grows, and the prospects of the future can never be foreseen. The best path of growth is the one that unfolds as the economy cuts its way through a jungle of ignorance, coming here and there and now and then onto places where the cutting is easier. These discoveries enable the economy to move more swiftly through the jungle if it is adventurous enough to explore for them in the first place and supple enough to exploit them when they are found. All the while, we remain in the jungle, seeing only a few feet ahead. We cannot know in advance the "optimum" way out or what lies on the other side. We grope our way forward.

Is this not what the philosophers of the Enlightenment mean by progress? Somehow, little by little, conditions were to get better because we would know more. We would approach closer to the Truth even though it would continue to elude us. The problem was to construct the social order most conducive to progress. That order was to be judged not by its efficiency in achieving predetermined concrete objectives but rather by the kind of people it created.

Turning to a different but related matter, we may observe that progress is not the only thing we cannot predict. Every economy is subject to unforeseen disturbances and stresses requiring response and readjustment. Often the problem, at least temporarily, is to keep things from getting worse, not to make them better. Here, too, the design of the economic system is critical. Constitutionally, a system may be more or less flexible and responsive to unforeseen demands placed on it, and economists should give more attention to this matter and less to working out specific remedies for specific crises. On the whole, it would seem better to have a system that corrects disturbances slowly without allowing them to degenerate into crises than to have one that lets crises develop but deals with them swiftly. In any event, the system is at least as much at issue as the details of specific corrective policies.

So much for these discursive comments on the desirable nature of welfare economics. Now let me consider briefly whether there is much hope that economists will move in this direction. I am not optimistic. We live in an age of fragmentation and estrangement. Specialization, the fetish of scientism and ethical neutrality, and the contradictory utopian spirit have moved most economists out of contact with reality. Although many economists are quick to label the considered opinions of others among them as mere prejudice (when they disagree), they cannot recognize ethical bias in themselves. They have convinced themselves that ethical bias is not there—because it "ought not" to be there: scientists "ought not" to allow ethical judgments of any kind to enter their work in any way, but instead "ought" to be objective and scientific.

The situation has become so bizarre that output and growth in output are often viewed as if they were ends in themselves, without regard to the uses to which they are put. What other meaning can be attached to the recent fashion of judging economies solely on the basis of how much they produce or how fast they grow? It is, of course, ethically neutral to count broken crockery or empty pyramids produced in one economy as equivalent to food and housing consumed in another. But such ethical neutrality removes all meaning from the question of how the two economies compare. The simple fact is that all such questions have implicit ethical content. We are asking whether one state of affairs is better than another, and the judgment of better or worse has to be made with reference to some normative standard.

Unless economists quit hiding their heads in the sand of pseudoscientism, economics will disintegrate altogether. Such practitioners as remain will be little more than social engineers or rationalizers, serving whoever will pay for their services. Perhaps that is just as well, but we should not delude ourselves that welfare economics will come to an end. It will merely pass into the hands of others with different training and qualifications, as we witnessed in the rise of the economic priesthood in the Soviet Union under Stalin.

Such a development would be unfortunate, for there is much to be gained by having persons who are thoroughly and expertly versed in economic analysis specialize in studying ways of achieving the good society. Of course, their views should not be treated as authoritative pronouncements from on high, but they should be welcomed into the arena of discussion as informed opinions deserving serious attention. In a market of ideas, competing ethical judgments have as important a place as competing interpretations of fact, provided care is taken to keep the two separated as much as possible.

I would conclude by urging the economics profession to wander back to the path laid out for it by the Enlightenment. Perhaps my condemnation of the profession has been too sweeping, consisting as it has of a blanket indictment of economists in general, without any accompanying bill of particulars. However, my aim has not been to indict or to condemn. It has been to stimulate economists to think about the state of their profession, which could stand improvement.

The essential step, it seems to me, is a bold confrontation of the real issues of social policy. Let economists seek more after policies which will make conditions better and less after policies which will make them best. Let economists think more about progress and less about growth. Let them look for ways of improving the economic system rather than for gimmicks and schemes that will "solve" narrow problems. In short, let them try to build a good society instead of trying to do good for society.

None of these tasks is easy. No simple standards are close at hand on which the necessary judgments can be made. They never have been and never will be. The problems will, however, always be with us, and they must be handled one way or another. We must simply apply reason and intelligence and do our best. At least we would be doing something important and fruitful.

Public Choice — Property Rights

Victor P. Goldberg

In recent years have emerged two overlapping bodies of literature concerned with the importance of legal institutions in the resource allocation process—the public choice and property rights schools. Both emphasize the importance of the institutional framework, the influence of incentives and constraints on all economic actors (for example, elected officials, bureaucrats, judges, employees, and managers), and the effect of transactions costs on allocation. In many ways the public choice-property rights literature (herefter PCPR) represents a revived interest in many of the questions that concerned institutionalists such as John R. Commons [1924] earlier in this century and is bringing back into fashion issues that economists, in their pursuit of quasi-concave reality, unwisely have pushed aside.

The concern here is with the normative biases that characterize much of the literature. To be sure, there are many practitioners in both fields to whom these criticisms will not apply.[1] Indeed, there will be few if any individuals to whom all the criticisms will be applicable. Nevertheless, there does exist a reasonably homogeneous

---

The author has a joint appointment with the Institute of Governmental Affairs and the Department of Economics, University of California, Davis. Helpful comments on earlier drafts came from Robert Curry, Rodolfo Gonzalez, Robert Goldfarb, Harold Hochman, Ronald Hunt, Thomas Mayer, William Moss, Lloyd Musolf, Alan Olmstead, James Roumasset, Werner Schink, David Tacy, David Warner, and the participants in Earl Rolph's Public Finance Seminar. I am especially indebted to James Buchanan, who has engaged in an extensive correspondence on this article and related issues.

group sharing most of the positions to be criticized below. Rather than attempt to define rigorously the bounds of this group, I will rely on two recent survey articles. Robert Tollison, in introducing a collection entitled *Theory of Public Choice,* describes the basic normative approach of the contributors:

> The writers in this volume basically adopt a modified Pareto-Wicksell framework in their approach to social analysis. The reason is simple—we are unwilling to play God. Given this constraint, we are forced to look at the revealed choice behavior of individuals as the basic informational inputs in determining "goodness" or "badness" of social policy . . . Consensus is the only standard by which "rightness" can be discerned under this approach. The application of nonuniversal principles to social problems is just another form of a social welfare judgement.[2]

In their review of the property rights literature, Eirik Furubotn and Svetozar Pejovich [1972, p. 1157] suggest the following as one of the central characteristics of that body of literature: "Strong concern is shown for the individualist basis of choice; the preferences or values of an individual are assumed to be revealed only through his market or political behavior. Social welfare functions are, therefore, either ignored or ruled out." The subset of the PCPR literature delineated by Tollison and Furubotn and Pejovich will be designated as the PCPR school for the purpose of this article.[3]

The central proposition of the PCPR school is that individual preferences are the ultimate data; we cannot use social welfare judgments not derived from individual preferences. Hence, changes in the institutional framework are unambiguously acceptable only if such changes could command unanimous consent (the Pareto criterion). A second criterion implicit in much of the work is that voluntary exchange (using the free market) is desirable. As Alan Peacock and Charles Rowley [1972] note, these two principles appear to be inconsistent. For example, a policy to eliminate a restriction on the free market will meet the second criterion, but will not meet the first if the elimination entails some group foregoing some special privileges.

The inconsistency does exist, but it is more complex than this simple example suggests. The PCPR approach is based on two notions. First, the complexity of the institutional framework is such that we can only analyze changes, not make *de novo* comparisons. Second, individuals will be able to attain gains from trade through voluntary exchange. Smith gives up something in exchange for Jones's apples, and in the process of exchange both parties end up at least as well off as before. A Pareto change rule for altering the institutional framework, then, will be analogous to private voluntary exchange. If Smith wants a certain change he will have to give up something to get it. If all parties find that in this complex trade they are at least as well off after the change, then the change will be made. Thus, the PCPR school makes the Pareto institutional change criterion a logical extension of the voluntary exchange concept.

The public choice approach explicitly recognizes two additional factors. First, decision making is costly; therefore, less-than-unanimity rules often might be preferable to unanimity rules. Second, it is not concerned solely with narrow rule changes such as "relegate A to the private market"; its focus is sometimes on broader "constitutional choice" rules. Thus, a general rule such as "use the free market for a wide range of activities, A, B, C" *might* command unanimous consent because an individual will feel that his loss of one special privilege will be more than compensated for by his gains due to the demise of other special privileges.

At the constitutional choice level, therefore, the two criteria are not necessarily inconsistent. While permitting a reconciliation of the two criteria, the constitutional choice approach entails a number of other difficulties which will be discussed below. For the moment it is sufficient to warn the reader that the constitutional choice approach appears to be evoked only on occasion and only, it seems, when it suits the author's purpose; this makes it much more difficult to distill the normative content of the PCPR literature.

The theme of the present article is this: The attempt by the PCPR school to develop normative rules based only on individual preferences is a failure. Value judgments are not avoided; indeed, implicit in much of the PCPR literature are some very strong value judgments which when made explicit probably would garner little support.

The argument below first will analyze the limits that the PCPR approach arbitrarily imposes on an individual's utility function and the methodological inconsistency that this entails. There will follow a discussion of some implications of the unanimity rule, particularly for this question: When should the government be required to compensate individuals for a change in the rules? Finally, the underlying difficulties with the constitutional choice approach will be discussed.

Boundaries on Utility Functions

Like most economists, the PCPR school considers tastes as given exogenously and adopts the satisfaction of individual preferences defined over goods as the ultimate goal. For James Buchanan, the boundaries of economics are delimited by individual preferences. ("When non-individualistic norms are introduced, the domain of economics, *as I define the discipline,* is abandoned" [1968, p. 188], emphasis in original.) In mainstream economics, the issues which would bring this goal into doubt rarely arise, and the failure to discuss them, if not admirable, is at least understandable. In the world that the PCPR school chooses to look at, however, the issues do arise, but their treatment leaves much to be desired.

Tullock on Ethics

In *The Logic of the Law* [1971b], Gordon Tullock attempts to build a normative framework for a legal system based on a modified Pareto criterion (pp. 6–7). He explicitly omits ethics in erecting the legal framework: "I shall attempt to deduce legal principles that are not based upon ethics, and then use these principles to produce a justification of ethics" (p. 5).[4]

In essence, he argues that the goal of public policy is to permit individuals to maximize utility (U) defined over goods (X); that is, maximize $U = U(X)$, subject to a number of constraints. Ethics appear among the constraints. Smith honors a contract or does not rob a candy store because his personal cost-benefit analysis suggests this to be the optimal course. The costs of conscience are part of the costs of antisocial behavior; people can be indoctrinated with ethical notions that will raise the costs of such antisocial behavior. This is the role of ethics in Tullock's scheme.

But if it is admitted that ethical principles affect people's behavior (positive) and their welfare (normative), why should ethics be treated differently than goods? That is, why not add additional arguments to the utility function to take into account the individual's ethical beliefs (E), so that $U^* = U^*(X, E)$. Surely, there is no *a priori* ground for treating Smith's preferences for deodorants and doodads as inviolable, while at the same time treating his preferences for integration or due process as of no consequence to his well-being.

Economists, following A. C. Pigou, have been content to argue that their concern was only with maximizing economic welfare, which was a subset of total welfare, and the maximization of which was not necessarily consistent with maximizing total welfare. As economists, led by the PCPR school, have expanded their domain, the line between economic and noneconomic welfare has been blurred. In Tullock's case, he argues that his broadly defined economic welfare is coextensive with total welfare, but he then explicitly excludes one set of arguments—ethical principles—from the utility function.

Tullock, then, is inconsistent. Some preferences will not count and will be considered manipulable as a matter of public policy; others will be taken as given. Thus, if Smith decides to sell himself into slavery to Jones, that decision is not questioned.[5] If that transaction upsets Brown—that is, violates his ethical code—his displeasure is of no consequence. If the net "efficiency" effects of slavery appeared to be undesirable,[6] it might be in the public interest to manipulate ethical principles to make it difficult for Smith to sell himself and/or more difficult for Jones to buy.

I am not arguing that we *should* treat ethics the same as goods (more precisely, as public goods) in individuals' utility functions and then determine the "optimal" ethical rules through the market—that is, by "selling" the right to determine which ethical codes are binding to the highest bidder. If Tullock were consistent, however, this is where he would end up. It is only because he *does use his own value judgments* to determine which preferences are to count that he avoids this *reductio ad absurdum.*

Not only does Tullock impose his value judgments upon others in his normative analysis, but also the value judgments he does impose do not appear particularly attractive. Slavery, for example, is to be judged primarily by its effects on the capital market, rather than against any moral standards.[7]

The integration of ethical concepts into welfare economics requires that we utilize some externally imposed ethical standards—a social welfare function[8]—to guide analysis.[9] Determining what these ethical standards should be is not within the scope of this article. It is fair to say, however, that neither the "highest bidder" rule nor Tullock's zero weighting are likely to be prime candidates.

As a final note on Tullock, consider the following statement [1971b, p. 256]: "[T]his book has been based upon the assumption that ethics are something we learn. If ethics are learned, then we can inquire about what would be the best ethics to teach . . . An ethical system that led to efficient behavior in society would presumably be superior to those that led to inefficient behavior." It would not seem unreasonable to suggest that tastes for goods also are, in part, learned. Does this mean that we then can inquire as to what would be the best tastes to teach? A consistent individualistic position would require that tastes for goods and for ethics be treated equally.

Self-Interest and Political Behavior

A salient feature of the PCPR literature is the extension of the notion of self-interest beyond the narrow confines of neoclassical economics. Legislators, bureaucrats, and judges pursue their own self-interest.[10] Individuals not only will follow their own self-interest within the rules, but also will invest resources to modify the rules.[11] The primary normative implication to the PCPR school of this extension is that the benevolent dictator model of government behavior is unrealistic;[12] consequently, the governmental solution to "market failure" problems might be much worse than the disease.

But the extension raises a question: If individuals do invest resources in order to attain institutional changes in their interest, how should the preference for institutional change be integrated into the normative analysis? If Smith wants a tariff on shoes and is willing to pay for it, from a *predictive* standpoint we certainly should take that preference into account. But how should that preference be treated for normative questions? This is precisely the same question as that we asked previously, and the answer also seems the same: Some preferences will not count. Not only will Smith's craving for tariff protection be unrecognized, but also the manipulation of individual tastes to decrease the likelihood that Smith actually will receive protection will be permissible.[13]

The arbitrariness of this dictum is compounded by the fact that in a complex world (incomplete information, nonzero transactions costs, free rider problems, and so forth) it is frequently difficult to disentangle institutional arrangements from goods. If Smith and Jones vote to keep blacks out of their neighborhood, should their success enter positively into their utility function? If they achieve the same result by entering into a series of restrictive convenants (that is, voluntary contracts) should *this* success count? If restrictive racial covenants are treated as legal, enforceable contracts (as they were until 1948[14]), then presumably entering into such a contract will be treated as pursuit of a legitimate, unchallengeable private interest. But if such contracts are not legal and enforceable, by what standards are we to judge attempts to make them so (or to enact substitute rules)?

It might be objected that the preference in both cases is simply for "distance from blacks" and that, however much we personally might dislike this preference, it is legitimate; the quarrel, then, would not be over *preferences* but over the legitimacy of certain *means* for achieving those preferences. But this can be said for *all* goods. Smith does not have a taste for deodorants firmly implanted in his psyche. Rather, he has desires for social acceptability, and so forth, which in part are satisfied by deodorants. That is, goods need not enter directly into any consumer's preference functions. They can be treated as "intermediate products" which are purchased and then yield a stream of utility to the consumer. An institutional change is just such an intermediate product. The link between the institutional change and the preference function might be a more involved, convoluted one than the link between most goods and the preference function, but this is a matter of degree. If one is to justify not including institutional changes as legitimate means for pursuing the individual's self-interest, then the grounds for including other means (goods) also must be questioned.

Again, the argument should not be taken as an endorsement for including institutional changes in utility functions for normative analyses. There are few value systems extant that would accept as an ethical guide the notion that institutional changes should be sold to the highest bidder, that is, that political power *should* determine how society's laws change. Consistency would require that the PCPR school adopt such an indefensible position. Only the imposition of implicit value judgments prevents it from reaching this conclusion.

Other Restrictions

The PCPR school has in mind a richer choice set than economists normally consider. Included as arguments of utility functions for *predictive* analysis are attractive working conditions, time to converse with fellow workers, aversion to blacks or other ethnic groups, and other peculiar "goods."[15] It is difficult to discern how the PCPR school has incorporated this into its normative framework. Yet, its analysis of behavior has at least an underlying *tone* of disapproval for the pursuit of these peculiar goods. It is "better" if the top management of the firm can channel the efforts of its subordinates toward maximizing profits rather than let them pursue their independent goals (see Alchian and Demsetz [1972]).[16] It is better if bureaucrats can be induced to produce government goods and services efficiently rather than allowed to satisfy their own preferences (see Niskanen [1968, p. 304]). In each case the no-social-welfare-function rule is violated. Also, and this is extremely important, in each case the violation makes more sense than the rule.[17]

Unanimity and Compensation

As noted previously, the PCPR proponents share two positions. First, the complexity of the institutional framework is such that we cannot compare completely different frameworks; we can only judge changes. Second, they have a great appreciation of the gains from trade due to voluntary exchange. While, as the discussion above showed, these two positions are not always mutually consistent, taken together they provide a voluntary exchange framework for institutional change. Only institutional changes that can muster unanimous support (that is, will be accepted voluntarily by all participants) can be recommended. If a proposal helped Smith but hurt Jones, it would not be acceptable; if, however, it were possible for Smith to compensate Jones for permitting the change, unanimous agreement on the compensated change might be forthcoming. Thus, concomitant with the unanimity rule is a compensation rule: Losers must be compensated.[18]

The compensation rule would be a guideline both for legislators in hammering out laws and for courts in deciding whether a taking is compensable. Furubotn and Pejovich state the PCPR position clearly [1972, p. 1142]: "For social policy, the fundamental issue reduces to this. At any moment of time there is a legally sanctioned structure of property rights in existence; thus, if the prevailing structure is to be modified by social action designed to reduce or eliminate the effects of an externality, taxes *must be* imposed on those who will gain from the proposed legal change, and compensation paid to those who will suffer capital loss or loss of satisfaction as a result of the new law" (emphasis added).

Compensation as a Rebuttable Presumption

But what does their statement mean? Must we compensate the shoemaker if we eliminate his tariff protection? Should a monopolist be compensated if his monopoly is dissolved? Should an influential lobbyist be compensated if a restrictive campaign spending law is enacted? Should criminals be compensated if the police enforcement budget is increased?[19]

In each case the value of a "right" is being lessened by state action. Which taking should be compensated? To answer this the PCPR school must call on some outside guidelines. Not all PCPR proponents will answer the question in the same way, but all will begin with an implicit value judgment giving extra weight to the status quo.[20] That is, there is a presumption that the status quo is legitimate, and we can justify disturbing it without compensation only if we can introduce some arguments (ethical or practical[21]) that will permit us to rebut that presumption.

The extreme position (which as far as I can tell is held by no one) is "what already is is legitimate." Buchanan's position is a small step down from this.[22] Compensation is required so long as the injured party previously was acting within the law. The shoemaker certainly should be compensated for the loss of his tariff protection, and the monopolist also should be compensated (if the monopoly previously had been legal). The criminal should not be compensated for the increased expenditure on police because his activity previously had been illegal. However, by extension, if looting heretofore had been a legal activity, then making it illegal would require compensation. If looting were illegal, but the penalty were raised by statute, it would appear that compensation also would be required. If a law exists but is unenforced and people come to make decisions on the assumption that it will remain unenforced, must a sudden attempt to enforce the law necessarily result in no compensation? If the police drastically reduce their expenditures on auto theft control and Smith's car (that he purchased on the good faith assumption that the police would maintain a "reasonable" level of enforcement) is stolen, should he be compensated?

The problem is defining what the law in fact is at a given moment. The law is, in Buchanan's conception, "a set of expectations, which include enforcement standards as traditionally observed, along with formal statute. A change in law, by my definition, involves an explicit modification of normal expectations."[23] Furubotn and Pejovich [1972, p. 1143] make a similar point: "The justification for compensation to B rests, ultimately, on the idea that, at any given time, individuals can have 'rights' to create certain types of 'diseconomies.' Thus, an individual (B) who is undertaking a lawful activity in good faith (e.g., generating smoke) must be compensated if there is to be a change in the law that will redefine property rights and reduce his welfare position." This approach then reduces to determining when in fact the law changes and in ascertaining what are legitimate expectations. I shall return to these issues later.

Harold Hochman [1974, p. 324] adopts a modified version of the Buchanan position: "Rules, even if unfair or inefficient, may as custom underlie reasonable expectations. Rule changes that disappoint such expectations may themselves be considered unjust." However, Hochman expresses greater willingness to impose outside value judgments to guide the compensation decision. Compensation need not be paid "if the present beneficiaries of an unjust practice have attained their positions through *illegitimate* means "[1974, p. 324] (emphasis added). He goes on to state that "it seems absurd to argue that individuals *unjustly* deprived of rights under an existing rule should compensate its beneficiaries if the rule is changed" [1974, pp. 326–27] (emphasis added). That is, the presumption for the status quo does not hold if the original position does not pass certain ethical criteria which, as the italicized words make clear, are loosely defined.[24]

The PCPR school does not, therefore, take the compensation requirement as literally as its bald statements of the requirement seem to suggest. Rather, it is a starting point for analysis, and its relative weighting is a matter for the various practitioners to determine. The criticism here is twofold. First, without explicitly adding additional value judgments the criterion will lead to the type of "absurdities" that Hochman warns against (and other types as well). Second, the criterion, by starting with the implicit value judgment that the status quo is legitimate, leads the practitioner to a policy of preserving existing power relationships and the results of the past use of power.

Acquiescence

The strong prejudice in favor of the existing structure of rights and power inherent in the unanimity-compensation rule goes far beyond ethical neutrality. This is not to say that the PCPR position is wrong, only that it is a much stronger (less appealing) position than that taken by most economists: Try for efficient allocations for any given income distribution—if you dislike the distribution, change it.[25] Here we have instead: Try for efficient allocation within the current rules—if you dislike the current distribution, you can change it, *provided* that no one is worse off than before.

The proviso is ambiguous. Suppose, for example, that a wealthy person was confronted with this question: Will you take a cut in income this year or do I knock your block off? He might be willing to consent to a decline in income. Since the haves always face the latent threat that the have-nots might decide to redistribute income or wealth by force, they might be willing to consent to some redistribution voluntarily to forestall the more painful redistribution. Would redistribution made under the explicit threat of force be Pareto optimal? What if the threat were less explicit? How subtle must the threat be before the resulting redistribution is acceptable?

Threats and power are relevant beyond the normal political arena. This poses an awkward question for the PCPR school. If the use of force to achieve agreement in the political arena is to be treated as illegitimate, will it be legitimate to use force in the private contract context? If, for example, a worker agrees not to participate in a union insurance plan as a condition of employment, is this a freely arrived at, voluntary agreement, or must we consider the effectiveness of the threats of the employer? A plausible argument can be made that in this situation, and in many others, the decision is voluntary in name only.[26]

The point of these last two paragraphs is this. The PCPR school's proposed standard for judging any exchange is acquiescence by the parties. This seems eminently reasonable until we realize that acquiescence can be attained—both in the political arena and in private contract—by the use of suspect means, for example, force. Acquiescence alone cannot be the standard for judging the desirability of exchange. Some externally imposed value judgments must be made concerning the reasonableness of the means by which agreement was reached.

Ignorance

Consider a further problem. Suppose that Smith will be hurt by a particular rules change, but he does not realize it (or he thinks that he will be helped by it).[27] Should he be compensated if the change is made? Or should we carry over the private contract analogy and argue that Smith has the right to make misjudgments and, consequently, should be compensated only for his perceived injury? This second rule is a substantial watering down of the Pareto criterion.[28] If Jones can fool Smith into thinking that a tariff or a minimum wage will not harm him, then the change is acceptable—what Smith does not know will not hurt him.

Taking this path creates difficulties for the definition of the *status quo* (existing legal framework) given by Buchanan (see above) and espoused by other PCPR proponents. If the current law is to be defined by "normal expectations," we must ask: whose expectations? Furthermore, we must decide how to treat incorrect expectations. If Smith has been dumping his garbage on Jones's land and Jones did not realize that he had a legal right to stop Smith (or to charge him a fee, or to collect damages), should Smith be compensated when Jones begins exercising his right?

We need not try to answer this or other similar questions to make the basic point. In the PCPR paradigm, the *status quo* is defined by what a *reasonable man* might regard as foreseeable results of the current law, whereas changes in that law—results the reasonable man would regard as unforeseeable—should be accepted if *actual men* perceive the consequences as being favorable (although a reasonable man would not).

If we take as our guide instead the perceptions of the reasonable man, then this further complicates the "acquiescence" guideline (see above). If, in the face of imperfect information, we must search for the acquiescence of the reasonable man, then we cannot deduce that a program is acceptable from the observation that actual men unanimously have agreed to it.

There are further complications arising from the imperfect perceptions of the consequences of instituitonal change. These will become important in the context of the "constitutional choice" problem of the last section, and discussion will be deferred until then. Next we will discuss a further difficulty in defining the status quo.

The Compensation Paradox

The rule that compensation always should be paid does not tell us whether compensation should be paid in a particular case. To understand this paradoxical claim, it is useful to first discuss a simple private contract example. Suppose that Smith sells Jones a table, but Smith reserves the right to reclaim it, if he sees fit. Would Jones be willing to enter such a contract? We would expect that his offer price would be less than if the sale had no such restriction. How much less would depend upon Jones's guess as to how likely it will be that Smith will act. So, if the contract were agreed to and Smith subsequently reclaimed the table, there would be no justification for compensation. Jones received the table at a price lower than the price of a table *sans* reclaim clause. The price differential was Smith's payment for the right to reclaim.

Compensation might be justified on other grounds. The reclaim clause might not be honored because the court felt that Jones was not aware of its existence or import,[29] or the court might rule that the clause carried with it an implicit guarantee that the reclamation must be based on reasonable grounds (even if the contract explicitly stated otherwise). But let us postpone all such questions of reasonableness for the moment. The point is that if the contract has such a reclaim clause in it, this will be given a value by the participants; the exercise of the reclaim clause is simply the exercise of an agreed upon right, and compensation to Jones would amount to a double payment to Jones.

If the government decrees that a chemical firm no longer can pollute the air, should the chemical firm be compensated for this taking of its right to pollute? If this entails a change in rights, then the PCPR position would be that compensation must be paid. But this raises a crucial question: What was the property right in the first place? In the United States, at least, a property right is a bundle of rights to do a, b, c, . . .; it also entails the (negative) right that, in effect, states that any or all of a, b, c, . . . are subject to an uncompensated taking under the police power. The police power is equivalent to the reclaim clause of the private contract example. The question of whether compensation should be paid, therefore, depends upon whether a taking of a property right actually has occurred or whether the taking was merely the lawful exercise of the police power clause inherent in the definition of a property right. The answer to *this* question depends on the boundary of the police power. When is the exercise of the police power reasonable? Thus, few would deny that increased expenditure on law enforcement is reasonable and the taking of the criminal's right to pillage and loot is, consequently, non-compensable.[30] Conversely, most would agree that if the government takes Smith's farm and continues to use it for farming, this taking would be compensable.

The argument here blends into the discussion of reasonable or normal expectations of the previous section. If Smith has no reason to expect the state to exercise its recall option (police power) and makes good faith purchases and investments on that basis, then, the PCPR school argues, he should be compensated. If, however, a reasonable man in Smith's position would have been able to perceive the exercise of the police power, there should be no compensation. The unanimity-compensation *principle* is vacuous if there is a police power clause. It conceivably could be consistent with a policy of never compensating. The *practical* decision of whether compensation should be paid in a given case (or class of cases) must be made within the PCPR paradigm through two means. (1) Define reasonable expectations. (If Smith buys a taxicab medallion which has value because of the restricted supply and the government decides to issue an unlimited supply of such medallions, should Smith be compensated? Would it make a difference if the legislation was pending when he bought the license or if he was one of the original recipients of the license?[31]) (2) Define a reasonable range of application for the police power. That is, application of the criterion requires a judicious admixture of expedient rules and of value judgments. The unanimity-compensation principle does not enable us to avoid making value judgments.

In Sum

It is conceivable that we can begin with the PCPR paradigm and come out with a rule which seldom leads to compensation; that is, the status quo can be defined very loosely, and/or the criteria for moving away from it can be easily met. While potentially there is room within the paradigm for a wide range of conflicting results, in fact there is a clustering around the position attributed above to Buchanan: Define the existing law narrowly, and require high standards for rebutting the presumption that the status quo is legitimate. While Buchanan is aware of many of the implications of this position and is willing to live with them, it is less clear that his followers have realized precisely what they were buying. This, I would hypothesize, is largely because the analytical convenience of assuming that we have an unambiguous status quo (that is not too outrageous) is so great that practitioners eagerly have adopted it and have not bothered to consider what problems are glossed over by the uncritical acceptance of this assumption. Furthermore, the problems raised are not amenable to analysis with the economist's traditional tools, and he, therefore, is quite willing to delegate such questions to other (unspecified) disciplines in the interest of intellectual comparative advantage. (It should be noted that Hochman [1974] does address questions of the sort raised here, and he does, in fact, arrive at conclusions that are much to the left of Buchanan.)

My complaint is not that the PCPR school fails to give an unambiguous answer to the question of when compensation is appropriate. Courts and scholars have wrestled with the issue for years with, at best, modest success. (For two studies which criticize the courts' treatment and which proffer alternative rules, see Joseph Sax [1971] and Frank Michelman [1967].) Nor will I offer a compensation rule which I regard as superior. The point is that the compensation rule follows from the Pareto criterion only if the status quo can be defined unambiguously. But as we have seen, this is not the case. To define the status quo we must first make a number of decisions based on expediency and on value judgments. Hence, even if we follow Buchanan et al. in agreeing that the Pareto change rule is a minimal value judgment,[32] implementation of the rule in actual compensation cases will entail the imposition of external value judgments (be they implicit or explicit).

Constitutional Choice

As noted in the first section, PCPR proponents often are concerned with constitutional choices—the establishment of rules for making rules.[33] Buchanan [1972b, pp. 123-24] likens this choice to individuals agreeing to the rules of a card game before the cards are dealt, that is, before they know which rules best serve their interest.

> It is surely reasonable to extend this essentially contractarian framework to an evaluation and analysis of the whole set of rules, formal and informal. . . . The appropriate question becomes: How would a group of individuals, no one of whom can predict his own position in any of the time segments over which the rules to be chosen are to be operative, go about setting up the socio-political rules of the game? The "veil of ignorance"

> or uncertainty is the device or requirement that forces participants to consider alternatives on grounds other than identifiable self-interest, narrowly interpreted (Buchanan [1972b, p. 125]).

We can look at constitutional choice in three ways: (1) The constitution is a set of rules already agreed to that governs *current* changes; (2) the constitution is a set of rules that individuals behind the veil of ignorance *should* adopt, and we can use those rules as a benchmark to evaluate what does happen; and (3) constitutional choice suggests a method for establishing rules to govern *future* changes in the rules. The three conceptions blend into each other.

We can argue (in the context of the previous section) that compensation is not required in a particular case because all parties already have agreed to the continuing operation of a rule-making process in which the interests of particular subgroups must, from time to time, be injured severely. That is, the parties have agreed in advance to a rule deciding when compensation should be paid (the police power?), and they should be better off if the rule is always followed, even though on occasion they will lose by its application.[34]

This approach, however, begs the question of the legitimacy of the rules agreed to. A narrow reading of this line of reasoning would lead us to validate the existing rules for making rules no matter how objectionable they might be. If we begin with a monarchy, for example, then rules for change within that framework would be legitimate. But no PCPR proponent would subscribe to this approach; at best the status quo constitution would have only a presumption of legitimacy, and, as in the previous section, this presumption could be rebutted. We must insist on the basic value judgment that individuals count; beyond that, virtually all PCPR proponents would agree with the value judgment that individuals affected by the constitutional rules should have acquiesced in some noncoerced fashion to the operation of those rules. (This is both a value judgment and an empirical question: How do we determine if there has been uncoerced acceptance? See the discussion above.) Buchanan also insists on the salience of a procedural value judgment: The legislature should legislate and the judiciary should settle individual conflicts within the rules and determine whether legislative enactments are consistent with the original constitution.[35]

The more constraints we place on the constitutional choice process, the more we shade over into the second conception: What rules should we adopt? This question is more in the spirit of the Buchanan quotation with which this section began. What rules would individuals behind the veil of ignorance choose? To answer this we first must decide how to characterize the choice at the constitutional level. Should we treat the constitutional choice problem as a decision made by *hypothetical* people acting behind the veil of ignorance or of *actual* people acting behind the veil?

If, following John Rawls [1971] and John Harsanyi [1955], we use hypothetical individuals, we essentially are asking what an *outside observer* expects a person behind the veil of ignorance to choose for rules of justice and for working constitutional rules. That is, if we take this approach we are imposing the value judgments of an outside observer in determining the rules (formal and informal) which henceforth will constrain the behavior of actual self-interest seeking individuals.[36] Consequently, if the PCPR school were to adopt this approach it would entail the very thing its methodology is designed to avoid—the imposition of outside value judgments. Acceptance of the Rawls-Harsanyi conception of the veil of ignorance would violate the basic normative principle of the PCPR school.

If instead we look to the decisions of actual people, we encounter different problems. For ''operational'' choice individuals will perceive their own short-run interest (for example, attaining a tax loophole),[37] and they will pursue this interest even if it means others will be worse off. As we move along the continuum from purely operational choice to purely constitutional choice,[38] the individual's perceptions of the effects of a change on him will become ever more clouded. In the extreme, the individual would have no idea of how the general rules being considered would affect him.

Buchanan and Tullock characterize the constitutional choice problem in this way:

> [We] try only to analyze the calculus of the utility-maximizing individual who is confronted with the constitutional problem. Essential to the analysis is the presumption that the individual is *uncertain* as to what his own precise role will be in any one of the whole chain of later collective choices that will actually have to be made. For this reason he is considered not to have a particular and distinguishable interest separate and apart from his fellows. This is not to suggest that he will act contrary to his own interest; but the individual will not find it advantageous to vote for rules that may promote sectional, class, or group interests because, by presupposition, he is unable to predict the role that he will be playing in the actual collective decision-making process at any particular time in the future. He cannot predict with any degree of certainty whether he is more likely to be in a winning or a losing coalition on any specific issue. Therefore, he will assume that occasionally he will be in one group and occasionally in the other. His own self-interest will lead him to

> choose rules that will maximize the utility of an individual in a series of collective decisions with his own preferences on the separate issues being more or less randomly distributed (Buchanan and Tullock [1962, p. 78]).

This characterization of the pure constitutional choice problem seems at least reasonable, but we might well ask: How do Buchanan and Tullock *know* that actual individuals in the hypothesized situation would or could make decisions in this way? This is not a frivolous question. In fact, Buchanan and Tullock engage in the same type of hypothetical exercise as Rawls, taking an individual in the original position and deciding what type of rules he would agree to. That is, they are not deriving constitutional rules from individual preferences in any sense; they have no observations on the behavior of individuals in a pure constitutional choice situation, nor do they pretend to. The constitutional rules are the product of an intellectual exercise—rules that Buchanan and Tullock presume reasonable people would agree to unanimously if given the chance. Their guesses as to what sort of rules would arise in a pure constitutional choice context are (or are strongly influenced by) value judgments.[39]

The pure constitutional choice case is a theoretical construct with no real world counterpart. As we move from the pure constitutional end toward the operational—to "real world" constitutional choices—individuals will be able to lift the veil of ignorance and will in some instances be able to make fairly sound judgments as to how a specific change will affect their interests. The veil of ignorance will be lifted differently for different individuals. While most people will not be able to tell how, for example, direct election of senators (rather than appointment by state legislatures) would affect them, some will have a fairly good idea of the gains and will consciously pursue these gains in their own self-interest. If, as a result, some of the blissfully ignorant end up net losers, can we consider the change desirable? This again raises the problem discussed briefly above. If Smith is ignorant of the consequences of a choice, while Jones is not (and Jones deliberately uses Smith's ignorance to his own selfish ends), of what normative significance is Smith's acquiescence?

Buchanan recently has come to this realization [1972b, p.127]:

> To the extent that rules are considered as permanent or quasi-permanent, designed for operation over a time sequence that remains perhaps open-ended, individual participants in the selection process must be uncertain as to just where their own self-interest lies. They will, to this extent, be motivated to opt for rules and rules changes that embody "fairness" or which at least contain

> "unfairness" within broad limits. . . . But despite all this, interests are identifiable even over long terms, and men will act to further them. Rules for social order . . . will reflect the struggle among interests, and will rarely, if ever, qualify as "just" in accordance with any idealized criteria.

From this, Buchanan concludes [1972b, p. 127] that "attainable consensus offers the only meaningful principle for genuine constitutional change." (This is essentially the third concept of constitutional choice noted above.[40]) But this is certainly a non sequitur. If a number of whites regard it as in their long-term interest that blacks be subjugated, must this preference be accepted?[41] If rules will rarely, if ever, qualify as just, then why give *any* weight to the status quo? It would be more reasonable for Buchanan to conclude that any change is as good (or as bad) as the status quo.[42] That is, his refusal to make value judgments coupled with the observation that institutional choice, even in the long run, will be influenced by self-interest should lead him to adopt a "plague on all their houses" normative position, rather than the one presented here.

The concept of constitutional choice was developed by Buchanan and Tullock in the context of a positive analysis. In that context the problems we are concerned with here are not very important. But applying the notion in a normative context raises difficulties not easily dealt with, as we have seen. If we consider the pure constitutional choice question we are in effect asking what ethical and legal rules would individuals agree to, *in the observer's opinion:* That is, we have a mechanism for generating value judgments. If, on the other hand, we realize that actual individuals will not, in general, act as if they were behind a veil of ignorance, and if we insist on *wertfrei* normative economics, then, aside from ranking a few positions which are unambiguously Pareto superior or inferior to the status quo, there is very little that can be done.

Conclusion

The foregoing remarks should not be construed as either a criticism of the *positive* theories of the PCPR school or as a defense of Pigovian welfare economics. Positive analyses with the PCPR tools can be (and are being) made independent of the normative position explicated here. Pigovian welfare economics is subject to many of the same criticisms (as well as others), although it is more likely to be guilty of errors of omission rather than commission.

The work of the PCPR school with its emphasis on transactions costs and self-interested behavior on the part of political actors points up the need for a more complex, eclectic welfare economics. Ethical judgments must be made concerning which preferences count (Should Smith be permitted to satisfy his desires for pornography or should Jones be permitted to satisfy his desire that Smith *not* read pornography?), which ways of achieving those preferences are reasonable (Can Jones use bribes, force, or boycotts to keep Smith from his pornography?), and so forth. True, this requires that we must to at least some extent "play God." But given the ungodly alternative, play we must.

Notes

1. Thus, such prominent public choice practitioners as Mancur Olson and Anthony Downs proceed from a very different value system than the one discussed here. The author considers himself to be at least a peripheral member of both schools and obviously does not share the value system criticized in the text.
2. Robert Tollison [1971, p. 4].
3. Olson and Christopher Clague [1971] characterize the school as the Virgina School or sometimes the Virginia-Chicago School; Peacock and Rowley [1972] refer to the Virginia Blend. The central figure in this literture is James Buchanan, and in some ways this article can be viewed as a critique of his work alone; however, the criticisms are, I believe, more general than that. Indeed, as I will note occasionally in the article, there are some points on which Buchanan and I would agree in criticizing a particular line of reasoning.
4. Buchanan is essentially in agreement with my criticism of Gordon Tullock's analysis.
5. See Tullock's discussion of slavery [1971b, pp. 52–54]; he eventually arrives at a "non-ethical" justification for antislavery laws.
6. He concludes that the net efficiency effects are probably undesirable [1971b, pp. 54].
7. See also Tullock [1971c] for his justification of inheritance. Tullock excludes the possibility that people might be willing to accept the existence of an unequal distribution of wealth while at the same time objecting to particular methods of wealth accumulation, such as inheritance.
8. Because welfare economics generally has been treated in mathematical form, the concept of the social welfare function has become a shorthand for all welfare judgments imposed from without.
9. For an analysis and conclusions bearing a close familial relationship to the one presented here, see Ezra Mishan [1972].
10. See also Downs [1957], Tullock [1971a], and William Niskunen [1968, 1971].
11. See G. J. Stigler [1971, pp. 265–66] and Buchanan [1972b, p. 127].
12. See Buchanan [1959, p. 134; 1962, p. 28].
13. But see Blaine Roberts [1973], who includes institutions in the utility function in determining conditions for Pareto optimality. Buchanan has

indicated to me that, in his conception, Smith's preference clearly should count.

14. In that year the Supreme Court ruled that restrictive racial covenants were legal but unenforceable in *Shelley* v. *Kraemer*, 334 U.S. 1 (1948) and *Hurd* v. *Hodge*, 334 U.S. 24 (1948).
15. See also Eirik Furubotn and Sevtozar Pejovich [1972] and Harold Demsetz [1964] for examples.
16. Armen Alchian and Demsetz do not explicitly state that such channeling is better. However, by labeling the pursuit of independent goals with the loaded term *shirking*, they imply that such behavior is less desirable.
17. Two points should be made. First, some preferences of managers and bureaucrats should be recognized in making policy; that is, there is no reason to take the extreme position that all such preferences should be ruled out of court. Second, if we apply the compensation or unanimity rule, we would be required to give full weight to their preferences; change would be accepted only if the public could bribe the bureaucrats to forgo satisfaction of these preferences. See the discussion in the "Unanimity and Compensation" section. (However, this need not be true in a constitutional choice framework; see the last section.)
18. "The unanimity test is, in fact, identical to the compensation test if compensation is interpreted as that payment, negative or positive, which is required to secure agreement" (Buchanan and Tullock [1962, p. 91]). A variant on the compensation rule is: unanimity for constitutional choice only. This is discussed in the last section.
19. Our concern here is with ethical questions, and we therefore will ignore the difficulties of identifying who should be compensated and how much.
20. For explicit statements in favor of the status quo, see Buchanan [1972b, p. 127; 1972a, p. 452] and Tollison [1972, p. 4]. For a criticism, see Warren Samuels [1972b, p. 458] and Amartya Sen [1970, pp. 24–25, 120–23].
21. I will ignore the practical problems here; one practical justification for compensation is that it requires the government to better take into account the costs of resources it uses. A second is that uncompensated takings will discourage the losers, who will perhaps be more reluctant to invest in the future. This problem is known as "demoralization costs." See Frank Michelman [1967], Oliver Williamson [1971], and Harold Hochman [1974].
22. This account of Buchanan's position is a synthesis of his numerous published writings in the area and his comments to me in personal correspondence.
23. Private correspondence dated 1 November 1973.
24. Note that Furubotn and Pejovich also qualify their position by requiring compensation for a polluter if he had been undertaking a lawful activity *in good faith*.
25. For criticism of this mainstream position, see Victor Goldberg [1974] and Samuels [1971, 1972a, 1972b].
26. For a case which fits the fact situation described in the text, see *Coppage* v. *Kansas*, 236 U.S. 1 (1915). The consumer frequently faces "adhesive contracts" which in the extreme are agreements with the terms imposed

by the producer; see Friedrich Kessler [1943] and W. D. Slawson [1971, pp. 549-61].

27. Most economists would agree that minimum wages and rent controls would be likely examples of this latter category.
28. The first rule also has problems. It weakens incentives to dispel ignorance of results (at least this would be so as long as individuals believed that decision makers would follow the rule faithfully).
29. See the discussion of the standard form contract in Goldberg [1974], Kessler [1943], or Slawson [1971].
30. Commenters on an earlier draft of this article were uneasy about recognizing a "right" to engage in illegal activities. In the amoral context which the PCPR school attempts to maintain, it appears reasonable to define *any* decrease in a person's future stream of net benefits due to a governmental action as the taking of a right which is potentially compensable.

    In general, our willingness to identify certain claims as "rights" depends on value judgments as to the legitimacy of those claims. Thus, Proudhon's well-known aphorism, "property is theft," would lead to identification of a very different set of rights.
31. See Hochman [1974, pp. 328-29].
32. "This Pareto rule is itself an ethical proposition, a value statement, but it is one which requires a minimum of premises and one which should command wide assent" (Buchanan, [1959, p. 125]).
33. Constitutional choice is more important in the public choice literature. For the property rights literature, the analysis is implicit: Beginning *de novo*, the market would be the most efficient method; therefore we should move toward it even if this entails some dislocations (or uncompensated takings). This position could be reconciled with that described in the previous section if inefficiency were considered to be one of the grounds for rebutting the presumption of compensation. My guess, however, is that many of the practitioners holding both views (the importance of efficiency and compensation) simply do not realize that the two positions quite likely conflict with each other—the positions are reconciled by neglect.
34. See Buchanan [1972a].
35. Buchanan's insistence upon the actual (as opposed to conceptual) separation of the legislative and judicial roles is puzzling. His entire constitutional choice analysis of *Miller et al.* v. *Schoene* turns on the question of whether the judiciary overstepped its boundaries: "The only role of the judiciary should have been one of determining whether or not the decision taken by the legislature was made constitutionally" (Buchanan [1972a, p. 450]). It is not clear to me why individuals acting behind the veil of ignorance would not permit the judicial and legislative roles to be performed by a single body for at least certain problems. This is, for example, the process of development of the common law.

    Consider the following two alternative arrangements: (1) the courts are very narrowly tied to precedent; (2) they are more loosely tied to precedent (that is, they can legislate more), but the legislature can pass legislation which is binding on the courts which can reverse (for the future) common law doctrine. (Or the courts can declare legislation unconstitutional on a wide variety of grounds, while the legislature and electorate have some process for amending the constitution and thereby overriding the court.) The second arrangement does not satisfy Buchanan's strictures, yet it is not *a priori* clear why one acting behind the veil of ignorance should prefer the first arrangement. The difference between the two rules is basically an operational one—parties with greater relative power in the judicial arena would prefer the second set of arrangements. Their advantage is increased if the rules require a greater than simple majority vote in the legislature. That is, the judiciary can redefine the legal status quo to favor one set of parties in a conflict situation and thereby shift the burden of legislative action.

My guess, although Buchanan denies this, is that his position stems in part from his personal distaste for the policies of the Warren court (see Buchanan [1972b, p. 127]) and that if his conception of judicial activism had been shaped instead by the doctrine of "substantive due process" (see Miller [1968, pp. 55-62]) of the period roughly from 1880 to 1930, he would have come out with a different position on the role of the judiciary.

36. This is not a criticism of John Rawls and John Harsanyi. Their goal *is* to produce value judgments.
37. Buchanan [1972b, p. 126] defines *operational choice* as "the choice of policy outcomes with a given constitutional order."
38. Buchanan [1972b, p. 126] defines *constitutional choice* as "the choice from among alternative sets of rules or institutions."
39. If viewed as a device for generating value judgments, the Buchanan-Tullock pure constitutional choice approach suffers from a defect not common to the Rawls-Harsanyi conception. By explicitly making their individual hypothetical, Rawls and Harsanyi can describe the characteristics that their individual would have behind the veil of ignorance; see, for example, Rawls's description of the individual behind the veil of ignorance who is to try and choose principles of justice (Rawls [1971, p. 137]) or the individual trying to choose appropriate constitutional rules once the conception of justice has been agreed upon (Rawls [1971, p. 197]). Buchanan and Tullock have no explicit conception, however, of what their man behind the veil of ignorance looks like and must resort, therefore, to ad hoc argumentation.
40. Buchanan [1967, pp. 299-300] suggests that we might be able to get a rough approximation of the veil of ignorance by increasing the waiting time between passage of legislation and its implementation. If we must wait, for example, one generation for the law to go into effect, then it will be difficult for the individual to determine whether he will receive benefits specific to his position in society. For criticism of this position, see Hochman [1974, p. x].

Dennis Mueller [1973, p. 61] provides a good illustration of the confusion engendered in the constitutional choice approach treating as "analytically equivalent" Harsanyi's approach and the notion that the constitution will be "drawn by a group of aging individuals for their descendants." Surely there is no reason to believe that the rules developed by hypothetical individuals in the original position will have much in common with rules chosen by actual people with their culturally determined tastes and prejudices and their familial links to members of future generations. An actual person will know whether he is a Catholic or a Hindu, black or white, rich or poor, and his decisions will be influenced by these factors both because such factors do influence the development of preference patterns and because such factors sometimes will mean that expected outcomes that will occur after an individual's death can influence his current utility and consequently his choices. (For example, an ardent white supremacist might feel that rules which gave blacks equal access to jobs, even three generations hence, were undesirable.)

It should be noted that Mueller's methodological position does differ from Buchanan's in that Mueller is explicitly seeking a justification for ethical rules; therefore, he cannot be criticized for using the constitutional choice approach as an attempt to avoid ethical judgments. However, his failure to see that the Rawls-Harsanyi approach is analytically distinct from the Buchanan-Tullock approach does lead him into unnecessary confusion.

41. The lengthy quotation in the text suggests that Buchanan and Tullock would not want such a preference to be accepted; yet, with the third approach to constitutional choice, it is likely that such preferences would exist.

42. It still would be possible to apply the Pareto rule to determine whether the status quo was unambiguously better or worse than alternatives, but there would be no way to compare it to cases in which that criterion is not met. Buchanan's rule as stated in the text suggests that if a change does not meet the Pareto rule, then it *should not* be made, which is far stronger than saying that a change cannot be recommended on the basis of the Pareto criterion.

References

[1] Alchian, Armen, and Harold Demsetz. "Production, Information Costs, and Economic Organization." *American Economic Review* 62 (December 1972): 777–95.

[2] ——. "Positive Economics, Welfare Economics, and Political Economy." *Journal of Law and Economics* 2 (October 1959): 124–38.

[3] ——. "Politics, Policy, and the Pigovian Margins." *Economica* 29 (February 1962): 17–28.

[4] ——. *Public Finance in Democratic Process*. Chapel Hill: University of North Carolina Press, 1967.

[5] ——. "What Kind of Redistribution Do We Want?" *Economica* 35 (May 1968): 185–90.

[6] ——. "Politics, Property and the Law: An Alternative Interpretation of Miller et al. v. Schoene." *Journal of Law and Economics* 15 (October 1972): 439–52(a).

[7] ——. "Rawls on Justice as Fairness." *Public Choice* 13 (Fall 1972): 123–28(b).

[8] —— and Gordon Tullock. *The Calculus of Consent*. Ann Arbor: University of Michigan Press, 1962 (paperback edition, 1969).

[9] Commons, John R. *Legal Foundations of Capitalism.* Madison: University of Wisconsin Press, 1924.
[10] Demsetz, Harold "The Exchange and Enforcement of Property Rights." *Journal of Law and Economics* 7 (October 1964): 11-26.
[11] Downs, Anthony. *An Economic Theory of Democracy.* New York: Harper, 1957.
[12] Furubotn, Eirik G., and Svetozar Pejovich. "Property Rights and Economic Theory: A Survey of Recent Literature." *Journal of Economic Literature* 10 (December 1972): 1137-62.
[13] Goldberg, Victor P. "Institutional Change and the Quasi-invisible Hand." *Journal of Law and Economics* [1974].
[14] Harsanyi, John C. "Cardinal Welfare, Individualistic Ethics and Interpersonal Comparisons of Utility." *Journal of Political Economy* 63 (August 1955): 309-21.
[15] Hochman, Harold M. "Transitional Equity." In *Redistribution Through Public Choice,* Harold M. Hochman and George E. Peterson, eds. New York: Columbia University Press, 1974, pp. 320-42.
[16] Kessler, Friedrich. "Contract of Adhesion—Some Thoughts About Freedom of Contract." *Columbia Law Review* 53 (July 1943): 629-42.
[17] Michelman, Frank L. "Property, Utility, and Fairness: Comments on the Ethical Foundations of 'Just Compensation' Law." *Harvard Law Review* 80 (April 1967): 1165-1258.
[18] Miller, Arthur S. *The Supreme Court and American Capitalism.* New York: The Free Press, 1968.
[19] Mishan, Ezra J. "The Futility of Pareto-Efficient Distributions." *American Economic Review* 62 (December 1972): 971-76.
[20] Mueller, Dennis C. "Constitutional Democracy and Social Welfare." *Quarterly Journal of Economics* 87 (February 1973): 60-80.
[21] Niskanen, William A. "The Peculiar Economics of Bureaucracy." *American Economic Review* 58 (May 1968): 293-305.
[22] ______. *Bureaucracy and Representative Government.* Chicago: Aldine-Atherton, 1971.
[23] Olson, Mancur, and Christopher K. Clague. "Dissent in Economics: The Convergence of Extremes." *Social Research* 38 (Winter 1971): 751-76.
[24] Peacock, Alan T., and Charles K. Rowley. "Pareto Optimality and the Political Economy of Liberalism." *Journal of Political Economy* 80 (May/June 1972): 476-90.
[25] Rawls, John. *A Theory of Justice.* Cambridge, Mass.: The Belknap Press of Harvard University Press, 1971.
[26] Roberts, Blaine. "An Extension of Optimality Criteria: An Axiomatic Approach to Institutional Choice." *Journal of Political Economy* 81 (March/April 1973): 386-400.
[27] Samuels, Warren J. "Interrelations Between Legal and Economic Processes." *Journal of Law and Economics* 14 (October 1971): 435-50.
[28] ______. "Welfare Economics, Power and Property." In *Perspectives on Property,* Gene Wunderlich and W. L. Gibson Jr., eds. State College, Pa.: Institute for Research on Land and Water Resources, 1972, pp. 61-148(a).
[29] ______. "In Defense of a Positive Approach to Government as an

Economic Variable." *Journal of Law and Economics* 15 (October 1972): 453-59(b).
[30] Sax, Joseph L. "Taking, Private Property and Public Rights." *Yale Law Journal* 81 (December 1971): 149-86.
[31] Sen, Amartya K. *Collective Choice and Social Welfare.* San Francisco: Holden-Day Inc., 1970.
[32] Slawson, W. David. "Standard Form Contracts and Democratic Control of Lawmaking Power." *Harvard Law Review* 84 (January 1971): 529-66.
[33] Stigler, George J. "Smith's Travels on the Ship of State." *History of Political Economy* 3 (Fall 1971): 265-77.
[34] Tollison, Robert D. "Involved Social Analysis." In *Theory of Public Choice,* James Buchanan and Robert Tollison, eds. Ann Arbor: University of Michigan Press, 1972, pp. 3-10.
[35] Tullock, Gordon. "Public Decisions as Public Goods." *Journal of Political Economy* 79 (July/August 1971): 913-18(a).
[36] ——. *The Logic of the Law.* New York: Basic Books, 1971(b).
[37] ——. "Inheritance Justified." *Journal of Law and Economics* 14 (October 1971): 465-74(c).
[38] Williamson, Oliver E. "Administrative Decision Making and Pricing: Externality and Compensation Analysis Applied." In *The Analysis of Public Output,* Julius Margolis, ed. New York: Columbia University Press (distributed for National Bureau of Economic Research), 1970, pp. 115-35.

Theory of Public Choice: A Review Article

A. Allan Schmid

How far can traditional economic postulates be extended to produce insights into public choice processes? Can theories of welfare maximization be applied to individual choices in politics as well as markets? A collection of articles edited by James Buchanan and Robert Tollison says yes.[1]

Two varieties of claims are made. One is a series of predictions of behavior under alternative sets of rules, and the second speaks to the appropriateness of a particular set. The editors assert that all the writers do not address the second because they are "unwilling to play God." This reviewer observes that varying degrees of "rightness" (if not righteousness) sneak into some of the articles nevertheless.

The various articles cover a broad range of topics from tax varieties, debt limits, and public utility pricing to intergovernmental fiscal relations. This review, however, will concentrate on the several articles that are applied to military conscription and education as representative of the approach which the book wishes to communicate to the profession.

Let us examine the book's prescriptive claims first. Richard Wagner says military "conscription will generate allocative inefficiencies" since the majority political coalition does not have to account for all of the costs. He likens conscription to a discriminatory tax. There

The author is Professor of Agricultural Economics, Michigan State University, East Lansing.

is a strong suggestion that economic science shows that the whole society would be better off with the efficiency of market purchased armies. However, it is clear that such a change is not Pareto-better, or no one would oppose it. Robert Tollison, writing on the same subject, offers an ingenious solution which makes future generations pay for the change via a bond (if in fact this is possible). Is there just a touch of Godlike activity in deciding that present generations may choose for future ones?

There is an assumption in both that costs exist in nature and that the rules of property must accommodate to them or risk being labeled inefficient. But, in fact, the decision on what effects are going to be costs to whom is the essence of public choice. The economist cannot instruct this choice without deciding who will count and who will choose. Whenever an effect is owned and barriers to trade exist, it is possible for restoration of trade to be Pareto-better. But this does not say whether those who want an army should have to pay to get labor, or whether they already own the labor and must be paid if that labor wants to escape its obligation.

Mark Pauly wants to be able to say something about optimum spending for education. If the consumption of education produces externalities for the community (and if free rider problems are solved), it may wish to buy more of the commodity than parents of children would buy in the market. Parents' decisions to buy education depend on how much community contribution they anticipate.

For a certain plausible set of parent and community demand curves, Pauly shows that different expenditure levels occur if the two groups adjust *independently* until each equates their marginal evaluation and cost, as opposed to *sharing* the cost of providing additional education for each child. He shows that only the latter is optimal and, furthermore, that optimal sharing involves an inverse relationship between community payments for a child's education and parents' income, as opposed to a flat tuition grant to all which can be supplemented privately at will. This is an important policy conflict in our society which Pauly wants to settle as a scientist. He fails to emphasize all of the underlying property rights assumption which made his conclusion true. He explicitly assumes a property rule where demand functions for a given group are revealed to the state so that they can be summed together with that of the state and the resulting marginal value then equated to marginal cost to determine optimal output. Then the effective private price necessary to achieve this quantity is determined and the difference between this price and marginal cost is the state subsidy. Given this, he shows that optimal choice requires that low demanders may get a completely free ride and the high demanders pay the whole shot for the quantity they purchase. However, this particular choice between proportional and flat rate subsidies is optimal only if certain other more basic property right questions are assumed.

Equal valued tuition certificates for all are not optimal if parents have no rights to state support and if the state has the right to prevent effective strategic bargaining. Once these critical rights are set, it does not make any sense for the state to offer subsidies to high demanders. But, expressed this way, it is a very obvious and uninteresting conclusion. It does not speak to who should have what basic rights or the results of alternative rights. It simply says, if you have them, do not waste them!

No tuition certificate is optimal if parents own their children and can reject the attempts of the community to adjust for the externalities of their underconsumption of education. The Amish are a case in point who would prefer this set of rights.

Pauly's analysis is no guide to ownership rules, but only to the conduct of the community choice *after* the rights of the community and parents are set. The community prefers to reach a chosen minimum level of education at minimum cost, while most parents want all the help they can get. Whose wants will predominate is a moral question only obfuscated by Pauly's would-be science.

The Pauly and Wagner analyses are representative of many of the chapters.[2] A fundamental set of property rights is assumed, and some additional alternative features are examined. A Pareto-better blessing then is given to one of them without ever calling much attention to the fact that the big policy game was over before the analysis started, which makes the Pareto-better calculation come out in the particular way it did. What often is forgotten is that all aspects of optimality are a function of the total set of property rights. Nothing can be said about optimality unless property rights are accepted or given (or hidden).

There is a tendency in this book and much of economics to take an undisputable, simple premise like utility maximization and deduce policy from it, that is, label certain things as inefficient. This exercise has little use in public policy since the key issue is *whose* utility is to count, that is, which people will have what options within which to maximize their utility. Even those who make an effort to be positivistic tend to fall into the efficiency trap of unexamined property rights premises.

So much for prescription. What does this collection offer for prediction? Let us return to the draft issue again. Wagner wants to predict what effect a change from the draft to a voluntary market army will have on the size of the military budget. He predicts that "conscription will produce both a larger, real-sized military budget and a less isolationist . . . military foreign policy." This conclusion follows from the application of welfare maximization theory to public choice, as noted above.

We can assume that this original contribution of the book, written in 1972, was made before Congress actually abolished the draft. If Wagner is correct, we could expect a contraction in the size of the budget. We have had an empirical test dumped in our laps. It is perhaps too early to be conclusive, but there is no sign that the military budget is shrinking, although we apparently are becoming more isolationist. Half of the prediction fails on its own grounds (besides not answering some important questions at all, such as what type of army results from volunteers). Several pieces in the book pride themselves on only requiring simple welfare maximization models rather than complex models of voter, legislative, or bureaucratic behavior. Supposedly this makes attention to the role of powerful congressional committees, the generals, and the military hardware interests unnecessary. Also unnecessary is any sense of history, of the impact of the Vietnam War. Simple welfare maximization models fail when the median individual is not doing the chosing and when the chooser has complex motivations and perceptions.

It is curious that in other places some of these same authors go to great lengths to point out the need to look at the decision rules (rights) which shape administrative behavior. Yet, here they do not seem to want to look at the particular legislative and voter expression rules.

If Wagner had stuck to just labeling the result of conscription as inefficient, he would have been alright, for the epithet has no empirical content capable of disconfirmation by experience. But he has a taste for more relevance than that, and his simple behavioral postulates get him into trouble.

Of course, experience is messy, and Wagner always could argue that the budget would have been even larger if conscription had continued. But at least this deals with the real world and the nitty-gritty of experimental design and data interpretation, instead of the elegance of the marginal calculus on cloud nine over Virginia.

The book also offers predictions with respect to educational funding under alternative rules. Craig Stubblebine does not ask about the optimum size of the budget, but about its actual size as a result of requiring public, private, or mixed financing. He sees institutional rules as changing product prices, which view enables a simple indifference map to be used to predict the majority vote or market choice, *if* you have such a map handy. He concludes that you cannot make any generalization that a given type of financing (public, private, or mixed) always will produce the largest budget, for it depends on the actual median preference for the amount of education (but mixed systems would give the largest budget in several plausible demand situations).

In passing, Stubblebine cannot understand why some people support state grants to public schools and colleges, but will not support Friedman type vouchers to any school "since the two are analytically equivalent." For this type of prediction, the simple behavioral assumptions he uses break down. Two people may perceive a given product differently. It is not merely that some people want children to receive more education than their parents might buy, rather, they want them to have a certain type of education. The types of financing and associated control may change the product or people's perception of it. This means that we need more detailed knowledge of human behavior than the drive to maximize some single dimensioned return. We cannot always take preference maps as given while we play with relative prices. The simple fact that people maximize utility does not tell us how they will define that utility.

This reviewer finds great value in the book's various attempts to trace through the effects of alternative property rights and public choice rules in the context of simple welfare maximization assumptions. But there is danger if this is used to beat off other efforts to insert voter, legislative, and bureaucratic behavior and to let simplified assumptions define *the* problem. One result of the latter, for example, is that you make the mistake of regarding all armies and schools as the same. This assumes away half of the policy issues that need illumination.

The book's opening and closing chapters provide one basis for its review. Tollison's introduction calls for "involved social analysis" and a positive scenario. The relevancy of the material for a wide range of public choices is impressive. The standard of positive prediction, however, is often broached. The calculation of efficient institutions sometimes begs the question of efficiency for whom and what. The big issue of public policy is: Whose utility counts? If this question is not faced explicitly, the statement that a given rule is the most efficient is just a name for hidden preferences.

The closing chapter by Gordon Tullock calls for a social science of two branches—one studying preferences and how they come about and one studying choice. He urges economists specializing in the latter to become great consumers of the output of the behavioral sciences, instead of the all too common habit of economists implicity taking their own personal tastes as typical. As this review notes, the pervading theme of the book is not receptive to Tullock's charge. There is a great preference (almost insistence) for simplistic views of human nature. Perceptions molded by choice experience itself tend to be ignored. The authors call for the next step of empirical testing of their predictions. I am afraid that if Tullock's call is not heeded, this testing will turn up empty handed.

The public choice theory of Buchanan and Tullock's *Calculus of Consent* was most useful in raising the level of public policy debate. If someone asserts that a free people never would voluntarily choose to be bound by a less than unanimity rule, this can be put to rest. This type of logic is continued here by reminding us that "the discovery of market failure by itself is not sufficient to invoke an unexamined alternative [government]." This attitude can do much to quiet unproductive arguments and simple policy prescription. But if public choice theory is to be truly predictive, economists will have to take off from Tullock's insistence on better understanding of how preferences and personalities form and change, rather than from the great bulk of this thought-provoking book.

Notes

1. James M. Buchanan and Robert D. Tollison, eds., *Theory of Public Choice* (Ann Arbor: University of Michigan Press, 1972 [pp. 329, $15.00]).
2. Pauly is more explicit than most. He notes his assumptions, but does not regard them as property rights issues in the same sense as the subsequent rights issues he examines.

The Economics of Property Rights: A Review Article

A. Allan Schmid

Pigouvian analysis implies that the existence of externalities requires government intervention. This conception seems to reverse the conventional wisdom of economics, which proved the maximization of wealth under competitive market conditions. The writers collected in *The Economics of Property Rights*[1] believe they have found a flaw in the Pigouvian derivations and indeed have turned the externalities conclusion around. Externalities frequently are reduced to their lowest economical level by the market, and, indeed, a good many externalities exist only because we have failed to leave the market alone to do the work for which it is uniquely qualified.

The authors believe they have found an objective benefit-cost analysis which gives answers to the age-old questions of how to choose among alternative property rights systems. The approach involves a conception of welfare improvement (social net benefit), although they specifically deny a social welfare function. The concept of total (social) cost minimization, or maximizing the value of production, enables the authors to critique some property rights rules as inefficient. The entire collection tends to support the glories of market capitalism and the inefficiencies of any other type of business organization, government ownership, or regulation.

The author is Professor of Agricultural Economics, Michigan State University, East Lansing.

The collection begins with Steven Cheung's analysis of market contracts in the context of the problem of ocean fisheries. This is a situation in which one fisherman's activity affects the return to another's efforts. No one has an incentive to invest and husband the resource, resulting in what some call the "tragedy of the commons." This view of externality leads many to suggest government regulation of numbers and fishing technique. Cheung argues that government is often the cause of the problem, if any, rather than the solution. He notes that the impact of a marginal increment of factor input on intramarginal returns is commonplace in firm economics, but causes no problem to maximizing total firm profit. That insight then forms the calculus of the book. Property rights can be chosen in terms of an aggregative or social view. When individuals do not own a resource, they have no incentive to invest. The answer is not government regulation, but the institution of private ownership rights (right to contract for the use of a resource) and appropriate firm size. The effect of one input on another would be accounted for if the effect were owned and traded. The only allowable consideration is whether it is economical to own and trade. In the case of the sea, it is difficult to police one person's use that steals from the owner. Also, one must have a considerable area before management becomes feasible. This would create high transaction costs in reaching agreement between numerous owners and in policing transgressors. These costs are a matter to be determined empirically. Sometimes the cost of private ownership prohibits exclusive rights and contracting. In that case, and only in that case, government regulation is efficient, says Cheung.

Here we have a microeconomics for determining the efficient system of rights as well as the efficient size of the firm. All is a matter of cost. Firms expand to the point where (among other production cost considerations) the marginal cost of enforcing exclusivity equals the associated marginal gain. If that means monopoly, than so be it, for it fosters efficiency and we all know that everyone is better off with the efficient solution.

The editors believe that property rights analysis as represented in this collection presents a unified approach. This belief is well founded, as the above conception is a common thread in the volume. In essence, all of the knotty problems of public debate over property issues, with all of its interpersonal utility comparisons, can be avoided by an examination of objective costs. Cost is seen as something that exists independent of the property rights system, and it thus can be a guide to choice of that system.

The analysis is used to suggest that a market solution not only is possible in ocean fisheries, but also would solve any problems in allocation of the radio-magnetic spectrum without resorting to the Federal Communications Commission (Ronald Coase). It would solve any problems of land and water use, such as pollution conflicts, without government regulation (Harold Demsetz). The analysis indicates why not-for-profit organizations such as hospitals are likely to be inefficient (M. Pauley and M. Redisch), and why socialist worker-owned firms are likely to underinvest to the detriment of the workers themselves (Eirik Furubotn). It indicates why price controls and licenses are bad since they lead to corruption of officials by bribes (N. Sanchez and A. R. Waters). It is truly a general and powerful conception.

What then are the essentials that these writers suggest in arranging property rights to maximize productivity? Costs and benefits must be brought to bear on those who create them. This is done by private ownership, whereby an actor has the right of residual profit and right of use or sale. This rules out any type of further government regulation or public ownership, which are labeled "rights attenuation."

The right to sell is the key. The authors emphasize that salability is necessary to assure use by the most valuable user. For example, Coase suggests that it prevents the use of the air waves by such deadbeats as the police, military, and educational groups who otherwise might lose out in competitive bidding. This applies to goods such as alternative radio channel uses, but also to bads such as one channel interfering with another. If interference is worthwhile to avoid, the market will so note. The same is true for all so-called negative externalities, such as pollution. Cheung, Demsetz, and others emphasize that sale internalizes all costs (externalities). Internalization is another word for obtaining a trade that allocates the resource to the most valuable use. If a resource or the effect of one aspect of its use has a higher value to another, the latter should be able to bid and obtain it. This makes both the former and new owner better off, while value of output increases. If a harmed party cannot make a sufficient bid, then of course the use is already in its most valued place (and the harmed one can only lick his wounds). We are not asked to inquire what affects the ability of the parties to make bids, as long as the reason is not the "artificial" one of legal barriers to trade or regulations, that is, other status quo rights are assumed.

Economists long have recognized the concept of gains from trade, and these authors have generalized it over a wide range of problems with the concept of internalization of relevant (to them) externalities, or as one author prefers to state it, with the concept of reducing the difference between social and private cost. This classic theme has been supplemented further by the concept of transaction cost.

A person with a better idea (way to increase resource rent) can have the net advantage disappear in a cloud of transaction costs as he tries to work out an exchange of ownership with the present owners. Prohibition of sale makes transaction costs nominally infinite. But even where sale is allowed, there is a particular problem in buying a resource owned in common by many individuals, all of whom must consent to the sale. Therefore, it follows that the world would be better off (rents maximized) if everything could be owned by individuals with unilateral rights to sell, which would keep transaction costs to a minimum. Transaction costs are seen as a pure waste with no benefit to anyone. However, the writers agree that the only valid basis for governmental involvement occurs when, for some resources and products, individual ownership is itself too costly because of exclusion (policing) costs. All of this is a straightforward matter of objective benefit-cost analysis unclouded by any apparent need to resolve interpersonal value questions.

It also follows that the size of the firm is controlled legitimately only by reference to the minimization of these net transaction costs. Unless there are offsetting internal coordination costs, all resources could be owned by one individual or group of stockholders (and this is suggested by Cheung in his analysis of the seas). The writers, notwithstanding their usual devotion to the competitive model, do not appear troubled by any other consequences of concentrated ownership. If costs that they recognize can be saved, the distributive consequences can be handled in a different context. Or, those harmed by monopoly always can try to buy out the monopolist and make it worth his while to act in a competitive manner. Affected people are limited in removing damage to the extent that the damage is not as valuable to them as it is to its creator, and thus society is served, according to several authors.

Closely related to the concept of transaction cost is that of information cost. Armen Alchian and Harold Demsetz present an argument for centralizing ownership of the residual rents and against worker-owned firms. First, there are high transaction-information costs if each resource owner (including labor) must make a simultaneous contract with every other resource owner needed in today's complex industry. These costs can be reduced by having one central contractor contract with all other factor owners individually.

Furthermore, in complex team production it is costly (transaction-information costs again) for everyone involved to determine the marginal product of each worker. It is too costly for each worker to monitor the performance of all other workers and determine the return appropriate for the marginal productivity of each worker. It is assumed that people will shirk if they can get away with it. The only way to prevent it is to make it worth someone's while to monitor their performance as a specialized function. This someone is the owner-directed manager, who will earn a higher income if he can prevent shirking through specialized information gathering. Never mind the problem of distinguishing shirking from revulsion at sweatshop conditions which also might enhance the residual; this is controlled by competition, although the authors do not inquire into how competition is affected by having a few managers dealing with many workers. Thus, again we have a maximization of product (saving of transaction and information cost) rationale for the specialization of ownership and for why worker-owned firms are likely to be uneconomic.

Several of the articles point up the key role of capital markets, which keep managers from shirking, and assure us all of least-cost output of the right products. Forms of business organization other than individual or corporate ownership with capital markets come in for much criticism. Without such a market, managers and residual return owners are not immediately reminded of the effects of decisions on future values, that is, future values are not capitalizable. It is certainly useful for substantive prediction to note what types of gains can be captured by people who make decisions, but the normative policy implications are another matter. What these arguments boil down to is this: If a firm is supposed to maximize those capital values which are seen in a given market, then it is inefficient to account for something else.

But who says that the rights now held and maximized are the correct ones? Could it be that we choose different kinds of business organizations to achieve a type of performance not obtainable in firms reacting to the rights embodied in current capital markets? Perhaps some would like the right to a different set of outputs which result from a different accounting of relevant costs. For example, one author notes that Yugoslav workers cannot sell their share of the firms they work for and shift the capital to a higher profit pizza parlor. But that is the point. Some groups feel that they have the right to direct the main flow of capital, and they prefer heavy industry and education to pizza. Salability is related to mobility, but anyone who has seen a town from which a major industry has moved knows that certain costs were ignored by market choosers as they sought the least cost (to them) location.

The above is a sample of the arguments for private corporate ownership and attendant markets and against rights attenuation in the form of government regulation, communal ownership, socialist and nonprofit firms, or any other form of business organization. Let us now look more closely at the underlying conceptualization.

One must admire the authors for dispassionately extending their logic to passionate areas, one of which is the right to labor power. If you believe that efficiency is unique and dependent upon the existence of a market after the original rights have been vested in one direction or another, you must accept a benefit-cost analysis of a situation beginning with slavery. Demsetz never strays from the logic of his conception and is willing to suggest that subsequent freedom depends upon the value to the slave of his freedom. He can make a bid, and its refusal or acceptance will maximize the value of labor to society. Recall that this analysis takes costs as given, and property rights issues, such as whether or not a market is permitted, follow from these costs. But must we not consider what it is that affects the ability of the slaves to buy their freedom? If the slaves have no other property, they have nothing to offer the owners in exchange, even if slavery is onerous to them. They could go to the capital market and borrow the present value of their future earnings. If the owner has put them to a low value use, this present value may give the owner more profit than if he keeps the slave in his current use. This is what Demsetz means by maximizing the value of product to society at the same time that both parties become better off in a Pareto-better trade. But if the owner already has put the slave in his highest MVP and is enjoying the maximum residual, the slave will not be able to make an effective bid. Well, the logic tells us that no further changes are Pareto-better or can increase the value of the product. Any further change involves a redistribution of income, and we all know that requires a social welfare function solution. But implicit acceptance of the status quo rights also requires a social welfare function.

A slave would not regard the right to buy his freedom as equal to the right to sell his labor. The movement from one rights situation to the other is not Pareto-better. Only if we accept the premise that the man does not own his labor (first order property rights question) can we say that subsequent trade would be viewed as better by both parties; for example, if the owner has the right to create a cost for the worker, then both are better off if second order trades can be made. If we say otherwise, it is equivalent to saying that the owner only has *some* rights as against the worker, who can create certain costs for the owner under the terms of the price regulation, licensing, and so forth. The only Pareto-better solution, given that starting place, is for the owner to buy these attenuations and privileges from the worker. If there are other third parties interested in whether their fellowmen are slaves, they may wish to prevent such sale or take advantage of high transaction costs to discourage sale. (This is a rationale for child labor laws which prevent parents from selling the labor of "their" child instead of sending her/him to school.)

Demsetz says "a primary function of property rights is that of guiding incentives to achieve a greater internalization of externalities." The statement would be more complete if he added: *given* the direction of the externality, namely, the question of who can create a cost for whom.

A person who owns nothing cannot create a cost for anyone else. A logic of cost minimization then will count this person for naught. The lack of human dignity, while an opportunity lost for the slave, is not a cost to the owner. Demsetz keeps our eye on cost minimization, whatever these costs may be. There is an implication that costs exist wholly in nature and technological relationships, but this is false. If the person owns his labor power, he is in a position to place a value on his dignity and other conditions for use of his resource, which then becomes a cost to other would-be users to be again minimized in Demsetz's calculations. *The point is that there is a cost minimization for each alternative property rights distribution. Cost minimization then cannot be a guide to the choice of that distribution.*

But, of course, Demsetz never set out to speak to the choice in initial rights distribution. Inquiry is not addressed to the broader questions of the original and subsequent vestures of property rights among people. It speaks only to the secondary question of carrying out the logic of the costs implicit in a given rights distribution. If we are all agreed that A owns all aspects of a good and may create costs for others with respect to its use, then it is of course illogical and inconsistent with this initial agreement to then reallocate some portion of these rights in the form of prohibitions of sale, price regulation, licensing, and so forth. But that is the point of conflict. People do not agree for all time as to what costs A can create for the B's of the world. When rights are attenuated (read: redistributed) this is not always done because people are stupid and do not know how to minimize given costs, but because they do not agree on what costs to minimize. As rights are changed (not exchanged) over time, the government may not wish to take all of a bundle of rights from A and give them to B, but it may wish to attenuate some of them (perhaps the right to sell or enter business) for the benefit of B.

None of these papers speaks directly to the question of the *distribution* of property as between A and B (except for reference to the Coase Rule). There is no argument as to why A should have much and B little. All attention is given to the *form* of property, such as salability, private versus public, or private stock corporations versus socialist worker-owned or not-for-profit firms. Is it possible to choose among even these limited alternatives without assuming or implying something about the distribution of rights among the A's and B's? The answer already has been suggested. If the nonsalability of a use is itself part of someone's property and income flow, then advocating trade which would ignore the loss of this income is a redistributive choice between A and B. The fact that A and C can make a Pareto-better trade does not tell us about the effect on B.

Third parties are often affected by sales and changes in uses and prices. For example, in Michigan, riparian rights are nonsalable or nonusable separate from the riparian lands. It is important to note that fishermen always support these nonsalable rights whenever they are challenged. Increased sales and diversions of water would affect the interests of fishermen. The fact that sales are prohibited (or that there are high transaction costs in getting the agreement of all communal owners on a stream) is to the benefit of fishermen. Water cannot be made salable without affecting their welfare and making their cost no longer a consideration in any cost minimization. But why not make this an explicit private right of fishermen instead of an indirect effect of the character of landowners' rights or a matter of enforcement by government regulation of migration? Then if someone could pay off the riparian plus all the fishermen and put the water to a higher use, all would be better off than if this is prohibited. The end result is likely to be the same. The transaction costs of dealing with many fishermen would forestall sale anyway. Third party effects have the tendency to be diffuse and nonseparable. If these effects are to be protected by property rights, they are going to be communal or governmentally administered.

The point is that attenuation of one person's rights is not always simply a loss to the world, that is, a waste. One person's attenuation is another person's bread! The right to market is the right to create costs for the parties not represented in the market (that is, to ignore costs not protected by a property right except that of nonmarketability). The right to market cannot be a value-free blanket policy recommendation unless the analysis is a partial one. In other words, the right to sell, and the existence of transaction costs, is like any other right which determines the content and direction of costs and welfare. Licensing, price control, communal ownership, contract rules, and the distribution of ownership between A and B are all alternatives to achieve a certain set of prices and other performance characteristics. Given the different starting places, each has its own subsequent Pareto-better result.

The authors deny that they have found a social welfare function (SWF) which can be used to decide between parties A and B. However, there are two senses to a SWF. One is an explicit weighting which says, for example, that a dollar received by A should count for 50 percent more than one received by B. This type of SWF is not used by these authors. But there is another sense of SWF which is already embodied in any status quo set of property rights which affect which costs count and who has to pay whom. The authors fail to see that this implicit SWF affects relative prices and income just as surely as does an overt weighting scheme. Any acceptance of status quo property rights distribution which is then given effect by the subsequent rights of salability and choice of business organization forms is an acceptance of a social welfare function.

The theoretical arguments supporting private markets, and so forth, dominate the book, but by no means are all of the book. The general empirical model is one of the interconnectedness of ownership rights, incentives, and economic behavior. Another major theme which affects the type of data collected is that people are observed to be utility maximizers with complex ends, of which profit is only one. As already noted, the way in which transaction, information, and policing costs fall are major variables affecting behavior. This produces insights into predicting specific performance characteristics of a host of different situations, some of which have been empirically tested. For example, there is some evidence that mutual savings and loan associations have higher operating costs than do stock firms. Predicting these specific variables is a different matter than proving that society is better or worse because of it.

Publication of this collection of articles, along with the earlier collection, *Theory of Public Choice*, edited by James Buchanan and Robert Tollison,[2] gives students easier access to a rich and useful literature. It would require another review to explore the similarities and differences between what these editors include under the terms *property rights analysis* and *public choice*. One similarity is an attempt to develop a social cost-benefit approach to choice of institutions, whose cost minimization calculus begs the question of what and whose costs are to be considered. Both books also contain articles that forget that one man's attenuated rights are another's bread and that nonsalability is a valuable property right in itself. Both constitute a narrow analysis of property and public choice, focusing as they do on internalization of previously selected rights.

Nevertheless, the two volumes, along with this *Journal,* which has yet to be subject to an anthology, constitute a rising and vibrant neoinstitutional economics addressed to the consequences of alternative institutions and rules of the game. If the pseudo-scientific global efficiency and welfare maximization material can be expunged and the questions broadened, we are well on the way to better informing an individual or like-minded group about which institutions will best further its interests, that is, an individual's calculus of consent.

Notes

1. Eirik Furubotn and Svetozar Pejovich, eds. Cambridge, Mass.: Ballinger Publishing Co., 1974. Pp. 367. $19.50.
2. See A. Allan Schmid, "Theory of Public Choice: A Review Article," *Journal of Economic Issues* 8 (June 1974): 519–24. See also Victor Goldberg, "Public Choice—Property Rights," *Journal of Economic Issues* 8 (September 1974): 555–79.

Economics and Public Policy for the Undergraduate: A Review Article

Alan Randall

The four books considered here,[1] while by no means perfect substitutes, share substantial common ground. They are aimed at the undergraduate and, to a lesser extent, the general interest reader. As pedagogical aids, they are intended to attract and hold the interest of the neophyte economics major, to entice the student receiving an exposure to elementary economics so that he may want to become an economics major, and to provide an insight into the purpose and the power of the economic way of thinking for students who may never take another course in economics.

For many years, the widely used principles texts have introduced economics along disciplinary lines with, for example, chapter headings in terms of the analytical subdivisions of economic theory and illustrated by examples which, it is hoped, will be sufficient to impress the student with the relevance of economics and to aid the learning process. The examples and applications are clearly subordinate to the theory of economics.

These books take the diametrically opposite approach. The central focus is on important contemporary social issues. Economics is introduced as an aid in understanding the problems and working toward solutions. Lest the student fail to get the message, these authors state, time and time again, that economics is socially useful because

The author is Assistant Professor of Agricultural Economics, University of Kentucky, Lexington.

it throws light on important problems. "The economic approach to policy is, in general, more comprehensive than any other and, while it has many half-filled boxes, it has no empty ones" (Culyer, p. 260).

All of this is not to say that there are no important differences in coverage and the level of exposition among these four books. Paul Heyne, alone, offers an introductory text providing balanced coverage of micro- and macroeconomics. The other books are almost totally concerned with introducing the student to microeconomics and what usefully might be called "social microeconomics." Heyne is also alone in introducing the subdivisions of economic theory in a relatively rigid predetermined sequence. The other books look at different social problems sequentially (usually one problem per chapter); however, the chapters are organized so that knowledge of economic theory tends to build up as one reads the books from beginning to end. Llad Phillips and Harold Votey have something of a problem in maintaining fluidity in a book consisting of twelve main chapters by different authors. This problem is overcome partially with brief "Commentaries" by the editors between chapters and a summary chapter and a sequential listing of "economist's tools" at the end of the book. Heyne and A. J. Culyer provide introductory chapters orienting the reader to the "way of thinking" to be found in their respective books and offer final chapters evaluating the power and scope of economics in solving social problems.

The level of presentation in Heyne and Douglass North and Roger Miller consistently is directed toward the student with no prior training in economics. Mathematics is scrupulously avoided, while graphs are used sparingly by Heyne and not at all by North and Miller. Esoteric economic jargon is minimized, and what little is used is introduced apologetically. Writing styles are conversational. Both of these books seem aimed at the one-semester introductory and service courses which are beginning to supplant, wholly or partially, the more traditional two-semester introduction at many colleges. Heyne would serve as a very adequate text for a one-semester beginning course, while North and Miller would be valuable supplementary reading. Phillips and Votey claim to have used their book successfully in both introductory and intermediate courses, but most chapters read like mini-research monographs, replete with economic terminology, graphs, simple mathematics, and empirical data. This reviewer sees the Phillips and Votey book as perhaps most useful in providing supplementary readings for intermediate level undergraduate courses. Culyer aims his book at the intermediate level undergraduate and uses simple mathematics, diagrammatic analyses, esoteric economic terminology, and quite sophisticated concepts from welfare economics. His work is perhaps best viewed as an attempt, admirable in many ways, to make the welfare economics literature of recent years accessible to the undergraduate student.

All these volumes are obedient to the dictates of current fashions in undergraduate teaching. Relevance and the needs of students are emphasized. In several cases, prefaces contain self-righteous pronouncements, such as "this book is rooted in the conviction that the principles of economics should be a tough course to teach and an easy one to take" (Heyne) and "I have offended against the cardinal rule of textbook writers by trying to appeal more to students than to their teachers" (Culyer). Fashion is also served, in three cases, by including chapters on such currently chic issues as energy, the environment, population growth, slum housing, and drug and crime control. The exception is Heyne.

Now, we are ready to focus upon the most important question about these books. What are they teaching our children? What kind of economic way of thinking do they promote? With the exception of some of the macroeconomic chapters in Heyne, the economics (or, more precisely, the social microeconomics) offered falls well within the mainstream of neoclassical micro- and welfare economics. The individualistic ethic prevails. What people want is considered a serviceable indicator of what is good. The individual is presumed to be motivated to maximize his utility, which function is for the most part purely self-interested (although Culyer considers the possibility of benevolence in his discussion of income redistribution). Given information about the range and cost of alternatives, this motivational assumption allows us to predict what choices the individual will make. If public policy influences the range and cost of alternatives, as surely it does, then this simple model is adequate to indicate the effect of alternative policies on individual choices and hence on aggregate economic variables.

While there is much of value in this kind of economic analysis of social issues which enables prediction of the outcomes from alternative policies, it seems to be human nature to want more, to want an actual answer. However, the contribution of neoclassical welfare economics has not been to provide a method of answering the question: "What is the best policy for society?" Rather, its contribution has been to deny the possibility of a unique answer, in the absence of recourse to a dictatorial decision maker. All of these books communicate this problem to their audience, Culyer in a manner much more formal than the others. He proposes the strict Pareto-improvement (allowing actual compensation, as a device to expand the set of strict Pareto-improvements) as the minimal criterion for an unambiguous welfare improvement. Given this criterion, it is not surprising that his analyses of specific social issues are long on social accounting and short on conclusions.

These volumes have, by and large, handled this difficulty in the traditional way. "Positive" economic analyses are performed, "the facts" are presented, and the individual is left to choose his preferred policy by filtering the facts through his value system and to pursue implementation of that policy through the political process. The inability of economic analysis, per se, to arrive at socially optimal policies is emphasized by all the authors.

In principle, this methodological approach is impeccable; in practice, difficulties abound. Some facts are more easily ascertained than others. Where price is the measure of value, some prices are revealed in the market, while others are not. The lack of hard information about some aspects of a decision problem will tend to make the more complete information about other aspects seem more impressive and more important, thus tending to push the decision in the direction indicated by the *weight of the available information* (which need not be the same direction as would be indicated by a complete set of information). In a positive economic analysis, nonmarket goods have a difficult time competing with market goods because of this information differential. Similarly, efficiency often has the upper hand over income distributional considerations because less information about distributional impacts is available. More fundamentally, efficiency analyses of alternative policies potentially are biased when economic data such as prices generated under existing policies are used to evaluate alternative policies, and the bias is inherently in favor of the status quo. Yet, one observes in these books little concern with such practical problems in empirical positive economics. Are these problems too esoteric to be of concern to beginning and intermediate level undergraduates?[2] The student reader should be informed of the difficulties inherent in applied economic policy analyses. The "here are the facts, now you make up your mind" tone of these books is a little misleading, glossing over, as it does, the loading of the dice of judgment by the presentation of an incomplete and imperfect array of information.

Since economic theory is both the product and the servant of economic ideology, it is appropriate to examine the economic ideologies these books promulgate. Mostly, the volumes are conscientiously nonideological in tone. The terms *good* and *bad* are avoided ostentatiously; North and Miller even provide a footnote pointing out that *efficient* is not equated with *good* in economics. Nevertheless, in the substance of these books some ideology creeps through. After one efficiency analysis piled upon another, the student surely must take the hint that even if efficiency formally cannot be equated with good it does seem a very important consideration to the authors.

Just as the analysis in these books tends to be consistent with the mainstream of current economic thought, so is the implicit ideology. Free markets lead to efficient allocation of resources, while government intervention in markets often leads to "solutions" worse than the original problem. Regulation is seen to lead to obvious and quantifiable misallocations, while the benefits of regulation, if any, are presented as vague. These books leave the impression that the noneconomists' fear of bigness, and particularly of big business, is for the most part uninformed and unnecessary. Heyne, for one, seeks to minimize the importance of economic power.

Distributional questions receive substantial attention from Culyer, North and Miller, and Phillips and Votey, while Heyne avoids in-depth discussion of distribution, leaving the clear implication that each receives the value of his marginal product. Culyer's analysis of distribution, in particular, is quite sophisticated. However, North and Miller and Perry Shapiro and Anthony Barkume (in Phillips and Votey) seem to derive pleasure from pointing out the apparent inconsistency between environmental quality and improvement in the incomes of the relatively poor, two popular goals among political liberals. The prominent position accorded this dilemma in these books is perhaps out of proportion to its importance in the broad constellation of distributional problems.

These comments on the economic methodology espoused and the economic ideology implicit in the volumes are intended neither to derogate the books nor indicate broad disagreements between the authors and this reviewer. All the works contain much sound analysis and a good deal of common sense. This reviewer finds the neoclassical methodology of social microeconomics very useful. He wishes, nevertheless, that some of the books under review had been a little more circumspect about the methodology, the way it is often used, and the conclusions it often generates.

There is a problem in writing issue-oriented textbooks: How quickly they seem to become outdated! North and Miller on population growth and resource scarcity and, to a lesser extent, Lloyd J. Mercer (in Phillips and Votey) on agriculture seem to be taking positions which rapidly are becoming outdated by the facts. Or, are current events mere aberrations and will these authors be shown (in a decade or so) to have been common sense voices temporarily drowned out by the tumult?

The major service performed by these books is to impress the student with the usefulness of economic analysis in confronting a wide variety of social issues, many of which previously were considered, to use a term which has become almost quaint, noneconomic. In so doing, these books quite accurately reflect the dominant view in the economic profession about the role and methodology of economic analysis of social policy issues. For the most part, they are well written, easy to read, and accessible to those with little or no prior economic education, Phillips and Votey and Culyer a little less so than the others. All of these volumes will find useful roles in the classroom. The issue-oriented mode of textbook writing has much to recommend it. Perhaps the time is not far away when that mode will be employed by other writers with even greater success.

Notes

1. Douglass C. North and Roger LeRoy Miller, *The Economics of Public Issues*, 2d ed. (New York, Evanston, San Francisco, and London: Harper and Row, 1973). Pp. viii, 184. $2.95, paper; Paul T. Heyne, *The Economic Way of Thinking* (Chicago, Palo Alto, Toronto, Henley-on-Thames, Sydney, and Paris: Science Research Associates, 1973). Pp. xiv, 289, paper; Llad Phillips and Harold L. Votey, Jr., eds., *Economic Analysis of Pressing Social Problems* (Chicago: Rand McNally, 1974). Pp. ix, 348. $5.95, paper; and A. J. Culyer, *The Economics of Social Policy* (New York: Dunellen, 1974). Pp. xii, 268. $15.00, cloth.
2. Formal proofs of the existence of these problems would be overwhelming for the beginning student, but these books do not present formal proofs of anything. It should be possible, nevertheless, to provide examples which suggest the nature of the difficulties.

On Lemmings and Other Acquisitive Animals: Propositions on Consumption

E. K. Hunt and Ralph C. d'Arge

Humans tend to anthropomorphize animals. Pigs and rats are seen as greedy, acquisitive, and voracious animals. They aggressively compete for more than their share. Lemmings are close first cousins of rats. The acquisitive behavior of rats reaches its most absurd extreme in the lemmings, who, in their recurrent migratory search for more, rush head-long into the sea in a mass orgy of societal suicide. (Biological reasons are still in dispute. We provide our own interpretation here.) In acquisitive societies, our views on pigs, rats, and lemmings are reasonably descriptive of much of human behavior. Greed and the desire for endless acquisition of material wealth and greater consumption are the motivating forces underlying American capitalism.

In our society, the desire for human inequality is intense. It is the most fundamental and overriding desire of most success-oriented individual maximizers. But what if a competitive economy were run by rats? Would we perceive a competitive equilibrium characterized as Pareto efficient? The answer is unquestionably "no." Rats immediately would recognize the stronger and weaker of their species, regardless of intraspecies utility comparisons. A pecking or survival

---

The authors are Associate Professors of Economics, University of California, Riverside.
This article was presented at the Annual Meeting of the Association for Evolutionary Economics, Toronto, Canada, 27-29 December 1972.

order would be established. The privileges that stem from this hierarchical order would be codified and legitimatized in a set of implicit property rights. These property rights would determine the initial endowments of income with which the competitive struggle for more, relatively and absolutely, would be combatted. Each rational, economizing economic rat or lemming would fight for his own private "optimum," as the entire society would be propelled irretrievably toward a deadly sea of environmental degradation. Gaps in intelligence, knowledge, abilities, and power immediately would be sensed, by action if not by instinct. The individual rat, sensing his own predicament and position, then would be confronted with the following alternatives: (1) Accept the preliminary pecking order and distribution of rights, ignore the impending disaster, and make the best of things within the context of the rat or lemming society; or (2) rebel against the established order and in so doing create notoriety and suspicion, ultimately either settling comfortably as a rebel without claws or being eaten by antagonized rat populations, but perhaps with some small but finite probability of contributing to the ultimate replacement of rat society by a more humane social system.

If the rat were a rational economizing sort, with risk aversion, he might likely choose the first option. But given that choice, what would his behavior pattern be following such a clearly "stated" desire for opting for the establishment. It is just such a case, with the individual rat pitted against a society composed of other coopted rats, that neoclassical welfare economics seeks to analyze. In so doing, neoclassical economics builds on a metaphysical intellectual base that is appropriate to its task. Analysis of the second alternative requires, we believe, a fundamentally different set of intellectual first principles.

The eminent philosopher, Stephen C. Pepper, wrote a survey of systems of metaphysics in which he showed that there are four general metaphysical world views which have provided relatively adequate bases for scientific inquiries, social and ethical philosophies, and theories of knowledge.[1] Most of the attempts to analyze the process of consumption and the nature of environmental externalities in orthodox economic literature have occurred within the general normative and analytical framework of competitive equilibrium. The metaphysical basis upon which the analysis of competition and, generally, neoclassical economics is constructed Pepper calls "mechanism"[2]; this is the metaphysical system upon which most of the other dominant strains of economic orthodoxy also have been based.

There is another metaphysical system, however, upon which many dissident economic theories have been constructed. This is the general

Weltanschauung that Pepper calls "contextualism."[3] In economic literature the intellectual traditions of institutionalism and Marxism fall within the broader world view of contextualism. In this article we shall attempt to impressionistically indicate a few highlights of the two general systems of thought and indicate some of the reasons why we believe the orthodox approach is almost useless as a basis for formulating a normative theory of consumption with externalities, which we believe to be the starting point for an understanding of consumptive behavior. We also briefly will outline our reasons for believing that the contextualism view offers far richer possibilities for constructing a much more serviceable theory of optimal consumption in the presence of externalities.

The Neoclassical Framework of Consumption Sketched

In the eighteenth century the cosmology implicit in Newtonian physics rapidly became the dominant intellectual framework for both the "natural sciences" and the "social sciences." The Newtonian concept is basically that of an atomistic world governed by eternal and immutable mechanical laws of motion. All change was governed absolutely by these laws. Change and movement in consumption could be understood as series of equilibria of atomistic elements, each self-contained and deterministically "programmed" by the totality of forces buffeting it about in accordance with the laws of mechanics. The basic Newtonian view is that which Pepper labels "mechanism."

This point of view rapidly came to dominate social inquiry in the eighteenth century. David Hamilton has shown the result of Newtonian mechanism in the social sciences:

> The eighteenth century viewed social forms as fixed in nature and what change took place was at most a quantitative one within fixed limits set by a natural order of things. The universe was a mechanical piece often likened to a clock whose moving parts, when once wound up by a devine Creator, would run eternally in the same pre-established mechanical arrangement. The best interest of man could be attained by an objective scrutiny of the workings of this mechanical universe. This inquiry was to be guided by reason, which would uncover the great principles by which the social universe was guided in its rhythmical pattern of movement. By laying bare these principles man would be able to conform to them and thus would enhance his contentment and happiness on earth. Misery and despair, the product of man's ignorance, which was also the source of his folly in flaunting these immutable natural principles, could be banished from the world.[4]

Adam Smith's *The Wealth of Nations* was the denouement of this eighteenth-century philosophy. In place of Newton's law of gravitation Smith substituted "self-interest." A society which operated in accordance with natural law would be a private property, capitalist, market system in which each atomistic individual exercised his "natural right" to seek his own self-interest. Each selfish-acquisitive individual simultaneously would promote the social good while he sought only his own welfare. The theory, of course, omitted social, political, and economic differences which lead to the establishment of "rights" and thereby consumption opportunities.

Smith's assertion that the Invisible Hand of the capitalist, market system would harmonize all individual egoistic actions and lead to an "optimal" allocation of productive resources has remained the most consistent theme for an ideological defense of market capitalism down to the present time. "The whole basis of modern price theory is to be found in Adam Smith without 'modern refinements.'"[5]

Orthodox economists of the last 150 years, like the medieval scholastics, accepted the basic axioms of their system almost without question. They have worked endlessly to create a brilliant deductive edifice on these axioms. By introducing complicated models of mathematical reasoning they have made it difficult, if not impossible, for all but the professional economist to follow the tortuous paths by which they arrive at their conclusions. Their conclusions are the same as Smith's: Inherent in the capitalist economic system are forces which, if nurtured properly, will tend to create an ideal consumption-oriented society.

The "common core" or ideological and cosmological framework of economics has been challenged only infrequently. Rather, with zeal, economists endlessly have produced esoteric trivia to embellish the decorative trim of their magnificent edifice. Milton Friedman succinctly has described modern economics and modern economists: "Economics is a scientific discipline that has a core that is common to almost all professional economists. *Naturally*, economists devote little professional research and writing—except in textbooks—to this common core. They concentrate on the issues that are on the frontier where economics is being made rather than taught or applied."[6]

The textbooks invariably begin with a very sharp, and perhaps cheap, dichotomy: the theory of the consumer and the theory of the firm.[7] Here we meet the homogeneous, maximizing, "economic man" with fixed budget, intent upon choosing commodities so as to maximize his individually inspired utility. This results in commodities being chosen in such proportions that the marginal rate of substitution between any pair will be equal to the ratio of their prices. Furthermore, these marginal rates of substitution between any pair of commodities will be the same for all consumers since they are confronted by more or less the same prices and not with each other. This allows an instantaneous transition to be made from individual preferences to those of the community—the community's marginal rate of substitution being equal to that of an individual—and from this it is concluded that what is being produced is in accordance with the community's preferences, with social needs.

Next, an individual firm is considered, confronted by given prices in a competitive market. A production function is postulated giving the greatest physical output for all possible combinations of inputs. With specified prices for both inputs and outputs, in order to maximize profits, the firm will follow a set of efficiency conditions: A point is chosen on the firm's production function such that the price of any factor (including labor) is equal to the value of its marginal product; the marginal rate of substitution between any pair of factors is equal to the ratio of their prices; the marginal rate of transformation between any two outputs is equal to the ratio of their respective prices. These conditions are the same for all firms since they all face the same input and output prices and implicitly the same amount of information, and they are located on top of each other at one point in space. They ensure both profit maximization and that all factors will be utilized as efficiently as possible. Now in equilibrium, since the prices facing the individual firm and the individual consumer are the same, an individual consumer's marginal rate of substitution is equal to any firm's marginal rate of transformation. At this point the neoclassical economists ecstatically proclaim: "Consumer Sovereignty"—"Pareto Optimality." Every resource is being used, every commodity is produced, in accordance with consumers' wants; it is not possible to reallocate without decreasing someone's "utility" subject to initial entitlement of resources and ownership.

The whole analysis is based on a set of assumptions that seldom are made fully explicit. The following are four of the most objectionable assumptions. First, there is acceptance of the socioeconomic institutional structure. Current capitalist institutions define the constraints, and the economist's task is clearly delimited within these bounds. Second, the premise of social harmony assumes that aside from a few "frictions" and difficulties, there are no irreconcilable conflicts of interest between social groups. There are, in fact, seldom any groups or classes of men at all. Third, differences between men disappear. They become simply homogeneous, utility-maximizing machines with sets of metaphysically given preferences. Veblen aptly summarized this view:

> [This] conception of man is that of a lightning calculator of pleasures and pains, who oscillates like a homogeneous globule of desire of happiness under the impulse of stimuli that shift him about the area, but leave him intact. He has neither antecedent nor consequent. He is an isolated definitive human datum, in stable equilibrium except for the buffets of the impinging forces that displace him in one direction or another. Self-imposed in elemental space, he spins symmetrically about his own spiritual axis until the parallelogram of forces bears down upon him, whereupon he follows the line of the resultant. When the force of the impact is spent, he comes to rest, a self-contained globule of desire as before.[8]

The fourth assumption is that the government has a shadowy existence. As long as Paretian optimality exists it is nowhere. When an externality occurs (it is generally an isolated occurrence in an otherwise perfect world) the government becomes a *deus ex machina* which restores the system to a state of bliss. It is an aloof, neutral, impartial arbitrator that descends on the scene and enacts an excise tax or gives a subsidy that re-creates competitive equilibrium. Vested interests? Economic and political power? Class control of government processes? These are the fuzzy notions of sociologists and political scientists. They have no place here. When the first order conditions are restored, or the new property rights to consume and pollute are established, the government discreetly recedes into the mystic mist.

The Contextualist Framework

Whereas the paradigm model of mechanism is the functioning of a machine, the paradigm model of contextualism is the "historical event." For the contextualist, the world of experience is not made up of immutable, fixed, atomistic elements that can be analyzed in complete isolation. Reality is a *process*. Our experience is the sum of on-going historic events and is not made up of atoms, lengths, heights, weights, numbers, and so forth. The most basic units of our experience are entire holistic events. They consist of such things as "making a boat, running a race, laughing at a joke, persuading an assembly, unraveling a mystery, emptying the garbage, removing an obstacle, exploring a country," discharging a whole amalgam of pollutants in a river, "communicating with a friend, creating a poem, re-creating a poem."[9]

The precise nature of a historical event depends on many things. First, events have a *texture*, that is, they have many particular things and processes which are contained within them. Second, they have an aggregate and individual quality that transcends the qualities of their textural components. Furthermore, the textural particulars are significantly affected by the total quality of the event. For example, in music the experienced quality of a particular chord depends upon the quality of the entire composition of which it is a part; similarly, the composition of solid waste odors depends not only on the dominant smelling component but also upon compaction, soil content, absorbtion, and other dimensions. Third, events have a *spread*. The present moment in any event contains elements of the *past* as well as elements of the future.[10] To consume a cluster of grapes now means a cost of soil, water, and human resources in the past, a bellyache in the near future (or headache if the grapes were pressed and fermented into wine), and a greater sludge load in secondary waste treatment plants for municipal organic waste.

Thus, *relationships* between objects, men, societies, and all other elements of reality are the essence of contextualism. The contextualist is "convinced that facts are never isolated appearances, that if they are produced together, it is always within the higher unity of a whole (although the whole may not be understood entirely), that they are tied to one another by internal relations, and that the presence of the one profoundly modifies the other."[11] The phenomenon of synergism, which is treated as something exceptional and strange in orthodox economics concerned with separability and linearity, is regarded as typical or normal in a contextualist framework because combinations or wholes are the most important ingredient for this theory.

Economic Growth and Consumption

The most important differences between contextualism and Newtonian mechanism are the notions of change or growth implicit in the two systems. Neoclassical growth theory is based upon the Newtonian notion of change. P. S. Laplace believed that if "we knew the configuration of matter in the whole universe at any one time and the precise laws of matter, or if we knew the configurations of matter at two times, so that we could deduce the laws which led from one configuration to the other, then we could deduce the configurations of matter for any other times whatsoever."[12] What better description could be given of neoclassical growth theory? A curvilinear line drawn between two points?

The neoclassical theory of optimal growth simply posits the existence of the necessary transformation and utility functions with the appropriate mathematical characteristics, generally ignoring the validity of the Sraffa inspired demonstration of the impossibility of empirically identifying such well-behaved transformation functions as well as the mountain of philosophical, methodological, and practical difficulties in specifying the existence of (much less the nature of) a dynamic utility function. From this point onward, with acceptance of a simple individual utility function and nonfinite resources, the analysis merely requires a few pages of mathematical deductions to "prove" the existence of a single optimal balanced growth path.[13]

From the same premises it is very simple to deduce the growth path of consumption when it is maximized (and, hence, in neoclassical economics, optimized): "To maximize consumption per man into perpetuity along a balanced growth path, choose that capital-labor ratio at which the marginal product of capital is equal to the rate of population growth."[14]

Externalities in Neoclassical Theory

In the neoclassical framework the processes of production and consumption were assumed to have "direct" effects on only the one or a few persons who do the consuming or producing.[15] Externalities occur when the utility function of one consumer is affected by the consumption or utility of another consumer, or the production function of one firm is affected by the production (or profits) of another firm, or the utility of an individual is affected by a production process with which he has no direct connection. The traditional neoclassical approach is to assume that, except for a single externality, Paretial optimality-cum-competitive equilibrium exists everywhere else.

The older policy measure (initiated by A. C. Pigou) which generally emerged was to tax and in so doing restore universal optimality. One of the newer policy prescriptions is to establish a "market for the right to pollute" and then let the Invisible Hand restore universal optimality. It generally is asserted that "failure to reach mutual agreement . . . can be regarded *prima facie* evidence that . . . a *net* potential Pareto improvement is not possible."[16] But this is too much for even the more candid neoclassical economists: "Rationalizing the *status quo* in this way brings the economist perilously close to defending it."[17]

The fantastically unrealistic assumptions upon which the Paretian analysis-cum-competitive equilibrium rests led J. De V. Graaf to declare that "the measure of acceptance . . . [this theory] has won would be astonishing were not its pedigree so long and respectable."[18] Furthermore, even if the analysis were not totally unrealistic, the ethical assumptions underlying the notion of competitive equilibrium-

Pareto efficiency are questionable, at best.[19] Joan Robinson calls the theory an "ideology to end ideologies,"[20] and S. S. Alexander notes that it "grants *our* social institutions immunity from criticism other than on grounds of efficiency."[21]

The critical *coup de grace* (if such is, indeed, needed) comes when one realizes that externalities are totally pervasive.[22] Most of the millions of acts of consumption (and production) in which we daily engage involve externalities. In a market economy *any* action of one individual or enterprise which induces pleasure or pain in any other individual or enterprise and is unpriced by a market constitutes an externality. Thus, if some guest at a formal dinner belches loudly and continuously, and this belching causes discomfort to other guests, then the economy is said to be in an inefficient state. Of course, we omit consideration of cultures where such behavior is taken as indicative of the superior quality of the meal.

A more incisive example of externality is the upwind factory that emits large quantities of sulfur oxides and particulate matter inducing rising probabilities of emphysema, lung cancer, and other respiratory diseases to residents downwind. This is clearly a case of undesired "consumption." The externality arises because the factory owners historically have not had to bear the burden of health and psychic damages which they cause.[23] In effect, their use of the air as a medium of waste disposal was (and in most areas still is) unrestricted and free.

These rather extreme examples underscore the difficulty of determining which social or private actions can be identified with externalities and which cannot. Unless people in modern societies are completely homogeneous, self-serving robots responding only to price and cost, practically *any* social behavior results in externalities. In fact, one of the reasons cited for the founding of societies is the common need for protection. Yet protection achieved by an individual through group participation is a form of reciprocal externality; I receive added protection by your presence as you receive added protection by mine. Such benefits of group participation are not priced at all or not by a well-defined market, but they are tantamount to identifying the *sine qua non* of societies in perhaps the most simplistic way! One therefore can argue that externalities are a normal and inherent part of societies and not some form of isolated, deviant behavior or exceptional outcome.

Returning to our first question of the mechanistic or neoclassical approach to the "decision" of rats as to where to "rip it off," let us start with the assumption that the rat is basically unsatisfied with income, God given endowments, and social position. The rat or lemming is confronted with a zero-sum game: What you have, if I take part of it, will be your loss and vice versa. If the rat were a rational self-economizing sort, with aversion to risk, he very well might opt for being a rebel without *identifiable* claws. However, normally we might expect the following behavior so that we denote this as our first proposition:

> I. Since economic behavior within broad social norms and statutes is determined by the marketplace, wages, and prices, the only way to advance oneself with some degree of self-decision and control is through *nonmarket transactions.* Thus, a feasible goal is to maximize (for each individual) either the number or expected value of nonmarket transactions subject to the initial allocation and consumption of goods as dictated by formal markets.

If property rights are somehow obscure or flexible in interpretation in some area of potential nonmarket transactions, then it pays (at least for individual gain) for the consumer (or producer) to exploit it. The long history of court cases on fee simple land entitlement, mineral rights, nuisance provisions, zoning laws and variances, special tax rebates, and practically every legal or jurisdictional decision can be traced to origins of nonmarket transactions. The market exists for establishing legal rights with regard to real property, but excluded are political patronage and nonrecorded payments (commonly described rather homily as *side-payments* in economic circles, where the word *bribe* is disliked). Anyone who has attended a county planning commission meeting on a zoning variance, observed the implicit relationships among judges and lawyers that decorate our courtrooms, or read about organized crime will not swallow easily the notion that nonmarket transactions do *not* pay. We all know that they do. Have you ever invested in stock without *inside* information, whether or not correct? Even economists cannot be categorized as fools in this sense. Those who know, win. But it might be added that if everyone knows, no one can win. Thus, we conclude that nonmarket transactions pay for those exploiting them. In a society dominated by a competitive ethic and pecking order with little chance for breaking out, which does the rebel do? If he is naïve, like Abbie Hoffman before 1971, he asserts "goodness" and revolutionary change. If not, if he lacks "Consciousness III," we would assert that if he were a self-maximizer he would ascribe to our second rather loose proposition:

> II. It is always in the interest of the self-maximizing individual in a market economy with incompletely specified property and user rights or differences in information available to create as many (in terms of value) nonmarket transactions as are possible.[24]

Given acceptance of this proposition, we should like to offer a third. What are the nature and textural content of nonmarket transactions? Some, if not all, are physical, social, biological, or other forms of interdependencies among individuals or groups where the market has, at least momentarily, overlooked such relationships. By definition, these are externalities of either a positive or negative sort.[25] Violent and nonviolent crimes are livid examples of such nonmarket interdependencies:

> III. There will be a tendency in market economies with incomplete information and unclear ownership rights for the value associated with the appearance of nonreciprocal external diseconomies and economies to be maximized.

Let us take E. J. Mishan's case of the individual's power lawnmower that disturbs a neighbor. The structure of incentives is as follows: Unless there are adequately specified nuisance ordinances on decibels of noise emission, it pays for the individual to mow his lawn in the *middle of the night* to create the strongest possible incentive for the neighbor to negotiate and offer a bribe. (We presume here that the neighbor cannot effectively retaliate in kind.) Once the "externality" appears or the neighbor is told of its potential existence, there is, of course, a transfer of wealth and consumption possibilities.

The transfer of wealth and consumption by "creating" external diseconomies for others needs little further elaboration. Creating these diseconomies, in effect, means "producing" a new good (or bad). The problem of such an incentive structure is its inherent ability to negate any efficiency associated with market economies. If through contrivance one man can impose an external diseconomy on other men knowing the bargaining will make him better off, he clearly will do so if he is a self-maximizing type described in the traditional economic literature. If all men attempt to impose external diseconomies on others for their own gain, then it cannot be said that the economy will be efficient since such imposed costs are market distorting, and there is no organized market to trade external diseconomies. As Kenneth Arrow recognized, there are not enough market traders, including third parties, to sustain efficiency (with only the externality generator and recipient) when there are information costs and inherent differences among intellectual capabilities.[26]

These very brief remarks lead us to the following proposition:

> IV. With incentives to generate external diseconomies and other potential nonmarket transactions in consumption or use of resources, the following efficiency principle will tend to be approximated: No one can be made more miserable without making someone else less miserable. This might aptly be called the Pareto misery principle.

To see why this principle has some validity, note that a self-oriented individual will maximize the value, to him, of participating in organized markets and creating nonmarket transactions. Taking this "production possibility" set for creating external diseconomies, he will select only those with a higher return than he could earn by engaging in market transactions. But by so doing, he will maximize the "cost" to others in that his gain is someone else's loss. All individuals acting independently to maximize the "cost" imposed on others will yield a "maximum" of these "costs" or payments to society, that is, by selecting only highly productive external effects. The recipient of contrived or inadvertent external diseconomies will undertake defensive expenditures or pay bribes until the usual marginal conditions of efficiency are fulfilled. Thus, the recipient's "cost" will be minimized for each external diseconomy, and an "efficient" pattern of external diseconomies will emerge.

But if external diseconomies, in terms of value to the generator, are maximized in the society and if they are efficiently contended with by recipients, then we have a mirror image of consumption theory and Pareto efficiency. That is, instead of allocation of a good to its highest value use with its production costs minimized, we have allocation of a "bad" (external diseconomy) to its most costly impact, with the impact being minimized in terms of recipient cost as well as production costs. The economy, of course, is efficient but efficient only in providing misery. To paraphrase a well-known precursor of this theory: *Every individual necessarily labours to render the annual external costs of the society as great as he can. He generally, indeed, neither intends to promote the public misery nor knows how much he is promoting it. He intends only his own gain, and he is in this, as in many other cases, led by an Invisible Foot to promote an end which was no part of his intention. Nor is it any better for society that it was no part of it. By pursuing his own interest he frequently promotes social misery more effectually than when he really intends to promote it.*

External economies also offer incentives for individual gain, but the incentive structure here is basically different than for external diseconomies. Without liability or nuisance rules that establish social responsibility, it is in the interest of both generator and recipient to negotiate on external diseconomies. However, with external economies the recipient gains more by attempting to be a free rider except, perhaps, at the margin. In consequence, the incentive for creating or producing external economies is less than that for external diseconomies, except perhaps for altruists. The policy presumptions for resolving external diseconomies by assigning property rights or using governmental taxing and subsidy powers are doomed to failure or, at best, limited success unless the viewpoint of contextual wholes is adopted and one analyzes all aspects of the underlying *incentive* structure in the competitive system. It appears to be an impossible task to develop legal rights on every type of physical, biological, and social interdependence, or a rational taxation system that will eliminate external diseconomies. Rather, to move toward a better efficiency of the economic system the incentive system itself needs alteration.

We have three suggestions utilizing the contextualist approach as regards resolution of externalities problems in consumption or use of goods. (1) The appearance of externalities should be recognized as a never-ending process unless certain types of external diseconomy generating laws or ethical values are introduced to stop it. (2) Laws and property rights systems not only must be designed to control behavior within the market but also must consider expectations on the value of nonmarket transactions. (3) Nonmarket economics should be concerned not only with the question of liability, which the rich can bid against, but also with the contextual content of rules systems, liability, and the basic incentive structure for nonmarket transactions.

Consumption and Externalities

Consumption to a rat or lemming is another ounce of grain. To humans in modern societies it is another XKE, Firebird, solid waste compacter, or deviant sexual act. All are costly and all are status symbols, either displayed in the parking lot or in the office for discreet viewers. All contribute to the GNP, but in a success-oriented economy, it is hard to argue that each contributes to the social welfare. With gross national product per capita of more than $5,600 and gross national waste per capita of about 11,000 pounds per year per capita, it is not hard to contrast us with Nero. What we have is too much to be appreciated, beyond adequate perception yet within our purchasing power at least partially because of the exploitative use of externalities. Our consumption is almost totally conditioned by an insatiable desire for individual advancement, invidious comparisons of the class immediately above, or a rat-like attempt at domination and sublimation. The result is a spiraling set of preferences conditioned by the surreal acts in TV and movies portraying desirable consumption. Everyone should have his (or her) San Simeon or Hyannis Port. What a Martian would perceive is not only an infinite desire for goods but an infinite desire gone mad! There is no longer a value to solitude or individual contemplation, health or human creativity.

Consumption formerly meant food, clothing, shelter, and a few amenities. No longer. Anyone traveling the streets of Georgetown or Beverly Hills will realize that consumption in the GNP accounts is a misnomer. Conspicuous demonstration, perhaps, but not consumption. What we see is a consumption pattern oriented toward externality yielding services of the following kinds: drugs; specialized prostitution currently called "massage parlors"; fast cars on crowded freeways; guarded apartments with stereos, educational television, and other equipment which make the home a self-contained "cultural center"; and a renewal of individual rights toward the principle of maximization of individual nonmarket negotiation or involuntary exchange. What we suggest is that, at least partially, the realization of the value that can be obtained from external diseconomies or other forms of involuntary exchanges has swamped the earlier value of external economies and cooperation. This change in incentive structure manifests itself in what is consumed and how it is consumed.

Conclusion

The contextualist framework does not provide any *a priori*, dogmatic answers to the problems of externalities. Yet, it does provide a frame of reference which seems to us to offer greater potential for coming to grips with the issues. The starting point in contextualist analysis is the recognition that both consumption and production are social activities involving the entire physical and social milieu and all persons within it. The basic cause of externalities is that, whereas the costs and benefits of economic activity are social, the laws of private property bestow the privileges and benefits on particular individuals while imposing only a part (and often a small part) of the social costs on these same individuals.

Moreover, the contextualist analysis of change stresses the fact that quantitative increases inevitably result in qualitative changes. The rates at which additional consumption will add to social benefits and social costs are bound to change. Furthermore, the changes will be qualitative; totally new kinds of social costs will be encountered. Some may involve irreversible damages. Orthodox economics has tended to ignore the ethical problems of inequality in the belief that continued economic growth would make everyone better off and obscure the inequities of the system.

Finally, contextualism rejects the notion that the government is a neutral *deus ex machina* which can be expected to charge excise taxes, bestow subsidies, or establish new markets which will cure the problems. The prime responsibility of government is the enforcement of private property rights, one of the most important sources of externalities. By forcing those who derive disproportionate benefits from production, by virtue of their ownership of capital, to pay a larger share of the social costs of production, the government would be biting the hand that holds its financial reins. If the bite were severe (as it would have to be to make significant progress in cleaning up our environment), the audacious administration that initiated this precipitous action surely would find that its financial support (the lifeblood of American politics) would be swiftly withdrawn.

The contextualist approach does show that to obtain satisfactory solutions to the problem of externalities there must be some way of altering the powers of private property and the vested interests. This may necessitate sweeping changes in the nature of property rights—the very foundation of a capitalist economy. The alternatives are violent self-destruction or the slower societal suicide of environmental destruction brought on by acquisitive, lemming maximizers.

Notes

1. Stephen C. Pepper, *World Hypotheses* (Berkeley: The University of California Press, 1961), pp. 1-348.
2. Ibid., pp. 186-231.
3. Ibid., pp. 232-79.
4. David Hamilton, *Evolutionary Economics* (Albuquerque: The University of New Mexico Press, 1970), pp. 19-20.
5. Ibid., p. 22.
6. Milton Friedman, "On Paul Samuelson," *Newsweek*, 9 November 1970, p. 80.
7. The following three paragraphs are from the introduction to E. K. Hunt

and Jesse G. Schwartz, *Critique of Economic Theory* (London: Penguin Books, 1972).
8. *The Portable Veblen*, ed. Max Lerner (New York: The Viking Press, 1948), pp. 232–33.
9. Pepper, *Hypotheses*, p. 233.
10. The terminology used is Pepper's.
11. Jean-Paul Sartre, *Search for a Method* (New York: Random House, 1963), p. 25.
12. Pepper, *Hypotheses*, p. 208.
13. See, for example, Kelvin Lancaster, *Mathematical Economics* (New York: The MacMillan Co., 1968), pp. 174–83. For a strong objection to this set of premises, see the article by R. C. d'Arge and K. C. Kogiku, "Economic Growth and the Environment," *Review of Economic Studies* (forthcoming).
14. Alvin L. Marty, "The Neoclassical Theorem," *American Economic Review* 54, no. 6 (December 1964): 1027.
15. By using the adjective *direct* we are following E. J. Mishan, "The Postwar Literature on Externalities: An Interpretative Essay," *Journal of Economic Literature* 9 (March 1971): 2. Excluded are "indirect effects" which obtain through changes in relative prices (or other means) in a Walrasian general equilibrium system.
16. Ibid., p. 17.
17. Ibid.
18. J. De V. Graaff, *Theoretical Welfare Economics* (Cambridge: The University Press, 1957), p. 142. For a survey of the objections to the neoclassical treatment of externalities see S. K. Nath, *A Reappraisal of Welfare Economics* (New York: Augustus Kelley, 1969); R. C. d'Arge and E. K. Hunt, "Environmental Pollution, Externalities and Conventional Economic Wisdom: A Critique," *Environmental Affairs* 1 (June 1971); and Hunt and Schwartz, *Critique.*
19. See d'Arge and Hunt, "Environmental Pollution."
20. Joan Robinson, *Economic Philosophy* (Garden City: Doubleday, Anchor Books, 1964), p. 64.
21. S. S. Alexander, "Human Values and Economists' Values," in Sidney Hook, ed., *Human Values and Economic Policy* (New York: New York University Press, 1967), p. 111.
22. See d'Arge and Hunt, "Environmental Pollution."
23. There have been, of course, a few extreme exceptions. Edward I once executed a coal burning violator in his politically and socially expedient but economically unsound attempt to reduce air pollutant emissions in London. The attempt had no long-term impact.
24. Actually, Samuelson and others forecast this proposition in some sense with their recognition that any public good would involve problems of "free riders" unless preferences were sufficiently altruistic.
25. For an argument that Coase and his predecessors had, at least implicitly, informational barriers or costs in mind in defining the *existence* of externalities, see R. C. d'Arge and W. D. Schulze, "The Coase Proposition, Information, and Long Run Equilibrium," *American Economic Review* (forthcoming).

26. See Kenneth Arrow, "The Organization of Economic Activity: Issues Pertinent to the Choice of Market Versus Non-Market Allocation," in *The Analysis and Evaluation of Public Expenditures: The PPB System*, Sub-Committee on Economy in Government, Joint Economic Committee, U.S. Congress, vol. 1 (Washington, D.C.: U.S. Government Printing Office, 1969).

Part V

Toward a Meaningful Political Economy

Introduction

One of the critical questions of methodology concerns the scope and central problem of economics. Is economics to be the study of markets and marketlike mechanisms? Or is it to be a political economy based on a broader conception of what the economy is all about and centering, say, on power and legal-economic interrelations? Orthodoxy largely is economics; heterodoxy largely is political economy. According to some heterodox economists, however, orthodox economics is in reality a subtle form of political economy: concentration upon a narrow economics means a concentration upon voluntary exchange in the market. This, in turn, means the selective creation of principles for the guidance of government that function, among other things, to protect the systemic distribution in a business society. The articles in this section are concerned with the creation and practice of political economy much more directly, although there are serious problems in its realization.

Joel Jalladeau examines the neoclassical paradigm as normal economic science and finds that its relative narrowness neglects the theory of the economic system *qua* system and socioeconomic change. He discusses instead a second tradition that explores the relations between the economy narrowly considered and the larger society. He holds that traditional economic theory and the theory of systemic evolution are less alternatives and more complementary avenues of study. The real need is to develop a science of the social system and its evolution, a difficult but not a futile endeavor.

Robert L. Heilbroner asserts the necessity for economics accurately to depict the structure and tendencies of the modern economy and reliably to guide efforts at improvement. He finds that conventional economics neglects man as both the product and producers of social forces that transcend the market and individual choice and thereby neglects political and sociological reality. (It can be argued, of course, that conventional economics does not neglect these topics but instead attempts to channel them in preferred directions.[1]) Heilbroner maintains that conventional economics is irrelevant in several senses: it fails to provide deep criticism of our present social and economic order in the face of serious difficulties; certain problems are not amenable to the limited tools of economic theory; and important problems are neglected through the omission of the political and social attributes of economic variables. The crux of the relevance issue, according to Heilbroner, is that economic systems are not merely functional with regard to the production of goods but are frameworks for the division of social prestige and power and mechanisms for the attainment of some postulated social end. Although Marxism has certain attributes centering upon its holistic view of the economy, he finds that it, too, is largely irrelevant as a political economics. Its key concepts are useless, its handling of technology is inadequate, its rigid *a priori* attitudes regarding classes and the state leads to fallacious conclusions, and, although it has provided many important insights, it has produced no satisfactory alternative paradigm.

Heilbroner calls for the creation of a political economics. Such a discipline would introduce political variables into economic theory and thereby explicitly incorporate the tensions and stresses of privilege, status, distribution, power, and change as well as formulate a theory of the economic behavior of the state. He would undertake this in a way that does not define the system on its own terms. The result would be greater realism regarding the mutual interdependence of public and private sectors. Such a discipline would recognize the centrality of the social valuational process and replace the conventional deterministic model with analysis of the really distinctive aspect of the social process, namely, social volition. Such a discipline would be, self-consciously and therefore candidly, an instrumentalist or goal-oriented science. Heilbroner defends the rationale for such a political economics against several charges. For example, against the charge that the intrusion of values would destroy its work as a science, he responds that traditional theory is not value free, because it accepts the ends and values implicit in the so-called laissez faire world and is drenched in unrecognized value judgments regarding the legitimacy of the existing institutional order, the distribution of power, and state of the economic process. He maintains that the scientific character of analysis is not a function of its being value free but of the character of its methods and that unmasking the frailty of the goal-choosing process will bring into the open what often has been a *sub rosa* process. What Lekachman calls the guilty little secret of power or what Schmid refers to as the process of determining whose interests are to count will be brought out into the open, and goal selection will be elevated to its proper, deliberative status rather than remaining latent in the exercise of asymmetrical power. Heilbroner also defends his instrumentalist approach against the charge that it will, by enlarging deliberative controls, open the way to totalitarianism. His response is that instrumentalism will clarify the now hidden opportunity costs of opting for a given degree of behavioral freedom or for a particular set of rights governing the distribution of behavioral freedom.[2]

Henry Oliver explores some of the problems that beset the practice of a meaningful political economy. He analyzes the ways in which questions about the relationships between economic and political systems differ and the methods of reasoning employed in analyses of these relationships. He stresses the great variation, open-endedness, and expansiveness of the questions and answers that can be posed about the interrelations of economic and politico-legal systems. Among the sources of differences are the direction of the flow of causation, the flexibility of the concepts of economic and political systems, concrete versus abstract environments, variable routes of the flow of causation, and others. The article is a sophisticated and comprehensive treatment of a complex and difficult subject.

The exchange of correspondence between James M. Buchanan and the editor reveals conflicting interpretations and positions on fundamental issues involved in creating and practicing political economy. These issues center on the meaning of positive versus normative work and their relation to the status of the status quo, all with regard to the economic role of government. The letters also present different attitudes toward the character of reality and the possible, toward continuity versus change, and about the significance of voluntary contractual change as the preeminent mode of altering the status quo. The correspondents believe that the problems with which they deal, and on which they cannot quite agree, are central to political economy.

Raymond S. Franklin and William K. Tabb advocate radical political economics as a viable form for political economy. The article articulates the major tenets and general orientation of radical political economics and its possibilities for application. Not unexpectedly, the authors are concerned with political and private economic power, income and wealth distribution, imperialism, market structure and stratification, and several recent and contemporary problems of the U.S. economy. In their view, radical political economy would live up to its name and support a fundamental change of the system.[3]

Arthur Schweitzer's article treats the work of Max Weber and Adolph Lowe (whose instrumentalist approach is used by Heilbroner). Both men are concerned with the political economy of the goal formation process in society and therefore with what Schweitzer calls social economics. Social economics is concerned with the penetration of noneconomic factors into the economy. It is through the lines of penetration that socioeconomic goals and attitudes as well as rules of conduct govern economic performance. Production, Schweitzer insists, is not a matter of purely isolated individual acts but depends upon and arises out of definite social relationships. These make their presence felt through several major social penetrators: recognition, or mutual or shared respect and expectations; emotions; institutional regularities, such as usage, custom, and constellations of interests; and codes of conduct, such as fashion, convention, and law. Society, as a process of goal formation and therefore an intrusion into economic life, is also a system of control, that is, the locus of forces responsible for the governing and channeling of interaction. Individual choice is conjoined with variable social determinants or regulators that constrain and channel individual choice. It is out of this process that private preferences and social goals are interactively formed. Part of Schweitzer's analysis echoes the early work of Adam Smith on the operation of approbation and disapprobation in the formation of social rules and, thereby, goals. In Schweitzer's view, political economy is a part of a larger social economy.

In the final review article, the editor returns to the problems raised in the correspondence between Buchanan and Samuels, in particular with regard to a book authored by Buchanan. He questions Buchanan's positive analysis in the light of a book by Arthur S. Miller that explores the power structure of the corporate system and that seems to limit severely Buchanan's argument. He also questions Buchanan's strategic argument regarding problems posed by its efforts to circumscribe the role of legal change. As in the correspondence, fundamental questions of positive and normative political economy are at stake. Buchanan and Samuels present alternative and quite different pictures of the nature of the political economy, and they do so using substantially different methodologies, raising many of the problems treated in earlier sections of this book.

Notes

1. *See* chapters 16, 17, and 20 in *The Chicago School of Political Economy* (East Lansing, Mich.: Division of Research, Graduate School of Business Administration, Michigan State University, 1976).
2. *See also* the Note by C.E. Ayres, September 1971.
3. *See* Frank Roosevelt, "Market Socialism: A Humane Economy?," December 1969, and the exchange between Martin Bronfenbrenner and Roosevelt, June 1971.

Restrained or Enlarged Scope of Political Economy? A Few Observations

Joel Jalladeau

W. E. Kuhn, translator

Today economics possesses the most elaborate theoretical structure of all the social sciences. But the change in name from *political economy* to *economic science* (economics) involves more than a semantic question. It is indicative of the transition from a social science to an ever more technical one; in other words, it manifests a more narrow focusing than originally, primarily with respect to the logic of resource and decision allocation, models of growth, and econometric studies.

In the scientific community a general consensus prevails concerning the theoretical foundations and the theoretical approach to economic problems. At the very time, however, when economic science is presenting its most brilliant appearance ever, a feeling of uneasiness regarding the actual condition of the discipline is manifested in the profession in two respects.

First, investigators have become less preoccupied with the discussion of the principal hypotheses and of their conformance to reality, and voices from among the most authoritative have arisen to issue forewarnings. Maurice Allais, for one, writes: "From the scientific point of view, incomparably greater care is brought to bear on the mathematical elaboration of models than on the discussion of their

---

The author is Maître Assistant, Faculty of Economic Sciences, University of Poitiers, France.

structure and of their hypotheses in the light of the analysis of facts."[1]

On a different level, Marxist economists, radicals of the New Left, and neoinstitutionalists protest against the narrowness of economics which tends to ignore the general movement of society. By confining itself to the more and more elaborate study of the mechanisms governing the functioning of a hypothetical economy, economics misses the dynamics of the evolution of contemporary societies. Now it so happens, as observed by Bernard Lassudrie-Duchêne,[2] that the absence of an economic interpretation of our times is deeply resented. Thus the problem of the aim of political economy, of its narrow or broad scope, is posed anew: Is it the theory of general equilibrium and/or study of the general movement of society?

Historically, political economy appears to have been a discipline of two traditions. Its major orientation has been economic theory, but a second orientation has focused on the theory of economic systems and of social change. Whereas the core component grew steadily richer and stronger and constituted the "normal" science, the second component became peripheral and gained the upper hand only after the inflexibility of the basic current of thought produced a vigorous protest.

The objective of this brief study is to assign to the second tradition of political economy its proper place in relation to the major tradition.

Normal Economic Science: The Neoclassical Paradigm

Thomas Kuhn, in *The Structure of Scientific Revolutions*,[3] examined the general conditions governing the extension of knowledge in the physical and natural sciences. Economists have been directed to examine their true science in the light of this new thesis.

Kuhn's Concept of Normal Science

Following Kuhn, every normal science is governed by a paradigm with, *inter alia,* the following properties: a "general metaphysical point of view" and a "universally recognized scientific activity." A paradigm provides the conceptual framework of scientific research; it delimits the nature of problems and the types of questions that can be grappled with; it determines the methods which can be utilized and the form in which the answers must be clothed in order that their validity can be ascertained. By furnishing to the investigator not merely a "map," but also "some of the directions essential for map-making," the paradigm exercises both a cognitive and a regulatory function.

Normalized science is not simply a fund of knowledge; as Kuhn specifies, the scientific community itself constitutes a social system. The researchers form a kind of "invisible college" founded in their commonly shared interests. They agree on the fundamental structure of their discipline, on the boundaries of their field of study, on the general theoretical approach to scientific problems, on the criteria used to validate their work. The members of the profession are the sole judges of the value of their scientific contributions. Standardized research favors the deepening and widening of knowledge pertaining to specific points rather than a fundamental questioning of the central theoretical core agreed upon by the community of scholars.

Application to Economics

If one transposes Kuhn's thesis to our discipline, he may join A. W. Coats in saying that, historically, political economy has been governed by a single paradigm: the theory of general equilibrium.[4]

The theory of economic equilibrium, as initially formulated by Léon Walras and in subsequent decades worked out minutely and elegantly by mathematical economists, has become, in G. L. S. Shackle's terminology,[5] the "Grand Theory" or the "Grand System of Economics," a fundamental theory which rests on two crucial suppositions: perfect competition and perfect rationality.

The paradigm rests on a strictly individualistic postulate, namely, that any and all conflicting components in the networks of relations between economic units and groups of economic units have been eliminated. Likewise, the stability of preferences constitutes a comfortable hypothesis. The economic system is conceived of as a self-regulating mechanism, with the role of government being most closely restricted and the interests of individual economic agents being well attuned to each other and to the general interest. This is a marvelously harmonious system.

Economic analysis applies itself foremost to questions of equilibrium and growth in an entirely mechanical fashion. Dynamics is thereby subjected to a strict limitation: Only those movements can be considered which can be integrated perfectly within the conceptual framework.

Economic theory, drawing its strength from a perfectly coherent perspective which rests on general equilibrium, thus establishes an intellectually irrefutable and enticing frame.

The analyst, by presupposing "a world governed exclusively according to economic logic,"[6] in which all similar agents evolve in a complete atomization of the economic sphere, in a way immunizes the theories which he designs against attacks from the world of reality.

The science of mechanics lends its configuration to economic science. This borrowing has allowed economics to make some extremely fruitful analytical advances: It is the asymptotic desire of every economist to arrive at formalized representations. Although the model building endeavor as such is praiseworthy, the economist may in the end become a victim of his own set of conceptual tools. With all due respect to the language of mathematics, it may be conducive to the study of only those questions which lend themselves to being treated with the technical instruments at our disposition, thereby conditioning the choice of factors which the analysis takes into account. Professor Germain Kreweras expresses the problem well: "In contemporary history we witness the institutional frameworks being modified with a rapidity that deters us more day by day from erecting on them the edifice of economic science."[7]

The formalization of economic relations constitutes an indispensable tool of coherent research and carries to its ultimate limit the advantage of logic. In the most extreme cases, however, it reduces to a "Ptolemaic economics,"[8] that is to say, to a continuous modification of variations and equations in areas of rapidly diminishing returns from the standpoint of knowledge as well as meaning. One is bound to encounter a kind of knowledge which is completely "esoteric."[9]

Mathematics is a highly appreciable servant, but a "very bad master,"[10] inasmuch as certain phenomena cannot be mastered by it. The economic and social totality is too rich. Yet, by virtue of the normalized character of the science, a question will be deemed economic only if it can be formulated in terms of the dominant paradigm. Neoclassical theory reasons in terms of stable structures. Relations of a type other than those of exchange are excluded therefrom. Its limitations stem from the fact that by reducing its subject matter to the calculus of economic efficiency, its field of inquiry is being cut off from its social substratum. Abstracting from the socioeconomic relations among the participants in the productive process is considered as "scientific advance" from a marginalist point of view, but as a "scientific retreat" from a Marxist point of view.[11]

Excluded from the "economy" are the mechanisms of want creation in a social system, the process by which preferences are formed, the distribution of power and its role in economic society, the interplay of social classes, the forces that tend to disrupt equilibrium, the conflicts, the contradictions, the structural changes. The examination of all these problems is abandoned to the other social sciences.

Normal economic science dodges the question of the evolution of systems, rejecting it as lying outside the scope of its scientific concerns.

It thereby bars itself as much from facing the problems of structural transformation in the industrialized economies as from tackling the question of the genesis of underdevelopment.[12] Conventional economics does not enlighten us to any great extent on these problems because they are thrust aside by the dominant paradigm.[13]

A theory of social change is tantamount to calling into question the invariance of structures in order to study the ongoing modification of structure versus mechanism. It is a matter of proposing a coherent explanatory system in terms of interdependence which cannot help but go beyond the traditional theoretical framework.

By abstracting from the relations between economy and society and by excluding from purview the genesis and the evolution of systems, the science of economics is losing its social status. In postulating a sociological void, it is ahistoric. But various currents of thought "in rebellion" have in the course of time attempted to restore to political economy the social status which it has lost by narrowing its focus and in the process becoming more and more a technique.

A Second Tradition: Relations between Economy and Society

The neoclassical conception which makes of economics the science of rational and efficient choice has meant, ever since *The Wealth of Nations*, an artificial restriction of the domain of the discipline. The great classical economists on the other side of the Channel adopted a broader perspective. It is above all the Marxist, historicist, and institutionalist movements which have emphasized the social nature of economic activity. However, certain neoclassical economists have greeted with enthusiasm the possibility of an economic sociology alongside economic theory.

For the representatives of this minor thought tradition the "noneconomic" factors—technology, institutions, classes, power, conflict—become the foundation stones of any theoretical structure.

Before examining in what terms to couch a theoretical approach to the problem of the relations between economy and society, a brief historical survey will permit placing this second tradition of political economy in proper perspective.

Economy and Society in the History of Economic Thought

John Stuart Mill, having studied the economic laws of a society which would undergo neither change nor motion, sought to state precisely "the economical condition of mankind as liable to change." This amounted to inquiring into such questions as the kinds of changes, the laws they follow, their ultimate directions, in other words, to uniting with the theory of equilibrium a theory of movement.[14]

In the end, Adam Smith, Thomas Malthus, David Ricardo, and Mill all examined the "uniformities of sequence" but took no unanimous position concerning the time of appearance of the stationary state and concerning whether or not the movement would be irreversible.

Karl Marx, in turn, in *Capital*, intended to "unveil the economic law of motion of modern society." For him, political economy was a "total science" ("science totale"),[15] the science of society in its historical development. The Marxist model of interpretation of the social system rests at once on both an economic and a sociological analysis tied closely together.[16] Political economy must reveal the true nature of the social relations of production in the contemplated social system. Viewed in this perspective, then, it is defined as the science of the social laws governing the production and distribution of the material means which serve to satisfy human wants.

The historical school, while clearly parting from the theory of historical materialism concerning the economic and social evolution, investigates "the laws of the historical development of nations" (á la Bruno Hildebrand). But in the 1870s, members of the younger branch of the historical school gave up the idea of deriving general laws of evolution, confining themselves to the study of facts and institutions and devoting bulky monographs to this task.

At the turn of the century Werner Sombart and Max Weber developed their famous propositions concerning the emergence and the growth of capitalism, and in the first decades of the twentieth century the protest movement against an economics severely limited in its scope appeared in the United States in the guise of institutionalism.

W. C. Mitchell, a positivist and institutionalist, defined *economics* as the science of the behavior of men in the social activities directed to the satisfaction of their wants. Its principal aim is to examine the interactions of the different economic institutions, to ponder their origin, to sketch the changes which they undergo. But it remained for Thorstein Veblen to lay bare the internal logic of the functioning of U.S. capitalism. His famous dichotomy between "Industry" and "Business" was meant to play as decisive a role as the Marxian concept of the mode of production.

Although this economic sociology has held mainly the attention of the heterodox economists, it is not a complete stranger to the concerns of orthodox economists.[17] Thus, at a time when, with the rising tide of marginalism, the science of economics contracted its domain, some from among the most eminent economists did not exclude the study of the economic order as a matter of secondary importance.

The Theory of Political Economy by W. S. Jevons is essentially an essay elaborating a pure theory of economic statics. Jevons thought, however, that it may be "legitimate to develop the branches of economic dynamics on the foundation of what has not been taken into account." In his Preface to the second edition (1879) he states the idea precisely by admitting the need for creating "a science of the development of economic forms and relations." Indeed, since a nation is not "a simple sum of individuals . . . but an organic whole held together by ties of infinite complexity," an economic sociology would be useful.[18]

As far as Carl Menger is concerned, there is a necessity to resort to a strictly individualistic ("atomistic") method of analysis. Wrongfully, the historicists have been led to maintain that the historical development of the economy should constitute the essence of economic science. The theoretical understanding of the origin and the changes of social structures is only a part of the science. It would be erroneous, however, not to recognize its import and its usefulness for grasping social phenomena in theoretical terms. This "comprehensive task of our science, relating to the formulation of the laws of economic development, although secondary, is by no means unjustified." Theoretical research must not neglect it, although it is the minor component of political economy.[19]

According to Friedrich von Wieser, the individualistic dogma does not permit accounting for the phenomenon of power. As a result, modern economic theory "requires a more profound theory of society." This means that a political economy "valid for our times is inconceivable without a social theory that is consistent with the fact of power."[20]

Joseph Schumpeter likewise was interested in economic sociology, this complementary field of economic analysis. In *Capitalism, Socialism, and Democracy* he envisaged the possibility of the evolution of capitalism not only by founding the analysis of it on the influence exerted by the economic base on the social whole, but also by strongly emphasizing the reverse impact of the institutional and mental structures on the prevailing economic order.[21]

Although this broadened approach has been marked by some grossly mistaken ideas, and although all the currents of thought have not produced the unifying theory for which they were searching, the foregoing brief survey of economic thought has revealed the existence of a second tradition in political economy.

In Search of a Theoretical Approach

What theoretical approach might lend itself to the formulation of a theory of social change? The labors expended upon conceptualization are certain to discover the method which meshes it with the economic and social reality under consideration. Finding the appropriate language is bound up with the nature of the problem under investigation: the relations between economy and society.

The theories of evolution give an account of the sum total of the interactions of all socioeconomic phenomena. The crossing over from one system to another implies a dynamics of the social structures and of the institutions. Such a theory must attempt to establish the conditions which govern the transition; their discovery must, in principle, make possible the reconstruction of a system's origin and the forecasting of its future development. To this end, autonomous concepts whose validity rests on their internal coherence must be worked out.

The study of a complex social system consists of an inquiry into the mode of connection between the different constituent subsystems. Explicitly or implicitly, the writers resort to the definition of a certain number of levels. The basement of the system is made up of the technico-economic floor (the productive forces of Marx). The socioeconomic level is characterized by the dominant social relations. The psychosocial level is defined by the motivations, behavior patterns, and lived values, while the level of expressed values (law, philosophy, politics) reveals the ideological forces. A privileged level gives the system its coherence. In the Marxist system, it is the social mode of production (productive forces and relations of production) which determines the essence and the structure of society. In a non-Marxist logical order, it is the levels of psychosocial forces and of expressed values, animated by the technico-economic dimension, which are given primacy.

Rather than interpret the relations of economy and society in terms of social relations of production, non-Marxist authors analyze the direct and indirect effects of the development of the productive forces on the social whole with the help of "transdisciplinary concepts."[22] Such concepts manifest, by themselves, hypotheses concerning the liaison between social forms and economic structures and involve the existence of a logic which is implicit in modern societies. The modern industrial system, for example, is being analyzed by contemporary institutionalists with the aid of concepts such as "logic of the industrialization process," "technostructure," and activities of the "instrumental type" versus activities of the "cermonial type"; associated with these concepts is a study of motivations. The interplay of propulsive and braking structures accelerates or retards the social evolution. Technology is, of course, the dynamic element, while the process of institutionalization in its entirety, oriented as it is to the past, constitutes the retarding element of social change. In this perspective, the interaction of structures leads, in constrast with the Marxist analysis, to an institutional "possibilism."

Thus, the schematized interpretation of economic and social processes gives rise to meaningful notions, brings to the fore characteristic relationships. These guiding principles aspire to making possible a better perception of the stage of evolution of the contemplated societies, but they may appear to be lacking in rigor. G. L. Back,[23] evaluating recent radical economic literature, holds the view that it proposes a new perception of reality, although not a substitute paradigm, as it is not clear how such a theory can be tested scientifically.

François Perroux,[24] in turn, some twenty years ago already had specified the conditions necessary for the validation of a theory of economic evolution. It should account for the transformation of structures of the same organizational type and for the transition from one type of organization to another. It should indicate how and why the succession of organizational types takes place according to the uniformities which can be set forth and verified with a sufficient degree of probability; it is on these terms that they might gain the rank of scientific propositions.

In attempting to explain how a society affected by qualitative changes, in particular, can pass from one stage to another, any evolutive model can be given an exact form only with difficulty. The model constitutes a specific thematic representation, and its understanding requires an independent effort of conceptual elaboration. By dint of their object as well as their representations, economic analysis and analysis of the relations between economy and society are not located on the same ground. That a theory of social systems does not take the same form and exhibit the same rigor as does normal economic science does not imply that it be supererogatory. Unlike current Marxist thought, contemporary institutionalism, for example, is certainly still far from offering a developed body of economic and sociological concepts. Even if a number of these theories are controversial, they nevertheless have the merit of inquiring into the direction of social change and even into the laws of economic evolution.

And the quest for these laws is "no less indispensable for being difficult if one does not have a prejudicial disclosure of the direction of the evolution."[25]

Although knowledge is of a different order than reality, it is, nevertheless, apprehension of the concrete. One must not "want to maintain a theory at all costs and make of it a Procrustean bed for the problems which transcend its field of application."[26] To recognize the difficulty of laying the foundations for theories of systems does not prove at all the futility of the step. A concept is a tool of understanding, the range of its validity residing in its explanatory power, in its capacity to apprehend the socioeconomic reality. In the final analysis, the problem is placed on the level of choosing which approach to retain: Marxist economic and sociological categories on the one hand, transdisciplinary concepts on the other. And on this there may be a legitimate divergence of views.

Neoclassical analysis constitutes the fundamental theory of the economic calculus, but it does not illuminate the relations between economy and society. Is it not possible to admit to an excess with regard to economic logic? A surplus which might perhaps be suitably expressed in a nonformalized language without eliminating the legitimacy of the query and the exigency provoking it?

That economic analysis in the narrow sense by virtue of its partiality leaves outside its field of observation a whole dimension of economic and social reality is not in itself open to criticism. The difficulty lies in the fact, however, that, considered as "normal" science, it becomes the one and only approach and path by which to attack the problems. The phenomena of power, class structure, conflict, and economic change which cannot be expressed in terms of the privileged paradigm have remained outside the scope of economics *qua* science.

Any theory aspiring to the rank of a paradigm will find it all the more difficult to assert itself the more it detaches itself from the logicomathematical method with a view of building upon a sociologicoeconomic vision, that is to say, on a focusing in depth which transgresses the actual boundaries of the various scientific disciplines. It is not a question here of criticizing the formalizing theory built on mathematical models, but of searching scientifically for a more comprehensive body of knowledge concerning the relations between economy and society.

If there is little reason to expect that the interest for the approach and the methods of conventional economics will weaken in the near future, the establishment of new associations of economists such as the Association for Evolutionary Economics (neoinstitutionalists) and the Union for Radical Political Economics (New Left) reflects the growing sentiment of dissatisfaction which is developing in certain areas of the profession.

The objective of the Association for the Critique of the Economic and Social Sciences (Association pour la Critique des Sciences Economiques et Sociales), recently launched in France, is a telling one in this regard: "to regroup the laborers in the social sciences who question the political neutrality and objectivity of these sciences and who are conscious of a rupture between themselves and the dominant economic tradition."

This state of crisis of political economy has led Professors Gunnar Myrdal and Martin Bronfenbrenner to agree in their diagnosis of the course of research on the relations between economy and society. In the view of the former, in the next ten or fifteen years the insitutional approach should become again a sweeping tide.[27] The latter believes that if the change which has occurred in the intellectual climate of the profession maintains its momentum for an entire generation, it might well amount to a scientific revolution.[28]

Apart from the radical criticism of the hypotheses and theorems of the neoclassical structure by Cambridge economists, beginning particularly with the concepts of capital and profit—a critique within the traditional field of economic knowledge—what is at issue here is the recognition of a socioeconomic research approach which takes into account a whole series of problems that so long have been considered "noneconomic," even "nonscientific."

The theoretical structure of a science depends upon the consensus of the interested scientific community; all the same, it appears that a theory of economic society and of social change is not incompatible with economic theory. The contemporary institutionalists do not gainsay the value of the fundamental economic calculus; what they dispute is that the axiomatic quality of the logicomathematical kind of reasoning constitutes all there is to political economy. According to certain Marxist authors such as Oskar Lange, and according to radicals of the New Left, economics, having lost its social nature, may be considered a "science of administration"; that is, it becomes an "auxiliary technique"—however important for the economic administration of a socialist economy—of Marxist political economy which must reveal the necessary consequences of the existing modes of production.

In conclusion, the reciprocal relations between the two traditions of political economy—economic theory and theory of social change—are less of an alternative than of a complementary nature.

Notes

1. "La théorie de l'équilibre général et de l'éfficacité maximale. Impasses récentes et nouvelles perspectives" [General equilibrium theory and maximum efficiency. Recent blind alleys and new perspectives], *Revue d'économie politique* (May/June 1971): 379. See also: Wassily Leontief, "Theoretical Assumptions and Nonobserved Facts," *American Economic Review* 61 (March 1971): 1-7; E. H. Phelps Brown, "The Underdevelopment of Economics," *Economic Journal* (March 1972): 1-10; and Norman Kaldor, "The Irrelevance of Equilibrium Economics," *Economic Journal* (December 1972): 1237-55.
2. Bernard Lassudrie-Duchêne, "Économie politique et sociologie" [Political economy and sociology], *Revue d'économie politique* (May/June 1968): 447.
3. (Chicago: University of Chicago Press, 1962). See also: D. F. Gordon, "The Role of the History of Economic Thought in the Understanding of Modern Economic Theory," *American Economic Review* 55 (May 1965): 119-27; and M. Bronfenbrenner, "The Structure of Revolutions in Economic Thought," *History of Political Economy* (Spring 1971): 136-52.
4. "Is There a Structure of Scientific Revolutions in Economics?" *Kyklos*, no. 2 (1969): 292.
5. *The Years of High Theory* (Cambridge: the University Press, 1967), pp. 4, 5, 286-96.
6. Roger Dehem, *L'utopie de l'économiste ou la rationalité économique collective* [The utopia of the economist or the collective economic rationality] (Paris: Dunod, 1969), p. 9.
7. "Dans l'histoire contemporaine nous voyons se modifier les cadres institutionnels avec une rapidité qui nous décourage chaque jour davantage de bâtir sur eux l'édifice de la science économique." "Science économique et mathématiques" [Economic science and mathematics], *Revue d'économie politique* (May/June 1968): 519.
8. Kenneth Boulding, "After Samuelson, Who Needs Adam Smith?" *History of Political Economy* (Fall 1971): 233.
9. Benjamin Ward, *What's Wrong With Economics?* (New York: Basic Books, 1972), pp. 12, 155.
10. Kenneth Boulding, *Economics as a Science* (New York: McGraw Hill, 1970), p. 115.
11. R. L. Meek, "Marginalism and Marxism," *History of Political Economy* (Fall 1972): 502.
12. Underdevelopment generally is considered as a contemporary phenomenon of the development of the industrialized economies. The theory of underdevelopment only can be a general theory. By the same token, it cannot be economic in the strict sense, that is, pertaining to economics

(reducing social facts to economic ones). Compare Samir Amin, *L'accumulation du capital à l'échelle mondiale* [The accumulation of capital on a global scale] (Paris: Anthropos publications, 1970); and Celso Furtado, *Développement et sous-développement* [Development and underdevelopment] and *Théorie du développement économique* [Theory of economic development] (Paris: Presses Universitaires de France, 1966; 1970).

13. Michel de Vroey presents "A Sociological Explanation for the Predominance of the Neo-Classical Paradigm in the Science of Economics" in *Proceedings of the Institute of Applied Economic Science* (August 1972): 1655-1702. He develops the idea that the logic of explanatory fertility ("la logique de la fécondité explicative") is not the only criterion to guide the development of science, which is equally influenced by factors outside the realm of knowledge.
14. *Principles of Political Economy*, in "Collected Works of John Stuart Mill," vol. 3 (Toronto: University of Toronto Press, 1965), p. 705.
15. Henri Guitton, *L'objet de l'économie politique* [The aim of political economy] (Paris: Rivière Publications, 1951), pp. 91-92.
16. For an examination of the economic categories of Marx, see Jean Ullmo, "Sur quelques concepts marxistes" [On some Marxist concepts], *Revue Economique* (January 1973): 109-38.
17. Warren J. Samuels, "The Scope of Economics Historically Considered," *Land Economics* (August 1972): 248.
18. W. S. Jevons, *La théorie de l'économie politique* [The theory of political economy] (Paris: Giard et Brière, 1909), pp. 3, 12, and *The Principles of Sciences* (New York: Dover Publications), p. 761.
19. Carl Menger, *Problems of Economics and Sociology* (Urbana: University of Illinois Press, 1963), pp. 117, 144, 147, 150, 119.
20. Friedrich von Wieser, *Social Economics*, Reprints of Economic Classics (New York: Augustus M. Kelley, 1967), pp. 11, 154, 319, 320, 158.
21. Pareto, the theoretician of pure economics, resorted to sociological categories in order to accommodate the nonlogical actions (residues and derivations) and exhibited in his treatise of general sociology the idea of an equilibrium of the social system.
22. Lassudrie-Duchêne, "Économie politique et sociologie," pp. 427, 444-47.
23. Symposium: "Economics of the New Left—Comment," *Quarterly Journal of Economics* (November 1972): 634.
24. *Les comptes de la nation* [The national accounts] (Paris: Presses Universitaires de France, 1949), p. 44.
25. Jacques Austruy, "Marginalia. Domaine et méthodes de la science économique" [Marginalia. Scope and methods of economic science], *Revue d'économie politique* (June 1969): 800-17. Research of this law is indispensable "surtout si elle est difficile à moins d'avoir la révélation préjudicielle du sens de l'évolution."
26. Furtado, *Development*, p. 78.
27. Gunnar Myrdal, "How Scientific Are the Social Sciences?" *Proceedings of the Institute of Applied Economic Science*, series H.S., no. 14 (August 1972): 1483.
28. M. Bronfenbrenner, "Radical Economics in America: A 1970 Survey," *Journal of Economic Literature* (September 1970); reproduced in *Problèmes économiques*, 30 December 1971, p. 3.

On the Possibility of a Political Economics

Robert L. Heilbroner

This essay is prompted by a profound sense of dissatisfaction with the state of contemporary economics, a dissatisfaction that finds its expression in the charge, voiced not only by a large number of students but by a growing body of economists, that conventional economic thought lacks "relevance" to the problems of our times. By this I believe most critics mean that conventional economics serves neither to depict accurately the structure or the tendencies of modern economic society, nor to guide reliably efforts to improve it. If this charge is true – and I believe that in large measure it *is* – an examination of the reasons for this lack of relevance would surely seem a matter of some importance. To provide such an examination is one purpose of this paper.

But I have a further end in mind, beyond a critique of conventional economic analysis. With all the risks that such an enterprise entails, I wish to use the occasion to suggest the direction in which I think that analysis must move if economics is to regain a sense of relevance. It should hardly come as a surprise that this direction is political – using the word in the broadest Aristotelian sense – for this is no more than to assert that the missing element in conventional analysis is any systematic consideration of man as the product and the producer of social forces other than those that can

The author is Professor of Economics in the New School for Social Research. *He wishes to thank Peter L. Bernstein, John Evans, Eugene Epstein, Arthur Ford, Stephen Hymer, Edward J. Nell, Frank Roosevelt, David Schwartzman, Thomas Vietorisz and, especially Adolph Lowe for their critique of an earlier version of this manuscript. An abbreviated version of this paper appeared in the Fall 1970 issue of The Public Interest.*

be detected by the narrow wave lengths of economic vision. To put it differently, what is required to rescue economics from a condition that I have described as "rigor, but alas, also mortis"[1], is to join the dimensions of political and sociological reality onto the flat-land models through which conventional economics seeks to explicate the nature of the existing social order. Hence my call for a "political economics", the nature of which I shall try to clarify as a second main purpose of this essay.

IRRELEVANCE – A PROBLEM OF SUBJECT MATTER

My aim is clearly an ambitious one, despite the cautious phrasing of my title. Tactically and strategically, then, I think it would be well to begin with the least troublesome aspect of the problem, by examining precisely what we mean when we claim that conventional economics is not "relevant" to the contemporary world. As we shall quickly see, the meaning of that critical word is neither simple nor single-valued, and a study of its definitions will lead us rapidly in the direction of the more difficult issues with which we must finally come to grips.

The first definition of irrelevance is perhaps the one that most closely expresses the impatience of many students with the discipline. It is the failure of the great majority of academic economists (as contrasted with "economics") to interest themselves in any deep criticism of our present social and economic order. A few instances may give substance to that general charge. One of them concerns the absence of professional economic interest in the phenomenon called "imperialism". Between 1950 and 1969, American direct foreign investment increased from less than $12 billions to over $65 billions, and the volume of sales of these foreign branches and subsidiaries ($120 billion in 1966) has mounted until, in Servan-Schreiber's well-known phrase, "Fifteen years from now it is quite possible that the world's third greatest industrial power, just after the United States and Russia, will not be Europe, but *American Industry in Europe.*"[2]

Whatever the accuracy of this prediction, there can be no doubt as to the importance of the American foreign economic expansion. Yet, a student of our times who depended for his knowledge of current economic trends on the main journals or books produced by the economics profession would be almost totally unaware of it. So far as I am aware, no analysis of the "imperial phenomenon" is to be found in the normal range of the professional literature. Until very recently, our knowledge of the extent, nature or consequences of the

American hegemony in foreign trade and investment, both in the underdeveloped and the developed world, has been gained almost entirely from Marxian economists or journalists.

There are other neglected subjects of similar importance. Poverty and environmental decay are probably the most striking. There is today a considerable discussion of poverty and ecology in the economic journals and scholarly books. But I think it is a fair charge to levy against the profession that neither of these critical issues first emerged as a consequence of its own researches, but rather from the inquiries of independent investigators, or from the actual disturbances caused by poverty and pollution themselves.[3]

THE THRALLDOM OF TECHNIQUE

The roster of ignored subjects could be easily expanded. What concerns us here, however, is not to chastize the profession, but to inquire into the reasons for this striking lack of interest in "relevant" issues. There are, I believe, two answers – one subtle, but easy to expound, another obvious, but not so easy to write about.

The first has to do with the current hegemony of the scientific method, or rather, with a particular model of that method that stresses avoidance of explicit value judgments and dependence on relationships capable of rigorous expression, preferrably mathematical notation. This particular paradigm of the scientific method has proved the most powerful intellectual tool that man has so far invented for the control of nature, and it is not surprising that economists should have borrowed it to forge similar tools for the control of society.[4]

The difficulty, however, is that this paradigm, applied to the field of social problems, tends to rule out of bounds those kinds of issues that resist accurate measurement, or that lend themselves only awkwardly or not at all to mathematical representation, or that contain a central and irrepressible value consideration. In a word, it tends to rule out most "political" matters. When confronted with their failure to initiate an examination of problems such as those mentioned above, most economists will reply that they have no "technique" capable of handling such problems, an answer that would imply that the paradigm itself may be a serious limitation to economic understanding. Instead, we find that the paradigm is unquestioningly retained, while those problems that do not yield to it tend to be relegated to the second rank of importance, or better yet, pushed off in the general direction of some other discipline.

So much has been written on the dangers inherent in the

thralldom of technique that I need not rehearse this familiar subject here.[5] Let me only add one remark of a general nature. It is that economists are apt to overlook that the powerful models of physical science, which they seek to imitate, exist for one purpose only – to offer patterns of interdependence or hypothesized relationships that can eventually be put to the test of empirical observation. That is, the main purpose of the model-building method of science is to facilitate the eventual testing of the *premises* on which these models are constructed. In economics, or in social science generally, it is not usually possible to utilize models in this way.[6] The controlled experiment that is the cornerstone of so much of physical science cannot be performed by the social scientist. Thus, models of economic relationships proliferate endlessly because they are not subject to the constraints of application and practice that ultimately winnow the hypotheses of physical science. This is a condition that encourages the exercise of economic imagination for its own sake, with a concommitant indifference as to whether or not the products explain or clarify the underlying social realities.

SOCIOLOGY OF ECONOMIC KNOWLEDGE

These very important questions will require further analysis, but first let me broach a second reason for the lack of interest of professional economists in "political" issues. It is quite simply that economists are mainly of conservative political orientations, and therefore do not *wish* to investigate these questions.

I am not the first to suggest that economists are conservative. In a well-known essay, "The Politics of Political Economists," George Stigler has written, ". . . the professional study of economics makes one politically conservative."[7] The reason for this, in Stigler's words, is "the effect of the scientific training the economist receives. It becomes impossible for the trained economist to believe that a small group of selfish capitalists dictates the main outlines of the allocation of resources. . . He cannot unblushingly repeat slogans such as 'production for use rather than for profit'. He cannot believe that a change in the *form* of social organization will eliminate basic economic problems."[8]

It may be however that there is another reason to which we must look for the prevailing conservatism of economic thought. Stigler refers to it, only to dismiss the thought: "The conservatism of economists cannot be explained by the vulgar argument of venality," he writes. ". . . The current rates of pay for good economists are much below what I would assume to be the going rate for a soul."[9]

I do not know the prevailing rates of pay for economists in 1959 when Stigler's essay was written, but the median going rate in 1967 for full professors was $18,000. In that year an income of $12,000 (just above the median for "superior assistant professors") put one into the top 15 percent of all taxpayers; an income of $14,000 (associate professors) into the top 10 percent; an income of $18,000 into the top 5 percent. "Superior" professors in that year averaged over $21,000 (not counting royalties, lecture or consultation fees), placing them in the top 2 percent.[10] One need not invoke venality to suggest that men who are placed in the upper income echelons of a society tend to share many of its values. What Malthus called "the insensible bias of situation and interest"[11] is a cast of mind that we recognize readily in others, including such august personages as the Justices of the Supreme Court.

In calling attention to the ideological pressures to which economists are consciously or unconsciously subject, I do not seek to impugn their intellectual integrity. The matter goes deeper. For the disturbing characteristic of the kinds of questions from which economists tend to shy away is that they concern problems for which there may be no solutions within the existing socio-political framework. That is, an explicit awareness of the political elements inextricably involved in economic change forces the analyst to the recognition that *powerful noneconomic constraints bound the domain of realistic economic theorizing.* With this recognition comes the unwelcome conclusion that many proposals for change are doomed to futility, and that certain attributes and tendencies of the system are beyond reform.[12]

The very awareness that limits do exist and must be taken into account acts as a powerful depressant on the state of mind of the would-be "value-free" investigator who senses that fatal inconsistencies of a political nature may invalidate the logic of his economic reasoning. A commitment to a political economics does not require that a hostile animus motivate the social analyst, but the questions that it poses serve unquestionably to try the faith of the partisan of the *status quo* or to reveal the disconcerting extent to which his economic conclusions rest on uncertain political assumptions.[13]

IRRELEVANCE AND INADEQUATE CONSTRUCTS

One reason that economics is "irrelevant" is thus that the majority of economists do not wish to make it relevant, partly due to the restrictive effects of the prevailing paradigm and its techniques, partly to an unwillingness to pursue inquiries whose outcome promises an increase in the psychic discomfort of the inquirer, possibly placing him in a position of acute conflict or political jeopardy. Although I cannot prove these assertions, it is my personal conviction that their deterrent effect is both widespread and deep-seated.

But there is a second and perhaps more fundamental meaning of irrelevance. This is a charge leveled not against the omissions of economists, but against those of economics. It is the contention that with the best will in the world, certain problems critical for an understanding of the social order remain irresolvable because the appropriate tools do not seem to be included in that famous tool kit of conventional economics.

The first deficiency is well known to conventional economists who spend a good deal of time trying to overcome it. It is the failure of present-day analytical techniques or conceptual schemes to present a consistent or integrated model of the economic system in the terms in which that system is usually perceived. Primary among these failings is the absence of a unified theoretical framework capable of explaining both macro and micro behavior. A second widely recognized lack is an adequate theory of the major agent of contemporary capitalism – the corporation. What is lacking is a set of premises concerning behavior, technology and organization from which reliable predictions can be made as to corporate behavior. Perhaps at an even more fundamental level are the misgivings expressed by some economists as to the validity of certain prime constructs of economic thought, such as "capital" or "welfare" or even "gross national product."

Certainly the inability of economic theory to cope with such problems lessens its effectiveness. Nonetheless, many of these particular failures of economics appear to be reparable. The gulf between micro and macro economics arises in large part from the different kinds of problems that each isolates, and there seems to be no intrinsic reason, rooted in the nature of economic reality, why a more unitary mode of reasoning should not eventually emerge. Work on the behavior of the corporation has proceeded apace, promising us a new model that seems to account for the observed tendencies toward concentration and oligopoly, and even yielding optimal strategies for growth. The problems of concept and measurement are much more obdurate, but once again, the difficulties do not seem to vitiate the core of economic theory itself, but rather to establish limits on the degree of exactness that can be expected of that theory in use.

I do not wish here to speculate on which areas of economics

will most readily yield to further refinements of conventional theory, but rather to point out a common denominator to be expected in all such advances. It is that *we can anticipate improvements in models that serve as ideal-typical representations of certain aspects of the system, but not in models that are intended to be used for "hard" prediction.*

IRRELEVANCE AND PREDICTIVE LIMITATIONS

The relevance of economic theory as an instrument of prediction depends on two interdependent but separable aspects of the process of theorizing itself. The first consists in the capacity of a theory to filter out from the immense field of our perceptions those attributes deemed significant. The second consists of subsequent efforts to link these mental constructs into a relational system.[14]

The first of these two tasks of theory is in some respects the more fundamental, for it prescribes the terms on which we come to grips with the unmanageable complexity of an unstructured reality. Some of the present lacunae of economic theory – the gap between micro and macro theory, for example – may well be repaired by the design of more "relevant" abstractions with which to handle the economic universe. More to the point, if it is possible to join a political element to the prevailing economic constructs, this would in itself radically alter the ideal-typical model of the economic system itself, perhaps changing very markedly our theoretical understanding of it. That is a matter of which we shall have more to say subsequently. But it is first necessary to examine certain intrinsic limitations within the second aspect of theorizing – to wit, attempts to join the given constructs into the kind of functionally related system that accords with the prevailing scientific paradigm.

These limitations are rooted in two indispensable assumptions that underlie all the functional relationships of conventional economics. One of these is that it is possible to describe in "law-like" terms the behavioral responses to certain critical changes in the economic environment, mainly the responses of buyers and sellers to changes in prices, or of consumers and investors to changes in income and/or interest rates. All models, macro or micro, are built on the bedrock of a presumed behavioral consistency, whether this be pictured as short-run maximizing, long-run satisficing, homeostasis, or whatever.

The second assumption underlying economic theory concerns the nature of the material relationships among the factors of production. Put concisely, economic theory builds its models on the premise that it is possible to describe "engineering" functions to serve as counterparts to the required behavioral functions. These engineering functions serve as necessary constraints on the forces of behavior, specifying the elasticities of substitution among goods or factors in the production process, the economies of scale for all inputs together and so on.

I think there can be no doubt that economic theory cannot build reliable – and in that sense, relevant – models that fit the reigning paradigm unless it can describe, with some degree of confidence, the nature of these essential behavioral and technical functions. Our textbook models of economic society are all grounded in the law of supply and demand, the law of variable proportions and so forth. Moreover, as Adolph Lowe has pointed out, it may well be that from an historical point of view economics was entirely justified in taking the reliability of these functions for granted.[15] In the environment of widespread poverty, small scale enterprise, uninhibited acquisitiveness, and "mechanical" technology characteristic of the middle 19th century, it is likely that both behavior and production displayed the reliable patterns of stimulus-response and change that economic theory attributed to and implicitly required of them.

The problem arises, however, when we ask whether that confidence can be justified in the altered environment of the latter 20th century. As Lowe has pointed out, the structure of a highly industrialized, oligopolistic system is such as to lengthen enormously the time-horizon applicable to "maximizing" decisions, while the concommitant rise of standards of living has greatly increased the importance of "discretionary" expenditure for the consumer. In this relaxed environment, the external pressures that once produced reliable patterns of behavior – short-run maximizing for the firm, negatively sloped demand curves for consumers – have given way to a much looser set of environmentally imposed constraints. As a result, "normal" economic behavior, both for the consumer and for the firm, becomes increasingly unpredictable. In Lowe's words: "[C]onsidering the state of uncertainty in the modern industrial market, opposite actions such as increasing or decreasing output, raising or lowering prices, can be defended in one and the same situation as the most promising step for profit maximization."[16]

Lowe's criticism deals a severe blow to the reliability of economic theorizing in the short run period in which the behavior function is critical. Recently, I have suggested that there is a second and no less substantial obstacle to reliable prediction in the long run, based not on the vagaries of behavior but of technology.[17] For over a long enough period it is possible to regard the perversities of behavior as essentially random departures from a trend line, while expecting the underlying trend to reassert itself persistently after each moment of perversity has passed. To put it differently, profit or utility maximizing may lead to differing actions in the short run, but over a longer period, it is at least plausible that a consistent pattern of behavior will emerge. But when we now examine the possibility of projecting long-run production functions, we find that the unpredictability of short-run individual or institutional behavior has been transferred to the "behavior" of technology. It is simply a fact that we cannot make predictions over a time span of as little as a decade with regard to the proportions of inputs – much less the kinds of inputs – that will be required to produce a unit of given output, or for that matter foresee the mix of outputs themselves. In this long run indeterminacy, changes in taste and motivation play their role, but the prime upsetting factor, including a main reason for changes in taste and motivation, is the unpredictable shape of the production function over time.

As a consequence of this increasing indeterminism of the basic premises on which predictive models are based, economics faces a genuine crisis. The seemingly capricious factor of behavior weakens the relevance of economic prediction in the short run; the unknowable path of technical change undermines it in the long run.

There is, however, a remedy – or at least a partial remedy – for the inadequacies of economics that stem from the erosion of the behavioral or technological determinism on which it was built. This is a reconstruction of economics along the lines that Lowe has described as "instrumental". By this Lowe means the deliberate abandonment of economics as a science that deduces its conclusions or predictions from secure premises of behavior and technology, and its replacement by a conception of economics as a policy-oriented instrument whose major theoretical purpose is to discover what "premises" – what behavioral forces, what technological constraints, what institutions – would be necessary to attain targets or goals. Economics thus overrides the indeterminacy of its behavioral or technological underpinnings by transforming them into the *dependent* variables of the economic model, the appropriate forms of which will be specified by whatever constraints or targets are introduced as parameters.

In this way economics regains relevance by becoming first and foremost a theory of planning, including above all the planning of the appropriate behavioral preconditions for the tasks determined by political choice. In the case of unruly economic behavior, for example, instrumental theorizing would consider what measures might be necessary to restore expectations to a state conducive to "normal" economic activity, while the disturbances inherent in unforeseeable leaps of technology could be minimized within the time spans of economic plans and projects by direct controls, to the extent that they would be necessary or feasible.

IRRELEVANCE OF NON-HOLISTIC THEORY

There are many problems associated with the construction of an instrumental economics, to which I will later revert, but its insistence on a political premise to economic theory brings us naturally to a third, and in some respects most far-reaching definition of the irrelevance of conventional economics. This is the charge that in concentrating on a narrowly defined set of problems, economics no longer asks the questions that are of greatest concern for contemporary society; that it elicits answers that are uninteresting because they do not take into account the political and social attributes of the economic variables on which they concentrate. To put the charge in the language in which it is frequently voiced, this aspect of irrelevance springs from the intellectual mistake of first wrenching the "economy" from the "society", and thereafter treating the abstractions of economics without regard for their inextricably linked noneconomic causes and consequences.

The antithesis to this narrow approach is, of course, the "holistic" approach of Marxian economics, and to a lesser degree the classical economists that preceded Marx. What is it that gives to these earlier doctrines their holistic quality? I believe the answer lies in three characteristics shared by all of them:

> 1. The holistic models treat as dependent variables (or as constants) aspects of the social process that modern theory treats as independent variables. For instance, a crucial element in Marxian and non Marxian models alike is a subsistence level toward which the wage level constantly tends. *This gives a basic social and political, as well as economic, parameter to the ensuing dynamics.*
> 2. Class interests are expressly recognized. The main dependent variables of the economic process – wages, rent, profits – are treated not merely as factor returns, but as class returns. *Economics thus emerges as the study of the changing fortunes of social classes under various assumptions concerning behavior, technology, and institutions.*
> 3. Definite, if sometimes only implicit, notions of welfare form an

> integral part of the model. Benign or otherwise, in every case a clear view of the desired social destination serves to join value judgments and economic analysis. *Economics thus becomes the willing servant of politics.*

Out of these assumptions emerge the "magnificent dynamics" of a great internal struggle within society that can be both clearly divined and unambiguously judged. These dynamics, it need hardly be said, depend on a number of critical assumptions. One of them, as we have already mentioned is the "driven" character of 19th century behavior, both of the worker and the capitalist, whence derives the strict determinism of the schemata. Another is the equally important presence within all these models of flexible wages and "inflexible" technology, which make possible the parameters of a wage level at or tending constantly toward subsistence and an employment level essentially determined by the stock of capital. A third essential premise is the rigid stereotype of class behavior in the political field, to which no modifications of nation or environment are admitted. A fourth is the uncluttered view of "human nature" and of social values in general characteristic of the age.

Alas for the latter day "classicist", none of these assumptions can be accepted today. The driven nature of economic behavior has altered with the shift from atomistic competition to oligopoly and with the appearance of discretionary spending power on the part of the consumer. The convenient relation between wages and population or surplus population no longer operates in the industrialized countries although the classical assumptions still provide important insights in the backward areas. Capital-labor coefficients can no longer be regarded as fixed, so that the employment effects of a changing capital stock cannot be unhesitatingly predicted. And finally, a century of political experience has dealt two severe blows to the political aspects of the holistic model. First, it has uncovered a wide range of variations in class attitudes and behavior among capitalist nations, and has thereby weakened the classical stereotypes of "fixed" economic-political reactions. Second, the experience with socialism has increased uncertainty, not only as to the nature of "human nature", but also as to the relation between economic change and human welfare.

For all these reasons, the goal of a "holistic" analysis is no longer seriously entertained by conventional economists. This carries with it both structural and political consequences for economic thought. On the structural side, the integral connection between economic growth and social change – the very heart of the classical model – has been largely abandoned in favor of models that explore various expansion "paths" for a few variables, with little or no concern for the meaning of whatever changes in the fortunes of the different elements of society are represented by those variables. On the political side, the tacit mutual support of political preferences and economic analysis has now given way to the indeterminate inquiry of "value-free" theory, or to the politically evasive premises of Pareto optima and social welfare functions. Thus, abandonment of the holistic goal has meant the deliberate constriction of economic theory from a discipline that aspired to the towering stature of a truly *social* science to the much more modest status of a science that explicates interactions of the economic elements within the social system, without regard to political or social ramifications.

However reluctantly, we have no choice but to accept much of this deliberate constriction, as more and more elements of the social process have become independent rather than dependent variables. Nonetheless, I am not so quick to acquiesce in the total abandonment of the aims of "holistic" theory, despite this inescapable restriction of its scope. For the loss of its social and political dimensions brings a truly devastating loss to economics as a social science. The difficulty with an "apolitical" economics is that it permits a proliferation of endless models or paths or strategies, all of which are equally plausible, since none have to conform to any requirements of social adaptability or political power, and all equally preferable since social values are rigorously excluded.

Here, I believe, is the crux of the issue of relevance. *It is the recognition, never to be lost to sight, that economic systems cannot be conceived merely as "functional" arrangements for the production and distribution of goods, but must also be seen both as frameworks for the division of social prestige and political power, and as mechanisms for the attainment of some postulated social destination.* In a word, both the "class" and the "welfare" aspects of society can be allowed to disappear from sight only at the cost of expunging the very elements that constitute the vital links between an "economy" and its surrounding social organization. The task for a political economics, then, is to find ways to reintroduce these essential elements into the body of economic analysis.

SHORTCOMINGS OF MARXISM

But are we not merely proposing a return to Marxism? Is not the integration of political and economic attributes the very essence of

Marxian social science? There is no question but that the articulation of a new political economics must use many of the insights of Marxian analysis. The fact remains, however, that a great deal of what passes as Marxian economics today is as irrelevant as neo-classical economics. Despite its political flavor and self-consciously political approach, Marxian economics has so far promised much more than it has delivered. Although it has identified certain problems to which conventional economics has been blind, it has been far from cogent in moving from general forebodings to specific predictions.[18]

In a word, Marxism has the aims but not the accomplishments of a genuine political economics. In particular, it has failed to present an operational model of society because of four major short-comings:

> 1. Some of the key formulations of Marxian economics – especially the labor theory of value and its related concepts – have proven awkward or useless as a "kit of tools" for analytical purposes.
> 2. The ramifications of technology, which Marxian analysis rightly places at the very center of the historic process, have not been adequately dealt with. In particular the physical and social side-effects of technology, from environmental decay to alienation and affluence, have been described in a doctrinaire fashion that fails to illumine the complex role played by science and technology in all industrial societies.
> 3. The Marxian treatment of social classes and the state has suffered from an excessively rigid aprioristic view. From this inadequate conceptual basis there have followed highly misleading or even outright fallacious conclusions.[19]
> 4. Ultimately, the Marxian model of society has not found a satisfactory paradigm of its own. Its economic core mechanism depends essentially on the same kinds of "mechanical" relationships as does the neo-classical. And whereas the method of dialectics is an effort to relate social and political events to this core in a "non-mechanical" way, the indeterminacy of these dialectical linkages has not permitted the model to serve as a basis for reliable social prediction or guidance.

To point out these serious deficiencies of Marxism serves two purposes. It makes clear that the traditional Marxian analysis must be vastly improved – even transformed – if Marxism is to have a claim to "relevance" that is demonstrably superior to that of orthodox analysis. But the second purpose served by an analysis of Marxian shortcomings is graver. For the most significant failures of Marxian analysis alert us to a more critical issue. *It is that the remedy for some of the faults of Marxian analysis lies beyond our present capabilities as social scientists.* Substitution of some of the more highly refined and flexible tools of conventional economics would add suppleness to Marxian technique. Yet they will not solve the problem of how to treat such semi-independent social variables as ideology, militarism and nationalism. Indeed, to include all these vital elements of the social process within a single model of sufficient particularity to yield reliable foresight seems well beyond our present abilities, at least within a paradigm of a functional model along conventional lines.

TOWARD GREATER RELEVANCE

It follows from my argument that the possibility of increasing the relevance of economics thus hinges on three kinds of changes, each with its own difficulties and likelihood of attainment: (1) the introduction of explicit political considerations into economic research: (2) the widening of the scope of conventional economic theory to include a political dimension; and (3) the supersession of the existing paradigm of "scientific" economics by another, more far-reaching one.

Of the three, the easiest to prescribe is the first. If economics is to become more relevant, economists must direct their energies into areas of the social order that they have heretofore overlooked, particularly areas in which political or sociological elements are intimately intertwined with strictly economic ones. Since I have already suggested some of these areas, I will only add that "institutional" economics would seem preeminently qualified to lead the expedition into this dangerous no-man's land.[20]

The second general remedy is the introduction of a political dimension into economic models to make explicit the tensions in an economic order that is both a functional mechanism and a vehicle for privilege and status. The difficulty is that the simplified class structure by which the classicists combined functional and political analysis seems no longer reliable as a basis for large-scale theorizing.

What can be done in the face of this impasse? First, the construction of models that reveal the political stresses of economic change by linking economic growth with changes in income distribution.[21] These must perforce be much more complicated models than those of the classicists, for the great simplifying triad of workers, capitalists and landlords does not begin to represent the politically active claimants to income under modern capitalism. Moreover the models should not be expected to predict the ultimate outcome of dynamic tendencies, but only to indicate the areas where the tension is likely to be greatest and where, accordingly, we can expect political intervention or collective private action of one kind or another.

An alternative to this "politicizing" of theory lies in the incorporation of *group consciousness* into the constructs whence behavioral functions are derived. An example is a behavioral model of Paolo Leon in which a key determinative factor is the notion of self-conscious class action undertaken by the managers of big corporations. Leon writes:

> Monopolists cannot individually remedy, by altering their investment decisions and wage scales, a disequilibrium in the economy as a whole. In this sense, monopolists and free competition entrepreneurs are not very different. Where they do differ is in the capacity of the former to anticipate events which pertain to the economy as a whole. Therefore if *all* monopolists are aware of a crisis that can damage each of them, it seems reasonable to assume that they will recognize themselves as a class, *or as a group of interests which becomes homogenous at a macroeconomic level.*[22]

It is not my purpose here to defend Leon's concept in particular or to expound the ways in which it affects the development of his model. But his approach – generalized to labor unions and other groups capable of collective action in response to perceived economic stress – opens a second possibility for a reorientation of conventional theory along political lines.

A third avenue of change is more difficult. It is an effort to formulate a theory of the economic behavior of the state. One of the most vitiating assumptions of present-day conventional economics is its tendency to treat government economic activity as either a wholly passive force – for example, the automatic stabilizers – or as a wholly unpredictable independent variable. Yet surely, without descending to the opposite, Marxian view of the state as the creature of a unified capitalist class, it should be possible to indicate the mutual interdependence of the public and private sectors in a more realistic fashion. Such an effort seems within the technical competence of conventional theory and would add immeasureably to the relevance of its models.

TOWARD A NEW PARADIGM

The foregoing suggestions are all intended to enrich the existing paradigm of economic theorizing, and to the extent that they can be implemented, should add a political flavor to the blandness of most present-day economic writing. Yet none of them transcends the paradigm itself. We are left with a representation of social processes that stresses functional relationships and a value-free approach to social problems, even though we know in our bones that society is not, and cannot be, adequately represented by a web of formulae and that value-considerations are clearly at the very heart of the social process itself.

One line of exploration suggests itself at once. It is the search for a new explanatory mode that would arch across the artificial divisions of "economics", "politics" and "sociology" to produce a unified conception of society as a seamless web. It would open up a topography of the social process more ramified than the one to which we are accustomed, thereby enabling us to comprehend the process of social change more thoroughly than is now possible. For example, looking down on society from this new vantage point we should be able to see a cross-linked matrix of activity somewhat like that shown below:

A TOPOGRAPHY OF SOCIAL PROCESSES

	Economics: production and distribution	**Political Science: governance**	**Sociology: social organ-ization**
Role of the individual	*factor of pro-duction*	*citizen*	*role-actor*
	consumer	*voter*	
Role of the state	*regulator of economic processes*	*source of force and authority*	*source of bureaucracy*
Role of the firm	*agency of production*	*lobbying and political influence*	*locus of industrial discipline*
Problems of growth	*intersectoral relations*	*planning*	*changes in motivation due to affluence*
Technological change	*effect on profit rates, structure of demand*	*control over externalities*	*changes in work patterns, life-styles*

Such a topographic or taxonomic approach has value because it forces the specialized observer to recognize the multiplicity of ways in which the simplest variable is embedded in society, and because the observation of these juxtapositions may open up new insights into social causality. Yet I do not believe that such an inquiry can take us beyond the limitations of the existing paradigm. For the topographic approach is limited in two ways. On the one hand, because we do not have the insight we seek from this new map of social activity, there is no systematic, ordered way of juxtaposing activities. Hence the taxonomic model yields no more than scattered, *ad hoc* insights, rather than systematic enlightenment.

On the other hand, to the extent that we *can* find behavioral regularities in and among the noneconomic spheres of life, we have not escaped from, but merely enlarged, the existing paradigm. We have then equated the idea of a unified social science with that of the representation of the social process as a system in *n* variables and *n* equations. That such a Laplacean fantasy is an adequate image of the social universe I find hard to believe. For quite aside from the difficulties presented by the vagaries of so many social processes (including, as we have seen, the best behaved of them, economics), such a "deterministic" model of society fails to come to grips with the aspect of the social process that, more than any other, sets it apart from physical processes – namely, the display of *social volition* as an integral part of the behavioral forces by which the system is set into motion.

ECONOMICS AS A GOAL-ORIENTED SCIENCE

This last conclusion points the way, I believe, for a genuine supersession of the existing paradigm. For what is ultimately constricting about the present conception of social "science" is that it plunges us into the free-will *vs* determinism dilemma from which there is no satisfactory exit so long as we conceive of functional relationships in terms of the unconstrained working-out of immutable behavioral forces. Once we drop this Laplacean conception, however, the dilemma disappears. For we can then retain the functional mode of explanation (which is, after all, the only method of causal analysis we possess) while ridding ourselves of its straitjacket implications *by using this mode as a goal-orienting device.* The new paradigm, in other words, consists in an abandonment of the view of social analysis as that of determining the immanent destination of a universe of goalless particles, and substituting a view of social science as the search for the means by which social goals can be attained.

As we have already seen, this instrumental reformulation, applied to economics, departs from the prevailing conception of the discipline by relinquishing the belief in dependable behavioral functions from which future configurations of the system can be deduced. In its place it elevates a desired terminus of the social process – steady growth, ecological balance and so forth – to the status of the initial premise of economic analysis, while relegating behavior, the premise of conventional theory, to the status of an "instrument" by which the terminus is to be attained. From this point of view, a search for the "laws" of behavior – political and social as well as economic – becomes a matter of secondary concern, and the study of modes of influencing behavior rises accordingly in importance.

To this instrumental reorientation of economics, which has been vigorously proposed by Lowe,[23] one can pose two principal objections. The first is that the intrusion of value-laden goals into the economic reasoning process destroys all hope of establishing a genuine science of economics, much less of political economics. To this objection two rejoinders can be made. The first is that so-called "value-free" economic theory in fact represents an acquiescence in the social termini implicit in a laissez-faire universe, and that even the most innocuous assumptions of "value-free" theory are in fact drenched in unrecognized value judgments as to the legitimacy of the institutional order and the starting position of the economic process.

The second rejoinder is that the scientific character of economic reasoning does not rest in its value-free or value-laden assumptions, but in the methods by which it proceeds from its premises to its conclusions. Whether the mode of scientific analysis be taxonomic or mathematical-functional,[24] essentially the claim to being a scientific procedure rests on nothing more than a subscription to orderly, repeatable methods and to the willing submission of hypotheses to empirical testing. These overriding requirements are in no way invalidated by the use of economic reasoning as a means of gaining a previously stated end, rather than as a means of deducing the trajectory of a system from assumed behavioral functions.

To be sure, in the initial selection of these social ends, the economists has no more claim to priority or expertise than any other educated member of the polity; and without question, the ends that will be selected cannot be invested with any more objective validity than the level of current wisdom affords. But this explicit unmasking of the frailty of the goal-chosing process does not worsen the chances that goals will be well-chosen. It merely brings into the open what was often before a *sub rosa* process. One might say that the ultimate political aim of instrumentalism is thus to elevate the process of goal selection to its proper status as the most important of all social activities.

The second major objection to instrumentalism is that it does not in fact offer us an escape from the reigning paradigm at all. If it throws our dependency on unreliable "laws" of behavior out the front door, it smuggles them in by the back. For it is argued, in selecting the appropriate economic or political or social means of influencing behavior to gain a desired end, must we not lean on behavioral regularities after all? Otherwise, how would we know that measure B would produce desired behavior A?

To this two answers can be given. One is that a main task of instrumental inquiry is not behavioral but structural – that is, inquiry into the allocations or technical sequencing needed to achieve a given economic target. Here, of course, instrumental analysis must deal with the unpredictable elements of the long-run production function, but insofar as its aim is to specify the technical preconditions for a postulated target it can legitimately confine itself to the "given" technology, permitting unpredicted technological change to improve on its bill of particulars.

But a second answer can also be given that directs itself specifically to the behaviorial problem. It is that instrumental analysis must depend on generalizations of differing probabilities with respect to behavior. But unlike conventional economics, the scientific application of instrumentalist theory does not collapse if these expectations of regularity prove unfounded. Instead, provided that the target remains the same, it now becomes the task of theory to discover other behavioral routes to the same goal, or to explore specific means of establishing the behavior that is required. Instrumentalism can thus be pragmatic rather than aprioristic with respect to the relevant "laws" of behavior.

Last, it may be objected that an instrumental orientation, by greatly enlarging the importance of controls over behavior, opens the way to a totalitarian drift for a society that practices such a boldly interventionist social science. To this the answer is easy. If a high ranking goal is freedom of behavior itself – that is, a decision not to permit intervention beyond such mild means as fiscal or monetary policy or the normal spectrum of political exhortation – it may then follow that other social goals become impossible to attain. In that case instrumentalism serves the purpose of making clear what opportunity costs must be borne by opting for a given degree of behavioral freedom.

I do not wish to gloss over the difficulties of instrumental analysis or to magnify unduly the possible gains to be had from its application. Our knowledge of social cause and effect is still very crude, and it is possible that an attempt to guide the social body by the rudder of behavioral control may result in wide tacks and little headway. But the purpose of instrumentalism, at this stage in the development of social science, is not so much to achieve an easy mastery over social processes as to free our minds from ways of thinking that prevent us from making our theories "relevant" to the problem of purposeful social change.

Instrumentalism, by placing the welfare of society as the initial premise of all subsequent analysis, opens a perspective from which not only economics but all social science suddenly takes on a new appearance. From this new perspective all the various disciplines fall into place as different ways of examining the means to given ends; "economics", "politics", "sociology" and so forth, each grappling with particular aspects of the overall problem of bringing about desired social change. In time, the refinements in technique needed to fill out this perspective will doubtless be added. In the meanwhile it is important to understand that the rigor of thought and the empirical basis of the conventional paradigm of scientific procedure are not discarded, but placed in the service of the goal-seeking propensities of the community. Since those propensities seem to be the very quintessence of social behavior, this is tantamount to saying that social science is thereby placed in the service of man.

FOOTNOTES

1. "Putting Marx to Work," *New York Review of Books,* Dec. 5, 1968, p. 10.

2. Servan-Schreiber, *The American Challenge* (New York: 1968) p. 3. (His italics).

3. A poll of members of the American Economic Association undertaken by Elmo Roper in 1959 revealed that only 52 percent of economists supported Galbraith's contention of a "unbalanced" public-private division of national effort. (*Saturday Review* June 6, 1959, p. 39.)

4. I use the expression "paradigm" in the fashion employed by Thomas Kuhn in his well known *The Structure of Scientific Revolutions.*

5. See, for example, the excoriating remarks by Kenneth Boulding, *Proceedings,* American Economic Association, May, 1966, p. 9.

6. See Joan Robinson, *Exercises in Economic Analysis,* p. xv-xvi.

7. *Quarterly Journal of Economics,* Nov. 1959; reprinted in Stigler's *Essays in the History of Economics* (Chicago, 1965) p. 52.

8. Ibid. (*Essays*), p. 60.

9. *Ibid.* p. 59.

10. Income figures for professors from annual surveys conducted by The American Economic Association; income brackets from *Statistics of Income,* Internal Revenue Service.

11. See *Works of David Ricardo,* (ed. Sraffa) Vol. II, p. 223.

12. Thus Robin Marris writes, in "Towards a Reform of the Big Firm," (*New Society,* Sept. 25, 1969), "We hope by the use of 'hard' disciplines, such as economics, to avoid the clumsiness of revolutionary improvisation. We shall certainly remain bourgeois; but, I believe, our methods may offer some possibility of salvation from present errors *if anyone of power and influence will listen to us and act on what they hear.*" (italics added). But the point is, of course, to ask why schemes for the "reform" of the big firm will in all likelihood not be listened to or acted on. Programs of improvement, calculated to appeal to the "public", or the "enlightened self-interest" of companies are as old as those of Robert Owen. The question for social science, including the "hard" discipline of economics, is not alone to criticize the content of these programs, but to understand and explain why the vast majority of them have come to naught.

13. It may be that my formulation is too mild and that at the very least a receptivity to the possibility of far-reaching structural change is a prerequisite for a willingness to undertake political-economic inquiry. I only mean to imply that such an attitude is by no means identical with a dogmatic or implacable rejection of the existing order – somewhere between the mild measures we call "reform" and the extreme ones we call "revolution" lies the little-explored territory of "radical reform" (A. Hirschman). This raises the difficult question as to what factors determine our position along this political spectrum. No doubt sheerly intellectual judgments play their part in this decision, but an unconscious identification with or rejection of the social order seems to exert an even stronger sway. The passion with which the existing order is defended or attacked suggests that "value-free" inquiry into the merits of society may ultimately be inconsistent with the internalization process by which social reality is apprehended. See Peter Berger and Thos. Luckman, *The Social Construction of Reality,* p. 119f.

14. See, *inter alia,* Fritz Machlup "Operational Concepts and Mental Constructs in Model and Theory Formation" *Giornale degli Economisti e Annali di Economia,* Sept-Oct. 1960.

15. *On Economic Knowledge* (New York, 1965) p. 68f.

16. Ibid, p. 48.

17. "On the Limits of Economic Prediction," *Diogenes,* April, 1970.

18. One of the main troubles in Marxist writing has been that the wish has been all too perceptibly father to the thought. The *Monthly Review,* for example, has predicted outright recession no less than six times between 1954 and 1963. (see issues of December 1954, October 1955, September 1956, November 1958, September 1962 and November 1963) and has failed to predict accurately the economic, political or social course of either the Soviet Union, China or Cuba. On a larger scale, a certain milennial strain continues to infuse socialist theorizing with regard to the long run future. (See my essay on "Socialism and the Future", *Commentary,* December 1969.)

19. One of the most important Marxist works of recent years has been *Monopoly Capital* by Baran and Sweezy. Its main purpose is to present a model of capitalism that will enable us to project the social and political as well as economic tendencies of the system. Two points are of interest in this regard. Although the book was published in 1966, there is no anticipation of inflation as a coming central issue within capitalism; rather, stagnation with its deflationary overtones continues to be the central focus of analytical attention. Second, the book contains statements such as the following: "Such planning and such action [mass low-cost housing], however, will never be undertaken by a government by and for the rich, as every capitalist government is and must be." (p. 300). Even granting the premise of the last clause, does it follow that a government of the rich might not find it politically useful to rid a nation of its slums? The examples of capitalist Switzerland, Netherlands and Scandanavia, are enough to prove that it may indeed. In other words, this

formulation of class interest and its consequences – both empirically and logically – is simply wrong. I should add that not all Marxist analysis is so simplistic, and that many insights of the Baran-Sweezy book are penetrating and powerful. Nevertheless, this kind of mechanical analysis is clearly "irrelevant" – not because it is apolitical, but because it is unpolitical.

20. I cannot refrain from mentioning once again the problem of "imperialism". The multi-national corporation is fast emerging as a major form of enterprise within all industrial capitalisms. Yet we still possess no full-scale study of the transition from national to international enterprise, and of the relationship of such enterprises with their "home" or their "host" governments. Important beginnings, however, may lie in the work of Stephen Hymer and others.

21. A beginning along these lines is to be found in the work of Joan Robinson, Kaldor, and Sraffa.

22. *Structural Change and Growth in Capitalism (1967)* p. 31. Author's italics.

23. Lowe, op cit. See also his essays in *Economic Means and Social Ends,* ed. R. Heilbroner, Prentice Hall, 1970.

24. "There do exist respectable sciences that have essentially no theory at all in the physicists' sense. Mineralogy, and to an even greater extent, taxonomy are primarily concerned with framing assumptions – for in essence a definition is an assumption and the naming of a species is a definition. . . . To say that all of biology [read *economics,*] should have an elegant mathematical framework is as much of an imposition of metaphysics on observation as it was to say that the only suitable astronomic observations must involve cycles and epicycles. . . ." L. S. Slobodkin, "on the Present Incompleteness of Mathematical Ecology," *American Scientist,* Sept. 1965. p. 351. 354.

Study of Relationships Between Economic and Political Systems

Henry Oliver

My article briefly describes and discusses certain variable characteristics of one great area of study coming under the general heading "comparative economic systems," namely, study of relationships between economic and political systems. More specifically, it concerns ways in which questions about these relationships differ and methods of reasoning employed in analyses of the relationships.

Questions About Systems' Interrelationships

Questions about relationships between economic and political systems can, of course, vary enormously in what they ask. Four major sources of difference are the direction of the flow of causation, the flexibility of the concepts of economic and of political system, the variability of the environments explicitly or implicity pictured in questions about systems' interrelationships, and the variability of the routes taken by the flows of causation inquired about, or, in other words, the intermediate variables inserted into the analysis. The general kinds of differences that these sources allow may be obvious. Briefly describing and illustrating them, however, may serve both to emphasize the vast scope of the field of potential study and the great variety of ways in which differences in the questions asked may keep seemingly conflicting analyses from truly being debated.

The author, prior to his death, was Professor of Economics, Indiana University, Bloomington.

Direction of Flow of Causation

Hypotheses can picture economic as affecting political systems, or political as affecting economic systems, or can describe a process of mutual interaction. When policy interests govern the questions asked, the flow of causation is, of course, that dictated by the nature of the decision considered. Whether a change in economic system or a change in political system is treated as the precipitant depends on the alternatives that potential decision makers are thought of as possibly pondering. But this still leaves wide latitude for analysis of systems' interrelationships, and policy interests presumably do not always dominate. Students of these interrelationships, like other categories of human beings, presumably often are interested in scientific or historical knowledge for its own sake, or because some combination of intellectual traditions, current intellectual trends, and self-interest dictates an attempt to learn.

Because of the road-to-serfdom controversy, the article's title probably most often brings to mind the flow of causation from the economic to the political side, that which the famous controversy emphasized. During the nineteenth century, however, thoughts about democracy and economic systems probably concerned the former's significance for the latter more often than the latter's for the former, and recent pleas for federalism often have stressed the way in which that form of political organization tends to limit state intervention in the economy. Similarly, in development literature the emphasis tends to be on governmental requisites of economic systems rather than on the economic systems needed to achieve political ones. Marx's and Schumpeter's theories of history describe mutual interactions, as do many historical studies of a less theoretical type. The social anthropologist's thesis of an integrated culture invites attempts of this kind.

Flexibility of Economic and Political System Concepts

The concepts of economic and political systems are so flexible that questions about systems' relationships can be highly varied for this general reason alone, without the benefit of other sources of difference. The categories that we call systems of various types can represent any pertinent level and any pertinent kind of abstraction, and the levels and kinds of abstraction that are pertinent depend on the precise questions that analysts wish to ask. The aspects of social life used as classificatory criteria can be few or many, broad or narrow, and, when either broad or narrow, can vary greatly in their characteristics. The combinations of criteria that can be used to classify systems especially are legion.

This flexibility is perhaps most easily seen when questions asked about systems are general in nature: for example, when we inquire whether abstract economic system S will result in abstract political system P in abstractly defined environment E. But the conclusion also holds when we inquire about effects within a concrete, historically observed society. When we say that the economic system of Ruritania changes, we may refer to any one or any combination of a large number of developments, and when we inquire about this change's significance for Ruritania's political system, the potential effects we have in mind similarly may represent any one or any combination of many aspects of Ruritanian life.

True, when policy interests dominate analysis, they impose certain restrictions. By definition, they lead to emphasis on "relevance," or, in other words, to reasoning intended to aid decisions. In ends-means analysis, the end is a desired change in a specified bundle of characteristics and, although the means that can be considered are not nearly so tightly restricted, even they must be changes in a "reasonably controllable" bundle of characteristics. In cause-and-effect reasoning of the opposite type, the cause is a potentially achievable change in a specified bundle of characteristics and, although the effects that can be considered are not nearly so tightly restricted, even they must be changes in a "reasonably interesting" bundle of characteristics. But these corollaries of "relevance" are not nearly as restrictive as they may seem at first glance. They leave quite a wide margin of leeway. Also, as is stated above, policy interests do not always dominate analysis.

Apparently the most frequent questions about economic systems classify them by reference to modes of ownership and/or ways in which allocational decisions are made. Analysis, however, may employ instead—or employ additionally—such criteria as various characteristics of the owners and allocators, or various characteristics of the available resources, the state of the arts, and the general social milieu. Examples of the former include owners' and allocators' social classes, income classes, ethnic groups, religions, places of residence, and national allegiances, and also their goals, taboos, codes of morals and manners, methods of calculation, other ways of thinking, and other customs. Examples of the latter include man-land ratios, the presence or absence of a frontier, and the state of "development" (that is, the sorts and extents of resources available for various activities). Kinds of writings that have distinguished between economies in these ways include not only the catholic bodies of literature that we call anthropology and history but also the more restricted literature dealing with the causes and effect of development, colonialism, and imperialism.

True, when such variables are introduced into the analysis they seem usually to be treated as characteristics of an economic system's environment rather than as characteristics of the system itself. This seems especially to be the case when questions make potential determinants, rather than potential resultants, of them. But to point out that characteristics of a system and characteristics of its environment are, at least in part, interchangeable concepts, is itself to emphasize the concepts' flexibility.

Moreover, even when we restrict our classificatory criteria to modes of ownership and methods of allocation, we do not thereby limit our system concepts to a few. Great variety still remains possible, partly because of quantitative distinctions between qualitatively identical mixtures, partly because mode of ownership and method of allocation are themselves concepts that can represent any of many levels and kinds of abstraction. One reason why the road-to-serfdom controversy was not a single debate was that the participants talked about a wide variety of kinds and degrees of state control over the economy.

So, too, on the political side. Apparently the most frequent questions about political systems classify them by referring to the number, structure, power, and sources of authority of chains of command. But these concepts too can represent any of many kinds and levels of abstraction; and quite a wide variety of other criteria can complement or replace them.

Concrete Versus Abstract Environments

The environments of the systems studied may be either concrete or abstract. When concrete, they are, of course, almost by definition highly varied. The details of history (and of the predicted immediate future) supply differences for the analysts' questions. When environments are abstract, they can, like systems themselves, represent any of many levels and many kinds of abstraction. As is stated above, the concepts of a system's characteristics and of its environment's characteristics are partly interchangeable. A description of a situation may take either form while being identical in substance.

When interest in a policy decision dominates thought about systems, "significant" differences in abstract environments are, of course, much less numerous than possible ones. To be "significant" they must be differences that would result in different policy choices. But, obviously, this does not rule out great variety in the abstract environments that we may picture. We do not know what differences are "significant" before we ask whether they have differential effects.

Indeed, perhaps the chief point to stress about environments is that, in studies of abstract systems' interrelationships, they often are not initially specified, or are described in only the vaguest of ways. The analyst's chief task is not to say whether economic system S will result in political system P in environment E but, instead, to discover the environments in which this result will, or will not, take place. Differences in the questions asked grow out of, instead of proceed from, the studies.

Parenthetically, this last, of course, is also often the case when differences between questions instead reflect variability in the *systems* concepts. Analysts often do not begin with a specified economic and a specified political system but, instead, inquire about the kinds of characteristics on one side that might have differential significance for specified kinds of characteristics on the other side; indeed, in the course of their analysis they sometimes alter even the systems concepts embodied in their initial, exploratory inquiries. In other words, systems concepts as well as environment concepts may undergo repeated transformations similar to those undergone by legal concepts in case law. But, in an article on systems' interrelationships, the role of search for differentially significant environments especially deserves stress.

Another, slighter point about systems' environments perhaps also merits attention. When certain classificatory criteria are used to distinguish between environments, interest may focus entirely on these criteria because of their special nature. Consider, for example, an effect of referring to voter preferences when classifying environments. To say that central planning requires nondemocratic rule when voters oppose such planning is to offer an unassailable thesis, but not one that seems to tell us much about systems' interrelationships. It does not seem quite parallel to such a similarly worded thesis as (in a non-Utopian society): A market economy requires "the rule of law."

Variable Routes of the Flow of Causation

Intermediate variables inserted into analyses of systems' interrelationships can differ radically even when system concepts, systems' environments, and direction of flow of causation are the same. In other words, when inquiring about these relationships, as well as when asking other questions, analysts may assign variable specific meanings to *ceteris paribus*. They automatically rule out all "independent" change other than that specified, and they similarly exclude all intermediate reactions except those described or implied, but they may differ substantially in their treatment of different potential reactions.

Consider, for example, the argument that "welfare states" and other "middle ways" eventually lead to thoroughgoing collectivism and therefore to serfdom. All but the final steps in the chain of reasoning may consist of quite familiar, quite traditional conclusions about micro and macro equilibria, plus the contention that policy makers try to "cure" the disequilibria by imposing more controls. At least one alternative line of analysis is available, however. Pessimists may instead talk about the impact of increasingly widespread intervention on such variables as voters' and legislators' expectations and political philosophies. When reviewing one of David McCord Wright's books about two decades ago, a British economist commended what he termed the author's "sociology." The literature on economic development similarly reveals this variability of routes, which, of course, is also what thoughts about economic anthropology would lead us to expect.

As this last remark may suggest, the multiplicity and variety of intermediate variables that have been inserted into analyses result, in part, from the multiplicity and variety of the classificatory criteria used to distinguish between environments and also from the flexibility of the system concepts themselves. They do not, however, entirely stem from these sources. To a considerable extent they reflect analysts' concentrating attention on different aspects of described systems or environments. In other words, they represent different uses of the information provided.

A corollary here concerns one of the purposes served by emphasizing how questions about systems' interrelationships may differ. As was stated above, one reason for describing and illustrating sources of difference is to show how analyses which at first glance seem to conflict may not truly constitute debate. This point is perhaps clearer when flexibility of system concepts and variability of systems' environments are the sources of difference, that is, when systems and environments either are vaguely described or differ only subtly from each other. Differences in paths of causation do not, like differences of these other two kinds, involve subtle alterations of either independent or terminally dependent variables. In a quite important respect, however, they may have the same significance. Unless we really define *ceteris paribus* to rule out only *independent* changes, we do not necessarily clash when we offer opposing conclusions. If we define the convenient Latin phrase more flexibly, implicitly all that we claim for our analysis is that our conclusion follows *if* the route of causation we describe is the only one, or the one that dominates. To repeat, differences between analyses' intermediate variables may represent different uses of the information provided. Two radically different conclusions may be correct as long as we safeguard them by assigning suitable specific meanings to *ceteris paribus* (or to *mutatis mutandis*).

Other Sources of Difference

Other, less noteworthy, sources of difference perhaps also deserve brief mention since they, too, can keep apparent conflict from truly being clash. Among these are: the distinctions between the past and the future and between the observed or predicted and the posited; the distinctions between necessary, sufficient, and contributory cause; and degrees of likelihood.

With respect to the first of these three sources, hypotheses about interrelationships can concern what was, what would have been, what will be, or what would be. The effects they picture can be those that did take place or will take place because of an observed change, would have taken place if a certain change had occurred in the past, will take place because of a predicted change, or would take place if a change would occur in the future. (These possible differences are, of course, closely related to, and substantially overlap, those in environments, which also can be past, past conditional, future, or future conditional. The variables of time and actuality in *systems' changes*, however, also deserve mention.)

With respect to the concept of cause employed, to say that, within a described environment, a certain characteristic in one system is a requisite of a certain characteristic in the other is not to say that it is a guarantee. To say that it is a guarantee is not to say that it is a requisite, even within that environment. To say that it is a contributory cause is not to say that it is either a guarantee or a requisite.

With respect to degrees of likelihood, even when hypotheses are not statistical—and, of course, most concerning systems' interrelationships are not—they may insert such semistatistical terms as *usually* and *rarely*, *probably* and *probably not*, and *more likely* and *less likely*. (This source of difference is, of course, a close cousin of the immediately preceding one.)

Again both the road-to-serfdom controversy and the literature on development come to mind. These last three sources of difference, like the earlier mentioned ones, help to account for the famous controversy's being a complex mixture, instead of a single debate, and for many variable features of the other body of writings.

But, for obvious reasons, these last three kinds of distinctions are less noteworthy sources of differences in questions than the first four. When we look at differences involving direction of flow of causation, flexible system concepts, variable environments, and variable routes that flows of causation take, we see not only how apparent conflict may not be true clash but also are impressed by the vast scope of study of economic and political systems' interrelationships. We are even more impressed by the scope of study that can come under the general heading "comparative economic systems."

Methods of Reasoning

Methods of reasoning employed by analysts of systems' interrelationships also have varied greatly. General types include: (1) tautology (for example, the thesis that if political federalism is real as well as formal it limits the scope of central planning); (2) inference from a case study (intensive study of a single country's or region's record, plus the drawing of a general conclusion therefrom); (3) deduction from generalizations about how persons, groups, organizations, and whole societies behave (for example, such chains of reasoning as those in Hayek's chapter on why the worst get to the top, Wright's passages on the role of financially independent political leadership, and many writings on the relationship between a market economy and the "rule of law"); and (4) a sort of statistical approach—more specifically, a search for associations, a systematic look at extensive bodies of complex historical evidence. (Wittfogel's *Oriental Despotism* is one of the books that comes to mind here.)

The weaknesses of the first two methods are perhaps easier to see than their merits. A tautological proposition is one that, in itself, says nothing about the universe but states only definitional relationships. A case study is precisely what its name implies, analysis that, in itself, reveals nothing about other cases. These limitations, however, do not signify sterility. The history of economics beautifully illustrates how tautological propositions can both guide and guard thought or, in other words, suggest nontautological hypotheses and help to discover error. Similarly, the study of an individual case many times has served the positive function of stimulating an hypothesis as well as the negative function of providing contrary evidence. It has suggested the questions to be asked in more comprehensive empirical studies. If one must utter a methodological stricture here, it is that students of systems should recognize tautological propositions and case study stimulated hypotheses for what they are, not that they should abjure them.

The third of the listed methods of reasoning, deduction from generalizations, is, of course, that which the term *theory* usually brings to mind, a method that mainstream economics long and brilliantly has employed. To date, the study of systems' interrelationships has not employed it nearly as successfully. The theses advanced seem, on the whole, to resemble the behavioral propositions of political science, sociology, and social anthropology much more than they do the behavioral propositions encountered in the theory of competitive markets, or in the theory of income, employment, and the price level. They tend to be somewhat fuzzy, not systematically integrated, and often not intellectually compelling. But, then, much the same can be said of the theory of development (which the analysis of systems overlaps) and of the other areas of economics stressing change in institutions. Perhaps the chief conclusion to draw here is that the limited success of employing this analytical method in the study of systems is further evidence for the thesis that mainstream economics is a social science sport.

Or, rather, the limited success of employing deduction in the study of systems' interrelationships is further evidence that what *used to be* mainstream economics is a social science sport. The last of the four methods of analysis mentioned above, the search for associations, is the closest approach to what perhaps should be called today's mainstream, the stream of econometrics. And this approach, obviously, is not a close one. Perhaps the most notable characteristic of this method of analysis, when employed in the study of systems' interrelationships, is the data's imprecision. Two other characteristics are the highly variable nature of the sets of variables associated and the strategic role that time lags logically play in the analysis. With respect to the former: The features of systems, and of their environments, to be correlated can be any of the many abstractly talked about above. With respect to time lags: The analysis concerns changes in institutions. The cause-and-retain effect period that most theses emphasize is a flexibly long long run.

On Some Fundamental Issues in Political Economy: An Exchange of Correspondence

James M. Buchanan and Warren J. Samuels

The letters printed below are published by the correspondents with the hope that they will stimulate discussion and creative rethinking about some fundamental and interesting issues that are often ignored in the conduct of economic analysis and research and the application of traditional tools and concepts. The issues, we are aware, are not novel. Our conflicts and apprehensions replicate, in varying degree, past methodological controversies. But we are convinced that the fundamental nature of the topics argued warrants continuing reexamination. Just as each generation of economists has the burden of interpreting for itself the history of the discipline, each generation also confronts, directly or indirectly, the problem of the methodological foundations of economic analysis. Moreover, as the discussions in the letters illustrate, methodological issues are closely related to normative or policy positions, although the relations are often ambiguous and equivocal.

Each reader will have to work out the problems raised in the letters and also interpret our respective positions. The issues are drawn in the letters in ways which represent our thinking during 1972 and

---

The authors, respectively, are Professor of Economics, Virginia Polytechnic and State University, Blacksburg, and Professor of Economics, Michigan State University, East Lansing.

1973 and also are not necessarily how they would be more widely formulated in the profession.

Among the issues raised and discussed in the correspondence are: the meaning of *positive* and *normative;* the role of antecedent specifications of property and other rights; the role of the status quo in positive science; the normative status of the status quo; the role of belief systems, social myths, and pretense in social science; the intrusion of additional normative premises into ostensibly positive analysis; the normative consequences of positive analysis; the attitude of the scholar to the world; the nature of liberal and conservative in economics; and, *inter alia,* what economics is all about. The most conspicuous substantive issue concerns the nature of public choice, specifically the economic role of government and how best to approach it as economists. While we both remain too ignorant in these fields, we have learned more about what each other, and ourselves, intends to accomplish therein.

The letters have been slightly edited, as indicated by elipses, primarily to exclude material irrelevant to our primary discussions. Publication of the letters does present ideas in a somewhat novel or unusual format, and they were not written with publication in mind and do not have the gloss of analytical rigor and polish usually found in journal articles. Rather, they are informal and exploratory ventures by two economists with clearly different points of view and approaches to government who nevertheless respect and are willing to learn from each other.

The correspondence began with a letter from Buchanan accompanying the draft of his "Politics, Property, and the Law,"[1] written in response to Samuels's "Interrelations Between Legal and Economic Processes,"[2] and which elicited a "Defense" by Samuels.[3] The letters, therefore, ideally should be read in conjunction with these and other materials referred to in the correspondence.[4]

Since the publication of the aforementioned articles, Buchanan has published his "Before Public Choice," in which he clarifies his position as follows:

> Where does this leave us in trying to discuss criteria for "improvement" in rules, in assignments of rights, the initial question that was posed in this paper? I have argued that the contractarian or Paretian norm is relevant on the simple principle that "we start from here." But "here," the status quo, is the existing set of legal institutions and rules. Hence, how can we possibly distinguish genuine contractual changes in "law". . . .

> Can we really say which changes are defensible "exchanges" from an existing status quo position? This is what I am trying to answer, without full success, in my paper in response to Warren J. Samuels' discussion of the *Miller et al. v. Schoene* case. There I tried to argue that, to the extent that property rights are specified in advance, genuine "trades" can emerge, with mutual gains to all parties. However, to the extent that existing rights are held to be subject to continuous redefinition by the State, no one has an incentive to organize and to initiate trades or agreements. This amounts to saying that once the body politic begins to get overly concerned about the distribution of the pie under existing property-rights assignments and legal rules, once we begin to think either about the personal gains from law-breaking, privately or publicly, or about the disparities between existing imputations and those estimated to be forthcoming under some idealized anarchy, we are necessarily precluding and forestalling the achievement of potential structural changes that might increase the size of the pie for *all*. Too much concern for "justice" acts to insure that "growth" will not take place, and for reasons much more basic than the familiar economic incentives arguments.[5]

On the other hand, Samuels, insensitive to neither the ethical limitations of assuming the propriety of the status quo system of working rules and rights assignments nor to the problem which Buchanan poses to orderly change and growth, prefers to analyze descriptively resource allocation as a function, proximately, of demand and supply, but more deeply as a function, in turn, of the power structure, rights, and the use of government. Samuels prefers to direct attention to such general interdependence dualisms as these: The power structure is a function of law *and* the use of government is a function of the power structure, and income and wealth distribution are a function of law *and* law is a function of income and wealth distribution. Samuels's interest is in the positive or objective comprehension of the interrelations between legal-political and economic (or nominally market) processes, in part for better understanding the chain of consequences of various government (and private) economic policies. As for the contractarian norm, Samuels finds it congenial but also finds a limited actual scope for Pareto-better adjustments and that such adjustments are always a function of the power structure as well as a wide range of non-Pareto optimal changes.[6]

In Buchanan's response to Samuels's initial article, in Samuels's defense, and in the early letters, the issue of positive versus normative, or of description versus prescription, was debated. The discussion quickly moved to various facets of the consequences of a positive analysis which posits the working rules of law and morals as contingent and subject to change and to concern with the consequences of an assumed propriety of the status quo system of power and use of government. We have somewhat different perceptions as to what order requires, as to what should be the "best" approach to the study of government as an economic variable (although neither would deny the other the opportunity to work as he pleases), and, *inter alia*, how these fundamental issues are to be reflected in the conduct of economic analysis. We agree with the Davenport-Samuelson principle that "there is no reason why theoretical economics should be a monopoly of the reactionaries,"[7] but we are quite far apart as to the nature of an economics (specifically the nature of the analysis of the economic role of government) which will both contribute to a free and open society and have meaning as knowledge. Needless to add, neither Buchanan nor Samuels takes one position or another in pure black-and-white terms. But just where we stand and the impact thereof for the issues debated will have to be assessed by others as well as by ourselves. It is our hope that more economists will once again turn to these important issues.

Notes

1. James M. Buchanan, "Politics, Property, and the Law: An Alternative Interpretation of Miller et al. v. Schoene," *Journal of Law and Economics* 15 (October 1972): 439-52.
2. Warren J. Samuels, "Interrelations Between Legal and Economic Processes," *Journal of Law and Economics* 14 (October 1971): 435-50.
3. Warren J. Samuels, "In Defense of a Positive Approach to Government as an Economic Variable," *Journal of Law and Economics* 15 (October 1972): 453-59.
4. James M. Buchanan, "The Limits of Liberty: Between Anarchy and Leviathan" (Chicago: University of Chicago Press, forthcoming). See also his "The Coase Theorem and the Theory of the State," *Natural Resources Journal* 13 (October 1973): 579-94. See Warren J. Samuels, "Welfare Economics, Power and Property," in *Perspectives of Property*, Gene Wunderlich and W. L. Gibson, Jr., eds. (University Park: Institute for Research on Land and Water Resources, The Pennsylvania State University, 1972), pp. 61-148, and "Public Utilities and the Theory of Power," in *Perspectives in Public Regulation*, Milton Russell, ed. (Carbondale: Southern Illinois University Press, 1973), pp. 1-27. See also Warren Samuels, "The Coase Theorem and the Study of Law and Economics," *Natural Resources Journal* 14 (January 1974): 1-33, "Law and Economics: Introduction," *Journal of Economic Issues* 7 (December 1973): 535-41, *Pareto on Policy* (New York: American Elsevier, 1974), and "Some Notes on Government as an Economic Variable" and "Government in the History of Economics" (in manuscript).

5. Gordon Tullock, ed., *Explorations in the Theory of Anarchy* (Blacksburg, Va.: Center for Study of Public Choice, 1972), pp. 36–37. Compare the review thereof by Samuels in *Public Choice* 16 (Fall 1973): 94–97.
6. Compare Samuels, "Welfare Economics," and "Some Notes on Government."
7. Paul A. Samuelson, "Maximum Principles in Analytical Economics," *American Economic Review* 62 (June 1972): 261.

18 May 1972

Dear Warren:

Thanks for sending me your draft response to my paper critical of your initial paper. I hope that Coase will decide to print it, since I think it does carry the discussion several stages along. And, after all, this is the purpose, to carry the discussion since neither of us would surely claim to have any of the final answers in these issues that have been discussed for centuries.

Let me make one or two more specific points by way of reaction. First, you protest too much your positivist stance. I agree that one can contrast a positivist and a normative stance, and I accept that my own is strictly normative in this context. But I submit that an unbiased reader of your piece would indeed read normative elements into it, and sometimes strong ones. And this through no necessary fault of your own. It is almost impossible to be purely positivist here, and, of necessity, we look at common facts through different windows, to use Nietzsche's term, and these windows are necessarily normative to a degree.

But, as I say, a good point can be made here.

I agree with may of the subcriticisms of my approach, which can be criticized on several grounds. I do not treat of property assignments, and this is what has been troubling me most this year. What can we say? I do not especially like the status quo defense that my methodology forces me into, but where can I go? I have been worrying about this for months now without much resolution or progress.

I should continue to insist that unanimity must remain the only acceptable rules for change, ideally, in any genuinely individualistic social order. And here is the problem. It is essential for social order, or a tolerable one at any rate, that men act as if and think as if the process works in a certain way even if, from another vision, the facts may seem so different. I do not really think that a viable social order that either of us would accept could exist if all men really looked on politics in the eyes of the elder Pareto, which sharply separated the rulers and the ruled. The basic and necessary myths of the free society. These are my main concern, and, admittedly, I have been partially concerned about my own little role in dispelling some of these. Once majority rule is shown to be the tattered relic that analysis must reveal it to be, what are we to think??? And of vital importance for our time (as surely is evidenced by the Wallace support) men must *not* see the judiciary as overtly legislating, even though, as scholars, we must recognize that judges do legislate and always have. But Earl Warren's tragic error was his failure to understand this.

These are but a few reactions. I should have more as I reread the paper and think about it more adequately.

Sincerely,

Jim

May 24, 1972

Dear Jim:

Thanks for your letter regarding my response to your paper.

Let me comment as follows:

I basically agree with you concerning the impossibility of a completely value-free positivism—but I think that the effort to generate as pure propositions as possible is desirable. People *will* read normative things from any positive proposition, but in reality they are adding their own normative premise and it is from that premise they draw their normative inferences. Thus, for example, my paper on government in the history of economics has made happy neither scholastic, libertarian, nor Marxist—but the central argument, despite its tautological element, remains intact!

Concerning the defense of status quo rights, the problem is that there is no agreement on the mechanism of change. Either we posit the status quo rights or some other structure of rights, or we posit some system for change. The problem has been discussed by Cardozo and Pound in books done years ago; see Cardozo's *The Growth of the Law, The Nature of the Judicial Process*, and, especially perhaps, *The Paradoxes of Legal Science*, and Pound's *Social Control Through Law*. The genius of the common law has been its gradualism, involving a balancing of continuity of rights against change of rights. The lawyers overdo the wisdom of their lady of the common law, but they have a point.

My own methodology forces me into allowing that an agnostic positive analysis opens the doors to change, to the lifting of the veil, so to speak. At the bottom of your first page, you say that, "It is essential for social order, or a tolerable one at any rate, that. . . ." Two points here: first, we must distinguish between seeing social order as a substantive attainment—i.e., as a set of particular relations—and seeing social order as a process of adjustment, including adjustment between continuity and change. Second, men (and women) do live by myths, but I dislike the game of pretending that things are otherwise than they are, that only safe things should be said in public, and so on. I dislike that with the admitted displeasure that there is only so much change that a society can put up with at one time or over a period of time. Here too we must distinguish between a particular structure and the process: In order for the pretense to have very much recommendatory forces, the status quo at stake must have some recommendatory force of its own—so that when I consider the function of pretense I try to examine it not only in the case of my own society but also in the case of societies of which I am not at all fond, e.g., the USSR, among others.

So there are dangers from an absolute and uncritical acceptance of the status quo *and* from an absolute and uncritical piercing of the veils and masks of society. This goes back, of course, to Plato versus Aristotle and their conflicting theories of the relation of knowledge to social action; to Mannheim on ideology and utopia; et al.

I think that this problem was the central problem which disturbed the late Frank Knight throughout his intellectual life. As for Pareto, what he said in the *Treatise on General Sociology* was said perversely but with much wisdom; but there has been much work done since then.

. . .

A last word: perhaps you are right about Earl Warren's error, I do not know; what I do know is that if he was in error, so was the "conservative" court in the 1890s and 1920s and early 1930s in so clearly doing the same thing, namely, reading *their* vision of good economic policy, their vision of the proper resolution of class and other interest conflicts, into the Constitution. What I also know is that the Constitution is only a framework and it is inevitable that different world views will read and interpret it differently. I think that one role of the scholar here is to articulate how that has been done and not to mask it or to read his own interpretation of the clauses involved into his own analytical work. That is the value of a positivist approach, so far as it will take one.

. . .

Yours sincerely,

Warren

16 August 1972

Dear Warren:

. . .

As we both realize, our basic positions differ substantially. Despite this, however, I think that your efforts in this, and other pieces, are extremely useful. Economists need to be pulled up short on just what it is they are assuming when they talk about government, about the state. And your piece ["Government in the History of Economics"] certainly accomplishes this.

My difference with you lies, I think, in what you have called my essentially normative position, which I do not, in turn, quite accept as such. I think that there are positive elements that can enable us to distingusih among governmental forms. It seems to me that we can derive a logical basis for government of what you call the Lockean variety from the simple calculus of free men, and that no similar logical basis can be so derived from alternative forms. Descriptively, of course, I agree with you. We can always look on government as the agency through which some men exert power over others, Pareto's position. But we need to do more than sit outside, so to speak, and describe. We need to work within a philosophy, or so it seems to me. And there are differences among the alternatives. This is where I categorically disagree with you I think. The alternatives are not equally weighted. The despotic government is "worse" by objective standards, or quasi-objective standards, then the free government. Hitler was worse than Churchill. We can apply positive analysis to derive a constitutional structure, and this structure will have many elements of what you label as Lockean that merely support middle-class interests and property. But property, correctly interpreted, is nothing other than the way we define a man, his ability to do things. Hence, any government must defend property. You slip too readily into meaningless terms when you talk about defense of classes and groups.

All of this relates quite closely to what I have been working on all summer. I have been trying, with only partial success, to derive a concept or theory of government as it might have emerged out of Hobbesian anarchy. This involves first a description of this anarchy and then a discussion of the basic contract, with its emendations. From this I get into the role of government in its various forms. I plan to then use this derivation as the basis for diagnosing what is wrong now. We agree, I suspect, on the fact that there is utter chaos in our thinking about most of these matters. And this is where I come full circle. Your paper can be of benefit in forcing economists and other scholars to think more clearly.

Sincerely,

Jim

August 23, 1972

Dear Jim:

. . .

Let me react to your letter as follows, all too briefly.

There are positive elements which *help* us to distinguish between forms of government; but is the differentiation to be normative or positive? You refer to objective standards and then qualify the argument by jumping to quasi-objective standards. Let's face it: whether you use logic or anything else, a logical basis for government of the Lockean variety is like any other normative, normative in its conception of what you call "the simple calculus of free men"—"free men," Jim, is too general, it avoids the problems arising when principles of freedom conflict and it avoids too specifying the underlying conception of "freedom." Furthermore, whatever the logic, as de Jouvenel put it (p. 249 of *Power*), "ideas get political meaning from the class which takes it over" (quote may not be exact; working from notes). But my main point is that your derivation of the logical basis of or for government will be normative. So that when you use this derivation (your last paragraph) as the basis for diagnosing what is wrong, you will be circular or tautological in that you will be applying the notion of wrong that is built into your logic or premises. You cannot derive an ought from an is alone and your analysis will not permit you to do so: you will be applying the ought built into your logical system or whatever you call it.

You cannot apply positive analysis to derive a constitutional structure *alone*: you need norms; implicit or explicit they are there, e.g., built into your concept of freedom or consent or what have you. I agree with you about the meaning of property but class is not entirely meaningless; you use it yourself three lines earlier.

I agree with you, too, about Hitler being worse than Churchill and about the need for working within a philosophy, and that there are differences—qualitative differences—between the alternatives. But: (1) there should not be an economic science built up pretending to be a science but which is only another ideology, and (2) there should be positive descriptive work (of my type) so that those who do want to construct normative systems will be better informed as to what is involved. Our norms are probably rather close; but we differ as to whether economics can be positive when it includes certain values which take on the luster of hard truth. I do not say that the alternatives are equally weighted; I am saying that we ought to know just what each one involves.

You earlier wrote me that your system favors established rights; when established rights are concentrated in relatively few hands, such concentration runs up against the notion of freedom involving a wide diffusion of rights and power; and it is exacerbated when the power holders use their power to further enhance their own capture of opportunities and inhibit the rise of the nonpowerful. The freedom for the few is wrong, just as the equality is wrong which is self-defeating in terms of the system.

Yours may well be an idealist position when mine, perhaps the realist position, says that you are trying to simulate with logic what is *in reality* a function of power, knowledge, and psychology. Or, whatever "the basic contract," it is only a framework within which power play etc. takes place. Yours is the attractive but utopian position, I think! Or, to the same effect, so long as anarchy without social control is repugnant, the problem boils down to what (whose) system of social control.

The real gut issues, which cannot be resolved once and for all time, are: whose values; the balancing of freedom and control; the balancing of continuity and change; the balancing of hierarchy and equality. There is no simple calculus of free men—or none that does not ignore important facets (someone's important facets) of what it means to be free. Thus Hayek emphasized the rule of law, but as one of his own students (I believe) put it, there can be a foul law which we would not want all to be equally subject to. Moreover, the tragedy is that perhaps every institutional arrangement which perfects or cements freedom in one regard or for some people can be used to tyrannize others.

I repeat: I do not deny the existence of qualitative differences between alternatives, but (a) let's think clearly about government, and (b) let's see exactly what those differences are. Perhaps what I dislike the most (relevant to this discussion) is the pretense of those who would enjoin others' use of government while denying their own use of government, when the heart of the matter is which (whose) use of government. Knight would insist that my analysis does not make a good propaganda for economic freedom (his words, from his review of Robbins on the classicists) but I do not intend it to be—except in the sense that I believe that open and full and free discussion is necessary for a free society, in large part as a check on the cupidity of the powerful and on the foolishness of many others.

Perhaps the best historical way of putting this is in the terms I heard some years ago about the Chicago School: in their zest to defend the business system they defended anything that businessmen did (and against all others, save the consumer). Well, there is more to the business system than optimal market adjustments—as you have read in my paper on welfare economics, power, and property, and perhaps in the one on utilities and the theory of power.

Apropos the utility paper "Public Utilities and the Theory of Power," I hope to prepare an appendix dealing with responses to the paper while in draft stage. Among other responses, I have one which presumes what Gray called the old public utility concept (which he says has been corrupted) and concludes that I show the utility system to be corrupt etc.; and I have another which says that since that is the way the system is, anything the utilities do is fine. Needless to say, given that my analysis is positive description (and correct—which I do not want to argue, at least here), in order to reach either of those positions, one needs an additional normative premise—which I did not provide!

I have gone on much longer than I had planned; I hope I have not bored you.

Yours sincerely,

Warren

27 March 1973

Dear Warren:

Gordon Tullock has showed me a copy of your review of the anarchy volume. It is a fine and perceptive review, and I shall find it helpful in my own efforts toward completing the book I am half-way through in draft.

Your response to the JLE paper was, also, very good. One of my projects, to be completed when I get the time, is to write a new paper, not in response to you so much, but one stimulated directly by your accusation that my position is normative. I found this at first amusing, since I had just returned from a conference on property rights in San Francisco where I was, literally, read out of court because I was "positivist" in refusing to allow ethical norms to enter explicitly into the analysis. At the conference, I had read essentially the same paper as that which you discuss at length in the review and the first of my two in the anarchy book.

But, in a sense, you are quite correct. But we do use the word "normative" in two quite distinct ways, that need to be carefully distinguished. My approach is not normative in any sense in which this term is most often used. I am not taking an advocacy position grounded on my own or anyone else's values. What I am doing, and explicitly, is to look at the universe of observations from a specific vision or window of social order, essentially the contractual one, in which men are free to trade. You are correct in that this way of looking at the world, either currently or historically as in the red cedar case, depends on my own private set of philosophical principles or tools. But most people would not call this normative, although it is personal, subjective, private. My main argument against you is that your position is, necessarily, also normative in this sense. At this level, positivism is impossible. You are, and you are of course allowed to do this, looking at essentially the same universe of observations, but with a different private, personal, subjective vision. You see different relationships because you look with different tools. Neither of us is normative, and both of us are positive, in the standard usage of these terms. But both of us are normative in the solipsist, subjective sense, as indeed all social science must by nature be.

I do bridle a bit at being labeled an establishmentarian. At a deep emotional level, I hate the "eastern establishment," far more, I am sure, than you do, and I suspect that, at base, I come much closer to the "revolutionary" than do you. One perceptive reader of our exchange in JLE interpreted you as defending the status quo, not me, and I think, correctly. In my vision, the status quo does have a unique place, for the simple reason that it exists, and hence offers the starting point for any peaceful (contractual) change. This is not properly labeled a defense of the status quo, as such. It seems to me that the establishmentarian would be one who defends the established way of doing things, which is far from my own position. We have gone far far away from the constitutional order that I should think essential, and my last chapter is, I hope, to be on "Prospects for Constitutional Revolution." I am, basically, a "constitutionalist" first of all, which is inherent in "individualism," terms that I gladly accept as descriptive of my position.

There is, at base, a faith here. If your "positivist" analysis of what we see is correct, and it may well be, then I simply cannot extrapolate this into a viable future social order at all. There will be collapse into anarchy, or tyranny, of one sort or another. I am by nature pessimist, but I must retain faith that what you describe is not basically descriptive, or at least need not be. I must hold onto the faith that individuals can live with one another, with at least the minimal respect for rights of others (minimal delineation of property rights) that makes society possible. My efforts are aimed at trying to analyze just how social order, to be viable at all, depends critically on a mutual willingness to accept individual rights, defined constitutionally, and enforced by the State. And how this might possibly be done without the state assuming powers of Leviathan. Perhaps you can call this a romantic attitude, perhaps it is. Your position, as I now interpret it, is closer to Hobbes than I had originally interpreted it. Incidentally, I was wrong in putting you in the "social welfare function" camp in the JLE piece, or at least I now think so.

But these are interesting issues, far more so than those with which most economists, or social scientists for that matter, deal. When and if I get my book in any sort of draft that I am ready to show to readers, I should greatly like to get your comments. I am shooting for September as the time for this, and I may send a copy along if my schedule is met.

Sincerely yours,

Jim

April 5, 1973

Dear Jim:

. . .

On the normativism issue: yes, we are both subjective and we are both making methodological judgments (see Tarascio, *Journal of Economic Issues*,

March 1971, 98–102). But you are deliberately building in—presuming the propriety of—the status quo whereas I am "only" providing for critical discussion of the status quo. Your specific vision builds in values on the most fundamental level; mine does not. If that is correct then the deepest normative element in my analysis is the provision I make for changing the status quo by building in the critical discussion of the status quo—but notice that this is open-ended, as no specific values are built in to guide change, only the door is opened. There is infinitely more implicit ethicizing in your approach than mine (selectively exercised, to be sure) as my paper on welfare economics, power, and property argues in regard to the ethical significance of the Pareto criterion. Further, I think that you are selective in what you accept from the status quo.

As for being establishmentarian: your writings seem to mix (a) the defense of the status quo and (b) an ideal system in which change comes from gains from contractual trade. Two points. First, it is hard to follow all this since you shift from a prejudice for existing rights to a desire to institute a new system of a particular genre. Part is against change and part is for change and the part that is for change is against all but contractual change thereafter. The second point has to do with your constitutionalism: whose constitution is it to be, since that will be of profound consequence in terms of results? Which rights will be protected and what provision for rights change in ways not loaded in favor of those in superior or advantageous positions in the status quo will be provided? I find, further, that in the real world of today you are more statist, Platonic, and authoritarian in your system than I am in mine: you want to establish a system whereas my analysis does not.

As for my own posture in re the status quo, I prepared a paper last summer on public utility regulation and power to which some responses had me convicting the utilities of social sins and others had me taking them off the hook. I urge that my analysis is strictly objective (given the subjectivity alluded to above) and that others' reactions involved *their* injection of an additional normative premise by which they read me as supporting or criticizing utilities, when all that I intended was to describe and nonnormatively interpret. My analysis, while it does open the door to critique of the status quo, does not presume its propriety nor does it abort any assumption of the propriety of any other system, including yours, insofar as it is normative. The reader of our exchange in JLE who saw me as defending the status quo either read certain normative elements into my analysis or juxtaposed my analysis to your proposed social order, a juxtaposition that was improper because my analysis is positive and not normative in regard to the status quo (and would be positive and not normative in interpreting your system if it existed) whereas yours is normative.

As for the problem of faith: you are, indeed, a pessimist by nature. I am not a pessimist by nature, though I am somewhat increasingly becoming a cynic. I always try to be an objective analyst—trying, whether optimistic or pessimistic about anything in particular. I do not see anarchy or tyranny, but much muddling through—though I must confess . . . that I dislike the state and the concentration of power via the war power. But I would guess that you elevate national security very highly and, while not in favor of the nation-state system, are prepared to live with it, with the war power of great moment necessarily. Also I would guess that while you may have second thoughts about the current administration and its corruption and arrogance (Watergate, ITT, etc.) you favor it versus a so-called liberal administration.

I would add that whatever the merits of your proposed system, and it has its attractions, its functional role in this world is to protect the status quo.

I am not sure, moreover, as to your meaning of "eastern establishment" and why you feel the way you do about it.

Also I would urge that society is comprised of more than property rights, that there are functional equivalents to property rights which your analysis neglects, e.g., regulation, because (at least in part) you prefer a once-and-for-all-time determination and assignment of rights by law.

. . .

Yours sincerely,

Warren

August 8, 1973

Dear Warren:

. . .

Now to your comments in the letter dated 5 April. The real issue concerns the place of the status quo in our respective scheme of things. I realize that my own position necessarily makes it seem that I am defending the status quo, and in a sense, I am doing so, not because I like it, I do not (and in this respect I am surely more radical than you are I think). But my defense of the status quo stems from my unwillingness, indeed inability, to discuss changes other than those that are contractual in nature. I can, of course, lay down my own notions and think about how God might listen to me and impose these changes on me, you, and on everyone else. This seems to me what most social scientists do all the time. But, to me, this is simply wasted effort. And explains much of the frustration. It seems to me that our task is really quite different, that of trying to find, locate, invent, schemes that change command unanimous or quasi-unanimous consent and propose them. Since persons disagree on so much, these schemes may be a very limited set, and this may suggest to you that few changes are possible. Hence, the status quo defended indirectly. The status quo has no propriety at all save for its existence, and it is all that exists. The point I always emphasize is that we start from here not from somewhere else. And as an economist, all I can do is to try to talk about and explain ways of changing that are conceptually contractual, nothing more.

This does allow me to take a limited step toward normative judgments or hypothesis, namely to suggest that the changes seem to be potentially agreeable to everyone, Pareto efficient changes, which must, of course, include compensations. The criterion in my scheme is agreement, and I cannot stress this too much. My approach is strictly Wicksellian here.

Having said all this, I realize that we are a long long way from ever defining properly just what is the status quo, and here I think my book goes a long way toward resolving some of your worries about my position. Given universal adult franchise, we had best start thinking in terms of just what this set of rights does via political process about the nominal claims to physical property that we talk about. "Ownership" is very fuzzy here, and needs clearing up, at least before we can so much as begin to suggest constitutional-legal changes.

Perhaps my own position is best summarized by a statement I made in the manuscript: viable society is impossible unless most people conceive political order in the consent paradigm. I am working always from this base.

Your position, as I now interpret it, is very close to Pareto, and I have much respect for it, and it holds continuing attraction for me, far more so than it does for the overwhelming majority of our colleagues in the profession. But aside from the necessary subjectivity in observation, which we both acknowledge, the positivist position is, at base, too cynical for me. As both Washington Irving and Joseph Conrad said, along with many others, it is nice to treat the world as if we were sitting in an observer's rocking chair and looking at its absurdities. But this is not enough. I think that I have, personally, some responsibility to do more than this.

As for your inferences about my current political attitudes, these are only partially correct. I do view the greatest danger to be Leviathan, the State, and I was strongly in Nixon's camp when he tried to make this the second-term theme, pre-Watergate disclosures. For these reasons, I tend to support whatever party or candidate that will promise to cut the size of government, central government in particular, down. I am not, as you infer, greatly interested in or concerned about national security issues. Perhaps I should be, but this is a point of continuing argument between Gordon Tullock and me.

My comments about the eastern establishment and my feelings toward it are based on a personal experience that has colored my attitudes. As a southerner, I was long ago explicitly and overtly subjected to discriminatory treatment of a particularly blatant sort. Hence, my broad sympathies with those who talk about the establishment. More soberly and rationaliy, I use the term pejoratively to refer to the dominant and pervasive attitude of the eastern-based media-intelligentsia axis. Exemplified now by the *Washington Post* treatment of Watergate.

. . .

Sincerely yours,

Jim

September 1, 1973

Dear Jim:

. . .

We apparently do not disagree as to the place of the status quo in your approach. Whether you defend the status quo for one reason or another it still has the position of being taken for granted. Moreover, you do more than say that it has to be reckoned with because it does exist; you go further and apply the unanimity or consent rule to any change from the status quo, thus giving it a preferred position normatively; it may not have any propriety at all save for its existence, as you put it, but the propriety which you give it because of its existence is all that is necessary. Change or continuity of the status quo *is* a normative matter and your approach builds in the continuity of the status quo.

You are quite right in stipulating (p. 2) that we are a long way from ever defining properly just what is the status quo. The status quo is selectively perceived and changed; it is differentially treated, depending upon the identification thereof. This is a point I made in my paper on welfare economics and power. The principle of selective perception, with regard to the status quo, freedom, coercion, government and so on, is very critical to the areas in which we are working.

You want only contractual changes from the status quo, i.e., consensual, unanimous (or quasi-unanimous) changes. But I find ubiquitous externalities produced by contractual changes. The Buchanan-Stubblebine Pareto-relevant and Pareto-irrelevant analysis obscures the importance of this (as I developed in the same paper). The problem with the consensus-unanimity-consent rule is that it neglects non-Pareto optimal changes through the market. It has a narrow identification of injury and of evidence of injury. The Pareto rule is thus itself applied only selectively and not to all changes or to all visitation of losses. The thrust of part of your analysis would also apply the consent rule unequally or selectively: only to government and not to market changes. The generalized externality problem is much greater, deeper, and more ineluctable, I fear, than you recognize.

Apropos the normative quality of your analysis, I reiterate my plea for a positive analysis of government and of public choice generally. The political economist, institutionalist or otherwise, must study more than choice from within opportunity sets (which is what the contractual model involves) and study the formation of the structure of opportunity sets, as they are in the real world. As you correctly perceive I am not trying to play God, only trying to study the legal-economic world as it is. It may shock you for me to say this but your endeavor to find or invent schemes that change through unanimous or quasi-unanimous consent is itself one form of playing God, Jim: for you are trying to reduce the set of change processes that are open to society, to subgroups within society, and to individuals. That the consent principle is attractive to me (whatever faults I find with it) does not obliterate that fact. Needless to say, I would not deny that the consequences of positive or descriptive, objective study of what is may have similar effects and that some of them may be untoward.

As for the status quo, it is not contractual and there is no justification for giving it such preeminent status simply because it is in existence and requiring contractual and only contractual (consensual, etc.) change from now on. Let me make a series of terse points about this:

1. Your approach to continuity versus change would very narrowly channel, indeed, very narrowly interpret, what Joe Spengler has called the problem of order. As a practical matter—not as a normative matter—I think that Pareto knew better, that while he was clearly sympathetic to the Pareto-rule he must be chuckling at the extent to which many people seem to think it empirically relevant. In a forthcoming book on Pareto one of the things I show is the extremely narrow empirical status of the Pareto rule according

to Pareto himself. I also show his great realism as to how the world really is, as well as his own use of the rule in a conservative manner. Normative predilections do have to come up against the real world—though you may feel that I am here decidedly much less radical than you, perhaps even reactionary.

2. Your approach to public choice (which defends the status quo indirectly, as you put it) neglects the hard decision-making society faces with regard to difficult issues of the power structure (the balance of freedom or autonomy and control, as Spengler puts it); or, rather, predisposes both normative and positive analysis along the lines of one strained (I think) solution or resolution thereof. It allows the privileged in the status quo to hold out and perpetuate themselves by being able to withhold their consent. As attractive as the consent (unanimity) rule is, it places too much power in the hands of the already privileged, indeed cementing their mortgage upon the future; and it fails to comport with the experience and realities of public choice, and is evasive of the real problems of public choice—which Tullock and others did get to in the *Explorations* book. In other words, in part, it reenforces the power of the powerful in the status quo to produce non-Pareto optimal changes not subject to controls exogenous to themselves, and it does this by giving them a veto (as Arrow and Baumol have commented).

3. Your approach, then, or so it seems to me, completely avoids the distributional issues: distribution of income, wealth, power, and so on. It epitomizes the rationale of a contractual age to the neglect of status or distributional realities in the status quo and thereby to the neglect of private power play factors; to the neglect, that is, of the fact that power operates *through* the contractual market even cet. par. government.

4. As for government, your once and for all time legal property rights identification and assignment process (quite a mouthful but very important) denies opportunity for future generations to review the social structure—even incrementally—and to revise institutions, including the Constitution. It perpetuates the past, which is to say, it perpetuates the decisions of those with power in the past (the status quo); it ignores non-Pareto optimal changes and their impact; it subjects the future to the system of the past. Continuity versus change *is* a problem and cannot readily be resolved through a unanimity rule; resolution through the market is only one narrow and incomplete solution.

5. I also must say that your disregard of the distributional issue takes for granted the existing pattern of interests which government has been used to support, whereas the rights identification and assignment process is a continuing one. There is something of fantasy here: a fantasy of a once and for all time rights identification and assignment process, a fantasy which parallels the fantasy (of the Coasian analysis) of ubiquitous markets for everything.

6. I would repeat the point which Al Schmid and I have repeatedly made: before Pareto efficient changes can be made, an antecedent determination of whose interests must be made. Your analysis seems to accept the status quo when it was not contractually produced or adopted, a major restriction upon your own principle.

7. I would add the point that you cannot derive an ought from an is: the fact that the status quo does exist does not mean that it ought to be defended by any rule like that of unanimity, does not mean that it should

be given, even indirectly, preeminent status. History involves a subtle value clarification process in which values are exploratory and emergent, and the changing status quo must be subjected to valuational analysis—and your unanimity rule is not the only component thereof.

Continuing, with regard to your statement on p. 2 that "viable society is impossible unless most people conceive political order in the consent paradigm," I suggest that you must have a special meaning of "viable" that becomes tautological with the consent paradigm: e.g., given viability requiring consent, it follows that only consent produces viability.

Returning to my emphasis on the positive (your p. 2, paragraph 4): I emphasize knowledge (positive analysis) is a basis for action, thereby making choice and the art of the possible more informed, trying to minimize or at least identify any values that creep in. This is hardly a cynical position (though I do have considerable cynicism in regard to power play in reality). If we do not follow a positive approach with students then we tend to make of ourselves high priests in respect to our own values and, moreover, we obscure the scope and meaning of the actual "public choice" processes that exist in society. Before we try to change those processes (there I go again, becoming a reactionary!) we had better learn how they work—which is the message long insisted upon by conservatives. My objection, then, to your scheme is that it is unrealistic in those respects—I think that I called it utopian in the best tradition in my response to your paper reacting to my JL&E paper.

I come next to your desire to cut the size of government, to reduce the power of government. I make the following points:

1. the power of alpha is relative to that of beta; if one's power is reduced, the power of the other is increased. Whose power is enhanced if government power—central government power—is reduced? That is an empirical question, in part at least.

2. De Gaulle wanted to "reform" the French senate ostensibly to diffuse power back to the localities; the French saw through that, I think: they saw that this meant that only he would have real power at the center and that the ostensible diffusion of power really meant further concentration of power.

3. Nixon's new federalism similarly may be seen—you will find this offensive, I am sure—as an attempt to reduce the use of government (the central or federal government) by certain groups by diffusing the power of government—but this would only mean that certain other groups in control at the state level and lower would have power. This is not diffusion of government as much as it is a restructuring of the control of government. It may also mean that government would be controlled by more concentrated power than—paradoxically—when it was centered in Washington, i.e., government in the aggregate becoming less responsive to the larger numbers or wider range of interests than formerly.

4. So that I suggest that the mere invocation of one change in the power structure without study of the total power structure may not and probably would not permit perception of just what power-diffusion or power-concentration consequences will follow.

5. I guess that we may differ in your eyes this way: that you oppose concentrated government power and my analysis looks to all concentrated

power and the two are different, government power being more malicious. That may be true to a point; but I would have you recall my argument that it is not a question of government or no government but which government or which interests government is to support. If Howard Hughes were the nation's or the system's sole capitalist we would be just as socialized as if we had a traditional socialist regime.

Finally, apropos Watergate: Jim, de Tocqueville inquired as to where the principle of authority in our system resided and he found it in public opinion and, upon seeking further, located it in the press; that is to say, he saw a tension between the politicians and the press when there was no alliance between them, both competing at times to influence public opinion. In my view, the *Washington Post* was doing precisely what it would have been doing following de Tocqueville: serving as a check on government. The pity is that more papers were not so inquisitive and that the *Post* stumbled on it all by accident almost. The press is a major check on the emergence of tyrannical power in our world—it is this despite its seeming and perhaps actual arrogance. (Social control institutions are, after all, power players themselves; the answer is in pluralism, but that is another story.)

Your attitude, Jim, toward the *Post* seems to me to presume too much in favor of governmental authority. You seem to identify with authority here, perhaps because you would prefer to think of Nixon as safe, perhaps not. I think that there is in your mental structure a subtle admixture of emphasis upon freedom and emphasis upon tradition and authority (see the first three papers in Meyer, ed., *What is Conservatism*?). Nixon-Agnew is a disaster for the moral fibre of this country. Knight said that there is precious little freedom even in a free society; I hope that we have what little there is now in 1984. Orwell was no fool; I think he sensed that tyranny would come from the right in the West.

I think that I share your dislike of the nation-state system; at any rate, I thoroughly dislike the nation-state system. Yet I have great concerns and fears about national security in the existing nation-state system. We are surely entrapped in a Greek tragedy. But I also fear the abuse of national security by political groups on the make and by self-serving politicians, as well as by those enamoured of nationalism and the like. We are caught in a web of dysfunctional psychology, misconceived and misapplied definitions of reality, and the machinations of those who play the game of power in the nation-state. With your views about the *Post* and Watergate I can only infer that you would excuse the Administration because it is "safe" insofar as socio-economic policy is concerned. If that is too strong, please excuse me for jumping to conclusions.

As for the discrimination you have suffered as a southerner: I lived in the South for something like seventeen years in Miami, one year in Missouri, and one year in Georgia. I can understand, perhaps, your feelings and sympathize with them, though I do not know of my having been discriminated against, at least on that account. I hesitate to say this, Jim, but the reputation of the South (which is admittedly not that much worse than the North) is deserved in the matter of slavery and segregation. I know that both are "solutions" to the problem of heterogeneous populations, but I think that the valuational process of society can and has come up with better solutions. Still, two wrongs do not make a right. Incidentally, this is a good example of how social-structure and power-structure factors can inhibit and impinge upon and operate through the contractualist marketplace.

In sum, then I would say the following. You are primarily normative and I am primarily positive in our respective endeavors; you are trying to indicate how things would go if they were organized in the manner you prefer (e.g., your interpretation of *Miller* v. *Schoene*) and I am trying to objectively describe (as objectively as I can at any rate) how things are going in the way they are presently organized. Curiously, you take the status quo for granted in your normative system and I take it only as the object of my positive study. Furthermore, with regard to your normative approach, while I am sympathetic I find problems with it, first, in juxtaposition to other normative considerations and, second, with regard to its feasibility in the world as I see it positively. Is this how you see our respective positions and relationship?

. . .

Yours sincerely,

Warren

16 November 1973

Dear Warren:

. . .

There is a basic philosophical difference between us; this we both acknowledge. There also remains some communication failure, but it seems unlikely that this can be cleared up in correspondence. The central point hinges around the discussion of the status quo, and about the humility required of the social scientist. Let me demonstrate by reference to one phrase in your letter of 1 September (bottom of page 2, middle of paragraph). You say that my position "places too much power in the hands of the already privileged." I accept this, and agree with it, as a value judgment. But who are you and I to impose our private values as criteria for social change. Each man's values are to count as any other's, at least in my conception, and what I am looking for are the implications of this genuinely "democratic" position for what we can, as social scientists, say about social change. This is the whole basis for the status quo and its uniqueness, and for the Wicksell-Pareto criterion for change. I can readily extend my conception to cover your worries about ubiquitousness of externality in market dealings. In an extremely abstract model, one in which the status quo is very well defined, and agreed on, all changes, in any form, must require unanimous consent, at least in the limit of rules.

Many of the points of disagreement will possibly be clarified, at least to the extent of knowing precisely where we disagree, when you get the opportunity to read my book, a manuscript of which I shall send you as soon as I get a copy available to send you.

. . .

Sincerely,

Jim

December 13, 1973

Dear Jim:

. . .

You are correct that we maintain our original differences but I think that now we are more informed about them. Perhaps there is communication failure also, I am not sure and tend to doubt it. Our differences are, first, over the valuational force of the status quo and, second, the role of positive and descriptive analysis.

I concur that the status quo is unique: it exists. But it is not humility to accept it: it is a valuational choice, a choice which constitutes the imposition of one's private values for (against) social change. Your private values (or mine, for that matter) with regard to the status of the status quo are no better than any change oriented one, notwithstanding that the status quo exists and has to be reckoned with.

The rationale that each man's values are to count as any other's is inaccurate and obscurantist in the context of any system of privilege. It presumes an equality that does not exist. There is coercion even in a market relying upon contracts; the problem is not coercion or no coercion but coercion within which institutional or power structure. The Wicksell-Pareto rule, as you call it, governs, but does not eliminate, the structure of coercion and sacrifice. Neither you nor Rothbard seem to want to recognize that structures of private privilege—particularly when ensconced in the Pareto criterion—can be just as damnable as government at its worst, especially when viewed from the perspective of those excluded from privilege. Moreover, the unanimous-consent-within-the-rules begs the substance of the rules as, say, imposed and/or administered by and in favor of the privileged.

Your position is clearly normative except in the context of a science (positivism) which studies the status quo only to cast luster on it, which gives effect to antecedent normative premises concerning the propriety of the status quo, in which case the normative character is present albeit not so clearly seen.

I find it hard to believe that you would have the Wicksell-Pareto criterion apply to any and all extant systems, to any status quo.

I also find that disciples of your position do not merely accept the status quo (and then proceed to exchange as the route to change) but only selective aspects of the status quo, e.g., accepting concentrations of power deemed hospitable to or consonant with capitalism but excluding others.

In short, I think you carry your acceptance of the status quo too far.

As for positive science, I still insist upon the possibilities of knowledge about legal-economic interrelations that can be gained from positive, objective descriptive analysis of the status quo, as in my original JL&E paper. I have further developed my ideas in the paper sent you earlier, comprising some notes on government as an economic variable.

Apropos the problems I find with your seemingly uncritical acceptance of the status quo, I find that positive study indicates that the world is an arena for struggling over continuity versus change and that the future, like the past, is made in the process. The reality is one of vast difficulties in adjusting the status quo to desired changes and that is an existential burden upon man, one not easily avoided by adopting the Pareto criterion.

Which brings me to Pareto himself: Pareto, in the *Treatise,* knew better, namely, that there is only a thin slice of social reality amenable to the Pareto criterion (as we have come to call it), and that most of the world is a matter of power play, the manipulation of derivations as vehicles for the manipulation of sentiments. My relation to you, in terms of principles, is much the same as the relation of Pareto's descriptive work to the Pareto criterion. Moreover, Pareto did not advocate the Pareto-rule as *the* criterion (as you do); he coupled it with the possibility of change in accordance with other decision rules based on values and/or sentiments; this notwithstanding that he strongly tended to conservatively apply the Pareto criterion himself.

In short, I think that we had best objectively analyze government as an economic variable, in part as an economic alternative.

. . .

Yours sincerely,

Warren

January 1, 1974

Dear Warren:

Thanks for your letter dated 13 December. Let me respond once again to your remarks on my interpretation of the status quo. Apologies if I seem to be repeating what I have said before, but mayhaps we are coming closer to an understanding of each other's position.

The key remark that you make, to me, is "in the context of any system of privilege." This implies that you, somehow, have already introduced some standard, some external criterion, to determine whether or not privilege exists. My approach requires, and allows, no such external criterion to be introduced. I say that I observe persons, as they exist, and as they are defined by the rights they possess. I do not place evaluation on relative positions, since, conceptually, I cannot know what relative positions should be in some normative sense. Note that I do not, repeat not, imply that persons are *entitled* to what they possess. (I use this word here because just yesterday I read Nozick's long piece on "Distributive Justice" in the new issue of *Philosophy and Public Affairs;* presumably a chapter from his forthcoming book *Anarchy, Utopia and the State.* Nozick does, in contrast to me, present an entitlement theory of justice.)

Persons possess rights, vis-à-vis each other in an observed social order of sorts. What is my role, as a specialist in *contract* here? Is it not to try to point out ranges of mutual gains from exchange, from trade, in whatever form? This is what I mean by humility, an unwillingness to go beyond the contractual limits imposed by the disciplinary specialization of economics.

By comparison, if I were a specialist in power relations among persons, I should look at the same set of interactions and try to suggest ways in which some persons may gain more power over others or may present others gaining power over them.

I do not see that these two roles need intersect in the same diagnosis or that the prescriptions be the same at all. Nor do I see that either approach necessarily involves evaluation in the sense that you suggest.

Consider the following mental experiment. You are allowed to observe, but not to be a participant in life on another planet. You observe two beings, which seem to be of different species, interacting one with another. You have no external criterion to tell you whether or not the observed interaction is imbedded in a system of privilege since you have no way of knowing much about alternative systems. As an economist, you observe what seem to be potential improvements, defined in the Pareto sense as providing more of everything to both parties. Your contribution lies in pointing this out, in explaining these possibilities.

I agree that, in a separate and distinct role, you may also make positive contributions, in the purely descriptive sense, in working out uniformities in the relationships that you observe, in delineating the structure of power. And, in offering some understanding of this set of relationships, you can be of assistance in the former and different role. Also your work may be of major help to the party whose power may be enhanced by greater understanding. (The Prince who followed Machievelli's precepts surely fared better than the one who did not. But this did not imply that Machievelli, himself, placed any normative evaluation on the role of one prince or the other.)

My distance from Pareto, or from you, is not nearly so far as you imply. Descriptively, most of what I see is explained precisely as you suggest Pareto explained most of what he saw. But this wholly detached role is simply not a responsible one until and unless one does something else. I go beyond this purely descriptive role in trying to find contractual improvements; that is all. You too, go beyond this role in talking about systems of privilege, etc. Pareto, in his old age anyway, more or less opted out, in my sense became irresponsible. Is this the ideal role you seek to play? I can respect this, but, if so, you need to rid yourself of evaluations, to quit talking about systems of privilege and the like, and to sit back, literally, in the scholar's rocking chair and do nothing but observe the world that you see.

. . .

Sincerely,

Jim

January 7, 1974

Dear Jim:

. . .

Perhaps we are coming closer to mutual understanding notwithstanding repetition.

Certainly I disagree with your view that specification of the power structure—say, system of privilege—requires a standard, some external criterion. I admit that it is a difficult task but positive (descriptive) and normative definitions or specifications of status quo power structures can be differentiated; one does not pass judgment, necessarily, upon a power structure by identifying it. As I perceive your position on this, it easily becomes useful as a stratagem to mask the existing system of privilege, to obscure it, or to permit selective alternation of it. Needless to say, the high priest function is repugnant to me, although I do acknowledge its function in legitimizing this or that system or subsystem.

I certainly do not totally object to seeking contractual solutions; but I do think that they cannot be projected in a vacuum which allows the status quo power structure to go unspecified and unexamined. As for economics as a discipline, I do not feel that the disciplinary specialization of the field mandates contractual limits. Economics does serve the high priest function (some economists perform very well at it) but I prefer to see economics as the objective study of the factors and forces governing resource allocation, income distribution, level-of-income determination, and the organization and control of the economic system. I do not feel that disciplinary specialization requires that I preach or preach only certain things—or study only certain things. As someone interested in power relations, furthermore, I am interested in description and not the advisory role.

With regard to your extra-terrestrial example, your argument rests upon ignorance by the observer, which further study can tend to correct; this same ignorance must tend to distort the substance and decrease the usefulness of any perceived potential improvements. Nothing wrong with making such suggestions, of course; but that is different from descriptive analysis. I question how wholly detached is the role you assume. I have in mind here not only that it takes the status quo power structure as given and operates to give it normative stature or propriety, but that as the position is usually employed it resonates with and serves to reenforce traditionalist or conservative arguments. Witness your dismay at liberalism, so-called, which I interpret as objection to certain uses of the state and not others. Your reliance upon the Pareto rule resonates very well with other anti-liberal or conservative arguments.

Upon reflection I find it interesting that you find my analysis of power to necessarily contain evaluations and I find your use of the Pareto or contractarian formula to necessarily contain evaluations. Your position is based upon the value-status of the contractarian principle—which I find admirable but capable of severe abuse—and my position is based upon the value-status of positive, neutral description—which you find, I think, acceptable but capable of severe abuse.

Perhaps we are each following a different strand of Knight's reasoning. You are concerned with order in the sense of stability, continuity, and reliance upon the market, as well as "minimizing" the economic role of government; and I am concerned with description on as fundamental a level as I can get to and master. Thus Knight could argue that there is precious little freedom even in a so-called free society and that religion is not only the opiate of the masses but the sedative of the classes.

(Apropos the last clause of the preceding sentence, I think that you would agree with me that Knight was not introducing external criteria when he recognized the existence of classes [however much they are difficult to precisely identify], that his was a most penetrating analysis of what I would call power.)

When you get a chance to read and reflect upon my paper on some notes concerning government as an economic variable I would appreciate your reactions, particularly as to how I handle the role of government as both a dependent and independent variable, but also the descriptive quality of the analysis given its level of generality.

Rereading your paper once again induces the following, though it is somewhat repetitive of an earlier letter of mine. On page one, paragraph three, you reiterate the humility argument; but on page two, paragraph three, you chastize me for taking a detached view which is not a responsible role (I extend your criticism of Pareto in his old age to me). The argument is—I think—contorted by introducing your perception of my need to rid myself of evaluations (see above); but you would have me not opt out. Two points here: first, I hardly think that an attempt at positive description is really opting out (though I do confess that it makes taking extreme positions for partisan purposes more difficult), rather it seems to me to perform one of the social roles of science; and second, it is not humility to be responsible according to your usage but activism—and an activism that, insofar as the Pareto rule is followed, gives effect to the interests of those with already dominant positions of power. Thus we have come back to where your letter starts, namely, with my interpretation of your posture with regard to the status quo!

. . .

Yours sincerely,

Warren

23 January 1974

Dear Warren:

. . .

Incidentally, our own extensive correspondence has been helpful, for I found very little to criticize in your last long letter to me, dated 7 January 1974. This seemed to me to be a good statement of our differences. With respect to the last paragraph of your letter, concerning my associating you with the aging Pareto's position, and with my own worries about this position, you will be perhaps amused to learn that the major criticism I got from Chicago Press referees was on my refusal to take an activist-partisan role and propose explicit reforms. If I had tried to stay all the way over to the position that you take, I should have brought down the house. Let us face it. People demand saviors, and they want all of us to show them the way. One of the readers for my book even said "he has showed us the way to the golden doors but he refuses to show us how to open them." So it goes.

Sincerely,

Jim

The Challenge of Radical Political Economics

Raymond S. Franklin and William K. Tabb

The following headline appeared in the 11 February 1972 issue of the *Wall Street Journal:* "The Unorthodox Ideas of Radical Economists Win A Wider Hearing." On 18 March 1972 the following appeared in *Business Week:* "Radicals gain professional chic. Their academic status rises as their critique of capitalism gains depth and new listeners." Whether radical economists are gaining professional chic or acquiring more status is less important than the fact that they are challenging mainstream views about the subject matter of economics and how the U.S. economy works. Mainstream orthodoxy not only is experiencing erosion as a result of its own inabilities to explain many current economic realities, but also is losing ground as a result of the emergence of new professional groups. Among these are the new grouping of institutional economists and the Union of Radical Political Economics (URPE), whose more than 1,850 members are devoted to radical scholarship and activities.[1]

Perhaps of even greater importance is the fact that the elementary economics course is no longer monopolized by mainstream economics

The authors, respectively, are Associate Professor of Economics, Queens College of the City University of New York, Flushing. *They would like to thank Professor Barbara Kaplan of the State University of New York, Purchase, and the referees of the JEI for their helpful suggestions concerning various aspects of this article.*

textbooks. This is due in no small part to the reasonably large quantity of new radical material and articles which have been published recently. This new state of affairs represents a sharp contrast to the 1950s, when departments of economics tended to be monolithically Keynesian. That bland Keynesianism complemented the consensus politics and blind optimism of the period.

This article is an interim summary of the major tenets and general orientation of radical political economy by two authors who are themselves radical economists. What is it? Why is it emerging now? What characterizes its political and ideological perspective?[2]

The second and third questions are perhaps easier to answer than the first. The emergence of a new radical political economy is related to a number of factors: the radicalization of the university campus in the 1960s, the persistence of deeply rooted social and economic problems which appear to transcend the purview of mainstream economics, and, finally, the shrinking confidence of establishment economists themselves.[3] These latter are losing faith in their ability to manage the economy and to cope with such problem areas as the twin processes of inflation and unemployment, imperialist involvements, racism in the marketplace, the fiscal crisis confronting our central cities, and the political barriers obstructing the achievements of modest economic reforms.

While the development of radical economics as a distinct approach was related to the radicalization process which occurred on the campuses in the mid- and late 1960s, it is also part of a more extensive intellectual tradition which can be traced to the contributions of Karl Marx. The immediate intellectual progenitors of the current crop of radical political economists are a handful of older Marxists. Among the Americans there are Paul Baran, Paul Sweezy, and Harry Magdoff; the main influences from abroad are Maurice Dobb, Joan Robinson, and Ernest Mandel. In addition, Herbert Marcuse (philosopher), William Appleman Williams (historian), and C. Wright Mills (sociologist), all rooted in the Marxian tradition, have had an important influence on many young radical economists. Thus, the current character of radical political economy has been shaped by young and old scholars from a variety of disciplines writing from within and without the orthodox Marxian framework.

This fact raises an important question concerning the relationship between the Marxian tradition and the younger, more eclectic radical political economists. While the matter is more complex than can be dealt with adequately in this article, it is our impression that the younger radical political economists, while receiving some of their inspiration directly from the works of Marx, derive most of their critical impetus from the muckraker's impulse to expose the system and its apologists. The radicals, especially those trained at major universities, often employ traditional mainstream tools and modes of analyses to derive very radical conclusions. In other words, they use mainstream economics against itself. Some have updated and applied the more orthodox Marxian concepts centering around alienation, commodity fetishism, social relations between capital and labor, the role of the property system, and the domination of society and government by the giant corporation. In our view, the various strands that make up radical political economics have not yet been consistently interwoven. Nevertheless, there is a growing literature which can serve as an exposition of recent developments in the radical argument.[4] It is also important to note that there are many differences among radicals and within the mainstream. We purposely have bypassed some of these differences. We also have omitted discussing areas in which mainstream and radical positions overlap. We do this for the purpose of clarity and realize that these simplifications are in need of modification in many instances.

The Scope of Radical Economics

Defining the *scope* of radical economics is more complex, but five major elements should be noted. These involve the structural transformation of society, centralized planning, the relationship between political and private economic power, wealth and income distribution, and participation in decision making.

Transforming Society

Unlike their welfarist, liberal mainstream counterparts who accept the broad institutional constraints of the existing system, radical economists are interested in the structural transformation of society. They see themselves as working toward ending, not stabilizing, monopoly capitalism, as working for the establishment of a socialist society which involves participatory planning, public ownership, the elimination of production for profit, and a genuinely egalitarian redistribution of income and wealth. They view theorizing not as an end in itself nor as an aesthetic ritual involving rigorous elegance, however irrelevant; rather, they see it as being linked to their advocacy of fundamental change or to their analysis of the barriers which obstruct such change. Economic analysis must deal with problems concerning political and economic power; rarely are solutions only technical in nature, unrelated to the ends or goals established by the given institutional arrangements. Radical economists, therefore, are devoted to providing the theoretical base for a social transformation; their politics are concerned with producing a political and ideological climate that would stimulate institutional changes.

Centralized Planning

While mainstream economists tend to view planning, especially centralized planning, as authoritarian and antidemocratic, radicals believe such a view is a gross oversimplification. They argue that we already have a great deal of such planning and regimentation in the economy, but it is mainly corporate planning for private ends done by a corporate oligarchy that is hierarchical, self-perpetuating, and largely invisible. Public planning with public ownership would broaden participation and widen the arena of public control over the economy. With respect to socialist planning, most radicals favor decentralized forms; decisions should be made as much as possible at the local level, and citizen-comsumer and worker-producer planning groups should decide what and how to produce. Many radicals fear centralized control, whether by large corporations, a powerful Council of Economic Advisors, a Wage-Price Control Board, or a GOSPLAN. Decentralization is a critical element because many radical political economists believe "production" should be concerned not only with the goods and services produced but also, and equally, with the work process itself.

Political and Private Economic Power

Radicals see an intimate relationship between the political apparatus that governs society and the economic concentration of private power. Except for periods of widespread mass agitation, the typical state of affairs is one in which the government does not direct but instead reflects or facilitates the interests of wealth and concentrated economic power. In general, the acquisition of political position and power is seen as something akin to the buying of commodities by the highest bidders.[5]

Income and Wealth Distribution

Because the connection of economic with political power is regarded as so crucial, radical economists assert that any basic understanding of the U.S. social order requires a careful analysis of the distribution of wealth and income and of its generation and transmission over time and between generations. They point to gross inequities in the distribution of wealth. Witness the well-known statistics reported not only in professional journals but also in the more popular business publications:

> In almost every year since 1947, the poorest fifth of American families has received only about 5% of the country's total family income while the top fifth got 42%—an 8:1 ratio . . . . From 1949 to 1969 . . . the gap between average real incomes of the poorest and richest fifths of the population widened from less than $11,000 to more than $19,000 in constant 1969 dollars. . . . According to the latest available survey, the top 20% of consumer units . . . owned 77% of all wealth. . . . The richest 2.5% of U.S. families own 44% of all private assets, while the poorest 25% have, on the average, no net worth at all . . . their total debts just equal their assets.[6]

From facts of this kind, which have been more or less permanent features of our system for the past fifty years, radical economists argue that the unequal distribution of income associated with an unequal distribution of wealth begets an unequal distribution of political power. This imbalance influences the political values, objectives, and policies of the government in ways which curtail social and economic justice and obstruct the economic system's ability to recognize and solve its plaguing problems. In other words, the system is flawed intrinsically by the nature of its hierarchical structure, not simply by the absence of "good" people in Congress or the presence of a "bad" president who did "wrong" things. Because mainstream economists either ignore or casually treat the relationship between political power and economic concentration, they do not understand the nature of the system's policy failures. The conscious overlooking of such interconnections, radicals believe, is *poor* not *pure* social science.

Mass Participation

The normative goals that guide the thinking of most radical economists are mass participation in decision making and the equal sharing of society's income and wealth. In practical terms, this implies that economic differences are to be kept to a minimum within a framework which gives cognizance to the variability in aptitudes, tastes, and psychological temperaments among individuals. This vision of society involves the rejection of the idea of individual gain without respect to the general gain or loss experienced by the group; it stresses the importance of moral over economic incentives.

The conception here is probably best expressed in terms of a "solidarity" principle, that is, one works for the benefit of group interests which need to be *consciously* understood by the individual.

In the radical vision, group competition is not to be eliminated completely; it is assumed that political and social restraints can be devised which prevent such competition from either turning into anarchy or resulting in the expansion and domination of some group clusters over others.

Community solidarity under capitalism is impossible, according to most radicals, because the life conditions of those who own and control the means of production are almost totally different from those of the people employed in the work places of the society. The use of private rationality by the owners of capital, given the maturation of our economic system, perpetuates an ever-widening gap between the technical means of providing a healthy and sane life for everyone and the alienating social relations of production which thwart the qualitatively more humane use of technical capacities.

This solidarity principle, moreover, leads radicals to reject the mainstream's concept of *efficiency,* which is defined in purely economic and technical terms and which necessitates inequality as a work stimulant. In contemporary U.S. capitalism, the important motivating force that keeps the system functioning "efficiently" is the maintenance of inequities which generate a fear of falling behind Smith and a desire to get ahead of Jones. In a good society, radical economists assert, *efficiency* should have far more than an economic meaning. In its profoundest sense it must involve self-realization through the work process, the worker's control over his own workspace, and a belief that the consumer goods being produced are needed and are important to a good life. These beliefs stem from the more encompassing view among radicals of the human condition: how man is socialized, what motivates him, what defines his welfare and well-being, what constitutes his potential for development and growth. Simply put, the rock upon which almost all mainstream economic thinking rests is that man is "naturally" acquisitive and is primarily motivated by his narrowly defined economic interests; absent is a recognition of the extent to which each man's emotions and values are socially rather than uniquely determined. Because of these beliefs, according to the radical, the mainstream economists obscure both the true potential of man and the social nature of the economic problems of our society.

Man's nature, in the sense that most radicals talk about it, is derived from his social relations in production and consumption. Imbuing man with a false vision which negates his social nature can only lead to alienation and breakdown. Radicals typically argue that the collective nature of production, which is ideologically "privatized" in the form of private ownership and self-interest motivation, is destructive to human development.

In a market-dominated society, cars are produced with built-in obsolescence in order to keep the wheels of profit rolling; the environment is polluted without consideration of its value to those who yearn for clean air and relish the beauty of a natural terrain; the "mere" sentimental value attached to an old landmark building and the security associated with stable neighborhoods is destroyed for the construction of an "efficient" superhighway needed by industry. Furthermore, man's morality, sexuality, and sensibility are manipulated for the purpose of the sale of commodities. In sum and substance, U.S. capitalism destroys human relations in order to maintain purely economic ones involving gain, getting ahead, and the private accumulation of things. To allow the market so much importance in the determination of a person's life-style is to attempt to make of man a one-dimensional creature.[7]

These five general propositions and values which relate to the scope of radical economics will be employed below in the analysis of specific areas and problems. For illustrative purposes, we have selected five topics: imperialism, market stratification, urban malaise, waste and the GNP mania, and inflation. Needless to say, there are other important areas with which radicals are deeply concerned, for example, the relationship among value, price, and wages,[8] racial and sexual discrimination,[9] and the origin and nature of "backwardness" in underdeveloped countries.[10]

Imperialism

Most mainstream economists have attributed the war in Vietnam to political drift, some gross error in judgment, or some kind of political-military miscalculation at the highest government level. Whatever the reason, most of them feel that the war has little to do with the nature of U.S. economic interests.[11]

Mainstream economists would disagree with the view of Henry Cabot Lodge, former U.S. Ambassador to South Vietnam and Paris peace negotiator, that the Vietnam War was related to Southeast Asia's "large storehouse of wealth" in the form of "huge rice surpluses . . . rubber, ore, and tin." Nor would they consider the fact that offshore oil exploitation by an oil consortium has been taking place for a number of years. Nor would they regard as relevant the following statement by the Vice-President of Chase Manhattan Bank in charge of Far Eastern operations:

> In the past, foreign investors have been wary of the over-all political prospect for the region. I must say, though, that the U.S. actions in Vietnam this year—which have demonstrated that the U.S. will continue to give effective protection to the free nations of the region—have considerably reassured both Asian and Western investors. In fact, I see some reason for hope that the same sort of economic growth may take place in the free economies of Asia that took place in Europe after the Truman Doctrine and after NATO provided a protective shield. The same thing also took place in Japan after the U.S. intervention in Korea removed investor doubts.[12]

This is not to say that radical economists accept the vulgar Marxism of the Lodges and Chase Manhattan bank officials. Most radical economists believe that the ideology of anticommunism, although serving economic interests, has an independent existence. They believe that military interests, however unrelated to the real national security of the United States, have combined with defense-oriented corporations to expand sales or to maintain corporate solvency. Furthermore, U.S. involvement in Vietnam is simply an extreme case of our general neocolonial entanglement in the affairs of Third World nations, a phenomenon dating back at least to the 1890s and the protracted U.S. war with Philippine guerillas.

Not all extended foreign entanglements, putting aside the initial reasons for the imperial impulse itself, are necessarily profitable from the point of view of the system or the capitalist class as a whole for any duration of time. As a matter of fact, U.S. Vietnam involvement, whatever specific advantages it has bestowed on particular interests, may have become counterproductive in terms of general business profitability; it has eroded our competitive international position *vis-à-vis* European and Japanese capitalism. This, in the radical view, represents one of the numerous contradictions of the imperialist expansionary process. It is not enough to say, as bourgeois economists are prone to do, that the social costs of an imperialist adventure like that in Vietnam are far greater than the private gain. An intrinsic feature of capitalism is its lack of a serious social accounting system; therefore, social costs—like Adam Smith's Invisible Hand—are invisible to the public.

Capitalism, in the radical view, has an expansionary impulse and a momentum which are driven by the logic of the profit motive. The effect on the economy is to enrich the colonizers and warp indigenous development of the colonized.[13] Dominant members of the corporate hierarchy desire the whole world as a market and wish to control as much of it as possible. Their search for investment opportunities and their need to protect established markets have pushed our economic interests far beyond our geopolitical boundaries. Thus, our government periodically is called into action to protect economic interests (however small they may be relative to the general economy of the United States), to control foreign territories, to subordinate areas, to manipulate weaker foreign ruling oligarchies, and to establish economic dependencies and appendages in ways which have very little to do with the security and sovereignty of the United States.

Latin America is a case in point. There, as in the case of other Third World areas, both liberals and conservatives seek to preserve U.S. ownership claims and to maintain valuable terms of trade advantages. Conservatives favor creating and strengthening military juntas; liberals prefer strengthening a local middle class as a buffer group. The latter policy, under the Alliance for Progress, failed because in the majority of cases it was difficult to create even the facade of bourgeois democracy against the entrenched local oligarchies. Faced with the choice of real reform or military rule, corporate interests accepted "friendly" dictatorships. Business views about Latin America are not based on abstract considerations; they are derived from corporate earnings of profit and interest from Latin America, currently exceeding investments by $1 billion annually.[14]

All this does not mean that the radical economists ignore the chauvinism of the Soviet Union, its bureaucratic styles, and the big-power game it plays in the context of the international nation-state system. But for the most part the Soviet Union's "expansionism" (not to exclude China's) is viewed as border oriented. It is, in other words, perimeter "imperialism" concerned with border security, perhaps pathologically so; it is not one that involves domination entanglements far beyond its frontiers. More often than not, the mainstream assertion that Russia or China is also guilty of imperialism is used as an excuse for ignoring or obscuring the nature of U.S. imperialism; it is rationalized that imperialism appears to be a "way of life" characteristic of all big powers.

In essence, the main area of imperialist penetration is in the underdeveloped world, and it manifests itself primarily in economic terms. It is here that the greatest danger comes from the United States, whose preoccupation with overthrowing "unfriendly" governments, even mildly democratic ones, has been well documented.[15] And while imperialism may be a more general problem which transcends capitalism, to U.S. radicals who live in the United States it is U.S.

imperialism against which they are most capable of taking action; therefore, it is U.S. imperialism to which radicals direct their analytic attention.

Market Structure and Stratification

Mainstream economists tend to argue that the individual's income and his position in society are directly related to his ability, that altering income and social position is simply a function of acquiring a better education or more skills through work experience.[16] Radical economists believe this is a gross oversimplification—so gross as to be erroneous. Far more goes into the determination of income and social position in the economy than education and work experience. A worker sweeping the floors of an automobile plant in Detroit earns much more than an identical worker sweeping the floor in a New York bank. Contrary to typical mainstream thinking on this matter, this difference has nothing to do with variations in education, work experience, native endowment, or I.Q.; it has little to do with the human capital explanation of the mainstream economists. This difference is a function of industry, location, unionism, and industrial structure.

In addition to institutional considerations, a basic part of the radical argument revolves about the role played by a stratified labor market. Because of the need to put people in various kinds of jobs that are undesirable, the system wittingly or unwittingly generates rules (based on race, sex, ethnic and class origin, and so forth) for allocating people to jobs.

At the bottom of the labor market are those who do the dirty work of the society—the lettuce pickers, chambermaids, dishwashers, janitors, messengers, car washers. For the most part these jobs are low paying, dead-end, and alienating. Such secondary jobs have an extremely high turnover rate; people work for awhile, quit or are fired, and then look for other similar jobs. These workers are mostly blacks, Puerto Ricans, Chicanos, women, or teenagers.

On the next rung up are workers who do routine primary work—tedious manual labor such as assembly-line work, construction work, menial sales or clerical work. Some of these jobs offer a chance for promotion, union protection, and better pay; these are mostly held by white ethnics.

The line between primary and secondary jobs is not always distinct; thus a typist in a typing pool or a keypunch operator is generally in the secondary job market, whereas a personal secretary would be in the primary one.

Below the secondary work force is the welfare population. Above the routine primary jobs are the creative workers, for example, professionals, media people, managers and executives. At the very top are those who receive their income from ownership rather than from participation in the labor market.[17]

While not immutable, such stratification has a strong propensity to maintain itself; it will not be altered without profound change in the rules of the game. If, for example, welfare payments rise to levels that people could live on, then the poorly paid low status job loses its stranglehold. Welfare payments (or any income maintenance or minimum income scheme) must not be too adequate, otherwise secondary workers will lose the incentive to work in those jobs.[18] Nor is it clear that a family assistance or negative income tax plan would overcome this incentive problem. If adequate income or decent housing is offered the very poor, then the working poor—who perceive themselves as bearing the tax burden of paying these costs—become upset. Therefore, the basic line for a negative income tax could not be set at livable levels. Again, when the unionized primary workers see government programs aimed at training secondary workers to compete for their jobs, they often turn to demagogues such as George Wallace. A real educational reform which would enable the sons and daughters of the poor and the working class to gain access in proportion to their numbers into Harvard, Yale, and Berkeley would, radicals believe, bring cries of outrage from upper-middle and high income groups.

The perspective of radical economists in examining institutions such as the educational system is that our economy needs stratification; therefore, it needs inequitable rules to maintain the economic privileges and social equilibrium of the existing order.[19] Segmentation in the economy leads to the "freezing" of social distinctions. Job career ladders are superficially contrived in order to nurture intra- and intervocational status preoccupations among workers who have neither job satisfaction nor control over work. Occupational divisions of the kind we have been discussing are structured for control. In the absence of more intrinsic work motivation, control is the route to efficiency and profit in a capitalist system.[20]

Mainstream economists, who tend to analyze the economy on the assumption that the structure of preferences and the distribution of income and wealth are exogenously determined, generally bypass the needs of those on the bottom of the economic and social ladder. This is not to argue that the class system is immutable, that its socializing institutions conform perfectly to its structure. To the contrary, a real source of pressure for change derives from the contradictions and dichotomies between the noneconomic and the economic components of the system. Unfortunately, because they lack "tidiness" for the use of "pure" economic tools and methods of measurement, the dynamics of such processes frequently are ignored by mainstream economists. When they make policy recommendations for upward occupational mobility, suggestions are linked closely to the changing economic requirements of the *given* system. This is illustrated by the efforts made over the past few years by human capital economists to justify modest improvements in the educational opportunities for minority groups; such changes are not aimed at eliminating an underclass or menial work. Mainstream economists simply do not think in such terms.

The radical solution to the "necessity" of menial work lies in two directions. As long as such work is required, a good society would undertake a more equitable sharing of it and would provide it with the social recognition which it deserves. It might be argued that a street cleaning job never could be respected or made meaningful. Perhaps this is true; however, in a society which takes pride in its public living space, in the beauty of its streets and roads and parks, workers devoted to the maintenance of the environment might not feel that their tasks are demeaning. The elimination of alienation might be even more possible if work roles were either to include a variety of activities or periodically were interchanged.

Radicals hope that technology ultimately will sweep away all remnants of menial work routines. Furthermore, radicals believe that work can be structured under a different system to make it meaningful and intrinsically satisfying; pride in one's work or its purposes can replace the present state of affairs where most individuals work only because it is necessary for survival or to enhance consumption. To mainstream economists the radical view of work is sheer utopian nonsense; as they see it, it violates human nature. The radical reply is that it is no trick to advocate that which already exists. As John Kenneth Galbraith cleverly pointed out with respect to the "virtues" of practical wisdom: "People who are concerned with being practical never urge anything that is new . . . . If you want to be practical, you should vehemently support what has already happened."[21]

Urban Malaise

Consider next the urban scene. Whatever might be said about the condition of U.S. cities today as compared with that of fifty or one hundred years ago, few would disagree with the statement that the gap between what "could be" and "what is" has widened. Why has this happened?

The radical answer starts with the generally recognized fact that those higher up on the stratified pyramid have moved to the suburbs, leaving the poor and their problems in the central cities. Rural and suburban controlled legislatures have aggravated matters by their unwillingness to offer effective help. The advice the urban economist has offered for remedying these circumstances often has been harmful to the powerless. Urban renewal frequently has meant tearing down the homes of the poor and building for those who add to the tax base of the city—the nonpoor.[22] In fact, the most sophisticated computer models often offer as policy the destruction of poor neighborhoods,[23] forcing residents to relocate elsewhere. Such a policy enables average per capita income in the city to rise.

The highway program, if it follows standard economic efficiency criteria, builds highways to and for upper income suburbanites, not for the benefit of low income city dwellers. This is because most of the benefit from highway construction is in the commuting time saved, and time saved for the rich is worth more than the same amount of time saved for the poor. This policy usually is followed because of technical calculations and, more important, because of the relative power of the two groups in influencing decision making.[24]

It is reasoned that the best highway route is the one which costs less; this usually means constructing the highway through the black ghetto, where property values allegedly are lower. The new mass transit systems planned for or presently under way in San Francisco, Atlanta, and Washington, D.C., are being built on the basis of economically efficient criteria. They will give best service to the relatively upper income suburbanites who will gain easier access to the central business district.[25] The logic of economic efficiency is the same logic which perpetuates the inequality of the system. Cities need good mass transit systems, but the system likely to be built will be one that meets the requirements of a stratified society. To build a system which meets the needs of lower income families and individuals, or one which might dramatically upset the automobile industry, would require that social and political struggles be waged against the class biases inherent in the system and against those interests which perpetuate a need for the given distribution of activities.

Mainstream's answer to many of these problems is governmental subsidies. When the radical looks at the nature of these subsidies, he finds that they frequently aid the rich rather than the poor. Contrary to official rhetoric, subsidy payments reflect biases similar to those discussed in relation to mass transit systems. It is not surprising to radicals that the largest single "welfare recipient" in recent times has been Lockheed Aircraft, which received a prize of $250 million for not being an efficient business; or that most farm subsidies go to agribusiness, very few to small farmers, and none to those in most need—the agricultural workers; or that the current methods of financing higher education lead to a redistribution of income from the bottom echelons to the middle and upper ones;[26] or that obsolescence in owning oil is given special tax consideration, but not obsolescence in owning a particular skill.[27] Nor is it surprising that the largest single federal housing program is the tax write-off to middle and upper income homeowners.[28]

The radical sees giveaway programs such as Telstar or the space buggy as a continuation of a long-standing tradition. He sees these subsidies as a logical continuation of a 130-million acre gift to the railroads in the last century (a land area as large as all of the New England states, New York, and Pennsylvania). He sees the defense corporation profiteers as the descendants of Commodore Vanderbilt, who sold leaky ships to the Union Army, or of Gustavus Swift, who sold rotten meat to the Union Army. In the radical view this is the way the state *normally* facilitates capitalist development. Such matters are ignored by mainstream economists, or they are viewed as deviations exposed by liberal muckrakers striving to make capitalism more honest.

Waste and the GNP Mania

Mainstream economists, at least until very recently, have never doubted the assumption that producing more goods and services automatically was good. John F. Kennedy's 1960 campaign was built around this unquestioned growth fixation. Behind him, giving intellectual credibility to his growth rhetoric, were the country's most prominent welfare liberal economists. Radical economists go beyond mere modification of the growth preoccupation; they see further growth of the kind that presently characterizes U.S. society as detrimental to the well-being of the American people.

The automobile industry is an example. This industry often has been identified as a symbol of the U.S. capacity for great physical output, the energy of its economy, and the well-being of its people. To the radical it has become a symbol of the opposite, a symbol of society's sickness. Much can be and has been said about the automobile. Ralph Nader's rise to fame followed his articulation of conditions which were known intuitively by millions. But there is an economic aspect of the automobile industry which has been less publicized, namely, the large amount of money spent for the construction of an inferior car.

A careful study made by a prominent group of mainstream economists estimated the cost of resources which would have been saved had cars with 1949 model lengths, weights, horsepower, transmissions, and so forth, been produced in each year up to 1960. They found that in that period it cost the U.S. public about $40 billion to produce a car which wears down sooner, uses more gas, is less safe, and costs more to maintain.[29] In other words, billions of dollars have been spent in order to make a product which is in many ways inferior to that which we already had. As if that were not enough, all this productive waste increased the Gross National Product and therefore was considered an improvement in our well-being and welfare. Forty billion dollars could have produced 2.5 million three-bedroom homes.

The automobile industry dramatically illustrates a phenomenon which occurs on a lesser scale in the production of many other goods. It is for good reason, therefore, that most radical economists believe that any serious analysis of the U.S. economy and social order which does not put the large corporation at center stage is irrelevant. To talk about the quality of American life as derived from some kind of value system which is unrelated to a corporation dominated society, as mainstream economists often do, is intellectually obscene.

Inflation

In the economic history of U.S. capitalism, inflation has been a problem only during periods of acute shortages of goods. These periods all have been associated with war. In the aftermath of World War II and with the assimilation of Keynesian wisdom consisting of monetary manipulation and budgetary deficits, the nature of and explanation for inflation has become a problem to mainstream economists. While government has managed to prevent drastic downward swings in the economy, it has not succeeded in bringing about a sustained high level of employment. Some mainstream economists have described the new situation as being one of "high level stagnation"; that is, an economy in which extreme unemployment such as that of the 1930s has been avoided, but one which does not achieve anything approaching the full utilization of the U.S. labor force. The definition of *full employment* opportunistically has been changed from 2 percent to 4 percent unemployment, and currently there is discussion among some mainstreamers in favor of using 5 percent as the definition.

In a situation of high-level stagnation, a new challenge to mainstream orthodoxy has arisen, a challenge which significantly has disillusioned many mainstream economists. Their numerous *ad hoc* inflation theories involving cost pushes, wage-price spirals, and changing price expectations have not explained the existing situation. Moreover, these numerous theories (despite the high-powered statistical techniques frequently employed to test them) have tended to move farther away from empirical validation and from the standard micro assumptions made by mainstream economists. It was not an accident that very few mainstream economists anticipated the period between 1965 and 1972. That is, very few economists at the time came to grips with the nature of the inflationary process.[30] Only in retrospect, after Richard Nixon did an about-face, did they tend to describe (without analyzing) something closer to the truth.

In a nutshell, the challenge stemmed from the simultaneous development of both inflation and unemployment. The current example of this dual process, which had its origin in the 1965 upsurge in military spending, illustrates what sent mainstream economists into a dither. Wanting to fight an unpopular war, but unwilling to tell the public what it eventually would cost them, the government not only continuously lied (as the Pentagon Papers show), but also did not raise taxes to pay for the war directly. The government feared that an increase in taxes would call attention to the real costs of the war and might lead to a taxpayer's revolt and a strengthening of the antiwar movement. Inflation, it must be noted, is a much less recognizable form of taxation. It not only transfers purchasing power from the general population to the government, but also transfers greater amounts from those who have the least power to hedge against it, such as pensioners.

As the inflationary process at home became more and more unruly, an international monetary crisis developed which reflected a growing competitive struggle among the capitalist nations of Europe and Japan. To cope with domestic inflation, Nixon initially pursued a right-wing Keynesian set of policies, tightening the money supply and trimming the federal budget by reducing needed nonmilitary programs. The Nixon effort at controlling inflation was, in fact, a governmentally induced recession to stabilize prices. Nixon essentially was saying that the cost of slowing down the economy must be borne by workers through unemployment and severely limited wage increases. What went wrong, of course, was that governmentally induced unemployment did not abate the inflation. With one eye on the 1972 elections and another on the international monetary crisis, the President and his conservative Keynesian advisors panicked. Within a short period of time, Nixon moved ideologically from the position of a free market, Milton Friedman type of monetarist to that of a liberal, deficit-oriented Keynesian and then to a Bismarckian, wage-price "socialist" controller. In retrospect it turns out that mainstream fiscal economists underestimated the inflationary dangers and that mainstream money managers underestimated the amount of money supply tightening and of unemployment which would be necessary to stabilize prices.

The final result of Nixonomics between 1968 and 1972 was the selective stimulation of those industries suffering from foreign competition, deficit spending, and monetary manipulation and an effort to increase the profit position of the largest corporations. When Penn Central fell and other giants were endangered by liquidity problems, emergency loans and accelerated depreciation allowances came to the rescue. Thus, the state again proved its biases as it intervened in order to save important cogs in the corporate machine.

Mainstream economists have no general explanation for the culmination of this process. At best, their views are *ad hoc* and fragmented. In contrast, the radical economist would point to the historical and structural context that defines the relations between the monopolistic, competitive, and public sectors.[31] The lead sector in this triad is the monopolistic one, with its ability to maintain or increase profits because of its market power even in the face of restricted demand. Wage patterns established in the more productive monopolistic sector to some extent spill over into less productive public and competitive sectors. The politics of the public sector have led to accelerated increases in costs without corresponding increases in output or improvement in services by the public sector. The rising costs experienced in the competitive sector tend to lower its profits since businessmen in this sector are unable to pass on cost increases in the form of higher prices. Workers in this sector find it difficult to make a decent living; many appropriately have been identified as "the working poor."

In the postwar period large amounts of government funds have been funneled into the defense and other concentrated sectors of the economy, but the main benefits of such public expenditure have been appropriated by those least in need. Even though the profits in the monopolistic sector have been large at various intervals, they have not stimulated the absorption of the unemployed or the movement of workers from low wage to high wage sectors. This condition has not led to a revolt against corporate privilege; rather, it has stimulated the middle layers of society to focus their anger downward against the lower class. For social class reasons, the middle class erroneously has come to believe that the bulk of its hard-earned taxable income is funneled into wasteful governmental programs to help "ungrateful" blacks. As a result, the government has found it increasingly difficult to justify its expenditures and tax collections and therefore has had to pursue excessive deficit spending in a context of high-level stagnation. The outcome, despite all the governmental hustling and bustling, has been unemployment and inflation.

The public's seemingly misallocated distrust of the public sector, at a time when more and more of our problems appear to require an increase in the public sector's direct involvement, may be perfectly reasonable. The government simply is not delivering the goods. What the public does not understand sufficiently is why this is the case and how the government's deficiencies are related to the needs, power, and policies of the giant corporations. On this question mainstream economists with their neoclassical focus have little to say.

Radicals believe that a simplified Marxian macro model which divides the economy into its class components (for example, workers and capitalists) in the context of a specified structure explains more than the Keynesian groupings of the economy into consumers, investors, and government. In the radical view the mainstream's glib dismissal of a class analysis represents a basic conceptual deficiency in their mode of analysis of both developed and underdeveloped societies. The radical response to mainstream's more "functional" categories is to ask: Should we treat both Jim Bass and David Rockefeller as consumers? Is the corner gas station owner an investor in the same sense as the committee that runs Texaco or General Motors?

The unfamiliarity with radical concepts and general categories on the one hand, and the almost unanimous acceptance of mainstream vocabulary and tools of analysis on the other, put radicals at a competitive disadvantage in many discussions about methodology. The mainstreamists draw on a widely known and axiomatically accepted structure of beliefs. The radical is granted none of his or her premises *a priori*. In a debate with mainstream professionals who have been nodding in agreement for years, radical statements that originate from outside the "monastery" appear clearly "foreign" and "invalid." However, outside the monastery there is a real and changing reality which will, in the radical view, eventually break up the monastic chanting of mainstream monks.[32] This will happen because, among other reasons, what is now labeled as radical critical sniping sooner or later will blossom into an integrated, formal alternative to mainstream's orientation to the world. This is why radical economists have been so involved in Thomas Kuhn's basic paradigm idea.[33]

Summary

Radical economists see the U.S. economy as primarily dominated by the monopolistic sector, consisting of corporate giants. While the government may not be simply the "committee" of this sector, the government certainly has and exhibits strong protective biases in its direction. More generally, the government acts to support class privilege and recreate it intergenerationally through the workings of its major institutions, for example, education, health, police, and the judiciary. This class bias on the part of the government does not necessarily eliminate the possibility of achieving modest reforms through the political process. But, from the radical perspective, reforms conceived within the *modus vivendi* of existing institutions cannot be consequential.

An example is the Nixon freeze of wages and prices, which has been criticized by welfare-liberal economists as working better in controlling wages than prices. From a radical viewpoint, even if liberal democrats were elected and seriously tried to limit profits, such a policy ultimately would fail. As Salvador Allende's government found in Chile, capital too can go on strike. If U.S. corporations actually were to feel the effect of higher taxes, the response might be "loss of confidence" and a slowdown in the economy, with the resultant demand for "stimulation" of the corporate sector. With an economic slowdown jobs are lost, tax revenues decline, and the pressures on politicians to "do something" intensify. In the short run, the only thing to do is to stimulate the economy. The right-wing Keynesian solution which has been followed in the United States consists of corporate tax credits and decreases in personal income taxes, or government work projects which, because they are poorly conceived, debase the image of government as producer and innovator and therefore accentuate the already noted problem of the government's justification of its social welfare expenditures.

The difficulty for those who would like to follow a more egalitarian economic policy, as George McGovern learned, is that such changes would take time and would require struggle against entrenched interests. At the same time, politicians need quick results if they wish to remain in office. Basic reforms which would restructure established patterns would meet tremendous resistance from those who stand to lose from such restructuring. A full-blown struggle against the maintenance of privilege means that during such a transformation economic conditions might get worse before getting better. Time would be needed before new power relations were established and new leadership groups not wedded to old ways emerged, until new methods and incentives operated well and people gained confidence. Few or no leaders operating in the U.S. political context of short-run political expediency would survive this kind of transition unless he or she were the representative and spokesman of a movement whose members had a long-term commitment, were aware of the cost of fundamental change, and understood the dimensions of an effort to overhaul the U.S. economy.

Most liberals and conservatives argue within a common framework. Both tend to accept as a premise that the key goal is economic growth, although they sometimes argue about how the benefits of this growth are to be distributed. For both, the key is how to use resources more efficiently. Since the basic instruments of economic growth in a capitalist economy lie within private corporations, the key to growth is to aid these corporations, a view concisely expressed by Nixon on 7 October 1971 when he said: "All Americans will benefit from more profits."[34]

Mainstream economists begin with the question of how, given the existing market structure, legal framework, and so forth, we can best stabilize capitalism (prevent economic crises, help it grow, and so forth). Radicals ask how society can be restructured to fulfill different goals and needs, those which relate to cultivating a different national style of life: a different work process, a different sense of community and neighborhood, different social relations, and a different mode of solving society's problems. To radical economists, such changes cannot occur until commerce, private property and its corresponding privileges, and profit cease to dominate the main aspects of U.S. society. Their politics revolve around class agitation and advocacy programs aimed at nurturing new centers of power among the less privileged members of society. Their intellectual labor is devoted to criticizing mainstream arguments, ideas, theories, and policy recommendations and to exposing the class biases of mainstream recommendations.

While part of what ails U.S. society may be related to industrialism per se, a significant part of the malaise is related to the characteristics of U.S. capitalism itself. It is the radical claim that many of these specific characteristics are not being seriously analyzed by mainstream economists. The persistence of grave economic and social problems capable of breeding social unrest is the basis for the belief that the growth of a new group of radical economists is permanent.

It is not without reason that Paul Samuelson, Nobel prizewinner and leading U.S. welfare-liberal economist, recently remarked: "Within American universities today the radical economists constitute an important trend and a serious research movement from which much will be heard in the future."[35] While our disagreements with Paul Samuelson are numerous, we believe that he is correct on this point. There is a future for radical economists.

Notes

1. URPE is involved in a variety of activities. It maintains its presence at professional gatherings by selling its journal, occasionally agitating for radical changes in the American Economic Association, and arranging sessions dealing with topics often avoided by mainstream economists. URPE also holds regional conferences and publishes a monthly newsletter and academic journal, *Review of Radical Political Economics.* Through its Movement Coordinating Committee, URPE works with community action groups in the interests of building a radical political movement.
2. The authors wish to warn the readers that we, as radical economists, have not always been able to separate our own interpretations of the radical position from others. It should be further noted that our understanding not only has been derived from published material, but also from oral history, where nuances that rarely are published are articulated, nevertheless. Finally, we have not developed some of the sharp differences that exist among radical economists themselves. Our excuses for these shortcomings are twofold: (1) the standard one, that is, any article has its limits because of time and space; and (2) in order to achieve a degree of coherence in the presentation of the contrast between radical and mainstream economics, it became necessary to subdue some of the differences within the radical camp.
3. See Wassily Leontief, "Theoretical Assumptions and Non-observed Facts," *American Economic Review* 61 (March 1971): 1-9; Kenneth E. Boulding, *Economics as a Science* (New York: McGraw-Hill, 1970); Benjamin Ward, *What's Wrong With Economics?* (New York: Basic Books, 1972); J. K. Galbraith, "Power and the Useful Economist," *American Economic Review* 63 (March 1973): 1-11; and Oskar Morgenstern, "Thirteen Critical Points and Contemporary Economic Theory; An Interpretation," *Economic Literature* 10 (December 1972): 1163-89.
4. See the following: Richard C. Edwards, Michael Reich, and Thomas E. Weiskopf, eds., *The Capitalist System: A Radical Analysis of American Society* (Englewood Cliffs, N.J.: Prentice-Hall, 1972); Tom Christoffel, David Finkelhor, and Dan Gilbarg, eds., *Up Against the American Myth* (New York: Holt, Rinehart & Winston, 1970); David M. Gordon, ed., *Problems in Political Economy: An Urban Perspective* (Lexington, Mass.: D. C. Heath, 1971); Milton Mankoff, ed., *The Progress of Poverty: The Political Economy of American Social Problems* (New York: Holt, Rinehart and Winston, 1972); David Mermelstein, ed., *Economics: Mainstream Readings and Radical Critiques,* 2d ed. (New York: Random House, 1973); Howard Sherman, *Radical Political Economy: Capitalism and Socialism from a Marxist-Humanist Perspective* (New York: Basic Books,

1972); and James H. Weaver, ed., *Modern Political Economy: Radical and Orthodox Views on Crucial Issues* (Boston: Allyn and Bacon, 1973).

5. The current *cause celebre,* as this article is being written, is the Robert Vesco bribe ($250 thousand to the Committee to Reelect the President), the attempted cover-up and alleged involvement of the Securities and Exchange Commission, the former Secretary of Commerce, and the former U.S. Attorney General. These, in the radical view, are not aberrations. Large contributions to political parties and causes by businesses normally are made with the expectation of a payoff (be it illegal in nature), a government contract, some hot information about a pending governmental decision conducive to land speculation, or the introduction of a bill granting some particular interest a special privilege. While the market may be the place where businessmen invest the bulk of their funds, the "parameters" that mainstream economists are so prone to ignore frequently are established in the political arena by an investment process that falls outside the purview of mainstream logic.
6. *Business Week,* 1 April 1972, p. 56. For more academic studies on which such statistics are based see Robert J. Lampman, *The Share of Top Wealth-Holders in National Wealth, 1922-1956* (Princeton, N.J.: Princeton University Press, 1962); Dorothy Projector and Gertrude Weiss, *Survey of Financial Characteristics of Consumers* (Washington, D.C.: Federal Reserve System, August 1966); and James D. Smith and Staunton K. Calvert, "Estimating the Wealth of Top Wealth-Holders from Estate Tax Returns," *Proceedings of the American Statistical Association* (September 1965): 248-65. Good summaries appear in Letitia Upton and Nancy Lyons, "Basic Facts: Distribution of Personal Income and Wealth in the United States" (Cambridge, Mass.: Cambridge Institute, May 1972); and Lester C. Thurow and Robert S. B. Lucas, *The American Distribution of Income: A Structural Problem,* a study prepared for the use of the Joint Economic Committee, Congress of the United States, 17 March 1972 (Washington, D.C.: U.S. Government Printing Office, 1972).
7. See Karl Polanyi, *The Great Transformation* (Boston: Beacon Press, 1957, paperback edition), chap. 6; and Herbert Marcuse, *One-Dimensional Man* (Boston: Beacon Press, 1964).
8. E. K. Hunt and Jesse G. Schwartz, eds., *A Critique of Economic Theory: Selected Readings* (London: Penguin Books, 1972).
9. William K. Tabb, *The Political Economy of the Ghetto* (New York: W. W. Norton and Co., 1970); Raymond S. Franklin and Solomon Resnik, *The Political Economy of Racism* (New York: Holt, Rinehart and Winston, 1973); and *The Political Economy of Women, Review of Radical Political Economics* (July 1972).
10. Andre Gunder Frank, *Capitalism and Underdevelopment of Latin America* (New York: Monthly Review Press, 1969).
11. Part of the analysis of imperialism represents the thinking of the authors. It is based on the work of many radical political economists, few of whom would agree with everything that is said, but most of whom would endorse the general line of argument.
12. Quoted in Harry Magdoff, *The Age of Imperialism* (New York: Monthly Review Press, 1969), p. 176.
13. Paul Baran, *The Political Economy of Growth* (New York: Monthly Review

Press, 1957); Frank, *Capitalism and Underdevelopment;* and Robert I. Rhodes, ed., *Imperialism and Underdevelopment: A Reader* (New York: Monthly Review Press, 1970).

14. See Thomas E. Weisskopf, "Capitalism, Underdevelopment and the Future of Poor Countries," *Review of Radical Political Economics* (Winter 1972): 1-35. See also two other issues of *Review of Radical Political Economics: Case Studies in Imperialism and Underdevelopment* 3 (Spring 1971), and *Capitalism and World Economic Integration: Perspectives on Modern Imperialism* 5 (Spring 1973). See also Magdoff, *Age of Imperialism*, chap. 4.
15. Andréas Papandreou, *Paternalistic Capitalism* (Minneapolis: University of Minnesota Press, 1972).
16. J. Mincer, "The Distribution of Labor Incomes: A Survey with Special References to the Human Capital Approach," *Journal of Economic Literature* 8, no. 1 (1970): 1-26.
17. For examinations of the labor force along these lines, see the following: Barry Bluestone, "The Tri-partite Economy: Labor Markets and the Working Poor," *Poverty, and Human Resources Abstracts* 5 (July-August 1970): 15-35; and David H. Gordon, *Theories of Poverty and Underemployment* (Lexington, Mass.: D.C. Heath, 1972).
18. Frances Fox Piven and Richard A. Cloward, *Regulating the Poor: The Functions of Public Welfare* (New York: Vintage Book, 1971).
19. Herbert Gintis, "Education, Technology and the Characteristics of Worker Productivity," *American Economic Review Papers & Proceedings* 61 (May 1971): 266-79; Samuel S. Bowles, "Unequal Education and the Reproduction of the Social Division of Labor," *Review of Radical Political Economics* 3 (Fall 1971): 1-30; and Christopher Jencks et al., *Inequality* (New York: Basic Books, 1972).
20. Stephen A. Marglin, "What Do Bosses Do? The Origins and Functions of Hierarchy in Capitalist Production," Harvard University, February 1971, mimeographed.
21. "Eleanor and Franklin Revisited," *New York Times Book Review*, 19 March 1972, p. 2.
22. See Alan A. Altshuler, *The City Planning Process: A Political Analysis* (Ithaca: Cornell University Press, 1965); and Jewel Bellush and Murray Hausknecht, eds., *Urban Renewal: People, Politics and Planning* (New York: Doubleday, 1967).
23. Jay Forrester, *Urban Dynamics* (Cambridge, Mass.: M.I.T. Press, 1970).
24. Frances Fox Piven, "Comprehensive Social Planning: Curriculum Reform or Professional Imperialism?" *Journal of the American Institute of Planners* 36 (July 1970): 16-29; and William K. Tabb, "Distributional Planning and Alternative Futures," *Journal of the American Institute of Planners* 38 (January 1972): 25-32.
25. Gordon Fellman, "Neighborhood Protest of an Urban Highway," *Journal of the American Institute of Planners* (March 1969); Ralph Ives, Gary W. Lloyd, and Larry Sawers, "Mass Transit and the Power Elite," *Review of Radical Political Economics* (Summer 1971): 68-77; and Larry Sawers, "Metropolitan Transportation Planning: A Primer of the Urban Transportation Problem," *Review of Radical Political Economics* (Spring 1970): 69-74.

26. W. Lee Hansen and Burton A. Weisbrod, *Benefits, Costs and Finance of Public Higher Education* (Chicago: Markham, 1970), p. 77.
27. The Oil Import Question," Cabinet Task Force on Oil Import Control (Washington, D.C.: U.S. Government Printing Office, 1970). See also "Oil Industry Paid 8.7 Percent in Federal Income Taxes in 1970," *Congressional Record,* 92d Cong., 1st sess., vol. 117, no. 159 (October 1971), pp. S16896-98.
28. "The U.S. Commerce Department estimates that the American public received $12.1 billion in imputed rent by owner occupied housing in 1968," B. Tuchman, "Economics of the Rich," unpublished manuscript, 1972.
29. Franklin M. Fisher, Zvi Grilliches, and Carl Kaysen, "The Costs of Automobile Model Changes Since 1949," *Journal of Political Economy* 64 (October 1962): 416-24.
30. *The New Economics and the Contradictions of Keynesianism, Review of Radical Political Economics* 4 (August 1972).
31. James O'Connor, *The Fiscal Crisis of the State* (New York: St. Martin's Press, 1973).
32. We are not suggesting here that radical economists are void of rhetoric and ritualizing and participating in professional seances. Our only point is that mainstream economists indulge far more than they are aware and care to admit.
33. Thomas S. Kuhn, *The Structure of Scientific Revolutions,* 2d ed. (Chicago: University of Chicago Press, 1970).
34. Quoted by Howard Sherman, "Inflation, Profits and the New Economic Policy," *Review of Radical Political Economics* 4 (August 1972): 113.
35. Paul A. Samuelson, "Liberalism at Bay," *Social Research* 39 (Spring 1972): 27-28.

Goals in Social Economics

Arthur Schweitzer

The theory of social economics by Max Weber is built upon the premise of an effective interplay between the economic and non-economic factors in the economy. Instead of supplying only the data for the pure economy, non-economic factors penetrate into the economy, interact with economic factors, and thus give rise to a distinct social economy. Since Weber could not complete his theory, it behooves us to build upon his foundations. Adolph Lowe, in his recent book, places great emphasis upon the interaction between the two kinds of factors so that his ideas fall within the scope of social economics. In the following pages we shall first examine Lowe's suggested theory and then seek to discover the relevance of some of Weber's economic ideas for our time.

Study of the social economy is concerned with two distinguishable sets of problems. One deals with the penetration of the non-economic factors into the economy; the other considers the interaction of the economic with non-economic factors within the economy. Non-economic factors penetrate into the economy along five different lines. Motives, approval, orientation, directives and regulations are not alien intruders but persuasive penetrators that in some form populate the social economy.

In specifying these penetrators, Weber came close to a definition of socio-economic action. In any society, provision of goods and services is not achieved by separate and isolated individual acts, but definite social relationships arise among the participants in the process of economic provisioning. As soon as economic provision becomes interconnected with social relationships, economic acts transform themselves into socio-economic actions. Instead of one uniform process of decision-making, interpenetration leads to socio-economic goals, socio-economic attitudes, socio-economic rules of conduct, socio-economic directives of the powerful, and to socio-economic regulation by governmental bodies. Rather than being composed of micro and macro mechanisms operating everywhere autonomously, interaction gives rise to socio-economic households and enterprises, socio-economic organizations and markets, distinctly different national economies and socio-economic systems. Any theory of penetration and interaction has thus always to explain the causes and effects of these coupled actions and institutions, culminating into divergent socio-economic systems.

One of Lowe's major concerns is to explain the nature of the genuine interaction between the extra- and the intra-systemic factors in the econ-

The author is Professor of Economics at Indiana University, Bloomington.

omy. These are his terms for economic and non-economic forces.[1] His central claim is that his theory of control locates the forces responsible for the patterns of interaction taking place within the political economy. "Control as an operational principle" not only replaces the principle of competition, but it is seen as the counterforce to the micro-autonomy of the private economy. Control takes the form of "public policy that concerns itself with the shaping of the behavioral patterns" of private economic actors. Control as the central principle leads to an "instrumental theory" that is largely normative in character and deals mainly with the rules of social engineering.

Unfortunately, formulation of the theory of interaction in terms of control leads to a confusion between the social and political economy. The entry of the penetrators and their role in the social economy is inadequately explained because they are seen mainly as stepping stones for, and justifications of, giving control the central place in the analysis. Since the control is mainly a political factor which cannot represent and explain the influence of social penetrators, it seems appropriate to distinguish between the social and the political economy. Consequently, I submit, economic actions influenced by the first four penetrators—motivation, approval, orientation and directives—belong to the social economy, while regulation and control of economic units by governmental bodies comprise the political economy.[2] In the following pages we shall examine mainly Lowe's suggested theory of social economics.

THE THREE-STAGE SYSTEM

Starting from conventional theory, Lowe subjects the law of supply and demand to a very detailed examination for two distinctly different purposes. One purpose is to bring into view the distinction between intra-systemic and extra-systemic factors and analyse their interaction. This distinction calls for condensing conventional theory into five postulates: profit maximization, stabilizing expectations, self-equilibriation in markets, full utilization of all available resources, and a macro-equilibrium that assures optimum provision for all consumers. In such a self-contained economy, implicit in these postulates, "intra- and extra-systemic forces associate without genuine interaction" (p. 60), since the latter are only adding or subtracting from the respective equilibrium quantities of the pure law. The task of the theory of social economics is to analyse the

[1]Adolph Lowe, *On Economic Knowledge: Towards a Science of Political Economics,* New York, 1965. Figures in parenthesis refer to the pages of this book.

[2]Business promotionalism by government may be initiated and pushed through by private groups so that it may be shifted from the political to the social economy. See my typology of government economic actions in *Big Business in the Third Reich,* Bloomington, Indiana, 1963, pp. 350-358.

markets in such a way that the effects of the economic laws are equally attributable to the interaction of both forces.

Lowe's other use of the conventional theory is to discover the relationship between the five postulates and actual economic systems. Pure theory "concerns itself almost conclusively with market economies," but "only within and between the modern national states of the Western world did market relations assume the dominant role in mass provisioning, culminating in the so-called free markets of the nineteenth century." That is, free "from governmental interference, from privileges of status, and from institutional restraints other than those laid down in the civil and criminal codes of law" (p. 28-29). While conventional theory arose with capitalism, theory and the actual system did not develop hand in hand. Since capitalism developed in successive stages, giving rise to early, industrial, and organized subsystems, Lowe investigates the question of whether and how far classical, neo-classical and modern theories succeeded in explaining the three stages of Western capitalist development.

While markets were central for and common to each stage, the extra-systemic forces differed significantly, so that the markets themselves changed their character. During the early stage, or industrial revolution, the principle of maximum profit "became the supreme maxim of market behavior" (p. 69). Markets were self-regulating and the all-round pressure of competition established a uniform price in each market that had to be accepted by all marketers. In spite of overlooking some essential details, classical theory succeeded in explaining the markets in early capitalism. In the industrial stage, however, small-scale technology was gradually replaced by large-scale technology, entailing large investments which gave rise to industrial markets. Being subject to cyclical fluctuations, these markets suffered from extreme price fluctuations and lost their capacity for self-adjustment. It was only "the automatic escape mechanism of economic growth" that "brought all downswings to an early stop and gave the secular movement of output and employment the appearance of a continuous boom" (p. 77). Economic growth minimized the impact of the mounting technological immobility upon the structure of markets. Neo-classical theory did not come to grips with the problems of growth and industrial technology. In the stage of modern capitalism, two different influences gave rise to organized markets. Governments supplied instruments of stabilization so as to support the too weak self-balancing tendencies of markets. At the same time, private business organizations introduced various elements of private control which were designed as measures of self-defense against the growing uncertainty of the ever more complex industrial markets.

Rather than modifying the law of supply and demand by accounting for the influences of cyclical fluctuations, secular growth, stabilizing influences of governments, and to counteract uncertainties by business, the supporters of micro-theory insisted on the distinction between competitive and monopolistic markets, thereby misunderstanding the motives leading to governmental and private interventions in the industrial markets. While Keynesian macro-statics did not come to grips with the increasing technological immobility, thereby missing a central characteristic of organized capitalism, the *General Theory* succeeded in "tracing the instability of income, output, and employment back to the fundamental psychological and institutional order of the core processes itself" (p. 220). Precisely these psychological and institutional entities—propensity to consume, long-term expectations, and liquidity preferences—and the institutions of wage unit and money supply provided the means by which one could explain why the rise in secular growth ceased to mitigate the length and severity of the cyclical downswings.

In confronting the three versions of conventional theory with the three stages of capitalism, Lowe comes to some important conclusions. In regard to social economics, central is the particular choice of the extra-systemic factors and their specific relationship to the intra-systemic factors. In micro-economic theory, "the notion of maximizing utility is much too general to have any concrete meaning" (p. 204), since the possible response of a buyer to a fall in price may be that he will raise his demand, reduce it, or leave it as it is. Macro-economic theory gives us only a catalogue of possibilities: Whether a particular volume of investment will reach or fall short of full employment depends upon the particular value of the marginal propensity to consume, the expected marginal efficiency of capital, and the liquidity preferences as well as upon the maneuverability of the institutional factors. The extra-systemic factors thus occupy a strategic position in any empirically relevant theory. Lowe implies that success in socio-economic theory depends upon (a) finding the empirically relevant propensities, (b) estimating accurately their "precise values" for the short and long runs, (c) discovering both the constant but strategic institutions, (d) stating the functional interrelationship between the propensities or preferences and the aggregate economic quantities, (e) locating the maneuverable institutional factors that have the capacity to mould the propensities and preferences in desired directions.

In regard to economic systems, Lowe's confrontation suggested that conventional theories provided an adequate criterion for discovering the stages of capitalist development but not for identifying correctly the factual characteristics of each stage. He felt that only the classical theory of markets found its empirical counterpart in the industrial revolution. Nothing corresponded in reality to the neo-classical theory of markets. In fact, this theory merely "covered up the ever-widening gap between theory and facts by distinguishing between 'pure' and 'applied' economics" (p. 211). While the Keynesian theory gives valid reasons for interventions by government, the role of the extra-systemic factors is misjudged, since their stimulating effect in a recovery is made dependent upon the physical fact of the average durability of capital (p. 255). Modern theory thus provides only an incomplete description and explanation of the present phase of organized capitalism.

Lowe thus implies that the factual characteristics of subsystems can be discovered by a critical examination of conventional theory. I am not persuaded by Lowe's argument that classical theory envisioned correctly the essential features of early capitalism. Nor does it seem adequate to equate organized capitalism with "mature industrialism." If the term "organized" is taken seriously, recent history records only two attempts for achieving an interplay between private and governmental organizations within the framework of capitalism. During the short period of the NRA, private trade associations were authorized by the government to fix prices and determine sales quotas for producers. In the first phase of the Nazi economy, markets were effectively controlled by the two reinforcing networks of compulsory cartels and compulsory trade associations, operating under a very loose supervision of the government. An ideology of self-government developed in the minds of business leaders, according to which the government should not use a rise in aggregate demand for directing the whole economy but should grant orders to specific concerns, thereby respecting the fixed prices and market organizations of private business.[3]

Actually, in Lowe's treatment there is no reference to specific organizations in markets so that the term organized capitalism is a misnomer. The entrance of public control becomes the central characteristic of his new subsystem. In consequence, it is not organized but controlled capitalism that is here under investigation.

There are thus two distinctly different lessons that one can learn from Lowe's brilliantly conceived critique of conventional economics. Negatively, neither the five postulates of conventional theory, nor the features of the three subtypes of private capitalism, reveal a clear and fruitful starting point for the analysis of economic systems. The whole book deals only with private capitalism, and the specific reasons for its three-stage development need further investigation. Positively, in making the distinction between an autonomous and a social (or political) economy, Lowe comes close to discovering the point of transition between these theoretical systems. Of the five postulates of modern theory, two depend upon quasi-sociological assumptions. The maximum goals of utility and profit require fully rational attitudes and actions, and the stabilizing expectations call for perfect foresight of the future. Only when these assumptions are empirically verified do the theories of profit and expectations admit of determinate solutions. One reason for examining the stages of capitalism is to show that these assumptions are empirically invalid. In abandoning maximum profit and perfect expectations, Lowe comes to his distinction

[3]Arthur Schweitzer, "Der organisierte Kapitalismus," *Hamburger Jahrbuch fur Wirtschafts–und Gesellschaftspolitik,* 1962, pp. 32-47, and Chapter VI of *Big Business in the Third Reich.*

between extra-systemic and intra-systemic factors of the economy. The former have to come from the social and political spheres, thereby leading to a shift from the autonomous to the social economy.

SOCIO-ECONOMIC GOALS

In the social economy, Lowe tells us, the social determinants of economic behavior are not constants, "but are variables the values of which may be drastically altered under the impact of an extra-systemic change" (p. 61). It is laid down as a general methodological rule that one can speak of social economics only if a genuine interaction takes place between the intra- and extra-systemic factors. Indeed, "the intra-systemic forces acquire their determinate strength and direction only if they are constantly exposed to the regulatory influence of the extra-systemic factors" (p. 62). These non-economic factors act as regulators because they exert a psychological constraint upon economic agents in selecting their micro-goals.

Surprisingly, the extra-systemic factors are not explicitly social but are all environmental in nature, and thus act as pressures upon economic actors. Depending upon their particular origin, Lowe distinguishes three types of such pressures. The stinginess of nature gives rise to "automatic pressures;" laws and ordinances of political bodies impose "contrived pressures;" organizational and cultural factors generate "institutional pressures." Acting as dynamic forces, these environmental factors alter the motivational patterns of actors, especially when they penetrate into the economy as "large and sudden changes" (p. 63). It is thus Lowe's "working hypothesis" that environmental pressures act as regulators or determinants upon economic actors that are in need of critical examination.

How do the pressures influence the motives that give rise to self-chosen goals by economic actors? We find in Lowe a very interesting and carefully reasoned critique of the motives of maximum utility and maximum profit. The conventional thesis that regularly and consistently consumers aim at maximum utility is said to be correct only in a situation of undersatiation. Only "destitution or unlimited appetition" (p. 209) provide evidence in support of the principle of maximum utility. This evidence was expected to be more common in early capitalism than in the subsequent phases of its development. A similar structure is also suggested for the principle of maximum profit. Industrial maturity and rising national wealth have evoked motivational changes in consumers and investors that make a uniform extremum incentive much less appealing to businessmen. In addition, the "defenses against excessive risks . . . weakened . . . one pressure toward extremum motivation that has hitherto acted upon all strata of marketers; the edge of competition" (p. 82). Finally, "new practical philosophies, which stress security and the enjoyment of a rising standard of living, are corroding the earlier virtues of acquisitive daring and parsimony" (p. 82).

The central thesis of this kind of social economics emerges here. Although different in their origin, the three types of pressure produce two different but uniform effects. In the period of poverty and early industrialization, the uniform effect of the pressures reinforces the motives of maximum utility and of maximum profit. Under conditions of increasing wealth and affluence, the automatic and institutional pressures lose much of their push so that the extremum motives of maximum utility and maximum profit are substantially modified, in some cases even replaced by motives of security and enjoyment. It is only the contrived pressure of government that increases in strength so that we experience in our time a shift from the autonomous to the political economy.

This central thesis is much more powerful and in effect replaces the rival theorem of the 'dependence effect' in the recent theory of economic affluence. The change in the structure of wants is to be attributed not merely to "production that creates the want it satisfies"[4] but lies in the decline of the extremum motivation itself. The declining impact of the two pressures and the gradual disappearance of undersatiation are responsible for the diminishing urgency or intensity felt by consumers. Diminishing urgency means that producers feel the need of luring buyers to their particular products by means of massive advertising. Putting the emphasis upon the manipulative rather than creative role of advertising also eliminates the implication that producers alone and deliberately, if not coordinately, "determine what the consumers will want."

The thesis of a diminishing significance of the extremum motivation applies also to the producer. His desire for a maximum of profit declines because with increasing wealth the volume of savings increases faster than the one of spontaneous investment opportunities. Under conditions of investment uncertainty, "a lower level of profits which can be expected with greater certainty becomes preferable to a higher but much less certain level" (p. 83). Even massive advertising does not have to be activated by the motive of maximum profit but could spring from reasons of prestige or relative standing among the very big in an industry.

In spite of this advance over the "dependence effect," it is my contention that the thesis of the diminishing significance of the extremum motivation cannot be accepted as an adequate explanation for the formation of goals in social economics. Nothing basically new has been discovered. There has been a shift only from the extremum to the medium ranges of the same utility and profit motives. Rather than a new or different theory of socio-economic goals, we find here an important but only a modification of the motivational postulate of conventional economic theory.

Such a modification does not meet Lowe's own requirement of a "genuine interaction" between the extra-systemic and intra-systemic factors.

[4]John K. Galbraith, *The Affluent Society*, Boston, 1958, p. 153.

[5]Friedrich A. Hayek, "The Dependence Effect," *Southern Economic Journal*, April 1961, p. 348.

Both automatic and institutional pressures impinge upon the intentions of actors only in the form of either restraint or of a declining push. Such an impact does not affect the desire for profit or utility but merely reduces the intensity of such an urge. If maximum is replaced by medium, there is only a change in the desired quantity but not in the quality of goals. The shift from a purely economic to socio-economic sets of goals is missing.

The cause of this failure seems to lie in misjudging the nature of the non-economic factors that enter into the formation of goals. If these factors act only as pressures, then they call only for a change in the intensity of economic motives and produce only a quantitative effect. There is no inherent need for reassessing the whole situation, for ascertaining the qualitative meaning of the penetrators, for internalizing this meaning and to come up with a goal that contains both economic and non-economic components. The lesson to be learned from this thesis of pressures is clear: Qualitative penetrators only can possess the capacity to induce economic agents of changing their motives and adopt new goals.

Lowe's concept of the nature of motives reveals the second reason why socio-economic goals could not come into view. The required theory has to be such that there is one set of motivational standards that remains constant over time, universally in scope, and general in significance. Such a standard functions as a guide for all possible economic actions. Social psychology has taught us that such a universally valid standard can hardly be found anywhere. It is precisely because the always present biological needs for goods and services are judged by different standards that a theory of social economics is called for.

This leads us to Max Weber's contribution to motives as a part of social economics. Our procedure can only be selective, bringing out the highlights of his line of argument. We shall discuss the issues of the empirical nature of the motives, of the identifiable meaning of the motives, of the basic contents of the motives, and of the situational patterning of motives and actions.

It is because of the empirical nature of motives that the concept of motivation in psychology differs from the one in social economics. In social economics, motives are not taken in their clinical isolation but are observed in concrete but typical situations. While psychology concentrates upon psychic capacities and feelings, social economics additionally includes intellectual purposes and various kinds of beliefs into the group of relevant goals. At the same time, there is an important restriction. Of the great variety of motives, emotional and otherwise, the social economist considers only those motives that function as potential or actual action-setters. Study of the various kinds of motives belongs to the various branches of psychology, but their findings are economically relevant only if they can be identified empirically and if such observed motives are oriented towards some form of traceable economic action.

In order to establish a clear meaning of particular motives, it is essential to establish a specific point of reference. According to Weber, the social economist recognizes the subjectively felt or held meaning which is attached to a contemplated or executed line of action by an acting individual.[6] It is thus not the general but the individual, not the abstract but the concrete meaning of the motives that is relevant in social economics. If no individual can be identified who holds a certain meaning, such a motive is irrelevant for the social economist. In addition to being individual, the meaning of the relevant motives has to be frequently observed so that many others hold similar opinions about the same kind of action. We also want to know who these others are and why they engage in similar action for similar or dissimilar reasons. The possibility of comparing these meanings and attributing them to particular individuals is one of the crucial preliminary tasks of social economics.

In particular situations, motives can have either single or multiple meanings for individuals. In order to come to grips with multiple meanings, it becomes necessary to typify the contents of meaning into certain categories. An extensive investigation of pre-industrial and industrial situations induced Weber to distinguish four different kinds of motives and actions. Emphasizing here only their motivational aspect, he speaks of (a) actions prompted by specific interests, (b) actions generated by ideological beliefs or religious faith, (c) actions motivated by habits or traditions venerated by the forefathers, (d) affectual actions springing from various kinds of emotions.[7] Weber's typification implies the thesis that the human motivational capacity regularly expresses itself along these four distinct lines of actions. Each of these four kinds of motives functions as a standard by means of which the economic agent orients himself in selecting his personal goals. These four observed standards imply a rejecting of the single standard of either utility or profit. Social economics has to be extensive enough to permit each and all of these motivational standards to play their role in the actual choices of economic actors.

In actual situations, particular actions are frequently prompted by a complex of motives. This complexity of motives came to Weber's attention in his empirical studies of large-scale agriculture, heavy industries, and stock exchanges in Imperial Germany.[8] The multiple motives tend to pattern themselves in two different ways. Either the relevant motives are oriented towards one standard but form different constellations in a par-

[6]Max Weber, *The Theory of Social and Economic Organization,* New York, 1947, 88ff.

[7]*Ibid.,* p. 112. Weber designated interest and belief goals as "rational" and traditional or emotional goals as "irrational." The reason why this distinction seems superfluous will be given later.

[8]I have tried to summarize Weber's motivational findings in these untranslated publications in my *The Method of Social Economics,* Bloomington, 1961, pp. 7-15.

ticular situation. For instance, interest similarity is accompanied by interest diversity in such a fashion that one can distinguish different modes of interest constellations. Or certain ethical or religious beliefs intermingle with certain emotions or interests so that actors orient themselves by several standards simultaneously.

In slightly modifying Weber's theory of motivation, I suggest three specific hypotheses. Taking their personal motives seriously, individuals will place considerable emphasis upon motive-oriented and self-selected goals. Of the many motives, individuals will regard economic self-preservation—including biological needs, shelter and comfort—and self-esteem as central in their economic activities, regardless of whether goods and jobs are scarce or abundant. Both desires are so much a part of human personality that these motives will be guiding actors in every economic system. Self-esteem may be considerably compressed but hardly ever permanently eliminated by destitution or dictatorial terror.[9]

It seems advisable to separate motives from goals. Motives arise out of feelings and urgings, while goals are in part the product of the intellect and thus include intentions as well as the decision-making capacity of actors. In addition to being influenced by the two central motives, goals can be oriented toward personal interests (gains), various kinds of beliefs, traditions, and other kinds of emotions. Experience induces individuals to prefer certain of these goal-orienting standards for particular situations so that certain standard-oriented goals are recognized and actualized at appropriate occasions. Such preferences—so runs our second hypothesis—form more or less definite patterns that can be quickly referred to without the actors having to consider all available alternatives prior to action.

Individual motives and goals are neither isolated nor independent from the corresponding intentions and actions of others.[10] Living within groups, eager or obliged to be accepted by others, most individuals find it desirable or advisable to take the motives or intentions of others into account when formulating their own goals. Our third hypothesis maintains that individuals have a greater chance of realizing most of their self-selected goals if they adjust themselves to the intentions and goals of others. Stated in this form, Weber's theory of motives and goals culminates into a search of the "interaction effect" between the individual and social components in economic goals.

[9]It is only in his political writings that Weber emphasizes the role of self-esteem, but it is equally relevant in economics. See his *Gesammelte Politische Schriften*, Tübingen, 1958, p. 122.

[10]It is precisely because Weber rejected the assumption of conventional theory that individuals act independently of each other than he concentrated upon the formulation of a social-economic theory. For a critique of the conventional assumption see James S. Duesenberry, *Income, Saving, and the Theory of Consumer Behavior*, Cambridge, 1949.

PRESSURES OR PENETRATORS

In using his distinction between extra- and intra-systemic factors, Lowe advances the working hypothesis that the non-economic factors take the form of three distinct environmental pressures that are persistently so strong as to either substantially modify or determine the content of the intra-systemic (economic) goals. Unfortunately, the explanatory capacity of the extra-systemic factor is very limited. While skillfully derived from conventional theory, each of the three pressures is so global in content and diverse in meaning that a link between the individual and social components cannot be established.

In addressing himself to the same question, Weber distinguishes carefully between "comprehending" objective pressures of nature and "understanding" the motives of others.[11] We can grasp the fact that the absence of coal seams prevents us from establishing coal mines, but we cannot discover any subjective intention in or behind this natural condition. When faced with human behavior, however, we have not only to identify specific actions but also seek to ascertain the underlying motive. The interpretation of the act and the motive together leads to our "understanding" of others. In comparing such a motive with our own motive and goals, we can arrive at the subjective meaning of the actions of others for ourselves. Explicitly or implicitly, a comparative interpretation leads us to classify the motives of others as being compatible or incompatible, acceptable or inacceptable, avoidable or unavoidable, with our own motives and goals. By means of an assessment we can decide whether and how far the motives of others can or must be allowed to influence our own motives and self-chosen goals.

We come here to the point of transition from the strictly individual to social goals and action. As soon as a person is thinking of motives, goals, and actions of others, he is developing a certain attitude—receptive, critical, alert—to others. This attitude turns into a social action if the expected motive or goal of others becomes a constitutive element of an individual's goal or if a person's goal seeks to achieve a change in the conduct of others. The social component thus penetrates already into individual goals as soon as an actor takes the motives and actions of others into account when making a decision, even though others are not aware that their motives are anticipated or that their actual conduct acts as a point of orientation in selecting individual goals.[12] Social action in this sense turns into a social relationship when actors do mutually orient their goals towards each others motives and actions. Social attitudes and social relationships constitute the social components entering into economic goals.

[11]Max Weber, *Gesammelte Aufsatze zur Wissenschaftslehre,* Tübingen, 1968, third edition, 93ff.

[12]Weber thus rejects the meaning of the term "social" in welfare economics in which "social welfare" is the sum of the individual satisfactions.

Interestingly enough, economic action can either be individual or social in nature. Economic action refers here to the provision of goods and services and thus includes such acts as producing and consuming, buying and selling goods, buying and selling services, earning and spending income, loaning and borrowing funds, saving and investing capital. Any of these actions can be strictly self-centered or it can be related to the motives, goals and actions of others. "The economic activity of an individual is only social if, and then only insofar, as it takes account of the behavior of someone else. Thus very generally it becomes social in so far as the actors's actual control over economic goods is respected by others."[13] Respect of each other's possessions and ownership rights is thus a general social condition for economic activity. Social attitudes and social relationships felt and acted upon by individuals effectuate the interaction between the social and individual components in goals.

In reconsidering goals, individuals will have to decide whether they want to pay the price of resentment of others, impose their will upon less powerful persons, or seek to adjust their own goals so as to make them acceptable to others. In each case, a social component enters into the act of reconsideration. Individual goals have to be opened up toward the concerns of others, even if this does reduce the benefit expected by the actor. The "incorporation effect" thus springs from the respect for the interests or feelings of others and leads to transforming the individual into socio-economic goals by single or corporate actors.[14]

While Weber did not spell out these two significant effects,[15] he clearly specified four major social penetrators that usually enter into the economy, and that need our special attention.

Recognition as a Penetrator. A self-centered economic actor may adopt a calculating attitude and an open mind toward all accessible opportunities. The self-selected interest goal leads to estimating prospective costs and gains and a selection of the potentially most profitable projects. In the pursuit of such economic self-interest, business firms usually find that others will respect their interests only if they themselves in turn respect

[13]Weber, *The Theory of Social and Economic Organization,* p. 113.

[14]Lower economic or social classes may suffer for long periods from the refused incorporation effect. But such refusal and the accompanying injury tend to play a major role in the rise of revolutionary or counterrevolutionary mass movements only if there is also a fear of a threat to the very economic existence of that class and an accumulated resentment. All four conditions are usually necessary for the rise of a defiant mass movement. Lack of two of these conditions explains the differences between neo-Nazism and the Nazi movement. See my forthcoming book on *Neo-Nazism—A Stifled Counterrevolution.*

[15]Neither in his interpretation of Weber's socio-economic ideas, (*Theory of Social and Economic Organization,* p. 30ff), nor in his own sociological economics (*Economy and Society,* 1956, 17ff), did Talcott Parsons discover the interaction injury and incorporation effects implicit in Weber's theory. This fatal omission prevents us from accepting Parson's work as laying out the path for social economics.

the interests of others. Self respect and mutual respect together tend to adjust the interest goals to each other. Mutual respect also gives rise to various forms of expectations and consent. For instance, partners in current exchanges hold the general expectation that circulating money will be accepted as means of payment in the future. Similar general expectations prevail in regard to most existing institutions of an economy which are shared in by most participants. Specific expectations arise in connection with individual exchanges. Sellers try to satisfy the buyers' interests in such a way that they will come back for future purchases. Continued trade and satisfactory treatment eventually crystallize into a feeling of goodwill of customers towards specific sellers. Such a feeling becomes a business asset for the firm assuring future sale and establishing a reserved area in the prevailing market.[16]

Recognition or implicit consent presuppose that sellers and buyers facilitate each others' interest realization without any consultation. Reciprocal recognition of interests calls for a modification of the respective profit goals.[17]

Consent by means of persuasion, however, usually modifies the profit goal by widening the profit horizon. Acts of persuasion bid for a policy of salesmanship and lead to selling costs. Extensive publicity may assume that buyers know their own interests, yet effective advertising can persuade them to shift their customs to one's own products. Goods must thus be attractive and possess mass appeal, in addition to usefulness. As a second goal, consent by persuasion internalizes mass appeal into the thinking of managers and establishes a second important condition for production.[18]

There thus arises a "patronage effect" that generates as much from satisfying the self-esteem and other desires of buyers as from the mass appeal of goods and the mass suggestion of advertising. Such a patronage effect, while desirable for any business in private capitalism, is an indispensable condition for modern mass production.

Emotions as Penetrators. Emotions may be temporary moods of individuals or states of feeling felt by members of groups for considerable periods of time. Such states of feeling include a long list of emotions, the gratification of which calls for certain goods and services. While Weber

[16]Independently of Max Weber, John R. Commons has identified the various forms of consent under the heading of goodwill, but without the Weberian distinction between the individual and social components in business goals and policies. John R. Commons, *Industrial Goodwill*, New York, 1919, chapter II.

[17]Means of deception also imply a consideration of others and thus constitute a social component that modifies the profit goal: Hiding the deception becomes the second goal, the success of which becomes a condition for making profits.

[18]Interestingly enough, mass appeal plays no role in Galbraith's list of causes for the preoccupation with production, although it is of prime concern to managers, and attraction influences greatly the purchases of our ladies.

speaks of "fear, anger, ambition, envy, jealousy, love, admiration, pride, vindictiveness, piety, submission, craving and greed,"[19] we shall use here only fear, craving for stimulants, and love of beauty to ascertain the peculiar relationship prevailing between feelings and goods and to assess the impact of both upon the formation of socio-economic goals.

Fear of death, a deep wish for vigorous health, are common characteristics of human life in industrialized societies. Since the link between diet and health has been recognized, consumers insist that food not only nourish biological needs but also contribute to the health of buyers. In turn, producers "enrich" milk with vitamins, "reinforce" bread with minerals, offer dietary products with reduced fat content. Restaurants serve "slenderized" dishes, and various health improvers enhance the mass appeal of cereals. While providing for the biological needs is still the main economic task, fear of sickness or concern for health supplies the emotions entering into the goals of buyers. The urge to live a diet-adequate life interacts with the individual's need of economic self-preservation. Both desires induce producers to add health-giving substances to their products as a typical procedure of production.

A quite different situation arises in the case of goods gratifying particular cravings for stimulants. Smoking and drinking of alcoholic beverages do not fill biological needs. The economic component in such products and acts of sensual consumption is often completely missing. As a substitute, advertisers claim certain health-giving qualities for their products, highlight it by a brand name, and treat the offered product as a source of great enjoyment. Deep emotions thus can crowd out the economic component in goals and substitute for it a psychological craving and social appreciation that are even more persistent than economic self-preservation.

The impact of love upon economic goals takes frequently an intermediate position between fear and craving. Items for the physical, emotional, or educational wellbeing of children have to be useful (for example, economic) as well as pleasing to children and parents (for example, social). Both considerations prevail also in the purchase of gifts for newlywed couples, especially when the bride also exercises the right to indicate the style or line of product she prefers. There is a wide range within which the useful and the loveable may mingle into socio-economic goals. The art of etiquette lies precisely in knowing which combination of economic need and social appreciation is appropriate in particular situations. The great variability of emotions and especially the susceptibility of some to external suggestions and enticements creates business opportunities for massive manipulation or even for creation of wants. Manipulating the female desire for beauty is the leading example. Mass appeal of artificial hair coloring was achieved only when the color did not wash out and the

[19]Weber, *The Theory of Social and Economic Organization*, p. 92.

treated hair looked "natural." Mass sale, however, was hindered by the prevalent belief that hair color was a natural endowment beyond artificial beautification. Advertising campaigns used mass suggestion and persuasion to convince ladies that their emotional craving for beauty could be gratified by staying young via a new color of their hair.

Institutional Regularities as Penetrators. It was Weber's important discovery that repetitive actions turn into institutionalized regularities. Actors orient their own goals by the repetitive behavior of certain persons or groups. Regularities become institutionalized through continuity over time as well as through the uniformity in their essential content. Weber regarded usage, custom and interest constellations as the most important examples of such regularities.

Usage grows out of particular habits. In having settled on one particular way of doing things, the inclination is to repeat the same acts without thinking of any specific goal. The habit takes over and in effect replaces the need to formulate goals. Much of our food consumption is habitual. Sellers can rely upon such habits for continued sales in the future. By the same token, established habits constitute a hurdle for advertisers if they seek to establish a market for a new product not yet falling within the range of habitual acceptance.

Custom as an institutional regularity establishes a certain routine of action that is repeated because of an expected or actual convenience. Getting the same kind of hair-cut, wearing the same kind of shoes, shopping at the same supermarket, bring the advantages of full familiarity and substantially minimize uncertainty. In production, custom brings the additional advantage of lower cost. Using the same outlay in all retail outlets, a chain store company saves design cost and facilitates check-up and supervision of stores. Workers can avoid the feeling of monotony if repeat performances are seen as a sign of convenience that assures continuity of work and piece rates offer the opportunity of higher pay. An internalized custom seems to mitigate against monotony and reduce the need for friendship cliques among workers. Such custom may also explain the empirical finding that repetitiveness of work is not a major incentive for the forming of small groups among workers.[20]

Interest constellations as an institutional regularity express themselves in four distinctly different patterns. Starting from the circle of self-interest, economic actors usually survey their opportunities for their accessibility. Readily attainable opportunities are regarded as a kind of private property that should be respected by others. If others grab these opportunities without consultation and compensation, a feeling of interest injury develops that usually prompts various kinds of countermoves. A second circle contains the interests of friends, collaborators, regular customers, or power-

[20]L. R. Sayles, *Behavior of Industrial Work Groups,* New York, 1958, Chapter 3.

ful neighbors. Such interests are not only respected but are either promoted jointly (for example, partnerships) or given favorable consideration whenever possible. In contrast, a third circle contains the interests of competitors, rivals, and outright enemies. Their interests usually collide with the self-interests so that either an interest collision or a complete avoidance of the disputed opportunities is the result of such interest conflict. Finally, there is the interest situation created by unknown others whose action is beyond control of single actors. The smaller the firm, the greater the need to adjust to the patterned interests of the unknown others if catastrophic consequences shall be avoided.[21]

One recent controversy illustrates well the emotional influence upon goals in the friendly interest circle. According to the SEC, the largest broker in the country informed 14 large customers of an expected profit decline in a manufacturing company but kept all other clients in the dark. Obviously, a distinction between insiders and outsiders had developed which were differentially treated by the broker. While a feeling of mutual trust prevailed between the brokerage house and its multitude of clients, a feeling of belonging together united the broker with the insiders. The brokerage house operated according to two different socio-economic interest goals. A goal of mutual interest provided services to outsiders strictly in accord with payments received, while a solidaric interest goal called for a sharing of exceptional profit opportunities with insiders. What appears as deliberate discrimination to outsiders and the SEC is defended by insiders as an outflow of their particular interest solidarity.[22]

It follows that even modern business men are not necessarily willing to merely observe and assess objectively the interest of others, but take special social components into account when determining their attitudes and policies towards the particular interests of others. There are thus observable two distinctly different interest constellations. In Weber's theory, this term signifies a fully purposive-rational assessment of interests, of one's own and of others, and their crystallizing into a definite interest constellation which actors take into account in formulating their interest goals.

As institutional regularities, usage, custom and interest constellations exert a three-fold influence upon goals. In bringing in a social component into economic goals, the regularities establish patterns of behavior that are readily repeated in similar subsequent situations. One goal can thus provide an action directive for a whole series of institutionalized actions by the same persons and groups. Mental energy can be saved for the really critical situations which require detailed assessment and specific decisions.

[21]Weber was still inclined to place the uncontrollable interest situation at the center and indicate the other circles only inferentially. See *Theory of Social and Economic Organization*, pp. 121-123.

[22]Similar interest groups have been empirically identified by L. R. Sayles among workers in industrial plants.

A long range time dimension is built into these institutionalized goals that stabilizes expectations and thus creates the social conditions for effective economic planning by others, but hardly ever by those who originate and live according to these regularities. As long range patterns, usage, custom, and interest constellations become standards of orientation for future actions. Accepting such standards is voluntary and is not binding on any one; mere convenience may be enough for adherence. A current custom tells us what certain buyers can be expected to do in the future and producers can orient their own production plans by such anticipated customary actions of others.[23] Prevalence of these institutional regularities in certain fields explains why a significant part of business transactions is carried on without reference to rationality or optimizing procedures.

Codes of Conduct as Penetrators. Weber distinguishes three kinds of codes that influence economic goals and enter into particular choices. Fashion, convention and governmental law share three common characteristics, although different in content. Each penetrator represents a form of conduct that is regarded as setting a standard for actors to select individual goals. Each code strikes an inner cord within an actor who feels obliged to accept the implicit norm, even if this should be harmful to his own interests. In addition, all of these penetrators are so closely related to prestige that any agent adhering to the norm can claim to have attained a certain status that is generally desired by one's equals and respected by one's superiors.

Actions are fashionable when they are guided by novelty and prestige. Novelty is indicated either by a new style or by a new way of expressing one's own individuality. A certain feature of a product, such as the length of women's apparel or the width of a car, connotes the acceptable style. All the style-conscious persons orient themselves by the particular indicator to such an extent that the setters of fashion practically determine individual goals. The desire to be in style is so great that millions of women have become steady inch worriers, busily engaged in shortening or lengthening their skirts from one season to the next. The wish to acquire the style-prestige is so great that conformity is forthcoming even when the particular product is uncomfortable to wear or fails to protect the human body against the hazards of nature.

In spite of their diverse effect upon production, style and vanity are subject to the same social condition. The respective products must be capable of indicating prestige and thus find the approval of others. Yet this condition fails to set either a qualitative limit for the same goods to be purchased or to reveal the relative importance of the various goods

[23]Since such standards are adhered to over longer periods of time, they do become the preliminary indicators for the feelings implicit in the institutional regularities. The criticism that such feelings can often not be observed prior to, or can be inferred only from the subsequent action, overlooks the role of the standards as preliminary indicators for motives hidden for a certain time.

selected. Mutual complementarity is the rule underlying the choice of prestigious goods insofar as a combination is required to indicate an adherence to a particular fashion or a certain style of life. In the field of fashion, the economic component in goals is frequently incidental, while the social components of novelty, prestige, and complementarity tend to be paramount.

Among the multitude of codes, five are especially relevant as guides for socio-economic conduct. Social amenities derive from common aspirations as to what is comfortable, pleasing, civilized, appropriate and attractive. Such aspirations lead to similar houses, lawns and driveways, to appropriate furnishings and modes of daily living, to goods indicating decency and decorum. Moral and ethical proprieties spring from religion as well as social philosophies that demand adherence to an appropriate conduct at specified occasions. A great volume of goods is devoted to these religious, charitable, ceremonial or devotional activities. Aesthetic sensibilities generate from prevailing opinions and preferences for certain forms and styles of artistic expression that influence in various ways the styles of products and the manifold modes of artistic or commercialized entertainment. Reputability as a convention hinges upon several norms. Repute can be built upon excellence of achievement, which has become the most important standard in modern production, education, and sports. Repute can also be derived from the desire to translate pecuniary privileges into standards of respectability. Finally, social honor depends upon a special claim to a position of personal and social dignity that is closely associated with a highly esteemed style of life cultivated by a superior group.

While Veblen and Weber agree that reputability and social honor are two distinct codes of normative conduct, they do disagree on the origin, content, and relative significance of these conventions in economic systems. As is well known, Veblen attributes the origin of honor to the predatory habit of life, leading to the norms of prowess and courage in battle, but he sees repute deriving mainly from the morals built upon the sacredness of property.[24] In contrast, Weber sees social honor as a dignity placed upon a distinguished style of life that depends as much on political authority as on legally monopolized economic opportunities, including property. For him, reputation is closely linked with social ranking within the status group which is derived as much from monopolized educational opportunities as from pecuniary decency.[25] This divergence in regard to the substrata of the norms underlying these two conventional codes of conduct is one of the most difficult and unresolved problems of social

[24]*The Theory of the Leisure Class,* New York, 1953, 29ff, 89ff.

[25]H. H. Gerth and C. Wright Mills, *From Max Weber: Essays in Sociology,* New York, 1958, 180ff and 300ff.

economics that urgently deserves detailed description and theoretical analysis.[26]

Whatever the content of the codes, conventions are relevant for economic goals in two ways. As standards, codes set patterns of desirable conducts which are readily available to actors as points of orientation when reflecting upon goals or anticipating the actions of others. While not totally binding, the normative core in the code contains a prescriptive range of recommended choices among which a specific selection has to be made. Foremen in industrial plants can assign work readily as long as they respect the conventional division of labor prevailing among different skill groups. When a particular convention is symbolized by one particular action or commodity, then the prescriptive range narrows down to one acceptable goal. In a unionized plant a newly hired worker either becomes a member of the union or he will be dismissed. The future task in the study of the conventions will be to search for the prevailing patterns of approved conduct in specific economic systems and to develop a theory of prescriptive socio-economic goals.[27]

TOWARDS A THEORY OF SOCIO-ECONOMIC GOALS

In the final analysis, the potential explanatory capacity of social economics may be large enough to reduce the gap between conventional and institutional economics. The purely economic laws have to be translated into socio-economic laws and the major propositions of institutional economics can and have to be incorporated into the motives, regularities, codes, and establishments of social economics. This potentiality can be realized if we keep in mind that social penetrators and subsequent patterns of economic behavior stay relatively stable only in certain periods and systems. Rather than leading to universal laws, social economics has thus a future if it becomes the theory of economic systems and subsystems.

[26]Veblen occasionally uses the term "social economy" (*Op. cit,* p. 29) and his theory of conspicuous consumption was fully recognized and partly accepted by Weber.

[27]Max Weber also included "law" as an important economically relevant code of conduct, thereby establishing the link between social and political economics. Limited space prevents us from pursuing here this line of thought.

The Myths of Liberty and the Realities of the Corporate State: A Review Article

Warren J. Samuels

The volumes reviewed here are quite disparate, but their joint consideration is useful to the understanding of both.[1] They differ in their purpose and in their comprehension of legal-economic reality. Arthur Selwyn Miller attempts a comprehensive description and interpretation of a system with which he is not entirely happy. James M. Buchanan, upon the identification of a situation with which he is quite unhappy, attempts to create a defensible case for certain principles and lines of reasoning intended conceptually to support a more congenial system. The authors perceive both the status quo and the nature of constitutional order quite differently. This is due in part to their conflicting preconceptions and values concerning the nature of a free society, its problems, and what enables its existence; to their (not unrelated) different specifications of the legal-economic world, its actualities, and possibilities; and to the difference in the tasks they have undertaken. Together the books raise the question of the relation of systemic myths to institutional realities, a question complicated by the problem of differentiating myth from reality.

Miller's *Modern Corporate State* has four basic descriptive and interpretive themes. The first asserts constitutional evolution: There has been continuing and inevitable constitutional development. The U.S. Constitution is a living instrument of governance; it is dynamic and organic, not static. Constitutional theory and law are both in a process of becoming, the latter being more a reflection than a determinant of changing social structure. The Constitution has been continually reinterpreted, and it has lasted because it has been flexible in the face of new problems.

The second theme asserts the reality of a broad constitutional system: The living, total constitution encompasses more than the written document. It deals with power wherever found, particularly power understood as the capacity to make or influence decisions that affect the values of social importance to others. The study of American constitutionalism requires scrutiny of the total flow of relevant decisions whenever made, including private decision making having constitutional consequences, for example, as made by political parties, large corporations, and unions. Received theory juxtaposes natural persons and the state, whereas in reality group action has grown in significance, and the individual increasingly is important only as a member of a group(s). The total, living constitution includes both public and private government.

The third theme, already anticipated, asserts the growth of the corporation and the correlative emergence of a new constitutional order largely through extraconstitutional development. The system has been transformed into one of nonindividual, nonstatist, nonpossessory economic and social power. The living constitutional law is increasingly dominated by fundamental societal decisions made by "nongovernmental" institutions: corporations, unions, foundations. Volitional (Buchanan's voluntary) contract has been largely replaced by adhesion (standardized) contracts.

The fourth theme asserts the fusion of economic and political power in the "corporate state, American style." There is symbiosis between the giant corporation and the national government (especially the executive branch), with the system run by an elite and the President largely a power broker.

These themes are presented in the first part of Miller's book, "The Argument Stated." In "The Argument Defined" he elaborates. The corporation, whose rise was abetted by the state, is increasingly in symbiotic relation with the state because of economic need and legal permissiveness. The role of law gradually has become derivative and less prescriptive or interdictional. The law has been used to permit and promote corporate development, and it has been predominantly influenced by the economically powerful. Power finds its ultimate statement in law, which has been used to protect and help established economic power. Even the courts have been, through litigation, an object of use in power play. The key has been the drive for economic wealth and power in and by business, with its utilization of technology, law, and public policy. The corporations have become instruments and agencies of governance which themselves use official government. On a world scale, the corporate system is a potential rival to and symbiotic partner with the nation-state system, following the logic of its domestic evolution.

The coming of the positive state has been another and, of course, related important constitutional change in U.S. history, and it too came without formal amendment (a view shared by Buchanan). The positive state has meant a shift from a government of limitations to one of powers, the growth of affirmative duties of government, and governmental promotion of associational activities. Furthermore, the intellectuals have become the servants of power in the legal-economic arena. There is a tension in Miller's analysis between his emphasis on the new positive state and his recognition of earlier deep uses of the legal system. Government power always has been the instrument of elite structures identified in terms of wealth and family. The positive state has old roots, but Miller stresses an exponential jump from negative to positive government, especially reckoned by the greater size of government (a view also shared by Buchanan). The origin of the positive state as we know it resulted from a confrontation of state promotion of business with egalitarian pressures, leading to the adoption and cooptation of welfare programs in a synthesis keeping the masses quiescent and enabling relatively free play for the economically advantaged. I will argue below that it is precisely to the terms of the bargain ensconced in this synthesis that Buchanan's book is ultimately addressed. So far as Miller is concerned, the rise of the corporate system and the positive state has meant a shattering of the politico-economic theory of U.S. constitutionalism: There is further blurring of private and public; government is increasingly of men and not of laws; and many of the rulers occupy corporate suites. The fusion of economic and political power into the "corporate state, American style" signifies a silent but profound constitutional revolution of the greatest magnitude. Corporations and unions dominate the system of private governance. The individual is submerged, ergo corporativism. A planning system exists through the influencing of economic habits and outlooks; although not necessarily involving the abolition of market forces, the system, while not fully centralized, channels the market.

In "The Argument Analyzed" Miller examines a wide range of constitutional problems and consequences of the new socioeconomic order. These include the mode of the determination of "problems" requiring collective action; the need for an ethic of change and pragmatism (which Buchanan decries as unfortunately already dominating the system);

the legitimacy and accountability of the corporate system; the formation of the "public interest" in such a system; the rise of the concept of corporate citizenship; the use of power to check power in the face of fusion; the relative roles of judicial and legislative controls; the significance of freedom, in the corporate system, largely being the attenuated liberty to decide which group to join or to which adhesion contract to "agree"; the increasing merger of "foreign" and "domestic," along with "private" and "public"; and the inability of a swollen, unresponsive, and increasingly repudiated official government to govern adequately (a view shared by Buchanan). Apropos of the latter, Miller perceives the decline of representative government (shared by Buchanan with a vengeance). Policy has become a function of elite interaction and decision making; democracy has become less a means of controlling state power than of organizing the masses; and governance has become a brokerage system.

In a brief epilogue, Miller argues that we have a syzygetic order: a conjunction of two organisms without the loss of their identity; but that constitutionalism requires the consideration of private government even though the corporation, as a private government, has not been formally constitutionalized by the Supreme Court.

Miller's book is a comprehensive, and necessarily somewhat repetitious, explorative memorandum rather than a systematic treatise. As he acknowledges through his references, his themes are by no means new. The ideas of John R. Commons and Robert Lee Hale, for example, pervade the book. The book has a brief introduction by Daniel Fusfeld which, after stressing the reality of symbiosis, fusion, and endemic conflict, suggests that there are three relevant alternative futures: fascist authoritarianism, a reformed corporate state, and democratic socialism. Buchanan, who is deeply pessimistic in his own right, would find this limited set of choices rather appalling. I find Buchanan's system too close to, or too capable of becoming, the first of the three for comfort.

Buchanan's *Limits of Liberty* is a very different volume. It is not only more complex in meaning but also different both in objective and its putative comprehension of legal-economic reality. Indeed, aside from some shared interpretations of developments, it is difficult to recognize that Miller and Buchanan are writing about the same subject. Perhaps they are not.[2] Inasmuch as I tend to agree with Miller's description of reality, I have a fundamental ambivalence in my evaluation of Buchanan's book. It is a brilliant, impressive, rewarding, and at times elegant restatement of the contractarian–natural rights position. But the conceptual gymnastics and casuistries which Buchanan perpetrates in order to erect defenses for his intellectual fortress are most irritating. An evaluation is all the more complex because I sympathize with his voluntaristic conception of freedom (which is why I can lament the description presented by Miller). It is further complicated by my understanding of the role which Buchanan undertakes in this book, a role which I find uncongenial for myself but all around me, namely, the role of high priest.[3] If one dislikes the picture Miller provides, is one to complain about the author or the reality he describes? If one is uncomfortable with the role Buchanan plays and the agenda he provides, can one not be skeptical of his formulations while acknowledging his contributions and important questions? The book is pure Buchanan: He is uncomfortable with conflict, conservative in regard to (some) established rights, and deeply pessimistic over events and trends. However much one may regret both his pessimism and his dogged conservativism, one must admire his talents.

Buchanan's objective is quite clear. He has a conception of the good society, and he is seeking certain constructions (call them fictions or myth, he would not disagree) with which to legitimize that society, that is, either to bring it about through a constitutional revolution (not likely) or to interpret and rechannel our own society in its image (not much more likely). His ideal is contractarian, consensual, and unanimity-based social action; the means are the myth or metaphor of social contract to limit legal change and to allow change through market contract. This is not a cynical misstatement of his aims and motivations, for references to his purpose are scattered throughout the book. He intends to "examine the bases for a society of men and women who want to be free but who recognize the inherent limits that social interdependence places on them" (p. ix). His is a search more for " 'getting to' the better society and less about describing" his own version of paradise once gained (p. x). He desires to " 'explain' some of the apparent sociopolitical malaise" that he observes "with the professional tools of the economist and from the value position" of "an individualist, a constitutionalist, a contractarian, a democrat—terms that mean essentially the same thing to me" (p. 7). He is interested in the analytic origins of conceptual contract in order to erect defensible principles for "conceptual constitutional foundations" no longer "highly vulnerable to positivist refutation" (p. 54; compare p. 51). He seeks to "locate the legitimacy of social order in implicit contract" (p. 74). He labors to remove "that continued misunderstanding and confusion" about "the separate constitutional and post constitutional stages of collective action" which "leads to disaster." The reform he seeks "lies first of all in attitudes, in ways of thinking about social interaction, about political institutions, about law and liberty. If men will only commence to think in contractarian terms, if they will think of the state in the roles as defined, and if they will recognize individual rights as existent in the status quo," he tells us, "I should not at all be insistent on particulars" (p. 176). The gravamen of the argument is that part which deals with the status quo: "Again it is necessary to repeat the obvious. The status quo defines that which exists. Hence, regardless of its history, it must be evaluated as if it were legitimate contractually" (p. 85).

The core of the "purely" analytical argument of the book involves a number of distinctions. One is the *precontractual* state of nature with its activities reduced to *production, predation,* and *protection,* and its *natural distribution* based on power, with a possible mutual disarmament agreement; the *constitutional* stage, also a function of bargaining and power play, with its eventual agreement on rights and rules governing individual and collective behavior; and the *postconstitutional* stage of trade in private and public goods in accordance with the rights and rules provided by the constitution (the explanation of which exchange has been the domain of economic theory, according to Buchanan). Another distinction involves the *protective* state, which seeks to maintain the integrity of the constitutionally provided rights and rules *vis-à-vis* the *productive* state. This latter is assigned the task of collective provision of public goods, according to the rights and rules stipulated in the constitution, but the productive state, in majoritarian democracy, readily degenerates into an activist force of constitutional revision and redistribution. A truly protective state should be *believed* by the public to be *external* to everyday life and limited in function. The limits of liberty, necessary to maintain balance between anarchy and Leviathan, involve restrictions on both self-government and legal change, the former being perceived as license for the latter, and the latter being seen as the threat to liberty in an individualist, orderly anarchy.

Although it is quite possible, if not necessary, to see vintage conservative wine in Buchanan's new bottles, the book does make interesting contributions to the extension and refinement of argument and issues. His schemas of constitutional stages, protective versus productive state, and government as external enforcer *vis-à-vis* internal participant are useful in focusing discussion among those who agree and disagree with his conservative uses thereof. The book is a suggestive if not important exploration in the theory of anarchism and of the economic role of government in a libertarian or market system (although at least some of what he says will be repugnant—too much an admission of legal complicity in the economic system—to libertarians either less perceptive or less candid than Buchanan). The work involves an interesting methodological individualism based on a particular normative individualism. Buchanan does offer a "solution" to the control of government, and he significantly stresses both the importance of agreement or covenant in the formation of rights and the role of power play in their formulation and constitutional adoption. The book makes important contributions to our understanding of individuals' constrained maximization response to law and extant contracts, for example, evasion; the cost and benefit factors involved in the allocation of resources to the procurement of redistribution, and thereby to legal change and to politics; the problem of differentiating between law determination and enforcement; fundamental aspects of the rights determination and redetermination process(es); the nature and the problems of self-government; law as a stock of social capital; the constitutional implications of the unanimity rule (whether one accepts it or not) *vis-à-vis* the pressure for collective action to produce legal change; the forces producing a unidirectional bias, as Buchanan sees it, toward expansion of government budgets; and to what he calls the punishment dilemma. Apropos of the last, Buchanan adroitly examines the certainty-severity tradeoff; variable individual behavior responses to alternative punishment strategies; large versus small numbers of violators; differential (or discriminating) punishment under factual circumstances wherein punishment is differential in individual effect whether nominally uniform or not; and, especially important to him, the dilemma wherein constitutionally intended punishment for law violations is subsequently coupled with citizen pain upon the perception of punishment of others. (An earlier semantics would have referred to this as matrism and a more recent one would have termed it permissivism—the latter until some of its advocates were themselves made subject to criminal prosecution.)

The complexity of Buchanan's book stems in part from his three-level analysis. At the first level, he presents a general theory of the contractarian society as a contribution to legal-economic philosophy. He takes as given a certain ideal or set of values and both seeks the means thereto and interprets significance on the basis of those values. Although his analysis is marked by the contractarian ideal, his handling of the Spenglerian problem of order (namely, the need for continuing reconciliation of autonomy and control, continuity and change, and hierarchy and equality) is relatively broad and open, that is, both sides of each dualism are given a place.

The second level of analysis involves a conservative formulation of both the problem of order and contractarian theory as well as of democracy. Whereas on the first level the inevitable role of law as a mode of change is formally recognized, here the conservative conception of law is stressed, and antipathy toward legal change is the major lesson. The relatively broad and open conception of the problem of order is replaced by selective conservative specification of each of the terms therein.

On the third level, the process of specification becomes even more idiosyncratic. Buchanan presents, often as *obiter dicta* but nonetheless passionately, his own conservative interpretation of events, especially those of the 1960s and early 1970s, although these are not carefully identified. He finds erosion of constitutional order, budgetary excesses, violations by the judiciary of the terms of its own (implicit) contract, and the flouting of customary modes of behavior. His antagonism to legislative majority voting seems matched by his antipathy to the federal judiciary. He rejects the workings of American self-government and democracy, for example, the vastness of legal change, the economic role of government, and the federal budget, on his own specific conservative and laissez-faire type of principles.

Discernment of the specific levels is impeded because of a technique of argument which Buchanan tends to use on all three. He is typically preoccupied with the construction of a theory of *conceptual* contract and its analytical implications. But he quite readily jumps from conceptual (hypothetical) analysis to evaluation of existing institutions based on the premise that they were founded on some *implicit* contract of the nature and with the terms lauded by Buchanan. It is one thing to evaluate existing arrangements by a particular normative criterion, however idiosyncratic; it is quite another to presume that these institutions are implicitly founded upon that criterion and are subject thereto inherently. Buchanan employs an "as if" model and argument and then concludes that the present situation violates the terms built into his model. Not only is the contractarian metaphor presumptuous in this use, but also, and especially, his specification and applications thereof. The problem is exacerbated when it is recognized that actual use of his theory in our society would constitute reinforcement of concentrated power in the private corporate and governing elite.

Buchanan's book is a fine example of normative motivation or metaphysics producing a by-product of important substantive contributions. However, his analytic work has some very serious defects and limitations.

One major defect is Buchanan's lack of truly fundamental attention to power. I should say that Buchanan, following Frank Knight, takes a very narrow approach in his treatment of the problem of freedom *vis-à-vis* power. Both men came to the conclusion that an effective propaganda for economic freedom requires the nonconsideration of power, and that conclusion informs Buchanan's analysis. Not that he fails to acknowledge facets of power in passing: Power and power play are held important in the formation of both the natural distribution and the constitution of rights and rules, an acknowledgement not common among conservatives. The producer interest is dominant in our society (p. 160). There is implicit but probably inadvertent recognition of adhesion contracts (p. 17). Asymmetrical influence over government policy is also recognized (p. 149). But these observations are found only in passing, and no general consideration or application is made of them. In Buchanan's system, power seemingly would disappear in a sea of voluntarism.

Compare his bountiful invocations of freedom, liberty, consent, and voluntarism with Miller's description: It is like a different world, and not merely because Buchanan is discussing a beautiful idea and Miller a somewhat sordid reality. Where in Buchanan's fantasia is Miller's groupism? Where is the corporate system? Where is power in the structure of ownership of the means of production? Where is the predominance of contracts of adhesion? Where is structure and exercise of private governance? Where is the fusion of private and public? Where is the system of freedom as a function and/or correlative of the system of control, mutual coercion, and of exposure to the freedom of others? Where is history as conflict over power and privilege? Where is man, with his quest for power for noble and ignoble motives? Buchanan's fantasy is predicated upon selective perception of freedom, voluntarism, and coercion, especially in a world of adhesion contracts. Mutual agreement exists only within a structure of power and mutual coercion which is asymmetrical. What is meaningful "consent" in a system of *private* governance, say, in a corporate system? Buchanan's system would only divert attention from power, privilege, benefits, and beneficiaries in the existing system, including asymmetrical access to and use of government.

The problem of maintaining a "free" society is deeper and more complex than invoking implicit social contracts, reviling democracy, and limiting legal change. The problem of freedom is, in part to be sure, the problem of the structure of power; otherwise it is freedom only, or largely, for the powerful. As Buchanan understands, liberty must be limited in order to have liberty. But there are many competing notions of freedom. The question is, which or whose liberty? One can believe in liberty, voluntarism, and consent in the abstract *and* also in the reality of the ubiquity of power and coercion. Buchanan seems to use voluntarism and unanimity (consent) as a strategem to limit change and to defend the existing structure of power, or those parts of it with which he identifies. What of power and coercion in the private sector "independent" of government?

One of Buchanan's deepest failures is in not recognizing the problem(s) of power and thereby not appreciating the realities of legal-economic interdependence and interpenetration, for it is in those domains, and not fictional implicit social contracts, that effective freedom is actually worked out in society. Or, rather, he is trying to mask those domains and salvage a particular system. One can sympathize with his fixation on the size of the federal budget, but one also can say that the budget has legal-economic sources and meaning with which his system fails to come to grips.

One of Buchanan's chief purposes is to counter the positivist argument that the state is in fact involved (as both a dependent and independent variable) in the definition and redefinition of rights. Thus he writes of

> a recurrent fallacy in many discussions of property rights and of the role of the state in enforcing these rights. Enforcement of claims is categorically different from defining these claims in the first place. Claims are conceptually agreed upon by all parties in the constitutional stage of social contract. The state is then called upon to monitor these claims, to serve as an enforcing institution, to insure that contractual commitments are honored. To say that rights are defined by the state is equivalent to saying that the referee and not the players chooses both the initial division of the marbles and the rules of the game itself (p. 68).

Similarly, he refers to "the familiar assertion that property rights are defined by and subject to change by the 'government' or the state. As noted in Chapter 3, this amounts to saying that only the government or the state has rights, and that individuals are essentially parties to a continuing slave contract" (p. 83). And again:

> The presence of ambiguity and conflict among individual claims is the source of major confusion about the protective-state role of government. To the extent that conflict emerges, adjudication of claims is necessary. Some search for the location of "the law" is required. In the process, the state, through its judicial arms and agencies, must make what appears to be quite arbitrary decisions of the either/or variety, decisions that are then imposed unwillingly on the losing parties to the dispute, and decisions which are subsequently enforced by the state. It is from ob-

> servations of this sort of activity that the state is often described as *defining* rights, as making basic law. But there is a vital difference between adjudicating conflicts among parties when ambiguities arise and in defining rights ab initio or in initiating explicit changes in rights when there is no conflict to be observed (pp. 88–89).

In Buchanan's system individuals "would no longer accept, implicitly, the positivist view that the state, and only the state, can define and redefine individual rights, and, by inference, its own. Democracy remains conceptually possible only if individuals view government in the consent paradigm" (p. 177).

Buchanan's distinctions are useful analytically to a point, but the errors he attributes to others and the uses to which he puts the distinctions are due to his own fallacies. He would separate the constitutional and postconstitutional stages and differentiate between the definition and enforcement of rights. These are analytically different, but in reality—our reality and any likely one—these are *not* separable, fortunately or otherwise. (Buchanan perhaps does not say they are separable, only that they should be *viewed* as separable. On the casuistry involved, see below.) There happens to be joint determination and enforcement of rights. Rights are enforced claims *vis-à-vis* claims not enforced. Rights are such because they are protected; they are not protected because they are rights. There is no complete *ab initio* determination, not to say definition, of rights, especially in a world of change. Fully defined rights are impossible. Also, rights can be defined such that any police power action can be seen as a destruction, taking, or violation thereof; or they can be defined such that future police power action can be understood to be built into the rights themselves. Moreover, in reality the constitutional and postconstitutional stages are not sequentially separable; they are simultaneous. Similarly, the conceptions of the internal versus external state and the protective versus productive state are fictional and misleading. In the real world of all actual and likely states, government is in fact internal and productive, like it or not.

Similar confusion is created by Buchanan with regard to constitutional law and property law. He seems to use the concept of constitutional contract to include property right definition and assignment, thereby telescoping constitutional law and common-cum-statute law as found in the real world. His analysis seems to demand the conversion of property law into constitutional law, apparently to further protect extant property rights from legal change. Additional and related confusion results from his recognition of a limited necessity for legal change, but ambiguity as to whether the change is to come through alternation of constitutional or property law. If the latter is the former there is no problem, except that all issues become *constitutional* issues, surely a dubious result by Buchanan's own criteria. A related problem, noted below, is his basic ambiguity as to how to differentiate permissible legal change from "social reform."

Buchanan desires to further finesse the problem of the initial definition and assignment of rights by placing more emphasis on the mutual gains from trade through voluntary contract than on concern over the initial assignment of rights among persons (pp. 8, 178). I do note that only once (pp. 22–23), thankfully, does Buchanan rely upon "efficiency" to judge rights, whereas analytically efficiency is itself a function of rights and not the other way around (except presumptively).

Buchanan's constitutional-postconstitutional and other dichotomies would function to obscure deep legal involvment in any status quo power structure, and through placing limits on legal change would protect it even further. Buchanan does recognize the importance of government in the formation of legal rights in the constitutional stage, in creating new rights, and, in passing, through legal change. But he adopts the dichotomies to try to finesse legal change in the real world, juxtaposing them against positive analysis of rights as actually a function of law and thereby subject to legal change. The goal is to channel legal change (what Buchanan laments as the activist state).

Apropos this issue more directly, Buchanan is too competent and candid a political economist totally to exclude or prohibit legal change in his system. At several points he explicitly recognizes that the necessity for it will exist (pp. 89, 108, 178, 180, and passim). Limits will have to be redefined (p. 20); new rights will have to come into effect (p. 179); and, presumably, future generations will be able to revise the fundamental contract. (I am not too certain of the latter. There would be a tendency in a Buchananite system for revolution to be the only avenue for major change open to dissidents, surely a somewhat paradoxical result.)

One problem with this recognition in the context of Buchanan's larger system is that the granting of formulation of a new right *necessarily* means infringing upon previously existing ones. The right of Alpha has meaning, in part, insofar as Beta is exposed to Alpha's right. To grant Beta a right means that Alpha is now limited by and/or exposed to Beta's right. Those imbued with the felicitous semantics of rights respond warmly to the idea of new *rights,* but analytically new rights are equivalent to much-maligned "regulation" insofar as both limit or "violate" previously existing rights.

Notwithstanding Buchanan's recognition of the necessity for legal change, the primary burden of his book is against it (for example, pp. 108, 128, 178). He is in favor of status quo rights (pp. 11, 82–83, 85, 136, 177, 178) and established order and culture (chapter 5 and pp. 5, 20, 49, 50, 117, 128, 129, 136, 177). One example occurs in a discussion of the punishment dilemma. Buchanan says that "the basic law enforcement policy and structure should be selected before explicit violation of law occurs" and "the instructions should ideally be given to an external agent, instructions which should be irrevocable once made" (p. 136). (The further significance of this will be made clear shortly.) The position most favored by Buchanan is that legal change should only come about through unanimous agreement (pp. 83–85, 178, and passim).

What is particularly striking, and irritating, is that Buchanan primarily uses a punishment model throughout to discuss *both* violations of criminal law *and* sought-after changes in constitutional and common law. He tends to see legal change as criminal, as a violation of constitution, rules, rights, and law as such (chapter 5). This is understandable: If a constitution and rights are given preeminent status and are not to be changed, regardless of the conditions of their origin and continued existence, in other words, if both are untouchable, then attempts to create change are sacrilegious and criminal. The punishment model is apposite; it is conservatism with a vengeance. Notice, too, the emphasis on authority, notwithstanding the parading of consent and voluntarism: Buchanan's state would seem to be strong and severe enough to protect established rights against all manner of reformers. Radicalism would seem to be unlawful *per se*.

Other points may be noted only in passing. Buchanan's analysis neglects not only legal-economic history and past social conflicts over rights and privilege but also the impact of nonlegal change, such as technology, on rights and/or the economic significance of rights. And nowhere is found the emergence of the corporate state, *à la* Miller. Nowhere is there acknowledgment of how much legal change has resulted from economic change, through the market, which has proven (in some sense, as to which Buchanan and I likely disagree) the capacity of the written Constitution to handle there given situations through application and interpretation by judiciary and legislature. If legal change is socialism, business has been its main promoter, both directly and indirectly. Nor is there meaningful acknowledgment of the realities of constrained maximization power play by business and other economic actors over legal change as an economic alternative. Granted, Buchanan grudgingly recognizes the need for new rights and legal change, but his preoccupation with a fairly rigid constitution or original contract prevents him from coming to realistic grips with the complexities of legal-economic change. But that is not his goal: He desires something else, namely, better to rationalize market change as *the* sanctioned mode and abort legal change as statist and coercive.

Despite his (necessary) recognition of the needs of constitutional and legal change, however minimized, his system does not solve the problem at which it is ostensibly aimed. The issue is not whether there is to be legal change, but *which* proposed change is to be permitted. I am *not* saying that he has failed to cope with the problem of change. He offers a solution: Build in constitutional-property rights (read: reinforce the status quo power structure or those parts of it with which he identifies) and allow change primarily through the market, quite a different situation than presently exists (or necessarily must exist even within his own system in practice). My point is a different one: Buchanan's analysis does not permit us to *differentiate* between permissible and impermissible legal change. It does not tell us when legal change is statism or "social reform" in his pejorative sense—certain people trying to impose their values on others—and when it is "genuine social reform" (p. 149) or "genuine constitutional change" (pp. 169, 178, 180). Even here he waffles, being willing to permit constitutional changes to which all individuals "might conceptually agree" (pp. 168–69). His system does not allow us unequivocally to differentiate "rebellious activity" from efforts to eliminate "unnecessary" social control, one of his examples being the universities in the late 1960s. Why can we not envision social reform as the complex, dirty, and often unreasoned process of effecting "constitutional revision" in the real world, or of "regulation" as changing rights in accordance with his system?[4] If law is social capital, why cannot it, too, be declared, from time to time, in principle, obsolescent? Is not *new* law also a candidate for such honorific treatment? Why cannot redistribution be held a public good? One need not advocate any particular regulation, but argue merely on the *conceptual* level. Compared to his stacking of the deck in favor of continuity, I would prefer the realistic conception of the system as a process of continuous renegotiation of the "social contract," a continuing constitutional revision, perhaps, a function of shifts in what Buchanan would call the natural distribution consequent to a change in the structure of power, a process he understands quite well. (On p. 79 Buchanan is Leninist regarding sought-after changes in constitutional arrangements in consequence of changes in the relative strengths of the parties.) Buchanan would undoubtedly say that I am opening the door to change, that is, to legal activism, or statism, but the door is there and already open. Buchanan realizes that but not only is unwilling to accept it as final, but also intends that his book should counteract it. It *is* perhaps unfair to criticize the work on grounds of its empirical and analytical defects; like Marx, his job is to change reality, not study it (as does Miller). But a neutral definition of the problem of order in regard to continuity versus change is preferable to one which defines order in terms of continuity alone. Moreover, Buchanan tends to see order as a condition, whereas I see it as a process undergoing evolution and transformation.

Another irritation is that Buchanan does not merely indicate problems with democracy and majoritarian decision making; rather, his analysis strikes at the heart of self-government. In order ostensibly to limit government, perhaps effectively to defend certain aspects of the power structure and uses of government, Buchanan denigrates self-government (democracy). True democracy, to him, means no or limited legal change, no or limited public choice after the (imaginary) constitutional stage. Buchanan fails to accept the predicament of self-government, that government *is* internal and not external. He would treat it, or have us treat it, as external ideologically (in the fine sense of the term) to influence the interests it would serve. But can the state *in fact* be "external to and divorced from the individuals or groups whose rights are involved" (p. 95)? Does not the very notion of self-government require the dismissal of all pretense of such absolutes and externals?

What Buchanan really objects to is policy consciousness, the perception of legal-economic arrangements as artifactual and thereby subject to change. Rather than try to obfuscate with regard to change, we should make the process enlightened, and on this Buchanan has much to offer as a conservative. But with unequal and partially obscured appreciation of the realities of legal-economic change in society, his system would enhance the opportunities of the more knowledgeable members.

As much as I can sympathize and even agree with Buchanan as to the problems of self-government, his analysis is dangerous: Its logical conclusion is the destruction of self-government. This is especially relevant if Miller's description of the corporate state is even remotely accurate. Buchanan's conception of external government also contradicts the actual historical origins and theorizing about the American experiment. Our government is to be internalized in the sense that it is to be made responsive to the people through various groups of representatives. Although

Madison and Hamilton, among others, saw problems consequent to that, including majoritarian democracy run rampant (whatever that may mean), Buchanan's formulation is extreme and antidemocratic. It would function to give effect to a private governing elite. I am not certain that is what Buchanan really wants, but that is what I find in his book.

On the subject of democracy, there are two further problems. First, when does limited government imply limited self-government and limited opportunity to use government to check concentrated private power (itself perhaps the result of past uses of government)? This question is not answered sufficiently by saying that private power tends to control government. Buchanan's system largely neglects the problem of private governance. Indeed, his system would divert attention from the system of power, privilege, benefits, and beneficiaries. Second, Buchanan is very selective about the utility functions and preferences to which his system is allowed to give effect: Preferences and utility functions concerning political activity, law, and change, that is, government as an economic variable, are severely constrained by him.

But at the heart of the book is not Buchanan's ambiguity about or bias against legal change, nor the argument as such. Rather, it is what Buchanan apparently wishes to accomplish with the argument. On this, to his credit, he is fairly candid.

He seems to know that the terms of social coexistence are actually our belief systems (which may include the myth of contract). The maintenance or achievement of a social scheme requires, then, the deployment of myths, symbols, and semantic contrivances. Pareto knew this, and Buchanan is a splendid Paretian in this and other respects. Many conservative myths have lost their hold, and Buchanan here seeks to resuscitate the contractarian metaphor and myth. The myth of divine rule would be acceptable, if not preferable, if only it would work (p. 130). From the 1920s and earlier he borrows the imagery of voluntary contract; he rejects the reliance of those times on the elitist Supreme Court to "protect rights" against legislative majorities. He is seeking defensible and salable principles of conservatism, intellectual weapons for his fortress. The semantics of laissez-faire will no longer suffice; something else must be found and substituted. Positive legal-economic analysis raises unsafe principles and objections; these must be defused and distinguished away. He does not insist on an authentic constitutional contract, not to say a continuing constitutional experience, only an implicit one; he seeks to legitimate a sham to rationalize the desired and the safe. He intends for the social contract myth to tie the hands of the present, especially of so-called judicial activists, legislative majorities, unsafe social reformers, and supposedly of government *per se*. The reality of concomitant constitutional and postconstitutional stages is unsafe; the reality of rights defined by the action of government is unsafe; both must be intellectually aborted. That government is fundamentally present in any case is irrelevant. It is more important that rights not be seen to be defined by government, for that would lead to their redefinition.

Either Buchanan is trying to salvage as much as he can in the actual process of continuing constitutional revision for certain established rights or that is the effective result of his system. The game is seemingly given away by his willingness (however reluctant) to have the rich buy off the poor to produce a new, acceptable constitutional order (pp. 85, 178). Political-economic philosophy is made instrumental in haggling over the price of social change. Buchanan is a participant, not an observer. Such, indeed, is the ideological role of economics: He decries the "public failure to understand the simple principle of laissez faire, the principle that results which emerge from the interactions of persons left alone may be, and often are, superior to those results that emerge from overt political interference." He laments the "loss of wisdom in this respect." The "message of Adam Smith requires reiteration with each generation. (Modern economics must stand condemned in its failure to accomplish this simple task, the performance of which is, at base, the discipline's primary reason for claiming public support)" (pp. 91–92). Such is Buchanan's own social welfare function. Needless to say, I believe Smith's message is not quite the one Buchanan describes.[5]

Buchanan's role is that of conservative high priest in a world of power play and the use of the state to defend and attack established positions of power (with certain uses defined as laissez-faire). This aspect of the natural state is forever with us, like it or not. What is important is what people believe. Beliefs can be manipulated by the generation of serviceable beliefs in order to influence attitudes toward, and thereby channel the performance of, legal-economic interactions. I shudder at the uses to which his ideas are capable of being put. I prefer to think that Buchanan might shudder too.

Buchanan decries any idea of "truth" in politics as well as the efforts of "social reformers" to impose their particularistic values. He argues that he is not imposing his own on others, only promoting a contractarian system wherein voluntarism, consent, and unanimity can reign supreme. I agree in at least one respect: He is not specific about the values he would have the social contract embody. But his is a *conservative* conception of contact. His is *a* reform scheme. His is readily and openly substitutable by a regime of only *implicit* contract. His regime is consonant with the interests of *certain* established power players, that is, a regime which promises to be power structure or dominance specific. He is playing God, a role he denigrates for others, but one performed by him on the *system* level. He is conservative and *he makes no bones about it*.

Buchanan offers some brilliant ideas, and the project required a great deal of work and confidence. Indeed, it is a feat of great imagination and noble conception. He has much to say regarding how governmental institutions actually tend to operate, his conservative uses of his more positive (descriptive) analysis notwithstanding. On balance, however, the book is neither philosophy nor science, but apologetics. When Buchanan argues that there is unidirectional bias in government spending, for example, he completely disregards lines of reasoning which suggest that there is under- rather than overspending (or a distorted structure of spending). I think that he probably is correct, but the discussion is one-sided if not casuistic. As apologist he is in good company, for it includes Locke. The role of apologist has a social function and importance. It is a part, although perhaps a distorted part, of the important social value clarification and selection process. What is disturbing is that Buchanan's interesting and important analytical points become casuistic distinctions with which to erect his ideological fortress, to defend against or finesse both liberal principles and positivist analysis, in sum to comprise a new chapter in the continuing conservative effort to formulate defensible principles and positions. I find his defenses insubstantial and shaky, notwithstanding my agreement that society requires principles of conservatism as well as of liberalism. My disturbance is due to what I see as his distortion of legal-economic reality, regardless of our agreements or disagreements as to values.

I also doubt whether pretense about conceptual contract will produce liberty by erecting meaningful limits to liberty. Preaching the virtues of voluntarism and consent will not suffice to obscure the essential coercive character of the system and the fundamental continuing economic role of government. (All systems are coercive, of course, but that is not at issue here.) Buchanan undoubtedly knows this, but perhaps he feels he has to finesse or ignore them in order to save the system (from itself). He may be correct: Our business civilization certainly has nurtured the view that we can change and recombine the elements of our world to make it better. But we could have an economic system dominated by the belief system prescribed by Buchanan which nonetheless might not look very different, to a relatively objective interpreter, from that described by Miller. Like it or not, Miller is largely descriptively correct. Buchanan's scheme would cement important parts of the status quo structure of private power, private governance, and private-public symbiosis, especially those elements generally thought of as "rightist." His analysis resembles an apologia for certain established private economic powers: perhaps it is not. But if a truly voluntaristic society cannot exist unless the corporate system is tamed, then preaching against social reformers will be to no avail. Will his contractarian myth be both the opiate of the masses and the sedative of the classes? I wonder, as a matter of *positive* analysis.

In all this I am the utopian, not Buchanan (however much he seems to be weak on providing a mode of legal change in his ideal system, a standard fault of the utopian literature). Why? Because I would prefer academics to be objective ends-means analysts (as far as possible), not ideological purveyors of particularistic or systemic values. I join Buchanan in applauding the creation of Pareto-better institutions, but *truly* Pareto-better institutions, not ones rationalized by narrow definitions of coercion, externalities, and so on, and certainly not entire systems of mutual coercion rationalized as voluntary in a world of adhesion contracts. I, too, dislike the state; but I do not believe in playing games about it, nor do I believe in sanctifying selected features of the status quo. Commons was correct: The state is an arena of collective bargaining. Buchanan's book is an attempt to channel the conditions and results of the bargaining, but the state would be no less an arena under his system.

Neither book is likely to become a classic. In Miller's case, professional and political socialization works so well that most economists will not be receptive to its description and implications, preferring instead the pseudo-comforts of sentiments such as Buchanan's. In the latter's case, his book's convoluted logic and strained application of distinctions do patent damage to legal-economic reality. It is, however, a worthy successor to Friedrich von Hayek's *Road to Serfdom.*

Notes

1. James M. Buchanan, *The Limits of Liberty: Between Anarchy and Leviathan* (Chicago: University of Chicago Press, 1975), and Arthur Selwyn Miller, *The Modern Corporate State: Private Governments and the American Constitution* (Westport: Greenwood Press, 1976).
2. It is not unlikely that each author would consider the other's book a fantasy and also possibly quite pernicious. Both may be guilty of another recent author's findings of a fallacy of rights. See Stuart A. Scheingold,

The Politics of Rights (New Haven: Yale University Press, 1974), Part One.

3. See Warren J. Samuels, in *The Chicago School of Political Economy* (East Lansing: Division of Research, Michigan State University, 1976), chapter 16.
4. Ibid., chapter 20.
5. See my "The Political Economy of Adam Smith," *Ethics* and *Nebraska Journal of Economics and Business,* forthcoming.